This project was carried out with the financial
support of
Deutsche Forschungsgemeinschaft
Bonn-Bad Godesberg
National Endowment for the Humanities
Washington, D.C.
State University of New York at Albany
and the cooperation of
Deutsche Bibliothek
Frankfurt/Main

Guide to the Archival Materials of the German-speaking Emigration to the United States after 1933

Verzeichnis der Quellen und Materialien der deutschsprachigen Emigration in den U.S.A. seit 1933

By John M. Spalek
in collaboration with
Adrienne Ash and Sandra H. Hawrylchak

Published for the Bibliographical Society
of the University of Virginia
by the University Press of Virginia
Charlottesville

THE UNIVERSITY PRESS OF VIRGINIA
Copyright © 1978 by the Rector and Visitors
of the University of Virginia

First published 1978

Library of Congress Cataloging in Publication Data
Spalek, John M.
  Guide to the archival materials of the German-speaking emigration to the United States after 1933 = Verzeichnis der Quellen und Materialien der deutschsprachigen Emigration in den U.S.A. seit 1933.
  Includes indexes.
  1. German Americans—Manuscripts—Catalogs.
2. Austrian Americans—Manuscripts—Catalogs. 3. Manuscripts—United States—Catalogs. I. Ash, Adrienne, joint author. II. Hawrylchak, Sandra H., joint author. III. Title. IV. Title: Verzeichnis der Quellen und Materialien der deutschsprachigen Emigration in den U.S.A. seit 1933.
Z6611.G46S62 [E184.G3]   016.973′04′31   78–10847
ISBN 0–8139–0749–7

CONTENTS / *INHALT*

PREFACE

The National Socialist takeover in 1933 caused an unprecedented exodus of the intellectual and scientific elite of Germany. The best talents in the humanities and the sciences, as well as leaders in public and professional life, were either expelled and deprived of their citizenship or chose not to remain in their own country. Five years after the Nazi takeover of Germany, Austria and Czechoslovakia (the latter with many German-speaking or German-educated individuals) suffered the same fate. Similarly affected also were a number of prominent Hungarians, for example Edward Teller and John von Neumann, many of whom were both educated and active at German universities during the Weimar Republic. The majority of the emigrés came to the United States between 1933 and 1942, and for many this country became their permanent home.

According to various statistics, more than 20,000 members of various professions emigrated to the United States in the course of their escape from National Socialism, and about 70 percent of this group came from the German-speaking area of Europe.[1] The stature of the emigrés is indicated by such names as Hannah Arendt, Bruno Bettelheim, Felix Bloch, Bertolt Brecht, Heinrich Bruening, Rudolf Carnap, Albert Einstein, Erik Erikson, James Franck, Erich Fromm, Walter Gropius, Hajo Holborn, Max Horkheimer, Paul Lazarsfeld, Thomas Mann, Ludwig Mies van der Rohe, Wolfgang Pauli, Max Reinhardt, Arnold Schoenberg, Paul Tillich, Bruno Walter, Max Wertheimer, and Billy Wilder.

Laura Fermi compares the mass exodus of science, art, and learning from Europe of the 1930s to the flight in the fifteenth century of the learned men of the dying Byzantine empire to Western Europe. She describes the wave of this cultural multitude as unique in the long history of American immigration.

The Guide is the first attempt to provide a comprehensive survey of the materials of this cultural and intellectual

---

[1] Laura Fermi, Illustrious Immigrants. The Intellectual Migration from Europe 1930-41 (Chicago and London: Univ. of Chicago Press, 1968), pp. 11-17, 93-95.

migration. Efforts to document this era have been until now mainly limited and individually sponsored projects on specialized subjects or individual emigrés. (For example, the collaborative project of the American Institute of Physics, the American Philosophical Society, and the Bancroft Library of the University of California at Berkeley to document quantum physics, and the establishment of the Arnold Schoenberg Institute at the University of Southern California.) One of the greatest obstacles to a comprehensive study of the immigration and its impact on this country was the fragmentary information available until now about the location and extent of source materials in this country (documents, manuscripts, correspondences).

By the time the Project started, forty years had passed since 1933, the year when many individuals were forced to leave Germany. As a result, firsthand sources, both archival materials and the emigrés themselves, have been decreasing in number as the years progressed. In a number of instances the Project came too late to prevent the loss of source materials discarded by heirs or friends unaware of their historic significance.

History of the Project

The project owes its inception to the Deutsche Forschungsgemeinschaft, which during the last decade has initiated and funded a large-scale inventory of manuscripts in German libraries and archives. In 1972 Professor John Spalek was approached about conducting a basic survey of archival materials of the German-speaking emigrés in the United States. The survey—begun in the fall of 1973—was initially projected for two years; however, because of the vast amount of materials uncovered, the project was extended for two additional years. The funds from the DFG were matched for two years by the National Endowment for the Humanities, and for the two other years by the State University of New York at Albany, which also provided generous support for various aspects of this undertaking throughout the four years.

Professor Spalek was joined in 1973 by Dr. Adrienne Ash and Ms. Sandra Hawrylchak, who conducted the main part of the survey and compiled the information contained in the Guide. Dr. Adrienne Ash was mainly responsible for travel and interviews, and Sandra Hawrylchak for the assembling and categorizing of materials, as well as the preparation of the manuscript of the Guide.

The project began with a list of several hundred prominent individuals that was prepared in consultation with experts on both sides of the Atlantic. This list was subsequently revised and expanded by specialists in various fields until it comprised approximately 700 names. This list, with only minor changes, remained the basis of the survey throughout its duration.

The first year of the Project was devoted to the survey of American libraries and archives, and this was substantially completed in the course of the second year. A total of over 400 libraries were contacted and ultimately about 200 proved to contain materials pertinent to the survey.

During the second year of the survey, the emphasis shifted to the contacting of private individuals who had or were expected to have collections in their private homes. This activity remained the main focus of the survey well into the fourth year (spring 1977). Since the survey of private collections could best be accomplished by personal contact, constant traveling throughout the country became a main feature of the Project. It can be said that, at least until the beginning of the survey, an estimated 40 percent of the collections were still in private hands. This ratio has been decreasing during the last few years through the acquisition of private collections by libraries and other institutions. The remainder of the fourth year was devoted to the preparation of the photo-ready copy of the manuscript of the Guide.

The unavoidable loose ends should be noted. Many individuals chosen as objects of the search could not be reached, or, if reached, had no materials to offer. Still others had returned materials to European archives, while the Project had limited itself to archives in the United States; in many cases, materials had simply been lost to posterity through circumstances following an individual's death. Lastly, when the Guide was assembled, it was discovered that a few individuals yielded extremely small amounts of historical material—such small amounts that it was decided a report on such an individual had limited usefulness. While notes on these "minimal finds" will be retained in the Project's offices, no archival summary appears in the Guide (see Appendix).

Although the compilers of the Guide were able to devote four years to this survey, it could have been continued for at least another year. It is hoped that an expanded version, both in detail and in additional names, can be produced within the next several years.

Criteria for Selection

The criterion for inclusion in the survey was basically the accomplishment of the individual, i.e., his or her importance to their respective professions.

Since the Guide is intended as a tool for both American and European researchers, the importance of an individual had to be assessed from both the American and the European point of view.

In most instances the American and European criteria for inclusion in the survey overlapped. Whenever the criteria diverged, the reason could usually be traced to the profession of the emigré. While the physical, natural, and social scientists, as well as the artists, are more important to the United States because of the impact they had in this country, writers and political figures are naturally of much greater interest for Germany and Austria. The selection of names for the Guide tried to do justice to both the American and European interests.

In the final analysis, however, the names included in the Guide represent a combination of the priorities that the Project set for itself as well as the actual results of a successful search.

Directions for Use

Individuals whose papers were surveyed are listed alphabetically. Under each individual's name are found the following:

Locations of materials (archives, libraries, private residences, etc.). Locations of large collections on an individual are listed first. Locations of smaller collections or individual items follow.

Descriptive paragraphs. These appear only after the locations of major collections. They include call numbers, restrictions, history of the collection, or any other pertinent information on the collection that might be helpful to the researcher.

PREFACE

Letter-number coded descriptions of materials. The letter-
    number codings in the left-hand margin are intended
    for quick reference to the type of material sought:
    e.g., B-1 indicates letters written by the individual
    in question to others (see the Coding Key for details).

Index. Because of the alphabetical arrangement of the Guide,
    there is no table of contents. Instead, individuals
    included are entered in capital letters in the index.

Additional Comments on Usage

1. Many archives provide a more detailed listing of papers
    than that provided by the Guide. In other cases, the
    Guide provides more detail than the actual repository.
    The availability of any and all such detail should be
    ascertained from the individual archive or institution.

2. Call numbers of collections cited by the Guide are gen-
    erally in-house references. However, when the Guide
    cites a call number that is preceded by the designation
    MS, this collection is registered and available through
    the National Union Catalog of Manuscript Collections.

3. Details of access and hours of availability as well as
    special regulations on individual collections should be
    obtained from each repository or its literature.

4. Descriptive paragraphs on a major collection (the Thomas
    Mann Collection, the Albert Einstein collection) are
    listed only once—under the individual in question
    (Thomas Mann, Albert Einstein). The collection itself,
    however, may be cited frequently under other individual
    emigrés for whom the collection yields letters, etc.
    Thus under Hermann Broch, the Thomas Mann Collection is
    listed as holding letters by Broch, but the researcher
    must refer back to Thomas Mann for important information
    on access, use, etc. of the Thomas Mann Collection.

5. As an aid to the researcher, the Project has noted,
    wherever obtainable, the ownership of the literary
    and publication rights to the materials surveyed.

Concluding Remarks

Though the publication of the Guide represents the culmination of four years of funding, footwork, and the elation of discovery, the work is not over. While resources will no longer permit an active search by the original staff, it is felt that inevitably the seeds of impetus have been sown, new materials will come to light, and fresh information will be added to the growing body of research. The scholarship that the Project hopes to stimulate in the future will have, among its many tasks, the casting of a wider net than that for which the Project had resources. The result will be countless pieces of new material to round out the study of this particular era of immigration to the United States. It is hoped that not only the history but the impact of this professional migration on the cultural growth and change of the United States will ensue, and such studies will of themselves cause the Project's legacies to grow. The vast network of contacts established by the staff between the research public and those who have materials of interest, whether institutional or private, assures that papers will be made available and, at the very least, saved from possible loss or destruction. To these ends the Project dedicates its work and now looks forward to biographic, descriptive, and interpretive scholarship on the German-speaking emigration to the United States 1933-1945.

Acknowledgments

In the first place, we wish to express our indebtedness to Dr. Werner Berthold of the Deutsche Bibliothek, Frankfurt/ Main, for his advice and support through the four years of the Project, in particular for his help in obtaining financial support from the Deutsche Forschungsgemeinschaft.

The Project owes thanks to individuals and institutions throughout the United States and West Germany. The particular, ongoing efforts of a few must be acknowledged: Mr. Rodney Dennis, Houghton Library, Harvard University; Dr. Wolfgang Elfe, The University of South Carolina; Dr. Ludwig Glaeser, The Museum of Modern Art, New York City; Ms. Christina Hanson, Beinecke Rare Book and Manuscript Library, Yale University; Mrs. Alice Loewy-Kahler, Princeton, New Jersey; Dr. Sibyl Milton, The Leo Baeck Institute, New York City;

PREFACE

Miss Pearl Moeller, The Museum of Modern Art, New York City;
Dr. Arthur Norberg, Bancroft Library, The University of
California, Berkeley; Dr. Dieter Oertel, Deutsche Forschungs-
gemeinschaft, Bonn-Bad Godesberg; Dr. Werner Röder, Institut
für Zeitgeschichte, Munich; Mr. Will Schaber, New York City;
Dr. Christa Sammons, Beinecke Rare Book and Manuscript
Library, Yale University; Ms. Judith Schiff, Sterling Memo-
rial Library, Yale University; Dr. Hans Staudinger, formerly
Dean of the Graduate Faculty of the New School for Social
Research, New York; Dr. Herbert Strauss and Mr. Steve Siegel,
The Research Foundation for Jewish Immigration, New York
City; Miss Hilde Waldo, Los Angeles, California; and Ms.
Joan Warnow, The American Institute of Physics, New York
City.

Special gratitude is owed to the institutions that pro-
vided financial support for the Project's work: The Deutsche
Forschungsgemeinschaft, Bonn-Bad Godesberg; The National
Endowment for the Humanities, Washington, D.C.; and The
State University of New York at Albany.

The explanatory paragraphs were translated into German
by Karin Isernhagen, Würzburg.

The photo-ready copy of the manuscript was prepared by
Marcella Curtright of Carson, California.

*Die Machtergreifung der Nationalsozialisten im Jahre
1933 bewirkte einen noch nie dagewesenen Exodus der geisti-
gen Elite Deutschlands. Hochbegabte Künstler, Wissenschaftler und Männer des öffentlichen Lebens wurden entweder aus-
gewiesen und ihrer Staatsangehörigkeit beraubt oder faßten
selbst den Entschluß, nicht in dem Land ihrer Geburt zu
bleiben. Fünf Jahre nachdem Deutschland unter Hitlers Gewalt
gefallen war, erlitten Österreich und die Tschechoslowakei
(letztere mit zahlreichen Deutschsprechenden und in deutscher
Tradition erzogenen) dasselbe Schicksal. Ein ähnliches Los
widerfuhr einer Anzahl prominenter Ungarn — Männern wie
Edward Teller und John von Neumann —, von denen viele während
der Zeit der Weimarer Republik an deutschen Universitäten
studiert und gelehrt hatten. Die meisten dieser außerordent-
lich befähigten Menschen kamen zwischen 1933 und 1942, besonders nach der Besetzung Frankreichs 1940, in die USA; viele
blieben für immer dort.*

*Die Zahl dieser Emigranten wird von verschiedenen Sta-
tistiken auf 20.000 geschätzt. Etwa 70 Prozent davon stam-
men aus den deutschsprachigen Gebieten Europas.[1] Ihr hohes
geistiges Niveau wird ohne weiteres offensichtlich, wenn man
Namen wie die folgenden hört: Theodor W. Adorno, Hannah
Arendt, Bruno Bettelheim, Ernst Bloch, Felix Bloch, Hermann
Broch, Bertolt Brecht, Heinrich Bruening, Rudolf Carnap,
Alfred Döblin, Albert Einstein, Erik Erikson, James Franck,
Erich Fromm, Walter Gropius, Hajo Holborn, Max Horkheimer,
Erich von Kahler, Paul Lazarsfeld, Heinrich Mann, Thomas
Mann, Herbert Marcuse, Ludwig Marcuse, Ludwig Mies van der
Rohe, Wolfgang Pauli, Erwin Piscator, Wilhelm Reich, Max
Reinhardt, Arnold Schoenberg, Paul Tillich, Bruno Walter,
Franz Werfel, Max Wertheimer, und Billy Wilder.*

Laura Fermi vergleicht in ihrem Buch Illustrious Immigrants *die Flucht dieser Künstler und Gelehrten von Europa*

---

[1] *Laura Fermi,* Illustrious Immigrants. The Intellectual
Migration from Europe 1930-41 *(Chicago and London: University of Chicago Press, 1968), S. 11-17, 93-95.*

nach Nordamerika mit der Auswanderung byzantinischer Wissenschaftler im 15. Jahrhundert von Konstantinopel ins westliche Europa. Einen derartigen Zustrom hochintelligenter Menschen in die amerikanische Gesellschaft betrachtet sie als einmalig in der langen Geschichte amerikanischer Immigration.

Das vorliegende Handbuch stellt einen ersten Versuch dar, das umfassende Material dieser Immigration[2] zu erfassen und unter bestimmten Gesichtspunkten zu ordnen. Bis vor kurzem beschränkten sich die Bemühungen, Art und Reichweite dieser einzigartigen Einwanderung darzustellen, nur auf individuell unterstützte Projekte, die bestimmte Immigranten oder spezifische Themen zum Gegenstand hatten, z.B. die Zusammenarbeit zwischen dem American Institute of Physics, der American Philosophical Society und der Bancroft Library an der University of California at Berkeley bei der Zusammenstellung einer Dokumentation der Quantentheorie in der Physik oder die Gründung des Arnold Schoenberg Instituts an der University of Southern California.

Eines der größten Hindernisse, eine umfassende Darstellung dieser Einwanderung mit ihren kaum übersehbaren intellektuellen und künstlerischen Auswirkungen zu geben, lag bislang in der fehlenden Kenntnis des Umfangs und der Standorte des Quellenmaterials.

Zum Zeitpunkt, als dieses Projekt in Angriff genommen wurde, waren schon vierzig Jahre vergangen, seitdem die ersten Gelehrten, Künstler und Politiker gezwungen worden waren, ihre Heimat zu verlassen. Aus diesem Grunde war es in einer Anzahl von Fällen schon nicht mehr möglich, authentische Informationen aus erster Hand zu erlangen. In anderen Fällen kam das Vorhaben zu spät, um den Verlust wertvollen Quellenmaterials zu verhindern, weil Erben oder Freunde von Immigranten Materialien, deren geschichtlicher Bedeutung sie sich nicht bewußt waren, schon vernichtet hatten.

Geschichte des Vorhabens

Das vorliegende Handbuch verdankt die Anregung zu seiner

---

[2]*Der Begriff "Immigration" wird aus amerikanischer Perspektive verwendet. Aus europäischer Sicht wird man von "Emigration" und sinngemäß von "Emigranten" — bzw. "Exilanten", soweit das Gastland als vorübergehendes Ausweichquartier, als "Exil", gesehen wird — sprechen müssen.*

*Entstehung der Deutschen Forschungsgemeinschaft, die während
des letzten Jahrzehnts eine Erfassung von Manuskripten in
deutschen und auch einigen anderen europäischen Bibliotheken
und Archiven auf breiter Basis sowohl angeregt als auch finanziell unterstützt hat. 1972 wurde Professor John Spalek
daraufhin angesprochen, eine Erfassung archivalischen Materials deutschsprachiger Immigranten in den Vereinigten Staaten durchzuführen. Die Bemühungen um eine solche Erfassung
begannen im Herbst des Jahres 1973 und waren ursprünglich
auf einen Zeitraum von zwei Jahren angesetzt. Aufgrund zu-
sätzlicher Funde wurde das Projekt um zwei weitere Jahre ver-
längert. Von amerikanischer Seite wurde das Vorhaben zwei
Jahre lang von dem National Endowment for the Humanities und
zwei Jahre von der State University of New York at Albany
unterstützt. Die State University of New York at Albany war
außerdem vier Jahre lang für verschiedene Nebenkosten des
Unternehmens verantwortlich.*

*1973 gewann Professor Spalek Frau Sandra Hawrylchak und
Dr. Adrienne Ash für die Durchführung des Projektes. Dr. Ash
war vorwiegend für die Interviews mit Immigranten und Biblio-
thekaren sowie für all die Aspekte des Projektes verantwortlich, die mit Reisen zusammenhingen. Frau Hawrylchak hin-
gegen oblag das Kategorisieren und die Zusammenstellung des
Materials sowie die Herstellung des Manuskripts.*

*Das Projekt begann mit einer Suchliste von mehreren hun-
dert Namen prominenter Immigranten, einer Liste, die nach
Rücksprache mit Fachleuten auf beiden Seiten des Atlantik
aufgestellt wurde. Diese Liste wurde im Laufe der Zeit durch
Spezialisten aus den verschiedensten Gebieten revidiert und
erweitert, bis sie ungefähr 700 Namen umfaßte. Sie bildete —
mit nur geringen Änderungen — bis zum Schluß die Basis dieses
Unternehmens.*

*Daß ein derartigen Vorhaben auch in einer vierjährigen
Arbeitszeit nicht abgeschlossen werden kann und das Handbuch
unvermeidlich Lücken aufweisen muß, versteht sich von selbst.
Viele Immigranten waren unerreichbar, und selbst dort, wo sie
erreichbar waren, fehlte es oft an authentischem Material.
Wieder andere hatten ihre Materialien bereits an europäische
Archive zurückgegeben, so daß das vorliegende Verzeichnis
notgedrungenerweise Lücken aufweisen muß, zumal wir uns in
unserer Erfassung auf Bibliotheken und Archive in den Vereinigten Staaten beschränkt haben. In vielen Fällen war auch
das Material nach dem Tode eines Immigranten verloren gegangen; und schließlich mußten wir feststellen, daß einige*

*Immigranten so wenig historisch bedeutsame Aufzeichnungen
besaßen, daß wir uns gegen ihre Aufnahme in das Handbuch
entschieden. Obwohl Anmerkungen im Hinblick auf die Mini-
malfunde in unserer Sammelstelle in Albany aufbewahrt werden,
haben wir uns gegen eine Zusammenfassung im Handbuch entschieden (siehe Anhang).*

Auswahlkriterien

*Das Kriterium für die Einbeziehung eines Immigranten
in das Verzeichnis war seine Leistung, z.B. seine (oder ihre)
Bedeutung innerhalb einer spezifischen Berufsgruppe.*

*Da das Handbuch amerikanischen und deutschen Forschern
als Hilfsmittel dienen soll, mußte die Bedeutung des Einzelnen sowohl von amerikanischer als auch von deutscher Warte
aus betrachtet werden. In den meisten Fällen stimmten die
amerikanischen und europäischen Kriterien überein. Wann
immer die Kriterien voneinander abwichen, war der Grund dafür
meist im Beruf des Emigranten zu suchen. Während die Natur-
und Gesellschaftswissenschaftler sowie die Künstler wegen
ihres starken Einflusses auf die hiesige Gesellschaft von
größerer Bedeutung für Amerika sind, gilt das Interesse der
Deutschen und Österreicher in stärkerem Maße den Schrift-
stellern und Politikern, die meist zur Gruppe der Exilanten
gehören. Mit der Auswahl der in diesem Handbuch aufgeführ-
ten Namen haben wir also versucht, sowohl dem besonderen
amerikanischen wie auch dem spezifisch europäischen Interesse
gerecht zu werden.*

Anleitungen zur Benutzung

*Personen, deren Dokumente erfaßt worden sind, werden in
alphabetischer Reihenfolge aufgeführt. Die folgenden Ein-
tragungen können unter dem Namen des Betreffenden gefunden
werden:*

*Standorte der Materialen (Archive, Bibliotheken, Privatadres-
sen usw.). Standortangaben größerer Sammlungen werden
stets zuerst aufgeführt, Standortangaben kleinerer Sammlungen schließen daran an.*

*Beschreibende Anmerkungen. Sie erfolgen nur nach den Stand-
ortangaben größerer Sammlungen und enthalten die*

Signatur, Benutzungseinschränkungen, Anmerkungen zur
Geschichte der Sammlung sowie andere sachdienliche
Informationen.

Kodifizierung durch Buchstaben und Zahlen. Die Buchstaben-
Zahlen-Kodifizierung am linken Rand einer Eintragung
ist als schnelle Orientierungshilfe im Hinblick auf die
Art des Materials gedacht: z.B. bezeichnet B-1 Briefe,
die von dem betreffenden Immigranten an andere geschrieben wurden. (Weitere Informationen hierüber können im
Kodifizierungs-Schlüssel gefunden werden.)

Register. Wegen der alphabetischen Einteilung des Handbuches
ist von einem speziellen Inhaltsverzeichnis abgesehen
worden. Statt dessen sind die Namen der im Handbuch
aufgenommenen Immigranten im Register groß geschrieben
worden.

Zusätzliche Hinweise zum Gebrauch des Handbuchs

1. In manchen Fällen besitzen die Archive weit detailliertere Aufstellungen des Materials, als dieses Handbuch
bieten kann. In anderen Fällen wiederum sind die Ein-
tragungen in unserem Register detaillierter. Auf alle
Fälle sollte die Möglichkeit des Vorhandenseins solch
detaillierter Aufzeichnungen in Archiven und Bibliotheken stets im Auge behalten werden.

2. Signaturen von Sammlungen, wie sie im Handbuch zitiert
werden, entsprechen im allgemeinen den Signaturen der
betreffenden Aufbewahrungsstellen. Wenn das Handbuch
jedoch eine Signatur angibt, der ein MS vorausgeht, so
heißt das, daß diese Sammlung im National Union Catalog
of Manuscript Collections aufgenommen und außerdem zugänglich ist.

3. Einzelheiten im Hinblick auf den Zutritt und die Zugäng-
lichkeit zu diesen Sammlungen sollten stets von den
betreffenden Aufbewahrungsstellen (oder den entsprechen-
den Veröffentlichungen) eingeholt werden.

4. Beschreibende Anmerkungen zu einer größeren Sammlung
(Die Thomas Mann Sammlung, die Albert Einstein Sammlung)
werden immer nur einmal aufgeführt, und zwar stets unter
dem Namen des in Betracht kommenden Immigranten (Thomas

*Mann, Albert Einstein). Auf die Sammlung selbst kann
jedoch des öfteren verwiesen werden, vor allem dann,
wenn sie wertvolle Aufschlüsse über einen anderen
Immigranten gibt. So findet der Forscher z.B. unter
Hermann Broch ein Hinweis auf die in der Thomas Mann
Sammlung enthaltenen Briefe von Broch. Um eingehen-
dere Informationen über die Thomas-Mann-Sammlung zu
erlangen, müßte er unter der Eintragung Thomas Mann
nachschlagen.*

5. *Als besondere Hilfe für den Forscher sind — wo immer es
möglich war — die Publikationsrechte der in Betracht
kommenden Materialien aufgeführt.*

Abschließende Bemerkungen

*Obgleich die Veröffentlichung dieses Handbuchs den
Höhepunkt eines vierjährigen, großzügig unterstützten Unternehmens darstellt, das mit mühseliger Kleinarbeit verbunden
war, oft aber auch echte Entdeckerfreuden einschloß, ist die
Arbeit noch nicht endgültig abgeschlossen. Auch wenn die
gegenwärtigen finanziellen Verhältnisse eine aktive Suche
nach noch unerfaßten Materialien durch die ursprüngliche
Arbeitsgemeinschaft nicht mehr zulassen, haben wir doch den
Eindruck, daß eine Anregung zu weiteren Nachforschungen
gegeben worden ist. Zweifellos wird noch unbekanntes Material entdeckt, werden neue Informationen an den Tag gebracht
werden. Richtung, Weite und Intensität der Forschung, wel-
cher dieses Handbuch zu dienen hofft, sind keine Grenzen
gesetzt; wir können nur hoffen, daß eines Tages als ihr
Ergebnis — zusammengesetzt aus vielen Einzelstudien — ein
Bild dieser einmaligen Immigration in die Vereinigten Staaten
entsteht, das unser gegenwärtiges an Genauigkeit und Voll-
ständigkeit bei weitem übertrifft. Auch hoffen wir, daß
eines Tages die Geschichte der Wirkung und des Einflusses
dieser außerordentlichen Europäer auf die gesellschaftliche
und kulturelle Entwicklung dieses Landes geschrieben wird.
Gewiß aber sollten die durch unsere Arbeitsgemeinschaft ge-
schaffenen weitverzweigten Verbindungen zwischen Forschern
und denen, die wertvolle Materialien besitzen — seien es nun
Institutionen oder Privatpersonen — dazu anregen, diese Dokumente zu gegebener Zeit der Allgemeinheit zugänglich zu machen
oder doch zumindest durch Deponierung in einem Archiv vor*

*ihrem endgültigen Verlust zu bewahren. Diesem weitgespann-
ten Ziel sei unsere eigene Arbeit gewidmet, deren größte
Belohnung einst darin liegen wird, Anstöße zu biographischer,
hermeneutischer und kulturgeschichtlicher Forschung über die
deutschsprachige Emigration in die Vereinigten Staaten (1933-
45) gegeben zu haben.*

Danksagungen

*Wir sind vor allem Herrn Dr. Werner Berthold von der
Deutschen Bibliothek in Frankfurt am Main für seinen Rat wie
für seine Unterstützung zu Dank verpflichtet, besonders für
seine Hilfe beim Erlangen der finanziellen Unterstützung
durch die Deutsche Forschungsgemeinschaft.*

*Unsere Arbeitsgemeinschaft möchte vielen Privatpersonen
und Institutionen hiermit ihren Dank abstatten. Die besonde-
ren noch andauernden Bemühungen einiger sollen hier aber
besonders erwähnt werden: Herr Rodney Dennis, Houghton
Library, Harvard University; Dr. Wolfgang Elfe, The Univer-
sity of South Carolina; Dr. Ludwig Glaser, The Museum of
Modern Art, New York City; Frau Christina Hanson, Beinecke
Rare Book and Manuscript Library, Yale University; Frau
Alice Loewy-Kahler, Princeton, New Jersey; Dr. Sibyl Milton,
The Leo Baeck Institute, New York City; Frau Pearl Moeller,
The Museum of Modern Art, New York City; Dr. Arthur Norberg,
Bancroft Library, The University of California, Berkeley;
Dr. Dieter Oertel, Deutsche Forschungsgemeinschaft, Bonn-Bad
Godesberg; Dr. Werner Röder, Institut für Zeitgeschichte,
München; Herr Will Schaber, New York City; Dr. Christa Sam-
mons, Beinecke Rare Book and Manuscript Library, Yale Uni-
versity; Frau Judith Schiff, Sterling Memorial Library, Yale
University; Dr. Hans Staudinger, ehemals Dekan der Graduate
Faculty of the New School for Social Research, New York; Dr.
Herbert Strauss und Herr Steve Siegel, The Research Founda-
tion for Jewish Immigration, New York City; Frau Hilde Waldo,
Los Angeles, California; Frau Joan Warnow, The American
Institute of Physics, New York City.*

*Eine besondere Danksagung gilt den Institutionen, die
unser Projekt finanziell unterstützt haben: Der Deutschen
Forschungsgemeinschaft, Bonn-Bad Godesberg; The National
Endowment for the Humanities, Washington, D.C.; The State
University of New York at Albany.*

xx

VORWORT

Die Übersetzung der erklärenden Paragraphen besorgte
Frau Karin Isernhagen, Würzburg. Das druckfertige Manuskript
des Handbuchs wurde von Frau Marcella Curtright, Carson,
California, hergestellt.

CATEGORIES FOR THE CLASSIFICATION OF ARCHIVE MATERIALS

KATEGORIEN FÜR DIE EINTEILUNG DER ARCHIV-MATERIALIEN

A. Autobiographical/*Autobiographisches*

    1. Diaries/*Tagebücher*
    2. Notebooks/*Notizbücher*
    3. Autobiographies, autobiographical writings of various kinds/*Autobiographien, autobiographische Dokumente verschiedener Art*

B. Correspondence/*Briefwechsel*

    1. Letters from e.g. Werfel/*Briefe von z.B. Werfel*
    2. Letters to e.g. Werfel/*Briefe an z.B. Werfel*
    3. Third-party letters/*Briefe Dritter*

C. Primary literature/*Primärliteratur*

    1. Novels/*Romane*
    2. Dramas/*Dramen*
    3. Poetry/*Gedichte*
    4. Short fiction/*kürzere Prosadichtung*
    5. Screen plays (film)/*Drehbücher*
    6. Radio plays/*Hörspiele*
    7. Essayistic/*Essayistisches*
    8. Scientific studies/*Wissenschaftliche Studien*
    9. Translations and adaptations of works by other authors/*Übersetzungen oder Bearbeitungen von Werken anderer Autoren*
    10. Political writings/*Politische Schriften*
    11. Biographies and monographs/*Biographien u. Monographien*
    12. Playscripts/*Regiebücher*
    13. Musical manuscripts/*Noten*
        a. Original compositions/*Original-Kompositionen*
        b. Adaptations or orchestrations of the works of others/*Bearbeitungen oder Orchestrierungen der Kompositionen anderer*
        c. Scores by others (with notations by the composer in question)/*Partituren anderer (mit Anmerkungen von z.B. Busch)*
    14. Drawings, sketches/*Zeichnungen*

D. Printed material (from newspapers and magazines)/*Gedrucktes (aus Zeitungen und Zeitschriften)*

CATEGORIES FOR THE CLASSIFICATION OF ARCHIVE MATERIALS

KATEGORIEN FÜR DIE EINTEILUNG DER ARCHIV-MATERIALIEN

1.-11., 13. und 14. according to the pattern of category C/*nach dem Muster von C*

12. Edited newspapers, magazines, etc./*Herausgegebene Zeitungen, Zeitschriften, usw.*

E. Adaptations (by others)/*Bearbeitungen (durch andere)*

F. Tapes, records/*Tonbänder, Schallplatten*

G. Interviews/*Interviews*

H. Secondary literature/*Sekundärliteratur*

1. Books/*Bücher*
2. Sections of books/*Buchbeiträge*
3. Newspaper and magazine articles/*Zeitschriften- und Zeitungsartikel*
4. Reviews of single works/*Rezensionen einzelner Werke*
5. Unpublished secondary literature/*Unveröffentlichte Sekundärliteratur*

I. Documents/*Dokumente*

J. Photographs/*Photographien*

K. Description of personal library, if intact/*Beschreibung der Bibliothek, falls noch erhalten*

L. Collections of materials used by the author/*Materialsammlungen des Autors*

M. Memorabilia/*Memorabilia*

N. Manuscripts of others in the collection/*Manuskripte anderer in der Sammlung*

O. Programs, posters/*Programme, Plakate*

ABBREVIATIONS / *ABKÜRZUNGEN*

A.	autograph/*Autograf*
Aug.	August/*August*
B.	archive box(es)/*Archivkarton(s)*
c.	copy(ies)/*Kopie(n)*
ca.	circa, approximately/*etwa, ungefähr*
cc.	carbon copy(ies)/*Durchschlag(¨e)*
chap.	chapter(s)/*Kapitel*
cl.	clipping(s)/*Zeitungs- oder Zeitschriftenausschnitt(e)*
cm	centimeter/*Zentimeter*
corr.	corrections/*Korrekturen*
D.C.	District of Columbia
Dec./*Dez.*	December/*Dezember*
E.	east/*ost*
ea.	each/*jeder*
ed.	edition, edited/*Auflage, herausgegeben*
F.	file folder(s)/*Ordner*
Feb.	February/*Februar*
ft.	foot(feet)/*ca. 30 cm.*
h.	handwritten/*handgeschrieben*
in.	inch/*ca. 2,5 cm.*
Jan.	January/*Januar*
L.	letter(s)/*Brief(e)*
m	meter/*Meter*
mimeo.	mimeographed/*hektographiert*
Ms.	manuscript(s)/*Manuskript(e)*
N.	north/*nord*
N.Y.	New York State
no.	number/*Nummer*

ABBREVIATIONS / *ABKÜRZUNGEN*

Nov.	November/*November*
Oct./*Okt.*	October/*Oktober*
Op.	opus/*Opus*
p.	page(s)/*Seite(n)*
pc.	photocopy(ies)/*Fotokopie(n)*
Prof.	professor/*Professor*
Ptc.	postcard(s)/*Postkarte(n)*
pub.	published/*veröffentlicht*
rev.	revised, revisions/überarbeitet, *Überarbeitungen*
S.	south/*süd*
Sept.	September/*September*
St.	Saint/*Sankt*
T.	typescript(s)/*Typoskript(e)*
Tel.	telegram(s)/*Telegramm(e)*
tr.	translated, translation/übersetzt, *Übersetzung*
U.N.	United Nations/*Vereinigte Nationen*
Univ.	university/*Universität*
unpub.	unpublished/*unveröffentlicht*
U.S.(A.)	United States (of America)/*Vereinigte Staaten*
W.	west/*west*
*	exact description of materials in question un-unavailable as of 1977/*eine genaue Beschreibung der Materialien war bis 1977 nicht erhältlich.*

REPORTS ON INDIVIDUALS IN ALPHABETICAL ORDER OF NAMES

BERICHTE ÜBER PERSONEN IN ALPHABETISCHER

REIHENFOLGE DER NAMEN

THEODOR W. ADORNO

Social Scientist, 1903-1969

Harvard University, Houghton Library, Cambridge, Massachusetts 02138.

LEO LOWENTHAL COLLECTION (bMS Ger 185): accessible only with the permission of Prof. Leo Lowenthal (Department of Sociology, University of California, Berkeley, California 94720). Otherwise closed until Dec. 31, 1998.

LEO LOWENTHAL COLLECTION (bMS Ger 185): zugänglich nur mit persönlicher Erlaubnis von Prof. Leo Lowenthal (Department of Sociology, University of California, Berkeley, California 94720). Im übrigen ist die Sammlung bis zum 31. Dez. 1998 gesperrt.

B1   149 L. 1935-1955, among them L. to: Max Horkheimer, Marie Jahoda, Paul Lazarsfeld, Leo Lowenthal, Friedrich Pollock.

B2   114 L. 1936-1955, among them L. from: Max Horkheimer, Leo Lowenthal, Friedrich Pollock.

C7   Introduction to "Prophets of Deceit." 1949. T.cc. 7p.

Leo Baeck Institute, 129 East 73rd Street, New York, N.Y. 10021.

B1,2 Unknown amount of correspondence with Leon Zeitlin.

D7   "Gedenkrede auf Theodor Heuss." 1 cl.

H3   1 cl. 1963.

H4   Jean Amery. "Anthropologie des Homo Faber." 1 cl.

J   3 photos of Adorno. 1966.

Southern Illinois University, Morris Library, Department of Special Collections, Carbondale, Illinois 62901.

ERWIN PISCATOR PAPERS

B1   1 L. to Piscator. 1963.

B2   3 L. from Piscator. 1963-1965. cc.

Harvard University, Harvard Divinity School, Andover-Harvard Theological Library, 45 Francis Avenue, Cambridge, Massachusetts 02138.

PAUL TILLICH COLLECTION

B1   1 L. to Paul Tillich. 1964.
      1 L. to Hannah Tillich. 1965.
B2   1 L. from Paul Tillich. 1964.

New York Public Library, Manuscript Division, Fifth Avenue and 42nd Street, New York, N.Y. 10018.

MAX WERTHEIMER PAPERS

C7   Essay on social psychology.

State University of New York at Albany, Department of Germanic Languages and Literatures, 1400 Washington Avenue, Albany, New York 12222.

KARL O. PAETEL COLLECTION

B1   1 L. to Paetel (xerox). 1952.

Dr. Friedrich J. Hacker, The Hacker Clinic, 160 Lasky Drive, Beverly Hills, California 90212.

B1,2 Correspondence between Friedrich Hacker and Adorno. 1963-1969.
C7   "The Stars Down to Earth." 20p.

Prof. Herbert Marcuse, Department of Philosophy, University of California San Diego, La Jolla, California 92037.

THEODOR W. ADORNO

B1,2   Lengthy correspondence between Adorno and Herbert
        Marcuse. Up to 1969.

H3   Marcuse, Herbert. "Nachruf auf Adorno." T. 4p.

University of Pennsylvania, The Charles Patterson Van Pelt
Library, Philadelphia, Pennsylvania 19104.

ALMA MAHLER-WERFEL COLLECTION

B1   1 L. and 1 short L. with poem to Alma Mahler-Werfel.
        A. 1925.

B2   Notes to a L. from Alma Mahler-Werfel.

Library of Congress, Manuscript Division, Independence Avenue
and First Street S.E., Washington, D.C. 20540.

HANNAH ARENDT PAPERS

B1,2   Unknown amount of correspondence between Arendt and
        Adorno.

ANNI ALBERS
Artist, Textile Designer, 1899-

<u>Archives of American Art</u>, Smithsonian Institution, National Collection of Fine Arts and National Portrait Gallery Building, Eighth and F Streets N.W., Washington, D.C. 20560. (Microfilms of collections are available in each of the branch locations: Boston, Massachusetts; New York, N.Y.; Detroit, Michigan; San Francisco, California.)

The ANNI ALBERS COLLECTION originated as a gift from Anni Albers in 1969 and consists of some 200 items in total.

Die ANNI ALBERS COLLECTION entstand aus einer Schenkung von Anni Albers im Jahre 1969 und besteht aus insgesamt etwa 200 Nummern.

D7   Articles by A. Albers. 1924-1969. Microfilm.

G   Interview with Anni Albers. 1968. Restricted.

H3   Articles about A. Albers. 1924-1969. Microfilm. Also articles concerning Bauhaus training, Black Mountain College weaving classes, and the history and function of weaving.

H4   Exhibition reviews and catalogs dating from the 1950s.

J   Photographs of her work, many used in her book <u>On Weaving</u>.

<u>Museum of Modern Art</u>, The Library, 11 West 53rd Street, New York, N.Y. 10019.

The ANNI ALBERS COLLECTION was received as a gift from Anni Albers and consists of 2 volumes of materials dating from 1933. Materials are readily available for study and reference purposes in the library.

Die ANNI ALBERS COLLECTION ist eine Schenkung von Anni Albers aus dem Jahre 1933 und besteht aus etwa 2 Bänden Material. Die Materialien sind für Forschungszwecke in der Bibliothek des Museums zugänglich.

D7   Articles, pamphlets.

H4   Exhibition catalogs.

ANNI ALBERS

<u>Yale University Library</u>, Manuscripts and Archives Research Room, 150 Sterling Memorial Library, New Haven, Connecticut 06520.

JOSEF ALBERS PAPERS

I   Certificate from the Philadelphia College of Art, June 8, 1962.

<u>State of North Carolina</u>, Department of Cultural Resources, Raleigh, North Carolina 27611.

BLACK MOUNTAIN COLLEGE ARCHIVES

I   "Hospitalization Anni Albers." Treasurer's file.

J   Portrait photo and 4 other photos of Anni Albers.

<u>Harvard University</u>, Houghton Library, Cambridge, Massachusetts 02138.

LYONEL FEININGER COLLECTION

B1   Several L. to Lyonel Feininger.

<u>Library of Congress</u>, Manuscript Division, Independence Avenue and First Street S.E., Washington, D.C. 20540.

PAPERS OF LUDWIG MIES VAN DER ROHE

B1,2 Correspondence with Ludwig Mies van der Rohe. 1949-1965.

JOSEF ALBERS

Painter, 1888-1976

<u>Yale University Library</u>, Manuscripts and Archives Research
Room, 150 Sterling Memorial Library, New Haven, Connecticut
06520.

JOSEF ALBERS. PAPERS AND MEMORABILIA. The major portion of
the collection was donated by Albers in 1960, with additional
materials donated by Albers in 1961, 1962 and 1963. Details
concerning access to the collection may be obtained from the
Yale University Library.

*JOSEF ALBERS. PAPERS AND MEMORABILIA. Der Hauptteil der
Sammlung ist eine Schenkung von Albers aus dem Jahre 1960;
zusätzliche kleinere Schenkungen, ebenfalls von Albers, stam-
men aus den Jahren 1961, 1962 und 1963. Auskünfte über den
Zugang zu dieser Sammlung können von der Yale University
Library eingeholt werden.*

A3   "Comments on my work." 83p.
B1   Christmas cards, 1950-1959.
      13 L. 1934-1953, among them L. to Lyonel Feininger and
      Piet Mondrian (cc.).
B1,2 Arp, Hans (Jean) and S. H. Arp-Tauber. L. 1933-1957.
      22p. + several rough drafts of L. by Albers.
      Black Mountain College. L. 1933-1934. 45p.
      Gropius, Walter and family. L. 1933-1950.
      Harvard University. L. 1936-1942, including L. to and
      from: Joseph Hudnut, Robert Field, Walter Gropius.
      89p.
B2   104 L. 1929-1958, including L. from: W. Kandinsky,
      Paul Klee, Lyonel Feininger, Willi Baumeister,
      László Moholy-Nagy, Kurt and Helma Schwitters, Piet
      Mondrian, and Thornton Wilder.
C7   Statements and formulations by Albers. T. 80p.
      "Erziehung zum Schöpfersein." Ms. of lecture. Prag,
      1928.
      2 lecture texts. Havana, Cuba, 1934 and 1935. German
      and Spanish texts.
      Talks at Black Mountain College, etc. May 1935 - July
      1946:
      American Federation of Arts, Annual Convention, May
      20-22, 1935. T. 3p.

6

"Abstract Art." Asheville, Aug. 1935. T. 4p. + cc.
Black Mountain College, Sept. 7, 1936. T. 2p.
"Conceiving Art Education." Black Mountain College,
Bulletin, No. 2, June 1934. 8p. + cc. Draft in Ger-
man. T. 5p. First draft with title: "Art Instruction
as Creative Education." 6p. + cc.
"A Second Foreword." Black Mountain College. T. 10p.
Black Mountain College luncheon. Harvard Faculty
Club, April 29, 1938. T. 10p.
"Continuations of the Bauhaus in the U.S.A.: Black
Mountain College." Sept. 1938. T. 9p.
Black Mountain College luncheon. Cosmopolitan Club,
N.Y., Dec. 9, 1938. "Last copy." T. 6p.
"Concerning Abstract Art." Speech. April 1939.
Greensboro, North Carolina, May 1939; Charlotte,
North Carolina, Feb. 1940. T. 11p.
Black Mountain College. First general meeting. Sept.
12, 1939. T. 5p.
"On Stage Design." Black Mountain College, Sept. 27,
1939. T. 5p.
"On Education and Art Education." Winnetka, Illinois,
Nov. 28, 1939. T. 11p. Excerpts. T. 5p.
Black Mountain College tea. Cambridge, Massachusetts,
Dec. 15, 1939. 2p. + cc.
"Art Instruction at Black Mountain College." Jan.
1940. 5p.
Black Mountain College meeting. Museum of Modern Art,
N.Y., Jan. 9, 1940. Mimeo. 5p.
"The Meaning of Art." Black Mountain College, May 6,
1940. 12p.
Alber's answer to questionnaire on value of art muse-
ums, from Rhode Island School of Design, April 1940.
T. and mimeo. 2p.
Black Mountain College. Statement for Design Class,
Jan. 1941. T. 4p.
Black Mountain College. New York City meeting, June
12, 1940. T. 9p. T. and A. 11p. Mimeo. 7p.
Black Mountain College. Speech for general meeting.
Sept. 22, 1941. T. 5p.
Remarks at funeral services for Mark Dreier. Oct.
1941. T. 4p.
Black Mountain College. New York City meetings, Jan.
5, 10-12, 1942. T. 8p. Annotations. A. 1p.

"Some Afterthoughts to the Meeting on Friday, 21 May 1943. To the Publicity Committee for information only, not for publication." T. 2p.
Office of War Information. Radio speech. Asheville, March 13, 1944. T. 3p. German, annotated. T. 3p.
Black Mountain College. Talk given at the opening of the new music room. June 8, 1945. T. 3p.
Black Mountain College. Speech at general meeting. July 4, 1945. T. 2p.
"Tradition and Experiment in Contemporary Art." Paper used in panel discussion. Women's College, Greensboro, North Carolina, summer 1945. T. 10p. (2c.). Revised draft. T. 10p.
"On Education." Black Mountain College, first general meeting, Oct. 6, 1945. T. 3p.
"Art at Black Mountain College." Written Dec.-Jan. 1945-1946, for Junior Bazaar. T. 4p.
"On General Education and Art Education." Denver Art Museum, July 1946. T. 28p.
"Abstract—Presentational." American Abstract Artists, Yearbook 1946. T. 3p.
Black Mountain College. Newsletter, Sept. 1946. T. 5p.
"Photos as Photography and Photos as Art." T. 10p.
"Fundamental Design of Today." Museum of Modern Art, New York City, July 16-22, 1941. T. 43p.
"Truthfulness in Art." Harvard Graduate School of Design, ca. 1937-1938. T. 11p.

D7   Offprints, cl., magazines containing articles by Albers.

D14   Numerous cover designs, reproductions of Albers' works and sketches.

H3,4 Magazine containing articles by Albers or reproductions of his works. 1930s-1960s. 7.5 archive boxes.
      Cl. of articles by Albers or reproductions of his works. Ca. 170p. 1 archive box.

H4   Catalogs of Albers exhibits. 1 archive box.

I   Documents re: closing of Bauhaus in Berlin. 10p.
      Yale University School of Art, Department of Design. Annual reports to President of the University, 1951-1958. 2 sets.

Univ. of Hartford. D.F.A. Diploma, June 8, 1958.
Universidad Católica de Chile. Diploma as Miembro
Académico, Aug. 19, 1953.
Yale University. Diploma. Master of Arts in privatim,
Oct. 9, 1950.
Bundesrepublik Deutschland. Certificate for the Ver-
dienstkreuz Erster Klasse. Oct. 17, 1957.
Landschaftsverband Westfalen-Lippe. Certificate for
the Conrad-von-Soest Preis. Jan. 10, 1959.
Diploma: Ehrenurkunde der Preußischen Staatsregierung,
1931.
Dessau. Magistrate's certificate. Dec. 24, 1932. Pc.
Family legal documents and L., family tree of Albers
family, etc.
"Early Weimar Years." Papers from the Weimar Bauhaus,
1921-1925, including L. and documents signed by
Gropius.
"Closing of Bauhaus Dessau." Documents, notes, L.
1932-1933.
"Breaking of Contract with City of Dessau." Notes, L.
and documents, 1933.
Yale career of Albers. L., records of departmental
chairmanship, annual reports, etc.
Yale University. Honorary degree, 1962.
Citation for J. Albers. Philadelphia Museum College of
Art, June 8, 1962.
Citation for A. Albers. Philadelphia Museum College of
Art, June 8, 1962.

K   20 books from Albers' personal library, including 4
with sections by Albers and 2 collections of Albers'
drawings.

L   General exhibition catalogs. 3.5 archive boxes.
Black Mountain College materials, 1933-1947. 1/2 archive box.

M   Medal, engraved: Josef Albers, 1957. Exhibition Contemporary Oil Paintings. The Corcoran Gallery of Art.

Archives of American Art, Smithsonian Institution, National
Collection of Fine Arts and National Portrait Gallery Build-
ing, Eighth and F Streets N.W., Washington, D.C. 20560.
(Microfilms of collections are available in each of the

branch locations: Boston, Massachusetts; New York, N.Y.;
Detroit, Michigan; San Francisco, California.)

The JOSEF ALBERS COLLECTION consists of approximately 400
items, donated by Anni Albers in 1969.

*Die JOSEF ALBERS COLLECTION umfaßt etwa 400 Nummern und ist
eine Schenkung von Anni Albers aus dem Jahre 1969.*

B1   L. to Archives of American Art. [1967-1970].
      L. to Neumann. A. 1933.

D3   Poetry of Albers from literary magazines.

D7   Critical articles by Albers.
      2 printed articles:
         "Concerning Art Instruction," Black Mountain College
            Bulletin (1934).
         "Art as Experience," Progressive Education (1935).

D14   Drawings by Albers in literary magazines.
      Reproductions in magazines of Albers works.

G   2 interviews with Josef Albers. 1968 and undated. Re-
         stricted. Permission required from Archives of Ameri-
         can Art.
      Interviews - from magazines.

H3   Articles re: Albers and the Bauhaus; Albers and Black
         Mountain College.
      2 articles about Albers.
      "Articles from various sources."
      Selective bibliographies of critical materials by and
         about Albers.

H4   Catalogs of Albers exhibitions, in many languages,
         some with introductions by Albers.
      Exhibition catalog [1967-1970].

I   Press release.

J   Photos of Albers taken by Henri Cartier-Bresson. 1968.
      Photo, before a square painting. 1952.

Albers materials located in other collections of the Archives
of American Art: AMERICAN ABSTRACT ARTISTS PAPERS, 1936-1959,

JOSEF ALBERS

ARTISTS GALLERY COLLECTION, JAMES BROOKS PAPERS, RAYMOND
JONSON PAPERS, MICHAEL LOEW PAPERS, ALICE TRUMBALL MASON
PAPERS, J. B. NEUMANN PAPERS, ARNOLD NEWMAN PAPERS, RECORDS
OF BLACK MOUNTAIN COLLEGE, ELSA SCHMID PAPERS, ESPHYR SLO-
BODKINA PAPERS, HARRIS STEINBERG PAPERS.

*Albers Materialien befinden sich in folgenden anderen Samm-
lungen der Archives of American Art: AMERICAN ABSTRACT ART-
ISTS PAPERS, 1936-1959, ARTISTS GALLERY COLLECTION, JAMES
BROOKS PAPERS, RAYMOND JONSON PAPERS, MICHAEL LOEW PAPERS,
ALICE TRUMBALL MASON PAPERS, J. B. NEUMANN PAPERS, ARNOLD
NEWMAN PAPERS, RECORDS OF BLACK MOUNTAIN COLLEGE, ELSA SCHMID
PAPERS, ESPHYR SLOBODKINA PAPERS, HARRIS STEINBERG PAPERS.*

B1   40 L. to J. B. Neumann. 1934-1947. Also 1 article
about Albers. (Xerox c. - originals in Brooklyn
Museum.)
L. in various collections by Albers. 1938-1947 and
undated, including L. to: Frederike Beer, James
Brooks, Michael Loew, Alice Trumball Mason, Elsa
Schmid, Hugh Stix.

B1,2 Correspondence with Raymond Jonson. 1937-1964.

B1,2 Microfilm of Josef Albers file from Black Mountain
I,   College Archive. 1933-1956. See description under
J   State of North Carolina, Department of Cultural
Resources.

B3   Several L. re: Albers' work.

C7   Speech on Black Mountain College. 1938. T. 6p.

D14   "Composure." Reproduction.

H3   Biographical data.
5 articles about Albers.
2 cl. of articles about Albers.
"Paintings by J. A."

H4   5 evaluations of Albers' work by 5 different individuals.
Catalogs concerning Albers' work.

I   "Data" file.
Invitation to Gallery Show. 1938.

JOSEF ALBERS

J   1 photo of a Josef Albers work.
1 photo of Josef Albers.

Museum of Modern Art, The Library, 11 West 53rd Street, New York, N.Y. 10019.

The JOSEF ALBERS COLLECTION, donated by Albers himself, consists of 9 volumes plus assorted miscellaneous materials. The materials are readily available for study and reference purposes in the Library.

Die JOSEF ALBERS COLLECTION, eine Schenkung von Albers selbst, besteht aus 9 Bänden sowie diversen vermischten Materialien. Diese Materialien können zu Studienzwecken jederzeit in der Bibliothek eingesehen werden.

B2   Invitations.

H4   4 volumes of cl. (programs, announcements, reviews) in Italian, English, Spanish, German:
1933-1940
1941-1949
1949-1950
1952-1954
1 volume of catalogs. 1929-1950.
4 volumes of catalogs of additional exhibitions.

J   Photos. Bauhaus faculty and others.

CURT VALENTIN PAPERS were a gift to the MOMA Library by the art dealer's Estate. Restricted Archive: Requirements for access upon written application to the Museum of Modern Art.

Die CURT VALENTIN PAPERS sind ein Geschenk an die MOMA-Bibliothek aus dem Nachlaß des Kunsthändlers; das Museum of Modern Art teilt auf schriftliche Anfrage mit, unter welchen Bedingungen die Papers eingesehen werden können.

B1   3 L. to Curt Valentin. A. 1946-1947.

B2   7 L. from Curt Valentin. T.c. 1946-1947.

JOSEF ALBERS

HANS RICHTER ARCHIVE: Written permission to use the Archive
is required in advance of visits to the Museum.

*HANS RICHTER ARCHIVE: Dieses Archiv kann nur mit vorher ein-
geholter schriftlicher Genehmigung eingesehen werden.*

B1   2 L. to Hans Richter. 1950 and undated.

State of North Carolina, Department of Cultural Resources,
Raleigh, North Carolina 27611.

BLACK MOUNTAIN COLLEGE ARCHIVES

B1,2   Correspondence, materials, re: Black Mountain College
       project undertaken by State of North Carolina with
       NEA. Access restricted.

I   "Josef Albers - Personal Sabbatical." Faculty file.
       "Summer Art Institute - 1946 - Albers." General file.

J   Photos, portraits, in classes, with students.
       Interior of room designed by Albers.
       Interior of Albers' living room.

Brooklyn Museum, Department of Prints and Drawings, Eastern
Parkway, Brooklyn, New York 11238.

A3   Technical notes by Albers, introduction, etc. to a
       monograph on his prints, prepared by the Museum
       (American Graphic Artists of the Twentieth Century,
       1973). 84p.

B1   13 L. to Brooklyn Museum. 1959-1973.

B2   24 L. from Brooklyn Museum. 1959-1973. Cc.

Library of Congress, Manuscript Division, Independence Avenue
and First Street S.E., Washington, D.C. 20540.

PAPERS OF LUDWIG MIES VAN DER ROHE

B1,2   Correspondence with Ludwig Mies van der Rohe. 1949-1965.

JOSEF ALBERS

Dr. Karl With, 3045 Kelton Avenue, Los Angeles, California
90034.

B1   Ca. 10 L. to Karl With. 1946-1950.

Flint Institute of Arts in the DeWaters Art Center, 1120 E.
Kearsley Street, Flint, Michigan 48503.

B1   1 L. to Dr. G. Stuart Hodge. 1966.

Museum of Fine Arts, Department of Paintings, Boston, Massachusetts 02115.

B1   1 L. to Mrs. Giese, Dept. of Paintings. 1967.
      2 L. to Boston Museum. 1967.

Harvard University, Houghton Library, Cambridge, Massachusetts 02138.

LYONEL FEININGER COLLECTION

B1   1 L. to Lyonel Feininger. 1952.

University of Texas, Humanities Research Center, Manuscripts
Collection, Box 7219, Austin, Texas 78712.

B2   1 L.

MARTHA ALBRAND

Suspense Writer, 1914-

Ms. Martha Albrand, 953 Fifth Avenue, New York, N.Y. 10021.

Private collection. / *Privatsammlung der Autorin.*

C1   Manuscripts (many ft.), primarily of published novels;
       also some manuscripts of unpublished works.

F   2-3 tapes.

G   Interviews. 1942-present.

H3   Cl. on Martha Albrand.

H4   Reviews of Martha Albrand's works.

J   Photos. 1930s-present.

K   Private personal library.

Boston University, Mugar Memorial Library, 771 Commonwealth
Avenue, Boston, Massachusetts 02215.

The major portion of the MARTHA ALBRAND COLLECTION was donated
by Ms. Albrand in 1968, with additional smaller amounts being
added to the collection in 1970 and 1973.

*Der größte Teil der MARTHA ALBRAND COLLECTION wurde 1968 von
Frau Albrand gestiftet. 1970 und 1973 wurde die Sammlung jeweils geringfügig vergrößert.*

B2   3 L. with accompanying T. from: Lucien Burstein (9p.)
      and "David" (7p.).

Cl   A Call from Austria. Novel, 1963. "Part of work." T.cc.
      with h. corr. 121p. "2/3 of original." T. with h.
      corr. 259p. A. 47p. "Final." T.cc. 207p.
      A Day in Monte Carlo. Novel, 1959. T.cc. with h. corr.
      173p.
      A Door Fell Shut. Novel, 1966. "Final." T. 258p. "Print-
      er's copy." T. and pc.,ea. 277p. 1 set of page proofs.
      And Gently Floweth the Rhine. Novel, 1969. "Original."
      T. with h. corr. 402p. A. 61p. "Working copy." T.
      with h. corr. 273p. A. 20p. Another copy. T. with h.
      corr. 264p. A. 5p.

The Ball. Novel, 1961. "Work on Ball." T.cc. with h.
corr. 150p. A. 24p. Another copy. T. with h. corr.
302p.
The Linden Affair. Novel, 1956. "Munich." T. with h.
corr. 23p. Affaire Linden. By Katrin Holland (pseu-
donym). German. T. 192p.
Manhattan North. Novel, 1971. T. pc. with h. corr. 230p.
T. pc. with additional h. corr. 230p.
The Mask of Alexander. Novel, 1955. T.cc. with h. corr.
219p.
Meet Me Tonight. Novel. "Original." 2 versions. T. with
h. corr. 143p. T.cc. 123p. "Final." T.cc. 173p.
"Original German translation." T. with h. corr. 275p.
"Final German translation." T.cc. 174p.
The Obsession of Emmet Booth. Novel, 1959. T.cc. with
h. corr. 258p.
Rhine Replica. Novel, 1969. "Setting copy." T. and pc.
6p. T. pc. with some h. corr. 264p. "1st 100 pages...
for jkt artist." T. pc. 100p. Layouts of title p.,
chap. headings, page design. 4p. Marked page proofs.
A Sudden Woman. Novel by Christine Lambert (pseudonym),
1963. "Original." T. with h. corr. 458p. A. 16p.
"Original changes." T.cc. with h. corr. 363p. A. 15p.
"Copy I." T.cc. with h. corr. 277p. A. 4p. "Partly
corrected work." T.cc. with h. corr. 465p. A. 5p.
"Final." T.cc. 275p. T. with printer's marks. 275p.
2 sets of page proofs.
Without Orders. Novel, 1943. T. pc. with h. corr. 258p.

C4   "Count Septimus and the Colonel." Short story, pub.
1947 in Town and Country. T.cc. 24p.
"London Fog." Short story, pub. in Town and Country. T.
cc. 22p.

C5   Desperate Hours. "Corrections." T.cc. 55p. "First draft
script." Mimeo. 125p. "Final." Mimeo. 119p.

C7   "Questions to Ned." A. 1p.
"Page 1, I..." Corr. to a Ms. T. and cc., ea. 2p.

D1   55 different editions of Albrand novels in 10 different
languages:
A Call from Austria. English.
A Day in Monte Carlo. German, English.
A Door Fell Shut. Danish, English.

16

MARTHA ALBRAND

A Sudden Woman. English, French.
After Midnight. English, French.
The Ball. English.
Desperate Moment. Belgian, German, English.
Ein Bild seiner Zeit. German.
The Hunted Woman. Belgian, English, Danish, Swiss.
Inferno. Portuguese, Swiss.
The Linden Affair. English, Swiss.
The Mask of Alexander. Belgian, English, Italian.
Nightmare in Copenhagen. Danish, English.
No Surrender. English.
None Shall Know. English.
The Other Side of the Moon. Condensed version in
    Ladies Home Journal (May 1947). English.
The Other Side of the Moon/Whispering Hill. German,
    Italian, Norwegian, Swiss.
Remembered Anger. Danish, English.
Romp les tiens. French.
Wait for Dawn. English, Swiss.
Without Orders. English.

D4   "Nightmare in Copenhagen." Tearsheets. John Bull, July
      3, 1954.
      "Remembered Anger." First of a 6-part serial. Austra-
      lasian, Feb. 16, 1946.

Academy of Motion Picture Arts and Sciences, Margaret Herrick
Library, 9038 Melrose Avenue, Hollywood, California 90069.

C5   Captain Carey, U.S.A. 1950. 2 F.

State University of New York at Albany, Department of Germanic Languages and Literatures, 1400 Washington Avenue,
Albany, New York 12222.

A3   Short autobiography. 1976. T. 5p.
      Bibliography prepared by Martha Albrand.

GÜNTHER ANDERS

Writer, 1902-

The major collection of archival materials by and about
Günther Anders is located at the author's home in Vienna.
Smaller amounts of materials, however, are to be found in
collections of other prominent individuals in libraries and
in private hands in the U.S.

*Der Hauptteil des Archivmaterials von und über Günther Anders
befindet sich in der Privatwohnung des Autors in Wien. Daneben finden sich jedoch in den U.S.A.—in Bibliotheken wie
auch in privater Hand—kleinere Mengen Materials in den Sammlungen berühmter Persönlichkeiten.*

<u>State University of New York at Albany</u>, Department of Germanic
Languages and Literatures, 1400 Washington Avenue, Albany, New
York 12222.

The ANDERS/BUDZISLAWSKI CORRESPONDENCE, ca. 90 items, was
donated by Mrs. Erna Budzislawski in March 1976.

*Die ANDERS/BUDZISLAWSKI CORRESPONDENCE, etwa 90 Nummern, ist
eine Schenkung von Frau Erna Budzislawski (März 1976).*

B1   53 L. and Ptc. from Günther and Charlotte Anders to
        Erna Budzislawski. 1955-1971.

B1,2   Transcriptions of correspondence between Günther Anders
        and Claude Eatherly. 5 L. (including tr. of 1 L. into
        German). 1959. Also 1 cl.

B2   32 L. from Erna Budzislawski to Günther and Charlotte
        Anders. 1959-1976.

B3   1 L. to Erna Budzislawski re: Günther Anders.

STORM PUBLISHERS ARCHIVE, KARL O. PAETEL COLLECTION

B1   2 L. to Alexander Gode von Aesch. 1948.
        1 L. to K. Paetel (xerox). 1946.

B2   1 L. from Alexander Gode von Aesch. 1948.

<u>Boston University</u>, Mugar Memorial Library, 771 Commonwealth

Avenue, Boston, Massachusetts 02215.

MENACHEM ARNONI PAPERS

B1   20 L. to Menachem Arnoni. 1963-1964.

B2   25 L. from Menachem Arnoni. 1963-1964.

C7   "We - the Sons of Eichmann." T. 10p.

H3   "Approved Killing in Mississippi," Look, Jan. 24, 1956.

Yale University, Beinecke Rare Book and Manuscript Library, New Haven, Connecticut 06520.

HERMANN BROCH ARCHIVE

B1   7 L. to Hermann Broch. 1947-1950.

University of Southern California, Lion Feuchtwanger Memorial Library, 520 Paseo Miramar, Pacific Palisades, California 90272.

B1   10 L. to Lion Feuchtwanger. 1941-1952.

B2   7 L. from Lion Feuchtwanger. 1941-1952.

Library of Congress, Manuscript Division, Independence Avenue and First Street S.E., Washington, D.C. 20540.

PAPERS OF SIEGFRIED BERNFELD, HANNAH ARENDT PAPERS

B1,2 Correspondence with Siegfried Bernfeld. 1937-1941.
      Unknown amount of correspondence with Hannah Arendt.

Southern Illinois University, Morris Library, Department of Special Collections, Carbondale, Illinois 62901.

ERWIN PISCATOR PAPERS

B1   1 L. to Erwin Piscator. 1939.

Leo Baeck Institute, 129 East 73rd Street, New York, N.Y. 10021.

J   1 photo of Anders. Undated.

Harvard University, Harvard Divinity School, Andover-Harvard Theological Library, 45 Francis Avenue, Cambridge, Massachusetts 02138.

PAUL TILLICH COLLECTION

B1   4 L. to P. Tillich. 1958.

New York Public Library, Manuscript Division, Fifth Avenue and 42nd Street, New York, N.Y. 10018.

EMERGENCY COMMITTEE IN AID OF DISPLACED FOREIGN SCHOLARS, 1933-1945

*   File compiled, no assistance given.

Mrs. Peter M. Lindt, 949 West End Avenue, New York, N.Y. 10025.

B1   Small amount of correspondence with Peter M. Lindt.

Mrs. Alice Loewy Kahler, 1 Evelyn Place, Princeton, New Jersey 08540.

ERICH VON KAHLER COLLECTION

B1   5 L. to Erich von Kahler. 1947-1952.

HERBERT S. ANKER

Biochemist, 1912-1976

Mrs. Herbert Anker, c/o Dr. Erin Novick, 3960 Blanton Road,
Eugene, Oregon 97405; Dr. Don Steiner, University of Chicago,
Department of Biochemistry, 920 East 58th Street, Chicago,
Illinois 60637.

The papers of Herbert Anker consist of 2 large cartons of
materials with Mrs. Anker and an undetermined amount of materials at the Department of Biochemistry, University of Chicago.

*Zwei große Kartons mit Herbert Anker Materialien befinden
sich im Besitz von Frau Anker; eine weitere unbestimmte Menge
Materialien befindet sich im Department of Biochemistry der
University of Chicago.*

A3   Bibliography, curriculum vitae.

B1,2   Correspondence with colleagues, other scientists, stu-
       dents. Ca. 100 L.

B3   Condolence L. after Anker's death.

C7   Notes and files.

D7,8   Nearly complete collection of offprints by Anker.

J   Photos. 1940-. (Both with Mrs. Anker and the Depart-
       ment of Biochemistry.)

K   Personal library.

L,   Manuscripts and articles by others, collected and used
N   by Anker in his work.

HANNAH ARENDT

Political Scientist, 1906-1976

Library of Congress, Manuscript Division, Independence Avenue
and First Street S.E., Washington, D.C. 20540.

The literary estate of Hannah Arendt was transferred to the
Library of Congress in 1977. The materials will remain completely closed until 1980. After that time, permission for
use of the materials must be obtained from Ms. Mary McCarthy,
literary executor of the estate.
  The collection consists of over 1,400 files, plus files
on individuals. These materials include correspondence,
manuscripts (published and unpublished), and student files.
Correspondence includes universities and colleges, publish-
ing houses (German, American, university presses, etc.),
radio, as well as other institutions, organizations and
associations. Individuals represented in the files include
notables from a wide range of disciplines and other emigrés
such as T. W. Adorno, Erich von Kahler, Hans Morgenthau,
Günther Anders (Stern), Paul Tillich, and Kurt Wolff. There
is a preliminary, 50-page typed listing of the materials,
prepared prior to the transfer of materials to the Library
of Congress.
  The Center for Advanced Research in Phenomenology,
Wilfried Lauriet University, Waterloo, Ontario, Canada, is
receiving a microfilm of materials in the Arendt Papers of
interest to its work. Dr. Huertas-Jourda, Department of
Philosophy, Wilfried Lauriet University, may be contacted
for further information. Inquiries concerning the Hannah
Arendt literary estate may be addressed to Mary McCarthy,
c/o Dr. Lotte Kohler, Department of German, City College of
the City University of New York, Convent Avenue and West
138th Street, New York, N.Y. 10031, or to Dr. Kohler.
  The collection of materials described below (2,137
items), designated as the HANNAH ARENDT PAPERS, was donated
to the Library by Dr. Arendt in 1965, with further additions
to the collection having been made in 1966. Permission to
use these materials may be granted by the Library of Congress.

Der literarische Nachlaß von Hannah Arendt wurde der Library
of Congress im Jahre 1977 übergeben. Diese Materialien sind
bis 1980 unzugänglich. Danach können sie mit Erlaubnis der

HANNAH ARENDT

Verwalterin des literarischen Nachlasses, Ms. Mary McCarthy,
eingesehen werden. Die Sammlung besteht aus mehr als 1400 Ordnern sowie
Ordnern über einzelne Personen. Die Materialien umfassen
Korrespondenz, Manuskripte (veröffentlichte sowie unveröf-
fentlichte) und Mappen über Studenten. Der Korrespondenzteil
umfaßt Briefwechsel mit Universitäten und Colleges, Verlags-
häusern (amerikanischen und deutschen), University Presses,
Rundfunkanstalten sowie anderen Institutionen, Organisatio-
nen und Gesellschaften. Daneben sind auch eine Reihe be-
rühmter Persönlichkeiten aus vielen universitären Diszipli-
nen sowie andere Emigranten vertreten, z.B.: Th. W. Adorno,
Erich von Kahler, Hans Morgenthau, Günther Anders (Stern),
Paul Tillich und Kurt Wolff. Es existiert noch aus der Zeit
vor der Übergabe der Materialien an die Library of Congress
eine vorläufige, 50 Schreibmaschinenseiten umfassende Liste
der Materialien.

Das Center for Advanced Research in Phenomenology der
Wilfried Lauriet University, Waterloo, Ontario, Canada, er-
hält Mikrofilmaufnahmen solcher Arendt-Materialien, die für
die Arbeit dieses Instituts von Interesse sind. Dr. Huertas-
Jourda, Department of Philosophy, Wilfried Lauriet Univer-
sity, erteilt genauere Auskünfte über die Art dieser Mate-
rialien.

Anfragen in Bezug auf den literarischen Nachlaß von
Hannah Arendt mögen entweder direkt an Dr. Lotte Kohler,
Department of German, City College of the City University of
New York, Convent Avenue and West 138th Street, New York,
N.Y. 10031, oder an Mary McCarthy c/o Dr. Kohler gerichtet
werden.

Die im folgenden beschriebene Sammlung (2137 Nummern),
die HANNAH ARENDT PAPERS, wurde der Library of Congress 1965
als Schenkung von Dr. Hannah Arendt übergeben; 1966 wurde
die Sammlung weiter vergrößert. Zugang zu diesen Materia-
lien kann durch die Library of Congress gewahrt werden.

A2   Notebook. German. 1935.

B1,2   Ca. 50 L. to and from Judah L. Magnes (and the Judah
       L. Magnes Foundation). 1948-1960.

C7   Miscellaneous memoranda and rough drafts.
      Unpub. lectures and speeches:
      "The Future of Freedom."

"Brecht."
"Concern with Politics in Recent European Thought."
"Ideology and Propaganda."
"Rand School Lectures 1948-9."
"Crisis in Zionism 1943."
"Brooklyn College Lectures 1942."
"Karl Marx and the Tradition of Western Political
    Thought." 2 versions.
"Odd Papers - Christian Gauss lecture."
"Philosophy and Politics."
"Die Judenfrage." Notes.
"Die Menschen und der Terror." Notes for 9 lectures.
"Die Protokolle."
Ms. of pub. articles:
"The Difficulties of Understanding."
"Karl Jaspers: Citizen of the World."
"Europe's Image of America."
"The Ex-Communists."
"Foreign Affairs in the Foreign Language Press."
"Gestern waren sie noch Kommunisten."
"Religion and Politics."
"Action in the Pursuit of Happiness."
"Algiers and the Cremieux Law."
Aufbau-articles.
Varia.
Ms. of unpub. articles:
"Antisemitismus. Einführung in die Politik."
"On the Nature of Totalitarianism."
"The Eggs Speak Up."
"Die weisen Tiere."
"Jewish History."
"Zur Minderheitenfrage."

C10   Between Past and Future. First draft and final version.
      Elemente und Ursprünge der totalen Herrschaft. Frag-
      ment.
      On Revolution. First and final versions. 1 B.

C11   Eichmann in Jerusalem. Notes by the author. Final ver-
      sion with corr. Outline of German tr. Final version
      of German tr.

L   Materials concerning the Eichmann trial: newspaper cl.,
      documents, police records (testimonies of witnesses,

etc.), press releases, notes of Eichmann. 8 B.

<u>Leo Baeck Institute</u>, 129 East 73rd Street, New York, N.Y.
10021.

The materials that comprise the Institute's HANNAH ARENDT
COLLECTION (AR-Z.81, 254) were donated by Dr. Arendt. Other
newspaper clippings are located in the Institute's LEO BAECK
NACHLASS. There are also letters to and from the Leo Baeck
Institute now in its business files that will eventually be
turned over to the Archive.

*Die Materialien, die die HANNAH ARENDT COLLECTION des Leo
Baeck Instituts ausmachen (AR-Z.81, 254) sind eine Schenkung
von Frau Arendt selbst. Andere Zeitungsausschnitte finden
sich im LEO BAECK NACHLASS des Instituts. Des weitern existieren in den Geschäftsordnern Briefe vom Institut und an
das Institut. Diese Briefe werden später in das Archiv ein-
gehen.*

B1,2   "Ein Briefwechsel." Pub. correspondence between Hannah
        Arendt and Hans Magnus Enzensberger. 3p.

B2   1 L. from Kurt May. 1963. T. pc.

B3   2 L. re: <u>Eichmann</u> book. 1963.

C11   <u>Rahel Varnhagen von Ense</u>. Text. T. 82p. Appendix. T.
        and pc., ea. 32p.

D7   Review of Rolf Hochhuth's <u>The Deputy</u>. 1 cl.

H3   7 cl. 1958-1964.

H4   <u>Eichmann in Jerusalem</u>. Reviews. 23 cl. 1963-1964.
        <u>Eichmann in Jerusalem. A Report on the Banality of Evil</u>.
        124 cl. (some pc.). 1963-1964.
        <u>The Human Condition</u>. 1 cl. 1959.
        <u>On Revolution</u>. 3 cl. 1963-1964.
        <u>Rahel Varnhagen</u>. 22 cl. 1958-1960.

<u>Yale University</u>, Beinecke Rare Book and Manuscript Library,
New Haven, Connecticut 06520.

HERMANN BROCH ARCHIVE

B1   10 L. to Hermann Broch. 1946-1951.

B2   5 L. from Hermann Broch. 1946-1951.

Harvard University, Harvard Divinity School, Andover-Harvard
Theological Library, 45 Francis Avenue, Cambridge, Massachusetts 02138.

PAUL TILLICH COLLECTION

B1   1 L. and 1 Ptc. to Paul Tillich. 1946, 1964.
       1 Tel. to Hannah Tillich. 1965.

B2   1 L. from Paul Tillich. 1962.

I   2 "Gutachten": Paul Tillich. 1958; Karl Jaspers. 1955.

American Academy of Arts and Letters/National Institute of
Arts and Letters, 633 West 155th Street, New York, N.Y. 10032.

B1,2 1 F. of correspondence re: business of the American
       Academy and the National Institute of Arts and Let-
       ters.

State University of New York at Albany, Department of Germanic Languages and Literatures, 1400 Washington Avenue,
Albany, New York 12222.

KARL O. PAETEL COLLECTION

B1   3 L. to Karl O. Paetel (xerox). 1944, 1952, 1954.

B2   1 L. from Karl O. Paetel (xerox). 1961.

New York Public Library, Manuscript Division, Fifth Avenue
and 42nd Street, New York, N.Y. 10018.

EMERGENCY COMMITTEE IN AID OF DISPLACED FOREIGN SCHOLARS,
1933-1945

HANNAH ARENDT

*   File compiled, no assistance given. 1942-1944.

Columbia University, Butler Library, New York, N.Y. 10027.

B1   1 L. to Kyrill Schabert. T. 1961.

Boston University, Mugar Memorial Library, 771 Commonwealth Avenue, Boston, Massachusetts 02215.

EUGENE BURDICK PAPERS

B1   1 L. to Eugene Burdick. T. Undated.

Mrs. Liselotte Stein, 115-25 Metropolitan Avenue, Kew Gardens, New York 11418.

FRED STEIN PAPERS

J   Photos of Hannah Arendt.

University of Wyoming, Archive of Contemporary History, The Library, Box 3334, Laramie, Wyoming 82071.

ALFRED FARAU COLLECTION

H5   Farau, Alfred. Lecture text on Hannah Arendt.

RUDOLF ARNHEIM

Psychologist of Art, 1904-

Archives of American Art, Smithsonian Institution, National
Collection of Fine Arts and National Portrait Gallery Build-
ing, Eighth and F Streets N.W., Washington, D.C. 20560.
(Microfilms of collections are available in each of the
branch locations: Boston, Massachusetts; New York, N.Y.;
Detroit, Michigan; San Francisco, California.)

The RUDOLF ARNHEIM PAPERS 1948-1974 (ca. 1,200 items) were
donated to the Archives in 1974 and 1976 by Dr. Arnheim.

*Die RUDOLF ARNHEIM PAPERS 1948-1974 (etwa 1200 Nummern) sind
eine Schenkung von Dr. Arnheim aus den Jahren 1974 und 1976.*

B1,2   Correspondence and legal papers. 1932-1973. Ca. 1,100
I   items. Restricted.

C7   Manuscripts of longer works:
           The Depth Effect of Two Dimensional Figures. A.
           The Autobiography of a Work of Art, Picasso's Guer-
               nica. A.
           The Disorder of Entropy and the Order of Art. A.
       "Is Modern Art Necessary?" T.
       "Emotion and Feeling in Psychology and Art." T.
       "Accident and the Necessity of Art." T.
       8 book reviews by Arnheim.
       3 convocation addresses given at Sarah Lawrence Col-
           lege, New York, 1956, 1968, 1974.

D7   30 printed articles by Arnheim.

F   Tapes.

G   Printed conversation between Arnheim and James R.
           Petersen. 1972.

H4   "Inverted Perspective in Art." 1 review.

New York Public Library, Manuscript Division, Fifth Avenue
and 42nd Street, New York, N.Y. 10018.

MAX WERTHEIMER PAPERS, EMERGENCY COMMITTEE IN AID OF DIS-
PLACED FOREIGN SCHOLARS, 1933-1945

B1   1 L. to Max Wertheimer. A. 1941.

*   File compiled by the Emergency Committee, no assistance
      given. 1940-1941.

Yivo Institute, 1048 Fifth Avenue, New York, N.Y. 10028

HORACE M. KALLEN PAPERS

B1,2   1 F. of materials.

American Philosophical Society, The Library, 105 South Fifth
Street, Philadelphia, Pennsylvania 19106.

WOLFGANG KÖHLER PAPERS

B1,2   Correspondence between Wolfgang Köhler and Rudolf Arn-
       heim. 2 L. 1962.

Museum of Modern Art, The Library, 11 West 53rd Street, New
York, N.Y. 10019.

HANS RICHTER ARCHIVE: Written permission to use the Archive
is required in advance of visits to the Museum.

*HANS RICHTER ARCHIVE: Vorherige schriftliche Genehmigung zur
Einsichtnahme ist erforderlich.*

B1   L. concerning Hans Richter. [1958].

B2   1 L. from Hans Richter. 1958.

EMIL ARTIN

Mathematician, 1898-1963

<u>Mrs. Natasha Artin-Brunswick</u>, 7 Evelyn Place, Princeton, New
Jersey 08541; <u>Mr. John Tate</u>, 28 Arlington Street, Boston,
Massachusetts 02140; <u>Mr. Michael Artin</u>, 41 Hyde Street, New-
ton Highlands, Massachusetts 02161.

Upon his return to Germany in 1950, Artin took most of his
materials with him. These remained in Germany after his
death. The remaining materials are divided among Mrs. Artin,
Artin's son and son-in-law.

*Bei seiner Rückkehr nach Deutschland im Jahre 1950 nahm Emil
Artin den größten Teil seines Materials mit nach Deutschland,
wo es auch nach seinem Tode verblieb. Das übrige Material
ist unter Frau Natasha Artin-Brunswick, Artins Sohn und seinem Schwiegersohn aufgeteilt.*

B2   Several L. to Artin.

C7   Lecture notes.

D8   Reprints of Artin's works. 1920-.

H3   Japanese article about Artin.

I   Documents re: Artin's dismissal from his teaching post
       (in Germany).
       Miscellaneous other documents.

J   Photos with wife, Natasha, and children.

K   Partial library (divided between his son and son-in-
       law). Remainder of library returned with Artin to
       Germany.

L   Reprints of articles by others. Ca. 10 ft.

<u>New York University</u>, Courant Institute of Mathematical Sci-
ences, Library, 251 Mercer Street, New York, N.Y. 10012.

B1,2   [Faculty] file: "Emil Artin." 1935-1938.

L   Lecture notes by Artin's students from his lectures at
       the Institute.

RAOUL AUERNHEIMER

Writer, 1876-1948

<u>University of California at Riverside</u>, Riverside, California
92502.

In the course of trying to set the Auernheimer papers in
order after Auernheimer's death in 1948, his widow sent
numerous packages of manuscripts to the Wiener Stadtbiblio-
thek, where they were placed in the Handschriftensammlung.
The substantial portion of the Nachlaß that remained in the
United States (over 5 ft.) was donated by Mrs. Irene Auernheimer before her death in 1967 to the University of California at Riverside. Written permission to use the materials
in the RAOUL AUERNHEIMER ARCHIVE is required. Information
concerning the collection is obtainable from Dr. Donald
Daviau (Department of German, University of California at
Riverside).

*Bei der Ordnung des Nachlasses von Raoul Auernheimer nach
seinem Tode 1948 sandte seine Witwe eine größere Anzahl von
Manuskripten an die Wiener Staatsbibliothek, wo sie in die
Handschriftensammlung aufgenommen wurden. Ein erheblicher
Teil des Nachlasses (über 1,50 m), der in den U.S.A. blieb,
wurde von Frau Irene Auernheimer vor ihrem Tod im Jahre
1967 der University of California at Riverside vermacht.
Das Material des RAOUL AUERNHEIMER ARCHIVS darf nur mit
schriftlicher Genehmigung eingesehen werden. Auskünfte über
die Sammlung erteilt Dr. Donald Daviau (Department of German,
University of California at Riverside).*

A2   Aphorisms, poems, personal reflections, dedications of
        works, birthday and special occasion poetry, pos-
        sible titles for future works, quotations of famous
        authors. Many of the aphorisms were intended for
        the collection "Was ich sagen wollte," which was
        never completed and remains unpub.
        Sketches and outlines to a planned Lassalle biography,
        with several loose pages and library slips inserted.
        Collection of cl. (various subjects), aphorisms, poems,
        primarily in German, some in English. 1943-1946.

A3   <u>Between Two World Wars. Autobiography of a Background.</u>
        Outline and detailed explanation of autobiography,
        projected length 80,000 words. T. 5p.

"A Brief Chronicle of My Life up to 1933." T. 8p.
"Mit mir in Amerika." Auernheimer's New York experi-
ences from the year 1939.
"News of My Death." Essay. T. 3c., ea. 5p.
Das Wirtshaus zur verlorenen Zeit. Outline of auto-
biography, projected length 80,000-100,000 words.
T. 2p.
"Noch einmal jung sein. Erlebnisse und Bekenntnisse."
1st chap. of autobiography. T. 18p.

B1 184 L., 1933-1948, including L. to: Barthold Fles,
Felix Guggenheim, Franz J. Horch, Hans Kafka, Rudolph
Kommer, Erich W. Korngold, Henry B. Kranz, Fritz H.
Landshoff, Emil Ludwig, Georg Marton, Dorothy
Thompson.
Hugo von Hofmannsthal. 4 L. (microfilm). 1910-1925.
Arthur Schnitzler. 38 L. (microfilm). 1906-1931.

B2 306 L., including L. from: Gustave O. Arlt, Vicki
Baum, Richard Beer-Hofmann, Felix Guggenheim, Oskar
Jellinek, Rudolph Kommer, L. Konstantin, Henry B.
Kranz, F. H. Landshoff, Ernst Lothar, Emil Ludwig,
Heinrich Mann, Thomas Mann, William Melnitz, Hein-
rich Schnitzler, Cornelia Otis Skinner, Friedrich
Torberg, Siegfried Trebitsch, Ludwig Ullmann, Alma
Mahler-Werfel, Anton Wildgans, Friderike Zweig,
Stefan Zweig.
Literary agents and agencies. 31 L. 1941-1948.
Organizations. 40 L. 1941-1946.
Radio and film companies. 9 L. 1942-1944.
Publishers. 93 L. 1939-1945.

B3 Auernheimer, Mrs. Irene. 4 L. to.

C2 Großmutter Mirjam oder Eden entdeckt Amerika. Story
for the Associated Press. Ein historisches Lustspiel.
T. 94p.
The Merry Wives of Reno. "Comedy." Written in German.
T. 22p.
The Merry Wives of Reno. Entwurf einer Komödie. T. 15p.
Metternich. Eine Komödie mit einem Vorspiel und Nach-
spiel. Vorspiel. T. 10p. & p. 22-67 (p. 1-21 missing).
Graduate of Love. Comedy. English version of Metter-
nich. T. 78p.
Le Chevalier de l'Europe. Abrégé de Scènes. T. 3p.

Metternich. Entwurf eines Drehbuchs. T. 27p.
The Romantic Case of Countess Rosalie. Comedy. Outline.
   T. 5p.

C3   Poems by Auernheimer. 54 poems and 8 epigrams in verse,
      in German.

C4   "Das Abenteuer." Novelle. T. 11p.
      Anecdotes. T. 7p.
      Aphorisms. T. 12p.
      "Between Neighbors." Anecdote. T. 1p.
      "Die Brieftasche." Novelle. T. 9p.
      Epigrams. T. 6p.
      Miscellaneous short stories. A. & T. 459p.
      "Der Geheimniskrämer." With the notation "Copyright
        1933 by European Books Ltd. (London-Berlin-Vienna)."
        T. 20p.
      "Die Geschichte mit Ottavio. Aus den 'Untersuchungen
        über das Privatleben des jungen Don Juan'. Novelle."
        T. with short h. description of the story by Auern-
        heimer. 2c. 19p., 18p.
      "Glück bei Frauen. Novelle." T. 2c. 12p.
      "Der glückliche verheiratete Molière. Novelle." T. 20p.
      "Gräfin Rosalie. Novelle." T. 2c. 21p.
      "Der Herr, der bitterlich weinte. Novelle." T. 17p.
      "Der höfliche Artur. Novelle." T. 2c. 11p.
      "Inhalt: Briefe, Wert: 0. Novelle." T. 9p.
      "Der junge Don Juan. Novelle." T. 2c. 12p.
        "The Young Don Juan." English version. T. 11p.
      "Lauretta's Bekehrung. Novelle." T. 45p.
      "Der Leichenbestatter von Ebenbrunn. Novelle." T. 23p.
      "Die Locke. Novelle." T. 12p.
      "Die Locke der Berenike. Novelle." T. 19p.
      "The Merry Wives of Reno." Story. T. 29p.
      "Der Mörder Babinsky. Novelle." T. 25p.
      "Der Nagel. Novelle." T. 12p. A. 1p.
      "Pfeifer und Sohn. Novelle." T. 16p.
      "Der Pferdejunge. Novelle." 3c. A. 21p. T. 15p. T. 13p.
      "Das schuldbeladene Paar. Novelle." T. 33p.
      "Das Wachs der Odysseus. Novelle." T. 20p.
      "Der Wahnsinnige. Novelle." T. 13p.
      "Zwei Frauen in Mariazell. Novelle." T. 11p.
      "Zwei Schwestern. Novelle." T. 20p.

C5 Es war die Kaiserin. Komödie für den Film. 3c. T. 71p.,
57p. and 50p.
The Friend of Her Youth. Film version of his story
"Thank You Mrs. Brown." T. 56p.
Thank You Mrs. Brown. Film story. T. 38p. Outline.
1p.

C7 Essays. A. & T. 345p.
Feuilletons. T. 83p.
Speech texts. T. 219p.

C9 Der Misanthrop. Komödie in fünf Aufzügen von Molière.
In deutschen Versen von Raoul Auernheimer. T. 67p.
Stille Nachtmusik. Rough drafts of an adaptation of
Erich W. Korngold's Singspiel. With Auernheimer's
notation: "Fertiges Exemplar mit Partitur bei dem
Verleger Weinberger, Frankfurt a. M. Aufgeführt in
Dortmund und im Wiener Radio (Rawag)." T. 109p.
Act II, Scene 3. A. 19p.
Act III, Scene 6. T. English. 20p

C11 Der Dichter Österreichs. Chap. 1: "Schule der Armut."
T. 13p. Chap. 9: "Die Grille." T. 19p. Corr. T. 2p.
Ferdinand Lassalle. Der romantische Sozialist. Bio-
graphical essay. T. 2c. 30p.
"Ein Kind hat Nasenbluten." Original first chap. of
Ferdinand Lassalle. A. 25p.
"Die Erweckung." Original chap. 2 of Ferdinand Las-
salle. A. 25p.
Lassalle. Outline in German. T. 2c. 14p. Detailed
notes. A. 13p.
Two Men in One. The Life of Ferdinand Lassalle, the
Romantic Socialist. T. 2c. 16p., 14p.
The Hapsburgs. Essay. T. 3c. 2p., 7p., 9p.
To Be or Not to Be an Emperor. Biography of a Family.
Outline of 10 chap. T. 1p.
The Hapsburgs. The Biography of a Family and a Polit-
ical Idea. Outline of 6 chap. T. 1p.
Mutter und Sohn. [Maria Theresa and Kaiser Joseph].
2c. A. 40p. T. 30p. Rough chap. T. 6p.
Joseph II. A. 26p.
Kaiser Joseph. T. 16p.
Maximilian of Mexico. Victim of Politics. Outline of a
biography, projected length 80,000 words. T. 2p.
Prinz Metternich. Staatsmann und Kavalier. Biography.
A. 303p.

Prince Metternich. Statesman and Lover. English version of first 2 chap. T. 3c. 23p.
Metternich. Staatsmann und Lebenskünstler. Outline. T. 7p.
Metternich. Statesman and Artist in Living. Outline. T. 2c. 6p., 11p.
The Unspeakable Austrian. Life of Franz Grillparzer. Outline of a biography, projected length 80,000 words. T. 3p.
Chap. 1: "The Immortal Austrian." T. 2c. 10p, 11p.

D7   878 feuilletons, including an almost complete collection of his contributions in the Neue Freie Presse (825; 1899-1938) and a number in the Basler National-Zeitung (35; 1938-1948).

E   A Maid of Honor. Prentiss Gilbert's version of Auernheimer's comedy Der gute König. T. 3c. 81p.

G   "Question: Why did you write a book just on Metternich?" T. 4p.

H3   19 articles on Auernheimer.

H4   Prince Metternich. Statesman and Lover. 3 reviews. Cl. 1940-1941.

Harvard University, Houghton Library, Cambridge, Massachusetts 02138.

RICHARD BEER-HOFMANN COLLECTION

B1   Beer-Hofmann, Richard. 5 L. 1941-1945.
      Lens, Miriam Beer-Hofmann. 2 L. 1946-1947.

B1,2 "My Life in Germany Before and After January 30, 1933." Correspondence concerning an essay contest in which Auernheimer was a contestant.

C7   "My Life in Germany Before and After January 30, 1933." Microfilm of Ms. 1940.

Leo Baeck Institute, 129 East 73rd Street, New York, N.Y. 10021.

B1   [Ludwig, Emil]. 1 L. A. 1938.

C7 "Lob des Schauspielers Alexander Moissi." 1927. T. 1p.
J   3 photos.

Mrs. Elisabeth M. Stoerk and Mrs. Susanne B. Hoeller, 288
Ocean Drive West, Stamford, Connecticut 06902.

FRIDERIKE ZWEIG ARCHIVE

B1 Zweig, Friderike. 1 L. 1943.
B3 5 L. from Irene Beate Auernheimer to Friderike Zweig.
    1948.

Southern Illinois University, Morris Library, Department of
Special Collections, Carbondale, Illinois 62901.

ERWIN PISCATOR PAPERS

B1 Piscator, Erwin. 2 L. 1939-1940.

Dr. Gustave O. Arlt, 13220-C Admiralty Way, Marina del Rey,
California 90291.

FRANZ WERFEL ARCHIVE

B1 Werfel, Franz. 2 L. 1926, 1942.

Mrs. Gertrude Urzidil, 83-39 116th Street, Richmond Hill,
New York 11418.

JOHANNES URZIDIL COLLECTION

B1 Urzidil, Johannes. 2 L. A. 1941.

University of New Hampshire, The Library, Department of Special Collections, Durham, New Hampshire 03824.

OSKAR MARIA GRAF COLLECTION

B1   Graf, Oskar Maria. 1 L. 1939.

University of Texas, Humanities Research Center, Manuscripts
Collection, Box 7219, Austin, Texas 78712.

B1   1 L.

C4   1 Ms.

University of Pennsylvania, The Charles Patterson Van Pelt
Library, Philadelphia, Pennsylvania 19104.

ALMA MAHLER-WERFEL COLLECTION

B1   2 L. to Alma Mahler-Werfel. A. 1941, 1943.
       2 L. to Franz Werfel. A. 1945.

C3   Poem, dedicated to Franz Werfel. 1944.

J   1 photo. Undated.

New York Public Library, Manuscript Division, Fifth Avenue
and 42nd Street, New York, N.Y. 10018.

EMERGENCY COMMITTEE IN AID OF DISPLACED FOREIGN SCHOLARS,
1933-1945

*   File compiled, no assistance given. 1940-1942.

Mrs. Peter M. Lindt, 949 West End Avenue, New York, N.Y.
10025.

B1   Small amount of correspondence with Peter M. Lindt.

SIEGFRIED AUFHÄUSER

Statesman, 1884-1969

Leo Baeck Institute, 129 East 73rd Street, New York, N.Y.
10021.

The SIEGFRIED AUFHÄUSER COLLECTION, at present uncatalogued,
consists of approximately 3 inches of materials.

*Die SIEGFRIED AUFHÄUSER COLLECTION, die z.Zt. noch nicht
katalogisiert ist, umfaßt etwa 8 cm.*

B1,2   Correspondence.

H3   C1.
       Ms. describing trade union work, career.
       Obituaries.

H5   Bibliography of Aufhäuser's writings.

KURT KERSTEN COLLECTION

B1   1 L. to Kurt Kersten. Undated.

State Historical Society of Wisconsin, 816 State Street,
Madison, Wisconsin 53706.

TONI SENDER PAPERS

B1,2   Correspondence with Toni Sender. 1942, 1949 and un-
       dated.

Mrs. Mary S. Rosenberg, 100 West 72nd Street, New York, N.Y.
10023.

ALBERT GRZESINSKI ARCHIVE

C7   "Gewerkschaften." T.cc. 12p.

H5   Grzesinski, Albert. "Aufhäuser-Gruppe 1944-45." Ca.
       50p.

State University of New York at Albany, Department of Ger-

SIEGFRIED AUFHÄUSER

manic Languages and Literatures, 1400 Washington Avenue,
Albany, New York 12222.

KARL O. PAETEL COLLECTION

B1   3 L. to Karl O. Paetel. 1947. Xerox.

JULIUS BAB

Writer, 1880-1955

Leo Baeck Institute, 129 East 73rd Street, New York, N.Y.
10021.

The JULIUS BAB COLLECTION consists of approximately 6 feet
of materials from the years 1895-1964 and was donated by
Mrs. Bab over a period of several years from 1958 to 1961.
The major collection of Bab materials is located in the
Akademie der Künste, West Berlin.

*Die JULIUS BAB COLLECTION besteht aus etwa 1,80 m Materia-
lien aus den Jahren 1895 bis 1964. Sie wurde dem Institut
in der Zeit von 1958 bis 1961 geschenkt. Der Hauptteil der
Bab-Materialien befindet sich in der Akademie der Künste,
West Berlin.*

A1   Diary. A. with h. enclosures. 1895.
      Diary, with detailed entries, including drafts of 6 L.
        A. 1899.
      Diary. 1902. 6 small notebooks. A. Sketches, May-
        Oct. 1902.
      Calendar diary, with h. daily entries. 1903. A.
      Calendar diary, with h. entries. 1904.
      Calendar diary, with h. entries. 1907.
      Diary. Notebook. A. 1908.
      Calendar diary, with h. daily entries. 1935.
      Calendar diary, with h. daily entries. 1938.
      4 calendar diaries, with h. daily entries. 1939.
      Diary. May - end 1940. A.
      Calendar diary, with h. daily entries. 1943.

B2   Ca. 600 L., including L. from: Hermann Bahr, Albert
      Bassermann, Richard Beer-Hofmann, Robert Breuer,
      Pearl S. Buck, Curt Goetz, Maximilian Harden, Ger-
      hart Hauptmann, Georg Hermann, Hermann Hesse, Hugo
      von Hofmannsthal, Arno Holz, Käthe Kollwitz, Gustav
      Landauer, Detlev von Liliencron, Thomas Mann, Fritzi
      Massary, Fritz Mauthner, Jacob Picard, Alfred Polgar,
      Walther Rathenau, Carl Sternheim, Siegfried Tre-
      bitsch, Fritz von Unruh, Franz Werfel, Carl Zuck-
      mayer, Stefan Zweig.
      "Bittschrift" of the Bab children to father Julius.
      Undated. A. 1p.

B3   L. from Franz Voigt to the Verein zur Abwehr des Antisemitismus. 1923.

C3   Poems. 1900-1923. T. 3p. A. 30p.

C7   Varia. Notes and summarizations. 1 F.
Essays. Jewish themes. 1917-1922 and undated. T. and A.
149p.
18 essays. General topics, including "Manuskripte für
Sonntags." T. All undated. 78p.
3 essays. 1902 and undated. A. 21p.

D7   24 cl., various themes. 1906-1920 and undated. 87p.

D7,   34 volumes (4 ft.) of newspaper cl. Primarily by Bab,
H3   some about Bab.

H3   11 articles about Bab. 1903-1916 and undated. 24p.

H5   Bibliography of the writings of Bab. T. 4p.

I   Printed thank you note from Julius Bab and siblings
after death of father. Undated. 1p.
German passport, with visa. Berlin, 1926.

J   3 different photos. Undated and 1947.

N   Poem and drawing by Peter Bab. 1906. 2p.
Poems and statements by unidentified authors. 8p.

O   16 programs. Miscellaneous topics. 1901-1917. 32p.
33 programs. 1913-1924 and undated. 52p.

Bab materials located in general files and in other collec-
tions at the Leo Baeck Institute: BERTHA BADT-STRAUSS COL-
LECTION, LEO BAERWALD COLLECTION, ERNST COLLIN COLLECTION,
SALAMON DEMBITZER COLLECTION, PAUL FECHTER COLLECTION, GEORG
HERMANN COLLECTION, HERSCH FAMILIE COLLECTION, KURT KERSTEN
COLLECTION, MAX LIEBERMANN COLLECTION, FRITZ MAUTHNER COL-
LECTION, JOHANNA MEYER COLLECTION, JACOB PICARD COLLECTION,
WALTHER RATHENAU COLLECTION, GEORGE BERNARD SHAW COLLECTION,
KURT SINGER COLLECTION, KAETE WOLFF COLLECTION. Letters are
found in the respective collections of the recipients.

A1   "12 Tage in England." Diary. 1937. 65p.

B1   Letters 1929-1955, including such correspondents as:
Walther Rathenau

Paul Fechter (8 L., 1929-1954)
G. Hermann (4 L., 1933)
Fritz Mauthner (26 L., 1904-1919)
Johanna Meyer (101 L., 1919-1954)
Kurt Kersten (20 L., 1946-1955)
Bertha Badt-Strauss (15 L., 1942-1953)
Albert B. Strauss (2 L., 1945-1946)
Hersch Family (1 L., 1936)
Kaete Wolff (5 L., undated)
Salamon Dembitzer (1 L., 1946)
Jacob Picard

B2   Letters from:
Max Liebermann (3 L., 1926-1927)
George Bernard Shaw (7 L.)
Gustav Landauer (2 L., 1906, 1915)

C3   "Ein Abend." 1901. T.
"Deutschland." 1919. A.
"Tod des Weimarer Goethehauses." 1945. A. pc. 2p.
"Goethe." 1941. T. pc. 1p.
15 poems. 1933-1940 and undated. 13p.

C7   Address to Kurt Singer. 1935. T. 2p.
"Ernst Collin. Gedanken." Undated. T.cc. 10p.
2 essays. 9p.
"Grabrede für Martha Kassel." 1952. T. and A. 4p.
Essay about Alexander Moissi. Undated. A. 1p.
"Weshalb Dichtkunst." Written c. of a speech by Bab.
Dec. 1935. 13p.

D7   2 essays. Cl.

H3   "Der literarische Nachlaß Julius Babs." 1964. 1 cl.
7 obituary notices or memorial addresses. 1955.
2 book lists. 1953.
1 cl. 1964.

H5   Short unpub. biography.
Picard, Jacob. "Julius Bab in Amerika." 2 versions.
5p., 6p.
"Anhang zum Lift für Julius Bab u. eigentlicher Lift
zum 70. Geburtstag." 3p.

I   1 F. of addresses.
Bill of loading for a bust. 1922. 1p.

Invitation from S. Fischer Verlag. 1911. 1p.
"Julius Bab 1880-1955 und das Theater der Republic
1918-1933." Exhibit by the Jewish community in Berlin. Invitation to opening, Sept. 27, 1967. 5p.

J   Photo of Bab on 80th birthday.

0   2 programs: Richard Dehmel matinee; "Das Tagebuch der
       Anne Frank."
       "Abschied von Julius Bab." Program. Feb. 16, 1955. 6p.

Harvard University, Houghton Library, Cambridge, Massachusetts 02138.

RICHARD BEER-HOFMANN COLLECTION, THEO FELDMAN PAPERS, AUTO-
GRAPH FILE

B1   14 L. to Richard Beer-Hofmann. 1918-1945 and undated.
       3 L. to Miriam Beer-Hofmann Lens. 1947-1948 and un-
       dated.

B2   10 L., including L. from: Hermann Bahr, Hugo von Hof-
       mannsthal, Walther Rathenau, Emile Verhaeren.
       33 L. and 25 Ptc. from Stefan Zweig. 1909-1934.

C3   1 poem. T.

C9   Tr. into German of 10 poems by Elinor Wylie.

New York Public Library, Manuscript Division, Fifth Avenue
and 42nd Street, New York, N.Y. 10018.

THEO FELDMAN PAPERS, EMERGENCY COMMITTEE IN AID OF DISPLACED
FOREIGN SCHOLARS, 1933-1945

B1   2 L. to Theo Feldman. 1951-1952. A.
       Correspondence with Henry Meier (Literarischer Verein,
       New York). 1942-1955.

B2   1 Ptc. from Richard Beer-Hofmann. 1932. A.

*   File compiled by the Emergency Committee, no assistance
       given. 1938-1944.

<u>Southern Illinois University</u>, Morris Library, Department of
Special Collections, Carbondale, Illinois 62901.

ERWIN PISCATOR PAPERS

B1   3 L. to Erwin Piscator. 1947-1948.

B2   2 L. from Erwin Piscator. 1948.

<u>University of Texas</u>, Humanities Research Center, Manuscripts
Collection, Box 7219, Austin, Texas 78712.

B1   2 L.

B2   5 L.

<u>Immigration History Research Center of the University of
Minnesota</u>, 826 Berry Street, St. Paul, Minnesota 55101.

AMERICAN COUNCIL FOR EMIGRÉS IN THE PROFESSIONS ARCHIVES

A3   Biographical sketch. 1p.
      Short description of planned lecture series. 1p.

B2   1 L. from Else Staudinger. 1942.

B3   2 L. by Alvin Johnson.
      1 L. by Toni Stolper.

<u>University of Pennsylvania</u>, The Charles Patterson Van Pelt
Library, Philadelphia, Pennsylvania 19104.

ALMA MAHLER-WERFEL COLLECTION

B1   3 L. to Alma Mahler-Werfel. T. and A. 1942-1944.
      2 L. to Franz Werfel. A. 1942, 1944.

B2   1 L. from Franz Werfel. T.c. 1942.

<u>State University of New York at Albany</u>, Department of Ger-
manic Languages and Literatures, 1400 Washington Avenue,
Albany, New York 12222.

KARL O. PAETEL COLLECTION

B1   3 L. to Karl O. Paetel (xerox). 1944-1946.

Princeton University, Firestone Library, Princeton, New Jersey 08540.

MISCELLANEOUS GERMAN MANUSCRIPTS COLLECTION

B2   2 Ptc. 1906 and 1925.

Mrs. Gertrude Urzidil, 83-39 116th Street, Richmond Hill, New York 11418.

JOHANNES URZIDIL COLLECTION

B1   2 L. to Johannes Urzidil. A. 1947.

Mrs. Elisabeth M. Stoerk and Mrs. Susanne B. Hoeller, 288 Ocean Drive West, Stamford, Connecticut 06902.

FRIDERIKE ZWEIG ARCHIVE

B1   1 L. to Friderike Zweig.

State University of New York at Binghamton, Center for Modern Theater Research, Binghamton, New York 13901.

MAX REINHARDT ARCHIVE

*   Materials in the uncatalogued portion of the Archive.

Mr. Francis Heilbut, 328 West 96th Street, New York, N.Y. 10025.

IVAN HEILBUT PAPERS

B1,2 Correspondence with Ivan Heilbut.

Barthold Fles Literary Agency, 507 Fifth Avenue, New York, N.Y. 10016.

B1   1 L. to Barthold Fles. 1944.

Mrs. Alice Loewy Kahler, 1 Evelyn Place, Princeton, New Jersey 08540.

B1   1 L. to Erich von Kahler. 1945.

C7   "Gedanken über Preußen (Mai 1945)." T.c. with h. corr.
       2p.

Mrs. Peter M. Lindt, 949 West End Avenue, New York, N.Y. 10025.

B1   Small amount of correspondence with Peter M. Lindt.

LUDWIG BACHHOFER

Art Historian, Orientalist, 1894-1976

Mrs. Ludwig Bachhofer, Box 3084, Carmel, California 93921.

The materials of historic interest from the estate of Ludwig
Bachhofer will be deposited at the State University of New
York at Albany. As of 1977, however, the ca. 5 ft. of materials (described below) are still with Mrs. Ludwig Bachhofer
and are inaccessible to researchers. Further information
concerning the career of Bachhofer may be obtained from his
daughter, Mrs. Else Regensteiner, 1416 East 55th Street,
Chicago, Illinois 60615.

*Materialien von historischem Interesse aus dem Nachlaß Lud-
wig Bachhofers werden der State University of New York at
Albany zukommen. Zum jetzigen Zeitpunkt (1977) befinden
sich die etwa 1,50 m Materialien (Beschreibung s.u.) noch
im Besitz von Frau Bachhofer und sind somit für Forschungszwecke nicht zugänglich. Genauere Angaben über die Laufbahn
Bachhofers können bei seiner Tochter eingeholt werden: Frau
Else Regensteiner, 1416 East 55th Street, Chicago, Illinois
60615.*

C7   Manuscripts by Bachhofer. A.

D7   Published articles and offprints by Bachhofer.

I   Documents: passports, financial papers, etc.

J   Numerous photos of art objects.
      Photos of the Bachhofers, their family and friends.

K   Private library.

M   Memorabilia.

New York Public Library, Manuscript Division, Fifth Avenue
and 42nd Street, New York, N.Y. 10018.

EMERGENCY COMMITTEE IN AID OF DISPLACED FOREIGN SCHOLARS,
1933-1945

*   File compiled, no assistance given. 1938-1939.

LUDWIG BACHHOFER

New School for Social Research, Office of the Dean of the
Graduate Faculty of Political and Social Science, 65 Fifth
Avenue, New York, N.Y. 10003.

RECORDS OF THE UNIVERSITY IN EXILE, 1933-45

A3   Curriculum vitae. 4p.

HANS BAERWALD

Mathematician, 1904-

Prof. Hans Georg Baerwald, 2732 Chama NE, Albuquerque, New
Mexico 87101.

Private collection. / *Privatsammlung.*

C8   Reports of Baerwald's work at Sandia, Clevite Corpora-
        tion, etc. Several thousand p.
      Copies of Baerwald's writings.

D8   Reprints of all of Baerwald's published works.

I   Collection of patents.
      Diplomas (Ph.D.), stipend award certificates, etc.

J   Personal photos.

K   Several hundred books. (The books will be given over to
        the University of New Mexico. The periodicals have
        already been donated to the University.)

University of Chicago, The Joseph Regenstein Library, 1100
East 57th Street, Chicago, Illinois 60637.

JAMES FRANCK PAPERS

B1,2 Correspondence between James Franck and Hans Baerwald.

New York Public Library, Manuscript Division, Fifth Avenue
and 42nd Street, New York, N.Y. 10018.

EMERGENCY COMMITTEE IN AID OF DISPLACED FOREIGN SCHOLARS,
1933-1945

*   File compiled, no assistance given. 1933-1940.

HANS BARON

Historian, 1900-

Prof. Hans Baron, 28 Huron Avenue, Cambridge, Massachusetts
02138.

The collection in Prof. Baron's possession comprises approximately 30 ft. of materials.

Die Sammlung von Professor Baron umfaßt etwa 9 m Material.

B1,2   Correspondence with colleagues and other scholars.
       1920s-1970s.

C7   German and English Ms. T. and A.
       Outlines and rough drafts for books, articles, speeches.

D7   Pub. versions (mostly offprints) of Baron's works.
       Nearly complete.

L   Materials used in his studies and for his courses.
       Numerous cl. and offprints of articles by others.

Immigration History Research Center of the University of
Minnesota, 826 Berry Street, St. Paul, Minnesota 55101.

AMERICAN COUNCIL FOR EMIGRÉS IN THE PROFESSIONS ARCHIVES

A3   Curriculum vitae, biographical questionnaires, etc.
       11p.

B1   1 L. to Emergency Committee in Aid of Displaced Foreign
       Scholars. 1943. 3p.

New York Public Library, Manuscript Division, Fifth Avenue
and 42nd Street, New York, N.Y. 10018.

EMERGENCY COMMITTEE IN AID OF DISPLACED FOREIGN SCHOLARS,
1933-1945

*   File compiled when assistance was granted. 1934-1944.

VICKI BAUM

Writer, 1888-1960

State University of New York at Albany, Department of Germanic Languages and Literatures, 1400 Washington Avenue, Albany, New York 12222.

The VICKI BAUM COLLECTION (ca. 500 items) was assembled by Doubleday Publishers and donated to the Department of Germanic Languages and Literatures in 1972.

Die VICKI BAUM COLLECTION (etwa 500 Nummern) wurde vom Verlagshaus Doubleday zusammengestellt und dem Department of Germanic Languages and Literatures 1972 vermacht.

B1   156 L. and Tel. 1930-1953, including L. to: Nelson Doubleday, Donald B. Elder, Lillian Glaser, Daniel Longwell, Ken McCormick.

B2   246 L. and Tel. 1931-1953, including L. from: Nelson Doubleday, Donald B. Elder, Lillian Glaser, Malcolm Johnson, Daniel Longwell, Ken McCormick.

B3   Publishers' correspondence concerning Baum and her works pub. by Doubleday. 1930-1953.

C1   A Tale of Bali. Synopsis entitled: "Das Ende der Geburt." T. 5p.
The Weeping Wood. Chap. outline. T. 4p.

KARL O. PAETEL COLLECTION

B1   2 L. to Karl O. Paetel (xerox). 1942.

New York Public Library at Lincoln Center, Library and Museum of the Performing Arts, 111 Amsterdam Avenue, New York, N.Y. 10023.

EDMOND PAUKER COLLECTION

C2   Divine Drudge. By Vicki Baum and John Golden. "Produced by John Golden at the Royale Theater, N3, 26. October 1933." Cc. 114p.
Das dumme Englein. Mimeo. 37p.

Grand Hotel. A Play by Vicki Baum. "Adapted from the
German by William A. Drake. American Version Pro-
duced by Herman Shumlin in association with Henry
Moses and directed by Mr. Shumlin." T.cc. 169p.
"Light Plot and Light. Clues Grand Hotel." T.cc. 7p.
"Property Plot of Grand Hotel." T.cc. 8p.
Grand Hotel. A Play. "Literal translation made by
Vicki Baum of her original German-language play pro-
duced by Max Reinhardt." T.cc. 146p.
Joujou. Outline for a musical comedy by Vicki Baum.
"Submitted to Oscar Strauss, as a basis for a French
operetta." T.cc. 20p.
Mitsou. A Comedy with Musicals. "Suggested by Vicki
Baum and Gina Kaus. After the novel by Colette."
T. 2c. 57p., 78p.
Pariser Platz 13. Drama in 3 Akten. Synopsis. T. 4p.
Pariser Platz 13. A Comedy in Three Acts. T. 128p.
No. 13, Paris Place. A Play in 3 Acts (4 scenes).
English version. T. 122p.
Saturday Night. By Vicki Baum and Benjamin Glaser.
"First Version." T.cc. 107p.

Yale University, Beinecke Rare Book and Manuscript Library,
New Haven, Connecticut 06520.

EDMOND PAUKER COLLECTION

A3   Bibliography of Vicki Baum's works, assembled and
      signed by V. Baum. Ca. 1959. 3 c.

B1   2 L. to Edmond Pauker.

B2   1 L. from Jean Benoit-Levy. 1957.
      7 L. from Edmond Pauker. 1957-1958.

I   Pariser Platz 13. Contracts.
      Saturday Night. Contracts.

Dr. George Froeschel, 1146 San Ysidro, Beverly Hills, California 90210.

B1   Several L. to George Froeschel.

University of Texas, Humanities Research Center, Manuscripts
Collection, Box 7219, Austin, Texas 78712.

B1   3 L.

B2   2 L.

C   1 Ms.

University of California at Riverside, Riverside, California
92502.

RAOUL AUERNHEIMER ARCHIVE

B1   2 L. to Raoul Auernheimer. 1943.

Harvard University, Houghton Library, Cambridge, Massachusetts 02138.

B1   1 L. to John P. Marquand. 1942.

B2   1 L. from John P. Marquand. 1942.

Academy of Motion Picture Arts and Sciences, Margaret Herrick
Library, 9038 Melrose Avenue, Hollywood, California 90069.

H3   Newspaper cl., including obituary notices. 1 F.

Leo Baeck Institute, 129 East 73rd Street, New York, N.Y.
10021.

GEORG HERMANN COLLECTION and general archives

B1   1 L. to Georg Hermann.

D7   1 cl. 1961.

H4   Es war alles ganz anders. 1 cl.

Columbia University, Butler Library, New York, N.Y. 10027.

VICKI BAUM

Bl   1 L. to Daniel Longwell. 1934.

Dr. Gustave O. Arlt, 13220-C Admiralty Way, Marina del Rey, California 90291.

FRANZ WERFEL ARCHIVE

Bl   1 L. to Franz Werfel. 1942.

University of California, Davis, Shields Library, Department of Special Collections, Davis, California 95616.

PAUL ELBOGEN PAPERS

Bl   1 L. to Paul Elbogen. 1952.

Mrs. Peter M. Lindt, 949 West End Avenue, New York, N.Y. 10025.

Bl   Small amount of correspondence with Peter M. Lindt.

HERBERT BAYER

Architect, 1900-

The papers of Mr. Herbert Bayer, consisting of manuscripts, notebooks, photographs, color slides, etc., will eventually be given to the Denver Art Museum, Denver, Colorado. The materials could not be described in greater detail as of publication date.

Die Materialien Herbert Bayers, die aus Manuskripten, Notizbüchern, Photographien, Dias usw. bestehen, werden später an das Denver Art Museum, Denver, Colorado gehen. Es war nicht möglich, rechtzeitig zur Veröffentlichung dieses Bandes genauere Angaben über die Materialien zu erhalten.

MAX BECKMANN

Painter, 1884-1950

Mrs. Max Beckmann, c/o Mr. Perry Rathbone, Christie, Manson
and Woods International Inc., 867 Madison Avenue, New York,
N.Y. 10021.

Private collection: inaccessible. Inquiries concerning
materials should be directed to Mr. Perry Rathbone.

*Unzugängliche Privatsammlung. Anfragen über Beckmann-
Materialien sind an Herrn Perry Rathbone zu richten.*

A1   Unpub. portions of Beckmann's diaries, dating from the
      1940s.

B1,2 Correspondence (personal and professional), dating
      from the 1920s. Includes correspondence with: Curt
      Valentin, Perry Rathbone, Washington University,
      Mills College, Stephens College, University of Colo-
      rado.

Museum of Modern Art, The Library, 11 West 53rd Street, New
York, N.Y. 10019.

The CURT VALENTIN PAPERS were a gift to the MOMA by the art
dealer's estate. Restricted archive: requirements for
access upon written application to the Museum of Modern Art.

*Die CURT VALENTIN PAPERS sind eine Schenkung aus dem Nachlaß
des Kunsthändlers an die Museum of Modern Art Library. Der
Zugang ist beschränkt; Zugangsbedingungen teilt das Museum of
Modern Art auf schriftliche Anfrage mit.*

A1   Short, elliptical diary of work on paintings. Nov. 15,
      1949 - Dec. 26, 1950. 4c. A. and T. 11p.

B1   65 L. and 15 Tel. to Curt Valentin..T. and A. 1937-1950.

B2   104 L. and 14 Tel. from Curt Valentin. T. and A. 1937-
      1950.

B3   Ca. 50 L., primarily re: Beckmann's work. 1950-1951.

C7   "My Theory of Painting." T.cc. 7p.

MAX BECKMANN

I   Lists of paintings, bills of lading, price sheets, etc. scattered through correspondence.

H4   Catalogs and cl., exhibition data:
    "Paintings 1936-39." New York City, 1940.
    (Paintings 1912-1939). New York City, 1941.
    "Max Beckmann Exhibition." Chicago, 1942.
    "The Actors by Max Beckmann." New York City, 1946.
    "Beckmann." New York City, 1947.
    "Beckmann." City Art Museum of St. Louis, 1948.
    Cl. re: exhibit of contemporary (entartete, non-Nazi) art in Boston. 1939.

Archives of American Art, Smithsonian Institution, National Collection of Fine Arts and National Portrait Gallery Building, Eighth and F Streets N.W., Washington, D.C. 20560. (Microfilms of collections are available in each of the branch locations: Boston, Massachusetts; New York, N.Y.; Detroit, Michigan; San Francisco, California.)

J. B. NEUMANN PAPERS, ULFERT WILKE PAPERS and miscellany

B1   3 L. to J. B. Neumann. 1926, 1927, 1945.

B1,2 Correspondence with Ulfert Wilke. 1954.

B2   3 L. from J. B. Neumann. 1929-1930.

C7   "On My Painting." (Original at NYPL.) New York, Buchholz Gallery, 1941.

H3,4 Catalogs, cl. and reproductions:
    St. Louis City Art Museum, 1948.
    Bowling Green State University, undated.
    Catherine Viviano Gallery, 1959, 1962, 1964-65, 1967 and 1968.

I   Contract for art work. 1925. Also transcript in English.

Mr. Stephen Lackner, 601 El Bosque Road, Santa Barbara, California 93105.

B1,2 Lengthy correspondence between Lackner and Beckmann.

57

RICHARD BEER-HOFMANN

Poet, Dramatist, 1866-1945

<u>Harvard University</u>, Houghton Library, Cambridge, Massachusetts 02138.

The RICHARD BEER-HOFMANN COLLECTION housed at the Houghton Library represents the largest single accumulation of archival materials by and about Richard Beer-Hofmann—47 archive boxes in total. The largest part of the collection (bMS Ger 131—29 boxes), containing the literary manuscripts, was purchased by Harvard in Jan. 1959 from Mrs. Miriam Beer-Hofmann Lens. The second part (bMS Ger 183—15 boxes), correspondence by and to Beer-Hofmann, was purchased from Mrs. Lens in June 1968. The third part (bMS Ger 131.2—1 box) contains mostly manuscripts by others that were in his possession at the time of his death and was donated by Mrs. Alice von Kahler in June 1971. In addition, Houghton Library also has in its possession 2 further archive boxes containing loose-leaf copies of letters and letter-books by Beer-Hofmann, all from his exile years, all uncatalogued. With the exception of the 2 boxes of uncatalogued materials referred to above, all materials have been catalogued and a bound, detailed inventory of the collection is available for use in the library.

Die RICHARD BEER-HOFMANN COLLECTION, die in der Houghton Library untergebracht ist, stellt die größte Ansammlung von Archivmaterialien von und über Beer-Hofmann dar - insgesamt 47 Archivkartons. Der größte Teil der Sammlung (bMS Ger 131 - 29 Kartons), der die literarischen Manuskripte enthält, wurde im Jahre 1959 von Frau Miriam Beer-Hofmann Lens käuflich erworben. Ein weiterer Teil (bMS Ger 183 - 15 Kartons), Briefe von und an Beer-Hofmann, wurde im Juni 1968 von Frau Lens erworben. Der dritte Teil (bMS Ger 131.2 - 1 Karton) umfaßt hauptsächlich Manuskripte anderer Autoren die sich zum Zeitpunkt des Todes von Beer-Hofmann in seinem Besitz befanden; diese Materialien sind eine Schenkung von Frau Alice von Kahler vom Juni 1971. Zusätzlich besitzt die Houghton Library 2 weitere Archivkartons mit losen Kopien von Briefen und Briefordnern Beer-Hofmanns, die alle aus seiner Exilzeit stammen. Dieses Material ist nicht katalogisiert. Abgesehen davon sind alle Materialien der Sammlung katalogisiert, und es ist ein detailliertes Verzeichnis der Sammlung in

RICHARD BEER-HOFMANN

gebundener Form erhältlich (zum Gebrauch in der Bibliothek).

A3 Daten. Autobiography. Chronological outline in note-
    book. T. 56p. Page proofs. 1 B.

B1 64 L. 1896-1943, including L. to: Marion Canby, Ernst
    Deutsch, Erich von Kahler, Peter M. Lindt, Richard
    von Mises, Thornton Wilder.
    1 archive carton of uncatalogued L. from Beer-Hofmann's
    exile years.

B2 2,671 L. 1896-1943, including L. from: Shalom Asch,
    Raoul Auernheimer, Julius Bab, Hermann Bahr, Gott-
    fried Bermann-Fischer, Ilse Blumenthal-Weiss, Georg
    Hermann Borchardt, Hermann Broch, Martin Buber,
    Marion Canby, Hans Carossa, Richard Coudenhove-
    Kalergi, Richard Dehmel, Ernst Deutsch, Theodore
    Dreiser, Tilla Durieux, Ludwig Edelstein, Albert
    Einstein, Curt von Faber du Faur, Sigmund Freud,
    René Fülöp-Miller, Manfred George, Max Graf, Maxi-
    milian Harden, Gerhart Hauptmann, Theodor Herzl,
    Hugo von Hofmannsthal, Franz Horch, Otto Kallir,
    Hans Kohn, Annette Kolb, Karl Kraus, Peter M. Lindt,
    Oskar Loerke, Otto Loewi, Ernst Lothar, Emil Ludwig,
    Thomas Mann, Fritz Mauthner, Richard von Mises,
    Caroline Newton, Theodor Reik, Max Reinhardt, Hein-
    rich Schnitzler, Oskar Seidlin, Johann Strauss,
    Richard Strauss, Helene Thimig, Robert Thoeren,
    Siegfried Trebitsch, Gottfried Reinhold Treviranus,
    Ludwig Ullmann, Jean Starr Untermeyer, Lesser Ury,
    Conrad Veidt, Karl Viëtor, Werner Vordtriede, Ernst
    Waldinger, Jakob Wassermann, Alma Mahler-Werfel,
    Franz Werfel, Thornton Wilder, Anton Wildgans, Vic-
    tor Wittner, Heinrich Zimmer, Arnold Zweig, Stefan
    Zweig.
    Rilke, Rainer Maria. L., 1902-1916. pc.

B3 195 L. to and from the Beer-Hofmann family, in particu-
    lar Paula Beer-Hofmann and Miriam Beer-Hofmann Lens.

C1 Herbstmorgen in Österreich (aus dem Fragment Paula).
    A. and T. 7 notebooks. 477p.
    Paula. Early sketches and notes. A. and T. 4 F. Frag-
    ments, outlines, notes, dates. 11 notebooks. 505p.

C2   Don Giovanni. Fragments, outlines, printed librettos
      in Italian and German. 1 F.
      Das goldene Pferd: Pantomime. 2 versions. A. 386p. T.
      43p. Rough drafts of texts, scenes, costumes. A.,
      some drawings. 1 F.
      Der Graf von Charolais. Drama in fünf Akten. Ms.,
      copies, sketches and drafts. A. 889p. plus 1 F. of
      sketches and drafts. Several tr.: Hungarian (by
      Sebesi Ernö), English (by Ludwig Lewisohn), Italian.
      Die Historie von König David. Outlines, rough drafts,
      sketches. A. and T. 977p. plus 1 F. of notes per-
      taining to biblical background: persons, places,
      tribes, David's city.
      Jaakobs Traum. Sketches, outlines, single acts. A. 3 F.
      Various anonymous tr. in English, Spanish, French,
      Hungarian. A. and T. 1 F.
      Jacob's Dream. English tr. by Ida Bension Wynn. T.
      with h. corr. 3 F. 4 additional versions. T. with h.
      corr. and rev. by Beer-Hofmann. 60p.
      Der junge David. List of characters, prologue, Acts I-
      VII, footnotes. A. 1,674p. Outlines, rough drafts,
      preliminary sketches, and later rev., unedited foot-
      notes, notes. A. 8 F.
      Pierrot, Hypnotiseur: Pantomine. A. 261p. French tr. by
      Beer-Hofmann and Hugo von Hofmannsthal. Scenario. A.
      122p.
      Der Tod Georgs. Acts I-IV, clean copy. A. 1,325p.
      Sketches and rough drafts, Acts I-IV. A. 3 F.
      Untitled dramatization. Rough draft. A.

C3   "Schlaflied für Miriam." 1915. T. 2p. English, Spanish,
      French and Czech tr. A. and T. plus cl. 1 F.
      Verses, 1924-1939. A. and T. 45p. plus 1 F.

C4   "Märchen (Drei Strahlen)." Rough draft. A.

C7   Rough drafts to essays, unpub-. fragments, papers,
      speeches, some newspaper cl., radio interview. A. and
      T. 174p. plus 4 F.

C9   Faust, von Goethe. Adaptation by Beer-Hofmann for the
      Burgtheater. T. 1 F.
      Macbeth. Preparatory work to stage version. A. and
      drawings. Accompanied by published German tr. 1 F.
      Überfahrt. Original English version by Sutton Vane. T.

German tr. by Otto Klement. T. with h. corr. and rev. by Beer-Hofmann. 3 F.

C12   Faust. Written suggestions to the producer of the Prag production. T. 1 F.
Iphigenie auf Tauris. Text with stage directions by Beer-Hofmann.

D3   "Schlaflied für Miriam." Offprints. 1 F.

D7   Newspaper and magazine cl. 1 B.

E   "Schlaflied für Miriam." Printed texts, musical versions by different individuals. 1 F.

H3   Newspaper and magazine cl. 1 B.

H4   Reviews (cl.):
Don Giovanni
Der Graf von Charolais. 1 F.
Herbstmorgen in Oesterreich. 1944-1945. 1 F.
Jaakobs Traum. German version. 1 F. English version. 1 F.
Der junge David. 1 F.
Paula. 1 F.
Der Tod Georgs. 1 F.

I   Document naming Erich von Kahler as "Nachlaßverwalter", dated Vienna, June 27, 1933. 1p.

J   Portraits of actors, different productions of:
Der Graf von Charolais.
Jaakobs Traum. 2 F., some cl.

L   Faust. Sketches of decorations by Alfred Roller, quotations from Goethe's correspondence, materials pertaining to a talk. T., A. and cl. 3 F.
Der Graf von Charolais. Sketches of different productions, costumes and decorations.
Die Historie von König David. Miscellany. 25p. Sketches, photos and cl. 4 F.
Iphigenie auf Tauris. Sketches, cl., programs. 1 F.
Jaakobs Traum. Music, sketches of decorations, costumes and biblical scenes. 3 F.
Der junge David. Background materials. 12 F. Sketches of decorations, costumes and scenes, cl., brochures. 3 F.

Richard II; Wintermärchen. Materials concerning Shakespeare productions in German, rev. tr., etc. 1 F.

N   17 Ms., dated around 1900. Various lengths, mostly
religious themes. A. and T. 17 F.

O   Theater programs, advertisements for:
Don Giovanni
Faust
Überfahrt. Vienna, 1924.

Leo Baeck Institute, 129 East 73rd Street, New York, N.Y.
10021.

The RICHARD BEER-HOFMANN COLLECTION (AR 910-43; Nachtrag AR
3081) contains primarily materials concerning the history of
the Beer-Hofmann family, dating as far back as the beginning
of the 19th century (1808-1962). This includes numerous family documents, as well as correspondence, photos and memorabilia and encompasses approximately 6 ft. of shelf space.
The largest part of the collection was donated in 1960 by
Mrs. Miriam Beer-Hofmann Lens, who still retains copies of
much of the collection in her possession.

*Die RICHARD BEER-HOFMANN COLLECTION (AR 910-43; Nachtrag AR
3081) enthält in erster Linie Materialien über die Beer-
Hofmann-Familiengeschichte (1808-1962): zahlreiche Familien-
dokumente, Briefwechsel, Photographien, Erinnerungsstücke
(etwa 1,80 m Materialien). Der größte Teil der Sammlung ist
eine Schenkung von Frau Miriam Beer-Hofmann Lens, die selbst
noch Kopien vieler Stücke der Sammlung besitzt.*

A3   "Daten" and "Vorbemerkung zu den Daten. Notizen vom
ersten bis letzten Lebensjahr." Dated 1944-1945. A.
58p.

B1   Beer, Sigmund and Agnes. 29 L., 17 Ptc. 1872-1909.
18 L. from Richard and Mirjam Beer-Hofmann to Antoinette Kahler. 1940-1945.

B2   222 L. from relatives:
64 L. from Sigmund and Agnes Beer. 1885-1908. Transcriptions of 70 L. 1872-1908.
88 L. from Alois and Bertha Hofmann. A. 1881-1905.

52 L. from friends.

B3 460 L. to and from members of the Beer-Hofmann family.

C4 "Der Tod Georgs." Dated Berlin, 1900. T. with numerous h. corr.

D1 Der Graf von Charolais.
Jaakobs Traum.

D2 Vorspiel auf dem Theater zu König David.

D3 Verse.

D4 2 offprints from Die Neue Rundschau: "Prosa" and "Das goldene Pferd."

H4 Richard Beer-Hofmann. Besprechungen seiner Werke. 29p.

I "Archiv R.B.H." and "Archiv Nachtrag." Beer-Hofmann's notes concerning his Nachlaß. Dated New York, 1940. A. pc. 7p and 4p.
Doctor diploma (Dr. juris). Vienna, May 31, 1890.
Family documents:
  Beer, Hermann (father). 104 documents. 1841-1902.
  Beer, Hermann Hieronymus (grandfather's brother). 101 documents. 1828-1868.
  Beer, Naphtali-Katherine (paternal grandmother). 10 documents. 1834-1855.
  Beer, Rosa (mother). 11 documents. 1843-1866.
  Beer, Sigmund and Agnes (uncle and aunt). 36 documents. 1843-1909.
  Hofmann, Albert and Anna (uncle and aunt). 34 documents. 1808-1854.
  Hofmann, Bertha (Pflegemutter). 9 documents. 1843-1891.
  Hofmann, Bertha and Alois (aunt and uncle, Pflegeeltern). 44 documents.
  Steckerl, Moritz and Sophie (maternal grandparents). 6 documents. 1861-1909.
  Beer family tree since 1713. A. 1p.
  Beer-Hofmann and Steckerl-Schmeichler family tree. A. 3p.

J Beer-Hofmann, Paula. 30 photos in album and 21 loose photos. 1900-1919.
Beer-Hofmann, Richard. 71 photos, portraits, etc. 1866-1945.

69 photos of family and friends of Beer-Hofmann.

M   Bible of Agnes Beer née Hofmann. Dated 1838.
Prayer book of the mother of Josefine Kahler née
   Sobotka. Dated 1867.
Embroidered coverlet (in poor condition).
Embroidered pouch with officer's sash of R. B. H.
Small leather box containing (10) stamps.
Lock of hair (R. B. H.).
Text on silver seal.
Talisman.

O   2 programs. 1921, 1932. 14p. and 28p.

SIEGFRIED ALTMANN COLLECTION, JULIUS BAB COLLECTION, KARL
D. DARMSTAEDTER COLLECTION, ERICH KAHLER COLLECTION

B1   Altmann, Siegfried. 19 L. 1922-1944.
Bab, Julius. 2 L. A. pc. 1 Ptc. A. 1 Tel. 1932-1933.
Broch, Hermann. 1 L. A. 1942.
Darmstaedter, Karl A. 1 L. 1944.
Kahler, Antoinette. 14 L., 6 cards. 1939-1943.
Kahler, Erich. 1 L. 1937. (2c.).
Kahler, Josefine. 2 L. 1918, 1933.
Loewy, Lilly, 2 L. 1941, 1942.
23 L. to various individuals. 1906-1944.

B2   1 L. 1945.

B3   Beer-Hofmann, Naemah and Mirjam. 1 L. ea. to Julius
   Bab.

C3   "Schlaflied für Mirjam." German version and English tr.
   Mimeo. 1p.
Poem to Antoinette Kahler. 1932. (2c.).

C4   Aphorisms. 1914-1942. T. 7p.

C7   "Einleitung zur: Hochzeit..." 1920. T. 62p.
Notes about converts to Judaism. Undated. 3p.

D3   Printed copy of "Schlaflied für Mirjam," with h. dedication.

H3   4 cl.

RICHARD BEER-HOFMANN

<u>Mrs. Miriam Beer-Hofmann Lens</u>, 412 Cathedral Parkway, New York, N.Y. 10025.

This private RICHARD BEER-HOFMANN COLLECTION, which contains over 45 ft. of materials (including his personal library), represents the remainder of the estate of Richard Beer-Hofmann still in Mrs. Lens' possession. Sales and donations of other materials from the estate have been made by Mrs. Lens over the past 15 years to Harvard University, Yale University and the Leo Baeck Institute, photocopies of much of which have been retained by Mrs. Lens.

Diese private RICHARD BEER-HOFMANN COLLECTION, die, einschließlich seiner Privatbibliothek, mehr als 13,50 m umfaßt, stellt den Rest des Nachlasses von Richard Beer-Hofmann dar und befindet sich noch in Frau Lens' Besitz. Frau Lens hat in den letzten 15 Jahren andere Materialien des Nachlasses der Harvard University, der Yale University und dem Leo Baeck Institute verkauft oder als Schenkung überlassen, wobei sie Photokopien eines Teils dieser Materialien behalten hat.

B1,2   Numerous L. between relatives of the Beer-Hofmann family, especially Beer-Hofmann, his wife and children. (The early family correspondence has already been donated to the Leo Baeck Institute.)
Additional L. of a personal nature.

C3   Original Ms. of poems by Beer-Hofmann.

C7   Original Ms. of essays.
Preliminary versions of essays, speeches, etc.

C14   Preliminary sketches of stage plans, costumes, scenes (for production of his plays).

H3   Printed copies of articles about Beer-Hofmann by various individuals.

J   Ca. 200 photos (many quite old) of family, friends (Erich von Kahler), theater personalities.

K   Beer-Hofmann's personal library, including many editions with dedications.
<u>Faust</u>-edition with notes by Beer-Hofmann for a stage production.

L   Ca. 8 F. with newspaper and magazine cl., used as

background materials for his works.
Photocopies of much of the material at Harvard University and the Leo Baeck Institute.

M   Embroidered items.
Sketches.
Oil paintings.
Household items (sewing basket, etc.).

Yale University, Beinecke Rare Book and Manuscript Library,
New Haven, Connecticut 06520.

Although the Beinecke Library possesses little or no original material by Beer-Hofmann, numerous letters to him from
famous German literary personalities are to be found in the
YALE COLLECTION OF GERMAN LITERATURE. These 973 letters,
from the years 1890-1929, were purchased from the daughter
of the late Beer-Hofmann, Mrs. Miriam Beer-Hofmann Lens,
who still holds all publication rights to the materials.

*Die Beinecke Library besitzt zwar kaum Originalmaterialien
von Beer-Hofmann, es finden sich aber in der YALE COLLECTION
OF GERMAN LITERATURE zahlreiche Briefe berühmter Persönlichkeiten den deutschsprachigen literarischen Szene an Beer-
Hofmann. Diese 973 Briefe aus den Jahren 1890 - 1929 wurden
von der Tochter Beer-Hofmanns, Frau Miriam Beer-Hofmann Lens,
käuflich erworben. Die literarischen Rechte ruhen bei Frau
Lens.*

B2   Bahr, Hermann. 35 L., 27 Ptc., 5 Tel., 2 calling cards
with notes. 1894-1925.
Hofmannsthal, Hugo von. 176 L., 117 Ptc., 25 Tel., 13
calling cards with notes. [1890]-1929.
Hofmannsthal, Gertrude von. 12 L., 12 Ptc., 3 Tel.
1904-1928.
Schnitzler, Arthur. 270 L., 214 Ptc., 22 Tel., 17
calling cards with notes. 1891-1928.
Schnitzler, Olga. 15 L., 9 Ptc., 2 calling cards with
notes. [1907-1914].

Princeton University, Firestone Library, Princeton, New Jersey 08540.

RICHARD BEER-HOFMANN

THE PAPERS OF ALBERT EINSTEIN (1879-1955). For details concerning the use of this collection, see description under
Albert Einstein.

*THE PAPERS OF ALBERT EINSTEIN (1879-1955). Angaben über den
Zugang zu der Sammlung finden sich unter "Albert Einstein."*

B1,2 Unknown amount of correspondence between Beer-Hofmann
       and Albert Einstein.

Mrs. Alice Loewy Kahler, 1 Evelyn Place, Princeton, New
Jersey 08540.

ERICH VON KAHLER COLLECTION

B1   2 L. to Erich von Kahler. 1935, 1936.

B3   22 L., 2 Ptc. from Mirjam Beer-Hofmann (Lens) to Erich
       von Kahler. 1923-1965.
       4 L., 3 Ptc. from Naemah Beer-Hofmann to Erich and
       Antoinette von Kahler.

H4   Kahler, Erich von. Introduction to Richard Beer-
       Hofmann's Der Tod Georgs for a new edition by S.
       Fischer Verlag (never pub.). T. pc. 17p.

H5   Kahler, Erich von. "Richard Beer-Hofmann. Diverse Vor-
       träge." Notes to 3 lectures. A. Ca. 150p.

Library of Congress, Manuscript Division, Independence Avenue
and First Street S.E., Washington, D.C. 20540.

BENJAMIN W. HUEBSCH PAPERS

B1   Huebsch, Benjamin W. 2 L., 1 Ptc. 1933-1934.

New York Public Library, Manuscript Division, Fifth Avenue
and 42nd Street, New York, N.Y. 10018.

THEO FELDMAN PAPERS

RICHARD BEER-HOFMANN

B1   Bab, Julius. 1 Ptc. A. 1932.
       Feldman, Theo. 2 Ptc., 1 L. A. 1932, 1944.

University of California at Riverside, Riverside, California
92502.

RAOUL AUERNHEIMER ARCHIVE

B1   Auernheimer, Raoul. 1 L., 2 Ptc. (microfilm). 1939-
       1945.

University of Wyoming, Archive of Contemporary History, The
Library, Box 3334, Laramie, Wyoming 82071.

ALFRED FARAU COLLECTION

H5   Farau, Alfred. "Richard Beer-Hofmann." Essay.

State University of New York at Binghamton, Center for Modern Theater Research, Binghamton, New York 13901.

MAX REINHARDT ARCHIVE

H3   Article by Harald Kreid on Beer-Hofmann.

J   1 photo of Reinhardt in Beer-Hofmann's *Graf von Charo-*
       lais. Berlin, 1904.

University of Pennsylvania, The Charles Patterson Van Pelt
Library, Philadelphia, Pennsylvania 19104.

ALMA MAHLER-WERFEL COLLECTION

B1   1 Ptc. to Franz Werfel. A. 1942.

Mrs. Peter M. Lindt, 949 West End Avenue, New York, N.Y.
10025.

B1   Small amount of correspondence with Peter M. Lindt.

C   Ms. submitted to Lindt for use on his radio program.

MARTIN BERADT

Writer, 1881-1949

<u>Leo Baeck Institute</u>, 129 East 73rd Street, New York, N.Y.
10021.

The major collection of Martin Beradt materials is located
at the Deutsches Literaturarchiv in Marbach, West Germany.
The materials at the Leo Baeck Institute in its MARTIN BERADT
COLLECTION, ca. 190 items, were donated by Mrs. Charlotte
Beradt, widow of Martin, in 1964-1965.

*Die wichtigste Sammlung von Martin Beradt Materialien be-
findet sich im Deutschen Literaturarchiv in Marbach. Die
Materialien im Leo Baeck Institute, die MARTIN BERADT COL-
LECTION (etwa 190 Nummern), wurden dem Institut von der
Witwe, Frau Charlotte Beradt, in den Jahren 1964, 1965 ge-
schenkt.*

B2   64 L., including L. from: Hermann Bahr, Max Brod,
      Martin Buber, Gerhart Hauptmann, Georg Hermann,
      Hermann Hesse, Walther Rathenau, Jakob Wassermann,
      Frank Wedekind.

B3   14 autographs collected by Beradt, including: Berthold
      Auerbach, Max Liebermann, Lesser Ury.

C4   Novellas with Jewish themes. Written in the 1940s. A.
      149p.

D4   3 cl. 1941-1943.

D7   3 cl. 1911-1913.

H3   1 obituary. 1 cl.
      3 cl. re: Martin Beradt lecture evening. 1911-1912.

H4   <u>Eheleute</u>. 36 cl. of reviews, etc. 1910-1911.
      <u>Die gesetzlichen Handhaben gegen Auswüchse der Kurier-
      freiheit</u>. Reviews. 2 cl. 1911.
      <u>Go</u>. Reviews. 10 cl. 1909.
      <u>Das Kind</u>. Reviews. 21 cl. 1911-1912.
      <u>Der Richter</u>. Reviews. 5 cl. 1909-1911, 1920.

I   Family documents, including 3 marriage certificates, 3
      death certificates, 1 birth certificate, family tree
      notes.
      Certified birth certificate of Martin Beradt. Magdeburg,
      1938. 1p.

3 gift certificates. Berlin, 1933.
University certificates: Friedrich Wilhelm-Universi-
tät, Berlin (1899, 1901, 1903); Ludwig-Maximilians-
Universität, Munich (1902); Seminar certificate,
Heidelberg (1902); Leaving certificate, Ruprecht-
Karls-Universität, Heidelberg (1902); Seminar cer-
tificate, Berlin (1903); 1st law exam, Berlin (1904);
Doctoral degree, Freiburg (1906).
School certificate. Gymnasium zum grauen Kloster, Ber-
lin. 1899. Print and A. 3p.
Certificate from Magistrate, Berlin-Schoeneberg. 1917/
1918.
Certificate of ownership of Verdienstkreuz für Kriegs-
hilfe, Berlin. 1920.

J   1 photo in album.
2 family photos.

M   Menu card for Martin Beradt. Dinner party at Marianne
Perl's, stepmother of Gertrud Perl, née Misch. Berlin, 1914. Printed. 2p.

Mrs. Elisabeth M. Stoerk and Mrs. Susanne B. Hoeller, 288
Ocean Drive West, Stamford, Connecticut 06902.

FRIDERIKE ZWEIG ARCHIVE

B1   L. to Friderike Zweig. 1944 (filed under the heading
Writers Service Center).

Library of Congress, Manuscript Division, Independence Avenue
and First Street S.E., Washington, D.C. 20540.

LITERARY ESTATE OF HANNAH ARENDT (closed until 1980)

B3   Beradt, Charlotte. Correspondence file.

GUSTAV BERGMANN

Philosopher, 1906-

Dr. Gustav Bergmann, Department of Philosophy, The University
of Iowa, Iowa City, Iowa 52240.

Dr. Bergmann still retains the greatest portion of his papers,
either at his home, or in his office at the University (inaccessible to researchers and scholars as of 1977). Of primary importance among his papers, Dr. Bergmann has designated
the following materials:

*Der größte Teil der Schriftstücke von Dr. Bergmann befindet
sich noch in seinem Privatbesitz (in seiner Wohnung und in
seinem Universitätsbüro) und ist für Forschungszwecke im
Moment nicht zugänglich. Dr. Bergmann hat folgendes Material
als besonders wichtig bezeichnet:*

B1,2   Several F. of selected L., selected on the basis of
       subject matter, as well as correspondents. 1940s to
       present.

C7   New Foundations of Ontology. Ms. of unfinished book,
       to consist of short preface, 7 chapters, and 4 appen-
       dices.

University of Iowa, The University Libraries, Special Collections, Iowa City, Iowa 52240.

B1,2   Correspondence in faculty information F., as well as
       possible additional materials in correspondence of
       University of Iowa President's Office.

Library of Congress, Manuscript Division, Independence Avenue
and First Street S.E., Washington, D.C. 20540.

OSWALD VEBLEN PAPERS

B3   1 L. in Veblen's "Refugees" file. 1939.

I   1 document in "Refugees" file. 1939.

GUSTAV BERGMANN

<u>New York Public Library</u>, Manuscript Division, Fifth Avenue
and 42nd Street, New York, N.Y. 10018.

EMERGENCY COMMITTEE IN AID OF DISPLACED FOREIGN SCHOLARS,
1933-1945

*   File compiled when assistance was granted. 1938-1944.

MAX BERGMANN

Chemist, 1886-1944

American Philosophical Society, The Library, 105 South Fifth
Street, Philadelphia, Pennsylvania 19106.

The MAX BERGMANN PAPERS were donated by the Rockefeller Institute for Medical Research together with the Simon Flexner
Papers in Jan. 1963. The ca. 8,500 items of the BERGMANN
PAPERS are arranged in folders, each folder containing 1-20
items. The folders are divided into such categories as
individuals, organizations and subjects, with multiple folders on some topics.

*Die MAX BERGMANN PAPERS sind (zusammen mit den Simon Flexner
Papers) eine Schenkung des Rockefeller Institute for Medical
Research vom Jan. 1963. Die etwa 8500 Nummern der BERGMANN
PAPERS sind in Mappen geordnet (1-20 Nummern pro Mappe). Die
Mappen sind nach Persönlichkeiten, Organisationen und wissen-
schaftliche Themenbereichen zusammengestellt; einige dieser
Untergruppen umfassen mehrere Mappen.*

B1,2 "Refugee Correspondence Since Nov. 1941." 1 F.
        Organizations, institutions, corporations, publishers,
          etc., including:
        Emergency Committee in Aid of Displaced Foreign
          Scholars.
        Loyalty Committee.
        National Research Council.
        Protein Committee.
        Rockefeller Institute.
        Selfhelp.

B1,2 Individuals' folders: Otto K. Behrens, Max Bergmann,
I   Konrad Bloch, Franz Boas, Erwin Chargaff, M. Demerec,
        Albert Einstein, Kasimir Fajans, Simon Flexner,
        Heinz Fraenkel-Conrat, Kurt Jacoby, Otto Loewi, O.
        Meyerhoff, Hans Neurath, Winthrop Osterhout, Erich
        Proskauer, Eugene Rabinowitch, Rudolf Schoenheimer,
        Curt Stern.

B1,2 Subject folders, including: Amino acids, ascorbic acid,
L   growth, peptides, proteins, Soviet relations, etc.

C7   Lecture texts and notes, including:
        7th National Organic Chemistry Symposium, American

Chemical Society, Dec. 29, 1937.
University of Michigan lectures. Summer school, July
5-8, 1938.

I   "Scientific Periodicals and Books from the Library of
       M. Bergmann." List of books in Bergmann's personal
       library.

SIMON FLEXNER PAPERS, W. J. VON OSTERHOUT PAPERS, F. P. ROUS
PAPERS, H. T. CLARKE PAPERS

B1,2   Correspondence with W. J. V. Osterhout.
       Correspondence with F. P. Rous.
       Correspondence with Simon Flexner.

H3   Obituary.

Rockefeller University, Library Archives, Welch Hall, 1230
York Avenue, Nr. 66, New York, N.Y. 10021.

B1,2   Small amount of administrative correspondence.
       Small amount of correspondence on immigration matters.

C8   Annual reports to Scientific Directors of Rockefeller
       University concerning work done in Bergmann's lab.

H3   Information on funeral of Bergmann, notices.

J   Photos.

Prof. Joseph S. Fruton, Department of Biochemistry, Yale
University, New Haven, Connecticut 06520.

Dr. Fruton has expressed his intention to deposit his Berg-
mann materials at the American Philosophical Society. The
Project was unable to obtain further information concerning
Prof. Fruton's materials.

*Prof. Fruton hat die Absicht geäußert, seine Bergmann-Mate-
rialien der American Philosophical Society zukommen zu lassen. Es war nicht möglich, weitergehende Informationen über
Prof. Frutons Materialien zu erhalten.*

MAX BERGMANN

University of California, Berkeley, The Bancroft Library,
Berkeley, California 94720.

EMIL FISCHER PAPERS

B1   6 L. to Emil Fischer. 1914-1918.

University of Illinois at Urbana-Champaign, University Library, University Archives, Room 19, Urbana, Illinois 61801.

ROGER ADAMS PAPERS

B1   1 L. to Roger Adams. 1928.

University of Chicago, The Joseph Regenstein Library, 1100
East 57th Street, Chicago, Illinois 60637.

JAMES FRANCK PAPERS

B1,2 Correspondence between Bergmann and James Franck.

Mrs. Agnes F. Peterson, Central and Western European Collections, Hoover Institution on War, Revolution and Peace,
Stanford, California 94305.

Private collection from the estate of O. L. Fischer, father
of Agnes Peterson

*Privatsammlung aus dem Nachlaß von O. L. Fischer, dem Vater
von Agnes Peterson.*

B1,2 Correspondence between O. L. Fischer and Max Bergmann.

GOTTFRIED BERMANN-FISCHER

Publisher, 1897-

The Project was unable to contact Mr. Bermann-Fischer (P.O.
Box 237, Old Greenwich, Connecticut 06807) in connection
with any materials of historical interest that he might have
in his possession.

*Es war nicht möglich, Herr Bermann-Fischer (P.O. Box 237,
Old Greenwich, Connecticut 06807) zu erreichen, um Auskünfte
über historisch interessante Materialien in seinem Besitz zu
erlangen.*

University of Pennsylvania, The Charles Patterson Van Pelt
Library, Philadelphia, Pennsylvania 19104.

ALMA MAHLER-WERFEL COLLECTION

B1   96 L., 3 Ptc., 1 Tel. to Alma Mahler-Werfel. 1924-1964.
      Includes business as well as personal correspondence.
      3 L. to Franz Werfel. 1943-1945.

B2   Drafts of 2 L. from Alma Mahler-Werfel. Undated.

B3   Bermann-Fischer, Tutti. L. and Tel. to Alma Mahler-
      Werfel. 11p.

I   Business contracts between Werfel and Bermann-Fischer.
      47p.

Mrs. Alice Loewy Kahler, 1 Evelyn Place, Princeton, New Jersey 08540.

ERICH VON KAHLER COLLECTION

B1   14 L. and 2 Ptc. to Erich von Kahler. 1940-1967.

B2   2 L. and drafts of 2 L. from Erich von Kahler. 1940,
      1941.

University of California, Los Angeles, Department of Special
Collections, 120 Lawrence Clark Powell Library, Los Angeles,
California 90024.

GOTTFRIED BERMANN-FISCHER

FRANZ WERFEL ARCHIVE

B2   6 L. from Franz Werfel. 1944, 1945 and undated.

Library of Congress, Manuscript Division, Independence Avenue
and First Street S.E., Washington, D.C. 20540.

BENJAMIN W. HUEBSCH PAPERS

B1   2 L. to B. W. Huebsch. 1963.

Harvard University, Houghton Library, Cambridge, Massachusetts 02138.

RICHARD BEER-HOFMANN COLLECTION

B1   Correspondence between Bermann-Fischer and Beer-
      Hofmann.

SIEGFRIED BERNFELD

Psychoanalyst, 1892-1953

Library of Congress, Manuscript Division, Independence Avenue and First Street S.E., Washington, D.C. 20540.

The PAPERS OF SIEGFRIED BERNFELD, which consist of approximately 6,000 items (9 shelf ft.), were donated to the Library of Congress in Sept. 1970 by his two daughters, Ms. Rosemarie Ostwald and Ms. Ruth Goldberg, who still retain all literary rights to the papers. A 35-page inventory of the Bernfeld Papers (prepared by C. Langston Craig, July 1975) is available upon request from the Library of Congress.

Die PAPERS OF SIEGFRIED BERNFELD, die aus etwa 6000 Nummern bestehen (etwa 1,80 m), sind eine Schenkung (Sept. 1970) seiner beiden Töchter, Frau Rosemarie Ostwald und Frau Ruth Goldberg, an die Library of Congress. Die literarischen Rechte für alles Material der Sammlung ruhen bei Frau Ostwald und Frau Goldberg. Auf Anfrage ist ein 35-Seiten Inventar der Bernfeld Papers erhältlich, das im Juli 1975 von C. Langston Craig erarbeitet wurde.

B1,2 Family correspondence. 1895-1958 and undated. 3 F.
      General correspondence. 1891-1959 and undated. 4 B.
      Includes correspondences with: Franz Alexander, Walter Benjamin, Edmund Bergler, Julie Braun-Vogelstein, Arnold Brecht, Else Frankel Brunswik, Martin Buber, Frances Deri, Helene Deutsch, Paul Federn, Otto Fenichel, F. W. Foerster, Anna Freud, Hilda Geiringer, Martin Grotjahn, Heinz Hartmann, Max Horkheimer, Hans Kohn, Ernst Kris, Karl Menninger, Caroline Newton, Herman Nunberg, Sándor Rádo, Otto Rank, Theodor Reik, Hanns Sachs, Raymond de Saussure, Ernst Simmel, Abraham Sonne, René Spitz, Richard Sterba, Günther Stern (Anders), William Stern, Ernst Waldinger, Arnold Zweig. 4 B.

B1,2 Professional files: Europe 1858-1942 and U.S. 1909-
D7,   1970. 5 B. Includes correspondence, memoranda, min-
H3,   utes, cl., notes, printed material, reports, etc.
L   Arranged alphabetically and chronologically by folder.

C7   Articles, lecture texts, etc. 1913-1962 and undated.
      4 B. Includes Ms. and T. of the following articles:
      "Begriff der Deutung."

78

"Bemerkungen über der Zusammenhang zwischen Person
und Bewußtsein."
"Beobachtung und Beeinflussung ins Psychoanalyse und
Selbstbeobachtung."
"Beobachtungsproblem in der Psychologie."
"The Concept of 'Interpretation' in Psychoanalysis."
"Deformation, Reizarbeit, und Unterschieschwelle."
"Der Erzieher."
"Geometrie der Organismen."
"Die Glaubwürdigkeit der Psychoanalyse."
"Die Individualpsychologie Adlers, die Sozialwissen-
schaften, und die Psychoanalyse."
"Die Kindheit."
"Klassenpsychologie."
"Das Modell."
"Moral Sadism."
On Adolf Hitler.
"On Classification of the Impulses."
On Christian Thomasius.
On interpretation of purpose.
On passions.
"Die Psychoanalyse in der Erziehungswissenschaft."
"Psychoanalyse und Soziologie."
"Psychologie des Säuglings."
"Psychologische Deutung des W.-Gesetzes."
"Die soziale Funktion der therapeutischen Psychoana-
lyse."
"Theorie des Bewußtseins."
"Über die Einteilung der Triebe."
"Über die Gleichzeitigkeit des Urbildes."
"Über die Unschärfe Relation in der Psychologie und
Psychoanalyse."
"Über die Zweckmäßigkeit der Natur."
"Zur Geometrie der Organismen."

C7,   Sigmund Freud biographical material. 1854-1958. 8 B.
L,   Includes collected writings and research files of
N   Bernfeld and his wife on Freud, notes and notebooks,
      c. of some Freud correspondence, articles by Freud,
      etc.

SIEGFRIED BERNFELD

<u>University of New Hampshire</u>, The Library, Department of
Special Collections, Durham, New Hampshire 03824.

OSKAR MARIA GRAF COLLECTION

Bl   1 L. to O. M. Graf. 1960.

<u>Harvard University</u>, University Archives, Widener Library,
Cambridge, Massachusetts 02138.

RICHARD VON MISES COLLECTION

Bl   1 L. to Richard von Mises. 1949.

<u>American Philosophical Society</u>, The Library, 105 South Fifth
Street, Philadelphia, Pennsylvania 19106.

WOLFGANG KÖHLER PAPERS

Bl   1 L. to Wolfgang Köhler. 1931.

EMIL BERNHARD (COHN)

Writer, 1881-1948

Rabbi Bernhard N. Cohn, 90 Riverside Drive, New York, N.Y.
10024.

Rabbi Cohn, son of Emil Bernhard, and 2 daughters of Bernhard, Mrs. Hanna Frenkel (Studio City, California) and Mrs.
Miriam A. Rochin (Los Angeles, California), each own a portion of the papers. Permission to see materials may be obtained from any one of the 3 heirs.

*Der Nachlaß von Emil Bernhard (Cohn) ist unter seinem Sohn
(Rabbi Cohn, N.Y.) und seinen beiden Töchtern (Frau Hanna
Frenkel, Studio City, California; Frau Miriam A. Rochin,
Los Angeles, California) aufgeteilt. Erlaubnis zur Einsicht
in die Materialien kann von den Erben eingeholt werden.*

A1   Diaries. Emil Bernhard kept a diary from his 17th
      year on. The first entry is dated March 13, 1898,
      the last Dec. 31, 1947.

B1   1 L. to Rabbi Bernhard Cohn. 1939.

B2   Professional correspondence. 1908-1912, including L.
      concerning Bernhard's activities as Rabbi in Kiel.
      5 L. from Albert Einstein. 1940-1948.
      5 L. from Thomas Mann. A. 1942-1946.
      3 L. from Selma Lagerlöf, Dr. Mendel (Essen), Joseph
      von Wildenbusch.

B3   4 L. from Albert Einstein to Grete Cohn, wife of Emil
      Bernhard.
      4 L. from Thomas Mann to Grete Cohn. 1950-1951.

C2   Eden Hotel. English version of Hotel Eden (1931). T.
      Mirabeau. English tr. of Mirabeau (1921). T.
      The Prisoner. English tr. of Das reißende Lamm (1926).
      T.
      Die Wolke von Puerto Santo. T. Also English tr. The
      Clouds of Puerto Santo. T.

C4   "Claude-Marie." Novelle, written in German under the
      pseudonym Elmer Brooks. T.
      "Jippenscha Ikku." Unpub. fairy tale. T.
      "Li T'ai Po." Unpub. fairy tale. T.
      "Das Märchen vom Glasauge." Unpub. fairy tale. T.

"Das weiße Mäuschen." Unpub. fairy tale. T.

C5   Der blinde Geiger. Film version of comedy, written in
      German. T.
      Pierre. T.
      Shadow Love. Exposé for a television program. T.
      The Written Word. Exposé for a planned film comedy. T.

C7   Talks and lectures. Ms., outlines, rough drafts, espe-
      cially from the years 1930-1932, as well as from his
      California period.

D2   The majority of Bernhard's pub. works are represented
      in his literary estate.

D7   Newspaper and magazine cl. of articles by Bernhard from
      his American years, including numerous articles from:
      Central Blad voor Israeliten (1937-1938), The New
      Palestine, Congress Weekly.

H4   Die Jagd Gottes. Drama review. 1926. 1 cl.

I   Inheritance documents.
      Marriage certificate for Bernhard and Grete Kaufmann.
      Mühlheim/Ruhr, Dec. 21, 1913.
      Medical inaugural dissertation of the father of Bern-
      hard. Berlin, 1867.
      School separation certificate for "Emil Cohn." Berlin,
      Sept. 19, 1899.
      Bernhard's testament. Amsterdam, March 10, 1937. A. pc.

J   Ca. 25 family photos, from the German as well as the
      American period.

Leo Baeck Institute, 129 East 73rd Street, New York, N.Y.
10021.

A3   "Steht still und schauet. Meine letzte Predigt im Dien-
      ste der Berliner Gemeinde." A. 1907. 8p.

B1   1 L. to Fritz Mauthner. 1923.

B2   9 L. from: Leo Baeck, Martin Buber, Ludwig Geiger,
      Theodor Heuss, Max Nordan, Dr. Ascher, Stefan Zweig.
      T. and A.

C7   "Worte gesprochen am Grabe des verewigten Herrn Levi

Schwarz." 1922. T. pc. 7p.

D7   2 cl. 1907.

H3   1 cl. 1948.

I   "Regierungskommissar des Freien Rheinischen Republik."
      Undated flier. 2p.

J   2 photos.

Mrs. Elisabeth M. Stoerk and Mrs. Susanne B. Hoeller, 288
Ocean Drive West, Stamford, Connecticut 06902.

FRIDERIKE ZWEIG ARCHIVE

B1   L. to Friderike Zweig, filed under the heading Writers
      Service Center. 1943.

C4   "Shadow Love." Short story. T. 8p.

University of Chicago, The Joseph Regenstein Library, 1100
East 57th Street, Chicago, Illinois 60637.

JAMES FRANCK PAPERS

B1,2 Correspondence with James Franck.

CURTIS BERNHARDT

Producer, 1899-

<u>Mr. Curtis (Kurt) Bernhardt</u>, 1350 North Berea Place, Pacific
Palisades, California 90272.

Private collection: several feet. / *Privatsammlung.*

B1,2   Correspondence.

C5   Scripts of the American films (MGM and Warner) done by
       Bernhardt (ca. 60%).

I   Contracts.

J   Large collection of photos of films and personal
       photos.

JULIUS BERSTL

Writer, 1883-

University of Southern California, University Library, Department of Special Collections, University Park, Los Angeles, California 90007.

The JULIUS BERSTL COLLECTION, which consists of approximately 6 ft. of materials, was donated to the University of Southern California by Julius Berstl in 1975.

Die JULIUS BERSTL COLLECTION, etwa 1,80 m Material, ist eine Schenkung von Julius Berstl aus dem Jahre 1975 an die University of Southern California.

A1   Diary. Begun May 27, 1897. 50p.

A3   "Bilanz. Gedanken - Erinnerung." T. 56p. and h. notes.
      2 cc. T. 60p. plus 1 cc. 1 fragment.

B1,2 Personal correspondence. Ca. 230p. (2 F.)
      Business correspondence. 400p. plus 1 small F.
      Correspondence with other authors. 50p.
      Correspondence concerning translations. 30p.

B2,   80th birthday materials. 30p.
H3   85th birthday materials. Ca. 120p. (2 F.)
      90th birthday materials. Ca. 50p.

B,   Miscellaneous correspondence and photos.
J

C1   A Roman Courtesan. T.cc. 293p.
      Adams Urgroßvater. Familienporträt aus der Steinzeit.
         T. 194p. plus several cc.
      Adam's Great-Grandfather. Family Portrait from the
         Stone Ages. Original T. and T.cc. 222p.
      Anthony und Hummel-Dummel. Eine Geschichte für Kinder
         von 8-80 Jahren. T.cc. 175p.
      Briefe an einen Toten. T.cc. 218p.
      Dissertation zur Erlangung des Grades eines Doktors der
         Philosophie. Vorgelegt von Peter Petronius Pütz. A.
         11p. T. 56p. Ms. fragments. Ca. 200p.
      Eine Prise Gold. Original T. 216p. T. 316p.
         A Pinch of Golddust. T.cc. 245p.
      Erst Brot dann Kuchen. T.cc. with corr. 327p.
         Bread before Cake. T. 88p. A. 83p. T.cc. plus addi-

tional T.cc. Original T. 288p.
Die Fahrt ins Rosenrote. T.
  Traveling into a Rosy Future. A. 89p. Dated 3.7.1973.
Der große Kean. 2c. 249p. ea. Notes. Also 1 F. music
  and various Ms.
Der heilige Zahn. T.cc. 240p. Another c. with corr.
  240p.
  The Sacred Tooth. Original T. and 2 cc. 235p. ea.
Hornißl. Reisen Abenteuer und unmaßgebliche Meinungen
  des letzten Individualisten. T.c. 127p. cc. 127p.
  Hornissl. Travels - Adventures and Unpretentious
  Opinions of the Last Individualist. Original T. with
  corr. 108p. Multiple c.
Irrgarten der Liebe. T. with corr. 276p. Another 2 cc.
  Labyrinth of Love. T.cc. with numerous corr. 251p.
  Another 2 cc.   .
Kaiserallee. T. with corr. 247p.
Marietta. Eine heitere Tier- und Menschengeschichte.
  T. 134p.
  Marietta, the Highbrow Hen. Story on Hens and Human
  Beings. T.c. 134p. and A. notes.
Strom ohne Ufer. Original T., no corr. T. with corr.
  240p. Alternate titles: Alarich, König der Lemminge.
  A Battling for Rome (River without Banks). T. 36p.
  River without Banks. Final version. T. with corr.
  225p. plus additions. 2 additional c.
Der Teufel in Berlin. T.c. 51p.
Tolstoy und Sonya. Several original T. versions, some
  with corr. 237p. H. original. 60+p.
Zeltmacher. T. 120p.
Untitled Ms. A. 300p.

C2   A Woman of Many Faces. T.c. 74p.
Chu the Sinner. T. Multiple c.
Dover-Calais. Lustspiel. 6c. ea. 85p. Bühnenmanuskript.
  Dover-Calais. Light Comedy. English adaptation by
  Eleanor Farjeon. T. 2c.
Feenhände. Schauspiel. Original T. and cc. 83p. ea.
Die Gräfin Lavalette. Schauspiel in drei Akten. T.cc.
  89p.
Mendelssohn und Malibran. Lustspiel. Original T. and cc.
  106p.
Die Nachtigall und der Pudel. Sinfonia Domestica. cc.
  81p.

Napi. 3cc.
Pinke & Co. Burleske in 3 Akten von Peter Pistorius.
Scribby's Suppen sind die Besten. A. notes, with nota-
tion "New Yorker Bearbeitung." Also printed version.
Der Teufel schläft nie. A. Ca. 200p. 2cc. 107p. ea.
The Devil Never Sleeps. Original T. 101p. Notes. A.
100p.
Die Venusfliegenfalle. Lustspiel in 3 Akten. T. 87p.
2cc.
Venus' Flytrap. Light Comedy. T.c. 79p. cc.
Von vorn anfangen. Cc. with numerous corr. 91p.
Begin from the Beginning. The tragic comedy of the
opportunistic politician. T. 104p. Corr. A. 30p.
The Widow of Ephesus. T. Several c. with notes.
Mimeographed acting versions of the following plays:
Napi, Penelope, Scribbys Suppen sind die Besten,
Endlich ein Käufer, Der lasterhafte Herr Tschu,
Der Flußgott, Hier bin ich, hier bleib ich, Mrs.
Cheney's Ende, Ein Monat auf dem Lande, Zur gefl.
Ansicht.

C3   Ein Menschenleben. Gedichtkreis. 1905-1965. T. 2cc.
       Ca. 50p. 2 notebooks of poems.

C4   "An Idyll with Ominous Undertones." A. 3p.
       "Idylle mit ominösen Untertönen." T. 3p. 2 T.cc.
       "Die große und die kleine Welt. Anekdoten, neu erzählt
       von J.B." T. and cl. (of pub. pieces).
       "The Rivergod." A. 6p.
       Synopses of short stories. German and English. 200p.
       Short stories. T. 200p.
       Short stories and fragments. T. 70p.
       Short stories. A. 50p.
       Miscellaneous short T. 70p.

C4,5   Short stories and film scenarios. 1 F.

C8   2 notebooks on graphology.

C9   3 plays tr. into German from French and English.
       Catto, Max. Das Blut singt. Tr. by Julius Berstl.
       Ich komme wieder. Komödie von John Copard. Tr. by
       Julius Berstl.

D4   Lichtenbergs Idyll. Liebesgeschichte. Reclam 1927. 71p.

2c.
Misc. magazine issues with contributions by Berstl.

H4   Berlin Schlesischer Bahnhof, Odyssee eines Theater-
      mannes. Reviews. 50p.
      Der große Kean. 40 cl.
      Paulus von Tarsus. 30 reviews, 50 cl., 1 envelope re-
      views.
      Materials on Berstl's plays tr. by Berstl and produced
      in the U.S.

H4,   Playbills and reviews of plays. Ca. 100 items.
O

I   Personal documents from high school, university.

J   3 albums with photos.

L   Miscellaneous cl. and short pieces. 100p. (2 F.)
      Bible quotations. 1 F.
      Miscellaneous World War II cl.

M   1 book of recipes.
      Ca. 100 picture postcards.

O   Collection of playbills.

Yale University, Beinecke Rare Book and Manuscript Library,
New Haven, Connecticut 06520.

EDMOND PAUKER COLLECTION

I   Napoleon der Zweite. Contracts.

Leo Baeck Institute, 129 East 73rd Street, New York, N.Y.
10021.

Bl   1 L. to Dr. Lutz Weltmann. T. 1953.

HANS A. BETHE

Physicist, 1906-

Dr. Hans A. Bethe, Newman Laboratory, Cornell University,
Ithaca, New York 14853.

Private collection: inaccessible. The materials will eventually be added to the HANS BETHE PAPERS already at Cornell
University.

*Unzugängliche Privatsammlung. Die Materialien werden später
einmal im Sinne der Erweiterung der HANS BETHE PAPERS, die
schon als Sammlung existieren, an die Cornell University
gehen.*

B1,2   Correspondence.

C8   Numerous scientific notes (several filing cabinets).
        Unpub. papers written for wartime secret projects.
        Ms. of pub. papers (few).

D8   Offprints of pub. articles.

I   Passports, documents, papers relating to appointment at
        Columbia.

J   Moderately large photo collection.

K   Personal library, with many complete sets of journals.

L   Numerous cl.

Cornell University, John M. Olin Library, Department of
Manuscripts and University Archives, Ithaca, New York 14850.

The HANS BETHE PAPERS 1935-1942, 16 archive boxes of largely
uncatalogued materials, were donated to the archives by Dr.
Bethe in 1964, 1966, 1970 and 1975 plus isolated individual
items at intervals. The greatest bulk of the collection
consists of notes and calculations related to highly technical and specialized areas of physics. Permission to use the
collection is obtainable from Dr. Hans A. Bethe.

*Die HANS BETHE PAPERS 1935-1942, 16 Archivkartons größten-
teils unkatalogisierten Materials, sind eine Schenkung von
Dr. Bethe (1964, 1966, 1970, 1975 sowie spätere kleine Ein-*

zelgaben). Die Sammlung besteht hauptsächlich aus Anmerkun-
gen und Berechnungen aus Spezialgebieten der Physik. Erlaub-
nis, die Sammlung einzusehen, kann von Dr. Bethe eingeholt
werden.

B1   Recommendations of various physicists for posts and
grants.

B1,2 Correspondence with colleagues concerning nuclear
physics, solar and stellar energy, radiation, con-
duction in metals, quantum mechanics, including correspondence with: Eugene Wigner, H. Shapley, J.
Robert Oppenheimer.
Correspondence dealing with Bethe's role in conference
for discontinuance of nuclear weapons tests.

C7   Outlines for courses.
Faculty Committee on Nuclear Peril. Lectures in Jan.-
April 1962.

C8   Calculations and research notes concerning nuclear
physics, solar and stellar energy, radiation, conduc-
tion in metals, quantum mechanics.

D7   Published papers.

F   Record of a talk (during intermission) at performance
of New York Philharmonic on Atomic Energy. Dec. 2,
1942.

G   T. of TV interview, re: science education in the U.S.

H3, Brochures, articles, newspaper cl. dealing with Bethe's
L   active role in conference for discontinuance of
nuclear weapons, etc.

H4   Reviews of Bethe's professional writing.

I   Materials concerning Cornell Physics Department.

L   Materials relating to Bethe's consulting activities
outside of Cornell.
Information on physics conferences and lectures, science conventions.

N   Theses.
Published papers by others.

HANS A. BETHE

American Institute of Physics, Niels Bohr Library, 335 East
45th Street, New York, N.Y. 10017.

NIELS BOHR CORRESPONDENCE, S. A. GOUDSMIT COLLECTION, PIC-
TORIAL FILE, ORAL HISTORY COLLECTION, FRITZ REICHE PAPERS

B1   10 L. to Niels Bohr. 1933-1954. Microfilm.
        2 L. to S. A. Goudsmit. 1936-1937. Pc.

B2   6 L. from Niels Bohr. 1932-1939. Microfilm.
        1 L. from S. A. Goudsmit. 1937. Pc.

F   Tapes of talks:
        "Energy Production in the Stars." 1968. Includes
        transcript.
        "Nuclear Matter." 1966.
        "Nuclear Matter." 1968.
        Film footage in the film The World of Enrico Fermi.

G   Taped interview. 5 hours.
        Taped interview. 15 hours with transcript.

H5   Reiche, Fritz. "Bethe and Weizsäcker - Nuclear Phys-
        ics." Ca. 250p. of notes on the work of Bethe and
        Weizsäcker. Undated. In German. A.

I   Explanation of travel expenses, trip to Copenhagen.
        1934. Microfilm.

J   Uncatalogued photos. Portraits and group photos.

Library of Congress, Manuscript Division, Independence Avenue and First Street S.E., Washington, D.C. 20540.

J. ROBERT OPPENHEIMER PAPERS: General case file (Bethe).
2 F.

B1   Ca. 30 L. and Tel. to J. Robert Oppenheimer. T. and A.
        1942-1966.
        4 L. 1943-1953.

B2   11 L. from J. R. Oppenheimer. T. and A. 1942-1966.

B3   L. between Bethe's lawyer and others re: reparation.

C8   "Reaction of Radiation on Electron Scattering and

91

HANS A. BETHE

Hitler's Theory of Radiation Damping." Written in
collaboration with J. R. Oppenheimer. [1948]. T.cc.,
with h. corr. 30p.
"The Hydrogen Bomb." [1950]. T.cc. 20p.

I   Recommendation for J. R. Oppenheimer. 1959. T.

Mrs. Alice Loewy Kahler, 1 Evelyn Place, Princeton, New
Jersey 08540.

ERICH VON KAHLER COLLECTION

B1   2 L. to Erich von Kahler. 1950, 1965.

B2   1 L. from Erich von Kahler. 1950.
     1 L. from I. I. Rabi. 1965.

B3   7 L. and 3 Ptc. from Rose Bethe to Erich von Kahler.
     1947-1968.

C7   "The Hydrogen Bomb." Mimeo. with h. notes and under-
     linings by Erich von Kahler. 20p.

H3   Edson, Lee. "Scientific Man for All Seasons," NYT
     Magazine, March 10, 1968, 28-29, 122-127. Cl.

American Philosophical Society, The Library, 105 South Fifth
Street, Philadelphia, Pennsylvania 19106.

W. J. VON OSTERHOUT PAPERS

B1,2 Correspondence with W. J. v. Osterhout.

Archive for History of Quantum Physics (locations in U.S.:
Bancroft Library, University of California, Berkeley; American Philosophical Society, Philadelphia, Pennsylvania; American Institute of Physics, New York, N.Y.).

B1   2 L. to Christian Møller. 1932.
     2 L. to Arnold Sommerfeld. 1933.

HANS A. BETHE

B2   1 L. ea. from Christian Møller and Arnold Sommerfeld.
      1931, 1946.

G   Transcript of interview. 1964. 22p.

University of California, Berkeley, The Bancroft Library,
Berkeley, California 94720.

E. O. LAWRENCE PAPERS

B1   9 L. to E. O. Lawrence. 1937-1956.

New York University, Courant Institute of Mathematical Sciences, Library, 251 Mercer Street, New York, N.Y. 10012.

B1,2 "Hans A. Bethe" file. 1942-1952.
I

Duke University, William R. Perkins Library, Manuscript
Department, Durham, North Carolina 27706.

FRITZ LONDON PAPERS

B1   1 L. to F. W. London. 1934.

B2   Draft of L. from F. W. London. 1934.

Smithsonian Institution, Dibner Library, Washington, D.C.
20560.

J   Photo from New York Times. 1960s.

California Institute of Technology, Robert A. Millikan Library, Pasadena, California 91109.

THEODOR VON KARMAN CORRESPONDENCE

B1,2   Correspondence with Theodore von Karman. 1940-1941.

New York Public Library, Manuscript Division, Fifth Avenue and 42nd Street, New York, N.Y. 10018.

EMERGENCY COMMITTEE IN AID OF DISPLACED FOREIGN SCHOLARS, 1933-1945.

*   File compiled, no assistance given. 1934-1940.

Leo Baeck Institute, 129 East 73rd Street, New York, N.Y. 10021.

MARTA FRAENKEL COLLECTION

J   Photo of Bethe. Cornell, 1935.

BRUNO BETTELHEIM
Psychoanalyst, 1903–

Dr. Bruno Bettelheim was interviewed by the Project concerning any materials of historical interest that he might have retained. At that time (1976) Dr. Bettelheim assured the Project that he had not kept such materials, but rather disposed of them prior to his move to California. The files of the Sonia Shankman Orthogenic School in Chicago do contain some information on Dr. Bettelheim; however, the work of the school is sensitive and there is no material available for research.

Als Dr. Bruno Bettelheim 1976 um Auskünfte hinsichtlich seiner historisch relevanten Materialien befragt wurde, versicherte er, er habe jegliches derartige Material vor seinem Umzug nach Kalifornien vernichtet. Die Akten der Sonia Shankman Orthogenic School in Chicago enthalten einige Materialien über Dr. Bettelheim, die allerdings wegen der empfindlichen Natur der Arbeit dieses Instituts nicht für Forschungszwecke zur Verfügung stehen.

Library of Congress, Manuscript Division, Independence Avenue and First Street S.E., Washington, D.C. 20540.

MAXWELL GITELSON PAPERS, DAVID RAPAPORT PAPERS

B1,2   Correspondence with Maxwell Gitelson.
        Correspondence with David Rapaport.

University of Iowa, The University Libraries, Special Collections, Iowa City, Iowa 52240.

B1   1 L. to Mrs. Delta Falvey. 1948.
      1 L. to James S. Schramm. 1948.

University of Chicago, The Joseph Regenstein Library, 1100 East 57th Street, Chicago, Illinois 60637.

LOUIS WIRTH PAPERS

B1   1 L. to Louis Wirth. 1952.

BRUNO BETTELHEIM

<u>Leo Baeck Institute</u>, 129 East 73rd Street, New York, N.Y. 10021.

H4   <u>The Informed Heart</u>. 1 cl.

FRANZ BLEI

Writer, 1871-1942

Leo Baeck Institute, 129 East 73rd Street, New York, N.Y. 10021.

The FRANZ BLEI COLLECTION (AR-B.319, 2933, uncatalogued) consists of ca. 330 letters and was donated in June 1963 by Dr. Joachim Schondorff (Munich).

Die FRANZ BLEI COLLECTION (AR-B.319, 2933, nicht katalogisiert) besteht aus etwa 330 Briefen. Sie ist eine Schenkung von Dr. Joachim Schondorff, München, aus dem Jahre 1963.

B1,2   Ca. 300 L. to and from the Georg-Müller Verlag, Munich. 1909-1915.

B3   Ca. 30 L. from Fritz Bley (editor of Zeitfragen) to the Georg-Müller Verlag. 1907-1911.

J   2 photos of F. Blei.

Yale University, Beinecke Rare Book and Manuscript Library, New Haven, Connecticut 06520.

KURT WOLFF ARCHIVE, HERMANN BROCH ARCHIVE

B1   8 L. to Kurt Wolff Verlag. 1913-1921.

B2   6 L. from Kurt Wolff Verlag. 1913-1921.

H4   Formen der Liebe. Review by H. Broch. T.cc. with h. corr. by Broch. 2p.

ERNST BLOCH

Philosopher, 1885-

Leo Baeck Institute, 129 East 73rd Street, New York, N.Y. 10021.

D7   "Die sogenannte Judenfrage." 1 cl. 1963.

H3   3 cl. 1957-1970.

J   3 photos of E. Bloch. 1956 and undated.

Harvard University, Houghton Library, Cambridge, Massachusetts 02138.

GEORGE SARTON PAPERS

B1   15 L. to George Sarton. 1924-1940.

B2   2 L. from George Sarton. [1925], 1940.

Harvard University, Harvard Divinity School, Andover-Harvard Theological Library, 45 Francis Avenue, Cambridge, Massachusetts 02138.

PAUL TILLICH COLLECTION

B1   1 L. to P. Tillich. A. 1962.

B2   1 L. from P. Tillich. T. 1960.

University of Texas, Humanities Research Center, Manuscripts Collection, Box 7219, Austin, Texas 78712.

B1,2 Uncatalogued and unsorted L.

C   1 Ms.

Prof. Adolf Lowe, 1125 Grand Concourse, The Bronx, New York 10452.

B1,2 Correspondence with Adolf Lowe. Ca. 10 L. 1940s.

98

ERNST BLOCH

Mills College, Library, Oakland, California 94613.

Bl   9 L. to Albert M. Bender. 1928-1930.
      2 L. to Frederick J. Koster. 1928-1930.

Yale University, Beinecke Rare Book and Manuscript Library,
New Haven, Connecticut 06520.

KURT WOLFF ARCHIVE, HERMANN BROCH ARCHIVE

Bl   1 L. to Kurt Wolff. A. 1921.
      6 L. to Hermann Broch. 1944-1949.

Indiana University, The University Libraries, The Lilly
Library, Bloomington, Indiana 47401.

LEWIS BROWNE MSS.

Bl   1 L. to Lewis Browne. 1924.

Library of Congress, Manuscript Division, Independence Avenue and First Street S.E., Washington, D.C. 20540.

BENJAMIN W. HUEBSCH PAPERS

Bl   2 L. to B. W. Huebsch.

American Philosophical Society, The Library, 105 South Fifth
Street, Philadelphia, Pennsylvania 19106.

SIMON FLEXNER PAPERS

Bl,2 Correspondence between Bloch and Simon Flexner.

Barthold Fles Literary Agency, 507 Fifth Avenue, New York,
N.Y. 10016.

Bl   2 L. to Barthold Fles. 1940 and undated.

99

ERNST BLOCH

<u>Mrs. Liselotte Stein</u>, 115-25 Metropolitan Avenue, Kew Gardens, New York 11418.

FRED STEIN PAPERS

J   Photos of Ernst Bloch.

FELIX BLOCH

Physicist, 1905-

Prof. Felix Bloch, Department of Physics, Stanford University, Stanford, California 94305.

Dr. Bloch has discarded all of his correspondence as well as the manuscripts of all of his writings. The remaining materials in his possession are, as of 1976, inaccessible to researchers and scholars.

Professor Bloch hat seine gesamte Korrespondenz sowie alle Manuskripte seiner Veröffentlichungen vernichtet. Die Materialien, die sich sonst noch in seinem Besitz befinden, waren zumindest 1976 für Forschungszwecke noch nicht zugänglich.

A2   Laboratory notes from before and shortly after the war only.

C7   Lecture notes.

D7   Offprint of speech given by Bloch upon acceptance of the Nobel Prize.

D7,8 Complete collection of offprints and xeroxes of Bloch's writings, bound. 3 volumes. Another 2 c. located in the Library of the Physics Department, Stanford University.

G   Transcripts of taped interviews with Charles Weiner and Thomas S. Kuhn.

I   Documents.

J   Photos.

K   Personal library, including scientific periodicals.

L   Miscellaneous newspaper cl. 1 B.
      Offprints by others, including many by Niels Bohr.
      Some valuable offprints included. Ca. 2 ft.

American Institute of Physics, Niels Bohr Library, 335 East 45th Street, New York, N.Y. 10017.

NIELS BOHR CORRESPONDENCE, S. A. GOUDSMIT COLLECTION, PICTORIAL FILE, ORAL HISTORY COLLECTION

B1 22 L. to Niels Bohr. 1931-1955. Microfilm.
2 L. to S. A. Goudsmit. 1936-1937.

B2 12 L. from Niels Bohr. 1931-1938. Microfilm.
3 L. from S. A. Goudsmit. 1936-1937. Cc.

F   Taping of a talk: "Reminiscences of Niels Bohr." 1963.
Film footage in a short film, produced by a Mr. Denni-
son. [1935].

G   Taped interview, plus transcript. 3 hours.

J   Photos, portraits and group. Unsorted and uncatalogued.

Library of Congress, Manuscript Division, Independence Avenue and First Street S.E., Washington, D.C. 20540.

J. ROBERT OPPENHEIMER PAPERS: General Case File (Bloch)

B1 7 L. and Tel to J. R. Oppenheimer. 1942-1943.

B2 6 L. and Tel. from J. R. Oppenheimer. 1942-1943.

I   Affidavit, swearing to maintain secrecy concerning details of the Los Alamos Project. 1943.

University of California, Los Alamos Scientific Laboratory,
P.O. Box 1663, Los Alamos, New Mexico 87544.

DIRECTOR'S PERSONNEL FILE

B1 Transcript of L. to John Wheeler. 1951.

B2 9 L. to Bloch. 1946-1950.

B3 16 L. re: Bloch's role as consultant at Los Alamos.

C8 Notebook of project activities, together with Hans
Staub. Restricted usage.

I   9 reports concerning work done at Los Alamos Scientific
Laboratory.
6 reports concerning work done at locations other than
Los Alamos.
Shipping orders, supply requests and invoices, Los Ala-
mos Scientific Laboratory. 1947. 4 items.

FELIX BLOCH

Stanford University Libraries, University Archives, Department of Special Collections, Stanford, California 94305.

WILLIAM WEBSTER HANSEN COLLECTION: collection closed

Bl   Ca. 15 L. to William Webster Hansen, concerning the development of the Stanford Microwave Laboratory. 1939-1948.

Duke University, William R. Perkins Library, Manuscript Department, Durham, North Carolina 27706.

Bl   2 L. to Marcus Edwin Hobbs. 1954.

Archive for History of Quantum Physics (locations in U.S.: Bancroft Library, University of California, Berkeley; American Philosophical Society, Philadelphia, Pennsylvania; American Institute of Physics, New York, N.Y.).

Bl   1 L. ea. to H. A. Kramers and Gregor Wentzel. 1938, 1933.

G   Transcript of an interview. 1964. 40p.

New York Public Library, Manuscript Division, Fifth Avenue and 42nd Street, New York, N.Y. 10018.

EMERGENCY COMMITTEE IN AID OF DISPLACED FOREIGN SCHOLARS, 1933-1945

*   File compiled when assistance was granted. 1933-1942.

University of Chicago, The Joseph Regenstein Library, 1100 East 57th Street, Chicago, Illinois 60637.

JAMES FRANCK PAPERS

Bl   1 L. to James Franck on Franck's 70th birthday. 1952.

KONRAD BLOCH

Biochemist, 1912-

Prof. Konrad Bloch, Conant Laboratory, 38 Oxford Street,
Harvard University, Cambridge, Massachusetts 02138.

Private collection: inaccessible. Dr. Bloch intends to
donate his materials to the Harvard University Archives.

*Unzugängliche Privatsammlung. Dr. Bloch hat vor, seine
Materialien den Harvard University Archives zu übergeben.*

A1   Desk calendars, appointment calendars (no diaries).

A2   Work notes (in notebooks).

B1,2 Correspondence, 1930-1935, concerning Bloch's attempts
      to find a position in the U.S.
      Correspondence, including c. of Bloch's own L. after
      1940.

C8   Teaching materials, including 25 years of lecture
      notes to 1 course.
      Manuscripts of lectures.
      Manuscripts of articles (only ca. 1/3 of total).

D8   Offprints of all of Bloch's articles.

H3, Cl. from newspapers, magazines.
L

I   Documents, awards, appointment L.

J   Photographs: family and other.

K   Personal library: scientific works and belles lettres.
     Journal of Biological Chemistry (30 years).

L   Files on international meetings and symposia, invita-
     tions.

N   Possible manuscripts of others.

American Philosophical Society, The Library, 105 South Fifth
Street, Philadelphia, Pennsylvania 19106.

MAX BERGMANN PAPERS, HANS T. CLARKE PAPERS

B1,2   Correspondence concerning U.S. citizenship and state
        of science. May 1941 - Oct. 1943 (Bergmann).
        Correspondence concerning Journal of Biological Chem-
        istry (Clarke).

ILSE BLUMENTHAL-WEISS

Poetess, 1899-

Leo Baeck Institute, 129 East 73rd Street, New York, N.Y. 10021.

This collection of approximately 178 items (AR 1020) was donated to the Institute by Mrs. Blumenthal-Weiss. These materials represent only a small portion of the total Blumenthal-Weiss collection, which has been retained by Mrs. Blumenthal-Weiss at her home in New York.

Diese Sammlung von etwa 178 Nummern (AR 1020) ist eine Schenkung von Frau Blumenthal-Weiss an das Institut. Diese Materialien stellen nur einen kleinen Teil der gesamten Blumenthal-Weiss Sammlung dar, die sich zur Hauptsache in der Wohnung von Frau Blumenthal-Weiss in New York befindet.

A3   "Im Auftrag des Reichskommissars." A. 1957. 81p.

B1   3 L. to Leo Baeck.
      1 L. to Rabbi Grünewald. 1970.

B2   4 L., including 1 ea. from: Max Brod and Franz Werfel.

C3   2 poems.

C7   1 report. 3p.
      1 lecture. 20p.
      5 Ms. of lectures, articles, etc., primarily on the
      Leo Baeck Institute, New York.

D3   "Heimkehr aus dem Konzentrations-Lager."
      Poems from an oral presentation. 18p.

D7   22 cl., various topics.
      9 cl., primarily on the Leo Baeck Institute.
      2 cl., on Hannah Arendt.

H3   14 cl.

I   Invitations, notices, etc. 6 items.

J   2 photos of Ilse Blumenthal-Weiss.

O   2 programs.

Further materials donated by Mrs. Blumenthal-Weiss were added to the following existing collections at the Institute.

106

ILSE BLUMENTHAL-WEISS

Zu folgenden schon bestehenden Sammlungen wurden Blumenthal-Weiss Materialien (Schenkungen der Autorin) hinzugefügt:

HERMANN HESSE COLLECTION: 6 L., 2 photos, 1 poem, 1 short
      text.
JACOB PICARD COLLECTION: 9 L., 1 text, 1 poem.
NELLY SACHS COLLECTION: 28 L. and Ptc., 1 poem, 5 photos.
MARGARETE SUSMAN COLLECTION: 36 L.

Harvard University, Houghton Library, Cambridge, Massachusetts 02138.

RICHARD BEER-HOFMANN COLLECTION, AUTOGRAPH FILE

B1 1 L. to Richard Beer-Hofmann. 1923.

C7 "Frauengestalten um Rainer Maria Rilke," and "Rainer
   Maria Rilke and Our Time." T.cc. with h. corr. 33p.
   "Kleine Variation aus einem Brief von R[ainer] M[aria]
   R[ilke]." A. 1951. 1p.

G   "Interview mit Ilse Blumenthal-Weiss anläßlich des 25.
   Todestages des Dichters Rainer Maria Rilke." T.cc.
   New York, Dec. 30, 1951. 3p.

Mrs. Gertrude Urzidil, 83-39 116th Street, Richmond Hill,
New York 11418.

JOHANNES URZIDIL COLLECTION

B1 6 L. to Johannes Urzidil. T. and A. 1951-1961.

B2 2 L. from Johannes Urzidil. T.cc. 1951.

Princeton University, Firestone Library, Princeton, New Jersey 08540.

ALLEN TATE COLLECTION

B1 1 L. to Allen Tate. 1951.

ERWIN BODKY

Musicologist, Harpsichordist, 1896-1958

Mrs. Angelica Lee, 353 School Street, Watertown, Massachusetts 02172.

This collection of Erwin Bodky materials has been assembled
by members of his family, in particular by his daughter, Mrs.
Lee, and represents the most complete collection of Bodky
materials in existence.

*Diese Sammlung von Materialien von und über Erwin Bodky ist
von Familienmitgliedern, insbes. von seiner Tochter, Frau
Angelica Lee, zusammengestellt worden. Sie ist die vollständigste Materialiensammlung über Erwin Bodky.*

B2   L. to Bodky, including a number of fan L.

C   Ms. of a book.

C13   Ms. of compositions by Bodky.

F   Recordings of Bodky's performances, playing. Ca. 12
       records.

H4   Newspaper reviews of concerts and performances. 1938-
       1958.

O   Posters and programs from concerts in Germany and Hol-
       land.

J   Numerous photos, including many of Black Mountain Col-
       lege.

M   Memorabilia, including Bodky's collection of instru-
       ments, which he had either built, played or collected.

State of North Carolina, Department of Cultural Resources,
Raleigh, North Carolina 27611.

BLACK MOUNTAIN COLLEGE ARCHIVES

I   Faculty file: "Erwin Bodky - Music."
       General file: "Summer Music Institute 1945 - Publicity
       - Erwin Bodky."

J   Portrait photo

ERWIN BODKY

New York Public Library, Manuscript Division, Fifth Avenue
and 42nd Street, New York, N.Y. 10018.

EMERGENCY COMMITTEE IN AID OF DISPLACED FOREIGN SCHOLARS,
1933-1945

*   File compiled when assistance was granted. 1934-1944.

Dr. Frank Borchardt, German Department, Duke University, Durham, North Carolina 27706.

The HERMANN BORCHARDT PAPERS in the possession of his son, Dr. Frank Borchardt, consist of approximately 6 ft. of materials. Additional materials, as well as copies of some of the items in Dr. Borchardt's possession, are located in the private collection of Kurt Schümann (Düsseldorf, Bilker Allee 136, West Germany), who was officially designated by the Borchardt family to act as executor of Borchardt's estate.

Im Besitz von Dr. Frank Borchardt, dem Sohn von Hermann Borchardt, befinden sich die HERMANN BORCHARDT PAPERS, etwa 1,80 m Material. Zusätzliche Materialien sowie Kopien einzelner Nummern der H. B. PAPERS befinden sich in der Privatsammlung von Kurt Schümann (Düsseldorf, Bilker Allee 136), der offiziell von der Familie Borchardt zum Testamentsvollstrecker bestimmt wurde.

A3   Der Club der Harmlosen: Wahre Lebensgeschichte in Geschichte meines Lebens.
     "The Holy Shammes." Borchardt's experiences in Minsk, 1934.
     Lagerbuch. Materials concerning Borchardt's experiences in German concentration camps.

B1   L. written from concentration camps: Sachsenhausen and Dachau. 1936-1937.
     3 L. to George Grosz. 1934-1935.

B2   67 L. and Ptc. from George Grosz. 1937-1950.

C1   Conspiracy of the Carpenters. Ms. in German.
     Die Verschwörung der Zimmerleute. Ms. in German.

C2   The Brethren of Halberstadt. Drama in 2 Acts. T.
     Bürger und Soldaten. Historisches Schauspiel aus der Hitlerzeit. "Geschrieben im Jahre 1939, mit Ausnahme des Singspiels im 2. Akt, das ich im Herbst 1938 auf Veranlassung eines Komponisten verfertigt habe." T.
     Fragments of dramas. Unsorted. 1 F.
     Die Frau des Polizei-Kommissars. Drama in 3 acts. T.

Der Gespensterseher, or Der Unterirdische, or Außerhalb
der Schöpfung. A comedy. English titles: The Ghost-
writer, or Outside of Creation. Ms.
The Lost Column. Play in 5 acts. T.
Das Mädchen von Reichenberg. Ms.
Pastor Muller's Redemption. T.
Der verlorene Haufe. Play in 5 acts. T.

C3   "Kunstgedicht gedichtet am 1. Juli 1937 auf Veranlas-
sung von George Grosz und für dessen Schwägerin,
Frau Charlotte Schmalhausen in Berlin, und sogleich
dorthin übersandt. von Hermann Borchardt." Satirical
poem.

C7   Commentary on the paintings of George Grosz. Unpub. A.
37p.
Six Lectures. Philosophical topics. T.
Traktat über die Unsterblichkeit. Incomplete version.
T. 492p. Second part. T.
"Die Zweiweltentheorie und John Locke." Probably
part of Traktat.
Treatise of Immortality. English Ms.
Miscellaneous unpub. fragmentary Ms. A.

H3   Schümann, Kurt. Lecture on Hermann Borchardt, held in
Düsseldorf. Oct. 24, 1960. 18p.

H4   The Conspiracy of the Carpenters. 1943. Collection of
American newspaper cl., collected in an album entitled "Vanity Fair."

I   Documents re: Borchardt's case against Ernst Toller in
connection with the drama Pastor Hall. Also correspondence concerning the case, to and from Toller's
lawyers.

M   Borchardt's address book from his American exile years.

O   Program. German American League for Culture, 45 Astor
Place, New York. March 7, 1942. Accompanied by bit-
ter antibolshevistic commentary by George Grosz.
Program. German American League for Culture. Goethe-
Tag, May 18, 1942. Accompanied by bitter antibolshe-
vistic commentary from George Grosz.

University of Pennsylvania, The Charles Patterson Van Pelt
Library, Philadelphia, Pennsylvania 19104.

ALMA MAHLER-WERFEL COLLECTION

B1   36 L. to Alma Mahler-Werfel. T. and A. 1940-1946.
      21 L. to Franz Werfel. T. and A. 1941-1945.
      1 L. to Prinz Hubertus zu Loewenstein. T. Undated.

B2   2 L. from Franz Werfel. 1943.

C7   "Germany Speaking." Lecture. T.cc. 4p.

Princeton University, Firestone Library, Princeton, New Jersey 08540.

BARROWS MUSSY COLLECTION

C1   The Conspiracy of the Carpenters. Tr. by Barrows Mussy.
      English tr. Ca. 400p.

State University of New York at Albany, Department of Germanic Languages and Literatures, 1400 Washington Avenue,
Albany, New York 12222.

STORM PUBLISHERS ARCHIVE

B1   3 L. and 4 Ptc. to Alexander Gode von Aesch. 1945.

B2   4 L. from Alexander Gode von Aesch. 1945.

University of California, Los Angeles, Department of Special
Collections, 120 Lawrence Clark Powell Library, and Dr.
Gustave O. Arlt, 13220-C Admiralty Way, Marina del Rey,
California 90291.

FRANZ WERFEL ARCHIVE

B1   4 L. to Franz Werfel. 1942-1945 and undated.

H4   Werfel, Franz. Introduction to Borchardt's novel Die
      Verschwörung der Zimmerleute. Undated [194-?]. 3

versions. 7p., 4p., 9p.

Immigration History Research Center of the University of Minnesota, 826 Berry Street, St. Paul, Minnesota 55101.

AMERICAN COUNCIL FOR EMIGRÉS IN THE PROFESSIONS ARCHIVES

A3   Biographical sketches. 7p.

B1   2 L. to Else Staudinger. 1943, 1947.

H4   Die Verschwörung der Tischler. 2 reviews.

Syracuse University, The George Arents Research Library, Syracuse, New York 13210.

DOROTHY THOMPSON PAPERS

B1   8 L. to Dorothy Thompson. 1947.

B3   1 L. re: Dorothy Thompson. 1947.

Harvard University, Houghton Library, Cambridge, Massachusetts 02138.

RICHARD BEER-HOFMANN COLLECTION

B1   1 L. to Richard Beer-Hofmann. 1912.

Mrs. Peter M. Lindt, 949 West End Avenue, New York, N.Y. 10025.

C   Ms. submitted to Lindt for use on his radio program.

GIUSEPPE ANTONIO BORGESE
Writer, 1882-1952

Yale University, Beinecke Rare Book and Manuscript Library, New Haven, Connecticut 06520.

HERMANN BROCH ARCHIVE

B1   2 L. to Hermann Broch. 1946, 1948.

B2   3 L. from Hermann Broch. 1946-1948.

Library of Congress, Manuscript Division, Independence Avenue and First Street S.E., Washington, D.C. 20540.

BENJAMIN W. HUEBSCH PAPERS

B1   2 L. to B. W. Huebsch. 1943, 1944.

B2   4 L. from B. W. Huebsch. 1943-1944.

Mrs. Alice Loewy-Kahler, 1 Evelyn Place, Princeton, New Jersey 08540.

ERICH VON KAHLER COLLECTION

B1   2 L. to Erich von Kahler. 1940.

B2   2 L. from Erich von Kahler. 1940.

C7   "First Memorandum." Dated Oct. 1940. Mimeo. 16p. "Manifesto." Mimeo. 2c. 48p., 49p. Accompanied by L. from secretary of Erich von Kahler.

D7   "Freedom and Discipline in a Vital Democracy." Offprint.

Columbia University, Butler Library, New York, N.Y. 10027.

B1   10 L. to Isabel Ireland and Justin O'Brien. T. and A. 1937-1941.

GIUSEPPE ANTONIO BORGESE

University of Chicago, The Joseph Regenstein Library, 1100
East 57th Street, Chicago, Illinois 60637.

JAMES FRANCK PAPERS and general archive files

B1,2   Correspondence with James Franck.
*   Materials relating to the Committee to Frame a World
        Constitution.

University of California, Santa Barbara, The Library, Santa
Barbara, California 93105.

F   "Republic of the Deep Seas." 1 tape. 1968.

University of Pennsylvania, The Charles Patterson Van Pelt
Library, Philadelphia, Pennsylvania 19104.

ALMA MAHLER-WERFEL COLLECTION

B1   1 L. to Franz Werfel. 1944.

KARL BRANDT

Agricultural Economist, 1899-1973

According to Mr. Klaus Brandt, son of Karl, his father completely destroyed all of his remaining materials shortly before his death in 1973. These materials were originally to
have been deposited at Mugar Memorial Library, Boston University, according to Brandt's will.

Nach Auskunft von Mr. Klaus Brandt, dem Sohn Karl Brandts,
hat sein Vater alles kurz vor seinem Tode noch vorhandene
Materials damals selbst vernichtet. Ursprünglich sollte
dieses Material laut Karl Brandts Testament der Mugar Memo-
rial Library der Boston University zukommen.

Stanford University Libraries, University Archives, Division
of Special Collections, Stanford, California 94305.

REPORT - VALUE OF SECULAR REALITY IN ISRAEL: Mi 230. This
collection of approximately 216 items (8 archive boxes, ca.
1 ft.) was donated in Jan. 1973 by Dr. Karl Brandt.

REPORT - VALUE OF SECULAR REALITY IN ISRAEL: Mi 230. Diese
Sammlung von etwa 216 Nummern (8 Archivkartons von etwa 0,30
m) ist eine Schenkung von Dr. Karl Brandt aus dem Jahre 1973.

C7   Bericht über den Wert von weltlichen Grundvermögen in
     Israel im Eigentum früher dort ansässiger Personen
     deutscher Staatsangehörigkeit oder deutscher Abstam-
     mung. Ms. of a book.

L   Maps:
     German Aryan property at Tira, Neuhardhof.
     Bethlehem, Waldheim.
     Wilhelma and outlying areas.
     Haifa. Notes containing comments on the land.
     Jerusalem. Notes containing comments on the land,
        charts and tables.
     Galilee.
     Jaffa. Charts and notes containing comments on the
        land.

Syracuse University, The George Arents Research Library,

116

KARL BRANDT

Syracuse, New York 13210.

DOROTHY THOMPSON PAPERS

B1   41 L. to Dorothy Thompson. 1938-1959.

B2   4 L. from D. Thompson. 1947, 1951, 1955, 1956.

B3   L. from D. Thompson re: Karl Brandt.

Yivo Institute, 1048 Fifth Avenue, New York, N.Y. 10028.

HORACE M. KALLEN PAPERS

B1,2   Items scattered throughout the collection. 1933-1942
       (folders 137, 232, 636, 810, 859).

Hoover Institution on War, Revolution and Peace, Stanford,
California 94305.

C7   "What to do with Germany." Speech, given at the Com-
       monwealth Club of California. June 22, 1945. 11p.

American Philosophical Society, The Library, 105 South Fifth
Street, Philadelphia, Pennsylvania 19106.

FRANZ BOAS PAPERS, L. C. DUNN PAPERS

B1,2   Correspondence with Franz Boas. 3 L. 1935.
       Correspondence with L. C. Dunn, filed under the headings
       "Victor Jollos" and "Harry Lydenberg."

New York Public Library, Manuscript Division, Fifth Avenue
and 42nd Street, New York, N.Y. 10018.

EMERGENCY COMMITTEE IN AID OF DISPLACED FOREIGN SCHOLARS,
1933-1945

*   File compiled, no assistance given. 1933-1943.

KARL BRANDT

Prof. Alfred Vagts, Sherman, Connecticut 06784.

B1   Several L. to Alfred Vagts.

ALFRED BRAUER

Mathematician, 1894–

Dr. Alfred Brauer, 300 Woodhaven Road, Chapel Hill, North Carolina 27514.

Although the actual size of the collection of materials in Dr. Brauer's possession (as well as a detailed inventory of its contents) has not been determined, the collection has been kept totally intact and therefore represents the most complete collection of materials concerning Dr. Brauer's career. The following is a cursory description of the collection's contents which will remain inaccessible to researchers and scholars for the present.

Das Material, das sich in Dr. Brauers Besitz befindet, ist weder genau inventarisiert noch in seinem Umfang bestimmt worden. Die Materialien wurden jedoch völlig intakt gehalten und stellen somit die vollständigste Sammlung von Material über Dr. Brauers wissenschaftliche Laufbahn dar. Das Folgende ist eine kursorische Beschreibung der Sammlung, die vorerst für Forschungszwecke nicht zugänglich ist:

B1,2   Small amount of correspondence, primarily professional in nature.

D7,8   Reprints or pc. of articles.

H3   Cl. concerning Brauer's career.

I   Numerous personal documents.

J   Photos.

K   Modest library of scientific periodicals.

Library of Congress, Manuscript Division, Independence Avenue and First Street S.E., Washington, D.C. 20540.

OSWALD VEBLEN PAPERS: folder "Refugee Brauer."

B1   1 L. to [Abraham] Flexner. T. 1939.
       5 L. to Hermann Weyl. T. and A. 1938–1939.

B2   5 L. and 1 Tel. from Abraham Flexner, Hermann Weyl.

B3   6 L. and 1 Tel. re: Alfred Brauer. 1938–1939.

H5   Biographical materials, references, publications lists,
      vitae.

Harvard University, University Archives, Widener Library,
Cambridge, Massachusetts 02138.

RICHARD VON MISES COLLECTION

B1   2 L. to Richard von Mises. A. 1934, 1935.

B2   1 L. from Richard von Mises. T.cc. 1946.

New York Public Library, Manuscript Division, Fifth Avenue
and 42nd Street, New York, N.Y. 10018.

EMERGENCY COMMITTEE IN AID OF DISPLACED FOREIGN SCHOLARS,
1933-1945

*   File compiled when assistance was granted. 1940-1943.

JULIE BRAUN-VOGELSTEIN

Writer, 1883-1971

Leo Baeck Institute, 129 East 73rd Street, New York, N.Y.
10021.

The JULIE BRAUN-VOGELSTEIN COLLECTION (Papers, 1834-1971),
partially catalogued (AR 2096), comprises approximately 45
shelf ft. and was donated from the estate of the Ludwig
Vogelstein Foundation. The collection includes family
papers of 5 generations of the Braun, von Kretschman and
von Gustedt-Pappenheim families and 4 generations of the
Vogelstein family. Various members of these families with
papers of interest include Heinrich Braun, Maria von
Kretschman, Ludwig Vogelstein, as well as Julie Braun-
Vogelstein. The Papers of Julie Braun-Vogelstein alone
comprise 7 ft. This summary reflects only the papers of
Julie Braun-Vogelstein except where otherwise indicated.

*Die JULIE BRAUN-VOGELSTEIN COLLECTION (Materialien aus den
Jahren 1834-1971) ist teilweise katalogisiert (AR 2096) und
umfaßt etwa 13,50 m Materialien; sie ist eine Schenkung aus
dem Besitz der Ludwig Vogelstein Foundation. Die Sammlung
besteht aus Familienunterlagen der Familien Braun, von
Kretschman und von Gustedt-Pappenheim aus 5 Generationen
sowie aus Unterlagen über 4 Generationen der Familie Vogelstein. Zu den Mitgliedern dieser Familien, von denen interessante Unterlagen vorliegen, gehören Heinrich Braun, Maria
von Kretschman, Ludwig Vogelstein sowie Julie Braun-Vogelstein. Die Julie Braun-Vogelstein Materialien allein umfassen gut 2,00 m. Die folgende Zusammenfassung gibt im
allgemeinen, von erkennbaren Ausnahmen abgesehen, nur Materialien von und über Julie Braun-Vogelstein selbst wieder.*

A3   Drafts of her memoirs, the Heinrich Braun biography.

B1,2 Correspondence of Julie Braun-Vogelstein with such
      emigrés as: Friedrich Stampfer, Arnold Brecht, Paul
      Tillich. Also with Henri de Man, Friedrich Adler
      and others.
      Correspondence of Heinrich Braun with Karl Kautsky,
      Max Weber (in HEINRICH BRAUN PAPERS).
      Correspondence with members of the family.

C7   Ms. about Adam von Trott zu Solz.

121

Ms. about art history. A. and T.

C14   Drawings.

D7,   Cl. by and about Julie Braun-Vogelstein.
H3

J   Photos.

*   Uncatalogued materials.

Library of Congress, Manuscript Division, Independence Avenue and First Street S.E., Washington, D.C. 20540.

PAPERS OF SIEGFRIED BERNFELD

B1,2   Correspondence with Siegfried Bernfeld. 1954.
       Correspondence with Sigmund Freud. 1927. c.

Yale University, Beinecke Rare Book and Manuscript Library, New Haven, Connecticut 06520.

HERMANN BROCH ARCHIVE

H5   Broch, Hermann. "Julie Braun-Vogelstein. Künstlerische
     Form des Abendlandes." T.cc. 7p.

Harvard University, Harvard Divinity School, Andover-Harvard Theological Library, 45 Francis Avenue, Cambridge, Massachusetts 02138.

PAUL TILLICH COLLECTION

B1   1 L. to Paul Tillich. A. [1956].

B2   1 L. from Paul Tillich. T. pc. 1956.

ARNOLD BRECHT

Political Scientist, 1884-1977

Prof. Arnold Brecht, 225 Central Park West, New York, N.Y.
10024.

Private collection: ca. 15 ft. Prof. Brecht plans for his
materials to go to the Deutsche Bundesarchiv in Koblenz.

*Privatsammlung, etwa 4,50 m. Prof. Brecht beabsichtigt,
seine Materialien dem Deutschen Bundesarchiv in Koblenz
zukommen zu lassen.*

A3   Autobiographical materials, dating from Brecht's school
       years to the 1920s.

B1,2   Correspondence 1933-present, largely with political
       figures, such as: Otto Braun, Heinrich Bruening,
       Jürgen Fehling, Theodor Heuss.

C7   Lecture notes (partially unorganized).
       Ms. of articles and books, including Ms. of works that
       have not yet been pub.

C7,   Cl. and notes on various topics and periods in German
L   history, in particular those relating to Brecht's
       own career.

D7   Cl. and offprints of all of Brecht's writings (bound).

J   Some photos.

K   Small private library.

L   Several newspaper cl. 1895-.

State University of New York at Albany, Department of Germanic Languages and Literatures, 1400 Washington Avenue,
Albany, New York 12222.

Before giving his materials to the Deutsche Bundesarchiv,
Dr. Brecht has allowed them to be photocopied by the State
University of New York at Albany. With the exception of the
personal library and several other items that could not be
photocopied, the University's ARNOLD BRECHT COLLECTION represents a nearly complete copy of the materials that were in
Prof. Brecht's private collection.

123

ARNOLD BRECHT

*Prof. Brecht hat gestattet, daß die State University of New
York at Albany seine Materialien photokopiert, bevor sie dem
Deutschen Bundesarchiv übergeben werden. Mit Ausnahme seiner
Privatbibliothek und einiger anderer Einzelstücke, die nicht
photokopiert werden konnten, stellt die ARNOLD BRECHT COLLEC-
TION eine nahezu vollständige Kopie der Privatsammlung Prof.
Brechts dar.*

<u>Library of Congress</u>, Manuscript Division, Independence Avenue
and First Street S.E., Washington, D.C. 20540.

PAPERS OF SIEGFRIED BERNFELD

B1,2   Correspondence between Bernfeld and Brecht.

<u>New York Public Library</u>, Manuscript Division, Fifth Avenue
and 42nd Street, New York, N.Y. 10018.

EMERGENCY COMMITTEE IN AID OF DISPLACED FOREIGN SCHOLARS,
1933-1945

*   File compiled, no assistance granted. 1934-1944.

<u>Yivo Institute</u>, 1048 Fifth Avenue, New York, N.Y. 10028.

HORACE M. KALLEN PAPERS

*   Materials in folders no.: 557-559, 640, 645, 905,
        1017, 1045. 1936-1951.

<u>Leo Baeck Institute</u>, 129 East 73rd Street, New York, N.Y.
10021.

JULIE BRAUN-VOGELSTEIN COLLECTION

B1,2   Unknown amount of correspondence with Julie Braun-
        Vogelstein.

BERTOLT BRECHT

Dramatist, 1898-1956

<u>Harvard University</u>, Houghton Library, Cambridge, Massachusetts 02138.

The Houghton Library, in addition to the materials located in its BERTOLT BRECHT/KARL KORSCH COLLECTION (bMS Ger 130), possesses other diverse Brecht materials, including photocopies of a major portion of the main Bertolt-Brecht-Archiv, Berlin N4, Chausseestraße 125, East Germany. Permission to use the materials may be obtained through the Houghton Library, which will forward all requests to Mr. Stefan Brecht (son of Bertolt), who still retains all rights to the materials.

Zusätzlich zu den Materialien in der BERTOLT BRECHT/KARL KORSCH COLLECTION (bMS Ger 130) besitzt der Houghton Library diverse andere Brecht-Materialien, einschließlich Photokopien eines großen Teils des Bertolt-Brecht-Archivs, Berlin N4, Chausseestraße 125, DDR. Erlaubnis, die Materialien zu benutzen, kann über die Houghton Library eingeholt werden, die alle derartigen Anträge an Herrn Stefan Brecht, den Sohn Bertolt Brechts, weiterleitet. Alle literarischen Rechte der Materialien ruhen bei Stefan Brecht.

A1   Diaries, 1940-1951. T. pc. 91p.

B1   14 L. to Karl Korsch. 1934-1938 and undated.
     1 L. to Liebling-Wood. 1949.
     11 L. to Ferdinand Reyher. 1949 and undated.

B2   3 L. from Karl Korsch. 1941, 1947, 1948.
     8 L. from Ferdinand Reyher. 1946-1949.

C2   "Der Hofmeister von Jacob Michael Reinhold Lenz."
       Mimeo. 1951. 98p.
     "Die Tage der Kommune." T.c.. 1954. 95p. Mimeo. version. 1954. 126p.

C5   <u>Lady Macbeth of the Yards</u>. Unpub. and never produced
       scenario of a <u>Macbeth</u> film. Written with Peter Lorre
       and Ferdinand Reyher. Mimeo. 32p.

C7   ["Bemerkungen über die Photographie"]. Addressed to
       Ferdinand Reyher. T. with h. corr. 7p.
     "Klassendefinition der Tuis." T. 1p.

"Die Kriegsfibel." Pc. 66p.
"Das Manifest." Pc. of T. with h. corr. 19p.
"Die proletarische Dialektik." T. 2p. Draft of English
version. T. 2p.

C12   In the Jungle of Cities. [Director's working copy].
       Printed edition, mounted on larger sheets with h.
       notes and direction by Thomas Babe. 79 leaves.
       (97p.).

D3   "Studien." Pc. 27p.

D7   "Manifest der kommunistischen Partei." 13p.

E   Fear and Misery of the Third Reich. Tr. by Clayton
       Talmadge Koelb and Kenneth Leslie Tigar. T. with h.
       corr. by Tigar. 153p.

I   Power of attorney to Ferdinand Reyher, with respect to
       Galileo and The Caucasian Chalk Circle. Zürich, Dec.
       2, 1947. 2p.
       Power of attorney, empowering Ferdinand Reyher to con-
       tract for a performance of Der gute Mensch von
       Setzuan. Berlin, Feb. 21, 1949. 1p.

Southern Illinois University, Morris Library, Department of
Special Collections, Carbondale, Illinois 62901.

ERWIN PISCATOR PAPERS

B1   19 L. to Erwin Piscator. 1936-1945.

B2   40 L. from Erwin Piscator. 1935-1949.

C2   The Private Life of the Master Race. T. with commen-
       tary by Erwin Piscator and Margarete Steffins. 109p.
       Incomplete English tr., individual scenes. Notes
       concerning the production by H. R. Hays and Ruth
       Norden. T. 40p. Notes by Erwin Piscator. A. 61p.
       Notes by Leo Kerz. A. 7p.
       The Rise of Arturo Ui. English tr. of Der aufhaltsame
       Aufstieg des Arturo Ui by H. R. Hays. T. 84p.

D2   Playscripts:
       The Horatians and the Curatians.
       The Private Life of the Master Race.
       The Threepenny Opera.

BERTOLT BRECHT

H5   Piscator, Erwin. Notes concerning Brecht and the Epic
      Theater. A. 14p.

Columbia University, Butler Library, New York, N.Y. 10027.

C2   Schweyk. T.c. 90p.

E   Galileo. English version by Charles Laughton. T.c.
      83p.
      Manual of Piety. English tr. by Eric Bentley, with h.
      annotations by Randall Jarrell, p. 2-96.
      Mother Courage and Her Children. English tr. by Des-
      mond I. Vesey. [193?]. 105p.

University of Southern California, Lion Feuchtwanger Memorial
Library, 520 Paseo Miramar, Pacific Palisades, California
90272.

B1   13 L. and 1 Tel. to Lion Feuchtwanger. 1934-1956.

B2   24 L. and 1 Tel. from Lion Feuchtwanger. 1934-1956.

University of Texas, Humanities Research Center, Manuscripts
Collection and Hoblitzelle Theater Arts Library, Box 7219,
Austin, Texas 78712.

B1   6 L.

B2   4 L.

C7   Tr. of an untitled article. Cc.

D7   Printed tr. of: "The Experiment" and "A Model for Epic
      Theatre."

I   1 document.

Museum of the City of New York, Fifth Avenue at 103rd
Street, New York, N.Y. 10029.

THEATRE AND MUSIC COLLECTION

H3   "Personality File."

H4   Production files on:
      Threepenny Opera (Beggar's Holiday).
      Mother Courage.
      Galileo.
      The Private Life of the Master Race.
      The Good Woman of Sezuan.
      The Rise of Arturo Ui.
      The Caucasian Chalk Circle.
      Man is Man.
      Baal.
      In the Jungle of the Cities.

Syracuse University, The George Arents Research Library,
Syracuse, New York 13210.

DOROTHY THOMPSON PAPERS

C4   Kinderkreuzzug. T.cc.

American Academy of Arts and Letters / National Institute of
Arts and Letters, 633 West 155th Street, New York, N.Y.
10032.

B1,2   1 F. consisting primarily of correspondence. Brecht
       was an awardee in 1948.

University of California, Los Angeles, Music Library, 405
Hilgard Avenue, Los Angeles, California 90024.

ERNST TOCH ARCHIVE

B1   Several L. to Ernst Toch.

Library of Congress, Manuscript Division, Independence Avenue
and First Street S.E., Washington, D.C. 20540.

BENJAMIN W. HUEBSCH PAPERS, HANNAH ARENDT PAPERS and general
archive files

BERTOLT BRECHT

B1   2 L. to B. W. Huebsch. 1935, 1941.

B2   1 L. from B. W. Huebsch. 1944. T.c.

C3   Eisler, Hanns. "Schweyk. Vorspiel zu den höheren Regionen." Libretto by Brecht. 1958.

H5   Arendt, Hannah. "Brecht." Unpub. essay.

New York Public Library at Lincoln Center, Library and Museum of the Performing Arts, 111 Amsterdam Avenue, New York, N.Y. 10023.

C2   Die heilige Johanna der Schlachthöfe. Schauspiel von Brecht. Mimeo. 101p.
      Schweyk. Rough tr. T. 43p.

State University of New York at Binghamton, Center for Modern Theater Research, Binghamton, New York 13901.

MAX REINHARDT ARCHIVE

J   Production photos:
      Baal. 7 photos of drawings by scenic designer Caspar Neher, 1 photo of Oskar Homolka as Baal. Berlin, 1926.
      Im Dickicht der Städte. 1 photo ea. of Fritz Kortner and Walter Frank.
      Trommeln in der Nacht. Scene design photos. 1922.

Boston University, Mugar Memorial Library, 771 Commonwealth Avenue, Boston, Massachusetts 02215.

VICTOR WOLFSON PAPERS, SAM WANAMAKER PAPERS

B1   1 L. to Mrs. Cooke. T. 1935.
      2 L. and 1 Tel. to Sam Wanamaker. T. 1955-1956.

Leo Baeck Institute, 129 East 73rd Street, New York, N.Y. 10021.

BERTOLT BRECHT

H3   1 cl. 1960.
O   2 theater programs. 1928, 1961/1962.

Academy of Motion Picture Arts and Sciences, Margaret Herrick
Library, 9038 Melrose Avenue, Hollywood, California 90069.

H3,4 Newspaper and magazine cl. 1 F.

Mrs. Liselotte Stein, 115-25 Metropolitan Avenue, Kew Gardens, New York 11418.

FRED STEIN PAPERS

J   Photos of Bertolt Brecht.

University of New Hampshire, The Library, Department of Special Collections, Durham, New Hampshire 03824.

OSKAR MARIA GRAF COLLECTION, FRIEDRICH SALLY GROSSHUT COLLECTION

H5   Graf, O. M. 3 essays on Brecht. 13p.
       Grosshut, F. S. Essay on Brecht.

Princeton University, Firestone Library, Princeton, New Jersey 08540.

THE PAPERS OF ALBERT EINSTEIN (1879-1955). For details concerning the use of this collection, see description under Albert Einstein.

THE PAPERS OF ALBERT EINSTEIN (1879-1955). Angaben über den Zugang zu der Sammlung finden sich unter "Albert Einstein."

B1,2 Unknown amount of correspondence between Brecht and Einstein.

MARCEL BREUER

Architect, 1902-

The Project was unable to contact Mr. Marcel Breuer (New
York, N.Y.) or to obtain further information regarding
Breuer materials of historical interest.

*Es war nicht möglich, Herrn Marcel Breuer (New York, N.Y.)
persönlich zu erreichen bzw. weitere Auskünfte über Breuer-
Materialien von historischem Interesse zu erhalten.*

Syracuse University, The George Arents Research Library,
Syracuse, New York 13210.

The MARCEL BREUER PAPERS consist of approximately 30 shelf
ft. of materials plus additional blueprints, sketches and
rough drafts. The materials were donated to the library by
Marcel Breuer in 1964 and 1967.

*Die MARCEL BREUER PAPERS umfassen etwa 9 m Materialien sowie
zusätzlich Entwürfe, Grundrisse und Skizzen. Die Materialien
sind eine Schenkung von Marcel Breuer aus den Jahren 1964
und 1967.*

B1,2   Correspondence to and from Breuer, primarily profes-
          sional, including memoranda. 1934-1953.
       Correspondence with museums, colleges and universi-
          ties, and other institutions.

C7   Ms. of pub. and unpub. articles.
       Ms. of lectures, speeches.

C14,   Drawings, blueprints, plans. Includes designs, sketches,
I   elevations, specifications, bids, estimates, con-
          tracts and numerous other materials.

I   Office materials. Internal workings of the office are
          represented, including correspondence, memorabilia,
          miscellaneous financial materials and documents.

J   Extensive black and white photo collection showing
          Breuer's work.
       Photographic plates.

L   Pub. materials used as reference items.
       Materials concerning Breuer House, Thompson House, etc.

Files on competitions.
114 blueprints and sketches of projects, including:
  Annunciation Convent.
  Bantom and Litchfield School.
  Brookhaven.
  Fairview Heights, Ithaca, New York.
  IBM, France.
  H.H.F.A.
  Hunter College, Bronx, New York.
  Krieger House.
  Koerfer.
  McMillan House, New Jersey.
  Passenger Station, New London, Connecticut.
  N.Y.U. Dormitory.
  El Recreo, Caracas, Venezuela.
  St. Francis Church.
  St. John's Abbey.
  Scarves by Vera.
  Temple B'Nai Jeshuren.
  Torrington Manufacturing Co.
  UNESCO.
  U.S. Embassy Office Building (The Hague).
  Ustinov House.
  Van Leer's.
  Whitby School, Greenwich, Connecticut.
  Whitney Museum.
  Yale Engineering Laboratory.

Harvard University, Houghton Library, Cambridge, Massachusetts 02138.

LYONEL FEININGER COLLECTION

B1   1 L. to Lyonel and Julia Feininger. A. 1928.

State of North Carolina, Department of Cultural Resources, Raleigh, North Carolina 27611.

BLACK MOUNTAIN COLLEGE ARCHIVES

I   [Treasurer's] file. "Gropius and Breuer."

HERMANN BROCH

Writer, 1886-1956

<u>Yale University</u>, Beinecke Rare Book and Manuscript Library, New Haven, Connecticut 06520.

The HERMANN BROCH COLLECTION was donated in July 1951, according to Broch's wishes, by his literary executor, Henry Seidel Canby. Additional materials have been donated at later times by friends and relatives of Broch. A detailed inventory of the collection has been published by Dr. Christa Sammons, "Hermann Broch Archive. Yale University Library," <u>Modern Austrian Literature</u>, V, No. 3/4 (1972), p. 18-69. The listing is incomplete, however, since materials are constantly being added to the collection. With the exception of a small amount of correspondence, the materials in the collection are accessible to qualified researchers and scholars. Written permission should be obtained from Broch's son, Mr. Hermann F. Broch de Rothermann (245 East 80th Street, New York, N.Y. 10021) and Mrs. Annemarie M.-G. Broch (Rampale, 83 Saint-Cyr-Sur-Mer, Var, France), Broch's widow.

Im Juli 1951 übergab der literarische Nachlaßverwalter Hermann Brochs, Henry Seidel Canby, entsprechend dem Willen Brochs der Yale University die HERMANN BROCH COLLECTION als Schenkung. Weitere Materialien sind später als Schenkungen von Freunden und Verwandten Brochs hinzugekommen. Frau Dr. Christa Sammons hat ein detailliertes Verzeichnis der Sammlung veröffentlicht: "Hermann Broch Archive. Yale University Library," <u>Modern Austrian Literature</u>, V, No. 3/4 (1972), S. 18-69. Dieses Verzeichnis ist jedoch unvollständig, da die Sammlung ständig um neue Materialien erweitert wird. Abgesehen von einem kleinen Teil der Korrespondenz sind die Materialien der Sammlung für Forschungszwecke qualifizierter Wissenschaftler zugänglich. Schriftliche Genehmigung zur Benutzung der Materialien ist von dem Sohn Hermann Brochs (Herr Hermann F. Broch de Rothermann, 245 East 80th Street, New York, N.Y. 10021) und von seiner Witwe (Frau Annemarie M.-G. Broch, Rampale, 83 Saint-Cyr-Sur-Mer, Var, Frankreich) einzuholen.

A2   Notebook [1912]. Poetry, philosophical notes, dreams.
     A. 93p.
     Notebook [1920]. Notes, aphorisms, statements of poetry

and literature. A. 9p.
Notebook. Nov. 1934 - Feb. 1935. Dreams. A. 19p.
Sealed.
Notebook. [1936]. Notes and drafts of poems. A. 46p.
Notebook. Undated. Notes on philosophical topics. A.
18p.
Notebook. Notes, bibliographical items, quotes. A. 96p.
Notebooks. Lecture notes. Philosophy and mathematics.
University of Vienna, 1915-1921. 34 volumes.

A3   Curriculum vitae. T.cc. 5p.

B1   Ca. 866 L., including L. to: Paul Amann, Joseph Angell,
Hannah Arendt, Aufbau-Verlag (Berlin), Bermann-
Fischer Verlag, Giuseppe Antonio and Elisabeth Mann
Borgese, Henry Seidel and Marion Canby, Franz Theo-
dor Csokor, Albert Einstein, Paul Federn, Theo Feld-
man, James Franck, René Fülöp-Miller, Iwan Goll,
Waldemar Gurian, Wieland Herzfelde, Franz Horch,
Benjamin W. Huebsch, Aldous Huxley, Alvin Johnson,
Alice Loewy Kahler, Erich von Kahler, Hermann Kasack,
Karl Kerenyi, Hermann Kesten, Alfred A. Knopf, Max
Krell, Elisabeth Langgässer, Emil Ludwig, James Hans
Meisel, Edwin and Willa Muir, Robert Musil, Rudolf
Pechel, Gustav Regler, Eleanor Roosevelt, Hans Sahl,
Leo Strauss, Peter Suhrkamp, Frank and Yvonne Thiess,
Bodo Uhse, Berthold Viertel, Ernst Waldinger, Her-
mann Weyl, Thornton Wilder, Helene and Kurt Wolff.
211 L. to Daisy and Daniel Brody, Rhein-Verlag. 1930-
1934 and 1943-1951.
48 L. to the S. Fischer Verlag (Gottfried Bermann-
Fischer and Peter Suhrkamp). 1930-1934.
L. to and from Jean Starr Untermeyer. Restricted.
Correspondence from the Estate of Hannah Arendt was
transferred to Yale University in July 1976.

B2   Ca. 1,700 L., including L. from: Günther Anders,
Joseph Angell, Hannah Arendt, Aufbau-Verlag (Berlin),
Bermann-Fischer Verlag, Ernst Bloch, Giuseppe Anto-
nio and Elisabeth Mann Borgese, Daniel Brody (Rhein-
Verlag), Henry Seidel and Marion Canby, Elias Ca-
netti, Franz Theodor Csokor, Kurt von Faber du Faur,
Paul Federn, Theo Feldman, Lion Feuchtwanger, S.
Fischer Verlag, James Franck, René Fülöp-Miller,

Albert Paris Gütersloh, Waldemar Gurian, Wieland
Herzfelde, Franz Horch, B. W. Huebsch, Aldous Huxley,
Alvin Johnson, Erich von Kahler, Hermann Kesten,
A. A. Knopf, Annette Kolb, Max Krell, Helen Tracy
Lowe-Porter, Emil Ludwig, Thomas Mann, Edwin and
Willa Muir, Rudolf Pechel, Alfred Polgar, Gustav
Regler, Hans Sahl, Frank and Yvonne Thiess, Berthold
Viertel, Ernst Waldinger, Hermann Weyl, Helene and
Kurt Wolff, Otto Zoff.

B1,2   Family correspondence. Over 600 L. to and from H.
Broch. 1925-1951, including L. to and from: Fran-
ziska Broch (von Rothermann), Friedrich Josef Broch,
Joseph and Johanna Broch, Hermann Broch de Rothermann. Portions still sealed.

B3   Ca. 235 L. to and from Erich von Kahler. 1940-1971,
including large amount of correspondence with Daniel
Brody and the Rhein-Verlag.

C1   [Filsmann. Roman-Fragment]. T. and cc. 38p. Fragmentary
second version. T.cc. 8p. Another fragmentary ver-
sion. T. and cc. 5p.
Die Schuldlosen. 1950. Numerous versions and tr. of
individual chapters and sections. 510p.
"Parabel von der Stimme."
"Cantos, 1913 (Stimme, 1913)."
"Mit schwacher Brise segeln (Ein Abend Angst)."
"Methodisch konstruiert (Eine methodische Novelle)."
"Cantos, 1923 (Stimmen, 1923)."
"Verlorener Sohn (Die Heimkehr; Spiegelbild des
Lichtes."
"Ballade vom Imker."
"Die Erzählung der Magd Zerline."
"Eine leichte Enttäuschung."
"Ballade von der Kupplerin."
"Erkaufte Mutter."
"Cantos, 1933 (Stimmen, 1933)."
"Steinerne Gast."
"Vorüberziehende Wolke."
"Inhaltsverzeichnis."
"Entstehungsbericht."
Die Schlafwandler. 1931-1932. Various versions of the
3 parts. 3,119p.

"I. Teil. Pasenow oder die Romantik."
"II. Teil. Esch oder die Anarchie."
"III. Teil. Hugenau oder die Sachlichkeit."
Der Tod des Vergil. Final version. T.cc. with corr.
3c. 527p., 668p. and 668p. Early version. T. with
some corr. 167p. English tr. by Jean Starr Unter-
meyer. 1945. 2 complete versions. 536p. and 535p.
and 2 incomplete versions. 73p. and 29p.
Essays and prose commentaries by Broch concerning
Vergil. 141p.
Die unbekannte Größe. 1933. T. with corr. (not Broch's).
150p. Another version. T. and cc. with corr. 172p.
Proofs for the S. Fischer edition, with corr. by
Broch and the proofreader. 2c., ea. 228p. "Grundzüge
zum Roman 'Die unbekannte Größe'." T. and cc. 3c.,
ea. 3p.

C2   Die Entsühnung. Several versions, including 2 mimeo.
stage versions. 590p.
Kommentar zu Hamlet. Satirisches Drama im Blankvers.
A. 15p. Fragmentary draft of beginning. A. 4p.
Morgenstern. 1917. T. with annotations by the editor.
6p.
Christian Morgenstern als Konstruktionstypus. T.cc.
with corr. 8p.

C3   Appendix to Gesammelte Werke, primarily poetry. T.cc.
19p.
"Broch as seen by himself." T. 1p.
101 different poems, some with multiple versions and
copies. T. and cc. 235p.

C4   "Der Meeresspiegel." T. and cc. 2c., ea. 31p.
["Noch immer bebt mir das Herz vor Fernweh..."].
Short story. T. with corr. 21p.
["Oh Vöglein Geschwindes..."]. Short story. T. and cc.
3p.
"Wer darf wagen." Story fragment. T. and cc. 2c., ea.
8p.

C5   Das unbekannte X. Der Film einer physikalischen Theorie ("Unter Anlehnung an Hermann Brochs Roman 'Die
unbekannte Größe'"). T.cc. with corr. 79p. "Vorbe-
merkungen [zu dem Filmprojekt der Unbekannten Größe]."
T.cc. 2c., ea. 4p.

136

["Film Scenario"]. Fragment. German text. A. 31p.

C7   Obituary notices, testimonial addresses. 64p.
Reviews. 325p.
Essays, articles, texts of speeches. Ca. 4,560p.

C8   Massenpsychologie. Fragmentary sections, numerous versions, tr. Ca. 2,300p.

C9   2 poems concerning Erich von Kahler, composed by Alice Kahler and adapted by H. Broch.
Star of the Unborn. A film exposé of Franz Werfel's last novel. Rough draft of a film version. T. 27p. German version. cc. 18p.

C10   "Die Aufnahmebereitschaft." Fragment. T. and cc. 3c., ea. 5p.
"Der russische Totalitätsstaat." Fragment. T. 26p.
"Demokratie vs. Faschismus. 1946. III. Amplifikation." Fragment. T. and cc. 78p. Fragment of second version. T. 4p.
Political fragments. T. 1 F.
"Strategischer Imperialismus." Various versions. T. 209p.
["Das System als Weltbewältigung"]. T. 60p. Another version as "System und Welt." 28p.
"Totale Humanität, unbequem aber möglich und notwendig." T. 11p.
"Trotzdem und trotzdem: Humane Politik." Several versions. T. 75p.

C11   Hofmannsthal und seine Zeit. Eine Studie. Multiple copies of several chapters, notes, etc. Ca. 1,440p.

N   1 essay. 10p.

Leo Baeck Institute, 129 East 73rd Street, New York, N.Y. 10021.

The HERMANN BROCH COLLECTION (AR-C.Z.228, 1022) was donated to the Institute by several individuals over the years 1959-1968. Other Broch materials are to be found in the SIEGFRIED ALTMANN COLLECTION, VICTOR POLZER COLLECTION, ERICH KAHLER COLLECTION, PAUL AMANN COLLECTION, GEORG LANDAUER COLLECTION.

Die HERMANN BROCH COLLECTION (AR-C.Z.228, 1022) ist das Ergebnis mehrerer Schenkungen aus den Jahren 1959 bis 1968. Weitere Broch-Materialien finden sich in den folgenden Samm-lungen: SIEGFRIED ALTMANN COLLECTION, VICTOR POLZER COLLEC-TION, ERICH KAHLER COLLECTION, PAUL AMANN COLLECTION.

B1,2   L. to and from Paul Amann.
Correspondence with Antoinette Kahler. 64 L., cards, poems. 1941-1951.
Unknown amount of correspondence with Georg Landauer.

B2   9 L., including L. from: Siegfried Altmann, Victor Polzer.
1 L. from Richard Beer-Hofmann. A. 1942.
1 L. from Albert Einstein, including 1 poem. C.
13 L. to Broch. 1940-1950.

B3   6 L., including L. from Viking Press re: Vergil and Verzauberung.
Correspondence between Irma Rothstein and the Insti-tute, re: bust of Hermann Broch. 1967. 4p.

C7   "Report on my activities in rescuing endangered Euro-pean writers June 1940 - October 1941." 2p.
"Worte des Abschieds." Obituary for Antoinette Kahler. 1951.

H3   5 cl. 1958-1970.

H5   1 article. 1964.

I   Book notices. 20p.

J   2 photos of H. Broch.
4 photos of Broch bust by Irma Rothstein.

Mrs. Joseph Bunzel, 1217 Delaware Avenue, Apt. 701, Buffalo, New York 14209.

B1   Ca. 100 L. and Ptc. from Broch to J. Bunzel.

C1   Der Tod des Vergil. A. and T. Ca. 200p., including approximately 10p. of totally unpub. manuscript.

Mr. Hans Sahl, 800 West End Avenue, New York, N.Y. 10025.

B1   41 L. and 10 Ptc. to Hans Sahl, many pertaining to
      Vergil and Massenwahn.

C3   1 poem dedicated to Hans Sahl.

Princeton University, Firestone Library, Princeton, New Jersey 08540.

HERMANN BROCH COLLECTION

B1   20 L., some with tr., to Sydney Schiff. T. and A.
      1938-1949.

B2   1 L. from Sydney Schiff. T.c. 1946.

B3   9 L. 1938-1945 and undated.

C1   "Narrative of death," from The Death of Vergil. T. 2p.
      The Bewitchment (A Novel). T. Summary. 2p.

C3   "The Divine Squandered——." English tr. T. 1p.
      "Five Elegies." 1939. English tr. T.

D7   "Bill of Rights—Bill of Duties. Utopia and Reality."
      34p.

Mrs. Alice Loewy Kahler, 1 Evelyn Place, Princeton, New Jersey 08540.

ERICH VON KAHLER COLLECTION

B1   1 L. to Erich von Kahler. 1940.
      1 L. to Ernst Schönwiese. 1947.
      Transcription of a L. to Hermann Kasack. March 1, 1950.

C7   "Geschichte als moralische Anthropologie (Erich Kah-
      lers scienza nuova." T.cc. with some h. corr. 18p.
      "Broch über Erich Kahler." Xerox c. of Ms. Original in
      Beinecke Rare Book Library, Yale University.
      Recommendation for Erich von Kahler for a Guggenheim
      Fellowship. Pc. 9p.

H4   von Kahler, Erich. Discussion of Broch's Vergil for
      Norddeutscher Rundfunk, April 1958. T. 4p.
      Critique of Broch's Tod des Vergil. T.cc. 5p.

H5   von Kahler, Erich. Statement about Broch. T.cc. 2p.
        Radio lecture on Broch for Österreichischer Rund-
            funk. T. 10p.
        Hermann Broch lecture. Various versions. A. ca. 75p.
        "The Epochal Innovations in Hermann Broch's Narra-
            tive." T.cc. with numerous h. corr. English tr.
        by Gisela Bahr. 10p.

Harvard University, Houghton Library, Cambridge, Massachusetts 02138.

AUTOGRAPH FILE, RICHARD BEER-HOFMANN COLLECTION, OSWALD
GARRISON VILLARD PAPERS

B1   13 L. 1936-1945, including L. to: Paul Amann, Richard
        Beer-Hofmann, Richard von Mises, Oswald Garrison
        Villard.

B2   1 L. from Oswald Garrison Villard. 1939.

New York Public Library, Manuscript Division, Fifth Avenue
and 42nd Street, New York, N.Y. 10018.

THEO FELDMAN PAPERS

B1   9 Ptc. and 1 L. to Theo Feldman. T. and A. 1940-1951.

H5   "Dem Andenken Hermann Brochs." Poem by Ernst Waldinger.

Mrs. Gertrude Urzidil, 83-39 116th Street, Richmond Hill,
New York 11418.

JOHANNES URZIDIL COLLECTION

B1   3 L. and 6 Ptc. to J. Urzidil. T. and A. 1946-1951 and
        undated.

H3   Printed copy of a radio speech by Johannes Urzidil on
        "Hermann Broch." 1951. 2p.

H5   Untermeyer, Jean Starr. Essay on her friendship with
        Hermann Broch. 1957. T. 9p.

HERMANN BROCH

Columbia University, Butler Library, New York, N.Y. 10027.

PANTHEON BOOKS COLLECTION

B,   File containing L. and documents concerning German and
I   English language versions of Broch's works. 1947-
        1964. Ca. 100 items. Also L. from Hans Staudinger.

University of Texas, Humanities Research Center, Manuscripts
Collection, Box 7219, Austin, Texas 78712.

B1   5 L.

B2   4 L.

B1,2   Uncatalogued and unsorted correspondence.

Immigration History Research Center of the University of
Minnesota, 826 Berry Street, St. Paul, Minnesota 55101.

AMERICAN COUNCIL FOR EMIGRÉS IN THE PROFESSIONS ARCHIVES

B1   6 L. 1942-1950, including 2 L. to Alvin Johnson.

B2   9 L. 1942-1949.

B3   13 L. concerning Broch including L. from: Jean Starr
        Untermeyer, Alvin Johnson, Max Krell.

University of Pennsylvania, The Charles Patterson Van Pelt
Library, Philadelphia, Pennsylvania 19104.

ALMA MAHLER-WERFEL COLLECTION

B1   3 L. to Franz Werfel. T. and A. 1941, 1943 and undated.
        4 L. to Alma Mahler-Werfel. T. and A. 1942-1950.

New School for Social Research, Office of the Dean of the
Graduate Faculty of Political and Social Science, 65 Fifth
Avenue, New York, N.Y. 10003.

RECORDS OF THE UNIVERSITY IN EXILE, 1933-45

B1,2   8 L. 1941.

University of New Hampshire, The Library, Department of Special Collections, Durham, New Hampshire 03824.

OSKAR MARIA GRAF COLLECTION

B1   3 L. to O. M. Graf. 1940.

Harvard University, University Archives, Widener Library, Cambridge, Massachusetts 02138.

RICHARD VON MISES COLLECTION

B1   1 L. to Richard von Mises. T. 1945.

B2   1 L. from Richard von Mises. T.cc. 1945.

Indiana University, The University Libraries, Music Library, Bloomington, Indiana 47401.

PAUL NETTL COLLECTION

H5   Eulogy on the death of Hermann Broch. T. 3p.

University of Southern California, Lion Feuchtwanger Memorial Library, 520 Paseo Miramar, Pacific Palisades, California 90272.

B1   1 L. to Lion Feuchtwanger. 1947.

B2   1 L. from Lion Feuchtwanger. 1947.

Mrs. Elisabeth M. Stoerk and Mrs. Susanne B. Hoeller, 288 Ocean Drive West, Stamford, Connecticut 06902.

FRIDERIKE ZWEIG ARCHIVE

B1   1 L. and 1 Ptc. to Friderike Zweig. 1943, 1947.

Prof. Kurt H. Wolff, 58 Lombard Street, Newton, Massachusetts 02158.

B1,2 Correspondence between Broch and Kurt H. Wolff.

Dr. Clementine Zernik, 225-10 106th Avenue, Queens Village, New York 11429.

B1   Several L. to Arnold Höllriegel. 1938-1939.

Mrs. Peter M. Lindt, 949 West End Avenue, New York, N.Y. 10025.

B1   2 L. to Peter M. Lindt.

State University of New York at Albany, Department of Germanic Languages and Literature, 1400 Washington Avenue, Albany, New York 12222.

STORM PUBLISHERS ARCHIVE

B1   1 L. to Alexander Gode von Aesch. Undated.

EBERHARD F. BRUCK

Lawyer, 1877-1960

Mr. F. Frederick Bruck, 148 Coolidge Hill, Cambridge, Massachusetts 02138.

Mr. F. Frederick Bruck, son of Eberhard, has preserved approximately 1.5 shelf feet of the materials of his father.

Mr. F. Frederick Bruck, ein Sohn von Eberhard Bruck, hat etwa 0,50 m Material über seinen Vater aufbewahrt.

B1,2   Correspondence with publishers, many concerning royalty questions.

B2   Collection entitled: "Wichtige Briefe."
       Miscellaneous L. to Bruck from the 1940s and 1950s.

B3   Condolence L. to the Bruck family.

C7   1 B. of manuscripts, including:
       "Might and Right." Speech. 7p.
       "Private Property." Speech. 7p.
       Reviews on Ernst Lewy.

D7   Printed copies of articles from all years.

H3   Numerous cl.

H4   1 B. of reviews on Bruck's work.

I   Tax, financial, personal documents.

L   Materials on the University of Bonn.

M   Memorabilia.
       Family history memorabilia.

New York Public Library, Manuscript Division, Fifth Avenue and 42nd Street, New York, N.Y. 10018.

EMERGENCY COMMITTEE IN AID OF DISPLACED FOREIGN SCHOLARS, 1933-1945

*   File compiled when assistance was granted. 1938-1944.

New School for Social Research, Office of the Dean of the

EBERHARD F. BRUCK

Graduate Faculty of Political and Social Science, 65 Fifth
Avenue, New York, N.Y. 10003.

RECORDS OF THE UNIVERSITY IN EXILE, 1933-45

B1,2   3 L. 1938.

FERDINAND BRUCKNER

Writer, 1891-1958

Southern Illinois University, Morris Library, Department of
Special Collections, Carbondale, Illinois 62901.

ERWIN PISCATOR PAPERS

B1   7 L. to Erwin Piscator. A. and T. 1941-1948.

B2   12 L. from Erwin Piscator. T.cc. 1941-1949.

C2   Chaff. Ca. 1946. T. with corr. 73p.

D2   Chaff. Playscript, sketches of costumes and scenes.
      The Criminals. Playscript.

I   2 contracts between Bruckner and Piscator. T.

Leo Baeck Institute, 129 East 73rd Street, New York, N.Y.
10021.

B1   1 L. to Berliner Tageblatt. 1929.

J   2 photos of scenes from Bruckner's Verbrecher.

University of Texas, Humanities Research Center, Manuscripts
Collection, Box 7219, Austin, Texas 78712.

B1   2 L.

B2   3 L.

State University of New York at Binghamton, Center for Modern
Theater Research, Binghamton, New York 13901.

MAX REINHARDT ARCHIVE

D2   Die Kreatur. Original promptbook for Reinhardt produc-
      tion. Berlin, 1930.

J   Production photos:
      Die Kreatur. Photo of Helene Thimig and Rudolf For-
      ster. 1930.
      Die Verbrecher. 4 photos. 1928-1929.

146

FERDINAND BRUCKNER

Mr. Hans Sahl, 800 West End Avenue, New York, N.Y. 10025.

B1   L. to Hans Sahl. Uncatalogued.

New York Public Library, Manuscript Division, Fifth Avenue and 42nd Street, New York, N.Y. 10018.

EMERGENCY COMMITTEE IN AID OF DISPLACED FOREIGN SCHOLARS, 1933-1945

*   File compiled when assistance was granted. 1942-1945.

Barthold Fles Literary Agency, 507 Fifth Avenue, New York, N.Y. 10016.

B1   1 L. to Barthold Fles. 1941.

Mrs. Peter M. Lindt, 949 West End Avenue, New York, N.Y. 10025.

B1   Small amount of correspondence with Peter M. Lindt.

147

HEINRICH BRUENING

Statesman, 1885-1970

Harvard University, University Archives, Widener Library,
Cambridge, Massachusetts 02138.

The HEINRICH BRUENING PAPERS, although officially the property of the Harvard University Archives, are presently in
the possession of Mrs. Claire Nix (Carpenter Street, Norwich,
Vermont). Mrs. Nix, editor of Heinrich Brüning: Briefe und
Gespräche 1934-1945 and Heinrich Brüning: Briefe 1946-1960
(Stuttgart: Deutsche Verlagsanstalt), is currently working
on an untitled publication that will be a selection from
lecture notes, correspondence, etc. from Dr. Bruening's
early years, planned as a supplement to the Memoiren (published in 1970, dictated by Bruening ca. 1935). After the
completion of Mrs. Nix's work (anticipated publication date
1979), the approximately 15 ft. of materials that constitute
the Bruening papers will be deposited in the Harvard University Archives. The materials will remain inaccessible to
researchers and scholars until such time as they are turned
over to Harvard University.

*Die HEINRICH BRUENING PAPERS, Besitztum der Harvard Univer-
sity Archives, befinden sich z.Zt. bei Mrs. Claire Nix (Carpenter Street, Norwich, Vermont). Mrs. Nix ist die Heraus-
geberin der Bände Heinrich Brüning: Briefe und Gespräche
1934-1935 und Heinrich Brüning: Briefe 1946-1960 (Stuttgart,
Deutsche Verlagsanstalt). Sie arbeitet z.Zt. an einer Publikation (noch ohne Titel) ausgewählter Vortragsnotizen, Briefe
usw. der frühen Jahre Brünings. Diese Publikation ist als
Ergänzungsband zu den Memoiren (veröffentlicht 1970, dik-
tiert von Brüning etwa 1935) geplant. Das voraussichtliche
Erscheinungsdatum ist 1979. Danach werden die Materialien
(etwa 4,50 m), die die Brüning Papers ausmachen, den Harvard
University Archives übergeben. Die Materialien bleiben bis
zu diesem Zeitpunkt für Forschungszwecke unzugänglich.*

A1   Diary. 1933-1934.

A3   Ms. of Bruening's memoirs to 1934. Cc.

B1,2 Over 10,000 L., of which nearly one-half are carbon
      copies of Bruening's own L., primarily postwar.

J   Several hundred photos of Bruening and friends.

L   Newspaper and magazine cl. (pre- and postwar) from the
        London Times, New York Times, Financial News, etc.
        on German politics.
        Materials pertaining to an economic history of Germany
        after the First World War. 1919-1933.

Dartmouth College, Baker Memorial Library, Hanover, New
Hampshire 03755.

B1   7 L. to Dr. Harold J. Tobin. T. and A. [1937].

B2   10 L. from Dr. Harold J. Tobin. T.cc. [1936-1937].

B3   37 L. [1937]. Includes L. to and from: George Shuster,
        Dr. Harold Tobin, Albert Dickenson, Ernest Hopkins,
        Robert George, etc.

C7   "4th Lecture." Bruening's notes to a lecture by Dr.
        H. J. Tobin on the relationship of church and state.
        1937. T. with h. corr. 4p. Also notes by Dr. Tobin
        for the lecture. A. 2p.
        "Attempts to Reestablish Authority in Democracy." Lec-
        ture. Dartmouth, March 16-17, 1937. T. 39p.
        "The Antagonism between Totalitarianism and Democratic
        Principles." Lecture. Dartmouth, March 16-17, 1937.
        T. 39p.

H3   14 cl. from the Dartmouth. 1937.

O   Program. Lowell Institute, Harvard. Summary of two
        lectures by Bruening.
        Program for the week March 15-21, 1937, Dartmouth Col-
        lege.

Swarthmore College, Swarthmore, Pennsylvania 19081.

SWARTHMORE COLLEGE PEACE COLLECTION: WILLIAM F. SOLLMANN
PAPERS

B1   46 L. and Ptc. to William Sollmann. 1939-1949 and un-
        dated. Includes some L. to and from Bruening's sec-
        retary, Mrs. Claire Nix.

B2   4 L. from William Sollmann. 1939-1944.

HEINRICH BRUENING

1 L. from Otto Strasser. 1941.

State Historical Society of Wisconsin, 816 State Street,
Madison, Wisconsin 53706.

LOUIS P. LOCHNER PAPERS

B1   10 L. to Louis P. Lochner. 1942-1945.

B2   10 L. from Louis P. Lochner. 1942-1945.

University of Iowa, The University Libraries, Special Collections, Iowa City, Iowa 52240.

B1   7 L. to George Sylvester Viereck. 1937-1939 and un-
      dated.

Harvard University, Houghton Library, Cambridge, Massachusetts 02138.

AUTOGRAPH FILE, OSWALD GARRISON VILLARD PAPERS

B1   4 L. including 2 L. to Oswald Garrison Villard. 1941.

B2   3 L. from O. G. Villard. 1941.

Leo Baeck Institute, 129 East 73rd Street, New York, N.Y.
10021.

B1   5 L. to Gustav Stolper. 1940 and 1947.

B2   2 L. from Gustav Stolper. 1940 and 1947.

Columbia University, Butler Library, New York, N.Y. 10027.

NICHOLAS MURRAY BUTLER PAPERS

B1,2 6 L. to and from N. M. Butler. 1936-1937.

150

Prof. Arnold Brecht, 225 Central Park West, New York, N.Y.
10024.

B1,2   Correspondence between Brecht and Bruening. Ca. 2 in.
        (5 cm).

Harvard University, Harvard Divinity School, Andover-Harvard
Theological Library, 45 Francis Avenue, Cambridge, Massachusetts 02138.

PAUL TILLICH COLLECTION

B1   1 L. to Paul Tillich. 1937. T.

Syracuse University, The George Arents Research Library,
Syracuse, New York 13210.

DOROTHY THOMPSON PAPERS

C7   Questionnaire on Nazi Germany. T.

Princeton University, Firestone Library, Princeton, New Jersey 08540.

THE PAPERS OF ALBERT EINSTEIN (1879-1955). For details concerning the use of this collection, see description under
Albert Einstein.

*THE PAPERS OF ALBERT EINSTEIN (1879-1955). Angaben über den
Zugang zu der Sammlung finden sich unter "Albert Einstein."*

B1,2   Unknown amount of correspondence between Bruening and
        Einstein.

University of Chicago, The Joseph Regenstein Library, 1100
East 57th Street, Chicago, Illinois 60637.

B1,2   Correspondence file relating to The Committee to Frame
        a World Constitution.

Mrs. Alice Loewy Kahler, 1 Evelyn Place, Princeton, New Jersey 08540.

ERICH VON KAHLER COLLECTION

B1   1 L. to Erich von Kahler. A. 1946.

MANFRED BUKOFZER

Musicologist, 1910-1955

University of California, Berkeley, The Music Library, Berkeley, California 94720.

The MANFRED BUKOFZER COLLECTION was formed as a result of a donation of more than 20 ft. of materials from Bukofzer's estate in the year 1955. The personal library of Bukofzer has been divided between the Music Library and the Bancroft Library of the University of California, Berkeley.

Im Jahre 1955 erhielt die University of California, Berkeley, eine Schenkung von mehr als 6 m Material aus Bukofzers Nachlaß. Aus diesem Material wurde die MANFRED BUKOFZER COLLECTION gebildet. Die Privatbibliothek von Bukofzer ging zum Teil an die Music Library und zum Teil an die Bancroft Library der University of California, Berkeley.

B1   Several L. from the 1930s.

B2   Ca. 150 L. and Ptc. from the 1930s, including L. from: Willi Apel, Karl Jaspers, Guido Adler, Alfred Einstein, L. Forster, C. G. Jung, Curt Sachs.

C7   26 notebooks containing: syllabi, lecture texts, notes, exams, course notes and outlines, bibliographies.
      Reviews and essays.
      Notes and fragments of musical compositions.
      Ms. of full-length works, including Bukofzer's book on music in Java.

C13   Transcriptions of compositions of others by Bukofzer.

D7   Reviews, newspaper cl. from the years 1929-1938. 2 F.
      Newspaper cl.

I   Documents, passport, etc.

J   Photos.

K   The personal library of Bukofzer has been divided between the Music Library and the Bancroft Library of the University of California, Berkeley.

L   Published materials such as compositions that he conducted.
      7 card catalog bibliographies to musical studies.

M   Memorabilia.

N   The Importance of Symbols for the Evaluation of Music.
       Author unknown.
     Exams and papers of former students.

University of Georgia, The University Libraries, Athens,
Georgia 30601.

OLIN DOWNES PAPERS

Bl,2   7 L.

New York Public Library, Manuscript Division, Fifth Avenue
and 42nd Street, New York, N.Y. 10018.

EMERGENCY COMMITTEE IN AID OF DISPLACED FOREIGN SCHOLARS,
1933-1945

*   File compiled when assistance was granted. 1940-1944.

FRITZ BUSCH
Conductor, Composer, 1890-1951

<u>Indiana University</u>, The University Libraries, School of Music
Library and Phonorecord Division of the Music Library, Bloomington, Indiana 47401.

The main portion of the FRITZ BUSCH COLLECTION was donated
to the library on Dec. 7, 1967 by the children and heirs of
Busch, Prof. Hans Busch, Mrs. Martial Singher and Gräfin
Gisela von Moltke. The collection has been totally catalogued and a published version of the catalog is available
from the library: Dominique René de Lerma, <u>The Fritz Busch</u>
<u>Collection. An Acquisition of Indiana University</u> (Blooming-
ton: Indiana University Libraries, 1972).

Der Hauptteil der FRITZ BUSCH COLLECTION ist eine Schenkung
(7. Dez. 1967) der Kinder und Erben von Busch (Prof. Hans
Busch, Frau Martial Singher, Gräfin Gisela von Moltke) an
die Bibliothek der Indiana University. Die Sammlung wurde
vollständig katalogisiert und ist in gedruckter Form durch
die Bibliothek erhältlich: Dominique René de Lerma, <u>The Fritz</u>
<u>Busch Collection. An Acquisition of Indiana University</u>
(Bloomington: Indiana University Libraries, 1972).

B2   1 L. from Max Reger. Undated.

B3   109 L. from Max Reger. 1914-1916. T. and cc.
      1 L. ea. from Hermann Abendroth and Olle Farrell.

Cl3a "Ritter-Marsch, op. 0. Bearbeitet für Klavier." May
      1909.
      "Variations pour orchestre sur une chanson enfantine
      française." Orchestration, incomplete. Undated.
      "Orchestral fragment in A, grazioso." Score, dated
      "Riverdale und auf See Ende Mai 1950."
      "String Quartett in G, presto." Clean copy plus rough
      draft with comments in German, not by Busch.

Cl3b Bach, Johann Sebastian:
      "In dir ist Freude."
      "Matthäus Passion."
      "Meine Seele erhebet dem Herren."
      "Nun ist das Heil und die Kraft."
      "H moll Messe."

"Wachet auf, ruft uns die Stimme."
Beethoven, Ludwig van:
  "Fourth Symphony."
  "Fifth Symphony."
  "Ninth Symphony."
  "Overture no. 2 to Leonore (Fidelio)."
Berlioz, Hector:
  "Overture to Benvenuto Cellini."
Brahms, Johannes:
  "Klavierkonzert, Re minor, op. 15."
  "Overtura academica."
  "Second Symphony in D major."
Bruckner, Anton:
  "VII Symphonie."
Dvořák, Antonin:
  "Symphonische Variationen."
Händel, Georg Friedrich:
  "Concerto grosso, op. 6, no. 8."
Josquin Despres:
  "La déploration de Jehan Okeghem."
Mahler, Gustav:
  "Second Symphony."
Mendelssohn-Bartholdy, Felix:
  "Sueno de verano, ouvertura and marscha."
Reger, Max:
  "Burlesque, op. 58, op. 94, no. 2, and op. 58, no. 3."
  "Im Spiel der Wellen, op. 128."
  "Phantasie über den Choral 'Ein feste Burg ist unser
    Gott', op. 27."
  "Phantasie über den Choral 'Wie schön leucht't uns
    der Morgenstern', für Orgel, op. 40, no. 1, für
    großen Orchester gesetzt von Fritz Busch."
Rotscher, J.:
  "Venetian Night Overture."
Schubert, Franz Peter:
  "Der treue Soldat."
  "Tanz Suite (Polonaise, op. 75; Ecossaison, Trio,
    Valses nobles, op. 77)."
Schumann, Robert Alexander:
  "Fuge über den Namen Bach, für Orgel oder Pedalflüge,
    für Orchester gesetzt von Fritz Busch."
Smetana, Bedrich:
  "II Vlatava."

Tallis, Thomas:
"Spem in alium."
Verdi, Giuseppe:
"Overture to Luisa Miller."
Victoria, Tomas Luis de:
"Hymn XXIV, tristes erant apostoli."
Wagner, Richard:
"Das Rheingold."
"Götterdämmerung."
Hindemith, Paul:
"Symphonic Metamorphosis of themes by C. M. von
Weber."

C13c   200 scores with annotations by Busch, including works
by: Johann Sebastian Bach (15), Ludwig van Beethoven (32), Hector Berlioz (2), Franz Adolf Berwald
(1), Georges Bizet (1), Aleksandr Porfirevich Boro-
din (1), Johannes Brahms (8), Max Bruch (2), Anton
Bruckner (1), Adolf Busch (1), Ferruccio Benvenuto
Busoni (1), Arcangelo Corelli (1), Ferdinand David
(1), Antonin Dvořák (20), Sir Edward William Elgar
(3), Paul Graener (1), George Friedrich Händel (3),
Joseph Haydn (2), Paul Hindemith (2), Arthur Honeg-
ger (1), Wilhelm Kenpff (1), Rudolf Immanuel Lang-
gaard (1), Lars-Erik Vilner Larsson (1), Franz Liszt
(1), Max Lobedanz (1), Stefan Lück (2), Gustav Mahler
(3), Felix Mendelssohn-Bartholdy (2), Johann Wolfgang
Amadeus Mozart (15), Johann Georg Leopold Mozart (1),
Gottfried Müller (1), Robert Müller-Hartmann (1),
Giovanni Battista Pierluigi da Palestrina (6), Henri
Constant Gabriel Pierne (1), Giacomo Puccini (1), Max
Reger (11), Lazare Saminsky (1), Paul Schierbeck (1),
Franz Peter Schubert (5), Robert Alexander Schumann
(5), Bedrich Smetana (2), Johann Strauss (1), Richard
Strauss (9), Joseph Suk (1), Sir Donald Francis Tovey
(1), Robert Calverley Trevelyan (1), Giuseppe Verdi
(7), Tomas Luis de Victoria (2), Richard Wagner (14),
William Turner Walton (1), Carl Maria von Weber (2),
Alberto Williams (1).

D13   Miscellaneous uncatalogued and unsorted materials, including fragments of unpub. works, photos, etc. 1 B.

F   "A New Year's Eve party given by Fritz Busch." Dialog
in French, German, Italian, English. Riverdale,
Dec. 31, 1950 and Jan. 1, 1951.

"Die Brüder Busch." The life and performances of the
Busch brothers, with excerpts from performances. Piano
Rudolf Serkin. Westdeutscher Rundfunk, Köln, Oct. 13,
1964.

Busch, Grete. "Memoirs: Chapter 1." Indiana Univ.
Audio-Visual Dept., March 1, 1956.

Busch, Grete. The reading of an early version of her
manuscript: Fritz Busch, Dirigent. Indiana Univ.
Audio-Visual Dept., March 1, 1956.

Freund, J. Helmut. "Gedenksendung des Hessischen Rundfunks in Frankfurt über Fritz Busch." Frankfurt,
1964.

Freund, J. Helmut. "Virtuos und Meister." Hessischer
Rundfunk in Frankfurt, March 13, 1970.

Freund, J. Helmut. "Zu Fritz Buschs Geburtstag." Monte-
video, March 13, 1952.

"Die Musikerfamilie Busch: Adolf, Fritz und Hermann
Busch." Südwestfunk, Baden-Baden, March 13, 1965.

"Ueber der Dresdner Staatsoper. Fritz Busch bis Karl
Böhm. Sendung des Süddeutschen Rundfunks." Stuttgart,
1964.

47 tapes of performances and rehearsals of Busch, in-
cluding performances of: Hugo Alfven (1), Johann
Sebastian Bach (3), Ludwig van Beethoven (7), Hector
Berlioz (1), Franz Berwald (2), Johannes Brahms (1),
Frederic Chopin (2), Joseph Haydn (2), Paul Hinde-
mith (1), Lars-Erik Vilner Larsson (1), Wolfgang Ama-
deus Mozart (8), Carl Nielsen (1), Juan Orrego-Salas
(1), Max Reger (2), Gioacchino Rossini (1), Franz
Peter Schubert (1), Robert Alexander Schumann (1),
Richard Strauss (2), Giuseppe Verdi (5), Richard
Wagner (3), Carl Maria von Weber (1).

K   Numerous scores, all without annotations by Busch.

L   Northlands Chamber Music Concerts. List of programs
and artists. Oct. 24, 1893 - July 17, 1914. 42p.

N   Danziger, Susie. Notes to an adaptation of Mahler's
"Urlicht."

Melotte, Henri. "Die Blasinstrumente in der Schubert-
schen Symphonie No. 7C dur." Dedicated to Fritz
Busch. Undated. Cc.
Mozart, Wolfgang Amadeus. "Zwei Fantasien für mechani-
sche Orgel (K. 594, 608), bearbeitet für Orchester
von Hans Eppstein." Score.
Ravel, Maurice. "Bolero."
Reger, Max. "Du bist mir gut, op. 66, no. 4."
"Präludium und Fuge (G moll)."
"Schönster Herr Jesu."
Sturzenegger, Richard. "Omaggio." Adaptation for piano.
Tovey, Sir Donald Francis. "Concerto for violoncello."
"Fuga a 3 voce."
"God Save the King."
Unidentified authors:
"Auszüge aus Aufsätzen über Aufführungspraxis Händel-
scher Werke, insbes. 'Messias'."
"Notes on organ part of Bach's B minor mass."

University of Georgia, The University Libraries, Athens,
Georgia 30601.

OLIN DOWNES PAPERS

B3   2 L.

University of Pennsylvania, The Charles Patterson Van Pelt
Library, Philadelphia, Pennsylvania 19104.

ALMA MAHLER-WERFEL COLLECTION

Bl   2 L. to Alma Mahler-Werfel. 1937, 1949.

JOSEPH BUTTINGER

Writer, 1906-

Prof. Joseph Buttinger, R.R. 1, Box 264, Pennington, New
Jersey 08534.

The large collection of papers, books, and other materials
accumulated by Joseph Buttinger since 1939 (his arrival in
the U.S.) remained intact until 1971-1972 when he began to
dissolve his holdings.

His library of over 60,000 books (socialistica, history, economics, political science, Vietnam, utopian literature) included the former libraries of Gustav Stolper,
Oskar Kurz, Otto Zelenka (nephew of Otto Bauer), Hermann
Broch, Karl Diehl, and Paul Levy. 44,000 volumes were
donated by Buttinger in 1971 to the new Hochschule für
Bildungswissenschaften in Klagenfurt; the Vietnam collection, utopian literature, and the literature on the American socialist communes (together ca. 9,000 vols.) went to
the City University of New York; duplicate copies of
socialistica (ca. 40 boxes) were given to the Verein für
Geschichte der Arbeiterbewegung in Vienna; additional duplicate titles (economics, political science, history, philosophy) were donated to the State University of New York
at Albany; and the Paul Levy papers and other political
materials were sent to the Friedrich-Ebert-Stiftung in
Bonn (Archiv für Soziale Demokratie). For a description
of the Buttinger library and its dissolution, see: Archiv.
Mitteilungsblatt des Vereins für Geschichte der Arbeiterbewegung, XIII, No. 1 (Jan.-March 1973), 3-11.

The remaining materials are in Joseph Buttinger's home
in Pennington, New Jersey. According to Mr. Buttinger, they
are arranged by topics and periods and are in relatively
good order.

*Die umfangreiche Sammlung von Büchern, Manuskripten und
anderen Materialien Joseph Buttingers stammt aus der Zeit
nach seiner Ankunft in den U.S.A. im Jahre 1939. Die Bibliothek und das Archiv befand sich in einem eigens dafür er-
bautem Gebäude in New York City bis zum Jahre 1971, als sich
Buttinger entschloß, seine Sammlung aufzulösen. (Siehe den
Bericht in: Archiv. Mitteilungsblatt des Vereins für Geschichte der Arbeiterbewegung, XIII, No. 1 (Jan.-März 1973),
3-11.)*

JOSEPH BUTTINGER

Seine Büchersammlung (Socialistica, Geschichte, Ökonomie, Soziologie, Vietnam, Utopienliteratur) wurde zum Teil durch den Ankauf von mehreren Privatbibliotheken aufgebaut: Gustav Stolper, Oskar Kurz, Otto Zelenka (Neffe von Otto Bauer), Hermann Broch, Karl Diehl, und Paul Levy. Davon wurden 44.000 Bände der neugegründeten Hochschule für Bildungswissenschaften in Klagenfurt übergeben; die Vietnam-Sammlung, sowie die Utopienliteratur wie die Literatur über die amerikanischen socialistischen Kommunen (zus. etwa 9.000 Bände) gingen an die City University of New York; Doubletten der Socialistica (etwa 40 Kartons) wurden dem Verein für Geschichte der Arbeiterbewegung in Wien geschenkt; weitere Doubletten (Ökonomie, Geschichte, Philosophie) gingen an die State University of New York at Albany; und der Paul-Levy-Nachlaß wurde der Friedrich-Ebert-Stiftung in Bonn (Archiv für Soziale Demokratie) übergeben.

Die übrigen Materialien befinden sich in Joseph Buttingers Privatbesitz in Pennington, New Jersey. Nach Aussage von Buttinger sind diese Materialien relativ gut geordnet, und zwar nach Themen und Personen.

A1   Diaries of all of Buttinger's official trips, starting with a trip to Germany in 1946 as member of a relief agency.

A3   Ms. of an autobiography in progress.

B1,2 Ca. 100,000 items of correspondence, organized roughly by subject and year. Includes extensive correspondence with: Paul Hagen (Karl Frank), Josef Moll (Podlipnik), Fritz Kolb, Herbert Steiner, Bruno Kreisky, Christian Broder, Hermann Langbein, Günther Nenning, Konrad Heiden, Karl O. Paetel, Fritz Sternberg, Norbert Leser, and various personalities connected with the Emergency Rescue Committee/ International Rescue Committee, Vietnam. Also ca. 2,500 L. from Germany, resulting from a C.A.R.E. package program in which Buttinger was involved.

C10 Ms. of all of Buttinger's writings (complete).

H4   Reviews of Buttinger's writings. Cl.

L   Materials used by Buttinger, in particular concerning his relief work for the International Rescue Committee, and Vietnam.

State University of New York at Albany, Department of Germanic Languages and Literatures, 1400 Washington Avenue, Albany, New York 12222.

KARL O. PAETEL COLLECTION

Bl   1 L. to Karl O. Paetel (xerox(. 1954.

RUDOLF CARNAP

Philosopher, 1891-1970

University of Pittsburgh Libraries, Department of Special
Collections, 363 Hillman Library, Pittsburgh, Pennsylvania
15260.

A large collection of materials pertaining to Rudolf Carnap
is located in the University of Pittsburgh Libraries, Department of Special Collections. The bulk of these materials were acquired from the Carnap family. As of 1977,
the materials remain uncatalogued because of difficulties
of the shorthand notation used by Carnap. Until the collection has been catalogued it will remain closed to researchers. The library, however, is vitally interested in making
the materials available for serious scholarship at the earliest possible time. The collection contains 172 cubic ft.
of material composed of 47 cubic ft. of manuscripts and 125
cubic ft. of books, periodicals and other printed matter
with extensive holograph and shorthand marginalia. The
collection will occupy approximately 235 linear ft. of shelf
space when processed.

*Eine umfangreiche Sammlung von Rudolf-Carnap-Materialien be-
findet sich im Department of Special Collections der University of Pittsburgh Libraries. Die meisten dieser Materialien wurden von der Familie Carnap erworben. Bis 1977 blieben die Materialien unkatalogisiert, da die Kurzschriftauf-
zeichnungen Carnaps schwer entzifferbar sind. Erst wenn die
Sammlung katalogisiert ist, wird sie für Forschungszwecke
zugänglich sein, wobei die Bibliothek in höchstem Maße daran
interessiert ist, die Materialien so schnell wie möglich für
engagierte Forscher freizugeben. Die Sammlung umfaßt 4,6 m³
Materialien, wobei 1,25 m³ auf Manuskripte und 3,35 m³ auf
Bücher, Zeitschriften und andere gedruckte Materialien ent-
fallen, die mit ausführlichen Lang- und Kurzschriftanmerkun-
gen versehen sind. Nach ihrer Durchsicht und Ordnung wird
die Sammlung etwa 70 laufende Meter umfassen.*

A2   Carnap kept detailed notes on almost everything he
       read, and these notes in his own shorthand are in
       the collection.

B1,2 The correspondence consists of an estimated 10,000 L.
       to and from hundreds of correspondents. There are

exchanges amounting to several hundred L. with each
of the following: Feigl, Hempel, Kaufmann, Neurath
and Schlick. There is also an extensive correspondence (ranging in number from 20 to over 100 L.)
with ea. of: Bar-Hillel, Bohnert, D. Kaplan, Lazero-
witz, R. M. Martin, Morris, Naess, Nagel, Ogden,
Popper, Quine, Reichenbach, Russell, Savage and
Stegmuller. Other important figures with whom there
is significant correspondence include: Ajdukiewicz,
Bernays, Beth, Church, Dewey, Einstein, Frankel,
Gödel, Goodman, Grünbaum, von Neumann, Waismann,
Wisdom, Wittgenstein, and von Wright.

C   The collection includes an estimated 30,000 manuscripts,
      many of which are notes from which papers and lec-
      tures were drawn, notes on discussions, readings,
      etc.

K   1,500-2,000 books and 1,400 issues of periodicals,
      many of which have extensive holograph notes and
      underlinings.

University of California, Los Angeles, Department of Special
Collections, 120 Lawrence Clark Powell Library, Los Angeles,
California 90024.

The CARNAP PAPERS, consisting of approximately 10 archive
boxes of materials, were donated to the University of California by Dr. Rudolf Carnap.

*Die CARNAP PAPERS, die etwa 10 Archivkartons Materialien
umfassen, sind eine Schenkung von Dr. Rudolf Carnap an die
University of California.*

A3   "Autobiography." First version with deletions and
       added h. pages. Also second version of Parts I and
       II and "Notes for Autobiography." 1958. With Car-
       nap's comment: "This is my own working copy with
       marginal remarks to be used for any further rewrit-
       ing."
       "Autobiography." 4th galley proofs. 1962.
       "Intellectual autobiography." 2nd proofs.

164

B1   1 L. to J. Schlaf. 1911.

B1,2 Correspondence with Julius Steinitz.
      Entire correspondence with Paul Schilpp. 1953-1959.
      Correspondence, notes and questions to Arthur Benson
      re: bibliography on Carnap.

B2   1 L. from Alfred Tarski. 1962. With Carnap bibliogra-
      phy attached.
      1 L. from Felix Kaufmann. 1927.

B3   Benson, Arthur. Correspondence re: Carnap bibliography.
      1954.

C7   Manuscripts in German shorthand:
      Review of [Hans] Reichenbach's Axiomatik. 1924.
      "Über den Goldbachschen Satz." Ms. with notations. 4p.
      "Beweis der Unmöglichkeit einer Gabelung der Arith-
         metik." 2c., 1 with h. corr.
      "Andere Geometrien 3, 4, 5." 1920.
      "Axiomsystem of Inductive Logic." Paragraphs 10-13
         of first version. 1961.
      "An Axiom System of Inductive Logic." 1959-1963. Ca.
         400p. (missing p. 45, 55, 78, 108). 7 extra c. of
         p. 299-399.
      "Axiomatik der Kausalität, 1923-27."
      "Alg. Begriffe d. Determination, 1923-27."
      "Begriffe, 1929-30."
      "Einführung in die Wissenschaft Philosophie." Plan
         of Vol. I and II.
      "Found. of Math, 1931."
      "Grundlegung der Geometrie." 1920.
      "Konstitution des Nichtgegebenen." 1929-30.
      Ms. on "Metalogic." 1931.
      "Modalities (1)." 1940-1942.
         "Modal Logic (2)." 1942.
         "Model Logic (3)." New and old.
      "Nicht-euklid. Geometrie." 1920-1922.
      "Physik I." 1919.
      "Semantica." 1938-40.
      "Topologie der Raum-Zeit-Welt." Parts I and II. 1923.
         Second version. 1924.
      Manuscripts for Schilpp volume:
      "Autobiography. Part I." In German shorthand.
      "Autobiography. Part II." In German shorthand.

"Carnap Replies." First version with changes, deletions and additions. A. Another first version. 1957. T. Revised version. 1958. T.

"Ayer on Other Minds." In German shorthand. Also copy of Ayer's "Carnap's Treatment of the Problem of Other Minds."

"Yehoshua Bar-Hillel on (Logical Syntax, Semantics and Pragmatics)." 1957. Also copy of Bar-Hillel's "Remarks on Carnap's Logical Syntax of Language" with "Notes." 1954.

"Beth on Constructed Language Systems." 1959. Also copy of Beth's "Carnap's Views on the Advantages of Constructed Systems over Natural Language in the Philosophy of Science."

C7,   Carnap's notes on articles for Schilpp volume, includ
H3   ing copies of most articles:

P. F. Strawson. "Carnap's Views on Constructed Systems versus Natural Languages in Analytic Philosophy."

Herbert G. Bohnert. "Carnap's Theory of Definition and Analyticity." 1955.

Arthur W. Burks. "On the Significance of Carnap's System of Inductive Logic for the Philosophy of Induction." 1954. 33p.

Robert S. Cohen. "Dialectical Materialism and Carnap's Logical Empiricism."

Donald Davidson. "The Method of Extension and Intension."

Herbert Feigl. "Physicalism."

Adolf Grünbaum's philosophy of time and space.

"Carl G. Hempel on Scientific Theories, 1954-1958."

Henle. "Meaning and Verifiability." Notes dated 1955.

"Reply to Abraham Kaplan on Value Judgments." 1958.

Kemeny. "Carnap's Theory of Probability and Induction." Notes dated 1957.

R. M. Martin. "On Carnap's Conception of Semantics." 1954. Corrections and changes, 1955.

Charles Morris. "Pragmatism and Logical Empiricism." Notes 1957.

Arthur Pap. "Reduction Sentences and Disposition Concepts." Notes 1954.

H. Putnam. "Degree of Confirmation and Inductive Logic." Notes 1957.

166

Karl R. Popper. "The Demarcation between Science and Metaphysics."
Quine. "Carnap and Logical Truth." Notes 1957.
Wilfred Sellars. "Empiricism and Abstract Entities." Notes and Carnap's reply.

D7   "Carnap Replies." 3rd proof. Aug. 1962. Selected sections of 4th galley proofs. 1962. Final version for printer. 392p.

F   "The Aim on Inductive Logic." Stanford Congress, Aug. 1960. Tape and transcript of tape.

H3   Benson, Arthur J. "Preface to the Bibliography of the Writings of Rudolf Carnap to the End of 1960" and "Bibliography of the Writings of Rudolf Carnap to the End of 1961." 4th galley proofs.
Schilpp, Paul A. "The Philosophy of Rudolf Carnap." 2nd galley proofs.
2nd galley proofs for Schilpp's The Philosophy of Rudolf Carnap, including articles by: A. J. Ayer, Y. Bar-Hillel, E. W. Beth, Herbert G. Bohnert, Arthur W. Burks, Robert S. Cohen, Donald Davidson, Herbert Feigl, Robert Feys, Philipp Frank, Nelson Goodman, Adolf Grünbaum, Carl G. Hempel, Paul Henle, Abraham Kaplan, John G. Kemeny, R. M. Martin, Charles Morris, John Myhill, Ernest Nagel, Karl R. Popper, Hilary Putnam, W. Quine, Wilfred Sellars, P. F. Strawson.
Galley proofs of essays in The Philosophy of Rudolf Carnap.
Part I: articles by: Y. Bar-Hillel, E. W. Beth, Carl G. Hempel, Karl R. Popper, John Myhill, Robert Feys, Donald Davidson, Ernest Nagel, Wilfred Sellars, W. Quine, Hilary Putnam, Charles Morris, P. F. Strawson, R. M. Martin.
Part II: A. J. Ayer, Herbert G. Bohnert, Nelson Goodman, Abraham Kaplan, Paul Henle, Adolf Grünbaum, Robert S. Cohen, Arthur W. Burks, Herbert Feigl.

N,   Minnesota Center Memoranda folders: papers by William
B1,2   S. Rozeboom, Grover Maxwell, Adolf Grünbaum, P. K. Feyerabend, H. Feigl. Includes notes by Carnap.

N   Nagel, E. "Carnap's Theory of Induction." 1957.

Steinitz, Julius. "Die Primär-Sekundäre Doppeltrilogie
der Zahlen als rationale Begriffe."
Goodman, Nelson. "The Significance of 'Der logische
Aufbau der Welt'." 1954.

University of California, Los Angeles, Lawrence Clark Powell
Library, Philosophy Reading Room, Los Angeles, California
90024.

The personal library of books as well as numerous reprints
of printed articles was donated to the university by Professor Carnap and is now housed in the Philosophy Reading Room.

*Professor Carnap hat der University of California seine pri-
vate Büchersammlung sowie zahlreiche Nachdrucke früher er-
schienener Artikel geschenkt; diese Sammlung befindet sich
im Philosophy Reading Room.*

G   17 recorded tapes of Carnap's talks and seminars.

K   Personal library of books and reprints.

Mrs. Maria Reichenbach, 456 Puerto Del Mar, Pacific Palisades, California 90272.

B1   Several L. to Hans Reichenbach.

D7   Rudolf Carnap reprint collection.

Indiana University, The University Libraries, The Lilly
Library, Bloomington, Indiana 47401.

ARTHUR FISHER BENTLEY MSS.

B3   L. from A. F. Bentley to Ernest Nagel. 1944.

H5   Bentley, Arthur Fisher. "Carnap." Ms., dated Feb. 10,
1949.
"Carnap's 'truth' vs. Kaufmann's 'true'." Ms., dated
1949.
"The positive and the logical." Ms., dated Aug. 1936.

RUDOLF CARNAP

["Unity of Science."] Ms. Sept. 1940.

Princeton University, Firestone Library, Princeton, New Jersey 08540.

THE PAPERS OF ALBERT EINSTEIN (1879-1955). For details concerning the use of the collection, see description under Albert Einstein.

THE PAPERS OF ALBERT EINSTEIN (1879-1955). Angaben über den Zugang zu der Sammlung finden sich unter "Albert Einstein."

B1,2   Unknown amount of correspondence between Einstein and Carnap.

Harvard University, University Archives, Widener Library, Cambridge, Massachusetts 02138.

RICHARD VON MISES COLLECTION

B1   6 L. to Richard von Mises. T. 1934-1947.

B2   1 L. from Richard von Mises. T.cc. 1947.

Harvard University, Houghton Library, Cambridge, Massachusetts 02138.

GEORGE SARTON PAPERS

B1   2 L. to George Sarton. 1942 and undated.

University of Minnesota, University Libraries, University Archives, Minneapolis, Minnesota 55455.

GEORGE P. CONGER PAPERS

B1   1 L. to George Conger. 1940.

169

ERNST CASSIRER

Philosopher, 1874-1945

<u>Yale University</u>, Beinecke Rare Book and Manuscript Library,
New Haven, Connecticut 06520.

The ERNST CASSIRER PAPERS have been deposited at the Beinecke Rare Book and Manuscript Library by the Yale University Press. Permission to see the papers is required from
the Yale University Press.

*Die ERNST CASSIRER PAPERS sind von der Yale University Press
der Beinecke Rare Book and Manuscript Library überlassen worden. Erlaubnis, die Papers einzusehen, muß von der Yale University Press eingeholt werden.*

B2   1 L. ea. to Hanna Hafkesbrink (1944) and Ake Petzält
      (1938).

C7   Ms., notes, drafts of longer works, including:
      <u>Aims and Avenues of the Knowledge of Reality</u>. German.
      <u>The Concepts of Substance and Form</u>. Voluminous notes
          and deleted drafts, original Ms. German.
      <u>Determinism and Indeterminism in Modern Physics</u>.
          Complete German Ms.
      <u>Essay on Man</u>. Outlines, notes, background material.
          A. Also original T. and cc. of individual chap.
          Mostly English.
      <u>Freedom and Form</u>. Ms.
      <u>Giovanni Pico della Mirandola</u>. Intro. and 3 chap.
      <u>Idea and Form (Gestalt)</u>. Essay collection.
      <u>Individuum und Kosmos / Individual and Cosmos in
          Renaissance Philosophy</u>. Several chap., outlines,
          some lectures, in German. Lengthy Ms.
      <u>Kant's Life and Teaching</u>. Extensive preliminary
          drafts and complete German Ms.
      <u>Language</u>. Notes, rough drafts, lengthy Ms.
      <u>Methodology</u>. Book II, chap. 1. German.
      <u>Myth of the State</u>. Individual chap. of Parts I and
          II, including corrected version of Part I. Numer-
          ous preliminary notes and background materials, as
          well as deleted sections. German and English. A.
          and T.
      <u>On the Einsteinian Theory of Relativity</u>. German.
          Partly cc., partly A.

170

Ontology. Book II, chap. 3. German. A.
Philosophy of Physics. Ms. 200p.
Philosophy of Symbolic Forms. Vol. I - IV. Extensive
preliminary drafts and complete Ms.
Philosophy of the Enlightenment. Vol. I and II.
Notes and drafts. English and German.
Problem of Consciousness. Book II, chap. 4. Notes,
mostly quotations.
The Problem of Knowledge in the Philosophy and Science of the Modern Age. Vol. I - IV. Preliminary
notes, background material and drafts. Also some
Ms.
Science and Knowledge. Notes, 1 chap., conclusion.
Shaftesbury and the Renaissance of Platonism in England. Lengthy Ms. A. and T.
Studies in Contemporary Swedish Philosophy: Axel
Hägerström. German. A. 129p. Also notes on Hägerström.
Thorild's Position in the History of Eighteenth Century Thought. German. A. 218p.
Ms., notes, drafts of shorter works, essays, lectures,
including:
"Albert Schweitzer as Critic of 19th Century Ethics."
Essay.
"The Ancient World and the Origin of Exact Science."
"Art."
"The Cambridge School."
"Carlyle."
"Changes in the Attitude Toward and Theory of the
State..." Lecture.
"Concept and Problem of Truth." Lecture.
"The Concept of Group and the Theory of Perception."
"The Concept of Philosophy as a Philosophical Problem." Göteborg lecture.
"The Concept of Symbolic Form in the Structure of
the Humanistic Sciences." Warburg Library Lecture.
"Content and Extension of the Concept."
"Critical Idealism as a Philosophy of Culture." Warburg Institute lecture.
Davos Conference lectures with Heidegger. March 1929.
"Descartes and Queen Christina of Sweden." Lecture.
Göteborg, 1938.
"Descartes - the Unity of Science." German. A. 30p.

"Descartes' Discours." Radio lecture in German.
Vienna, Jan. 1937.
"The Development of Modern Science and the Basic
Principles of Critical Idealism." Lecture. London,
1927.
"The Educational Value of Art."
"The Expression Function. Philosophy of Culture."
"Forms and Transformations of the Philosophical Con-
cept of Truth." Speech upon the acceptance of the
rectorate of the Univ. of Hamburg, Nov. 2, 1929.
"Galileo's Platonism."
"Goethe and Plato."
"Goethe and the Eighteenth Century."
"Goethe and the Historical World."
"Goethe and the Kantian Philosophy."
"Goethe's Idea of Edification (Culturedness) and
Education."
"The Group Concept" or "The Concept of Group and the
Theory of Perception."
Hegel lectures and seminar courses.
"Henri Bergson's Ethics and Philosophy of Religion."
Lecture. Univ. of Prague, Jan. 22, 1933. 36p.
Hermann Cohen articles, papers, etc.
"Hölderlin and German Idealism." German. A. 56p.
"Humanistic and Naturalistic Founding of the Philoso-
phy of Culture." Lecture. Vienna, 1936.
"The Idea of the Republican Constitution." Lecture
for Constitution Day, Aug. 11, 1928.
Inaugural lecture at Göteborg Univ., Oct. 1935, on
the nature of philosophy.
"Influence of Language upon the Development of Scien-
tific Thought."
"Judaism and the Contemporary Political Myths."
Kant lectures and seminars (numerous). Also many
notes.
"Kristeller."
"Language and Art." Lecture. Columbia Univ., 1941-
1942. Also seminar notes.
"Language and Myth."
"Language and the Structure of the Objective World."
"The Law of Number" / "The Development of Critical
Philosophy."

Leibniz articles, lectures, Cassirer's commentaries
for his edition of Leibniz's works, extensive notes
on Leibniz.
Leibniz and Newton lectures. 1936. Also English arti-
cle. Ms.
"Logos, Dike, Kosmos in Greek philosophy."
"Mathematical Mysticism and Mathematical Science."
"Middle Ages." Lecture series. German.
"Myth of the State." Seminar at Columbia Univ., 1944-
1945. English.
"On Aesthetics." Seminar, 1942-1943.
"On the Concept of Nation. A Rejoinder to Bruno
Bauch."
"On the Epistemology of the Humanistic Sciences." Lec-
ture. Göteborg and Lund, 1941.
"On the Logic of the Symbol Concept."
"On the Nature and Development of Natural Law." Lec-
ture text.
"The Opposition of 'Spirit and Life' in Modern Philo-
sophical Anthropology." Lecture. Frankfurt, Oct. 3,
1928.
"Perspectivism." Notes and short text.
"Philosophical Anthropology." Lecture series. Göte-
borg, 1939-1940. German.
"Philosophy of History." Graduate seminar lectures
and reworked lectures. Yale Univ., 1941-1942. A.
Plato lectures. Oxford, 1935 and Yale, 1943-1944.
Also numerous lectures and notes on Greek philoso-
phers.
"The Problem of Jean Jacques Rousseau." German.
Dated Dec. 21, 1931. 102p.
"Problems of the Philosophy of Culture." Lecture,
Göteborg Univ., 1939-1944. A.
"Relation of Philosophy and Scientific Thought and
Their Historical Development." Lectures at Bedford
College, Univ. of London, 1934-1935.
"Report on Epistemological Literature."
"Schiller and Shaftesbury." German. A. Also lectures
and notes on Schiller.
"Spinoza's Position in the General History of
Thought." German. A. 37p. Also offprint, miscella-
neous notes.

"Structuralism in Modern Linguistics." Essay. Ms.
English notes and first draft.
"Symbolism and Philosophy of Language." Seminar
notes. Yale, 1941-1942.
"Symbolproblem." Lecture and essay. German.
"Theory of Knowledge and Philosophy of Nature."
Lecture, outline and background material. A. 143p.
"Thomas Mann." Notes and drafts. A. German.
"Thomas Mann's Picture of Goethe." Ms. in German.
"The Unity of Science." 2 radio lectures. Berlin,
Oct. 21 and 28, 1931.
"What is Subjectivism?" German. A. 63+p.
"William Stern." Lecture. Durham, North Carolina,
March 27, 1938.
"Young Goethe." Lecture. Göteborg, Oct. 2, 1940. 70p.
Princeton, Jan. 18, 1945. 93p.
Extensive notes and drafts (lectures) on such subjects
as: the causal problem, determinism, induction,
field theory, dynamics, continuity, substance, think-
ing, subject-object, concept of number and group,
consciousness, form, the state, Enlightenment, spirit,
sensuality, knowledge, biology and its concepts,
goal and cause, geometry, physics, history and philosophy of science, aesthetics.
Voluminous package of notes and connected texts (lectures) on figures throughout the history of philosophy and thought. German. A. Includes: Descartes,
Leibniz, Galileo, Kant, Kepler, Herder, Goethe, Lessing, Schiller, Spinoza, Nicholas of Cusa, Bacon and
Hobbes, Locke, Giordano Bruno, Berkeley, Hume,
Burckhardt, Carlyle, Chamberlain.
Notes on works of others.
Lecture series on the history of idealism, compiled
between 1925 and 1937.

D7   Offprints of several articles.

Columbia University, Butler Library, New York, N.Y. 10027.

C7   "Ficino's Place in Intellectual History. Some comments
on P. O. Kristeller's book: The philosophy of Marsi-
lio Ficino." 1943. A. 58p.

"Kant and Rousseau." Undated. T. 47p.

Princeton University, Firestone Library, Princeton, New Jersey 08540.

THE PAPERS OF ALBERT EINSTEIN (1879-1955). For details concerning the use of the collection, see description under Albert Einstein.

THE PAPERS OF ALBERT EINSTEIN (1879-1955). Angaben über den Zugang zu der Sammlung finden sich unter "Albert Einstein."

B1,2   Unknown amount of correspondence between Einstein and Cassirer. 1920, 1927, 1937.

Leo Baeck Institute, 129 East 73rd Street, New York, N.Y. 10021.

H3   "Vom Philosophentag in Halle." 1 cl. 1927.

J   1 photo of Cassirer. Ca. 1931.

Immigration History Research Center of the University of Minnesota, 826 Berry Street, St. Paul, Minnesota 55101.

AMERICAN COUNCIL FOR EMIGRÉS IN THE PROFESSIONS ARCHIVES

A3   Curriculum vitae. 2p.

B3   1 L. 1945.

Yivo Institute, 1048 Fifth Avenue, New York, N.Y. 10028.

HORACE M. KALLEN PAPERS

B1,2   1 F. of materials. 1940.

American Philosophical Society, The Library, 105 South Fifth Street, Philadelphia, Pennsylvania 19106.

FRANZ BOAS PAPERS

B2   1 L. from Boas. 1937.

ERWIN CHARGAFF

Biochemist, 1905-

American Philosophical Society, The Library, 105 South Fifth Street, Philadelphia, Pennsylvania 19106.

The ERWIN CHARGAFF PAPERS, approximately 75 boxes of materials, were placed on deposit at the American Philosophical Society by Dr. Chargaff in 1976. All rights to the materials were retained by Dr. Chargaff. The papers are unsorted as of 1977 and unavailable to researchers except with written permission from Dr. Chargaff (Department of Biochemistry, Columbia University, 630 West 168th Street, New York, N.Y. 10032).

Die ERWIN CHARGAFF PAPERS, etwa 75 Kartons Materialien, wurden von Dr. Chargaff im Jahre 1976 bei der American Philosophical Society deponiert. Alle Rechte ruhen weiterhin bei Dr. Chargaff. Die Materialien waren 1977 noch unsortiert und stehen für Forschungszwecke nur mit schriftlicher Genehmigung von Prof. Chargaff zur Verfügung (Department of Biochemistry, Columbia University, 630 West 168th Street, New York, N.Y. 10032).

B1,2 Personal and professional correspondences, especially L. to Chargaff.

C8 Scientific Ms. and notes from his years at Columbia University, 1935+.

D8, Newspaper and magazine cl.
H3

J Photos.

K Personal library. Ca. 90 shelf ft.

M Memorabilia.

H. T. CLARKE PAPERS, MAX BERGMANN PAPERS

B1,2 Correspondence, uncatalogued.
3 L. concerning Chargaff's employment in the U.S.

American Institute of Physics, Niels Bohr Library, 335 East 45th Street, New York, N.Y. 10017.

B1,2 Cassettes and correspondence with Chargaff concerning
F   DNA.

RICHARD COUDENHOVE-KALERGI

Statesman, 1894-1972

Columbia University, Butler Library, New York, N.Y. 10027.

NICHOLAS MURRAY BUTLER PAPERS: 2 F.

B1   35 L. to N. M. Butler. 1925-1945.
B2   41 L. from N. M. Butler. 1925-1944.
D7   "The Future of Europe and America." 1941. 14p.

Harvard University, Houghton Library, Cambridge, Massachusetts 02138.

RICHARD BEER-HOFMANN COLLECTION, OSWALD GARRISON VILLARD PAPERS

B1   2 L. to Richard Beer-Hofmann. 1941.
      56 L. to Oswald Garrison Villard. 1940-1947.
B2   4 L. from Oswald Garrison Villard. 1940-1947.

University of Pennsylvania, The Charles Patterson Van Pelt Library, Philadelphia, Pennsylvania 19104.

ALMA MAHLER-WERFEL COLLECTION

B1   1 Ptc. and 2 L. to Franz Werfel. A. 1934-1945.
      1 Ptc. and 4 L. to Alma Mahler-Werfel. A. 1927-1956.
      1 L. to Riddelberger. c. 1945.
C7   "Deutschland zwischen Paris und Moskau." Undated. 6p.

New York Public Library, Manuscript Division, Fifth Avenue and 42nd Street, New York, N.Y. 10018.

EMERGENCY COMMITTEE IN AID OF DISPLACED FOREIGN SCHOLARS, 1933-1945

*   File compiled, no assistance given. 1940-1944.

179

Yale University, Beinecke Rare Book and Manuscript Library,
New Haven, Connecticut 06520.

KURT WOLFF ARCHIVE

B1   1 L. to the Kurt Wolff Verlag. 1921.

B2   1 L. from the Kurt Wolff Verlag. 1921.

Library of Congress, Manuscript Division, Independence Avenue
and First Street S.E., Washington, D.C. 20540.

BENJAMIN W. HUEBSCH PAPERS

B2   1 L. from B. W. Huebsch. T.c. 1942.

Bruno Walter Memorial Foundation, c/o Miss Susie Danziger,
115 East 72nd Street, New York, N.Y. 10021.

BRUNO WALTER COLLECTION

B1,2   Correspondence with Bruno Walter.

RICHARD COURANT

Mathematician, 1888-1972

<u>Mrs. Richard Courant</u>, 142 Carlton Road, New Rochelle, New York 10804.

This private collection of materials from the estate of Richard Courant consists of some 10 boxes of letters, approximately 400-500 volumes from Courant's personal library, and an unestimated amount of additional diverse materials. Questions concerning the collection may also be directed to Prof. Ernst David Courant (owner and legal executor of the materials), 109 Bay Avenue, Bayport, New York 11705.

Diese Privatsammlung aus dem Nachlaß von Richard Courant besteht aus etwa 10 Kartons mit Briefen, etwa 400-500 Bänden aus seiner Privatbibliothek sowie einer unbestimmten Menge verschiedener anderer Materialien. Fragen in Bezug auf die Sammlung können auch an Prof. Ernst David Courant, 109 Bay Avenue, Bayport, New York 11705, gerichtet werden. Prof. Courant ist Nachlaßverwalter und Besitzer der Materialien.

A1   Several diaries. 1914-1915.

A2   Materials from early school days (notebooks).

B1,2 10 B. of correspondence from the 1930s plus a few earlier L. Filed by name of author, alphabetically. Also includes some of Courant's own L.:
      1. Up to 1920.
      2. 1920-1934, including L. to Mrs. Courant and Otto Neugebauer, concerning: Courant's first visit to the U.S. (1932); Courant's appointment to the Mathematische Institut Göttingen; Courant's efforts to procure work for colleagues in the U.S. (1933-1934).
      3. 1934-1938. Primarily L. concerned with Courant's rescue efforts for fellow mathematicians, including K. O. Friedrichs.
      4. 1938-. Personal L. (The professional correspondence dealing with New York University is located at the Courant Institute.)
      5. Correspondence with fellow mathematicians from all years.

B2   Ca. 6 L. from Albert Einstein.

B3   Correspondences of Mrs. Courant with her family, primarily from the early years in the U.S. (1934-1939).

C7   Lecture notes from Göttingen (as lecturer).

C8   Several Ms.

D7,8 Offprints and cl. of numerous Courant articles.

H3,   Numerous cl., including many from 1933 that are of
L   historical significance.

I   Documents.

J   Several photos.

K   A number of early runs of journals (German, European).
      Many were sold to a dealer.
      Personal library. Ca. 400-500 volumes. Some volumes
      have already been sold, others given to the library
      at the Courant Institute.

New York University, Courant Institute of Mathematical Sciences, 251 Mercer Street, New York, N.Y. 10012.

RICHARD COURANT PAPERS: The filing cabinets of the Courant Institute of Mathematical Sciences contain over 800 files of Dr. Courant containing correspondence with individuals, laboratories, universities, publishers, as well as many subject headings and items related to teaching. There are also files of materials on international conferences and symposia, government agencies, etc., illustrating the broad spectrum of Dr. Courant's interests, contacts and work. Many major figures of twentieth-century science (Max Born, Albert Einstein, Edward Teller) and figures of political interest (Alger Hiss) are represented in the materials. A detailed listing of the headings of the file folders is available through the Courant family or through Ms. Frances Adamo at the Institute. The materials date roughly from 1935 and form the basis of Ms. Constance Reid's study, Courant in Göttingen and New York, published by the Springer Verlag in 1976. The following is a brief summary of the collection:

RICHARD COURANT PAPERS: Die Aktenschranke des Courant Institute of Mathematical Sciences enthalten über 800 Ordner

RICHARD COURANT

Briefwechsel zwischen Courant und verschiedenen Persönlich-
keiten, Laboratorien, Universitäten, Verlegern sowie weitere
mit seiner Unterrichtstätigkeit verbundene Materialien. Es
existieren daneben Ordner mit Materialien über internationale
Konferenzen, Symposien, Regierungsbehörden usw., die Courants
weitgespannte Interessen und Verbindungen widerspiegeln.
Viele bedeutende Wissenschaftler (Max Born, Albert Einstein,
Edward Teller) sowie Persönlichkeiten aus der Politik (Alger
Hiss) sind in den Materialien vertreten. Eine genaue Auf-
zeichnung der Ordnertitel ist sowohl bei der Familie Courant
als auch durch Ms. Frances Adamo am Mathematischen Institut
erhältlich. Die Materialien beginnen etwa in der Zeit von
1935 und bilden die Grundlage für eine Studie von Ms. Con-
stance Reid, Courant in Göttingen and New York, die 1976 im
Springer Verlag veröffentlicht wurde. Es folgt eine kurze
Zusammenfassung der Sammlung:

B1,2   Correspondence. 1935-1960.
        Memoranda.

C8   Manuscripts.

D8   Offprints (very few).

I   Documents. 1935-1960.

J   Photos.

American Philosophical Society, The Library, 105 South Fifth
Street, Philadelphia, Pennsylvania 19106.

L. C. DUNN PAPERS, NIELS BOHR CORRESPONDENCE

B1,2   Correspondence with L. C. Dunn in file "Emergency Com-
        mittee in Aid of Displaced German Scholars."
        Correspondence with Niels Bohr. 1926-1962.

Archive for History of Quantum Physics (locations in U.S.:
Bancroft Library, University of California, Berkeley; American Philosophical Society, Philadelphia, Pennsylvania; American Institute of Physics, New York, N.Y.).

B1   1 L. to Walther Gerlach. 1922.

11 L. to H. A. Kramers. 1948-1950.

B1,2   Correspondence with Niels Bohr. 1922.

G   One interview. 1962. Also transcript. 16p.

Library of Congress, Manuscript Division, Independence Avenue and First Street S.E., Washington, D.C. 20540.

OSWALD VEBLEN PAPERS

B1   4 L. to Carl L. Siegel. 1946.

B1,2   Correspondence with Oswald Veblen.

B2   1 L. from Carl Siegel. 1939.

California Institute of Technology, Robert A. Millikan Library, Pasadena, California 91109.

PAUL S. EPSTEIN PAPERS, THEODORE VON KARMAN CORRESPONDENCE

B1   5 L. and 1 Tel. to Paul S. Epstein. 1929-1944.

B1,2   Correspondence with Theodore von Karman. 1921-1955.
       3 F.

University of Chicago, The Joseph Regenstein Library, 1100 East 57th Street, Chicago, Illinois 60637.

JAMES FRANCK PAPERS

B1,2   Lengthy correspondence between Courant and James
       Franck. 1932-1958.

B1,   L. of congratulations to James Franck on 70th birthday.
J   1952. Accompanied by photo of Courant and wife.

J   Photo with Niels Bohr. Rockefeller University, New
       York, June 5, 1962.

Harvard University, University Archives, Widener Library,

RICHARD COURANT

Cambridge, Massachusetts 02138.

RICHARD VON MISES COLLECTION

Bl   5 L. to Richard von Mises. T. 1920-1944.
B2   1 L. from Richard von Mises. T.c. 1943.

New York Public Library, Manuscript Division, Fifth Avenue
and 42nd Street, New York, N.Y. 10018.

EMERGENCY COMMITTEE IN AID OF DISPLACED FOREIGN SCHOLARS,
1933-1945

*   File compiled when assistance was granted. 1933-1944.

Columbia University, Butler Library, New York, N.Y. 10027.

Bl   1 L. to D. E. Smith. T. 1936.

HANS THEODOR DAVID

Musicologist, 1902-1967

Baldwin-Wallace College, Riemenschneider Bach Institute, Berea, Ohio 44017.

HANS T. DAVID COLLECTION: A detailed inventory of the collection is available from the Riemenschneider Bach Institute.

HANS T. DAVID COLLECTION: Ein detailliertes Verzeichnis der Sammlung ist beim Riemenschneider Bach Institute erhältlich.

A2   5 notebooks.

C7   1 unpub. essay.

C13a   21 pieces of original music.

C13b   Ca. 30 arrangements of music by others.

D7,8   Published materials by David include:
        5 books;
        34 journal articles;
        25 reviews of books, editions of music and performances;
        20 sets of program notes.

I   Degrees and honors received.

K   The Hans David Library consists of:
        78 items of raria;
        716 musical scores;
        491 books of music literature and theory;
        80 historical sets, collected editions and/or monuments;
        3 archive boxes of monographs;
        58 printed editions of music, including a 40-volume edition of Mozarts Werke by Alfred Einstein, as well as music from the Moravian Church.

M   Portrait painted by Mrs. Hans David in the spring of 1957.

Dr. Elinore Barber, Riemenschneider Bach Institute, Berea, Ohio 44017.

HANS THEODOR DAVID

Dr. David's family gave his personal microfilm collection (mostly films of Renaissance and Baroque manuscripts and prints), his teaching materials, and some of his personal correspondence to his former student, Dr. Elinore Barber, in whose possession they still remain. The correspondence includes a number of carbon copies of letters written to various colleagues and some of their replies.

Dr. Davids Familie übergab dessen persönliche Mikrofilm-Sammlung (in erster Linie Filme von Renaissance- und Barockmanuskripten und Drucken), sein Lehrmaterial und einen Teil der Privatkorrespondenz an seine Schülerin, Frau Dr. Elinore Barber; Frau Barber befindet sich noch im Besitz dieser Materialien. Dieser Teil der Korrespondenz schließt eine Reihe von Briefdurchschlägen an verschiedene Kollegen sowie deren Antworten ein.

<u>Dr. Edward E. Lowinsky</u>, Prof. Emeritus, Department of Music, University of Chicago, Chicago, Illinois 60637.

B1   13 L. to Edward E. Lowinsky. 1962-1967.

B2   21 L. from Edward E. Lowinsky. 1962-1967.

<u>Library of Congress</u>, Reference Department, Music Division, Independence Avenue and First Street S.E., Washington, D.C. 20540.

C13   "Sonata" [Sonata, viola]. 9p. Undated.

MAX DEHN

Mathematician, 1878-1952

Dr. Wilhelm Magnus, 11 Lomond Place, New Rochelle, N.Y. 10804.

Dr. Magnus, a former student and later close friend of Dehn, became the keeper of Dehn's mathematical papers immediately after Dehn's death in 1952.

Nach Max Dehns Tod im Jahre 1952 übernahm Dr. W. Magnus, ehemaliger Student und späterer enger Freund von Dehn, Dehns wissenschaftlichen Nachlaß.

B1   1 L. to Wilhelm Magnus.

C8   H. notes by Dehn, nearly incomprehensible.
      1 short unpub. Ms.

D8   Complete collection of the published works of Dehn.

H3   Obituary of Dehn by Wilhelm Magnus and Ruth Moufang.

J   Photographs.

Library of Congress, Manuscript Division, Independence Avenue and First Street S.E., Washington, D.C. 20540.

OSWALD VEBLEN PAPERS: 1 F.

B1   6 L. and 1 Tel. to Hermann Weyl. T. and A. 1942-1944
      and undated.
      2 L. to Oswald Veblen. 1938, 1941.

B2   3 L. from Hermann Weyl. T.c. 1938-1942.
      3 L. from Oswald Veblen. T.c. 1938, 1941.

B3   91 L. in Veblen's "Refugee File" concerning Dehn.
      1938-1945.

I   Documents in Veblen's "Refugee File," many biographical
      in nature.

Ms. Hanna H. Meissner, 176 East Stadium Avenue, West Lafayette, Indiana 47906.

Ms. Meissner is the sister of the late mathematician, Ernst

David Hellinger. The Dehn materials in her possession, from the estate of Dr. Hellinger, are the result of the collaboration of Dehn and Hellinger during the 1940s.

Frau Meißner ist die Schwester des verstorbenen Mathematikers Ernst David Hellinger. In ihrem Besitz befindet sich einiges Material über Max Dehn aus dem Nachlaß von Dr. Hellinger. Dieses Material datiert aus der Zeit der Zusammenarbeit von Dehn und Hellinger in den vierziger Jahren.

B1,2   Correspondence between Dehn and Hellinger, 1940s, re: article on James Gregory.
　　　　Inestimable amount of correspondence by Dehn.

C7   Ms. of articles written in collaboration with E. D. Hellinger:
　　　 "Certain Mathematical Achievements of James Gregory." 1943.
　　　 "On James Gregory's Vera Quadratura." 1939.

State of North Carolina, Department of Cultural Resources, Raleigh, North Carolina 27611.

BLACK MOUNTAIN COLLEGE ARCHIVES

I　　　[Faculty] file. "Max Dehn - Mathematics."
　　　 [General] file. "Toni Dehn" (wife of Max).

Northwestern University, Mathematics Department, Evanston, Illinois 60201.

B1   1 L. to H. T. Davis. Undated.
　　　1 L. from W. T. Reid re: Ernst David Hellinger. 1950.

New York Public Library, Manuscript Division, Fifth Avenue and 42nd Street, New York, N.Y. 10018.

EMERGENCY COMMITTEE IN AID OF DISPLACED FOREIGN SCHOLARS, 1933-1945

*   File compiled when assistance was granted. 1933-1944.

MAX DELBRÜCK

Biophysicist, 1906-

<u>California Institute of Technology</u>, Robert A. Millikan
Library, Pasadena, California 91109.

MAX DELBRÜCK CORRESPONDENCE: 13 manuscript boxes of materials.   (More materials are expected.)   The materials were
donated by Prof. Delbrück in 1968; he still retains all
literary rights to the papers.   A small amount of correspondence is restricted.

*MAX DELBRÜCK CORRESPONDENCE: 13 Manuskriptkartons mit Mate-
rialien.   (Weiteres Material wird erwartet.)   Die Materialien
sind ein Schenkung von Prof. Delbrück aus dem Jahre 1968.
Alle Rechte ruhen noch bei Prof. Delbrück; ein geringer Teil
des Briefwechsels ist im Moment noch nicht zugänglich.*

A3   List of Delbrück's publications. 1929-1946. Dated Aug.
        13, 1946.

B1   213 L. 1943-1968, including L. to: T. F. Anderson,
        G. W. Beadle, S. Benzer, G. Bertani, P. M. S. Black-
        ett, Niels and Aage Bohr, John Cairns, A. H. Doer-
        mann, R. Dulbecco, W. D. Fraser, A. D. Hershey, S. E.
        Luria, Wolfgang Pauli, R. B. Setlow, D. Varju, J. D.
        Watson.

B1,2   Correspondence files relating to the Institut für Gene-
        tik (Cologne):   P. Abel, H. Bank, C. Bresch, E.
        Brüche, Dekan Köln, H. Dernbach, Düsseldorf, Gipfel-
        konferenz, L. Grossman, W. Harm, A. Haug, G. Hotz,
        O. Kuhn, G. Leibholz, W. Menke, G. Rassow, W. Sauer-
        bier, P. Starlinger, J. Straub, H. G. Zachau.
        Correspondence files concerning the following subjects:
        Immigration. 1931-1939.
        Harold Johns. 1960-1964.
        Wagner Kangler. 1959-1967.
        E. Kellenberger. 1956-1969.
        A. Kelner. 1948-1949.
        Nato.
        Rockefeller Fellowship. 1936-1939.
        R. Sinsheimer. 1950-1957.
        George Streisinger. 1951-1959.
        H. Stubbs. 1962-1967.

190

Sundials.
UV Luncheon Club Seminar.
Vanderbilt Appointment. 1939-1947.
Warren Weaver. 1967.
National Foundation for Infantile Paralysis:
Correspondence and miscellany concerning grants.
1951-1964.
R. S. Edgars file. Correspondence re: phage research
grant. 1961-1964.

B2 511 L. 1943-1966, including L. from: T. F. Anderson, S.
Benzer, G. Bertani, P. M. S. Blackett, Niels and
Aage Bohr, John Cairns, A. H. Doermann, R. Dulbecco,
W. D. Fraser, A. D. Hershey, S. E. Luria, Wolfgang
Pauli, W. Reichardt, R. B. Setlow, D. Varju, J. D.
Watson.

B3 Ca. 35 L. Includes L. to and from: T. F. Anderson,
G. W. Beadle, S. Benzer, N. Bohr, J. Cairns, W. M.
Elsasser, W. D. Fraser, A. D. Hershey, W. Pauli, W.
Reichardt, J. D. Watson, C. Worthingham.

C7 "A conducted tour by easy stages to the last para-
graph." 1946. Ms.
Comments by Delbrück and A. Bohr concerning N. Bohr's
Cologne lecture.
National Foundation for Infantile Paralysis. Progress
Reports. 1948-1960. 5 F.
Comments on paper by A. D. Hershey and Davidson. 1951.
Delbrück statement to California Institute of Technol-
ogy faculty. Dated March 14, 1960.
"Reduction of Dimensionality in Biological Diffusion
Processes." Written together with G. Adam.

L Reprints by R. B. Setlow.

N Anderson, T. F. "Types of Morphology Found in Bacterial
Viruses." Undated. 2 c.
Bohr, Niels. "Quantum Physics and Biology." Ms. Dated
Sept. 7, 1959.
Dulbecco, R. "A Study of the RNA of an Animal Virus."
Ms. Undated. "Abstract of Progress Report." July 1 -
Dec. 31, 1955.
Hellwig and Gerhard. "Ist der Trainingseffekt und sein
Zusammenhang mit der Entropieabgabe lebender Orga-
nismen ein allgemeines Prinzip?" 1965.

Hershey, A. D., F. Kimura and J. Bronfenbrenner. "Uniformity of Size of Bacteriophage Particles."
Watson, J. D. and O. Maaløe. "The Transfer of Radioactive Phosphorus from Parental to Progeny Phage."
1951.

Prof. Max Delbrück, Division of Biology, California Institute of Technology, Pasadena, California 91125.

The materials in Prof. Delbrück's possession are to be deposited eventually in the Archives of the California Institure of Technology Library. At present the materials are inaccessible.

Die Materialien in Prof. Delbrücks Besitz sollen ihren endgültigen Platz in den Archiven der California Institute of Technology Library finden; z.Zt. sind diese Materialien nicht zugänglich.

A2,   Work notes and materials.
L

B1,2   Current correspondences in which Prof. Delbrück is
       engaged.

D8   Complete collection of offprints and cl. of Delbrück's
       writings.

J   Photos.

American Philosophical Society, The Library, 105 South Fifth Street, Philadelphia, Pennsylvania 19106.

MILISLAV DEMEREC PAPERS, WARREN STURGIS MCCULLOCH PAPERS, NIELS BOHR CORRESPONDENCE

A3   Autobiographical questionnaire.

B1   42 L. to Niels Bohr. 1932-1962.

B1,2   Correspondence with Milislav Demerec.
       Correspondence with Warren S. McCulloch.

Archive for History of Quantum Physics (locations in U.S.:
Bancroft Library, University of California, Berkeley; American Philosophical Society, Philadelphia, Pennsylvania; American Institute of Physics, New York, N.Y.).

B1   1 L. to H. A. Kramers. 1936.
      1 L. to Christian Møeller. [1931].
B2   1 L. from Christian Møeller. 1931.

Indiana University, The University Libraries, The Lilly
Library, Bloomington, Indiana 47401.

HERMANN JOSEPH MULLER MSS.

B1   7 L. to Hermann Joseph Muller. 1939-1951.
B2   6 L. from Hermann Joseph Muller. 1941-1951.
B3   1 L. from Muller to Carl Hartman re: Delbrück. 1945.

University of Missouri Library, Western Historical Manuscript
Collection/State Historical Society Manuscripts, Columbia,
Missouri 65201.

L. J. STADLER PAPERS

B1   1 L. to L. J. Stadler. 1946.

New York Public Library, Manuscript Division, Fifth Avenue
and 42nd Street, New York, N.Y. 10018.

EMERGENCY COMMITTEE IN AID OF DISPLACED FOREIGN SCHOLARS,
1933-1945

*   File compiled when assistance was granted. 1939-1944.

University of Chicago, The Joseph Regenstein Library, 1100
East 57th Street, Chicago, Illinois 60637.

JAMES FRANCK PAPERS

J   2 group photos:
      Institute for Theoretical Physics. Copenhagen, 1935.
      Ninth Washington Conference on Theoretical Physics.
      Washington, D.C., Oct. 31 - Nov. 2, 1946.

FELIX DEUTSCH

Psychoanalyst, 1884-1964

Dr. Helene Deutsch, 44 Larchwood Drive, Cambridge, Massachusetts 02138.

The materials in the possession of Dr. Deutsch, widow of
Felix, are from the estate of Deutsch. Information concerning the papers may also be obtained from Dr. Martin
Deutsch (son of Felix and Helene), Massachusetts Institute
of Technology, Cambridge, Massachusetts 02138.

*Ein Teil des Nachlasses von Felix Deutsch befindet sich im
Besitz von Frau Dr. Deutsch, der Witwe von Felix Deutsch.
Auskünfte über die Materialien können auch von Dr. Martin
Deutsch (dem Sohn von F. u. H. Deutsch) eingeholt werden:
Massachusetts Institute of Technology, Cambridge, Massachu-
setts 02138.*

B1,2   Some correspondence.

C7,8   Work notes.
       Scientific materials, composed mainly of unpub. mate-
       rials.

K   Personal library. (It is intended that the library be
       sent to Jerusalem.)

Yivo Institute, 1048 Fifth Avenue, New York, N.Y. 10028.

HORACE M. KALLEN PAPERS

B1,2   Miscellaneous correspondence materials. 1935. 1 F.

HELENE DEUTSCH
Psychoanalyst, 1884-

Dr. Helene Deutsch, 44 Larchwood Drive, Cambridge, Massachusetts 02138.

Questions concerning the materials in the private collection of Dr. Deutsch may also be directed to Dr. Martin Deutsch (son of Helene and Felix), Massachusetts Institute of Technology, Cambridge, Massachusetts 02138. Although the future of the collection has not been definitely decided as of 1976, the collection of Freudiana will probably go to the Freud Archives at the Library of Congress, Washington, D.C.

Fragen in Bezug auf die Privatsammlung von Frau Dr. Deutsch mögen auch an Dr. Martin Deutsch (Massachusetts Institute of Technology, Cambridge, Massachusetts 02138), den Sohn von Felix u. Helene Deutsch, gerichtet werden. Obwohl bis 1976 über den zukünftigen Verbleib des Materials insgesamt noch keine endgültige Entscheidung getroffen war, dürfte zumindest die Sammlung der Freudiana wahrscheinlich an die Freud-Archive der Library of Congress, Washington, D.C. gehen.

B1,2 Correspondence from many years.

L   Large Freudiana collection.
      Additional collections of materials on psychoanalysis.

Dr. Martin Grotjahn, 416 North Bedford Drive, Beverly Hills, California 90210.

B1,2 Letters to and from Martin Grotjahn.

University of Texas, Humanities Research Center, Manuscripts Collection, Box 7219, Austin, Texas 78712.

I   24 documents re: Helene Deutsch.

Library of Congress, Manuscript Division, Independence Avenue and First Street S.E., Washington, D.C. 20540.

PAPERS OF SIEGFRIED BERNFELD

B1,2 Correspondence with Siegfried Bernfeld. 1925-1935.

RENÉ D'HARNONCOURT

Art Museum Director, Historian, 1901-1968

Museum of Modern Art, The Library, 11 West 53rd Street, New
York, N.Y. 10019.

René D'Harnoncourt was Director of the Museum of Modern Art
from 1949 to 1968.

*René D'Harnoncourt war von 1949-1958 Direktor des Museum of
Modern Art.*

*   Two microfilms, 1930-1967, contents as follows, are on
       deposit in the Library, available for study and refer-
       ence purposes upon written application:
       Original sketches of exhibitions, graphic work, draw-
          ings.
       Photos showing D'Harnoncourt's installations and
          exhibition techniques, designs, plans, in U.S.,
          Mexico, and Europe.

B   Business correspondence, belonging to the Museum of
       Modern Art, from D'Harnoncourt's years as Director.
       Restricted and confidential.

J   Photos of D'Harnoncourt at work, exhibition catalogs.

Columbia University, Butler Library, New York, N.Y. 10027.

ORAL HISTORY COLLECTION

G   Tape concerning relations between the Carnegie Corpora-
       tion and the American Federation of Art. 1968. Also
       transcript. 65p. Permission required for use.

Harvard University, Fogg Art Museum, Cambridge, Massachusetts
02138.

B1,2   Correspondence with Dr. Paul Sachs. 1954-[1959].

197

WILLIAM DIETERLE

Film Director, 1893-1972

University of Southern California, University Library, Department of Special Collections, University Park, Los Angeles, California 90007.

The WILLIAM DIETERLE COLLECTION was donated to the Library in 1967 by William Dieterle and consists of 10 boxes of materials. A 10-page inventory of the collection is available from the Department of Special Collections.

Die WILLIAM DIETERLE COLLECTION ist eine Schenkung von William Dieterle aus dem Jahre 1967; sie enthält 10 Kartons Material. Ein 10seitiges Inventar der Sammlung ist über das Department of Special Collections erhältlich.

C12, Scripts, photographs, costume designs, advertisements
J,   and publicity materials, etc. for the following
L   films:
    The Story of Louis Pasteur.
    The White Angel.
    The Life of Emile Zola.
    Blockade.
    Juarez.
    The Hunchback of Notre Dame.
    The Story of Dr. Ehrlich's Magic Bullet.
    Dispatch from Reuters.
    All That Money Can Buy.
    Tennessee Johnson.
    Kismet.
    September Affair.

Dr. Marta Mierendorff, 8633 West Knoll Drive, Hollywood, California 90069.

INSTITUT FÜR KUNSTSOZIOLOGIE

C7   Radio speech. Introduction for the Continental Players.

State University of New York at Binghamton, Center for Modern Theater Research, Binghamton, New York 13901.

MAX REINHARDT ARCHIVE

C12   Hands Across the Sea. Script used in student workshop
       supervised by Dieterle. Ca. 1940.

J   11 photos of Dieterle as an actor. 1922-1925.

O   1 program.

Southern Illinois University, Morris Library, Department of
Special Collections, Carbondale, Illinois 62901.

ERWIN PISCATOR PAPERS

B1,2 Correspondence with Erwin Piscator.

ALFRED DÖBLIN

Writer, 1887-1957

Leo Baeck Institute, 129 East 73rd Street, New York, N.Y.
10021.

The primary collection of Döblin materials is located at
the Deutsches Literaturarchiv, Marbach am Neckar. Döblin
materials at the Leo Baeck Institute are found in the following collections: GEORG HERMANN COLLECTION, FRITZ
MAUTHNER COLLECTION, KURT KERSTEN COLLECTION and general
archive files.

*Die wichtigste Döblin-Sammlung befindet sich im Deutschen
Literaturarchiv in Marbach am Neckar. Döblin Materialien
im Leo Baeck Institute finden sich im allgemeinen Archiv
und in folgenden Sammlungen: GEORG HERMANN COLLECTION,
FRITZ MAUTHNER COLLECTION, KURT KERSTEN COLLECTION.*

B1   1 L. ea. to: Paul Fechter (1931), Rudolf Grossman
      (1932), Dr. Isador Kaslan (1936), Fritz Mauthner
      (1930), Kurt Kersten (1954).
      1 L. and 1 Ptc. to Georg Hermann. 1939, 1936.

C7   "Der Eid ist radikal abzuschaffen." 1928. A. 7p.

D7   "Der Eid ist radikal abzuschaffen." 1928. 1 cl.

H3   6 cl.

H4   Book advertisement: Alfred Döblin. Ausgewählte Werke
      in Einzelbänden. 1960. 17p. with biography.

J   Photo of Döblin. Ca. 1930.

Elvira and Arthur Rosin, 14 East 75th Street, New York, N.Y.
10021.

B1   47 L. to Arthur and Elvira Rosin. 1933-1957.

Dr. Harold von Hofe, Department of German, University of
Southern California, Los Angeles, California 90007.

LUDWIG MARCUSE PAPERS

B1   27 L. to Ludwig and Sascha Marcuse. 1946-1957.

B3   13 L. from Erna Döblin to L. and S. Marcuse.

Mr. Peter Döblin, 500 West End Avenue, New York, N.Y. 10025.

Peter Döblin is the son of Alfred.

B1   26 L. to Peter Döblin. 1936-1951

Library of Congress, Manuscript Division, Independence Avenue
and First Street S.E., Washington, D.C. 20540.

BENJAMIN W. HUEBSCH PAPERS

B1   8 L. and 1 Ptc. to Benjamin W. Huebsch. 1931-1941.

B2   3 L. from B. W. Huebsch. 1941.

B3   13 L. between B. W. Huebsch and Peter Döblin.
       2 L. from Erna Döblin to Huebsch.

I   Affidavit for Klaus Döblin, from B. W. Huebsch to the
       U.S. Department of State.

Mrs. Erna Budzislawski, 2040 Rodney Drive, Los Angeles, California 90027.

B1,2   Correspondence between Erna Budzislawski and Alfred
       Döblin. Ca. 30 L., including 12 by Döblin. 1947-1948.

Mrs. Elisabeth M. Stoerk and Mrs. Susanne B. Hoeller, 288
Ocean Drive West, Stamford, Connecticut 06902.

FRIDERIKE ZWEIG ARCHIVE

B1   4 L. to Friderike Zweig. 1944.

B2   2 L. from Friderike Zweig. 1945.

B3   1 L. re: Alfred Döblin.

University of Southern California, Lion Feuchtwanger Memorial Library, 520 Paseo Miramar, Pacific Palisades, California
90272.

B2   6 L. and 1 Tel. from Lion Feuchtwanger.

Barthold Fles Literary Agency, 507 Fifth Avenue, New York,
N.Y. 10016.

B1   4 L. to Barthold Fles. 1944 and undated.

Yale University, Beinecke Rare Book and Manuscript Library,
New Haven, Connecticut 06520.

KURT WOLFF ARCHIVE

B1   3 L. to the Kurt Wolff Verlag. 1913-1921.

B2   1 L. from the Kurt Wolff Verlag.

State University of New York at Albany, Department of Germanic Languages and Literatures, 1400 Washington Avenue,
Albany, New York 12222.

HELMUT HIRSCH COLLECTION

B1   1 L. to Helmut Hirsch. c. 1951.

B2   1 L. from Helmut Hirsch. 1951.

B3   1 L. from Döblin's secretary to Hirsch. 1951.

University of California, Los Angeles, Music Library, 405
Hilgard Avenue, Los Angeles, California 90024.

ERNST TOCH ARCHIVE

C3   Toch, Ernst. "Das Wasser, op. 53. [Kantata nach Worten
        von Alfred Döblin für Tenor, Bariton, Sprechen und
        Chor mit Instrumenten; Flöte, Trompete, Violinen,

ALFRED DÖBLIN

Violoncelli, Kontrabass und Schlagzeug. 1930]." 29
leaves. Microfilm.

University of California, Los Angeles, Department of Special
Collections, 120 Lawrence Clark Powell Library, Los Angeles,
California 90024.

FRANZ WERFEL ARCHIVE

B1   1 L. to Franz Werfel. 1943.

University of New Hampshire, The Library, Department of Special Collections, Durham, New Hampshire 03824.

OSKAR MARIA GRAF COLLECTION

B1   1 L. to Oskar Maria Graf. 1926.

University of Pennsylvania, The Charles Patterson Van Pelt
Library, Philadelphia, Pennsylvania 19104.

ALMA MAHLER-WERFEL COLLECTION

B1   1 L. to Alma Mahler-Werfel. A.

Mr. Francis Heilbut, 328 West 96th Street, New York, N.Y.
10025.

IVAN HEILBUT PAPERS

H5   Heilbut, Ivan. Essay on Döblin.

ALBERT EHRENSTEIN

Writer, 1886-1950

The ALBERT EHRENSTEIN ARCHIVE, containing unpublished writings of Ehrenstein as well as published and secondary materials, is located in the Jewish National and University
Library in Jerusalem.

*Das ARCHIV ALBERT EHRENSTEIN befindet sich in der Jewish
National and University Library in Jerusalem und enthält
unveröffentlichte und veröffentlichte Schriften Ehrensteins
sowie Sekundärmaterial.*

Leo Baeck Institute, 129 East 73rd Street, New York, N.Y.
10021.

JACOB PICARD COLLECTION, KURT KERSTEN COLLECTION

B1   1 Ptc. to Kurt Kersten. 1947.
      1 L. and 1 Ptc. to Kurt Kläber. A. 1945, 1941.

B1,2 Uncatalogued correspondence between Jacob Picard and
      Albert Ehrenstein.

C3   "Melancholie."
      "Meinem ermordeten Bruder Otto."
      "Der grüne Salamander spricht."
      "Trinklied für Pe-Lo-Thien." Accompanied by drawing by
      Oskar Kokoschka and notes by Charlotte Beradt.

H5   Picard, Jacob. "Abschied von Albert Ehrenstein." 2p.

Yale University, Beinecke Rare Book and Manuscript Library,
New Haven, Connecticut 06520.

KURT WOLFF ARCHIVE

B1   8 L. to Kurt Wolff Verlag. 1910-1923.
      8 L. to Walter Hasenclever. 1910-1923.

B2   1 Ptc. from Theodor Däubler.

B3   2 L. between Walter Hasenclever and the Kurt Wolff Ver-
      lag re: Ehrenstein.

ALBERT EHRENSTEIN

Mrs. Elisabeth M. Stoerk and Mrs. Susanne B. Hoeller, 288
Ocean Drive West, Stamford, Connecticut 06902.

FRIDERIKE ZWEIG ARCHIVE

B1   8 L. to Friderike Zweig. 1942, 1946, 1950.

B3   1 L. from the Relief Committee re: Ehrenstein.

H5   Writers Service Center. Materials in folder entitled
        "Lives and Outlines."

State University of New York at Albany, Department of Germanic Languages and Literatures, 1400 Washington Avenue,
Albany, New York 12222.

STORM PUBLISHERS ARCHIVE

B1   3 L. to Alexander Gode von Aesch. 1946.

B2   3 L. from Alexander Gode von Aesch. 1946.

University of Pennsylvania, The Charles Patterson Van Pelt
Library, Philadelphia, Pennsylvania 19104.

ALMA MAHLER-WERFEL COLLECTION

B1   3 L. to Franz Werfel. A. 1931-1942.
        2 L. to Alma Mahler-Werfel. T. and A. 1944, 1947.

B2   7 Ptc., 1 Tel. and 4 L. from Franz Werfel. A. 1915-
        1919. Also several c.

Harvard University, Houghton Library, Cambridge, Massachusetts 02138.

C7   Essays on individuals:
        Franz Kafka. A. 1942. 9p.
        Lothringer. A. and T. 1944. 11p.
        Peter Altenberg. A. 1944. 3p.

205

ALBERT EHRENSTEIN

New York Public Library, Manuscript Division, Fifth Avenue
and 42nd Street, New York, N.Y. 10018.

THEO FELDMAN PAPERS, EMERGENCY COMMITTEE IN AID OF DISPLACED
FOREIGN SCHOLARS, 1933-1945.

B1   1 Ptc. to "Gruppe für Literatur." A. 1927.
       2 L. and 3 Ptc. to Theo Feldman. A. 1944, 1947.
*   File compiled by the Emergency Committee when assist-
      ance was granted. 1942-1944.

University of New Hampshire, The Library, Department of
Special Collections, Durham, New Hampshire 03824.

OSKAR MARIA GRAF COLLECTION

B1   4 L. to O. M. Graf. 1938-1941.

Library of Congress, Manuscript Division, Independence Avenue and First Street S.E., Washington, D.C. 20540.

PAPERS OF SIEGFRIED BERNFELD

B1   1 L. to Sigmund Freud. 1912. c.

Indiana University, The University Libraries, The Lilly
Library, Bloomington, Indiana 47401.

MAX EASTMAN MSS.

B3   1 L. from Max Eastman re: Ehrenstein. 1929.

New School for Social Research, Office of the Dean of the
Graduate Faculty of Political and Social Science, 65 Fifth
Avenue, New York, N.Y. 10003.

RECORDS OF THE UNIVERSITY IN EXILE, 1933-45

A3   Curriculum vitae.

B1   2 L. 1940-1941.

Dr. Clementine Zernick, 225-10 106th Avenue, Queens Village,
New York 11429.

B1   Unknown amount of correspondence with Arnold Höllrie-
     gel. 1938-1939.

ALBERT EHRENZWEIG

Lawyer, Professor of Law, 1906-1974

Mrs. Maria Rosenthal, Boalt Hall, School of Law, University
of California, Berkeley, California 94720.

Mrs. Rosenthal was the secretary of Prof. Ehrenzweig until
his death in 1974. Ca. 12 ft. of materials from the 1940s
to the present make up the collection. Mrs. Rosenthal is in
the process of preparing a catalog of the papers. At the
present time, access to the materials is limited to Mrs.
Rosenthal and the immediate Ehrenzweig family.

*Frau Rosenthal, die Sekretärin Prof. Ehrenzweigs bis zu sei-
nem Tode 1974, ist im Begriff, einen Katalog seines Nachlasses zu erarbeiten (etwa 3,60 m Material aus dem Zeitraum
vierziger Jahre bis heute). Zur Zeit haben nur Frau Rosenthal und Mitglieder der Familie Ehrenzweig Zugang zu dem
Material.*

B1,2 Correspondence with the Kelsen Institute (Konrad Lorenz
      and others) re: Hans Kelsen.

J   Photos.

L   Background materials used in his work.
      Materials on Max Radin. (Ehrenzweig had intended to
      collaborate with Max Radin.)

University of California, Berkeley, School of Law, Boalt
Hall, Berkeley, California 94720.

K   Personal library of Ehrenzweig.

Mrs. Joan von Kaschnitz, 2411 Santa Clara Avenue, Alameda,
California 94501; Mrs. Elizabeth Steffan, 989 Overlook Road,
Berkeley, California 94708.

I   Files, containing documents on personal and financial
      affairs of Ehrenzweig. Unsorted.

New York Public Library, Manuscript Division, Fifth Avenue
and 42nd Street, New York, N.Y. 10018.

208

ALBERT EHRENZWEIG

EMERGENCY COMMITTEE IN AID OF DISPLACED FOREIGN SCHOLARS,
1933-1945

*   File compiled, no assistance given. 1938-1941.

Prof. Kurt Steiner, Department of Political Science, Stanford University, Stanford, California 94305.

B1,2 Correspondence with Kurt Steiner.

New School for Social Research, Office of the Dean of the Graduate Faculty of Political and Social Science, 65 Fifth Avenue, New York, N.Y. 10003.

RECORDS OF THE UNIVERSITY IN EXILE, 1933-45

A3   Curriculum vitae.

B1,3   L. of recommendation, L. by Ehrenzweig.

ALBERT EINSTEIN

Physicist, 1879-1955

Princeton University, Firestone Library, Princeton, New Jersey 08540.

THE PAPERS OF ALBERT EINSTEIN (1879-1955), comprising scientific, nonscientific and personal papers, are available on microfilm at Princeton University Library and the Institute for Advanced Study. In addition, there is an "Einstein Guidebook" that may be consulted by responsible scholars at Princeton University Library. All details concerning access to the papers, conditions of use, rights of publication, etc. are described in the explanatory note to the guidebook. The trustees of the estate of Albert Einstein retain all discretionary power over the papers themselves and any use of them. The Princeton University Library will give access to the scientific papers of Albert Einstein to recognized scholars under the rules prevailing at the Library for such purposes. Any scholar who would like to consult the nonscientific material of Einstein should request permission from the trustees of the estate of Albert Einstein before visiting the Library.

THE PAPERS OF ALBERT EINSTEIN (1879-1955) bestehen aus naturwissenschaftlichen, nicht naturwissenschaftlichen und persönlichen Materialien und sind auf Mikrofilm in der Princeton University Library und dem Institute for Advanced Study erhältlich. Außerdem existiert eine "Einstein Guidebook", die von Forschern in der Princeton University Library eingesehen werden kann. Einzelheiten über Zugang zu den Papers, Benutzungsbedingungen, Publikationsrechte, usw. finden sich in einem erklärenden Kapitel der Guidebook. Die Verwalter des Nachlasses von Albert Einstein behalten sich unbeschränkte Verfügungsgewalt über die Materialien und ihren Gebrauch vor. Die Princeton University Library gewährt anerkannten Wissenschaftlern entsprechend den in der Bibliothek für solche Zwecke geltenden Bestimmungen Zugang zu den wissenschaftlichen Materialien von Albert Einstein. Wissenschaftler, die die nicht-wissenschaftlichen Materialien Einsteins einsehen möchten, sollten die Erlaubnis der Verwalter des Nachlasses einholen, bevor sie die Bibliothek besuchen.

Leo Baeck Institute, 129 East 73rd Street, New York, N.Y. 10021.

ALBERT EINSTEIN COLLECTION (Ar-C.Z.44, 136 and AR-B.80, 1147), as well as several items from the ERICH KAHLER, VIERFELDER, BERNHARD KAHN, KURT GROSSMANN and JACOB PICARD COLLECTIONS. The main portion of the collection was purchased in 1960/ 1961 from Erich von Kahler, Princeton, New Jersey, with additional materials donated in later years.

ALBERT EINSTEIN COLLECTION (AR-C.Z.44, 136 und AR-B.80, 1147) sowie mehrere Nummern der folgenden Sammlungen: ERICH KAHLER, VIERFELDER, BERNHARD KAHN, KURT GROSSMANN und JACOB PICARD COLLECTIONS. Der Hauptteil der Sammlung wurde 1960/61 aus dem Besitz Erich von Kahlers, Princeton, New Jersey, erworben; spätere Schenkungen erweiterten die Sammlung.

B1   40 L. 1922-1953, among them L. to: Hermann Broch and Erich von Kahler.
       2 L. to Erich Leyens. 1929, 1930.

B1,2 Uncatalogued and unsorted L. to and from: Jacob Picard and Kurt Grossmann.

B2   1 L. from Antoinette von Kahler.
       2 L. from Erich Leyens. 1929.

B3   3 L. of Leyens about Einstein.

C3   1 poem, dedicated to Hermann Broch. [1944].
       1 poem. 1935.

C7   Text on Germany.
       Introduction or discussion of a book. 1p.

C8   Mathematical formulas. 1p.

D7   4 newspaper cl., 2 written in collaboration with Erich von Kahler. 1920, 1925, 1944.

H1   <u>Albert Einstein.</u> "Festschrift." 1949. 20p. in print.

H2   Reichenbach, Hans. "The Philosophical Significance of the Theory of Relativity." 23p.

H3   43 newspaper cl. about Einstein.

I   Einstein family tree. 1p.
       Ancestors of Albert Einstein. From the birth registers of the city of Buchau (c.). 2p.
       "Stammbaum des Herrn Prof. Dr. Albert Einstein seit

1754." Family tree. Göppingen, 1930.
Family tree of Albert Einstein since 1759 (c.).
"Aufruf der überparteilichen Vereinigung zu Wahlen am
30.11.1930." Signed by Albert Einstein.
"A Forum on 'The Message' of Albert Einstein." An-
nouncement of the Jewish Club of 1933 and the Leo
Baeck Institute.
Power of attorney from Einstein for Robert O. Held.
1952. (c.).

J   7 photos of Einstein, paintings, portraits.
Photo montage of Einstein photos, by Trude Fleischmann.
2 photos of Einstein. 1931.

M   Postage stamps: Israel, Poland, Ghana, United States;
newspaper notices concerning postage stamps.
Bronze bust of Albert Einstein. Sculpture by Dr. Helmut Nathan.

Brandeis University, Goldfarb Library, Special Collections,
Waltham, Massachusetts 02154.

THE ALBERT EINSTEIN PAPERS, which contain approximately 4 ft.
of archival materials, represent a compilation of materials
from varied sources (many unidentified, some as yet unsorted
and uncatalogued). One portion was received as part of the
STEVEN WISE COLLECTION.

THE ALBERT EINSTEIN PAPERS, die etwa 1,20 m Archivmaterialien umfassen, sind eine Zusammenstellung von Materialien
aus verschiedensten Quellen. Ein Teil gehörte zur STEVEN
WISE COLLECTION, viele andere Quellen sind nicht bekannt.
Einige der Materialien sind noch nicht sortiert und katalogisiert.

A3   Autobiographical speech. Undated. T.c. 2p.

B1   53 L. to Rabbi Steven Wise. 1934-1939. T. and A., some
with English tr.
Many pc. of Einstein L.

B1,2   1 album of family correspondence. 1934-1937. T. and A.,
some with English tr.
Miscellaneous and scientific L. 1896-1915.

B2   2 L. from Rabbi Steven Wise.
       2 autograph books, including Käthe Kollwitz, Anna
       Seghers.

L   Ca. 2.5 in. of miscellaneous materials.

American Philosophical Society, The Library, 105 South Fifth
Street, Philadelphia, Pennsylvania 19106.

LETTERS OF SCIENTISTS COLLECTION, FRANZ BOAS PAPERS, MISCEL-
LANEOUS MANUSCRIPT COLLECTION, ALBERT F. BLAKESLEE COLLEC-
TION, NIELS BOHR CORRESPONDENCE, MAX BERGMANN PAPERS

B1   6 L., including 1 L. to F. Boas.
       8 L. to Niels Bohr. 1920-1955.

B1,2   1 F. in Bergmann Papers designated "Albert Einstein."

B2   6 L. from: Niels Bohr, E. C. Kemble, Wolfgang Pauli,
       Arnold Sommerfeld. 1920-1946.

H3   Materials concerning: A. Einstein, Cordell Hull, Andrew
       F. West William S. Dix and Drake deKay. 1921-1956.
       T. 19 items.

Archive for History of Quantum Physics (locations in U.S.:
Bancroft Library, University of California, Berkeley; American Philosophical Society, Philadelphia, Pennsylvania; American Institute of Physics, New York, N.Y.).

B1   1 L. ea. to: F. Haber, Pascual Jordan, A. Sommerfeld,
       Alfred Landé, W. Wilson.
       75 L. to Paul Ehrenfest. 1915-1933 and undated.
       8 L. to Erwin Schrödinger. 1936-1953.

B1,2   Microfilm of correspondence between Einstein and Paul
       Ehrenfest. Ca. 50 items. [1917-1922]. Restricted.
       "Correspondence with E. J. Gumbel."
       Microfilm of correspondence with H. A. Lorentz and
       Heike Kamerlingh-Onnes. 1911-1926. Ca. 56 items.

C8   "Elementare Überlegungen zur Interpretation der Quan-
       tenmechanik." Undated. A. 10p.

<u>Smithsonian Institution</u>, Dibner Library, Washington, D.C.
20560.

The materials represented here were donated to the Smithsonian Institution by Burndy Library (Norwalk, Connecticut) in
Sept. 1976. The assembling of the ALBERT EINSTEIN PAPERS
was begun by Dr. Bern Dibner during Einstein's lifetime,
obtained partially through purchases, partially from gifts.
It is made up of 2 archive boxes of materials. Additional
materials are located in the library's WEINER COLLECTION and
MISCELLANEOUS COLLECTION.

*Diese Materialien sind eine Schenkung der Burndy Library
(Norwalk, Connecticut) an die Smithsonian Institution vom
Sept. 1976. Die Zusammenstellung der ALBERT EINSTEIN PAPERS
wurde von Dr. Bern Dibner zu Einsteins Lebzeiten begonnen.
Die Materialien wurden teils gekauft, teils handelt es sich
um Geschenke; sie umfassen 2 Archivkartons. Weitere Materia-
lien befinden sich in der WEINER COLLECTION und in der MIS-
CELLANEOUS COLLECTION der Dibner Library.*

B1   2 L. 1909-1950, among them L. to: Franklin Delano
     Roosevelt, Arnold Sommerfeld, Oswald Veblen.

B2   3 L. 1947, 1948, 1971.

C7   Essay on Isaac Newton. 9p.

C8   "Über eine naheliegende Ergänzung des Fundaments der
     allgemeinen Relativitätstheorie." 1920. 5p.
     "The Essence of the Theory of Relativity." 1946-1948.
     8p.
     Mathematical notes. A. and c. Ca. 12p. Notes and
     equations on the theory of relativity. Ca. 1925. 1p.

C14 Drawings.

D8   Proofs.

F   Records.

H3   2 cl. with quotes by Einstein.
     Numerous cl. about Einstein.

J   Photos.

L   Materials concerning an Einstein exhibition.

M   Ephemera.

University of Texas, Humanities Research Center, Manuscripts Collection, Box 7219, Austin, Texas 78712.

B1   121 L.

B2   1 L.

C3,8   11 uncatalogued items, including poems and notes.

C8   3 Ms.

University of Chicago, The Joseph Regenstein Library, 1100 East 57th Street, Chicago, Illinois 60637.

The JOSEPH SCHAFFNER PAPERS contain approximately 125 Einstein items.

Die JOSEPH SCHAFFNER PAPERS enthalten etwa 125 Einstein Nummern.

B1   58 L. to Walter Mayer (Einstein's assistant). 1930-
       1933. Also additional correspondence to Mayer, in-
       cluding Ms. material, photos and reproduction of a
       cartoon. 34 items.
       4 L. 1925-1946, including 1 L. to Joseph H. Schaffner.

B2   28 L. from Walter Mayer. 1930-1933.

B3   Schaffner correspondence and other miscellaneous mate-
       rials concerning Einstein. 1 F.

C7   "Gruß an Amerika." Radio text upon Einstein's arrival
       in U.S. Dec. 1930. A. 1p. with mathematical calcula-
       tions on reverse side.

I   Document dealing with dangers of atomic weapons.

J   Framed photo of Einstein by Jousef Karsh, dedicated
       to Schaffner.
       Photo clipped from magazine showing Einstein playing
       violin.

Additional Einstein materials are located in the following

collections: EMERGENCY COMMITTEE OF ATOMIC SCIENTISTS, FED-
ERATION OF AMERICAN SCIENTISTS, JAMES FRANCK PAPERS, SALMON
O. LEVINSON PAPERS, EUGENE RABINOWITCH PAPERS, JULIUS ROSEN-
WALD PAPERS.

*Weitere Einstein Materialien befinden sich in den folgenden
Sammlungen: EMERGENCY COMMITTEE OF ATOMIC SCIENTISTS, FED-
ERATION OF AMERICAN SCIENTISTS, JAMES FRANCK PAPERS, SALMON
O. LEVINSON PAPERS, EUGENE RABINOWITCH PAPERS, JULIUS ROSEN-
WALD PAPERS.*

B1   4 L. 1949, 1954.

B1,2   Correspondence to and from Einstein, as well as L.
        from his secretary, 1946-1949. Re: Einstein's accep-
        tance of the Foreign Press Award, 1947.
        Lengthy correspondence between Einstein and James
        Franck. 1921-1955.

B1,   L. of congratulations to Franck on Franck's 70th birth-
J   day. 1952. Accompanied by photo of Einstein.

B2   4 L. 1934, 1941, 1954.

C7   Statement of the goals of the Emergency Committee of
        Atomic Scientists, 1946 (c.).
        "Physics and Reality." Original T. and cc.

H3   2 press releases and numerous cl. 1929-1931, 1945,
        1949-1950, 1955.

J   Group photo. Berlin-Dahlem, 1920.

Indiana University, The University Libraries, The Lilly
Library, Bloomington, Indiana 47401.

Einstein materials are located in the following collections:
ARTHUR FISHER BENTLEY MSS., CYRIL CLEMENS MSS., MAX EASTMAN
MSS., HERBERT FLEISCHMAN MSS., UPTON BEALL SINCLAIR MSS.,
VACLAV HLAVATY MSS., VIKING PRESS MSS., DEWITT MSS.

*Einstein Materialien finden sich in den folgenden Sammlungen:
ARTHUR FISHER BENTLEY MSS., CYRIL CLEMENS MSS., MAX EASTMAN
MSS., HERBERT FLEISCHMAN MSS., UPTON BEALL SINCLAIR MSS.,
VACLAV HLAVATY MSS., VIKING PRESS MSS., DEWITT MSS.*

B1   64 L. 1937-1954, among them L. to: Vaclav Hlavaty and
      Upton Sinclair.

B2   28 L. (cc.) 1942-1954, among them L. from: Vaclav Hla-
      vaty and Upton Sinclair.

B3   8 L. to and from Vaclav Hlavaty concerning Einstein.
      1952-1960.

H5   Bentley, Arthur Fisher. "Examination of Einstein's
      term 'space'." Dated Jan. 1931.
      Sinclair, Upton Beall. "The Einstein I Knew." Cc.

Stanford University Libraries, University Archives, Department of Special Collections, Stanford, California 94305.

SIR ISAAC NEWTON COLLECTION (Ne 132), SCIENTISTS AND SCIENCE
COLLECTION (M 133)

B1   3 L. 1926, 1927, 1947.

B2   1 L. from F. E. Brasch. 1927.

B3   10 L. 1927-1941.

C7   "Allgemeines über die Schule." Lecture, Oct. 15, 1936.
      German text with English tr.

D8   4 newspaper cl. of articles by Einstein, 1905-1930.

H3   2 newspaper cl. 1921.

H5   "Alfred E. Cohn an A. E." Cc. of a poem.

I   Invitation for F. E. Brasch to A. E.'s lecture series
      "Theory of Relativity." 1921.
      Death certificate of Anita N. McGee. 1940.

N   Brasch, F. E. Page proofs of introduction of the tr. of
      an Einstein L.

Columbia University, Butler Library, New York, N.Y. 10027.

SPANISH REFUGEE COLLECTION, ORAL HISTORY COLLECTION, N. M.
BUTLER PAPERS and general archive files

ALBERT EINSTEIN

*SPANISH REFUGEE COLLECTION, ORAL HISTORY COLLECTION, N. M.
BUTLER PAPERS und allgemeine Archivordner.*

B1   52 L. and Tel. 1929-1953.

B2   L. from N. M. Butler. 1936.

H5   Interview with William Fondiller: recollections of
       Einstein and others. 1970.

I   Pc. of transfer of securities to Princeton Bank and
       Trust Co. 1938.

Library of Congress, Manuscript Division, Independence Avenue
and First Street S.E., Washington, D.C. 20540.

The ALBERT EINSTEIN PAPERS consist of 7 L. by Einstein, as
well as pc. of L. by and to Einstein and 3 mathematical Ms.
The remaining Einstein materials are found in various other
larger collections: PAPERS OF SIEGFRIED BERNFELD, FELIX
FRANKFURTER PAPERS, FLORENCE TAFFREY HARRIMAN PAPERS, BENJA-
MIN W. HUEBSCH PAPERS, J. ROBERT OPPENHEIMER PAPERS, OSWALD
VEBLEN PAPERS.

*Die ALBERT EINSTEIN PAPERS bestehen aus 7 Briefen von Ein-
stein, Photokopien von Briefen von und an Einstein sowie 3
mathematischen Manuskripten. Die übrigen Einstein Materialien finden sich in verschiedenen anderen größeren Sammlungen:
PAPERS OF SIEGFRIED BERNFELD, FELIX FRANKFURTER PAPERS, FLOR-
ENCE TAFFREY HARRIMAN PAPERS, BENJAMIN W. HUEBSCH PAPERS,
J. ROBERT OPPENHEIMER PAPERS, OSWALD VEBLEN PAPERS.*

B1   1 L. to Sigmund Freud. 1936. c.
       Ca. 30 L. by Einstein, including L. to: Felix Frank-
          furter, Benjamin W. Huebsch, J. Robert Oppenheimer,
          Oswald Veblen.
       Pc. of L. by Einstein.

B2   Ca. 20 L. to Einstein, including L. from: Felix Frank-
          furter, J. Robert Oppenheimer, Oswald Veblen.
       Pc. of additional L. to Einstein.

C8   3 mathematical Ms.

218

ALBERT EINSTEIN

<u>American Institute of Physics</u>, Niels Bohr Library, 335 East 45th Street, New York, N.Y. 10017.

ZVI GEZARI COLLECTION, NIELS BOHR CORRESPONDENCE (on microfilm), FRITZ REICHE PAPERS, ALFRED LANDÉ COLLECTION, PICTORIAL FILE (uncatalogued)

B1   3 L. to John R. Lamarsh. 1945. pc. (Originals with
        John R. Lamarsh).
        8 L. and 1 Ptc. to: Niels Bohr, Alfred Landé. 1914,
        1920-1949.

B1,2   Correspondence between Einstein and Zvi Gezari. 1953-
        1954. pc. (Originals in Gezari's possession.)

B2   11 L., including 10 L. to Niels Bohr. 1920-1954.

C7   Notes, in German, for radio address in appreciation for
        his American reception, March 14, 1933. A. pc. (Orig-
        inal in possession of William J. Numeroff.)

C8   Notes by Einstein. pc. 6p.

F   Film footage. [1950]. 11 minutes.
        16mm color film of Einstein.

H5   Recollections by Gezari about Einstein.
        Reiche, Fritz. "Different explanations, evaluations,
        Einstein's equation, etc." Notes and calculations
        by Reiche. A. Ca. 75p.

J   Portraits and group photos.
        Black and white photos (Gezari Collection).

<u>Boston University</u>, Mugar Memorial Library, 771 Commonwealth Avenue, Boston, Massachusetts 02215.

FREDERICK FISHER PAPERS, MILDRED BUCHANAN FLAGG PAPERS, MAXWELL GEISMAR PAPERS, NUNNALLY JOHNSON PAPERS, JOSHUA LOTH PAPERS, ROBERT LEWIS SHAYON PAPERS, MENACHEM ARNONI PAPERS

B1   20 L. 1934-1955.

B2   1 L. from Harlow Shapley. 1946.

Harvard University, Houghton Library, Cambridge, Massachusetts 02138.

AUTOGRAPH FILE, RICHARD BEER-HOFMANN COLLECTION, GEORGE SARTON PAPERS, OSWALD GARRISON VILLARD PAPERS

B1   18 L., including 3 L. to Richard Beer-Hofmann. 1926-
      1949.

B2   2 L. and 2 Tel. 1931-1942.

New York Public Library, Manuscript Division, Fifth Avenue and 42nd Street, New York, N.Y. 10018.

MAX WERTHEIMER PAPERS, EMERGENCY COMMITTEE IN AID OF DISPLACED FOREIGN SCHOLARS, 1933-1945

B1   5 L. to Wertheimer. 1922-1939 and undated.

B2   6 L. from Wertheimer. 1922 and undated.

*   File compiled by the Emergency Committee, no assist-
      ance given. 1933-1943.

Mrs. Maria Reichenbach, 456 Puerto del Mar, Pacific Palisades, California 90272.

B1   Ca. 20 L. to Hans Reichenbach. 1919-1940.

D8'   Albert Einstein reprint collection.

David Rothman, c/o Rothman Department Store, Southold, Long Island, New York 11971.

B1   Ca. 20 L. to David Rothman. Undated.

Rabbi Bernhard N. Cohn, 90 Riverside Drive, New York, N.Y. 10024.

EMIL BERNHARD PAPERS

B1   5 L. to Emil Bernhard. 1940-1948.
      4 L. to Grete Cohn, wife of Emil Bernhard.

University of New Hampshire, The Library, Department of Special Collections, Durham, New Hampshire 03824.

OSKAR MARIA GRAF COLLECTION

B1   7 L. to O. M. Graf. 1940-1954.

B2   2 L. from O. M. Graf. 1949, 1954.

Wesleyan University, Olin Library, Middletown, Connecticut 06457.

B1   1 L. to Dr. Freundlich. 1931.

C7   Birthday greeting to Edison, broadcast from Germany,
      Oct. 21, 1929.

C8   "Zur einheitlichen Feldtheorie." 1929. 10p.
      "Das Raum-, Aether-, und Feld-Problem der Physik."
      1929. 15p.
      "Riemann-Geometrie mit Aufrechterhaltung des Begriffes
      des Fern-Parallelismus." 1930. 7p.

Yivo Institute, 1048 Fifth Avenue, New York, N.Y. 10028.

HORACE M. KALLEN PAPERS, CARL SCHURZ COLLECTION and general files

B1,2 Correspondence. 1933-1951.

B1   Isolated L. to the Carl Schurz Foundation.

B1   12 L. (mostly c.). 1929-1947.

C4   "Jeder zeigt sich uns heute..." 1929. A. 1p.

University of California, Berkeley, The Bancroft Library, Berkeley, California 94720.

E. O. LAWRENCE PAPERS, TOM MOONEY PAPERS, GILBERT N. LEWIS
PAPERS, LEAGUE OF AMERICAN WRITERS PAPERS

B1   6 L. and 3 Tel. 1931-1932, 1945-1947.

C7   Statement to be read at Congress of American Authors,
        May 21, 1939. 1p.

H4   Newspaper cl.

University of Minnesota, University Libraries, University
Archives (and Social Welfare History Archives Center), Minneapolis, Minnesota 55455.

GUY STANTON FORD PAPERS, SURVEY ASSOCIATES PAPERS

B1,2   4 L. to and from Einstein.

B3   2 L. re: Einstein's arrival in the U.S.

I   Documents. 1944-1946.

Franklin Institute, The Library, Philadelphia, Pennsylvania
19103.

B1   5 L. re: receipt of Franklin medal. 1935.

I   Certificate of award of the Institute's Franklin medal.
        1935.

University of Iowa, The University Libraries, Special Collections, Iowa City, Iowa 52240.

B1   6 L. 1934-1949.

Southern Illinois University, Morris Library, Department of
Special Collections, Carbondale, Illinois 62901.

ERWIN PISCATOR PAPERS

B1   4 L. (1 c.) and 1 Tel. to Erwin Piscator. 1939-1947.

ALBERT EINSTEIN

B2   3 L. (c.) from Piscator. 1940-1945.

Harvard University, University Archives, Widener Library, Cambridge, Massachusetts 02138.

RICHARD VON MISES COLLECTION

B1   3 L. to Richard von Mises. T. 1919, 1929.

Prof. Konrad Wachsmann, 805 South Genesee, Los Angeles, California 90036.

B1,2 Correspondence with Wachsmann. 6 L. 1929-.

Mrs. Richard Courant, 142 Carlton Road, New Rochelle, New York 10804.

B1   Ca. 6 L. to Richard Courant.

Yale University Library, Manuscripts and Archives Research Room, 150 Sterling Memorial Library, New Haven, Connecticut 06520.

DECISION: A REVIEW OF FREE CULTURE. CORRESPONDENCE AND PAPERS OF KLAUS MANN

B1   2 L. to Klaus Mann. 1941.

Duke University, William R. Perkins Library, Manuscript Department, Durham, North Carolina 27706.

SOCIALIST PARTY OF AMERICA PAPERS

B1   2 L. 1946-1947.
       "Dear Friend" L. from Emergency Committee of Atomic
       Scientists, signed by Einstein (similar L. found
       also at the Johns Hopkins University, The Milton S.
       Eisenhower Library, Baltimore, Maryland 21218, and

223

at Oberlin College Library, Oberlin, Ohio 44074).

University of Southern California, Lion Feuchtwanger Memorial
Library, 520 Paseo Miramar, Pacific Palisades, California
90272.

B1   1 L. to Lion Feuchtwanger.

B2   2 L. and 1 Tel. from Lion Feuchtwanger.

University of Kansas, Kenneth Spencer Research Library,
Department of Special Collections, Lawrence, Kansas 66045.

B1   2 L. to Lloyd Biggle.

New York University, Courant Institute of Mathematical
Sciences, Library, 251 Mercer Street, New York, N.Y. 10012.

B1,2 File "Albert Einstein Professor." 1949.

State University of New York at Albany, Department of Germanic Languages and Literatures, 1400 Washington Avenue,
Albany, New York 12222.

STORM PUBLISHERS ARCHIVE

B1   1 L. to Alexander Gode von Aesch. 1949.

B2   1 L. from Alexander Gode von Aesch. 1949.

Dr. Gertrud Weiss-Szilard, 8038 El Paseo Grande, La Jolla,
California 92037.

B1,2 Correspondence with Leo Szilard.

Barthold Fles Literary Agency, 507 Fifth Avenue, New York,
N.Y. 10016.

ALBERT EINSTEIN

B1   2 L. to Barthold Fles. 1935, 1939.

B2   1 L. from Barthold Fles. c. 1939.

California Institute of Technology, Robert A. Millikan Library, Pasadena, California 91109.

PAUL S. EPSTEIN PAPERS, THEODORE VON KARMAN CORRESPONDENCE and general archive files.

PAUL S. EPSTEIN PAPERS, THEODORE VON KARMAN CORRESPONDENCE und allgemeine Archivordner.

B1   1 L. to Paul Epstein. pc.

B1,2 Correspondence with Theodore von Karman. 1921-1946.
        1 F.
      Individual item(s) in 5 folders. 1923-1945.
      Pc. of materials in Princeton, including ca. 20 L. to
        Paul Epstein concerning Einstein. 1919-1957.

Wallace R. Rust, 523 Britton Road, Rochester, New York 14616.

Pc. of materials also in possession of Mr. Gerald Holton, Harvard University.

B1   Correspondence with "Mr. Moore."

Mrs. Liselotte Stein, 115-25 Metropolitan Avenue, Kew Gardens, New York 11418.

FRED STEIN PAPERS

J   Photos of Albert Einstein.

Syracuse University, The George Arents Research Library, Syracuse, New York 13210.

B1   L. to "Dear Friend."

C8   "On symmetrically rotating stationary gravity fields."
      Written in German. A. 11p.

University of California, Los Alamos Scientific Laboratory,
P. O. Box 1663, Los Alamos, New Mexico 87544.

H5   "Who Would Hire Albert Einstein." Essay. 18p.

University of Wyoming, Archive of Contemporary History, The
Library, Box 3334, Laramie, Wyoming 82071.

ALFRED FARAU COLLECTION

H5   Farau, Alfred. "Albert Einstein." Essay.

Hoover Institution on War, Revolution and Peace, Stanford,
California 94305.

FRANZ SCHOENBERNER COLLECTION

B1   L. to F. Schoenberner. 1952.

University of California, Los Angeles, Department of Special
Collections, 120 Lawrence Clark Powell Library, Los Angeles,
California 90024.

FRANZ WERFEL ARCHIVE

B1   1 L. to Franz Werfel. 1944.

Mrs. Erich (Louise) Mendelsohn, 1101 Green Street, San Francisco, California 94109.

ERICH MENDELSOHN ARCHIVE

B1   1 L. to Erich Mendelsohn. 1941.

ALBERT EINSTEIN

Minnesota Historical Society, 690 Cedar Street, St. Paul, Minnesota 55101.

JAMES GRAY PAPERS

B1   1 L. to Gray. 1946.

Rockefeller University, Library Archives, Welch Hall, 1230 York Avenue Nr. 66, New York, N.Y. 10021.

B1   L. to Jacques Loeb. Undated. T.c.

Mrs. Elisabeth M. Stoerk and Mrs. Susanne B. Hoeller, 288 Ocean Drive West, Stamford, Connecticut 06902.

FRIDERIKE ZWEIG ARCHIVE

B1   L. to Friderike Zweig. 1944.

Yale University, Beinecke Rare Book and Manuscript Library, New Haven, Connecticut 06520.

HERMANN BROCH ARCHIVE

B2   1 L. from Hermann Broch. 1947.

University of Michigan, Bentley Historical Library, Michigan Historical Collections, 1150 Beal Avenue, Ann Arbor, Michigan 48105.

KASIMIR FAJANS PAPERS

B1,2 Xerox c. of correspondence of Kasimir Fajans and Albert Einstein concerning the immigration of Helm Blume to Canada in 1942.

Dr. Edward E. Lowinsky, Prof. Emeritus, Department of Music, University of Chicago, Chicago, Illinois 60637.

B1   1 L. to Edward E. Lowinsky. A. Plus 1p. of mathemati-
      cal calculations.

B2   2 L. from Edward E. Lowinsky.

University of Pittsburgh Libraries, Department of Special
Collections, 363 Hillman Library, Pittsburgh, Pennsylvania
15260.

RUDOLF CARNAP PAPERS

B1,2 Correspondence with Rudolf Carnap.

Dr. Clementine Zernik, 225-10 106th Avenue, Queens Village,
New York 11429.

B1   L. to Arnold Höllriegel. 1938-1939.

Mrs. Peter M. Lindt, 949 West End Avenue, New York, N.Y.
10025.

B1   Small amount of correspondence with Peter M. Lindt.

Mrs. Alice Loewy Kahler, 1 Evelyn Place, Princeton, New
Jersey 08540.

ERICH VON KAHLER COLLECTION

B1   1 L. to Erich von Kahler. 1950.

ALFRED EINSTEIN

Musicologist, 1880-1952

<u>University of California, Berkeley</u>, The Music Library, Berkeley, California 94720.

The major portion of the ALFRED EINSTEIN COLLECTION was purchased in 1954 by the library from the estate of Alfred Einstein. The collection consists of ca. 5 1/2 ft. of materials in addition to the EINSTEIN MOZART COLLECTION (15 archive boxes), of which a 28-page inventory is available: John Emerson, <u>Materials for Mozart Research. An Inventory of the Mozart Nachlaß of Alfred Einstein</u>. University of California, Berkeley, 1963. Permission to use the materials is obtainable from the heirs (through the University of California, Berkeley).

Der Hauptteil der ALFRED EINSTEIN COLLECTION wurde 1954 von der Bibliothek der University of California, Berkeley, aus dem Nachlaß von Alfred Einstein aufgekauft. Die Sammlung besteht aus etwa 1,60 m Material. Daneben existiert die EIN-STEIN MOZART COLLECTION (15 Archivkartons), zu der ein 28seitiges Inventarverzeichnis erhältlich ist: John Emerson, Mate-rials for Mozart Research. An Inventory of the Mozart Nachlaß of Alfred Einstein. University of California, Berkeley, 1963. Erlaubnis zur Einsicht des Materials wird von den Erben gewährt. (Auskünfte darüber erteilt die University of California, Berkeley.)

B1,2 Correspondence between Einstein and Theodor Kroyer.
     1915-1933. Ca. 50 L. and Ptc.
    Correspondence between Einstein and Fritz Stiedry.
     1938-1952. Ca. 6 in. (15 cm).

B3 "Italienische Briefe." Transcriptions. Undated. Ca. 100
    items.
    Correspondence between J. v. Widmann and E. Frank.
     1877-1888. c. Ca. 1 in. (2.5 cm).

C7 <u>The Italian Madrigal</u>. 300p. with some corr.
    "Italian Madrigal Verse." Ms. A. 1937. Ca. 20p.
    <u>Gluck</u>. Undated. T. Ca. 180p.
    <u>Viola da Gamba</u>. A. Ca. 300p.
    Ms. Fragment on history of music. Undated. Ca. 200p.
    "Einstein notes." 4 small boxes (1 ft.) with list of
    themes.

Notes, lists, dates, fragments of Italian texts, materials for a study. 1 in. (2.5 cm).
Notes for a study. Undated. Ca. 80p.
Notes on Italian opera. Ca. 50 leaves.
Notes, lists and dates for a "Madrigal" study. Ca. 1
in. (2.5 cm).
2 notebooks. 1940.
1 notebook containing notes and fragments. Undated.
A. 1 1/2 in. (4 cm).

D7   Printed articles, notices, yearbooks. 10 items.
Proofs:
Golden Age of the Madrigal. 1941. Ca. 50p.
Breve storia della musica. Undated. Ca. 160p.

K   Einstein's personal music library.
75 facsimiles by 44 composers including: Bach, Beethoven, Brahms, Boni, Bossinensis, Compère.

L   Transcriptions. Ca. 10 small notebooks, plus 1 archive
carton, plus 1 notebook with some loose pages.
Chansons, Vivaldi, Bach, Madrigals, Canzonette. Tran-
scriptions accompanied by partial listing. Ca. 3 in.
(7.5 cm).
Vocal music, Gluck, Madrigals, Carmen. Transcriptions.
Ca. 3 in. (7.5 cm).
"Bologna March - April 1902" and "Listen der Komponi-
sten." 1 notebook.
Microfilm entitled "Viola da Gamba, Sources."
1 untitled microfilm.
"Steffani Transcriptions." Includes L., as well as
materials concerning the publication.
"Madrigal Materials." Transcriptions in large notebook.
Ca. 1 1/2 in. (4 cm).
Bibliography of compositions from the "Orlando furioso"
and from the "Gerusalemme liberata" in the 16th and
17th centuries. 1950. T. 10p.
Notes and texts for a study. English and Italian. Un-
dated. Ca. 75p. in notebook.
Card catalog bibliography of dates, compositions, works.
"Geistlicher und weltlicher Vokalkompositionen des 16.
und 17. Jh. in (zumeist italienischen) Originalaus-
gaben." 2c. Köln, Musikhistorisches Museum, 1922.

ALFRED EINSTEIN

Materials for Mozart research, including numerous pc.
of Mozart manuscripts, and 35 transcriptions of
Mozart fragments from the Salzburg Mozarteum by Einstein. 1951.

MANFRED BUKOFZER COLLECTION

B1   1 L. to M. Bukofzer. Ca. 1930.

Columbia University, Butler Library, New York, N.Y. 10027.

W. W. NORTON PAPERS

B1   11 L. to W. W. Norton. 1943-1944.
      45 L. to Norton Publishers (A. C. Burnham, Storen Lunt,
      Katherine Barnard). 1945-1952.

B2   17 L. from W. W. Norton. T.c. 1943-1945.
      Ca. 80 L. from Norton Publishers. T.c. 1945-1952.

B3   Correspondence between A. C. Burnham (Norton Publish-
      ers) and translator Willis Wager. 1945-1946.
      Condolence L. from Norton to Einstein family. 1952.

I   Contracts:
      The Relations Between Poetry and Music. 1949.
      The Romantic Era in Music. 1943.

Smith College, Music Library, Northampton, Massachusetts
01060.

ALFRED EINSTEIN COLLECTION: donated by Einstein to the
library

C13   120 Ms. scores, all copies of Einstein's transcriptions
      of vocal and instrumental music of the 16th-18th cen-
      turies used for his Italian Madrigal.

Dr. Edward E. Lowinsky, Prof. Emeritus, Department of Music,
University of Chicago, Chicago, Illinois 60637.

B1   104 L. to Edward E. Lowinsky. 1941-1952.

B2   59 L. from Edward E. Lowinsky. 1941-1952.

University of Georgia, The University Libraries, Athens, Georgia 30601.

GUIDO ADLER PAPERS, OLIN DOWNES PAPERS

B1,2   87 L. to and from Guido Adler.
       7 L. to and from Olin Downes.

Mrs. Elisabeth M. Stoerk and Mrs. Susanne B. Hoeller, 288 Ocean Drive West, Stamford, Connecticut 06902.

FRIDERIKE ZWEIG ARCHIVE

B1   7 L. to Friderike Zweig. 1943-1946.

B2   51 L. from Stefan Zweig. c. 1930-1941.
       T.c. of L. from Friderike Zweig. 1943-1946

B3   1 L. from Hertha Einstein to Friderike Zweig. 1952.
       .

Princeton University, Firestone Library, Princeton, New Jersey 08540.

C7   "The Italian Madrigal." Ms. in German.

THE PAPERS OF ALBERT EINSTEIN (1879-1955). For details concerning the use of this collection, see description under Albert Einstein.

THE PAPERS OF ALBERT EINSTEIN (1879-1955). Angaben über den Zugang zu der Sammlung finden sich unter "Albert Einstein."

B1,2   Unknown amount of correspondence between Alfred and
       Albert Einstein.

Mrs. Lotte Lenya Weill-Detwiler, 404 East 55th Street, New York, N.Y. 10022.

ALFRED EINSTEIN

B1   Correspondence with Kurt Weill.

Dr. Eric Werner, 900 West 190th Street, New York, N.Y. 10040.

B1,2 Correspondence between Alfred Einstein and Eric Werner.

Bruno Walter Memorial Foundation, c/o Miss Susie Danziger, 115 East 72nd Street, New York, N.Y. 10021.

BRUNO WALTER COLLECTION

B1,2 Correspondence with Bruno Walter. 1940s and 1950s.

Leo Baeck Institute, 129 East 73rd Street, New York, N.Y. 10021.

JACOB PICARD COLLECTION and general archive files

B1,2 Correspondence with Jacob Picard.

J   1 photo of Einstein.

Mrs. Vally Weigl, 50 West 95th Street, New York, N.Y. 10025.

B1,2 Correspondence with Karl Weigl.

New York Public Library, Manuscript Division, Fifth Avenue and 42nd Street, New York, N.Y. 10018.

EMERGENCY COMMITTEE IN AID OF DISPLACED FOREIGN SCHOLARS, 1933-1945

*   File compiled, no assistance given. 1934-1942.

Harvard University, Houghton Library, Cambridge, Massachusetts 02138.

LYONEL FEININGER COLLECTION

B1   L. to Lyonel and Julia Feininger. A. 1949.

University of California, Los Angeles, Music Library, 405
Hilgard Avenue, Los Angeles, California 90024.

ERNST TOCH ARCHIVE

B1   1 L. to Ernst Toch.

Metropolitan Opera Association, Inc., The Archives, Lincoln
Center Plaza, New York, N.Y. 10023.

H3   2 newspaper cl.

HANNS EISLER

Composer, 1898-1962

<u>Southern Illinois University</u>, Morris Library, Department of
Special Collections, Carbondale, Illinois 62901.

ERWIN PISCATOR PAPERS

B1   9 L. and 1 Tel. to E. Piscator. A. and T. 1936-1943.

B2   13 L. from E. Piscator. 1936-1943.

<u>University of Southern California</u>, Lion Feuchtwanger Memorial
Library, 520 Paseo Miramar, Pacific Palisades, California
90272.

B1   5 L. to Lion Feuchtwanger. 1941-1950.

B2   6 L. from Lion Feuchtwanger. 1941-1950.

<u>Library of Congress</u>, Manuscript Division, Independence Avenue
and First Street S.E., Washington, D.C. 20540.

C13   "Schweyk. Vorspiel zu den höheren Regionen." Libretto
      by Brecht. Ms. c. 1958.

<u>Yale University Library</u>, Manuscripts and Archives Research
Room, 150 Sterling Memorial Library, New Haven, Connecticut
06520.

ERNST TOLLER COLLECTION

C13   Musical score to Ernst Toller's <u>Draw the Fires! An His-
      torical Play</u>. 20p.

<u>Academy of Motion Picture Arts and Sciences</u>, Margaret Herrick
Library, 9038 Melrose Avenue, Hollywood, California 90069.

H3   Newspaper cl.

HANNS EISLER

University of New Hampshire, The Library, Department of Special Collections, Durham, New Hampshire 03824.

OSKAR MARIA GRAF COLLECTION

B1   1 L. to Oskar Maria Graf. Undated.

University of Georgia, The University Libraries, Athens, Georgia 30601.

OLIN DOWNES PAPERS

B3   6 L.

RUDOLF EKSTEIN

Psychoanalyst, 1908-

Dr. Rudolf Ekstein, Reiss-Davis Child Study Center, 9760 Pico Boulevard, Los Angeles, California 90035.

Private collection: inaccessible. / *Unzugängliche Privat-sammlung.*

A3   Autobiographical essay. A.

B1,2   Correspondence files from the 1940s, 1950s and 1960s.
       Correspondence with professional organizations:
         Los Angeles Psychoanalytic Society.
         Southern California Psychoanalytic Society.
         The American Psychoanalytic Association.

C7,8   Ms. of articles, book reviews, books and textbooks (4)
       on: philosophy, education, problems of psychoanaly-
       sis, schizophrenia, children's literature, Greek
       mythology, etc.

D7   Offprints of articles.

F   Tapes and videotapes.

I   Documents from Ekstein's professional life, concerning
       lecture tours, speeches, etc. 1962-.

J   Photos of Ekstein over the years.
       Photos of youth movements in Austria.

K   Bound volumes of psychoanalytic periodicals.
       Personal library specializing in psychoanalysis, art,
       gardening.

L   Freudiana. Includes some L.

Library of Congress, Manuscript Division, Independence Avenue and First Street S.E., Washington, D.C. 20540.

PAPERS OF SIEGFRIED BERNFELD

H5   Bio-bibliographical data on Ekstein in Bernfeld's "Pro-
       fessional File."

PAUL ELBOGEN

Writer, 1894-

University of California, Davis, Shields Library, Department
of Special Collections, Davis, California 95616.

The PAUL ELBOGEN PAPERS were donated to the library by the
author over a period of several years (1970s). The materials
represent a mixture of original manuscripts and photocopies
of originals that Mr. Elbogen still retains in his possession.

*Die PAUL ELBOGEN PAPERS wurden der Bibliothek der University
of California, Davis, nach und nach in den siebziger Jahren
vom Autor selbst geschenkt. Die Materialien umfassen sowohl
Originalmanuskripte als auch Photokopien von Originalen, die
sich noch in Paul Elbogens Besitz befinden.*

A1 Diaries of trips:
    Trip to Germany, Italy, Greece and France. 1960. 63p.
    Trip to Spain and Portugal. 1963. 25p.
    Trip to Japan. 1968. 37p.
    Trip to Morocco. 1969. 35p.
    Trip to Italy. 1970. 100p.
    Trip to Guatemala. 1972. 30p.

A3 Reisen - eine bildende Kunst. Series of reflections
    and anecdotes about Elbogen's travels on 5 continents
    over 50 years. T. 199p.

B1 6 L. 1958-1970.

B1,2 Correspondence between Elbogen and Harvey Einbinder.
    Correspondence between Elbogen and Arno Schmidt.

B2 9 L., including L. from: Vicki Baum, Aldous Huxley,
    Robert Neumann.

C1 Herzen im Bernstein. T. 1 notebook.
    Rettung aus dem Fegefeuer. T. 4 notebooks.
    Der Schatten Gottes. An historical novel on "Blue-
    beard."

C3 Ca. 30 unpub. poems.

C4 Unpub. stories. T. 31 items.

C5 Honorable Outlaw. Outline of film story.

238

C7   Essays and articles. A. and T. 11 items.
     Essays and reviews. T. several hundred items.

C11 Comte Leon, der erste Sohn Napoleons. A biography. T.
     163p.

D1   Zwischen den Mühlsteinen. Serialization of a novel in
     82 parts, Basler Nachrichten, Sept. 27 - Dec. 31,
     1966.

D7   Cl. from Berlin and Viennese magazines and newspapers.

H3   Assorted cl. from German newspapers.

J   1 photo with Mickey Rooney.

Mr. Paul Elbogen, 218 21st Avenue, San Francisco, California,
94101.

Mr. Elbogen still retains the original manuscripts of much of
the photocopied material now at the Library of the University
of California, Davis. In addition, Mr. Elbogen has the original manuscripts of several of his later longer works.

*Zusätzlich zu den Originalmanuskripten, deren Photokopien sich
nun in der Bibliothek der University of California, Davis,
befinden, besitzt Paul Elbogen die Originalmanuskripte mehrerer seiner langen Spätwerke.*

A3   Vom Hundertsten ins Tausendste. "Selbstbiographisches
     Mosaik." T. 200p.

C1   Zwillingsroman. Ms. of Elbogen's latest novel. A. Ca.
     600p.

University of Pennsylvania, The Charles Patterson Van Pelt
Library, Philadelphia, Pennsylvania 19104.

ALMA MAHLER-WERFEL COLLECTION

B1   1 L. to Alma Mahler-Werfel. T. 1959.

ERIK ERIKSON

Psychoanalyst, 1902-

Dr. Erikson has expressed his intentions to donate the papers in his possession to the Countway Library, Harvard University Medical School. The papers remain, as of 1977, in the hands of Dr. Erikson in California.

Dr. Erikson hat die Absicht geäußert, die Materialien in seinem Besitz der Countway Library der Harvard University Medical School zukommen zu lassen. Zum jetzigen Zeitpunkt (1977) befinden sie sich noch in Händen von Dr. Erikson in Kalifornien.

Columbia University, Butler Library, New York, N.Y. 10027.

W. W. NORTON COLLECTION and general archive files

B1 1 L. ea. to Robert Brunner and Dover Publications.
   T. 1950 and 1951.
   66 L. and 4 Tel. to W. W. Norton & Co. 1948-1965.

C7 Childhood and Society. Jacket text. 1950. A. 3p. Also
   typed copy. Outline. 1948. T. with corr. 51p.
  Young Man Luther. Advertising text. 1958. A. 3p.

Erikson Institute for Early Education, 1525 East 53rd Street, Chicago, Illinois 60637.

Personal collection of Gerhard and Maria Piers.

Privatsammlung von Gerhard und Maria Piers.

B1,2 Lengthy correspondence with Gerhard and Maria Piers,
   primarily during recent years.

C7 Young Man Luther. Ms.
  Identity Youth and Crisis. Ms.

University of Iowa, The University Libraries, Special Collections, Iowa City, Iowa 52240.

B1 4 L. to Clyde Kluckholm. 1947-1948.

Library of Congress, Manuscript Division, Independence Avenue and First Street S.E., Washington, D.C. 20540.

HELEN M. LYND PAPERS

B1,2 Correspondence between Erik Erikson and Helen M. Lynd.

Dr. Friedrich Hacker, The Hacker Clinic, 160 Lasky Drive, Beverly Hills, California 90212.

B1,2 Correspondence between Hacker and Erikson.

RICHARD ETTINGHAUSEN
Educator, Art Historian, 1906-

Dr. Richard Ettinghausen, 24 Armor Road, Princeton, New Jersey 08541.

Private collection. / *Privatsammlung.*

B1,2   Correspondence, primarily of a scholarly nature, including correspondence with: Dr. Otto Kurz, Prof. Klaus Brisch, Dr. Oleg Graber, Dr. Myriam Ayalon.

D7   Nearly complete collection of offprints.

J   Several photos of Ettinghausen.
Visual materials on archeological, historical sites, subjects, etc.
Art collection (primarily Near Eastern).

K   Extensive art library, particularly in Near Eastern studies.

Smithsonian Institution, Freer Gallery of Art, Washington, D.C. 20560.

E. E. HERZFELD COLLECTION

C8   List of archeological artifacts with detailed descriptions of each, compiled by Ettinghausen. Wood, stone, metal, pottery, glass, stucco, bone, ivory, painted plaster, etc. H-1 through H-101 plus several unnumbered artifacts.

New York Public Library, Manuscript Division, Fifth Avenue and 42nd Street, New York, N.Y. 10018.

EMERGENCY COMMITTEE IN AID OF DISPLACED FOREIGN SCHOLARS, 1933-1945

*   File compiled when assistance was granted. 1933-1944.

Harvard University, Houghton Library, Cambridge, Massachusetts 02138.

242

RICHARD ETTINGHAUSEN

GEORGE SARTON PAPERS

B1   2 L. to George Sarton. 1950.

KASIMIR FAJANS

Physical Chemist, 1887-1975

University of Michigan, Bentley Historical Library, Michigan
Historical Collections, 1150 Beal Avenue, Ann Arbor, Michigan 48105.

The KASIMIR FAJANS PAPERS consist of approximately 10 ft. of
materials, which were donated by Mrs. Kasimir Fajans from
1975-1977. A detailed inventory of the collection is available from the Bentley Historical Library.

*Die KASIMIR FAJANS PAPERS umfassen etwa 3 m Materialien, eine
Schenkung von Frau Fajans aus den Jahren 1975-1977. Ein detailliertes Verzeichnis der Sammlung ist von der Bentley
Historical Library erhältlich.*

A3   Bibliographies.
       Biographical articles.

B1,2   Substantial amount of correspondence with scientists
         (ca. 40% of entire collection), arranged alphabetically by correspondent, primarily after Fajans'
         immigration to the U.S. Includes: Lawrence Badash,
         Norman Bauer, Theodore H. Berlin, Max Born, C. J. F.
         Böttcher, Max Bredig, Otto Hahn, George Hevesy, Oliver Johnson, Donald Morris, Newton Ressler, Ernest
         Rutherford, Glenn Seaborg, Arnold Sommerfeld, W. A.
         Weyl, Richard Willstatter.
       Correspondence with editors, publishers. 1919-1973.
       Miscellaneous correspondence on various topics, including: thorium lead, Manhattan Project, quanticle theory, naming of brevium, Owens-Illinois, Minnesota
         Mining and Manufacturing Company, Shell Development
         Company, protactinium, Society for the Protection of
         Science, radioactivity, history of science, boron
         compounds, etc.
       Congratulations on the occasion of Kasimir Fajans Day
         in Ann Arbor, Michigan, May 27, 1974.
       Letters from students and colleagues from Munich and
         Karlsruhe.
       Letters from students at the University of Michigan.
       Helfman Scholarships (financial aid for European scholars, 1940).
       Correspondence with U.S.S.R. Embassy in Washington and

244

with Profs. Kedrov, Frankel, Skriabin and Starosel-
skia-Nikitina of the Soviet Union, 1970-1974.
Xerox c. of correspondence of Fajans and Albert Einstein on immigration of Helm Blume to Canada in 1942.

C7,8   U.S. lectures. 1928-1930.
Lecture notes. 1930-1966.
Papers related to lectures. 1918-1975.
Articles, reviews and papers. 1913-1971 and undated.
   5 F.
"History of Binding Theories." Draft.
Refractometry. Draft by Norman Bauer, K. Fajans and
   S. Z. Lewin.
Electronic Structure of Molecules and an introductory
   lecture, "The Development of Views Regarding the
   Nature of Chemical Forces."
Articles co-authored by Chien-Hon Chu and Kasimir
   Fajans.
"Applications of the Quanticle Theory to Biochemistry."
   Draft.
"Special Configurations and Interatomic Binding."
   Draft.
2 articles on properties and structure of vitreous,
   liquid and crystalline boron oxide by S. W. Barber
   and K. Fajans.
"New Confirmations of the Quanticle Theory."
Chemical Bonding. Chp. 4. Drafts and computations.
   Additional notes and computations on bonding and
   valence.

D8   Fajans reprints. 1908-1970s.
Books by Kasimir Fajans.

H4   Reviews of doctoral dissertations performed in Kasimir
   Fajans' laboratory, Germany.

H5   Biographical information, including data on publications, students and careers.

I   Invitation to the Professorship at the University of
   Freiburg.
Invitation to the Professorship at the University of
   Michigan.
Kasimir Fajans Award, University of Michigan.

N   Papers by students and colleagues.

Reprints of others. 1908+.
Reprints signed by Rutherford.
German dissertations.

<u>American Philosophical Society</u>, The Library, 105 South Fifth
Street, Philadelphia, Pennsylvania 19106.

MAX BERGMANN PAPERS, MISCELLANEOUS MANUSCRIPTS COLLECTION

B1,2   Correspondence with Max Bergmann.

B2   1 L. to James Franck.

ALFRED FARAU

Writer, 1904-1973

<u>University of Wyoming</u>, Archive of Contemporary History, The
Library, Box 3334, Laramie, Wyoming 82071.

The ALFRED FARAU COLLECTION, 93 folders of materials plus
several books and other published items, was donated to the
library in 1973 by Mrs. Sylvia Farau, widow of Alfred. All
literary rights to materials in the collection have been retained by Mrs. Farau.

*Die ALFRED FARAU COLLECTION (93 Materialmappen, mehrere
Bücher und anderes publiziertes Material) ist eine Schenkung
(1973) von Frau Sylvia Farau, der Witwe des Autors. Die
literarischen Rechte in Bezug auf alles Material der Sammlung ruhen bei Frau Farau.*

A1   Diaries. 1921-1938.
     "Triester Chronik 1939/40."
     "Tagebücher 1943-1947." Later incorporated into <u>Auto-
         biographisches</u>.
     "Tagebücher 1949. Europe 1953, '56, '57, '58, '60."
     Later incorporated into <u>Autobiographisches</u>.
     "Tagebuch eines Emigranten."

A3   Chronological index of works.
     Graphological, palmistry, astrological, medical opin-
         ions.
     "Journalistische Tätigkeit." Funk Express.
     Biographical dates.

B1,2 Correspondence with theaters, record and film compa-
         nies, newspapers and magazines.
     Correspondence with publishers.
     Correspondence with radio stations. 1940-.
     Correspondence from Künstlerkreis Wien.
     Miscellaneous correspondence.
     Correspondence concerning "Adler lectures."
     Correspondence with parents until 1927, 1927-1929,
         1940-1942.
     Miscellaneous correspondence with psychologists.
     Correspondence concerning contracts.
     Correspondence with Harry Zohn until 1970.
     Correspondence with friends.
     Correspondence with "Professor h.c."

247

B2   Congratulatory L. on Farau's 60th birthday.

B3   Correspondences of Sylvia Farau. 1921-1956. 4 F.

C1   Der Sohn der Erde. Versions 1931-1936, final version
         and copy. 3 F. First version. 1928. 1 F. Final ver-
         sion. 1958. 1 F.
      Stoliumtod. Novel 1929/1930. 107p.
      Wettlauf mit dem Weltuntergang. Die unverlogene Liebe.
         1935-1936.

C3   "Sprüche des Kosmos." 1925.
      "Frühlingslied." 1926.
      "Das Frühlingslied und Gedichte."
      "Gedichte 1926-1939." A.
      "Gedichte 1939-1941."
      "Gedichte 1941-1946." A.
      "Die Bartholomäusnacht." A. and c.
      "Der Einzug des Gewaltigen."
      "Der Narr von Bergen-Belsen." A. and T.
      "Optimistisches Manifest." Final versions.
      "Schatten sind des Lebens Güter." Rollenhefte für die
         Lese-Aufführung. 1962. Final version. 1954.

C6   "Märchen vom kleinen Opichi." Final version and Eng-
         lish tr.
      Another copy of final version and optical version.
      "Radio Parodien (Übertragung aus dem ersten oesterr.
         Providelbergwerk)." 1937-1944.
      "Der Ruf der Sterne." Several versions and transla-
         tions.

C7   Numerous lecture texts and articles on psychologists
         and psychological themes, including several on Alfred
         Adler. Ca. 10 F.
      Reviews and critiques, until 1933, 1933-1935, 1935-
         1946, 1946-1953, 1953-1955, 1951-1961, 1961-1962.
         4 F.
      "Das Buch über Laienanalyse."
      "Kleinere Schriften vermischten Inhaltes bis 1944."
      "Kleinere Schriften vermischten Inhaltes seit 1944."
      "Report on Our Time, 1939-1958." 4 volumes. Original
         T., cc., newspaper cl.
      Lecture texts on: Alfred Polgar, Albert Einstein,
         Richard Beer-Hofmann, Peter Altenberg, Hannah Arendt,

Raimund, Nestroy, Grillparzer. 5 F.
"Jugend-Schriften vom 6-18. Lebensjahr."
Lectures and essays on literary topics. 8 F.
Miscellaneous lectures and essays, including:
  "Abschied von Wien."
  "Auswanderung unter Hitler in Oesterreich."
  "Eindruck von einer Europareise."
  "Radiostationen in Deutschland u. Oesterreich vor
    1938" und "Europäische Radiostationen vor 1938."
  "Die Schicksalsfrage unserer Zeit."
  "Vom Wesen des genialen Menschen."
  "Die Welt von 1913."
  "Wo ist die Jugend die ich rufe?"
  "Die Prophezeiungsschrift."
  "Der Untergang einer Stadt."
  "The Twentieth Century and I."
  "Dichter des Weltraums."
  "Reise ins Wiener Kaffeehaus."
  "Aus dem Tagebuch eines skeptischen Optimisten."
  "Vom alten Österreich und der neuen Welt."
  "Von Babenberger bis Bürckel."
  "Kindheit und Pubertät."

C9   Faust-parody.

C11   "Grillparzer." Original plus later versions. 1934-1964.
      2 F.

D7   Miscellaneous published materials.

I   Diploma and membership cards.
      Medal for art and science.
      Contracts. Including critiques, biographies and corres-
      pondence. 2 F.

J   Photos of Farau and parents. Also obituaries.

L   "Hitler Aufzeichnungen (Material für spätere Arbeiten
      1947-50)."
      Austrian Institute, Consulate and Forum materials.
      "Geburtstag 60 Jahre." 1 F.
      "Silver Anniversary." 1 F.

N   Grossberg, Mimi. "Geschick der österr. Emigration."
      Lecture at Austrian Institute.

ALFRED FARAU

California Institute of Technology, Robert A. Millikan Library, Pasadena, California 91109.

THEODORE VON KARMAN CORRESPONDENCE

B1   1 L. to Theodore von Karman. 1955.

PAUL FEDERN

Psychoanalyst, 1872-1942

<u>Mrs. Annie Urbach</u>, 691 Roble Avenue, Apt. 3, Menlo Park,
California 90425.

Mrs. Urbach is the daughter of Federn. The materials in her
possession are from the estate of her father. Mrs. Urbach
intends the materials to go to the Freud-Archiv, Vienna, and
perhaps copies of the materials to the Freud Archives at the
Library of Congress, Washington, D.C.

*Frau Anni Urbach ist die Tochter von Paul Federn. Die Mate-
rialien in ihrem Besitz stammen aus dem Nachlaß ihres Vaters.
Frau Urbach hat vor, diese Materialien dem Freud-Archiv in
Wien zukommen zu lassen (Kopien werden eventuell an die Freud
Archives der Library of Congress, Washington, D.C. gehen).*

A3   Federn's last words before committing suicide. A.pc. 1p.
     Family history and family tree.
     Bibliography with 1p. autobiography.

B1   2 L. concerning practicing medicine in the U.S.

B2   1 L. from Freud. pc. 1931.

B3   Correspondence between Annie Urbach and Kurt Eissler
     concerning Federn materials.

C3   Poems. 2p.

C7   Notes by Federn on his grandchildren. 1935-1941. T.
     German. Ca. 20p.

D7   1 offprint. German. 1919.

H3   Memorial address.
     Lecture by Edward Hitschmann on P. Federn. T.

H5   Memoirs of Annie Urbach on Federn. T.pc. Ca. 10p.
     Memoirs of Annie Urbach on Freud and Federn. 3p.
     Biographical sketch of Federn by his son for a 100th
     birthday publication. T.cc. 1961. 7p.

I   Miscellaneous documents including naturalization cer-
     tificate. 1938.
     Doctor's degree.
     Gutachten by Freud. T. 1926.

Library of Congress, Manuscript Division, Independence Avenue and First Street S.E., Washington, D.C. 20540.

The PAUL FEDERN PAPERS, 1871-1950, consist of approximately 7,000 items, which are uncatalogued (as of 1976). The papers were donated by Ernst Federn, son of Paul. Access to the papers is restricted until 1987; however, permission to use the papers may be obtained from Ernst Federn.

Die PAUL FEDERN PAPERS, 1871-1950, bestehen aus etwa 7000 Nummern, die 1976 noch nicht katalogisiert waren. Die PAPERS sind eine Schenkung von Ernst Federn, dem Sohn von Paul Federn. Der Zugang zu den PAPERS ist bis 1987 beschränkt, es kann jedoch eine Sondererlaubnis von Ernst Federn eingeholt werden.

A1   Appointment books.

A2   Notebooks.

B1,2   Professional and personal correspondence, including
       correspondences with: C. G. Jung, Karl Menninger,
       George M. White, and various publishers.

C7,8   Manuscripts.
       Research papers and notes.

H3,   Newspaper cl.
L

I   Passport.

N   Blanco, Ignacio N. "Studies on the Foundations of
       Psychoanalytical Psychiatry." 1 c.

PAPERS OF SIEGFRIED BERNFELD

B1,2   Correspondence with Siegfried Bernfeld. 1925-1937 and
       undated.

C8   "Psychoanalyse und Erziehung." T.

H3   Bernfeld, Siegfried. Article on Paul Federn. 1950.

Dr. Ernest Lewy, 1585 Manning Avenue, Los Angeles, California 90024.

PAUL FEDERN

B1,2   Several L. to and from Ernst Lewy.

Yale University, Beinecke Rare Book and Manuscript Library,
New Haven, Connecticut 06520.

HERMANN BROCH ARCHIVE

B1   L. to Hermann Broch.

B2   3 L. from Hermann Broch.

C7   Commentary on H. Broch's essay "Bemerkungen zur Utopie
        einer 'International Bill of Rights and Responsibili-
        ties'." T. 11p.

ARTHUR FEILER

Economist, 1879-1942

Hoover Institution on War, Revolution and Peace, Stanford,
California 94305.

The ARTHUR FEILER COLLECTION: 5 archive B.

L   Collection of newspaper and magazine cl. by Feiler,
     including primarily articles on German economics and
     politics. 1930-1938.

Leo Baeck Institute, 129 East 73rd Street, New York, N.Y.
10021.

C7   Articles, pub. and unpub.

D7   Proofs of works not yet pub.

K   Over 40 books from the personal library of Feiler.

Harvard University, Houghton Library, Cambridge, Massachusetts 02138.

OSWALD GARRISON VILLARD PAPERS

B1   1 L. to Oswald Garrison Villard. 1937.

B2   1 L. from Oswald Garrison Villard. 1937.

Yivo Institute, 1048 Fifth Avenue, New York, N.Y. 10028.

HORACE M. KALLEN PAPERS

B1,2 Individual items located in folders (345, 668). 1925,
     1942.

Columbia University, Butler Library, New York, N.Y. 10027.

B1   1 L. to John Maurice Clark. T. 1938.

New York Public Library, Manuscript Division, Fifth Avenue
and 42nd Street, New York, N.Y. 10018.

254

ARTHUR FEILER

EMERGENCY COMMITTEE IN AID OF DISPLACED FOREIGN SCHOLARS, 1933-1945.

*   File compiled, no assistance given. 1934.

LYONEL FEININGER

Painter, 1871-1956

Harvard University, Busch-Reisinger Museum, Cambridge, Massachusetts 02138.

The major portion of the LYONEL FEININGER COLLECTION was
donated by Julia Feininger from the estate of Lyonel Feininger to the Busch-Reisinger Museum. The Museum retained the
graphics and related materials for its own collection and
transferred the materials comprising the literary estate of
Feininger to the Houghton Library of Harvard University in
June 1963. Busch-Reisinger has retained approximately 20
ft. of materials in its collection.

*Der Hauptteil der LYONEL FEININGER COLLECTION ist eine
Schenkung an das Busch-Reisiger Museum von Julia Feininger
aus dem Nachlaß von Lyonel Feininger. Das Museum behielt
Grafiken und damit verbundene Materialien für seine eigene
Sammlung, während es die zum literarischen Nachlaß gehören-
den Materialien an die Houghton Library der Harvard University weitergab (Juni 1963). Das Busch-Reisinger Museum hat
etwa 6 m Materialien in seiner Sammlung behalten.*

B1   6 albums of transcribed excerpts from L. from Lyonel
        Feininger to Julia Feininger. English and German
        versions. 1905-1935. 640p.

B1,   4 albums of Feininger's letters with woodcuts. 1919-
C14   1952 and undated.

C14   Etchings, woodcuts, paintings (some from the Bauhaus).
        1919.
        5 albums of "folio" drawings. 1903-1944 and undated.
        125 albums of drawings, sketches. 1892-1955 and un-
        dated. Ca. 18 ft.

H3,4   479 exhibition catalogs, folders and magazines.
        13 envelopes of cl. 1905-1962 and undated.

J   452 photographs, mostly of Feininger's oil paintings.
        Album of photos from all years (people and works of
        art).

L   Offprints and individual issues of periodicals.

M   1 volume of primarily children's drawings (Feininger

children).
Invitations.

N   Ca. 10 sketches by other artists.
     1 album of letters with woodcuts by various artists.
     Art by other artists including: K. P. Röhl, Rudolf
     Baschant.

O   Programs of the American Academy.

Harvard University, Houghton Library, Cambridge, Massachusetts 02138.

The LYONEL FEININGER COLLECTION: bMS Ger 146 (8 archive
boxes); bMS Ger 146.1 (20 archive boxes). The collection
represents the literary estate of Feininger and was transferred to the Houghton Library from the Busch-Reisinger
Museum of Harvard University in June 1963. The literary
rights are still retained by Mr. Theodor Lux Feininger (22
Arlington, Cambridge, Massachusetts 02138).

*Die LYONEL FEININGER COLLECTION: bMS Ger 146 (8 Archivkar-
tons); bMS Ger 146.1 (20 Archivkartons). Die Sammlung stellt
den literarischen Nachlaß Feiningers dar; sie wurde der
Houghton Library im Juni 1963 vom Busch-Reisinger Musuem der
Harvard University überlassen. Die literarischen Rechte
ruhen bei Theodor Lux Feininger (22 Arlington, Cambridge,
Massachusetts 02138).*

A3   Autobiographical essay. T. Undated. 7p.

B1   122 L. 1903-1956, including L. to: Andreas Feininger,
     Lawrence Feininger, Jenny and Bernhard Lilienfeld
     (63), Galka Emma Schreyer (14), Curt Valentin.
     Ca. 1,200 L. to Julia Feininger. 1905-1946.

B2   Ca. 1,050 L. from Julia Feininger. 1905-1935. Includes
     some pc.
     1 package of birthday congratulatory Tel.
     Ca. 1,490 L. 1889-1959 and undated, including L. from:
     Anni Albers, Josef Albers, Willi Apel, Alfred Ein-
     stein, Willi Grohmann, Isa Gropius, Walter Gropius,
     Wassily Kandinsky, Paul Klee, Siegfried Kracauer,
     Alfred Kubin, Karl Loewenstein, Edward Lowinsky,

Alma Mahler-Werfel, Erich Mendelsohn, Alfred Neu-
meyer.

B3   399 L., primarily to Julia Feininger. T. and A. 1879-
1960 and undated.
Correspondence of the Lyonel Feininger family and
friends. 1905-1946. Transcripts of original L. now
in Baden-Baden. Edited by Julia Feininger.
Correspondence of the Lyonel Feininger family. 1907-
1908. Transcript of original L. now in Baden-Baden.
Edited by Julia Feininger.

H3,4 Newspaper cl. on Lyonel Feininger and his work. 2
archive B.

I   1 notice for a Karl Feininger presentation.
Form, signed by Feininger. Undated.
2 lists of Feininger's works. 1944 and undated.
Contract between Feininger and the City of Dessau.
1925. Accompanied by cashier's receipt. 1929.

J   1 photo of Andreas Feininger house.
14 photos of Lawrence Feininger.
1 photo of Bernhard Lilienfeld.

N   21 Ms. by Karl Feininger, primarily on musical topics.
A. and c. 160p.
3 Ms. by Alfred Hamilton Barr and Mark Tovey. A. and T.
12p.
7 Ms. by Andreas Feininger, Lawrence Binyon, Anita
Elisabeth Hess, Adolf Knoblauch, Richard Mansfield.
A. and T. 69p.
2 drawings by Anita Elisabeth Hess for L. Feininger.
2 drawings by Andreas Feininger.

Archives of American Art, Smithsonian Institution, National
Collection of Fine Arts and National Portrait Gallery Build-
ing, Eighth and F Streets N.W., Washington, D.C. 20560.
(Microfilms of collections are available in each of the
branch locations: Boston, Massachusetts; New York, N.Y.;
Detroit, Michigan; San Francisco, California.)

The LYONEL FEININGER PAPERS 1887-1920 consist of a microfilm
collection (732 frames) of materials, some of which were

lent to the Smithsonian for the purpose of microfilming. Other Feininger materials are located in the following collections at the Archives: AMERICAN ABSTRACT ARTISTS PAPERS, 1936-1959, LOUISE BRUNER PAPERS, CLEVELAND PRINT CLUB PAPERS, L. A. FLEISCHMANN PAPERS, ALICE TRUMBALL MASON PAPERS, ARNOLD NEWMAN PAPERS, ULFERT WILKE PAPERS, WILLARD GALLERY SCRAPBOOKS and miscellany.

Die LYONEL FEININGER PAPERS 1887-1920 bestehen aus einer Mikrofilmsammlung (732 Aufnahmen); die Filme wurden von Materialien aufgenommen, die der Smithsonian Institution zum Zweck des Abfilmens zur Verfügung gestellt wurden. Andere Feininger Materialian befinden sich in den folgenden Sammlungen des Archivs: AMERICAN ABSTRACT ARTISTS PAPERS, 1936-1959, LOUISE BRUNER PAPERS, CLEVELAND PRINT CLUB PAPERS, L. A. FLEISCHMANN PAPERS, ALICE TRUMBALL MASON PAPERS, ARNOLD NEWMAN PAPERS, ULFERT WILKE PAPERS, WILLARD GALLERY SCRAPBOOKS u.a.

B1   2 L. to Marian Willard. 1937.
        Numerous L. including L. to galleries, institutions (American Abstract Artists, etc.), individuals.

B1,2 Correspondence between Feininger and the Institute of Contemporary Art, Boston (known as Institute of Modern Art until 1948). Original located at the Institute.
        Correspondence between Feininger and the Willard Gallery. 1936-1969.
        Correspondence with the Cleveland Print Club. Also possibly photos, biographical data, miscellany.

C14   Drawings (graphics) by Feininger.

D14   Reproductions of Feininger's graphic works.
        Prints from Art News. 1955.
        Scrapbook containing sketches, cl. and illustrations from German periodicals: Jugend, Das Narrenschiff, UIK, Lustige Blätter, etc. 1893-1901.
        Scrapbook(s) of cl., catalogs and photos, compiled by Jerome Milkman of Feininger and other artists. 1930-1950.

H3   Articles.
        Materials from the artists files of the Whitney Museum

of American Art.

Printed matter: 1941, 1955 and undated.

Microfilm of files of the materials at the Pennsylvania Academy of Fine Arts (photos, correspondence, newspaper cl., biographical materials, press releases, published brochures, catalogs, etc.).

I   Item in Roy R. Neugebauer birthday book. 1953.

J   Photo(s) of Feininger's work.
    Photo of Lyonel Feininger (beside easel). 1945.

Museum of Modern Art, The Library, 11 West 53rd Street, New York, N.Y. 10019.

The CURT VALENTIN PAPERS were a gift to the MOMA Library by the art dealer's estate. Restricted Archive: requirements for access upon written application to the Museum of Modern Art.

Die CURT VALENTIN PAPERS sind eine Schenkung aus dem Nachlaß des Kunsthändlers an die Museum of Modern Art Library. Der Zugang ist beschränkt; Zugangsbedingungen teilt das Museum of Modern Art auf schriftliche Anfrage mit.

B1   38 L. and 1 Ptc. to Curt Valentin. T. and A. 1939-1950.

B2   76 L. (cc.) from Curt Valentin. 1939-1953.

B3   Correspondence between Curt Valentin and Julia Feininger. Ca. 100 L. 1939-1953.

I   Contracts.
     Lists of paintings with dates and prices.

Yale University Library, Manuscripts and Archives Research Room, 150 Sterling Memorial Library, New Haven, Connecticut 06520.

JOSEF ALBERS PAPERS

B1   18 L. to Josef Albers. 1934-1953.

LYONEL FEININGER

Mrs. Louise Mendelsohn, 1101 Green Street, San Francisco,
California 94109.

ERICH MENDELSOHN ARCHIVE

B1   7 L. to Erich Mendelsohn. 1920-1946.

Leo Baeck Institute, 129 East 73rd Street, New York, N.Y.
10021.

GEORG HERMANN COLLECTION and general files

B1   1 L. to Georg Hermann. A. 1903.
J   1 photo.

University of Minnesota, University Libraries, University
Archives, Minneapolis, Minnesota 55455.

H3   "Presenting Lyonel Feininger; a retrospective exhibi-
      tion at the University of Minnesota, 1938."

OTTO FENICHEL

Psychoanalyst, 1898-1946

HANNA FENICHEL

Psychoanalyst, 1897-1975

Dr. Andreas Aebi, Department of German, Rutgers, The State
University, Newark, New Jersey 07102.

The materials in Dr. Aebi's possession (3 large cartons, ca.
1 m.) are from the estate of Hanna and Otto Fenichel. Dr.
Aebi is in the process, as of 1977, of preparing an index to
the papers. The following cursory summary of the materials
was prepared by Dr. Aebi.

*Die Materialien in Dr. Aebis Besitz (3 große Kartons, etwa 1
m) stammen aus dem Nachlaß von Hanna und Otto Fenichel. Dr.
Aebi ist z.Zt. (1977) im Begriff, ein Verzeichnis der Materialien zu erstellen. Der folgende Überblick wurde auch von
Dr. Aebi angefertigt.*

A1   Diaries. 1911-1946.

A3   Autobiographical account of the Fenichel travels from
      Vienna to California via Berlin, Oslo and Prague.

B1,2 Correspondence from the 1940s, including L. to and
      from: Kurt Eissler, Erich Fromm, Karl Menninger,
      etc. Numerous c. of Fenichel's own L. (nearly com-
      plete). Also a complete listing of Otto Fenichel's
      correspondence, including names of correspondents,
      places and dates, record of replies. Over 10,000
      entries. 1911-1946.

C3   Poems by Otto Fenichel. Several Ms.

C8   Manuscripts of articles.
      Notes to speeches and seminars.

L   Clinical materials.

M   Autograph collection.

N   Max Kohen manuscripts:
      Numeri 25.
      Spiegelworte.
      Licht auf Altertümer.
      Dokument eines Tyrannenmord.

262

OTTO FENICHEL / HANNA FENICHEL

Manuscript of a drama or film.

<u>Library of Congress</u>, Manuscript Division, Independence Avenue and First Street S.E., Washington, D.C. 20540.

DAVID RAPAPORT PAPERS, PAPERS OF SIEGFRIED BERNFELD

B1,2   Correspondence between Hanna Fenichel and David Rapaport.
        Correspondence between Otto Fenichel and Siegfried Bernfeld. 1915-1947.

C8   Research notes by Hanna Fenichel and Siegfried Bernfeld concerning a Freud biography.
        Fenichel, Otto. "Der Begriff der 'Realität' und seine Entstehung durch Projektion." T. Undated.
        "Esoterik." T. 1918.

<u>New York Public Library</u>, Manuscript Division, Fifth Avenue and 42nd Street, New York, N.Y. 10018.

ERICH FROMM PAPERS

B1,2   Correspondence between Otto Fenichel and Erich Fromm.

C7   Unidentified Ms. by Otto Fenichel.

<u>Dr. Martin Grotjahn</u>, 416 North Bedford Drive, Beverly Hills, California 90210.

B1,2   Correspondence between Otto Fenichel and Martin Grotjahn.

<u>Dr. Friedrich J. Hacker</u>, The Hacker Clinic, 160 Lasky Drive, Beverly Hills, California 90212.

B1,2   Correspondence between Otto Fenichel and Friedrich Hacker.

263

<u>Dr. Ralph R. Greenson</u>, 902 Franklin Street, Santa Monica, California 90403.

I   Clinical records of Hanna Fenichel.

<u>Dr. and Mrs. Alfred Goldberg</u>, 801 Broom Way, Los Angeles, California 90049.

I   Clinical records of Hanna Fenichel, some notes.

<u>Ms. Lilly Lampl</u>, Huntington Beach, California

B1,2 Correspondence, dealing primarily with the emigration of Ms. Lampl's parents to the U.S.

J   Photos.

LION FEUCHTWANGER

Writer, 1884-1958

<u>University of Southern California</u>, Lion Feuchtwanger Memo-
rial Library, 520 Paseo Miramar, Pacific Palisades, California 90272.

On April 22, 1960 Mrs. Marta Feuchtwanger, widow of Lion
Feuchtwanger, donated both the Feuchtwanger house and Lion
Feuchtwanger's personal library (more than 30,000 volumes)
and literary estate (ca. 90 ft.) to the University of
Southern California. It is known today as the LION FEUCHT-
WANGER MEMORIAL LIBRARY of the University of Southern California. Feuchtwanger's personal library, the third such
library assembled by him during his lifetime, was begun in
1943 and contains manuscripts, incunabula, first editions,
as well as materials used by him in writing his novels and
dramas.

*In Form einer Schenkung überließ Frau Marta Feuchtwanger,
die Witwe von Lion Feuchtwanger, am 22. April 1960 der University of Southern California das Feuchtwanger-Haus, Lion
Feuchtwangers Privatbibliothek (über 30.000 Bände) sowie
seinen literarischen Nachlaß (etwa 30 m). Diese Schenkung
trägt den Namen LION FEUCHTWANGER MEMORIAL LIBRARY. Feuchtwanger hatte 1943 mit dem Aufbau dieser Privatbibliothek,
der dritten, die er im Laufe seines Lebens zusammenstellte,
begonnen. Sie enthält Manuskripte, Inkunabeln, Erstausgaben
sowie Material, das er bei der Anfertigung seiner Romane und
Dramen verwandte.*

B1,2 48 ring binders containing correspondence (ca. 200
      items per binder) and several folders with corres-
      pondence. Altogether over 10,000 L. to and from
      Feuchtwanger, including:
      Correspondence between Feuchtwanger and Huebsch. Ca.
      1,000 L.
      L. and Tel. from Feuchtwanger to: Günther Anders, Ber-
      tolt Brecht, Hermann Broch, Helene Deutsch, Alfred
      Döblin, Albert Einstein, Hanns Eisler, Elow, Bruno
      Frank, George Froeschel, Manfred George, Oskar Maria
      Graf, Alexander Granach, Hans Habe, Wieland Herzfelde,
      Stefan Heym, Max Horkheimer, Heinrich Eduard Jacob,
      Leopold Jessner, Alfred Kantorowicz, Kurt Kersten,
      Erich Korngold, Leo Lania, Emil Ludwig, Erika Mann,

265

Heinrich Mann, Katia Mann, Thomas Mann, Ludwig Marcuse, Walter Mehring, Ernst Erich Noth, Kurt Pinthus, Hans Reichenbach, Fritz Sternberg, Robert
Thoeren, Walther Victor, Berthold Viertel, F. C.
Weiskopf.

L. and Tel. to Feuchtwanger, including L. from: Günther
Anders, Bertolt Brecht, Hermann Broch, Helene Deutsch,
Alfred Döblin, Albert Einstein, Hanns Eisler, Elow,
Bruno Frank, George Froeschel, Manfred George,
Claire Goll, Iwan Goll, Oskar Maria Graf, Alexander
Granach, Hans Habe, Wieland Herzfelde, Stefan Heym,
Heinrich Eduard Jacob, Alfred Kantorowicz, Kurt Ker-
sten, Erich Korngold, Leo Lania, Emil Ludwig, Erika
Mann, Golo Mann, Heinrich Mann, Katia Mann, Thomas
Mann, Ludwig Marcuse, Walter Mehring, Ernst Erich
Noth, Kurt Pinthus, Erwin Piscator, Wilhelm Speyer,
Fritz Sternberg, Robert Thoeren, Ernst Toch, Walther
Victor, Berthold Viertel, F. C. Weiskopf, Franz Wer-
fel, Victoria Wolff, Stefan Zweig.

Cl Goya oder Der arge Weg der Erkenntnis. Several different versions denoted by T. of different colored
paper. T. with numerous h. and stenographic corr.
Ca. 1,880p.

Die häßliche Herzogin. A. with stenographic corr., the
last pages totally in stenography. 166p.

Das Haus der Desdemona oder Größe und Grenzen der
historischen Dichtung. 2 parts in F. 217p. Tables of
contents, notes for further chapters, several incomplete versions.

Jean-Jacques [Rousseau]. Plan for a story or play.
June 1944. T. 10p.

Jefta und seine Tochter. Several different versions.
Ca. 750p. Final version. T. 275p. Notes on charac-
ters, plot. 25p.

Jud Süß. A.

Die Jüdin von Toledo [Spanische Ballade]. Early versions, final version, character descriptions, index,
dates, notes.

Narrenweisheit oder Tod und Verklärung des Jean-Jacques
Rousseau. Several versions, index with character descriptions, table of contents. Ca. 900p. Proofs for
first 2 parts.

Die sieben Weisen. Rough outline for a contemporary
   novel. 6p.
Simone. 2 final versions. 345p., 347p. English tr.
   331p. Proofs, English. 256p.
Der Tag wird kommen. Third part of Josephus-trilogy.
   455p. Table of contents. 9p.
Unholdes Frankreich (working title: Der Teufel in
   Frankreich). Final version. 245p. Parts of an earlier
   version.
Waffen für Amerika. Final version. 1,250p. Notes. 106p.
Wahn oder Der Teufel in Boston. Next to final version.
   118p. English tr. and final English version. Mimeographed. Character descriptions, outline.

C2   Friede. Ein burleskes Spiel. Nach den "Acharnern" und
       der "Eirene" des Aristophanes. 54p.
     Julia Farnese. Ein Trauerspiel in drei Akten von Lion
       Feuchtwanger. 2 c., ea. 56p.
     Der König und die Tänzerin. Ein heiteres Spiel in 4
       Akten. Nach dem Indischen des Kalidasa. 80p.
     Prisoners of War. "Agent's copy." 62p.
     Vasantasena. (Nach dem Indischen). Incomplete copy.
       59p.
     Waffen für Amerika. Play, preliminary work for novel.
       Early version with h. corr. by the author. 158p.

C4   "Cleopatra." Outline. 12p.
     "Ester." Rough draft. 28p.
     "Velazquez." Rough table of contents. 23p.

C5   Bolivar. Ein Heldenleben. Plan for a film. 96p. Draft
       of English version. 71p.
     Jud Süß. "Film Szenarium Nr. 32." Gaumont British Pic-
       ture Corp. Ltd., London. 698p.

C7   Zwölf Dokumente. Rough version of introduction. 6p.

D7   "Gesammelte Aufsätze." Quarto volume containing:
       1. Pasted cl. with h. entries of date, volume and no.
          Begun in 1908, p. 1-184.
       2. Plays or parts of plays, printed in newspapers.
          Begun in 1919, p. 185-324.
       3. Dust jackets and title pages of plays and the
          novel Der tönerne Gott, p. 325-327.

4. Playbills, from the first performances of König
Saul and Prinzessin Hilde to 1923.

F　　Tapes:
Lion Feuchtwanger for a Bertolt Brecht program for
the BBC, Oct. 4, 1958.
Lion Feuchtwanger speech in memory of Thomas Mann,
Jewish Club of 1933, Ebert Concert Hall, Oct. 15,
1955.
Lion Feuchtwanger Library. Interview for CBS. Ralph
Kaplan, Marta Feuchtwanger, Dr. Lewis F. Steig,
Hilde Waldo, Oct. 7, 1963.
Lion Feuchtwanger. Interview with Bayrischer Rund-
funk on the occasion of the Münchner Kulturpreis,
July 27, 1957.
Lion Feuchtwanger. Reading from Die Jüdin von
Toledo.
KPFK-FM. Brecht in Hollywood. Included in the Memoirs
of Brecht's American Years. John Houseman, Marta
Feuchtwanger, Elsa Lanchester, William Melnitz,
. 1963.
Review House of Desdemona. Books unlimited no. 8.
Lion Feuchtwanger in seinem Heim. Color film by Al-
brecht Joseph. German and English versions.
Lion Feuchtwanger Memorial Library. Film. Robert Cohen
Productions, Hollywood, California.

H4　　Over 3,000 reviews, primarily from German and American
sources, a few French, English and Italian. Very few
prior to 1941.

J　　Numerous photographs of Feuchtwanger, wife and friends.

K　　Lion Feuchtwanger's private library. Over 30,000 volumes, including rare editions, manuscripts, as well
as works he used to write his novels and dramas.

N　　Mann, Heinrich. Die Jugend Heinrich IV und Die Vollendung des Königs Heinrich IV. Complete h. Ms.

Library of Congress, Manuscript Division, Independence Avenue
and First Street S.E., Washington, D.C. 20540.

LION FEUCHTWANGER

The Library of Congress possesses ca. 6 ft. of Feuchtwanger
materials in its LION FEUCHTWANGER PAPERS (donated by Mrs.
Marta Feuchtwanger) and the BENJAMIN W. HUEBSCH PAPERS.

*Die Library of Congress besitzt etwa 1,80 m Feuchtwanger
Material in ihren LION FEUCHTWANGER PAPERS (eine Schenkung
von Frau Marta Feuchtwanger) und in den BENJAMIN W. HUEBSCH
PAPERS.*

B1	54 L., 2 Ptc. and 4 Tel. to Benjamin W. Huebsch. 1926-1958 and undated. 1 L. to Jewish Book Council of America. T.c. 1957.
B2	17 L. and 1 Tel. from B. W. Huebsch. T.c. 1938-1958. 1 L. ea. from: Harold Guinzburg (1957), Jacques Chambrun, Inc. (1943), James B. Pond (1933).
B3	13 L. between Huebsch and Marta Feuchtwanger. 4 L. to and from Huebsch. 6 L. from Hilde Waldo (Feuchtwanger's secretary) to Huebsch.
C1	Simone. T. with h. corr. by Feuchtwanger.
C5	Jean-Jacques. Draft of a play or film script. Undated. T.c. 9p.
I	2 references from B. W. Huebsch.
J	2 photos and a drawing of Feuchtwanger.

Leo Baeck Institute, 129 East 73rd Street, New York, N.Y.
10021.

The LION FEUCHTWANGER COLLECTION was donated by Mrs. Marta
Feuchtwanger in 1960. A few additional items are located in
the GEORG HERMANN COLLECTION, FRITZ MAUTHNER COLLECTION, KURT
KERSTEN COLLECTION. One additional, as yet unsorted, box of
materials was added to the collection in 1975.

*Die LION FEUCHTWANGER COLLECTION im Leo Baeck Institute ist
eine Schenkung von Frau Marta Feuchtwanger aus dem Jahre
1960. Einiges zusätzliche Material findet sich in der GEORG
HERMANN COLLECTION, der FRITZ MAUTHNER COLLECTION und der*

LION FEUCHTWANGER

KURT KERSTEN COLLECTION. Der Sammlung wurde im Jahre 1975 ein weiterer, bis jetzt noch ungeordneter, Karton mit Materialien hinzugefügt.

B1   20 L. 1918-1954, including L. to Georg Hermann, Kurt Kersten, Fritz Mauthner, Arnold Zweig.

C2   Lysistrata. II. Akt. T.c. with h. corr.

D7   3 articles on Jewish themes. 1957-1958.

H3   7 cl. 1959-1970 and undated.

I   Invitation to Lion Feuchtwanger lecture and exhibit. 1964.

J   Photo Ptc.
      1 photo of Feuchtwanger.

O   Program: "Kalkutta." 1929.

Boston University, Mugar Memorial Library, 771 Commonwealth Avenue, Boston, Massachusetts 02215.

The materials that make up the LION FEUCHTWANGER PAPERS were donated to the library in 1964 by Marta Feuchtwanger. Additional materials are located in the following collections: MICHAEL BLANKFORT PAPERS, HELEN DEUTSCH COLLECTION, HANS HABE COLLECTION.

Die Materialien, aus denen die LION FEUCHTWANGER PAPERS in der Mugar Memorial Library zusammengestellt wurden, sind eine Schenkung von Frau Marta Feuchtwanger aus dem Jahre 1964. Weitere Materialien finden sich in den folgenden Sammlungen: MICHAEL BLANKFORT PAPERS, HELEN DEUTSCH COLLECTION, HANS HABE COLLECTION.

A3   2 bibliographies. T. 2p., 1p.
      Curriculum vitae. T. 2p.

B1   1 L. ea. to Michael Blankfort, Helen Deutsch and Hans Habe.

B2   3 L. from Helen Deutsch. Pc. 1947-1951.

LION FEUCHTWANGER

C1   <u>Jud Süß</u>. First 2p. A. pc.

C7   "Ghost train." Lecture. 1940. T. 11p.

J   1 photo of Feuchtwanger.
      1 photo of Feuchtwanger's death mask.

<u>Indiana University</u>, The University Libraries, The Lilly Library, Bloomington, Indiana 47401.

LEWIS BROWNE MSS., UPTON BEALL SINCLAIR MSS., VIKING PRESS MSS.

B1   3 L. to Lewis Browne. 1933-1944.
      5 L. to Upton Sinclair. 1941-1953.
      2 form L. (to Browne and Sinclair), signed also by B.
      Frank, M. Horkheimer, T. Mann, E. M. Remarque, F.
      Werfel.

B2   1 L. from Upton Sinclair. T.c. 1942.

B3   1 L. from Thomas Mann to Lewis Browne. 1942.

<u>Viking Press, Inc.</u>, 625 Madison Avenue, New York, N.Y. 10021.

H4   Nearly complete collection of reviews of Feuchtwanger's
      works that were published by Viking Press.

<u>New York Public Library</u>, Manuscript Division, Fifth Avenue
and 42nd Street, New York, N.Y. 10018.

THEO FELDMAN PAPERS

B1   7 L. to Theo Feldman. T. 1947-1953.

<u>University of New Hampshire</u>, The Library, Department of Special Collections, Durham, New Hampshire 03824.

OSKAR MARIA GRAF COLLECTION, FRIEDRICH SALLY GROSSHUT COLLECTION

271

B1   8 L. to Oskar Maria Graf. 1937-1958.
      50 L. to F. S. Grosshut. T. and A. 1945-1958.

B2   1 L. from O. M. Graf. 1954.
      1 L. from F. S. Grosshut. T.cc. 1949.

B3   5 L. from Hilde Waldo (Feuchtwanger's secretary) to
      F. S. Grosshut. 1958-1969.

University of Pennsylvania, The Charles Patterson Van Pelt
Library, Philadelphia, Pennsylvania 19104.

ALMA MAHLER-WERFEL COLLECTION

B1   8 L. to Alma Mahler-Werfel. T. and A. 1930-1964.
      2 L. to Franz Werfel. T. and A. 1943, 1944.

B2   1 L. from Franz Werfel. T. (plus c.). 1942.

Columbia University, Butler Library, New York, N.Y. 10027.

B1   9 L. to Marie M. Meloney. T. 1933-1934.
      1 L. to Emil Lengyel. T. 1932.

University of Texas, Humanities Research Center, Manuscripts
Collection, Box 7219, Austin, Texas 78712.

B1   1 L.

B2   2 L.

C   1 Ms.

Southern Illinois University, Morris Library, Department of
Special Collections, Carbondale, Illinois 62901.

ERWIN PISCATOR PAPERS

B1   1 L. to E. Piscator. T. 1947

B2   2 L. from E. Piscator. 1936, 1948.

Cornell University, John M. Olin Library, Department of Manuscripts and University Archives, Ithaca, New York 14850.

B1   1 L. to Theodore Dreiser. 1932.

Minnesota Historical Society, 690 Cedar Street, St. Paul,
Minnesota 55101.

JAMES GRAY PAPERS

B1   1 L. to James Gray. 1947.

Yale University, Beinecke Rare Book and Manuscript Library,
New Haven, Connecticut 06520.

HERMANN BROCH ARCHIVE

B1   1 L. to Hermann Broch. 1947.

Syracuse University, The George Arents Research Library,
Syracuse, New York 13210.

FRANZ WAXMAN PAPERS

B1   1 L. to Franz Waxman. 1956.

University of California, Los Angeles, Department of Special
Collections, 120 Lawrence Clark Powell Library, Los Angeles,
California 90024.

FRANZ WERFEL ARCHIVE

B2   1 L. from Franz Werfel. 1944.

Dr. Marta Mierendorff, 8633 West Knoll Drive, Hollywood,
California 90069.

INSTITUT FÜR KUNSTSOZIOLOGIE

C7   Speech in honor of Leopold Jessner's 65th birthday,
      Los Angeles. Pc.

State University of New York at Binghamton, Center for Modern Theater Research, Binghamton, New York 13901.

MAX REINHARDT ARCHIVE

*   Materials in uncatalogued portion of the archive.

Mrs. Peter M. Lindt, 949 West End Avenue, New York, N.Y.
10025.

B1   Small amount of correspondence with Peter M. Lindt.

C   Ms. submitted to Lindt for use on his radio program.

RUTH FISCHER

Political Figure, 1895-1961

Harvard University, Houghton Library, Cambridge, Massachusetts 02138.

The RUTH FISCHER PAPERS, which comprise over 150 shelf ft.
of materials, were received by Houghton Library from the
estate of Ruth Fischer in 1962. The Library has now undertaken the sorting and cataloguing of the collection. Completion of this work is not foreseen before 1978. Until
such time, the collection will remain closed.

*Die RUTH FISCHER PAPERS, die aus über 45 m Materialien be-
stehen, wurden der Houghton Library im Jahre 1962 aus dem
Nachlaß von Ruth Fischer überlassen. Die Sammlung wird
jetzt durch die Bibliothek sortiert und katalogisiert.
Diese Arbeit wird wohl nicht vor 1978 beendet sein; die
Sammlung bleibt dementsprechend bis dahin unzugänglich.*

Leo Baeck Institute, 129 East 73rd Street, New York, N.Y.
10021.

HELMUT HIRSCH COLLECTION, KURT GROSSMANN COLLECTION

B1,2   2 F. of correspondence between Hirsch and Ruth Fischer.

*   Materials concerning Ruth Fischer from the files of
       the Zionist Organization of America.

Hoover Institution on War, Revolution and Peace, Stanford,
California 94305.

KARL BOROMAEUS FRANK COLLECTION

B1,2   Correspondence between Ruth Fischer and Karl Frank.

D7   Attacks against Karl Frank.

New York Public Library, Manuscript Division, Fifth Avenue
and 42nd Street, New York, N.Y. 10018.

RUTH FISCHER

EMERGENCY COMMITTEE IN AID OF DISPLACED FOREIGN SCHOLARS, 1933-1945

* File compiled when assistance was granted. 1943-1945.

Mr. Hans Sahl, 800 West End Avenue, New York, N.Y. 10025.

B1   Many L. to Hans Sahl.

State University of New York at Albany, Department of Germanic Languages and Literatures, 1400 Washington Avenue, Albany, New York 12222.

HELMUT HIRSCH COLLECTION

B1   1 L. to Helmut Hirsch. 1958.

University of New Hampshire, The Library, Department of Special Collections, Durham, New Hampshire 03824.

OSKAR MARIA GRAF COLLECTION

B2   1 L. to O. M. Graf. 1934.

ERNST FRAENKEL

Political Scientist, 1898-

Leo Baeck Institute, 129 East 73rd Street, New York, N.Y.
10021.

The MARTA FRAENKEL COLLECTION (AR 4348) was donated to the
Leo Baeck Institute by Dr. Gertrud Mainzer, executrix of the
estate of Marta Fraenkel. It contains approximately equal
amounts of papers of Marta Fraenkel and her brother Ernst.

*Die MARTA FRAENKEL COLLECTION (AR 4348) ist eine Schenkung
von Dr. Gertrud Mainzer, der Nachlaßverwalterin von Marta
Fraenkel. Sie besteht zu etwa gleichen Teilen aus Materialien von Marta Fraenkel und von ihrem Bruder Ernst.*

B1   61 L. from Ernst Fraenkel to his sister, Marta. 1946-
      1947 and undated.
      6 L. 1946-1947.

B2   8 L. to Fraenkel. 1946-1973 (5 L. upon Fraenkel's 75th
      birthday).

H3   7 cl. 1967-1973.

I   Documents, including school certificates, doctoral
      degree, etc. 1915/1916-1965. 17 items.

J   Photos.

New York Public Library, Manuscript Division, Fifth Avenue
and 42nd Street, New York, N.Y. 10018.

EMERGENCY COMMITTEE IN AID OF DISPLACED FOREIGN SCHOLARS,
1933-1945

*   File compiled, no assistance given. 1941-1942.

State University of New York at Albany, Department of Germanic Languages and Literatures, 1400 Washington Avenue,
Albany, New York 12222.

HELMUT HIRSCH COLLECTION

277

B1   1 L. to Helmut Hirsch. T. 1962.

B2   1 L. from Helmut Hirsch. 1961.

Harvard University, Harvard Divinity School, Andover-Harvard
Theological Library, 45 Francis Avenue, Cambridge, Massachusetts 02138.

PAUL TILLICH COLLECTION

B1   1 L. to Paul Tillich. A. 1962.

JAMES FRANCK

Physicist, 1882-1964

University of Chicago, The Joseph Regenstein Library, 1100
East 57th Street, Chicago, Illinois 60637.

The main portion of the JAMES FRANCK PAPERS was donated to
the library by the family of Franck in 1972 and 1973. Additional materials that were donated by friends and colleagues
have been added to the main collection, including the Robert
Platzman editorial papers, which were donated by the Platzman family in 1975. A detailed inventory of the 26 boxes of
materials that comprise the collection is available on microfilm from the library: Mary Janzen, Guide to the James
Franck Papers (University of Chicago, 1975). 124p. Additional Franck correspondence is located in other collections
of the library: MAX RHEINSTEIN PAPERS, DEPARTMENT OF PHYSICS
PAPERS, EUGENE RABINOWITCH PAPERS, SAMUEL KING ALLISON PA-
PERS, PRESIDENTS PAPERS 1924-45, PAPERS OF THE ATOMIC SCIEN-
TISTS OF CHICAGO, PAPERS OF THE BULLETIN OF THE ATOMIC SCIEN-
TISTS, and the ARCHIVAL PHOTOFILES (photos). The JAMES
FRANCK COLLECTION OF SCIENTIFIC OFFPRINTS, a collection of
103 boxes of offprints that were sent to James Franck during
his lifetime, was given by Franck to Robert Platzman in the
1950s, who in turn later donated them to the University of
Chicago. The following is a short description of the JAMES
FRANCK PAPERS.

*Der größte Teil der JAMES FRANCK PAPERS ist eine Schenkung
der Familie Francks aus den Jahren 1972 und 1973. Weitere
Materialien, Geschenke von Freunden und Kollegen, sind der
Sammlung hinzugefügt worden; dazu gehören auch die Robert
Platzman editorial papers, eine Schenkung der Familie Platz-
man aus dem Jahre 1975. Ein detailliertes Inventar der 26
Kartons Materialien ist als Mikrofilm erhältlich: Mary
Janzen, Guide to the James Franck Papers (University of Chi-
cago, 1975), 124 S. Weitere Franck-Korrespondenz befindet
sich in anderen Sammlungen der Bibliothek: MAX RHEINSTEIN
PAPERS, DEPARTMENT OF PHYSICS PAPERS, EUGENE RABINOWITCH
PAPERS, SAMUEL KING ALLISON PAPERS, PRESIDENTS PAPERS 1924-
45, PAPERS OF THE ATOMIC SCIENTISTS OF CHICAGO, PAPERS OF
THE BULLETIN OF THE ATOMIC SCIENTISTS und die ARCHIVAL PHOTO-
FILES (Photokopien). Die JAMES FRANCK COLLECTION OF SCIEN-
TIFIC OFFPRINTS, eine Sammlung von 103 Kartons mit Sonder-*

drucken, die James Franck während seines Lebens erhalten hat, ist Robert Platzman in den fünfziger Jahren von James Franck überlassen worden; Platzman hat sie dann später der University of Chicago als Schenkung vermacht. Im Folgenden findet sich eine knappe Beschreibung der Materialien der JAMES FRANCK PAPERS.

B1,2   Correspondence. 1915-1964. 10 B. Includes lengthy correspondences with: Niels Bohr, Max Born, Richard Courant, Paul Ehrenfest, Albert Einstein, Philip Elkan, Hans Gaffron, Fritz Haber, Otto Hahn, Gustav Hertz, Helmut Hertz, Werner Kroebel, Walter Lochte-Holtgreven, Rudolph Ladenburg, Lise Meitner, Otto Oldenburg, Grete Paquin, Wolfgang Pauli, Max Planck, Robert Pohl, Peter Pringsheim, Eugene Rabinowitch, Gert Rathenau, Otto Stern, Edward Teller, Max von Laue, Wilhelm Westphal.
Additional L. from: Leo Baeck, Hans Baerwald, Walter A. Berendsohn, Max Bergmann, Emil Bernhard (Cohn), Curt Bondy, Antonio Borgese, Carl Cori, Eduard Heimann, Paul Hertz, Otto Klemperer, Otto Loewi, Thomas Mann, Maria Goeppert Mayer, Otto Meyerhoff, Rudolf Minkowski, Otto Neugebauer, Fritz Reiche, Hans Reichenbach, Max Rheinstein, Eugen Rosenstock-Huessy, Leo Spitzer, Herta Sponer, Gustav Stolper, Hildegard Stücklen, Leo Szilard, Arthur von Hippel, Victor Weisskopf, Hermann Weyl, Eugene P. Wigner, Otto Zoff.

B2,   James Franck, August 26, 1952. Seventieth birthday
J   book, containing L. of congratulations and photos, including: Felix Bloch, Max Born, Richard Courant, Albert Einstein, Fritz London, Maria and Joseph E. Mayer, Ulrich Middeldorf, Wolfgang Pauli, Peter Pringsheim, Otto Stern, Edward Teller, Arthur von Hippel, Victor Weisskopf, Eugene Wigner.

B3,   Selected Papers of James Franck. Editorial papers of
D8,   Robert L. Platzman. Includes correspondences of
H3,   Platzman, articles and critical essays, Franck off-
L   prints, bibliographies of Franck's works, etc. 3 B.

C8   14 notebooks containing laboratory notes, primarily by Franck. Includes notes by Gustav Hertz, Eva von Bahr, Hilde Levi. Also contains loose Ms.

Ms. and T. of articles by Franck (some co-authored by Franck), speeches, notes to articles, etc. concerning Franck's work on photosynthesis at Johns Hopkins, after 1948, etc. 4.5 B.

D7   Cl. of articles by Franck, primarily biographical in nature. 5 cl.

F   Tape recording of talk by Franck on his memories of the early history of quantum physics. Chicago, Oct. 19, 1960.
4 tapes of talks at James Franck Memorial Symposium. Chicago, May 12-13, 1966.
Tape of talk by Friedrich Hund: "Paths to Quantum Theory, Historically Viewed."

H3   Miscellaneous cl. Ca. 30 items.
Obituaries. Ca. 20 items.

I   Documents, including: birth certificates, marriage certificate, family tree, army documents, appointment papers, passports, registration papers, etc. 30 items.
Certificates. 2 F.
Diplomas. 2 F.
Doctorate degrees. 2 F.

J   58 photos of Franck, colleagues and friends, as well as photos of special occasions (Nobel Prize).
Herta Sponer's photograph album. Göttingen, 1920-1933. Includes photos of Franck, Herta Sponer, colleagues, friends. 55 photos with captions.

L   4 reports of the Samuel S. Fels Fund.
Papers of the Jeffries Committee. 8 F.
Papers of the Franck Committee, including several drafts of the "Franck Report." 11 F.
Papers of the Franck Memorial Symposium. Chicago, May 12-13, 1966.

M   Medals: Alessandro Volta medal (1927), National Academy of Sciences Centennial Medal (1963), Benjamin Count Rumford medal (1955), Max Planck medals (1951 and 1958), Nobel Prize medal (1925).

N   Ms. and T. by other scientists, including: William A. Arnold, Norman I. Bishop, G. I. Brealey, Warren Butler, Roderick K. Clayton, E. W. Fager, C. S. French,

Hans Gaffron, Lionel Goodman, M. Gouterman, Gerhard Herzberg, W. H. Jennings, D. Kearns, L. M. Kosbut- skaya, A. A. Krasnovskii, Robert Livingston, Rufus Lumry, Berger Mayne, R. A. Olson, R. H. Potterill, Jerome L. Rosenberg, Erich Schneider, Harrison Shull, J. D. Spikes, Herta Sponer, Per S. Stensby, Bernard L. Strehler, Shiro Takashima, Norbert Uri, O. J. Walker, J. Weiss, Paul Weiss, W. Wiessner.

American Institute of Physics, Niels Bohr Library, 335 East 45th Street, New York, N.Y. 10017.

Franck materials are located in the following collections: NIELS BOHR CORRESPONDENCE, S. A. GOUDSMIT COLLECTION, ALFRED LANDÉ COLLECTION, FRITZ REICHE PAPERS, PICTORIAL FILE.

B1 39 L. to Niels Bohr. 1920-1948. Microfilm.
  11 L., including L. to: S.A. Goudsmit, Alfred Landé, Fritz Reiche.

B2 34 L. from Niels Bohr. 1920-1946. Microfilm.
  1 L. ea. from S. A. Goudsmit and J. A. Wheeler.

J Photos, catalogued and sorted.

American Philosophical Society, The Library, 105 South Fifth Street, Philadelphia, Pennsylvania 19106.

MISCELLANEOUS MANUSCRIPT COLLECTION, OSWALD HOPE ROBERTSON COLLECTION, NIELS BOHR CORRESPONDENCE

B1 4 L., including L. to Kasimir Fajans.
  23 L. to Niels Bohr. 1923-1948.

B1,2 Correspondence between Oswald Hope Robertson and James Franck.

B2 14 L. from Niels Bohr. 1923-1957.

Archive for History of Quantum Physics (locations in U.S.: Bancroft Library, University of California, Berkeley; Ameri- can Philosophical Society, Philadelphia, Pennsylvania;

JAMES FRANCK

American Institute of Physics, New York, N.Y.).

B1   16 L., including L. to: S. A. Goudsmit (3), Alfred
       Landé (1), Walther Gerlach (9), E. C. Kemble (1),
       H. A. Kramers (1), Arnold Sommerfeld (1).
       18 L. to Niels Bohr. 1920-1922.

B2   20 L. from Niels Bohr. 1920-1922.
       2 L. from S. A. Goudsmit. 1927.
       1 L. from H. A. Kramers. 1924.

G   6 sessions of interviews. 1962. Transcript. 116p.

Princeton University, Firestone Library, Princeton, New Jersey 08540.

THE PAPERS OF ALBERT EINSTEIN (1879-1955). For details concerning the use of this collection, see description under Albert Einstein.

THE PAPERS OF ALBERT EINSTEIN (1879-1955). Angaben über den Zugang zu der Sammlung finden sich unter "Albert Einstein."

B1,2   Unknown amount of correspondence between James Franck
       and Albert Einstein. 1921-1952.

University of California, Berkeley, The Bancroft Library, Berkeley, California 94720.

E. O. LAWRENCE PAPERS, GILBERT N. LEWIS PAPERS

B1   12 L. (4 restricted). 1938-1944.

B1,2   4 L. concerning Franck's visit to Berkeley.

Yale University, Beinecke Rare Book and Manuscript Library, New Haven, Connecticut 06520.

HERMANN BROCH ARCHIVE

B1   1 L. to Hermann Broch. 1946.

283

B2   2 L. from Hermann Broch. 1946.

Leo Baeck Institute, 129 East 73rd Street, New York, N.Y.
10021.

B1   1 L. to A. Sommerfeld. T. 1933.

J   1 photo.

Duke University, William R. Perkins Library, Manuscript
Department, Durham, North Carolina 27706.

B1   2 L. to F. W. London. A. 1930, 1947.

B2   2 L. from F. W. London. A. 1936, 1946.

New York University, Courant Institute of Mathematical Sciences, Library, 251 Mercer Street, New York, N.Y. 10012.

B1,2   File: "Professor James Franck." 1939-1958.

H3   Obituary.

University of Illinois at Urbana-Champaign, University Library, University Archives, Room 19, Urbana, Illinois 61801.

ROGER ADAMS PAPERS

B1   1 L. to Roger Adams.

Johns Hopkins University, The Milton S. Eisenhower Library,
Baltimore, Maryland 21218.

B1   1 L. to J. H. Hollander. 1938.

Massachusetts Institute of Technology, Research Laboratory of
Electronics, Cambridge, Massachusetts 02139.

284

D7   Reprint of speech given Dec. 1945 (under the auspices
      of U.S. Rubber Co.). New York Philharmonic Symphony
      Program.

Smithsonian Institution, Dibner Library, Washington, D.C.
20560.

C8   "Photosynthesis." 1946.

California Institute of Technology, Robert A. Millikan Library, Pasadena, California 91109.

THEODORE VON KARMAN CORRESPONDENCE and general archive files

B1,2 Correspondence with Theodore von Karman. 1922-1948. 1 F.
      Individual items in 1 folder, dated 1933.

University of California San Diego, Mandeville Library,
Department of Special Collections, La Jolla, California 92037.

MARIA GOEPPERT MAYER COLLECTION

H3   5 articles on Franck; 1 includes bibliography.

New York Public Library, Manuscript Division, Fifth Avenue
and 42nd Street, New York, N.Y. 10018.

EMERGENCY COMMITTEE IN AID OF DISPLACED FOREIGN SCHOLARS,
1933-1945

*   File compiled when assistance was granted. 1934-1944.

Dr. Friedrich Kessler, Boalt Hall, School of Law, University
of California, Berkeley, California 94720.

Private personal collection.

B1,2 Correspondence between Kessler and James Franck.

<u>Mrs. Alice Loewy Kahler</u>, 1 Evelyn Place, Princeton, New Jersey 08540.

ERICH VON KAHLER COLLECTION

B1   1 L. to Erich von Kahler. 1956.

BRUNO FRANK
Writer, 1887-1945

Library of Congress, Manuscript Division, Independence Avenue and First Street S.E., Washington, D.C. 20540.

BENJAMIN W. HUEBSCH PAPERS

B1   3 L. to Benjamin W. Huebsch (one signed also by T. Mann, E. M. Remarque, F. Werfel, L. Feuchtwanger, M. Horkheimer). 1940-1943.

B2   2 L. from Benjamin Huebsch. T.c. 1940.

J   2 photos of Bruno Frank.

University of Texas, Humanities Research Center, Manuscripts Collection, Box 7219, Austin, Texas 78712.

A. A. KNOPF ARCHIVE

B1   5 L.

B2   7 L.

C   1 Ms.

Viking Press, Inc., 625 Madison Avenue, New York, N.Y. 10021.

H4   Reviews of works by Bruno Frank that were published by Viking.

Yale University, Beinecke Rare Book and Manuscript Library, New Haven, Connecticut 06520.

KURT WOLFF ARCHIVE

B1   4 L. to Kurt Wolff Verlag. 1913.

B2   1 L. from Kurt Wolff Verlag. 1913.

University of New Hampshire, The Library, Department of Special Collections, Durham, New Hampshire 03824.

BRUNO FRANK

OSKAR MARIA GRAF COLLECTION

B1   10 L. to Oskar Maria Graf. 1933-1942.

B2   3 L. from O. M. Graf. 1933, 1942.

Leo Baeck Institute, 129 East 73rd Street, New York, N.Y. 10021.

LEOPOLD SCHWARZSCHILD COLLECTION and general archive files

B1   L. to [Kurt] Korff. A. 1924.

B1,2 Correspondence with Leopold Schwarzschild. 1940-1941.

J   6 photos of Frank. 1904-1934 and undated.

Mr. Francis Heilbut, 328 West 96th Street, New York, N.Y. 10025.

IVAN HEILBUT PAPERS

B2   7 L. from Ivan Heilbut.

Southern Illinois University, Morris Library, Department of Special Collections, Carbondale, Illinois 62901.

ERWIN PISCATOR PAPERS

B1   3 L. to Erwin Piscator. A. 1940-1941.

B2   1 L. from Erwin Piscator. T.c. 1941.

Mr. Hans Sahl, 800 West End Avenue, New York, N.Y. 10025.

B1   Many L. from B. Frank to Hans Sahl.

University of Southern California, Lion Feuchtwanger Memorial Library, 520 Paseo Miramar, Pacific Palisades, California 90272.·

288

BRUNO FRANK

B1   1 L. to Feuchtwanger.
B2   1 L. from Feuchtwanger.

University of Southern California, University Library, Department of Special Collections, University Park, Los Angeles, California 90007.

WILLIAM DIETERLE COLLECTION

C5   The Hunchback of Notre Dame. 2 synopses.

Dr. Harold von Hofe, Department of German, University of Southern California, Los Angeles, California 90007.

LUDWIG MARCUSE PAPERS

B1   1 L. to Ludwig Marcuse. 1944.
      1 L. to Sascha Marcuse. 1942.

University of Pennsylvania, The Charles Patterson Van Pelt Library, Philadelphia, Pennsylvania 19104.

ALMA MAHLER-WERFEL COLLECTION

B1   2 L. and 1 Tel. to Franz Werfel. A. 1940-1945.

Indiana University, The University Libraries, The Lilly Library, Bloomington, Indiana 47401.

LEWIS BROWNE MSS., UPTON BEALL SINCLAIR MSS.

B1   1 L. ea. to Lewis Browne and Upton Sinclair (signed also by L. Feuchtwanger, M. Horkheimer, T. Mann, E. M. Remarque, F. Werfel).

B3   1 L. from T. Mann to Lewis Browne.

Yale University Library, Manuscripts and Archives Research
Room, 150 Sterling Memorial Library, New Haven, Connecticut
06520.

DECISION: A REVIEW OF FREE CULTURE. CORRESPONDENCE AND PAPERS
OF KLAUS MANN

B1   1 L. to Klaus Mann. 1941.

Columbia University, Butler Library, New York, N.Y. 10027.

B1   1 L. to Bernardine Kielty Scherman. A. 1944.

Dr. Friedrich Hacker, The Hacker Clinic, 160 Lasky Drive,
Beverly Hills, California 90212.

B1,2 Correspondence between Hacker and Bruno and Liesl
        Frank.

Barthold Fles Literary Agency, 507 Fifth Avenue, New York,
N.Y. 10016.

B1   2 L. to Barthold Fles. 1945.

Mrs. Lotte Lenya Weill-Detwiler, 404 East 55th Street, New
York 10022.

B1   Correspondence with Kurt Weill.

Mrs. Peter M. Lindt, 949 West End Avenue, New York, N.Y.
10025.

B1   Small amount of correspondence with Peter M. Lindt.

C   Ms. submitted to Lindt for use on his radio program.

KARL FRANK (PAUL HAGEN)
Writer, 1893-1969

Hoover Institution on War, Revolution and Peace, Stanford,
California 94305.

KARL BOROMAEUS FRANK COLLECTION: 10 archive boxes of materials. Information is based on a 5-page inventory of the
collection available from the Hoover Institution.

*KARL BOROMAEUS FRANK COLLECTION: 10 Archivkartons Materia-
lien. Die Informationen darüber beruhen auf einem fünfseiti-
gen Inventarverzeichnis der Sammlung, die von der Hoover
Institution erhältlich ist.*

A3   Autobiographical notes and project notes, Office of
        Strategic Services.

B1,2   Correspondence, 1939-1958, including L. to and from:
        Fritz Erler, Willy Brandt, Carl Zuckmayer, Thomas
        Mann, Hans E. Hirschfeld, Hans Gerth, Albert
        Grezesinski, Arkadij Gurland, Ruth Fischer. 2
        archive B.

B2   Statements and L. from Hagen defenders. 1937, 1940-
        1941, 1961.

C7   Manuscripts of books and articles. 1939-1945. 1 archive
        B.
        "What Not to Do with Germany; a Critical Review of Our
        Present Peace Plans."
        Speaker's engagements. 1939-1942.
        Lectures. 1943-1944.
        Speeches. 1944.
        Lectures. 1945.
        Lectures on "Political Irrationality." 1958-1960.
        "Germany after Hitler." Ms. 1944. Also reviews.
        "Will Germany Crack?" 1942. Also reviews.

D7   Printed articles.

H3   Attacks on Karl Frank in newspapers, by Günther Rein-
        hardt, Walter Winchell and Ruth Fischer.
        Investigation of Paul Hagen. 1940.

H4   Reviews.

I   Department of Justice. Foreign Agents Registration

Section.
The trip to Germany.
Visa question and congressional action (lecture trip
   to Canada).
Immigration and Naturalization Service (trip to Europe).
Selected credentials.
Applications for teaching position in social psychol-
   ogy. 1946-1947.

L   Two courses taught by Frank at Knox College, Galesburg,
   Illinois, 1945.
Materials (cl.) for further studies:
   "Psychological Interpretations of History."
   "The Archaic: 1. West, 2. East."
   "German Psychology."
Newspaper cl. on topics for lecture talks.
Society for the Prevention of World War III, Inc., New
   York. Materials.
"Neu beginnen" materials.
Writers' War Board materials.
Formation of a Council for a Democratic Germany, in-
   cluding L. to and from: Th. Mann, Louis Lochner.
Voice of Freedom. Issues, 1941-1942.
American Association for a Democratic Germany. Mate-
   rials.
Pamphlets and other materials on post-war Germany.

N   Klein, Lt. Col. Julius. "A plan to make contact with
   the German underground movement."

University of Minnesota, University Libraries, Social Welfare History Archives, Minneapolis, Minnesota 55455.

SURVEY ASSOCIATES PAPERS, PAUL U. KELLOGG PAPERS

B   60 L. from, to and concerning Frank.

C7   3 Ms.

I   4 documents, 1940-1949.

State University of New York at Albany, Department of Germanic Languages and Literatures, 1400 Washington Avenue,

KARL FRANK (PAUL HAGEN)

Albany, New York 12222.

HELMUT HIRSCH COLLECTION, KARL O. PAETEL COLLECTION

B1   2 L. to Helmut Hirsch. 1946-1947.

B2   1 L. from Karl O. Paetel (xerox). 1963.

C7   "Deutschland nach Hitler. Um die Vollendung der demo-
      kratischen Revolution." Mimeo. 54p.

H3   "Zur Abwehr der Angriffe gegen Paul Hagen / Replies to
      the Attacks on Paul Hagen." Pamphlet. xv, 16p.
      Bilingual edition.

Prof. Joseph Buttinger, R.R. 1, Box 264, Pennington, New
Jersey 08534.

B1,2 Extensive correspondence with Joseph Buttinger.

LEONHARD FRANK

Writer, 1882-1961

Yale University, Beinecke Rare Book and Manuscript Library, New Haven, Connecticut 06520.

KURT WOLFF ARCHIVE, EDMOND PAUKER COLLECTION

B1   2 L. to the Kurt Wolff Verlag. 1912-1917.

B2   1 L. from the Kurt Wolff Verlag.

I   Contract for Die Ursache.

New York Public Library at Lincoln Center, Library and Museum of the Performing Arts, 111 Amsterdam Avenue, New York, N.Y. 10023.

EDMOND PAUKER COLLECTION

C2   Hufnägel. Mimeo. copy. Production rights: Felix Bloch
      Erben.

Academy of Motion Picture Arts and Sciences, Margaret Herrick Library, 9038 Melrose Avenue, Hollywood, California 90069.

C5   Homecoming. Film script. 1928. Usage restricted.

University of New Hampshire, The Library, Department of Special Collections, Durham, New Hampshire 03824.

OSKAR MARIA GRAF COLLECTION

B1   2 L. to Oskar Maria Graf. 1952-1953.

University of Texas, Humanities Research Center, Manuscripts Collection, Box 7219, Austin, Texas 78712.

B1   1 L.

B2   1 L.

LEONHARD FRANK

<u>Leo Baeck Institute</u>, 129 East 73rd Street, New York, N.Y. 10021.

KURT KERSTEN COLLECTION

B1   1 L. to Kurt Kersten. 1956.

<u>Dr. Friedrich Hacker</u>, The Hacker Clinic, 160 Lasky Drive, Beverly Hills, California 90212.

B1,2 Correspondence between Hacker and Leonhard Frank.

<u>Mrs. Liselotte Stein</u>, 115-25 Metropolitan Avenue, Kew Gardens, New York 11418.

FRED STEIN PAPERS

J   Photos of Leonhard Frank.

PAUL FRANK

Writer, 1885-

New York Public Library at Lincoln Center, Library and
Museum of the Performing Arts, 111 Amsterdam Avenue, New
York, N.Y. 10023.

EDMOND PAUKER COLLECTION

C2 Die Attraktion. 81p.
  Elegante Welt. 106p.
  Ein Herr zu viel. 87p.
  Der Mantel. 18p.
  Zehn Millionen Dollar. 86p.
  Written in collaboration with Hans Adler:
   The Golden Letter. 188p.
   Journey to Sorrento/The Trip to Sorrento. 249p.
   The Lady in White. 143p.
   Premiere. 207p.
   Wir werden beobachtet. 128p.
  Written in collaboration with Georg Bittner:
   Magic Fire. 116p.
  Written in collaboration with Julius Bittner:
   Im Namen des Kaisers. 169p.
  Written in collaboration with Ladislaus Fodor:
   Poor Little Church Mouse. 112p.
  Written in collaboration with Georg Fraser:
   And Such Men Are Called Heroes. 112p.
  Written in collaboration with Siegfried Geyer:
   Die Baronin. 86p.
   Monsieur Helene. 63p.
  Written in collaboration with László Gorog:
   White Cyclamens. 101p.
  Written in collaboration with Ludwig Hirschfeld:
   Geschäft mit Amerika/Business with America. 3p.
   Das Mädchen aus der Fremde. 122p.

C5 Refugees/Flüchtlinge. Synopsis of a film, written with
  Felix Basch. 26p.

Yale University, Beinecke Rare Book and Manuscript Library,
New Haven, Connecticut 06520.

EDMOND PAUKER COLLECTION

PAUL FRANK

I   Contracts between Paul Frank and Edmond Pauker:
     Fahrt nach Sorrent.
     Geschäft mit Amerika.
     Der goldene Leiter.
     Premiere.

Mrs. Elisabeth M. Stoerk and Mrs. Susanne B. Hoeller, 288
Ocean Drive West, Stamford, Connecticut 06902.

FRIDERIKE ZWEIG ARCHIVE

B1   1 L. to Friderike Zweig. 1947.
     Additional L. to Friderike Zweig in file under "Writers
        Service Center." 1944.

H5   Materials in folder marked "Lives and Outlines."

Mr. Gerard W. Speyer, 117 Overlook Road, Hastings-on-Hudson,
New York 10706.

C4   "Melody of Life." Original story by Wilhelm Speyer and
     Paul Frank. Undated. T. 26p.

Prof. Harry Zohn, Department of German and Slavic Languages
and Literatures, Brandeis University, Waltham, Massachusetts
02154.

B1   2 L. to Friderike Zweig. 1944.

PHILIPP G. FRANK

Physicist, Philosopher, 1884-1962

Harvard University, University Archives, Widener Library, Cambridge, Massachusetts 02138.

The following materials were donated by Mr. Stan Fraydas (nephew of Philipp Frank) in 1975 (1 B.).

Die folgenden Materialien sind eine Schenkung von Mr. Stan Fraydas, dem Neffen von Philipp Frank, aus dem Jahre 1975 (1 Karton).

B1,2   "Exchange with Melania Serbu." 1960.
        "Correspondence about lectures and meetings." 1960.
        "Unanswered letters." 1960.
        Correspondence between Philipp Frank and wife. 1952.

C8   Ms. of writings by Frank, including some unpub. items.

J   Photos, including several unidentified photos.

RICHARD VON MISES COLLECTION

B1   Ca. 15 L. to Richard von Mises. T. 1939-1952.

B2   3 L. from Richard von Mises. T.c. 1939-1951.

Mr. Stan Fraydas, 34 East Stanton Avenue, Baldwin, New York 11510.

K   Small collection of books from the personal library of
        Philipp Frank, including:
        Books written by Frank, including one co-authored
        with Richard von Mises.
        Pamphlets about Frank.
        One volume of Boston Studies in Philosophy of Science
        published in honor of Frank.

California Institute of Technology, Robert A. Millikan Library, Pasadena, California 91109.

THEODORE VON KARMAN CORRESPONDENCE and general archive files

B1,2   Correspondence with Theodore von Karman. 1922-1943.
         1 F.
       Individual item(s) in folder, dated 1940.

United States Army Missile Command, Headquarters, Redstone
Scientific Information Center, Redstone Arsenal, Alabama
35809.

C8   "Vorschlag einer einfachen Methode zum Ausschalten von
       Querbeschleunigung." June 1944. 9p.

American Philosophical Society, The Library, 105 South Fifth
Street, Philadelphia, Pennsylvania 19106.

WARREN STURGIS MCCULLOCH PAPERS

B1,2   Correspondence with Warren Sturgis McCulloch.

Archive for History of Quantum Physics (locations in U.S.:
Bancroft Library, University of California, Berkeley; American Philosophical Society, Philadelphia, Pennsylvania; American Institute of Physics, New York, N.Y.).

G   Transcript of interview. 1962. 16p.

University of California, Los Angeles, Department of Special
Collections, 120 Lawrence Clark Powell Library, Los Angeles,
California 90024.

THE CARNAP PAPERS

D7   "The Pragmatic Components in Carnap's 'Eliminations of
       Metaphysics'." 2nd galley proofs of article for
       Schilpp-volume: The Philosophy of Rudolf Carnap.

New York University, Courant Institute of Mathematical Sciences, Library, 251 Mercer Street, New York, N.Y. 10012.

PHILIPP G. FRANK

B1,2 [Faculty] file: "Philipp Frank." 1937-1939.

Harvard University, Houghton Library, Cambridge, Massachusetts 02138.

GEORGE SARTON PAPERS

B1   1 L. to George Sarton. 1941.

Mrs. Gertrude Urzidil, 83-39 116th Street, Richmond Hill,
New York 11418.

JOHANNES URZIDIL COLLECTION

B1   1 L. to Johannes Urzidil. 1958.

Library of Congress, Manuscript Division, Independence Avenue
and First Street S.E., Washington, D.C. 20540.

OSWALD VEBLEN COLLECTION

B3   1 L. concerning Frank in Veblen's "Refugee File." 1939.

American Institute of Physics, Niels Bohr Library, 335 East
45th Street, New York, N.Y. 10017.

PICTORIAL FILE (uncatalogued)

J   Photos in photo file.

New York Public Library, Manuscript Division, Fifth Avenue
and 42nd Street, New York, N.Y. 10018.

EMERGENCY COMMITTEE IN AID OF DISPLACED FOREIGN SCHOLARS,
1933-1945

*   File compiled when assistance was granted. 1936-1943.

PHILIPP G. FRANK

Princeton University, Firestone Library, Princeton, New Jersey 08540.

THE PAPERS OF ALBERT EINSTEIN (1879-1955). For details concerning the use of this collection, see description under Albert Einstein.

THE PAPERS OF ALBERT EINSTEIN (1879-1955). Angaben über den Zugang zu der Sammlung finden sich unter "Albert Einstein."

B1,2   Unknown amount of correspondence between Einstein and Philipp Frank. 1919-1949.

KURT OTTO FRIEDRICHS

Mathematician, 1901-

Prof. Kurt Otto Friedrichs, c/o New York University, Courant
Institute of Mathematical Sciences, 251 Mercer Street, New
York, N.Y. 10012.

Private collection: inaccessible. / *Unzugängliche Privatsammlung.*

B1,2   Several L. from Friedrich's time at the Institute,
       preserved mostly out of personal interest.

C7   Several Ms.
       Lecture Ms. and course materials, often mimeo.

D7   Offprints, cl. of all pub. articles by Friedrichs.

G   Interview of Friedrichs by Ms. Constance Reid concern-
       ing Richard Courant.

I   Documents concerning Friedrichs' career, employment.

J   Photos.

L   Offprints and cl. of articles by others.

New York University, Courant Institute of Mathematical Sciences, Library, 251 Mercer Street, New York, N.Y. 10012.

B1,2   File "K. O. Friedrichs." 1955-1961.

Harvard University, University Archives, Widener Library,
Cambridge, Massachusetts 02138.

RICHARD VON MISES COLLECTION

B1   1 L. to Richard von Mises. T. 1943.

B2   1 L. from Richard von Mises. T.cc. 1943.

American Philosophical Society, The Library, 105 South Fifth
Street, Philadelphia, Pennsylvania 19106.

L. C. DUNN PAPERS

Bl,2   Correspondence with L. C. Dunn in file marked "Emer-
          gency Committee in Aid of Displaced German Scholars."

California Institute of Technology, Robert A. Millikan Library, Pasadena, California 91109.

THEODORE VON KARMAN CORRESPONDENCE

Bl,2   Correspondence with Theodore von Karman. 1927-1962.
          1 F.

New York Public Library, Manuscript Division, Fifth Avenue
and 42nd Street, New York, N.Y. 10018.

EMERGENCY COMMITTEE IN AID OF DISPLACED FOREIGN SCHOLARS,
1933-1945.

*   File compiled when assistance was granted. 1937-1944.

GEORGE FROESCHEL

Screen Writer, 1891-

.

Dr. George Froeschel, 1146 San Ysidro, Beverly Hills, California 90210.

Private personal collection: inaccessible at present. According to the wishes of Froeschel, all his possessions, including his house, land, furniture and archive, will be willed to Brandeis University, Waltham, Massachusetts. The cataloguing of the archive is to begin in the course of the next few years.

Im Moment noch unzugängliche Privatsammlung. Dem Wunsche George Froeschels entsprechend, sollen all seine Besitztümer (Haus, Grund und Boden, Mobiliar, Archiv) nach seinem Tode der Brandeis University, Waltham, Massachusetts, zukommen. Die Katalogisierung des Archivs soll im Laufe der nächsten Jahre beginnen.

A2   Notebooks.

B1,2   Correspondence over many years, including L. to and from Vicki Baum.

C1   Complete collection of Ms. of all of Froeschel's novels.

C2   Ms. of dramatic works, including:
       One Big Family. 1940. Never produced. T. 99p.
       Der Tapferste der Tapferen. "Typoskript für Bühnen."
         Wien: Rausch, 1961. Also earlier version with many
         h. corr.
       Wann wurde die letzte Hexe verbrannt? Bound Ms. 1955-
         1956. Never produced.

C4   Complete collection of Ms. of short stories.

C5   Complete collection of all film scripts.

C7   Complete collection of prose writings, from age 18 to present.

D4,7   Collection of newspaper and magazine cl. of Froeschel's writings.

H4   Reviews of films, mostly cl.

I   Contracts and other documents.

J   Photographs, including photos from his films.

K   5,000-volume library, including many foreign-language
      editions of Froeschel's works.

O   Programs from film showings.

University of Southern California, Lion Feuchtwanger Memorial
Library, 520 Paseo Miramar, Pacific Palisades, California
90272.

B1   2 L. to Lion Feuchtwanger. Undated.

B2   2 L. from Lion Feuchtwanger. Undated.

BELLA FROMM

Journalist, 1900-1971

<u>Boston University</u>, Mugar Memorial Library, 771 Commonwealth Avenue, Boston, Massachusetts 02215.

The BELLA FROMM COLLECTION (Collection 531) is contained in 64 manuscript boxes, 15 of which were catalogued in May 1976. The major portion of the collection (catalogued prior to 1976) was donated to the library by Ms. Fromm before her death; the remaining materials were received by the library from the estate of Bella Fromm. A detailed inventory of the entire collection is available from the Mugar Memorial Library.

Die BELLA FROMM COLLECTION (Collection 531) ist in 64 Manuskriptkartons aufbewahrt, von denen 15 im Mai 1976 katalogisiert wurden. Der Hauptteil der Sammlung (schon vor 1976 katalogisiert) ist eine Schenkung von Frau Fromm persönlich an die Bibliothek. Die übrigen Materialien stammen aus dem Nachlaß von Bella Fromm. Ein detailliertes Verzeichnis der vollständigen Sammlung ist von der Mugar Memorial Library erhältlich.

A1   Diaries. 1922-1937. A. and T. Ca. 40p.
       Diaries. 1917-1932. T. with h. corr. Ca. 125p., including several L., photos, cl., invitations.
       Diary. 1933. A., T. and cc. with h. corr. Ca. 150p.
       Diaries. 1934-1935. A., T. and cc. with h. corr. Ca. 200p.
       Diaries. 1936-1938. A., T. and cc. with h. corr. Ca. 200p.
       Diaries. 1938-1940. A., T. and cc. with h. corr. Ca. 200p.
       Diary. 1947. A., T. and cc. with h. corr. Ca. 200p.
       Diaries from the 1940s, 1950s and 1960s. A., T. and cc. with h. corr. Ca. 100p.

A3   Curriculum vitae. Several versions, drafts. T. with h. corr. A. and cc. Ca. 30p.

B1,2 Correspondence 1930-1939, primarily business interactions between Bella Fromm and her publishers.
      Correspondence 1939-1970, including L. to and from: Marian Anderson, Willy Brandt, Pearl S. Buck, Ralph

J. Bunche, Nicholas Murray Butler, John Chafee,
Erich Fromm, Manfred George, Albert Grzesinski,
Hans Habe, Averell Harriman, Konrad Heiden, J. Edgar
Hoover, Jacob Javits, Rudolf Katz, Helen Keller,
Robert Kempner, Robert Kennedy, Alfred C. Kinsey,
Louis P. Lochner, James H. Meisel, George S. Messer-
smith, Carl Misch, Edward R. Murrow, Pastor Martin
Niemoeller, Otto Rank, Nelson Rockefeller, Eleanor
Roosevelt, Gerhart Seger, Anna Seghers, Sigrid
Schultz, William Shirer, Hans Simons, Cardinal
Spellman, Leopold Stokowski, G. R. Treviranus, von
Hindenburg, Robert Wagner, Bruno Weil, Sumner Welles.
Publishers' correspondence. Ca. 95 L.
Lecture correspondence. Ca. 60 L.

B3   26 L., including L. from: Leo Baeck, Louis Lochner,
George Messersmith, J. Edgar Hoover, Dorothy Thomp-
son. 1933-1952.
Pc. of L. from Goebbels to General Blomberg, exempting
Bella Fromm from the Aryan laws and allowing her to
continue work.

C1   Blood and Banquets. Ms.
Die Engel weinen. Ms.

C7   Articles written by Bella Fromm in America for German
readers.
Essays and articles on various topics. 1930s-1960s. T.
and cc. with h. corr. Ca. 500p.
Trip to Germany. 1954-1955. Notes. A. Ca. 125p. Also
ca. 100 cl.
Unfinished articles and notes on articles. A., T. and
cc. 1930s-1960s. Ca. 300p.
Lecture notes from the 1940s and 1950s. T. with h.
corr. Ca. 300 3" x 5" cards.

D7   1 archive carton of newspaper and magazine cl., including cl. from B-Z am Montag, Berliner Morgenpost,
Wochenend, etc.
Excerpts from Blood and Banquets in Harper's.
Germany articles. Ca. 50 cl.
Niemoeller articles. 16 cl.
7 scrapbooks of newspaper cl. 1929-1933. Ca. 100p. ea.
2 scrapbooks of newspaper cl. 1933-1936. Ca. 100p. ea.
6 cl. from PM, Redbook, True Detective.

F   Records:
     Interview with Bella Fromm by Dick Osgood. WXYZ,
        Detroit, Nov. 30, 1944.
     "The Master Race." Oct. 1944.

G   Radio interview in England. Undated. T.cc. 3p.

H4   Blood and Banquets. 2 scrapbooks of reviews, etc. Also
     another scrapbook with cl. and publicity materials,
     1942-1957.
     6 advertisements for Blood and Banquets.

I   Blood and Banquets. Contract with Harper & Bros., May
     29, 1942.
     German Society of New York. Membership card. 1959.
     5 documents and several L. re: confiscation by the
     Nazis of Bella Fromm's private property; efforts to
     obtain work permit in Germany after 1933; efforts to
     obtain travel permit in 1938.
     Warrant for Bella Fromm from the Reichsschrifttums-
     kammer for literary activities. April 27, 1937.
     Dr. Peter Wolfheim. Documents from the 1930s.

J   19 photos of Bella Fromm. 1940s.
     1 photo of Sybille von Kies.
     4 photos of George Messersmith.

L   "Abschrift (der) Besprechung des Regierungspräsidenten
     in Ansbach mit dem ihm unterstellten Behörden in
     Ansbach am 30.7.45." 12p.
     American and German women of the 1940s and 1950s. 2
      archive B.
     Antisemitism in Germany. 5 items.
     "Berliner Gesellschaft der dreißiger Jahren." Scrap-
     book of cl.
     German and American youth and schools of the 1940s and
     1950s. 2 B.
     German officials from prewar and Nazi times. 2 B.
     Lists of Nazi officials of the 1930s. Ca. 10 items.
     Miscellaneous materials. 16 B., 1 F. and ca. 50 loose
     items.
     "Vorträge und Anerkennungen." Scrapbook of cl., post-
     war lectures.

M   "Adressen- und Fernsprech-Verzeichnis für die Redak-
     tion der Tageszeitung." Ullstein Verlag, Oct. 1932.

Autograph book. 1944-1946. Ca. 50p.
Berlin telephone book. 1948.
Verein der Ausländischen Presse zu Berlin. Membership
    book. 1934.
Overseas Press Club. 2 menus.

N   Lecture text by Walther Leisler Kiep.

O   Programs and social invitations from 1920s-1960s. Ca.
        400 items.

<u>Mrs. Elisabeth M. Stoerk and Mrs. Susanne B. Hoeller</u>, 288
Ocean Drive West, Stamford, Connecticut 06902.

FRIDERIKE ZWEIG ARCHIVE

B1   6 L. to Friderike Zweig. 1948.

C1   <u>Die Engel weinen, oder Aus meinen großen Schmerzen</u>
      <u>macht ich ein kleines Lied, oder Nicht mit den Händen</u>
      <u>halten, im Herzen bewahren</u>. T. 226p.

<u>Columbia University</u>, Butler Library, New York, N.Y. 10027.

NICHOLAS MURRAY BUTLER PAPERS

B1   13 L. to N. M. Butler. 1944-1946. Also several cl.

B2   14 L. from N. M. Butler. 1944-1946. Also several cl.

<u>State University of New York at Albany</u>, Department of Ger-
manic Languages and Literatures, 1400 Washington Avenue,
Albany, New York 12222.

KARL O. PAETEL COLLECTION, STORM PUBLISHERS ARCHIVE

B1   3 L. to Karl O. Paetel (xerox). 1956-1959.
      2 L. to Alexander Gode von Aesch. 1950.

ERICH FROMM

Psychoanalyst, Writer, 1900-

New York Public Library, Manuscript Division, Fifth Avenue
and 42nd Street, New York, N.Y. 10018.

The ERICH FROMM PAPERS (57M26), which consist of approxi-
materly 9 archive cartons of materials, were received by the
New York Public Library in 1957. The collection is restricted
until 1987.

*1957 hat die New York Public Library die ERICH FROMM PAPERS
(57M26), etwa 9 Archivkartons Material, erhalten. Die Sammlung ist bis 1987 nur beschränkt zugänglich.*

B1,2   Correspondence. 1932-1943. Ca. 1 1/2 B., including L.
        to and from: Max Horkheimer, Paul Lazarsfeld, Wil-
        helm Reich, Raymond de Saussure, Karl A. Wittfogel,
        Otto Fenichel.

C2   Scenario of an untitled drama. T.cc. 12p.

C7,8   Notes on: authoritarian character, conscience, values,
        ethics, ethnology and psychoanalysis, the family,
        Nazism, Hitler, the Sabbath, sado-masochism, miscel-
        laneous notes.
        "Anti-Semitism - Spearhead of Naziism." Undated. T. 3p.
        "Changing Concepts of Homosexuality in Psychoanalysis."
            T.cc. 10p.
        "Faith as a Character Trait." A. 11p.
        "Psychoanalysis and Society." Outline. A. 8p.
        "Psychology of Authority." Notes. A. 37p.
        "Psychotherapy and Social Psychology." A. 13p. and 8p.
        "The Self." T. 12p.
        "Sex and Character." A. 35p.
        "The Social Limitation of Psychoanalytical Therapy."
            T.cc. 53p.
        "Some Remarks Concerning the Psychoanalytic Viewpoint
            on War." T.cc. 4p and 3p.
        "What Claims Has a Refugee." A. 5p.
        "What's Wrong with the Interventionist, by an Interven-
            tionist." T.cc. 13p.
        Paper on the nature and development of psychoanalysis.
            T., p. 6-54.
        Book reviews. 1935-1937. Works by: Conrad Aiken, R. W.
            Babson, G. Britt, J. F. Brown, M. Mead, E. J. Warden,

P. T. Young.
"Proposed Project on the Study of the National Charac-
ter of the English-Speaking World." T. 8p.
The German Workers under the Weimar Republic. Chap.·1,
2, 5. T.
Escape from Freedom. Chap. 5-7, various versions. T.
and A. 162p.
"The History of the Concept of Freedom." Notes.
Man for Himself. Chap. 1-5 plus index, notes. Various
versions. T. and A.
"Zur Dynamik des jüdischen Geschichtsprogresses" [sic].
T. with corr. 1926. 14p.
"Zum Gefühl der Ohnmacht." T.cc. 34p.
"Die gesellschaftliche Bedeutung der Autorität in der
gegenwärtigen Familie." T.cc. Dated 10/16/34. 9p.
"Zur Methode und Aufgabe einer analytischen Sozial-
psychologie." T.cc. 83p.
"Notizen über den Stand der Untersuchungen über die
Familie. Ende Juni 1934."
"Zur Psychologie der Einstellung zur Autorität." T.
99p. T.cc. with h. corr. 77p.
"Zur psychologischen Struktur der Autorität." T.cc.
with corr. 73p.
"Die [----] Schöpfung." Undated. A. 64p.
"Volksgemeinschaft als Schuldgemeinschaft." T. 3p.
"Nie wieder Krieg!" T. 20p.
"Die wirtschaftsgeschichtliche Grundlage der Entwick-
lung der Familienautorität." T.cc. 133p.

D7   "Should We Hate Hitler?" 1 cl.

I   Papers relating to Fromm's lectureship at Univ. of
Frankfurt. 1929-1932.
List of students registered in course at New School for
Social Research: "Society and Psychoanalysis."
Advisory Panel on Research in Human Relations, Navy
Dept., New York, Oct. 3-4, 1946. Notes, reports,
memoranda.
Minutes of Fromm's Round Table at the Washington Meet-
ing of the F.W.A.A. T. 9p.
William Alanson White Institute of Psychiatry. Fromm's
seminar notes and bibliography.

Personal financial documents: unsorted bills, receipts, bank statements. 1936-1949.

L   Transcripts of students' compositions prepared for Fromm for unidentified study on authority.
Materials relating to the Institute for Social Research.
"Die Autorität in der Familie." T.cc. 126p.
Research material on the family including typed transcripts of replies to questionnaires from European informants.
The German Workers under the Weimar Republic. Varia. T. Also statistical tabulations of questionnaires used. T.cc.

N   Manuscripts by: E. W. Burgess, A. D. Chandler, Otto Fenichel, Max Horkheimer, Lois Barclay Murphy, Progressive Education Association, unknown author.

Duke University, William R. Perkins Library, Manuscript Department, Durham, North Carolina 27706.

SOCIALIST PARTY OF AMERICA MANUSCRIPTS

B1   16 L. primarily to Irwin Suall. 1950-1960.

B2   Ca. 18 L. to Erich Fromm. 1948-1960.

C7   "Why Join the SP-SDF?" Ca. 1960. T.
"A Proposed Socialist Manifesto." Ca. 1960. T.
"Luncheon Speech for Independent Voters for Thomas." New York, Oct. 16, 1948. T.
"Let Man Prevail. A Socialist Manifesto and Program." 1960. T.
"Draft of Platform, 1964, on Foreign Affairs."

Columbia University, Butler Library, New York, N.Y. 10027.

HARPER & ROW COLLECTION, W. W. NORTON PAPERS

B1   55 L. and 5 Tel. to Harper & Row. T. 1956-1961.
2 L. and 1 Tel. to W. W. Norton. 1946-1952.

ERICH FROMM

Library of Congress, Manuscript Division, Independence Avenue
and First Street S.E., Washington, D.C. 20540.

HELEN M. LYND PAPERS, BINGHAM R. NIEBUHR PAPERS

B1,2   Correspondence between Helen M. Lynd and Erich Fromm.
       Correspondence between Fromm and Reinhold Niebuhr.

University of Texas, Humanities Research Center, Manuscripts
Collection, Box 7129, Austin, Texas 78712.

B1   5 L.

Harvard University, Harvard Divinity School, Andover-Harvard
Theological Library, 45 Francis Avenue, Cambridge, Massachusetts 02138.

PAUL TILLICH COLLECTION

B1   2 L. to Paul Tillich. 1961, 1962.
      Condolence Tel. to Hannah Tillich. 1965.

Boston University, Mugar Memorial Library, 771 Commonwealth
Avenue, Boston, Massachusetts 02215.

ROBERT RIMMER PAPERS, J. SHERLOCK PAPERS

B1   1 L. ea. to Robert Rimmer and J. Sherlock. T. 1968,
      1964.

Prof. Andreas Aebi, Department of German, Rutgers, The State
University, Newark, New Jersey 07102.

PAPERS OF HANNAH AND OTTO FENICHEL

B1,2 Correspondence between Erich Fromm and Hannah and Otto
      Fenichel.

Mrs. Alice Loewy Kahler, 1 Evelyn Place, Princeton, New Jersey 08540.

ERICH VON KAHLER COLLECTION

B1   6 L. to Erich von Kahler. 1963–1965.

B2   1 L. from Erich von Kahler. 1965.

RENÉ FÜLÖP-MILLER
Writer, 1891-1963

Mrs. Erika Renon, 624 University Drive, Menlo Park, California 94025.

Mrs. Renon, the widow of Fülöp-Miller, retains approximately 9 ft. of materials from the estate of Fülöp-Miller in her possession. At present Mrs. Renon is using the materials to write her autobiography.

Frau Erika Renon, die Witwe von René. Fülöp-Miller, befindet sich im Besitz von etwa 1,80 m Material aus dem Nachlaß von Fülöp-Miller. Zur Zeit benutzt Frau Renon die Materialien bei der Erarbeitung ihrer Autobiographie.

A3   Autobiographical notes on childhood.

B1,2   Correspondence with publishers and literary agents. 1935-.
        Correspondence between Stefan Zweig and Fülöp-Miller.

B2   "Letters from friends and important people."

C1   Triumph over Pain. Ms.

C5   "Hollywood Movie Outlines." 1 archive B.

C7   Numerous lecture Ms.

C8   Science and Faith. 3 volumes of unpub. essays.

D7   Offprints of articles.
        Newspaper cl.

F   "The World as Metaphor." Tape of radio interview. 1957.

G   Interviews.

H4   Reviews of articles, books and criticisms of art by Fülöp-Miller.

I   Contracts for film stories and books. 25 years.

J   Photos.

L   Materials on art-related subjects.
        Russian legend texts.
        Horoscopes.

Dartmouth College, Baker Memorial Library, Hanover, New Hampshire 03755.

The RENÉ FÜLÖP-MILLER PAPERS (1 box of materials) were donated to the library by Mrs. Erika Renon.

*Die RENÉ FÜLÖP-MILLER PAPERS (1 Karton Materialien) sind eine
Schenkung von Frau Erika Renon.*

B2   1 L. from "Dick." T. Undated.

C1   Adam Ember (The Night of Time). 2 complete copies. Un-
dated. T. and T. with corr. Ca. 400p. ea.
Two Napoleons. German draft. A. Ca. 60p. English draft.
T. and 2 cc., ea. 16p.

C2   Two Napoleons. "Ein Drama in drei Akten." T. 126p.

C7   Reviews and book critiques. T. with corr. 165p.
Notes to lectures. T. Ca. 60p.
The Symbolic World of Color. Publisher's copy of a book
never released.
Lectures and essays. German and English. Ca. 300p.

C8   Science and Faith. Collection of essays. T. with h.
corr. Ca. 500p. Proofs, correspondence between Fülöp-
Miller and publisher, translator. T. and A. Ca. 40p.
Science and Poetry. Ms. of an unpub. work. T. with h.
corr. Ca. 200p.
Transactional Psychology and its implications for
Psychiatry. 1951. T. 48p.

L   Newspaper cl. of poems by Mrs. Erika Renon.

N   Poems by Erika Renon:
"Small Harvest."
"Silk and Rough Love."
"Dartmouth Poems."

Mrs. Elisabeth Stoerk and Mrs. Susanne B. Hoeller, 288 Ocean
Drive West, Stamford, Connecticut 06902.

FRIDERIKE ZWEIG ARCHIVE

B1   4 L. to Elisabeth Stoerk. 1944-1945.
34 L. to Friderike Zweig. 1941-1962. Additional L.
filed under "Writers Service Center." 1943.

B2   5 L. from Friderike Zweig. 1944-1945.

B3   3 L. to Friderike Zweig re: Fülöp-Miller. 1949, 1961, 1962.

C1   Brouillon d'une synopsis du roman en conter. A. 8p.

C7   "Credo." T. English. 8p.

D7   1 cl.

H3   6 cl.

H4   2 cl.

State University of New York at Albany, Department of Germanic Languages and Literatures, 1400 Washington Avenue, Albany, New York 12222.

STORM PUBLISHERS ARCHIVE

B1   21 L. and 1 Ptc. to Alexander Gode von Aesch. 1944-1950.
      1 L. to Patrick Mahoney. 1949.

B2   11 L. from Alexander Gode von Aesch. 1946-1948.

B3   16 L. and 3 Ptc. from Mrs. Erika Fülöp-Miller to Mr. and Mrs. Alexander Gode von Aesch. 1946-1959.
      Publishers' correspondence. 7 L. 1944-1947.

C4   "Count Koritzky. (Help Wherever You Can Without Hesitation)." T. with h. corr. 14p.

D1   The Saints That Moved the World. Introduction to the book, published as a pamphlet by Thomas Y. Crowell Company. 6 c., ea. 18p.

Syracuse University, The George Arents Research Library, Syracuse, New York 13210.

DOROTHY THOMPSON PAPERS

B1   23 L. to Dorothy Thompson. 1949-1960.

317

B2   1 L. from Dorothy Thompson. 1950.

B3   L. by Dorothy Thompson concerning Fülöp-Miller. 1949, 1950 and undated.

Library of Congress, Manuscript Division, Independence Avenue and First Street S.E., Washington, D.C. 20540.

BENJAMIN W. HUEBSCH PAPERS

B1   11 L. to B. W. Huebsch. T. and A. 1929-1955.

B2   4 L. from B. W. Huebsch. T.c. 1938-1941.

B3   5 L. from Erika and Heddy Fülöp-Miller to B. W. Huebsch. A. 1933-1963.
      2 L. from the American Committee for Emigré Scholars, Writers and Artists concerning Fülöp-Miller. 1950.

Mrs. Gertrude Urzidil, 83-39 116th Street, Richmond Hill, New York 11418.

JOHANNES URZIDIL COLLECTION

B1   7 L. to Johannes Urzidil. T. 1950-1963 and undated.

B2   1 L. from Johannes Urzidil. T.c. 1961.

University of Pennsylvania, The Charles Patterson Van Pelt Library, Philadelphia, Pennsylvania 19104.

ALMA MAHLER-WERFEL COLLECTION

A3   "Jugenderinnerung." Ms.

B1   5 L. to Alma Mahler-Werfel. 1941-1957 and undated.

Yale University, Beinecke Rare Book and Manuscript Library, New Haven, Connecticut 06520.

HERMANN BROCH ARCHIVE

RENÉ FÜLÖP-MILLER

B1   3 L. to Hermann Broch. 1944-1950.
B2   1 L. from Hermann Broch. 1944.

Leo Baeck Institute, 129 East 73rd Street, New York, N.Y. 10021.

KURT KERSTEN COLLECTION

B1   3 L. to Kurt Kersten. 1958, 1961.

Harvard University, Houghton Library, Cambridge, Massachusetts 02138.

RICHARD BEER-HOFMANN COLLECTION

B1   2 L. to Richard Beer-Hofmann. 1927, 1944.

Academy of Motion Picture Arts and Sciences, Margaret Herrick Library, 9038 Melrose Avenue, Hollywood, California 90069.

H3   Obituary.

Columbia University, Butler Library, New York, N.Y. 10027.

OSCAR JASZI COLLECTION, 1876-1968

B1,2 Many items of correspondence.

New York Public Library, Manuscript Division, Fifth Avenue and 42nd Street, New York, N.Y. 10018.

EMERGENCY COMMITTEE IN AID OF DISPLACED FOREIGN SCHOLARS, 1933-1945.

*   File compiled, no assistance given. 1943-1944.

<u>Mrs. Peter M. Lindt</u>, 949 West End Avenue, New York, N.Y. 10025.

B1   Small amount of correspondence with Peter M. Lindt.

KARL GEIRINGER

Musicologist, 1899-

Dr. Geiringer is living, as of 1977, in Santa Barbara, California where it is presumed he also has his literary papers. The project was unable to reach Dr. Geiringer because of scheduling difficulties.

Dr. Karl Geiringer hat z.Zt., 1977, seinen Wohnsitz in Santa Barbara, California, wo sich wahrscheinlich auch seine literarischen Materialien befinden. Dr. Geiringer konnte wegen Terminschwierigkeiten nicht persönlich kontaktiert werden.

University of Georgia, The University Libraries, Athens, Georgia 30601.

GUIDO ADLER PAPERS, OLIN DOWNES PAPERS

B1,2   Correspondence with Guido Adler. 2 L.
       Correspondence with Olin Downes. 24 L.

Columbia University, Butler Library, New York, N.Y. 10027.

B1   16 L. to Daniel G. Mason. T. and A. 1943-1952.

University of California, Los Angeles, Music Library, 405 Hilgard Avenue, Los Angeles, California 90024.

ERNST TOCH ARCHIVE

B1   13 L. to Ernst Toch.

New York Public Library, Manuscript Division, Fifth Avenue and 42nd Street, New York, N.Y. 10018.

EMERGENCY COMMITTEE IN AID OF DISPLACED FOREIGN SCHOLARS, 1933-1945

*   File compiled when assistance was granted. 1940-1944.

<u>Library of Congress</u>, Reference Department, Music Division, Independence Avenue and First Street S.E., Washington, D.C. 20540.

C7   "A thematic catalogue of Haydn's settings of folksongs from the British Isles." Microfilm of original.

N   Haydn, Joseph. "Notturno no. 4. Partita in F." Partial Ms. 1937.

<u>Bruno Walter Memorial Foundation</u>, c/o Miss Susie Danziger, 115 East 72nd Street, New York, N.Y. 10021.

BRUNO WALTER COLLECTION

B1,2   Correspondence with Bruno Walter.

<u>Prof. Gerhard Herz</u>, University of Louisville, School of Music, Department of Music History, Louisville, Kentucky 40208.

B1,2   Correspondence with Gerhard Herz.

<u>New School for Social Research</u>, Office of the Dean of the Graduate Faculty of Political and Social Science, 65 Fifth Avenue, New York, N.Y. 10003.

RECORDS OF THE UNIVERSITY IN EXILE, 1933-1945

B1,2   3 L. 1938.

MANFRED GEORGE

Journalist, Editor, 1893-1965

The MANFRED GEORGE ARCHIVE was purchased in 1974 by the
Deutsches Literaturarchiv, Marbach, West Germany, from Mrs.
Jeannette George, widow of Manfred. Materials in this country concerning George are primarily isolated individual
items located in larger collections of other exiles or prominent Americans.

*1974 hat das Deutsche Literaturarchiv, Marbach, West Germany,
das MANFRED GEORGE ARCHIVE von Frau Jeannette George, der
Witwe Manfred Georges, käuflich erworben. In den U.S.A.
finden sich Materialien über George in erster Linie als Einzelstücke innerhalb größerer Sammlungen anderer Exilkünstler
oder berühmter amerikanischer Persönlichkeiten.*

University of Southern California, Lion Feuchtwanger Memorial
Library, 520 Paseo Miramar, Pacific Palisades, California
90272.

B1   29 L. and 2 Tel. to Lion Feuchtwanger. 1940-1958.

B2   20 L. and 4 Tel. from Lion Feuchtwanger. 1940-1958.

Harvard University, Harvard Divinity School, Andover-Harvard
Theological Library, 45 Francis Avenue, Cambridge, Massachusetts 02138.

PAUL TILLICH COLLECTION

B1   9 L. and 1 Tel. to Paul Tillich. T. 1955-1965.

B2   5 L. from Paul Tillich. T.c. 1955-1965.

Leo Baeck Institute, 129 East 73rd Street, New York, N.Y.
10021.

JACOB PICARD COLLECTION, KURT GROSSMANN COLLECTION and
general archive files

A3   Curriculum vitae. T. Undated. 1p.

MANFRED GEORGE

B1   1 L. to Georg and Edith Tietz. A. 1959.
      1 L. to Jacob Picard.

B2   1 L. from Johannes Urzidil. T. 1955.

H3   Collection of biographical materials on Manfred George
      assembled by Kurt Grossmann.

J   5 photos of George. Undated.

Mrs. Gertrude Urzidil, 83-39 116th Street, Richmond Hill,
New York 11418.

JOHANNES URZIDIL COLLECTION

B1   3 L. to Johannes Urzidil. T. 1962-1965.

Harvard University, Houghton Library, Cambridge, Massachusetts 02138.

RICHARD BEER-HOFMANN COLLECTION, LEO LOWENTHAL COLLECTION

B1   2 L. to Richard Beer-Hofmann. 1944-1945.
      1 L. to Max Horkheimer. 1952. Pc.

Mr. Hans Sahl, 800 West End Avenue, New York, N.Y. 10025.

B1   Several L. to Sahl.

American Philosophical Society, The Library, 105 South Fifth
Street, Philadelphia, Pennsylvania 19106.

FRANZ BOAS PAPERS

B1   1 L. to Franz Boas. 1938.

B2   1 L. from Franz Boas. 1938.

State University of New York at Albany, Department of Germanic Languages and Literatures, 1400 Washington Avenue,

MANFRED GEORGE

Albany, New York 12222.

The MANFRED GEORGE COLLECTION is primarily a photocopy collection of clippings by George, assembled from scrapbooks
housed at the Aufbau office, 2121 Broadway, New York, N.Y.
10023.

*Die MANFRED GEORGE COLLECTION ist in wesentlichen eine Samm-
lung von Photokopien der Zeitungsausschnitte von George,
zusammengestellt nach Sammelmappen, die sich im Aufbau-Büro
(2121 Broadway, New York, N.Y. 10023) befinden.*

D7   6 notebooks containing xerox c. and cl. of articles
      by Manfred George. 1940-1965. Ca. 2,000p.

F   3 tapes of lectures by George (reproduced from records
      in the possession of the George family).

L   German American Writers Association (GAWA). Cl. and
      other materials assembled by Manfred George. Ca.
      150p.

HELMUT HIRSCH COLLECTION, STORM PUBLISHERS ARCHIVE, KARL
O. PAETEL COLLECTION

B1   52 L. to Karl O. Paetel (xerox). 1943-1957, 1960-1965.
      1 L. to Helmut Hirsch. 1964.

B2   2 L. from Alexander Gode von Aesch. 1948-1949.
      6 L. from Karl O. Paetel (xerox). 1960-1963.

Mr. Francis Heilbut, 328 West 96th Street, New York, N.Y.
10025.

IVAN HEILBUT PAPERS

B2   2 L. from Ivan Heilbut. 1942.

Library of Congress, Manuscript Division, Independence Avenue
and First Street S.E., Washington, D.C. 20540.

BENJAMIN W. HUEBSCH PAPERS

MANFRED GEORGE

B1   1 L. to B. W. Huebsch. 1944.

B2   1 L. from B. W. Huebsch. 1944.

Boston University, Mugar Memorial Library, 771 Commonwealth
Avenue, Boston, Massachusetts 02215.

BELLA FROMM COLLECTION

B1   1 L. to B. Fromm. T. 1942.

Dr. Gustave O. Arlt, 13220-C Admiralty Way, Marina del Rey,
California 90291.

FRANZ WERFEL ARCHIVE

B1   1 L. to Franz Werfel. 1940.

University of Pennsylvania, The Charles Patterson Van Pelt
Library, Philadelphia, Pennsylvania 19104.

ALMA MAHLER-WERFEL COLLECTION

B1   1 L. to Alma Mahler-Werfel. T. 1947.
      2 L. and 1 Tel. to Franz Werfel. 1942-1943.

B2   2 L. from Franz Werfel. T.c. 1942-1943.

Mrs. Peter M. Lindt, 949 West End Avenue, New York, N.Y.
10025.

B1   Small amount of correspondence with Peter M. Lindt.

CURT GLASER

Art Critic, 1879-1943

Leo Baeck Institute, 129 East 73rd Street, New York, N.Y.
10021.

The materials (AR 1240) located at the Leo Baeck Institute
were donated by Dr. Ernst Asch in 1961 and 1965.

*Die Materialien im Leo Baeck Institute sind eine Schenkung
von Dr. Ernst Asch aus den Jahren 1961 und 1965.*

A3   Curriculum vitae. T. Undated. 2p.

B2   2 L. from Adolf Goldschmidt and Heinrich Wölfflin.
        1942, 1922.
        2 L. from Wilhelm von Bode. 1922.
        1 L. from Max J. Friedlaender. 1941.

B3   3 L.

C8   "Materialien zu einer Kunstgeschichte des Quattrocento
        in Italien." T.cc. 687p.

D7   "The Louvre Coronation and the Early Phase of Fra
        Angelico's Art." 1942. Offprint. 16p.

H3   2 cl. 1929, 1943.
        2 obituaries.

H5   List of publications. Undated. T.cc. 1p.

J   Photo in photo album.
        Photo from newspaper cl. 1923.
        Photo in Berlin home. 1923.

N   Pencil drawing by Th. Heine. 1933.

Mr. Hans Sahl, 800 West End Avenue, New York, N.Y. 10025.

B1   Several L. to Hans Sahl.

Mary S. Rosenberg, 100 West 72nd Street, New York, N.Y. 10023.

ALBERT GRZESINSKI ARCHIVE

B1   1 L. to A. Grzesinski. T. 1944.

B2   1 L. from A. Grzesinski. T.c. 1945.

Harvard University, Houghton Library, Cambridge, Massachusetts 02138.

LYONEL FEININGER COLLECTION

B1   1 L. to L. Feininger. T. Undated.

Mrs. Alice Loewy Kahler, 1 Evelyn Place, Princeton, New
Jersey 08540.

ERICH VON KAHLER COLLECTION

B1   4 L., 1 Ptc. to Erich von Kahler. 1938-1940, 1949.

NAHUM NORBERT GLATZER
Historian, 1903-

Prof. Nahum Norbert Glatzer, Department of Religion, Boston
University, Boston, Massachusetts 02215.

Private personal collection, accessible with permission from
Dr. Glatzer. Although no detailed inventory of the collection has been made, it is completely sorted and organized.

Diese Privatsammlung ist mit Erlaubnis von Dr. Glatzer zu-
gänglich. Es wurde zwar noch kein detailliertes Verzeichnis
der Sammlung erstellt, die Sammlung an sich ist jedoch sor-
tiert und geordnet.

B1,2   Correspondence, from 1920s to date. Thousands of L.,
       in alphabetical order. Also c. of important Glatzer
       L. Includes correspondence with:
       Martin Buber. 148 L. 1945-.
       Leo Baeck. 20 L. 1945-.
       Franz Rosenzweig. Ca. 50 L. 1925-1929.

C7   Ca. 100 F. containing Ms. of essays, articles, books
       and anthologies. Mid-1920s to date.
       Class notes from courses taught.
       Lecture notes.

D7   Offprints of all of Glatzer's writings.

E   Transcripts of several interviews.

H4   Reviews of Glatzer's published works.

I   Passports.
       Awards, certificates of honor, certificates of merit,
       honorary documents.

K   8,000-volume library. Also complete index to collection.

L   Large collection of Rosenzweig materials.
       Cl. collections, including: World War II, persecution
       of Jews, European and American papers, dislocation
       of populations, Arnold Toynbee, art, science, Second
       Vatican Council.
       10 F. concerning work done with students.

N   Rosenzweig, Franz. Stern der Erlösung. Ms.
       Buber, Martin. Ms.

<u>Mrs. Alice Loewy Kahler</u>, 1 Evelyn Place, Princeton, New Jersey 08540.

ERICH VON KAHLER COLLECTION

B1   1 L. to Erich von Kahler. 1964.

MORITZ GOLDSTEIN

Writer, 1880-1977

Prof. Moritz Goldstein, 895 West End Avenue, New York, N.Y.
10025.

Private collection: inaccessible. / *Unzugängliche Privatsammlung.*

A1   "Journale." 10 diaries, dating from 1902.

A3   Ein Mensch wie ich. Autobiography. 1948. 227p.

B1,2 Sizable correspondence, primarily with publishers,
      organized by works. Many L. from the years 1919-
      1933, including: Ullstein-Verlag, Sibyllen-Verlag,
      Wasservogel-Verlag, Kiepenheuer-Verlag, Vertrieb-
      stelle des Verbandes Deutscher Bühnenschriftsteller.

B1,2 Folders pertaining to the works that were produced,
H4,   including correspondence, reviews, theater programs
I,   and financial documents:
O   Alessandro und der Abt. 1913.
          Die Gabe Gottes. 1918-1920.
          Der verlorene Vater. 1926-1932.

C1   Viktoria-Palast. Before 1933. Unpub. 416p.
      Die Götter in Manhattan. 1954. Unpub. 529p.

C2   Ms. of unpub. dramas:
      Menschen. Tragödie in 3 Aufzügen. 1902.
      Der Herzog von Orvieto. Drama in 5 Aufzügen. 1903.
      König Morung. Tragödie. 1908.
      Melissas Schatten. Tragödie in 5 Aufzügen. 1922.
      Unheilige Dreieinigkeit. Schauspiel in 3 Akten. 1924.
      Die Besiegten. 3 Einakter. 1911-1912.
      Abdullahs Esel. Schauspiel in 5 Akten. 1937. 109p.
      Ein wildfremder Mensch. Komödie in einem Vorspiel
          und 3 Akten. 1957. 75p.
      Blitz und Donner. Zauberposse in 3 Akten (5 Szenen).
          1965. 51p.
      Küot oder Ein Tagelied. 1906.
      Knabe im Park oder Die Gehirnparalyse. Undated.
      Ermanarich. Fragment of a tragedy.

C3   "Gelegentliches." Occasional poetry. 1 F.
      "Gedichte." Ca. 1908-1962. 1 F.

C4   "Kleine Erzählungen." Ms. of 28 stories, most written
        prior to 1933.
        "Aufstieg zum Olymp." Unpub. story. 1970. 42p.
        "Das jüdische Lager." Unpub. story. 1968. 23p.
        "Aphorismen zur Gegenwart und Zukunft der Juden."
        Formulierungen. Aphorisms. 1968. 216p.

C4,7 Ms. of articles, stories.

C7   Zeitgenossen und Mitmenschen. Collection of feuille-
        tons from the American exile years.
        Philosophic writings (all unpub.):
        Gedankengänge. 1960-1962. 257p.
        Sexualästhetik. 1919. 263p.
        Widerlegung der Macht. 467p. (part pub. in 1947).
        "Vision der Zukunft." Originally intended as part of
        Macht-book. 1947. 70p.
        Die Sache der Juden. 1938. 183p.

D1   Complete collection of his books.

D4,7 Collection of offprints. 1901-1933 (many from the
        Vossische Zeitung).

D7   Cl. and offprints of articles that appeared in news-
        papers and magazines, postwar period (Neue Zeitung,
        Aufbau, Pariser Tageszeitung).

L   Collections of materials used in writing the following
        works:
        Widerlegung der Macht.
        "Das jüdische Lager."
        "Aufstieg zum Olymp."
        Ermanarich.

Boston University, Mugar Memorial Library, 771 Commonwealth
Avenue, Boston, Massachusetts 02215.

BELLA FROMM COLLECTION

B1   4 L. 1933-1960.

IWAN GOLL

Writer, 1891-1950

Princeton University, Firestone Library, Princeton, New
Jersey 08450.

ALLEN TATE COLLECTION

Bl   15 L. to Allen Tate. 1942-1955.

State University of New York at Albany, Department of Germanic Languages and Literatures, 1400 Washington Avenue,
Albany, New York 12222.

STORM PUBLISHERS ARCHIVE

Bl   5 L. to Alexander Gode von Aesch. 1948.

B2   4 L. from Alexander Gode von Aesch. 1948.

Yale University, Beinecke Rare Book and Manuscript Library,
New Haven, Connecticut 06520.

HERMANN BROCH ARCHIVE, KURT WOLFF ARCHIVE

Bl   1 L. to Kurt Wolff. A. 1913.

B2   12 L. from Hermann Broch. 1939-1948.

Mrs. Gertrude Urzidil, 83-39 116th Street, Richmond Hill,
New York, N.Y. 11418.

JOHANNES URZIDIL COLLECTION

Bl   1 L. to Johannes Urzidil. T. 1945.

B2   5 L. from Johannes Urzidil. A. c. 1945-1947.

Boston University, Mugar Memorial Library, 771 Commonwealth
Avenue, Boston, Massachusetts 02215.

WALLACE FOWLIE PAPERS

B1   2 L. to Wallace Fowlie. T. and A. 1944 and undated.

Southern Illinois University, Morris Library, Department of Special Collections, Carbondale, Illinois 62901.

ERWIN PISCATOR PAPERS

B1   1 L. to Erwin Piscator. T. 1940.

B2   2 L. from E. Piscator. T.cc. 1936, 1941.

Columbia University, Butler Library, New York, N.Y. 10027.

B1   2 L. and 2 Ptc. to Henri-Martin Barzun. A. 1941.

University of Pennsylvania, The Charles Patterson Van Pelt Library, Philadelphia, Pennsylvania 19104.

ALMA MAHLER-WERFEL COLLECTION

B1   1 L. to Franz Werfel. T. 1942.

B2   1 L. from the Bermann-Fischer Verlag. T.cc. 1946.

I   Receipt for royalties (Werfel's *Bernadette*) from the Bermann-Fischer Verlag.

University of Kansas, Kenneth Spencer Research Library, Department of Special Collections, Lawrence, Kansas 66045.

HENRY SAGAN COLLECTION

B1   1 L. to Henry Sagan.

Mr. Hans Sahl, 800 West End Avenue, New York, N.Y. 10025.

B1   Several L. to Hans Sahl.

<u>University of Southern California</u>, Lion Feuchtwanger Memorial
Library, 520 Paseo Miramar, Pacific Palisades, California
90272.

B1   1 L. to Lion Feuchtwanger.

<u>Leo Baeck Institute</u>, 129 East 73rd Street, New York, N.Y.
10021.

B1   1 L. to A. R. Meyer. A. 1921.

OSKAR MARIA GRAF
Writer, 1894-1967

University of New Hampshire, The Library, Department of Special Collections, Durham, New Hampshire 03824.

The OSKAR MARIA GRAF COLLECTION, more than 47 archive boxes of materials, was purchased by the University in 1970 from Mrs. Gisela Graf. Mrs. Graf, widow of Oskar, still retains all publication rights to the materials. In addition to a 286-page detailed index of the collection, microfilms of the collection in its entirety may be either purchased or borrowed from the University of New Hampshire.

Die University of New Hampshire hat 1970 die OSKAR MARIA GRAF COLLECTION (mehr als 47 Archivkästen) von Frau Gisela Graf käuflich erworben. Die literarischen Rechte zu diesem Material ruhen bei Frau Graf, der Witwe Oskar Maria Grafs. Neben einem 286igseitigen ausführlichen Index der Sammlung können von der University of New Hampshire Mikrofilme der gesamten Sammlung ausgeliehen oder käuflich erworben werden.

A3   Fruehzeit. 141p.
     Wir sind Gefangene. Bekenntnis dieses Jahrzehnts. 431p.
     Wunderbare Menschen! 119p.
     3 short curricula vitae. 16p.
     Fragments and untitled autobiographical essays. Ca. 30p.
     Gelächter von Außen. 429p. plus numerous fragments.
     Rußland Reise. 1934. 165p.
     20 shorter autobiographical pieces. Ca. 290p.
     "Werke von Oskar Maria Graf." List of works up to 1949, with short biography.

B1   373 L. 1920-1967, including L. to: Johannes R. Becher, Heinrich Böll, Albert Einstein, Hans Magnus Enzensberger, Julius Epstein, Lion and Marta Feuchtwanger, Ernst and Ruth Fischer, Bruno Frank, Günther Grass, Friedrich Grosshut, Hans Habe, Hermann Hesse, Theodor Heuss, Rolf Hochhuth, Prinz Hubertus zu Loewenstein, Heinrich Mann, Katia Mann, Thomas Mann, Robert Neumann, Otto Preminger, Erich Maria Remarque, Luise Rinser, Will Schaber, Anna Seghers, Luitpold Stern, Fritz von Unruh.
     Ca. 206 L. to publishers. 1938-1967.
     8 "Offene Briefe." 1966.

B2   Ca. 644 L. 1933-1966, including L. from: Raoul Auern-
heimer, Johannes R. Becher, Walter Berendsohn, Hein-
rich Böll, Hermann Broch, Franz Theodor Csokor,
Alfred Döblin, Albert Ehrenstein, Albert Einstein,
Hanns Eisler, Julius Epstein, Lion and Marta Feucht-
wanger, Bruno and Elisabeth Frank, Leonhard Frank,
Friedrich Sally Grosshut, E. J. Gumbel, Hans Habe,
Wieland Herzfelde, Hermann Hesse, Theodor Heuss,
Paul Hindemith, Richard Katz, Kurt Kersten, Prinz
Hubertus zu Loewenstein, Erika Mann, Heinrich Mann,
Katia Mann, Klaus Mann, Thomas Mann, Ludwig Marcuse,
Walter Meckauer, Alfred Neumann, Robert Neumann,
Jacob Picard, Kurt Pinthus, Erich Maria Remarque,
Roda Roda, J. Luitpold Stern, Fritz von Unruh, Bert-
hold Viertel, Ernst Waldinger.
Ca. 375·L. from publishers. 1940-1967.
Ca. 30 open L. directed to Graf. 1966.
8 form L. from: P.E.N. Club, Reichsstelle zur Förderung
des deutschen Schrifttums, Schutzverband deutscher
Schriftsteller. 1933.
19 L. concerning Prisoners All! 1963-1967.
55 L. concerning Altmodische Gedichte. 1963-1964.

B3   81 condolence L. on the death of Graf. 1967.
22 L. from and 20 L. to Gisela Graf. 1965-1970.
8 L. from and 16 L. to Mary Graf. 1941-1959.
26 L. 1919-1968, including L. from: Kurt Pinthus, Rainer Maria Rilke.

C1   Published novels:
Der Abgrund: ein Zeitroman. A. 540p. Another copy
with the title: Die gezählten Jahre. 540p.
Banscho oder die Freiheit: der Roman einer Gegend.
471p.
Another version. T. and pc., ea. 519p. "Exposé."
8 p.
Banscho; or, The Fight for Freedom: the novel of a
village. "Outline of the novel." 2c., ea. 8p.
Die Chronik von Flechting. Ein Dorfroman von Oskar
Maria Graf. 163p.
Entdeckung der Welt: Roman einer Zukunft. 366p.
Die Heimsuchung. Bound Ms. 217p.
Das Leben meiner Mutter. Exposé. 14p. Outline. 9p.

Der mißlungene Roman; oder, Die Flucht ins Mittel-
mäßige. 360p. Odd chapters, exposé. 30p.
Unruhe um einen Friedfertigen. 2 c., ea. 1p.
Unpub. novels:
Dämmerung, Nacht und Morgengrauen. Roman. 2 c., ea.
viii, 360p.
"Kurzer Inhalt des II. Bandes 'Geliebte Johanna'."
2 c., ea. 3p.
Dusk, Darkness, Dawn. Exposé. 2p.
Geliebte Johanna. 2nd volume. 2 c., ea. 75p.
[Der Intourist]. "Skizzen zum Roman Der Intourist."
2 c., 2p. and 3p.
[Joseph Hasicek]. Fragments.
[Lehrer Torberger]. Fragment. 11p. 3c.
"Material zum Roman des franz. Bauerns Dominice."
Fragments. 5p.
Menschen aus einer anderen Welt; oder, Das Testament
des Malers Lechner. 111p. Another version: Das
Testament des Kaspar Heimrath; die Geschichte einer
großen Liebe. 54p.
Mir geht nichts über mich! Aufzeichungen eines Nihi-
listen. "Exposé des Romans." 2 c., ea. 2p.
"Schon oft im Laufe der Jahre ist mir der Gedanke
aufgestiegen, die Geschichte meines Schulkameraden
Joseph Sittinger zu schreiben." 2 c., 42p. and 39p.
[Unbekannte Kameraden]. 3 different parts. 5p, 2p.,
8p.
Der Untergang. "Romananfang." 3 c.: p. 9-62; p. 19-
53, 56-64; p. 19-53, 56-62.
Untitled Ms. 2 c., 5p. and 2p.

C3   Published poems:
Altmodische Gedichte eines Dutzendmenschen. 20 poems,
some with multiple c. Table of contents. 5p.
Old-fashioned Poems of an Ordinary Man. 2 poems.
Amen und Anfang. 4 poems.
Ring des Jahres, ein lyrisches Kalendarium. Pub. as:
Der ewige Kalendar. 2 c., ea. 27p. Extra c. of poem
"Der August."
2 poems.
Unpub. poems:
"Gedichte eines unbekannten jungen Mannes." 124 poems.
121p.

"Gedichte im Exil. 1933 bis 1941." 32 poems. 67p.
"In den Wind gesprochen... Gedichte im Exil 1941/42."
  25 poems. 34p.
"Meine Lieblingsgedichte; was wir liebten und noch
  lieben!" Outline and table of contents.
"Worte an den einen. Versuche 1920-21." 30p.
"Zurück zur Sentimentalität. Sonderbares Vorwort zu
  einer geplanten Sammlung alter und neuer Lyrik."
  Published posthumously. Introduction. 22p.
89 unpub. poems, some with several c.

C4   Aphorisms. 205 pieces plus 58 loose p.
Das bayrische Lesebücherl. Kulturbilder von einst bis
  jetzt. Title p., table of contents, introduction.
  28p.
Dunkel strömt das Leben... fünf Erzählungen. 1926-27.
  109p.
Finsternis. 6 "Bayrische Dorfgeschichten." 155p.
Fünf Novellen. 99p.
Die große Bauernfibel: Dorfgeschichten und Begebnisse
  von einst, gestern und jetzt. Title p., dedication,
  table of contents.
Jedermanns Geschichten. Introduction.
Kalendergeschichten. Title p.
"Kleiner bayrischer Dialektspiegel; verdeutscht für
  meine werte Kundschaft aus dem geliebten Norden
  Deutschlands und anderswo." 10p.
Kleines Angebot; Legenden, Sinngeschichten und Märchen
  mit Moral. 1964. Title p., table of contents.
Zur Jugend gesprochen. 2 c., ea. 115p.
3 fragments, 3 outlines to stories.
132 individual stories, fairy tales, novellas, etc.
  Also numerous cl. 7 B.
Translations of stories: 3 Russian, 20 English.

C5   David gegen Goliath; oder, Stärker als Hitler. Film
  story. 43p.

C7   4 book reviews. 10p.
Essays, speeches, etc. on literary figures:
  Bertolt Brecht. 3 essays. 13p.
  Willi Bredel. Essay. 4p.
  Fritz Brügel. Essay. 3p.
  Theodore Dreiser. Essay. 2p.

Il'ia Ehrenburg. Essay. 4p.
Maxim Gorki. Essay. 3p.
Detlev v. Liliencron. Fragment. 1p.
Klaus Mann. 2 essays. 4p.
Thomas Mann. 2 essays, 1 speech. 85p.
Rainer Maria Rilke. Essay. 33p.+
Alexander Roda Roda. Essay. 2 c., ea. 3p.
Ludwig Thoma. Essay (4 versions), fragment. 26p.
Ernst Toller. Speech. 2 c., ea. 4p.
Leo Tolstoy. 2 essays. 4p.
Sergei Tret'iakov. Essay (2 versions). 4p.
4 essays, 2 fragments on literary topics. 48p.
20 essays, speeches, open letters on various topics.
    Ca. 360p.
32 political essays, speeches. Ca. 1,010p. Including:
    "Das deutsche Volk und Hitlers Krieg."
    "Der Moralist als Wurzel der Diktatur. Eine geistes-
        politische Betrachtung."
    "November Rede."
    "Verbrennt mich!"

D4   2 scrapbooks with newspaper cl. of Graf's stories
        pasted in.

D7   40 newspaper cl. of 34 different autobiographical
        essays.
    Miscellaneous literary topics. 5 cl.
    Miscellaneous themes. 19 cl. of 13 different articles.
    Essays on literary figures:
        Bertolt Brecht. 20 cl. of 5 different articles.
        Heinrich Heine. 3 cl. of 2 different articles.
        Thomas Mann. 2 cl.
        Rainer Maria Rilke. 1 cl.
        Ludwig Thoma. 6 cl. of the same article.
    Political essays. 22 cl. of 17 different essays.
    Reviews. 2 cl.

E   [Bolwieser]. Kleinstadttragödie. Drama adaptation by
        Walter Schröder. 2 c. 133p.
    Bolwieser. Radio play adaptation by Edmund Steinberger.
        80p.
    [Bolwieser]. Kleinstadt-Tragödie. Drama adaptation by
        Walter Kiewert.
    Harter Handel. Radio play adaptation by Edmund Stein-
        berger. 60p.

F   Records and tapes of Graf reading his poems, stories, or informal talks. Some professional, some by Gisela Graf.

       TV film for Bayerische Rundfunk of Graf in his home town, Berg am Starnberger See. 1964.

G   "Oskar Maria Graf über Sowjetrußland. Ein Gespräch mit dem bekannten Schriftsteller."

       Radio Interview. New York City, May 1944. 6p.

H3   General articles about Graf. 1928-1968. 63 newspaper cl., 2 F. of typewritten articles.

       Articles in which Graf is mentioned. 1939-1971. 81 cl.

       Graf's 50th birthday. 1944. 2 articles.

       Graf's 60th birthday. 1954. 26 cl.

       Graf's 65th birthday. 1959. 104 cl.

       Graf's 70th birthday. 1964. 125 cl.

       Graf's 74th birthday, burial in Germany. 1968. 29 cl.

       Graf's 75th birthday. 1969. 22 cl.

       Obituaries. 1967. 146 cl.

       Graf's trip to Germany. 1958. 21 cl.

       Graf's trip to Germany. 1960. 7 cl.

       Graf's trip to Germany. 1964. 24 cl.

       Graf's trip to Germany. 1965. 3 cl.

       German American Writers' Association. 4 cl.

       Graf's honorary doctorate. Wayne State University, 1960. 4 cl.

       Graf's speeches in U.S. 1938-1963. 40 cl.

H4   Der Abgrund. 11 cl., several advertisements.

       Altmodische Gedichte eines Dutzendmenschen. Ca. 15 reviews, orders for the book.

       Amen und Anfang. Reviews, advertisements. 1 F.

       An manchen Tagen. 32 reviews, several advertisements.

       Anton Sittinger. 67 reviews, several advertisements, book jacket sketch.

       Banscho. 11 reviews.

       Bayrischer Bauernspiegel. 1 review.

       Bayrisches Dekameron. 24 reviews, 1 advertisement, 1 document.

       Bayrisches Lesebücherl. 5 reviews.

       Bolwieser. 8 reviews, book jacket, advertisements.

       Die Chronik von Flechting. 2 reviews.

       Dorfbanditen. 1 review.

       Einer gegen alle. 2 reviews, book jacket.

Die Erben des Untergangs. Die Eroberung der Welt. 44
reviews.
Der ewige Kalender. 2 reviews, 1 advertisement.
Die Flucht ins Mittelmäßige. 54 reviews, advertise-
ments.
Gelächter von Außen. 61 reviews.
Der große Bauernspiegel. 20 reviews.
Größtenteils schimpflich. 6 reviews, advertisements.
Der harte Handel. 1 review.
Die Heimsuchung. 1 advertisement.
Kalendergeschichten. 7 reviews, advertisements.
Das Leben meiner Mutter. 82 reviews, 1 collection of
reviews, book jacket, advertisements.
Mitmenschen. 10 reviews, 1 advertisement.
Der Quasterl und andere Erzählungen. 2 reviews, 1 book
jacket.
The Stationmaster. 1 review.
Unruhe um einen Friedfertigen. 26 reviews, 1 advertise-
ment.
Wir sind Gefangene. 81 reviews, advertisements, book
jacket.
Wunderbare Menschen. 3 reviews, advertisements, book
jacket.
Miscellaneous collections of reviews, including 2
scrapbooks of reviews and advertisements.

H5 Dabringhaus, Erhard. "The works of Oskar Maria Graf as
they reflect intellectual and political currents of
Bavaria, 1900-1945." Dissertation.
Dietz, Wolfgang. "Untersuchungen zum Erzählwerk Oskar
Maria Grafs; die Erzählungen und Romane der zwanziger
Jahre (1918-1933)."
Weber, Erwin. "The influence of Tolstoy on Oskar Maria
Graf." M.A. thesis.

I Graf's X-rays.
Russia trip documents: itinerary, meal tickets, receipts, etc.
Personal documents: passport, marriage certificate,
divorce papers, death certificate, visiting and membership cards, testament, doctorate degree, contracts, etc.

J Pictures of personalities admired by Graf.

Photos of Graf, his family, friends, colleagues. Several envelopes and albums.

L   Akademie der Künste, Berlin. Papers.
Miscellaneous materials on cultural, literary, political topics. 5 F.
Materials on Arizona and the American Indians. 3 F.
Miscellaneous newspaper cl., notes, etc. 29 F.
Miscellaneous invitations, announcements, etc. Ca. 13 items.
Newspaper cl. on Bruno Gröning. 5 F.
Notes for novellas, newspaper cl. 1 F.
2 scrapbooks, autobiographical and biographical materials.
"Studien-Material." 2 F.
"Yearbook, 1954." Newspaper cl. with notes by Graf. 2 F.
"Zum Umarbeiten." Short stories and newspaper cl. 4 F.

M   Address books, addresses.
Bayrischer Dekameron. Copy of the book that was found by an American soldier beside the body of a dead German soldier and sent to Graf.

O   Posters, a few designed by Graf.

FRIEDRICH SALLY GROSSHUT COLLECTION

Bl   20 L. to F. S. Grosshut. T. and A. 1950-1964.

University of Pennsylvania, The Charles Patterson Van Pelt Library, Philadelphia, Pennsylvania 19104.

ALMA MAHLER-WERFEL COLLECTION

Bl   22 L. to Alma Mahler-Werfel. A. and T.

Leo Baeck Institute, 129 East 73rd Street, New York, N.Y. 10021.

KURT KERSTEN COLLECTION, JACOB PICARD COLLECTION

B1   12 L. to Kurt Kersten. 1940-1954.

B1,2   Correspondence with Jacob Picard.

H3   1 cl. 1948.

University of Southern California, Lion Feuchtwanger Memorial
Library, 520 Paseo Miramar, Pacific Palisades, California
90272.

B1   8 L. to Lion Feuchtwanger. 1953-1958.

B2   7 L. from Lion Feuchtwanger. 1953-1958.

State University of New York at Albany, Department of Germanic Languages and Literatures, 1400 Washington Avenue,
Albany, New York 12222.

STORM PUBLISHERS ARCHIVE, KARL O. PAETEL COLLECTION

B1   20 L. to Karl O. Paetel (xerox). 1941-1965.
        4 L. to Alexander Gode von Aesch. 1945-1947.

B2   2 L. from Alexander Gode von Aesch. 1947.
        1 L. from Karl O. Paetel (xerox). 1964.

New York Public Library, Manuscript Division, Fifth Avenue
and 42nd Street, New York, N.Y. 10018.

THEO FELDMAN PAPERS

B1   3 L. to Theo Feldman. 1943.

Harvard University, Houghton Library, Cambridge, Massachusetts 02138.

RILKE COLLECTION

B2   2 L. from Rainer Maria Rilke. 1919.

Library of Congress, Manuscript Division, Independence Avenue
and First Street S.E., Washington, D.C. 20540.

BENJAMIN W. HUEBSCH PAPERS

Bl   1 L. (together with Curt Riess and Thomas Mann) to
        B. W. Huebsch. T. 1939.

Southern Illinois University, Morris Library, Department of
Special Collections, Carbondale, Illinois 62901.

ERWIN PISCATOR PAPERS

Bl   1 L. to Erwin Piscator. 1942.

University of Kansas, Max Kade German-American Document and
Manuscript Center, Watson Library, Lawrence, Kansas 66044.

Bl   1 L. to Erich A. Albrecht. T. 1939.

Johns Hopkins University, The Milton S. Eisenhower Library,
Baltimore, Maryland 21218.

Bl   1 L. to William Kurrelmeyer. 1944.

Mrs. Peter M. Lindt, 949 West End Avenue, New York, N.Y.
10025.

Bl   Small amount of correspondence with Peter M. Lindt.

ALEXANDER GRANACH
Actor, 1890-1945

State University of New York at Albany, Department of Germanic Languages and Literatures, 1400 Washington Avenue,
Albany, New York 12222.

DOUBLEDAY PUBLISHERS ARCHIVE (xerox)

B1   1 L. to Bucklin Moon. 1944.
      1 Tel. to Henri Verstoppen. 1944.

B2   7 L. from Ken McCormick and Bucklin Moon. 1943-1945.

B3   Publisher's correspondence concerning Granach and his
      book: There Goes a Man.

H3   4 cl.

Southern Illinois University, Morris Library, Department of
Special Collections, Carbondale, Illinois 62901.

ERWIN PISCATOR PAPERS

B1   12 L. to Erwin Piscator. A. 1938-1945.

B2   10 L. from Erwin Piscator. T.cc. 1938-1945.

H5   Piscator, Erwin. Draft of memorial speech for Granach.
      A. 1945. 1p.

University of Southern California, Lion Feuchtwanger Memorial
Library, 520 Paseo Miramar, Pacific Palisades, California
90272.

B1   1 L. to Lion Feuchtwanger. 1940.

B2   1 L. from Lion Feuchtwanger. 1942.

Mr. Hans Sahl, 800 West End Avenue, New York, N.Y. 10025.

B1   Several L. to Hans Sahl.

Leo Baeck Institute, 129 East 73rd Street, New York, N.Y.
10021.

346

O   1 program on the occasion of the opening of the
Alexander-Granach-Archive.

Mrs. Erna Budzislawski, 2040 Rodney Drive, Los Angeles, California 90027.

Bl   1 L. to Erna Budzislawski. 1945.

Mrs. Liselotte Stein, 115-25 Metropolitan Avenue, Kew Gardens,
New York 11418.

FRED STEIN PAPERS

J   Photos of Alexander Granach.

WALTER GROPIUS

Architect, 1883-1969

Mrs. Ise Gropius, Lincoln, Massachusetts 01773.

The estate of Walter Gropius consists of over 50,000 items, including his personal library, which will remain in the Gropius house. The house will eventually be taken over by the New England Society for the Preservation of Antiquities. A two-volume study of Gropius (to be published by the MIT Press) is being prepared, as of 1977, by Mr. Reg Isaacs with the aid of Mrs. Gropius and the materials from the Gropius estate. The first volume is a biography of Gropius, and the second volume will present his principles, influence and views.

Der Nachlaß von Walter Gropius umfaßt mehr als 50.000 Nummern, darunter seine Privatbibliothek, die im Gropius-Haus verbleiben wird. Das Haus wird später einmal von der New England Society for the Preservation of Antiquities übernommen werden. Unter der Mithilfe von Frau Gropius und anhand der Materialien aus dem Nachlaß von Gropius soll bis 1977 eine zweibändige Studie über Walter Gropius vorbereitet werden; der Autor ist Reg Isaacs, die MIT Press wird die Studie verlegen. Bei dem ersten Band handelt es sich um eine Biographie Gropius', wohingegen der zweite Band sich mit seinen Prinzipien, seinen wichtigsten Ansichten und seinem Einfluß auseinandersetzt.

A1   Diaries and appointment calendars.

B1,2 Correspondences with Harvard University, with students,
      with other Bauhaus members. 4 file cabinet drawers.
      "Important letter" file.
      Correspondences with publishers.

C7   Ms. of lectures and speeches.

C14   Graphics by Gropius and by his students.

F   Tapes

I   Documents re: prizes and awards received by Gropius.
      Certificates: marriage, divorce, etc.

J   4 cabinet drawers of photos.

L   Copies of Alma Mahler-Werfel L., lectures, articles.

WALTER GROPIUS

M Memorabilia.
   Artifacts.

Harvard University, Busch-Reisinger Museum, Cambridge, Massachusetts 02138.

The WALTER GROPIUS COLLECTION at Harvard, 83 boxes of unsorted materials, was donated by Mrs. Ise Gropius, widow of
Walter. Attempts are being made to establish a Walter Gropius Archive at Harvard and access to materials at the present time is restricted to Mr. Reg Isaacs, executor of the
Gropius estate, and Mrs. Ise Gropius.

*Die WALTER GROPIUS COLLECTION der Harvard University (83
Kartons unsortierten Materials) ist eine Schenkung der Witwe
Gropius', Frau Ise Gropius. Man hat vor, ein Walter Gropius
Archiv einzurichten; zur Zeit haben jedoch nur Mr. Reg
Isaacs, der Nachlaßverwalter, und Frau Ise Gropius Zutritt
zu diesen Materialien.*

B Correspondence.

C14 Graphics:
     90 tubes with graphics, rough sketches, blueprints.
     Gropius/Breuer collaboration from the TAC years.

J Photos.

The Architects' Collaborative (TAC), 46 Brattle Street, Cambridge, Massachusetts 02138.

J Ca. 300 negatives, mostly from American years. Primarily of Gropius' work, a few personal. 1906-1968.
   Many used as the basis for a Gropius exhibit.

L Job files of Gropius' years at TAC. 1945-1968. Being
   microfilmed. 70+ reels. Correspondences, contracts,
   cost estimates, invoices, etc.

University of Illinois at Chicago Circle, The Library, Box
8198, Chicago, Illinois 60680.

INSTITUTE OF DESIGN RECORDS, 1927-1970

B1   1 L. to Nathan Lerner. 1946. Restricted.
        2 L. to Walter P. Paepcke. 1946, 1948. Restricted.
        Correspondence. 1945-1955, including L. to: Nathan
        Lerner, Nathaniel Owings, John T. Rettaliata.

B1,2 Correspondence with Henry T. Heald. 1942-1951.
        Correspondence with Walter Paepcke. 1951-1955.
        Correspondence with Serge Chermayeff. 1946-1967.

C7   Address on the Institute of Design, together with Lud-
        wig Mies van der Rohe and Serge Chermayeff. April
        1950.
        Text of speech. Civic dinner, Feb.-April 1950.

Harvard University, Houghton Library, Cambridge, Massachusetts 02138.

LYONEL FEININGER COLLECTION, GEORGE SARTON PAPERS, general
archive files

B1   12 L. to Lyonel and Julia Feininger. 1919-1954.
        22 L. to Harper & Row. 1952-1956.
        1 L. to George Sarton. 1953.

B2   107 L. from Harper & Row concerning Gropius' book: The
        Scope of Total Architecture. 1952-1956.

C8   The Scope of Total Architecture. Revisions and notes.
        T. with h. corr. 23p.

Columbia University, Butler Library, New York, N.Y. 10027.

B1   12 L. to W. W. Norton. T. 1937-1944.
        15 L. to Frank S. MacGregor. T. 1956-1962.
        3 L. to John Appleton. T. 1958-1960.
        1 L. ea. to Ruth Hill and Virginia Olson. T. 1961.

University of Pennsylvania, The Charles Patterson Van Pelt
Library, Philadelphia, Pennsylvania 19104.

WALTER GROPIUS

ALMA MAHLER-WERFEL COLLECTION

B1   19 L. to Alma Mahler-Werfel. T. and A. 1918-1958.
      3 L. to Franz Werfel. T. and A. 1942 and undated.
B2   1 L. from Alma Mahler-Werfel. Draft. A. Undated.
H3   3 cl.

State of North Carolina, Department of Cultural Resources,
Raleigh, North Carolina 27611.

BLACK MOUNTAIN COLLEGE ARCHIVES

B1,   Correspondence and materials in reference to Black
I   Mountain College project undertaken by the State
         of North Carolina with NEA. Restricted.

I   [Treasurer's] file: "Gropius and Breuer."
       [General] file: "Walter Gropius."
       [Faculty] file: "Walter Gropius, Art."

Yale University Library, Manuscripts and Archives Research
Room, 150 Sterling Memorial Library, New Haven, Connecticut
06520.

JOSEF ALBERS PAPERS

B1,2   Correspondence with Josef Albers. Ca. 1936-1942. Re-
         stricted until 1981.
       Correspondence with Josef Albers. 1933-1950. Unre-
         stricted.

I   "Early Weimar Years." Documents and L. from the Weimar
       Bauhaus. 1921-1925, many signed by Gropius.

Archives of American Art, Smithsonian Institution, National
Collection of Fine Arts and National Portrait Gallery Build-
ing, Eighth and F Streets N.W., Washington, D.C. 20560.
(Microfilms of collections are available in each of the
branch locations: Boston, Massachusetts; New York, N.Y.;
Detroit, Michigan; San Francisco, California.)

B1   Correspondence in records of the Institute of Contemporary Art, Boston.
Correspondence, representing The Architects' Collaborative in: Herbert Ferber Correspondence 1966-1969.

Southern Illinois University, Morris Library, Department of Special Collections, Carbondale, Illinois 62901.

ERWIN PISCATOR PAPERS

B1   7 L. to Erwin Piscator. T. 1940-1967.

B2   12 L. from Erwin Piscator. T.cc. 1940-1966.

Prof. Konrad Wachsmann, 805 South Genesee, Los Angeles, California 90036.

B1,2 Correspondence with Konrad Wachsmann. Ca. 25 L. 1934-1960.

H5   Character analysis of Gropius. 1975.

Library of Congress, Manuscript Division, Independence Avenue and First Street S.E., Washington, D.C. 20540.

PAPERS OF LUDWIG MIES VAN DER ROHE

B1,2 Correspondence with Ludwig Mies van der Rohe. 1938-1969.

H5   Writings by Mies van der Rohe re: Walter Gropius.

Harvard University, Harvard Divinity School, Andover-Harvard Theological Library, 45 Francis Avenue, Cambridge, Massachusetts 02138.

PAUL TILLICH COLLECTION

B1   1 L. to Paul Tillich. T. 1958.

B2   1 Tel. from Hannah Tillich. 1965.

Dr. Gustave O. Arlt, 13220-C Admiralty Way, Marina del Rey, California 90291.

FRANZ WERFEL ARCHIVE

B1   1 L. to Franz Werfel. 1933.

Boston University, Mugar Memorial Library, 771 Commonwealth Avenue, Boston, Massachusetts 02215.

MENACHEM ARNONI PAPERS

B1   1 L. to Menachem Arnoni. T. 1963.

Mrs. Liselotte Stein, 115-25 Metropolitan Avenue, Kew Gardens, New York 11418.

FRED STEIN PAPERS

J   Photos of Walter Gropius.

University of Texas, Humanities Research Center, Manuscripts Collection, Box 7219, Austin, Texas 78712.

B1   3 L.

Harvard University, University Archives, Widener Library, Cambridge, Massachusetts 02138.

H3   Numerous press cl.

Museum of Modern Art, The Library, 11 West 53rd Street, New York, N.Y. 10019.

HANS RICHTER ARCHIVE: Written permission to use the Archive is required in advance of visits to the Museum.

HANS RICHTER ARCHIVE: Vor Besuch des Archivs muß eine schriftliche Genehmigung eingeholt werden.

H3   1 cl.

FRIEDRICH SALLY GROSSHUT
Writer, 1906-1969

University of New Hampshire, The Library, Department of Special Collections, Durham, New Hampshire 03824.

The FRIEDRICH SALLY GROSSHUT COLLECTION consists of 14 archive boxes of materials, the personal library of Grosshut, and additional loose manuscripts. It was purchased by the library from Mrs. Sina Grosshut in 1971.

Die FRIEDRICH SALLY GROSSHUT COLLECTION umfaßt 14 Archivkartons Materialien, die Privatbibliothek von Grosshut sowie weitere ungebundene Manuskripte. Die Bibliothek hat diese Sammlung 1971 von Frau Sina Grosshut gekauft.

B1   4 L. to: Lion Feuchtwanger, Hermann Kesten, Erika Mann, Statesman and Nation.

B2   50 L. from Lion Feuchtwanger. 1945-1958. Also 5 L. from Feuchtwanger's secretary. 1958-1969.
20 L. from Oskar Maria Graf. T. and A. 1950-1964.
10 L. from Robert M. W. Kempner. T. 1950-1965.
15 L. and Ptc. from Hermann Kesten. T. and A. 1949-1963.
14 L. and 1 Ptc. from Peter M. Lindt. T. and A. 1950-1957.
12 L. from Erika Mann. T. and A. 1949-1966.
23 L. from Heinz Politzer. T. and A. 1942-1949.
260 L. 1917-1969, including L. from: Walter A. Berendsohn, Max Brod, Marta Feuchtwanger, Emil Gumbel, Ossip Kalenter, Hans Kelsen, Katia Mann, Thomas Mann, Ludwig Marcuse, Alfred Neumann, Erwin Piscator, Nelly Sachs, Gabriele Tergit, Friedrich Torberg, Ernst Waldinger, Arnold Zweig.

B3   3 L. 1950-1956.

C1   Reeducation in der Wüste. Undated. T.cc. 285p.
Der Schwitzkasten. Undated. T.cc. 474p.
Staatsrat Geer. Undated. T.cc. 500p.
Tanz um Paris. Undated. T.cc. 638p.

C2   Abderitisches Capriccio. Ein heiteres Märchenspiel in fünf Akten. Undated. T.cc. Ca. 60p.
Der fünfte Stand. Undated. T. 6p.

Go Ahead, Hoax! Undated. T. 28p.
Maskenball. Undated. T. 5p.
Quer. T. 6p.
Der Regenmacher. T. 30p.
Der Rezensent. T. Ca. 50p.
Es geschieht in Ohio. 1938. T. 74p. Also a second copy.
Writer's Dilemma. T. 7p.

C3   139 loose sheets with poems. Undated. T. and A.
Die besinnlichen Gedichte: Zwanzig unzeitgemäße Gesänge. Undated. T.c. 50p.

C4   "Österreichische Novelle." [1938]. T. 108p.
"Schauspieler Bortum." Undated. T. 113p.
"Student Müller." T. 57p.
"Schiedsrichter Rissing leitet ein Spiel." T. 43p.
"Lassalle bei Richard Wagner." T. 127p.
"1812." T. 53p. Also second copy.
"Das letzte Lied." T. 44p.
15 additional prose pieces. 133p.

C7   26 essays on famous personalities, including: B.
Brecht, L. Feuchtwanger, R. Wagner, T. Mann, H. Mann,
K. Mann, W. Whitman, O. M. Graf, M. Brod. Ca. 225p.
14 reviews. Ca. 100p.
33 essays. 360p.

C10   Die Menschwerdung des Staats. 1940. T.cc. 338p.
Märchen, Sagen und Autokraten. [1969]. T. Ca. 170p.
Polizei und Lichtspielzensur in der Weimarer Republik.
Undated. T. 145p.
"Organische Staatslehre und drittes Reich." T. 9p.
"Gleichgeschaltete Vergangenheit." T. 12p.
Unsorted and untitled Ms. on political themes. 370p.
plus 7 archive B.

D7   Newspaper cl. from all years. 1 archive B. plus 20 cm.

H4   Shirer, William L. Review of Staatsnot, Recht und
Gewalt.

I   Invitation to opening of Feuchtwanger Memorial Library.

K   Entire personal library of F. S. Grosshut. Over 20
shelf ft.

L   Collection of materials re: Oskar Maria Graf. 1958.

N   Ms. by unknown author. Anthology of German poems. T.
       40p.

OSKAR MARIA GRAF COLLECTION

B1   1 L. to O. M. Graf. 1962.

B2   21 L. from O. M. Graf. 1950-1964.

Leo Baeck Institute, 129 East 73rd Street, New York, N.Y.
10021.

The F. S. GROSSHUT COLLECTION (AR 1559) was donated to the
Institute by Friedrich Sally Grosshut in 1961.

*Die F. S. GROSSHUT COLLECTION (AR 1559) ist eine Schenkung
an das Institut von Friedrich Sally Grosshut aus dem Jahre
1961.*

C7   "Max Tau: Glaube an den Menschen." [1949]. 4p.
       "Wiesbaden." 1949. 5p.
       "Nordisches Nocturno." 1951. 6p.
       "Begegnung mit Else Lasker-Schüler." 1951. 4p.
       "Deutsche Literatur in Israel." Undated. 6p.
       "Wiedersehen mit Alfred Neumann." Undated. 3p.
       "Der Fall Klaus Mann." 5p.

D7   "Lion Feuchtwanger." 1949.

H3   13 cl.

I   Program. Volksbühne, 1927.

Immigration History Research Center of the University of
Minnesota, 826 Berry Street, St. Paul, Minnesota 55101.

AMERICAN COUNCIL FOR EMIGRÉS IN THE PROFESSIONS ARCHIVES

A3   Curriculum vitae and short autobiographical sketch.

B2   2 L. from Otto Zoff. 1950.

B3   1 L. 1950.

KURT GROSSMANN

Writer, 1897-1972

Leo Baeck Institute, 129 East 73rd Street, New York, N.Y.
10021.

The KURT RICHARD GROSSMANN PAPERS, 1933-1969 (MS 75-713),
comprise approximately 51 ft. of materials. They were received as a result of gifts and purchases from Kurt Grossmann before his death and later from his widow (1967-1973).
Ca. 5 ft. of materials are closed until 1980.

*Die KURT RICHARD GROSSMANN PAPERS, 1933-1969 (MA 75-713)
umfassen etwa 15 m Materialien. Es handelt sich um Geschenke
und Ankäufe von Grossmann selbst und später von seiner Witwe
aus den Jahren 1967 bis 1973. Ein Teil der Materialien (etwa
1,50 m) ist bis 1980 nicht zugänglich.*

B1,2   Correspondence. 1938-1966, including L. to and from:
       Victor Basch, Arnold Bergsträsser, Sol Bloom, Emanuel
       Celler, Albert Einstein, Friedrich Wilhelm Foerster,
       Manfred George, Nachum Goldmann, Robert M. W. Kemp-
       ner, Thomas Mann, Otto Strasser, Paul Tillich, Ernst
       Toller, Kurt Tucholsky, Veit Valentin, Stefan Wise.
       Correspondence with: Hans Egon Holthusen, Julius Klein
       (1966), Franz Josef Strauss (1953). Closed.
       Correspondence with publishers, newspapers, including:
       Der Spiegel, Bundestag protocols, Deutsche National-
       und Soldatenzeitung (1966).

C7   Reports on lectures given in Germany after World War II.
       Die Ehrenschuld. Ms. Restricted.
       Carl von Ossietzky. Ms. Restricted.
       Ms. of articles.

D7   Newspaper cl. of articles.

L   Books, cl. and other printed materials relating mainly
       to: human rights, prosecution of Nazi criminals,
       refugee and immigration problems, restitution cases,
       and German-Israeli agreement of 1954.
       Travel notes and research materials about Germany and
       Israel. 1966-1968.
       Materials on Manfred George.

Diverse materials, located at the Institute, but not part of the KURT GROSSMANN PAPERS.

Verschiedene Materialien, die sich im Institut befinden, aber nicht Teil der KURT GROSSMANN PAPERS sind.

C7   "Antisemitism in the last two decades." 1961. Mimeo. 13p.

D7   "Die deutsch-jüdische Symbiose." Cl. 1968.

H3   5 cl.

H4   1 cl.

L   Grossmann files from the Zionist Organization of America, New York, N.Y. (deposited Feb. 1977): pamphlets, cl. about Ruth Fischer (1941-1943); Ms. files from World Jewish Congress about refugees (1945); assorted refugee leaflets.

Harvard University, Houghton Library, Cambridge, Massachusetts 02138.

OSWALD GARRISON VILLARD PAPERS

Bl   2 L. to Oswald Garrison Villard. 1939.

Yivo Institute, 1048 Fifth Avenue, New York, N.Y. 10028.

HORACE M. KALLEN PAPERS

Bl,2 Individual item(s) in folder no. 416. 1943.

State University of New York at Albany, Department of Germanic Languages and Literatures, 1400 Washington Avenue, Albany, New York 12222.

KARL O. PAETEL COLLECTION

Bl   1 L. to Karl O. Paetel. 1962. (xerox)

B2   1 L. from Karl O. Paetel. 1962. (xerox)

GEORGE GROSZ

Painter, 1893-1959

Archives of American Art, Smithsonian Institution, National
Collection of Fine Arts and National Portrait Gallery Build-
ing, Eighth and F Streets N.W., Washington, D.C. 20560.
(Microfilms of collections are available in each of the
branch locations: Boston, Massachusetts; New York, N.Y.;
Detroit, Michigan; San Francisco, California.)

L. A. FLEISCHMANN PAPERS, ULFERT WILKE PAPERS, FERNANDO FUMA
PAPERS, JULIAN LEVI PAPERS, HARRIS STEINBERG PAPERS, WHITNEY
MUSEUM PAPERS, ALFREDO VALENTE PAPERS, EMILY GENAUER PAPERS,
CLEVELAND PRINT CLUB PAPERS, HARRY WICKEY PAPERS

B1   10 L. 1940-1957, including L. to: Morris Kantor,
        L. A. Fleischmann, Henry Schnakenberg, Elizabeth
        Navas.
        13 L. to Ulfert Wilke. 1938-1956.

B1,2   Correspondence with Fernando Fuma.
        Correspondence with Emily Genauer.
        Correspondence with Julian Levi. Ca. 1922.

B3   Correspondence of Harris Steinberg concerning Grosz'
        work.

D7   "A Piece of My World Without Peace." Essay by Grosz
        on his own work. 1946.

F   Tape recording made at Skowhegan School of Painting
        and Sculpture. Aug. 27, 1957.

H3   Associated American Artists Scrapbooks. 1941-1948.
        Ca. 100 items, mostly cl.
        "Clippings and reproductions."
        Clippings. 1947, 1954.

H3,4   Associated American Artists Scrapbooks. Postcards,
        invitations, biographical data, catalogs of exhi-
        bits, price lists, etc.

H4   Cl. on Grosz' work, assembled by Harris Steinberg.
        Catalogs of exhibits of Grosz, assembled by Harris
        Steinberg.
        Exhibition catalog to George Biddle.
        Exhibit at Associated American Artists. 1954.
        Materials from artists' files of the Whitney Museum

359

of American Art.
Exhibit at Donald Morris Gallery, Detroit 1968.

J   Photos of Grosz' work.
Photos of George Grosz.

Dr. Frank Borchardt, German Department, Duke University,
Durham, North Carolina 27706.

HERMANN BORCHARDT PAPERS

B1   67 L. to Hermann Borchardt. 1934-1950.

B2   3 L. from Hermann Borchardt. 1934-1950.

H4   Borchardt, Hermann. Commentary on paintings by Grosz.
37p.

O   2 programs of the Deutsch-Amerikanische Kulturverband,
with bitter anti-Bolshevist commentary by Grosz. A.

Southern Illinois University, Morris Library, Department of
Special Collections, Carbondale, Illinois 62901.

ERWIN PISCATOR PAPERS

B1   5 L. to Erwin Piscator. T. and A. 1945-1951.

B2   9 L. from Erwin Piscator. T.cc. 1940-1949.

J   Photos of sketches by Grosz from the Epic Theatre Exhibit at the Piscator Institute, New York, Jan. 19,
1960.

Mr. Hans Sahl, 800 West End Avenue, New York, N.Y. 10025.

B1   19 L. and 46 Ptc. to Hans Sahl.

Yale University, Beinecke Rare Book and Manuscript Library,
New Haven, Connecticut 06520.

KURT WOLFF ARCHIVE

GEORGE GROSZ

B1,2   Correspondence with the Kurt Wolff Verlag. 8 L. 1920-
       1921. Also 1 cl.

Museum of Modern Art, The Library, 11 West 53rd Street, New
York, N.Y. 10019.

HANS RICHTER ARCHIVE, CURT VALENTIN PAPERS: Written permission to use each of these collections is required in advance
of visits to the Museum.

*HANS RICHTER ARCHIVE, CURT VALENTIN PAPERS. Um diese Samm-
lungen einzusehen, ist eine vorherige schriftliche Genehmigung des Museums erforderlich.*

B1   4 L. to Curt Valentin. T. 1939-1942.
      1 L. to Hans Richter. T. 1958.

B2   2 L. from Curt Valentin. T.c. 1939, 1941.
      1 L. from Hans Richter. T. 1958.

H3   10 cl.

American Philosophical Society, The Library, 105 South Fifth
Street, Philadelphia, Pennsylvania 19106.

FRANZ BOAS PAPERS

B1,2   Correspondence with Franz Boas. 2 L. 1933.

Library of Congress, Manuscript Division, Independence Avenue
and First Street S.E., Washington, D.C. 20540.

BENJAMIN W. HUEBSCH PAPERS

B1   1 L. and 1 Ptc. to B. W. Huebsch. A. 1927, 1933.

Indiana University, The University Libraries, The Lilly
Library, Bloomington, Indiana 47401.

MAX EASTMAN MSS.

GEORGE GROSZ

B1   1 L. to Max Eastman. 1934.

Leo Baeck Institute, 129 East 73rd Street, New York, N.Y. 10021.

KURT KERSTEN COLLECTION

B1   1 L. to Kurt Kersten. 1948.

University of Texas, Humanities Research Center, Manuscripts Collection, Box 7219, Austin, Texas 78712.

C   1 uncatalogued Ms.

University of Pennsylvania, The Charles Patterson Van Pelt Library, Philadelphia, Pennsylvania 19104.

ALMA MAHLER-WERFEL COLLECTION

B1   1 L. to Franz Werfel. A. 1940.

Newark Museum, 43-49 Washington Street, Newark, New Jersey 07101.

I   "Artist Information Form" of the Newark Museum, filled
        out by Grosz. 1944. 2p.

University of Iowa, The University Libraries, Special Col-lections, Iowa City, Iowa 52240.

H3   Death notice. 1 cl. 1959.

State University of New York at Binghamton, Center for Mod-ern Theater Research, Binghamton, New York 13901.

MAX REINHARDT ARCHIVE

*   Materials in uncatalogued portion of archive.

MARTIN GROTJAHN

Psychoanalyst, 1904-

Dr. Martin Grotjahn, 416 North Bedford Drive, Beverly Hills,
California 90210.

Private collection: inaccessible. / *Unzugängliche Privatsammlung.*

A1   Diaries.

A3   Memoirs as an analyst. Unpub. Ms.

B1,2 Correspondence from Grotjahn's American years, includ-
      ing L. from: Sigmund Freud, Helene Deutsch, René
      Spitz, Otto Fenichel.

C7   Ms. of all books and articles.

D7,8 Cl. and offprints of all of Grotjahn's articles, etc.

F   Several tapes of lectures given by Grotjahn.

H3   Files of biographical data collected by Grotjahn.

J   Photos.

L   Newspaper cl. collected by Grotjahn.

Reiss-Davis Child Study Center, 9760 West Pico Boulevard,
Los Angeles, California 90035.

F   Tapes of lectures by Grotjahn.

Library of Congress, Manuscript Division, Independence Avenue
and First Street S.E., Washington, D.C. 20540.

PAPERS OF SIEGFRIED BERNFELD

B1,2 Correspondence with Siegfried Bernfeld. 1947-1957.
      Includes some reprints by Grotjahn.

VICTOR GRUEN

Architect, 1903-

Victor Gruen Center for Environmental Planning, Pepperdine
University, 8035 South Vermont Avenue, Los Angeles, California 90044.

The VICTOR GRUEN CENTER FOR ENVIRONMENTAL PLANNING was
founded by Victor Gruen in 1968. Dr. Gruen still retains a
portion of his collection in Vienna, where he established a
Victor Gruen International Foundation in 1968.

*Das VICTOR GRUEN CENTER FOR ENVIRONMENTAL PLANNING wurde
1968 von Victor Gruen gegründet. Dr. Gruen behält einen
Teil seiner Sammlung noch in Wien, wo er 1968 die Victor
Gruen International Foundation ins Leben rief.*

B1,2   "Washington D.C. World's Fair Correspondence." 1959.
        "1970-71 Univ. of Lovan" correspondence.

C7   Ms. of pub. articles, speeches, essays. 1943+. 23
        spring binders.

H3,4   Brochures describing projects.
        Pub. articles about Victor Gruen Associates Projects.
        Victor Gruen Foundation materials (Vienna, Los Ange-
        les). Articles, cl.

I   Awards.
        Licenses.
        Membership certificates, etc.

J   Photos.
        Blueprints.
        Slides.

K   Gruen's library of books, offprints. In-depth acquisi-
        tions on various subjects.

Syracuse University, The George Arents Research Library,
Syracuse, New York 13210.

The VICTOR GRUEN COLLECTION was donated by Gruen to the
library in 1963.

*Die VICTOR GRUEN COLLECTION ist eine Schenkung Gruens aus dem
Jahre 1963.*

C7 Texts of speeches:
  "An Appraisal and a Proposal." Undated.
  "Environmental Architecture." 1961.
  "Hearts of Our Cities." 1962.
  "The Land Wasters." 1961.
  "Metropolitan Area Planning." 1958.
  "Urban Planning for the Sixties." 1958.
  Testimony. 1959.

D7 How to Live with Your Architect. 1949.
  Reprint of speech given by Gruen over "The Voice of
   America."

D7, Magazine articles by and about Gruen. 1/2 B.
H3

H3 Biographical materials dealing with many of the projects upon which Gruen worked. Undated. 1 F.

J 1 photo of Gruen.

GUSTAVE E. VON GRUNEBAUM

Islamist, Arabist, 1909-1972

Mrs. Gustave von Grunebaum, 251 Veteran Avenue, Los Angeles, California 90024.

The materials in Mrs. von Grunebaum's possession are from the papers of Gustave von Grunebaum (inaccessible to researchers at present).

Die Materialien, die sich im Besitz von Mrs. von Grunebaum befinden, stammen aus der Sammlung von Gustave von Grunebaum und sind z.Zt. für Forschungszwecke nicht zugänglich.

A3   Calendar diaries, dating from the 1930s on.

B1,2   Lengthy correspondence between von Grunebaum and his father.
        Correspondence with friends, University of Chicago, University of California, etc.

C1   4 novel Ms. T. Dating prior to 1938.

C7   2 large envelopes of notes to previous publications, recent unpub. writings, etc.

D7   Offprint collection. Complete after 1938, a few before.

H3,   Near East Center: honorary degrees, cl. about Grune-
I   baum.

H4   Reviews of his works.

I   Documents: naturalization papers, baptismal certificate, several awards, family tree, memorial article, etc.

J   Photos of von Grunebaum at conferences.

K   Von Grunebaum's professional library was sold to the von Grunebaum Center at the University of California, Los Angeles. The remainder of his library (history collection) remains with the family.

University of California, Los Angeles, Department of Special Collections, 120 Lawrence Clark Powell Library, Los Angeles, California 90024.

GUSTAVE VON GRUNEBAUM CENTER

B1,2   Correspondences of von Grunebaum with friends and
       colleagues.

C7   3 Ms. of pub. books (drafts).

H3   Cl. about von Grunebaum.

K   Personal and professional library of von Grunebaum.

M   Memorabilia, such as honorary doctorate, etc.

New York Public Library, Manuscript Division, Fifth Avenue
and 42nd Street, New York, N.Y. 10018.

EMERGENCY COMMITTEE IN AID OF DISPLACED FOREIGN SCHOLARS,
1933-1945

*   File compiled when assistance was granted. 1938-1944.

ALBERT GRZESINSKI
Political Figure, 1879-1947

<u>Mary S. Rosenberg</u>, 100 West 72nd Street, New York, N.Y.
10023.

Mrs. Rosenberg obtained the ALBERT GRZESINSKI ARCHIVE, ca.
3 ft. of materials, through purchase.

*Frau Rosenberg hat das ALBERT GRZESINSKI ARCHIVE (etwa 0,90
m Material) käuflich erworben.*

B1   19 L. 1939-1941, 1945, including L. to: Curt Glaser,
      Horace M. Kallen.

B2   13 L. 1940-1945, including L. from: J. W. Gerard, Curt
      Glaser.

B3   12 L.

C7   Ms. of essays. Ca. 525p., including the following
      topics:
      Ribbentrop.
      Postwar Germany.
      Hitler, Nazis, Nazis in America.
      Association of Free Germans.
      Siegfried Aufhäuser.
      World War II.

D7   "Auslandsorganization der NSDAP." 31p.

I   Documents concerning rationing in Germany during World
      War II.
      Tables on food and commodities in Germany.
      Documents concerning Nazi organizations in U.S.

L   Pamphlet on Poland. 31p.
      Pamphlet on Rudolf Hess. 1934.
      Ca. 1,700 newspaper cl., primarily concerning World
      War II and the Nazi regime. German and English.

N   Katz, Rudolf. "Übergangs-Verfassung." T.cc. 6p.
      Aufhäuser, Siegfried. "Gewerkschaften." T.cc. 12p.
      6 Ms. by Hamburger, Braunthal, Wachenheim, Fränkel.
      T. 62p.
      10 "Resolutions" concerning the New Germany.

<u>Yivo Institute</u>, 1048 Fifth Avenue, New York, N.Y. 10028.

HORACE M. KALLEN PAPERS

B1,2   Individual items in folders: 57, 353, 354, 608, 656, 700-703, 707, 808.

Hoover Institution on War, Revolution and Peace, Stanford, California 94305.

KARL BOROMAEUS FRANK COLLECTION

B1,2   Correspondence with Karl Frank.

State Historical Society of Wisconsin, 816 State Street, Madison, Wisconsin 53706.

TONI SENDER PAPERS

B1,2   Correspondence with Toni Sender. 1940, 1942.

Immigration History Research Center of the University of Minnesota, 826 Berry Street, St. Paul, Minnesota 55101.

AMERICAN COUNCIL FOR EMIGRÉS IN THE PROFESSIONS ARCHIVES

B1   1 L. to Hans Staudinger. 1941.

B2   1 L. from Alvin Johnson. 1941.

Boston University, Mugar Memorial Library, 771 Commonwealth Avenue, Boston, Massachusetts 02215.

BELLA FROMM COLLECTION

B1   1 L. to Bella Fromm. 1942.

EMIL J. GUMBEL

Mathematical Statistician, 1891-1966

University of Chicago, The Joseph Regenstein Library, 1100
East 57th Street, Chicago, Illinois 60637.

The EMIL J. GUMBEL PAPERS, 4 archive boxes of materials,
were donated to the Library by Mr. Ludwig Rosenberger in
1974, who had acquired the materials at an earlier date from
the Argosy Bookshop of New York.

*Die EMIL J. GUMBEL PAPERS, 4 Archivkartons Materialien, sind
eine Schenkung von Herrn Ludwig Rosenberger aus dem Jahre
1974. Herr Rosenberger selbst hatte die Materialien zu einem
früheren Zeitpunkt vom Argosy Bookshop of New York erworben.*

A3   Curriculum vitae and bibliographies of Gumbel's publi-
       cations, to ca. 1939. 1 F.
       Short memoir containing Gumbel's reflections on his
       life. Undated.

B1,2   Correspondence, primarily from the 1940s, including L.
       to and from: Johannes R. Becher, Alfred Falk (numer-
       ous), Paul and Rosi Fröhlich, Robert M. W. Kempner,
       Otto Lehmann-Russbüldt (numerous), Otto Nathan,
       Albert Norden, Karl O. Paetel, Frederick Pollock,
       Kurt Rosenfeld, Arthur Schwarz (numerous), as well
       as institutions, organizations, etc. 1.5 B.

B1,2   Correspondence and papers relating to Gumbel's position
H3   at the New School for Social Research and other in-
I   stitutions. Ca. 1940-1946. 8 F.
L   Correspondence, statements and cl. relating to Gumbel's
       role in the investigations of Arnold Bergsträsser.
       Ca. 1940-1945. 12 F.
       Correspondence and papers relating to Gumbel's work
       for the Office of Strategic Services. Ca. 1940-1945.
       Correspondence, papers and cl. relating to Gumbel's
       association with: École Libre des Hautes Études
       (1942-1943); Hamburger Universität (1964); Ligues
       des Croits de l'Homme, Congress at Lyon (1934). 4 F.

C7   Statement on German reconstruction. Undated.
       "Erklärung gegen die deutsche Aufrüstung." Drafts and
       related correspondence. Co-signed by many prominent
       German scholars.

E   Transcript of radio interview with Gumbel on the sub-
        ject of prewar German politics. 1944.
        Dialog between Gumbel and Dr. Siegfried Aram concern-
        ing prewar German politics. Undated.

I   "Der Tod des Hermann Friede." Unidentified document.
        Public statement on necessity of German reconstruction,
        signed by many prominent German immigrants.

Leo Baeck Institute, 129 East 73rd Street, New York, N.Y.
10021.

The EMIL GUMBEL PAPERS, 1928-1960 (MS 72-231) contain approximately 6 ft. of materials, half of which pertain to the
scientific writings of Gumbel and the other half to his
political writings. The materials were received as a gift
of Gumbel's estate, through his son, in 1967. All publication rights to materials in the collection remain with the
Gumbel family. No xeroxing of the scrapbooks is possible
because of their fragility. Similarly, copying of the clippings is partially restricted.

*Die EMIL GUMBEL PAPERS, 1928-1960 (MS 72-231) umfassen etwa
1,80 m Materialien, von denen die eine Hälfte in den wissenschaftlichen, die andere in den politischen Bereich fällt.
Die Materialien sind ein Geschenk (1967) von Gumbels Sohn
aus dem Nachlaß seines Vaters. Alle Rechte der Veröffentlichung ruhen bei der Familie. Wegen ihres brüchigen Zu-
stands können die Sammelalben nicht photokopiert werden.
Auch dürfen nicht von allen Ausschnitten Abschriften angefertigt werden.*

C10   Wegbereiter des deutschen Faschismus. Ms.
        Die deutschen Militärbünde 1919-1923. Ms.
        The Black Reichswehr - Conspirators Against the Weimar
            Republic. Ms.
        Bavarian History November 1918 - November 1919. Ms.
        Miscellaneous Ms. and notes:

D8,10   Reprints of scientific papers, political articles and
        lectures in various languages.

D12   Microfilm of Die Menschenrechte, journal edited by Gum-
        bel.

H3   Scrapbooks with articles relating to Gumbel's scien-
      tific and political activities.

H4   Cl. of reviews of Gumbel's scientific and political
      writings.

J   Photos.

L   Reviews of works by others.
      Technical and scientific reports, 1953-1962.
      Proceedings of statistical and other scientific sympo-
          sia, conferences and conventions; Columbia University
          teaching bulletin.
      Materials on Berthold Jacob case and the Reichstag
          arson trial at the German Supreme Court, Leipzig 1933.
      Collections of materials on statistics, mathematics,
          economics.

KURT KERSTEN COLLECTION

Bl   1 L. and 1 Ptc. to Kurt Kersten. 1948, 1953.

American Philosophical Society, The Library, 105 South Fifth
Street, Philadelphia, Pennsylvania 19106.

L. C. DUNN PAPERS

Bl,2 Correspondence with L. C. Dunn. 7 L. 1940-1942.

H3   Newspaper cl.
      Printed materials concerning Gumbel's "case." Pamph-
          lets, cl. 1925. Ca. 6 items.

I   File containing documents, curriculum vitae, etc.

State University of New York at Albany, Department of Germanic Languages and Literatures, 1400 Washington Avenue,
Albany, New York 12222.

KARL O. PAETEL COLLECTION

Bl   21 L. to Karl O. Paetel (xerox). 1942, 1954, 1965.

EMIL J. GUMBEL

<u>University of New Hampshire</u>, The Library, Department of Special Collections, Durham, New Hampshire 03824.

FRIEDRICH SALLY GROSSHUT COLLECTION, OSKAR MARIA GRAF COLLECTION

Bl   3 L. to F. S. Grosshut. T. 1962-1964.
        1 L. to O. M. Graf. 1927.

<u>Yivo Institute</u>, 1048 Fifth Avenue, New York, N.Y. 10028.

HORACE M. KALLEN PAPERS

Bl,2   Individual items in folders: 704, 859, 897, 938. 1942-
        1949.

<u>Library of Congress</u>, Manuscript Division, Independence Avenue and First Street S.E., Washington, D.C. 20540.

OSWALD VEBLEN PAPERS

B   Correspondence by, to and concerning Gumbel in file
        marked "Refugee File."

<u>Harvard University</u>, University Archives, Widener Library, Cambridge, Massachusetts 02138.

RICHARD VON MISES COLLECTION

Bl   1 L. to Richard von Mises. T. 1947.

<u>Immigration History Research Center of the University of Minnesota</u>, 826 Berry Street, St. Paul, Minnesota 55101.

AMERICAN COUNCIL FOR EMIGRÉS IN THE PROFESSIONS ARCHIVES

C7   "Funeral speech for Warner F. Brook." 1p.

Duke University, William R. Perkins Library, Manuscript
Department, Durham, North Carolina 27706.

FRITZ WOLFGANG LONDON PAPERS

B1   1 L. to F. W. London. 1943.

New York Public Library, Manuscript Division, Fifth Avenue
and 42nd Street, New York, N.Y. 10018.

EMERGENCY COMMITTEE IN AID OF DISPLACED FOREIGN SCHOLARS,
1933-1945

*   File compiled when assistance was granted. 1940-1944.

WALDEMAR GURIAN

Political Scientist, 1902-1954

<u>Mrs. Edith Gurian</u>, 2617 Fernway, South Bend, Indiana 46615.

The Project was unable to obtain a description of the ca. 6
ft. of Gurian materials in the possession of Mrs. Gurian.
These materials from the estate of Gurian will eventually be
deposited at the Library of Congress.

*Es war nicht möglich, eine Beschreibung der etwa 1,80 m
Materialien zu erhalten, die sich im Besitz von Frau Gurian
befinden. Diese Materialien aus dem Nachlaß von Waldemar
Gurian werden später der Library of Congress zukommen.*

<u>Library of Congress</u>, Manuscript Division, Independence Avenue
and First Street S.E., Washington, D.C. 20540.

HANNAH ARENDT PAPERS

B1,2   "Waldemar Gurian" file. Uncatalogued materials.

<u>Yale University</u>, Beinecke Rare Book and Manuscript Library,
New Haven, Connecticut 06520.

HERMANN BROCH ARCHIVE

B1   4 L. to Hermann Broch. 1946-1947.

B2   6 L. from Hermann Broch. 1946-1947.

<u>Cornell University</u>, John M. Olin Library, Department of Manu-
scripts and University Archives, Ithaca, New York 14850.

B1   3 L. to Wyndham Lewis. 1943-1944.

<u>State University of New York at Albany</u>, Department of Ger-
manic Languages and Literatures, 1400 Washington Avenue,
Albany, New York 12222.

KARL O. PAETEL COLLECTION

B1   2 L. to Karl O. Paetel (xerox). 1945-1946.

University of Notre Dame, Archives, Box 513, Notre Dame,
Indiana 46556.

B2   1 L. from Robert Maynard Hutchins. 1943.

HANS GUTERBOCK

Hittitologist, 1908-

Prof. Hans Guterbock, 5617 Drexel, Chicago, Illinois 60637.

The materials in Dr. Guterbock's possession represent materials primarily from his professional life, and especially concerning his work on the Hittites. The materials are at present inaccessible to the public.

Professor Guterbocks Material ist in erster Linie solches, das mit seinem wissenschaftlichen Werk, und da besonders mit seinen Arbeiten über die Hethiter, in Verbindung steht. Zur Zeit ist das Material nicht zugänglich.

B1,2   Family correspondence (to remain private).
Professional correspondence, including lengthy correspondence with one colleague. Very few early L., primarily from 1960 to the present.

C7   Notes for a lecture.

C8   Ms. of several articles.
Working notes for various later published works.

D7,8   Nearly complete collection of Guterbock's writings (offprints, cl.).

I   Miscellaneous documents: diploma, proof of ancestry, etc.

J   Photographs of work, including collection of Hittite monument photos.
Personal photos.

K   Personal library, including many professional periodicals such as: Istanbuler Schriften, Journal of Turkish Historical Society, etc.

L   Collection of articles by others (cl., offprints).
Materials on German expeditions on the Hittites (property of the individual expeditions).

ARTHUR E. HAAS

Physicist, 1884-1941

Dr. Arthur G. Haas, Department of History, 1101 McClung Tower, University of Tennessee, Knoxville, Tennessee 37916.

Dr. Arthur G. Haas is the son of the late Arthur E. Haas.

Dr. Arthur G. Haas ist der Sohn des verstorbenen Arthur E. Haas.

A3   Fragment of an autobiography. 1884-1920. T. 70p.

B1   Numerous personal L. to wife.

B1,2 "Professional correspondence." Ca. 100 L.

Harvard University, Houghton Library, Cambridge, Massachusetts 02138.

GEORGE SARTON PAPERS

B1   1 L. to George Sarton. 1924.

Princeton University, Firestone Library, Princeton, New Jersey 08540.

THE PAPERS OF ALBERT EINSTEIN (1879-1955). For details concerning the use of this collection, see description under Albert Einstein.

THE PAPERS OF ALBERT EINSTEIN (1879-1955). Angaben über den Zugang zu der Sammlung finden sich unter "Albert Einstein."

B1,2 Unknown amount of correspondence between Einstein and Haas. 1936.

C8   "Unpublished material."

American Institute of Physics, Niels Bohr Library, 335 East 45th Street, New York, N.Y. 10017.

NIELS BOHR CORRESPONDENCE (Microfilm)

378

B1   3 L. to Niels Bohr. 1914, 1922.

B2   1 L. from Niels Bohr. 1922.

American Philosophical Society, The Library, 105 South Fifth
Street, Philadelphia, Pennsylvania 19106.

NIELS BOHR CORRESPONDENCE

B1   2 L. to Niels Bohr. 1927, 1959.

B2   1 L. from Niels Bohr. 1927.

HANS HABE

Writer, 1911-1977

Boston University, Mugar Memorial Library, 771 Commonwealth
Avenue, Boston, Massachusetts 02215.

The HANS HABE COLLECTION, 14 archive boxes of materials plus
numerous books, was donated by the author between the years
1965 and the present. Habe still retains much of his collection at his home in Switzerland.

*Die HANS HABE COLLECTION (14 Archivkartons und zahlreiche
Bücher) ist eine Schenkung des Autors aus der Zeit von 1965
bis heute. Ein großer Teil der Sammlung von Hans Habe befindet sich noch in seiner Privatwohnung in der Schweiz.*

A3   Ich stelle mich. Incomplete Ms. of autobiography. A.

B1   3 L. 1939-1943.

B2   8 L. including L. from: Lion Feuchtwanger, Robert F.
      Kennedy, Erich Maria Remarque.

B3   6 L. including L. by: Erika Mann, Erich Maria Remarque.

C1   Christoph und sein Vater. Incomplete versions, notes.
         107p.
      The Devil's Agent. Original incomplete version. 51p.
      The Mission. English Ms., first drafts. 324p. Proofs.
         4 sets.
      Off Limits. Incomplete Ms. A.
      Die Tarnowska/The Countess. Incomplete Ms. A.
         "Die Gräfin Tarnowska." Part I. T.cc.
         "Der Tatbestand." Part II. T.cc.
      Der Tod in Texas. Early version. A. 58p. Later version.
         T.cc. Notes. A. 33p.
         The Wounded Land. English tr. and pc. of tr. 406p.
         and 407p.

C3   2 poems from Das Netz/The Poisoned Stream. A. 2p.

C7   Lecture texts:
         "Unser Kulturkampf mit dem Osten." May 13, 1963.
            T.cc. 22p.
         The Devil's Agent. Munich. T.cc. 21p.
         Universität für Zeitungswesen. Munich. T.cc. 15p.
         University of Heidelberg. T. 26p.

D1   <u>Off Limits</u>. Serialization of the novel in <u>Revue</u>.

D7   3 cl.

E   <u>The Mission</u>. Television program by Jochen Huth. March
      1967. Mimeo. 216p. Another copy. T.cc. 214p.

F   Record. Hans Habe on his book <u>Christoph und sein Vater</u>.

G   "Gesprek met Hans Habe." Interview with Habe in Dutch.

H3   Biography of Habe, from a publication of Austrian emi-
      grés in the U.S.
      Advertising brochures on Habe. Kurt Desch Verlag,
      Munich.
      3 scrapbooks of cl. by and about Habe and his works.
      1941-1942.
      "Über mich." 2 notebooks with newspaper cl. by and
      about Habe. 1954-1962.
      6 cl.

H4   <u>Ilona</u>. 1 Dutch advertising brochure.
      <u>Im Namen des Teufels</u>/<u>The Devil's Agent</u>. Reviews in a
      scrapbook. 1956-1962. Also scrapbook of reviews of
      the movie. 1962-1963.
      <u>Kathrine</u>, <u>Walk in Darkness</u>, <u>Aftermath</u>, <u>Black Earth</u>.
      Reviews in a scrapbook. 1943-1952.
      <u>Off Limits</u>. Reviews in a notebook. 1955-1958.
      <u>Die Tarnowska</u>. Reviews. 1 F.
      <u>Der Tod in Texas</u>/<u>The Wounded Land</u>. 3 advertising bro-
      chures.
      Miscellaneous reviews of works. 1 F.

I   Bronze Star from the U.S. Army for Habe. Pc.
      Oakleaf Cluster to Bronze Star from U.S. Army. March
      19, 1946. Pc.
      Croix-de-guerre de Luxembourg from the Herzogin Char-
      lotte von Luxembourg. Aug. 8, 1945. Pc.

J   3 photos of Casa Acacia, Habe's home in Ascona, Swit-
      zerland.
      <u>The Countess</u>. 3 photos on location in Venice.
      3 film photos from Habe's filmed works:
      <u>Seduction of the Minors</u>, <u>The Ambassadrice</u>, <u>The</u>
      <u>Countess</u>.
      Photos of Habe and his home.
      3 photos of Habe's private art collection.

K   62 different editions and translations of Habe's
       works:
       Black Earth
       Christoph und sein Vater
       Ilona
       Im Jahre Null
       Im Namen des Teufels
       Kathrine
       Meine Herren Geschworenen
       Die Mission
       Ob Tausend fallen
       Off Limits
       Die Tarnowska
       4 books containing contributions by Habe.
       5 books containing references to or articles about
       Habe.

L   6 American propaganda brochures.
       The Countess/Die Tarnowska. Background material. 6 F.
       Ilona. Background materials. 1 F.
       28 dust jackets from Habe's novels.
       Walk in Darkness. Advertisements for the dramatized
       version by William Hairston.
       2 cl. on assassinations. 1933-1934.

N   An unpub. Ms. by Thomas Mann. 1961. A. Pc. 2p. Accom-
       panied by statements by Erika Mann.

O   Ilona. Playbill.
       Advertisement for Habe lecture. Tukan Literary Circle,
       Munich.
       "Showcard." Program for dramatized version of Walk in
       Darkness.

MICHAEL BLANKFORT PAPERS, ALLAN KNIGHT CHALMERS PAPERS,
BELLA FROMM COLLECTION

B1   6 L. 1951-1966, including 3 L. to Bella Fromm.

B3   12 L., 1 Tel. and 1 Ptc. from Marina Habe to Michael
       Blankfort. T. 1966-1968.

H3   "Hounding Axel Springer." 1 cl.

Harcourt Brace Jovanovich, Inc., 757 Third Avenue, New York, N.Y. 10017.

B1,2   Publisher's correspondence between Harcourt Brace
       Jovanovich and Habe concerning the American editions
       of The Countess and Ilona. 48 L.

University of Southern California, Lion Feuchtwanger Memorial Library, 520 Paseo Miramar, Pacific Palisades, California 90272.

B1   11 L. to Lion Feuchtwanger. 1947-1958.

B2   8 L. from Lion Feuchtwanger. 1954-1958.

University of Pennsylvania, The Charles Patterson Van Pelt Library, Philadelphia, Pennsylvania 19104.

ALMA MAHLER-WERFEL COLLECTION

B1   6 L. to Alma Mahler-Werfel. T. and A. 1947-1949 and
       undated.
       1 L. to Franz Werfel. A. 1942.

University of New Hampshire, The Library, Department of Special Collections, Durham, New Hampshire 03824.

OSKAR MARIA GRAF COLLECTION

B1   3 L. to O. M. Graf. 1965-1966.

B2   1 L. from O. M. Graf. 1965.

Dr. Gustave O. Arlt, 13220-C Admiralty Way, Marina del Rey, California 90291.

FRANZ WERFEL ARCHIVE

B1   1 L. to Franz Werfel. 1941.

Leo Baeck Institute, 129 East 73rd Street, New York, N.Y. 10021.

Bl   1 L. to "Mein lieber Joss." T. 1939.

University of Texas, Humanities Research Center, Manuscripts Collection, Box 7219, Austin, Texas 78712.

Bl   1 L. plus miscellaneous unsorted materials.

FRIEDRICH J. HACKER

Psychoanalyst, 1914-

Dr. Friedrich J. Hacker, The Hacker Clinic, 160 Lasky Drive,
Beverly Hills, California 90212.

Private personal collection: inaccessible.

Unzugängliche Privatsammlung.

A2   School notebooks from youth.

B1,2 Correspondence, in German and English. 1940s-1960s. Ca.
      4 ft. Includes L. to and from: Theodor W. Adorno,
      Erik Erikson, Otto Fenichel, Bruno and Liesl Frank,
      Leonhard Frank, Thomas Mann and family, Gerhard and
      Maria Piers, Otto Preminger, Ernst Simmel, Bruno
      Walter, Hans Weigl.

C7   Notes from his lectures and workshops. 1960s-1970s. T.
      German and English. Ca. 5 ft.

C7,8 Ms. of longer works. Ca. 1,000p. Including Ms. of:
      Terror.
      Aggression.
      Ms. of articles.

D7,8 Complete collection of offprints, some mimeo. Several
      hundred.

F   Several tape recordings from public appearances plus
      transcripts.

G   Interviews.

H3   Cl. concerning Hacker's public appearances on radio
      and television. Ca. 3 ft.

H4   Reviews of Hacker's works.

I   Numerous documents.

J   More than 100 photos.

K   Sizable personal library.

L   Notes and materials used in his writings.
      Cl. on the field of psychology.
      Information notebooks on Hacker's patients.

N   Adorno, Theodor. "The Stars Down to Earth." 20p.

FRIEDRICH J. HACKER

Reiss-Davis Child Study Center, 9760 West Pico Boulevard,
Los Angeles, California 90035.

F   Tapes of Hacker's lectures.

IVAN HEILBUT

Writer, 1898-1972

Mr. Francis Heilbut, 328 West 96th Street, New York, N.Y. 10025.

Mr. Francis Heilbut, the son of Ivan, possesses approximately 60 ft. of materials from the estate of his father.

Mr. Francis Heilbut, der Sohn von Ivan Heilbut, besitzt etwa 18 m Material aus dem Nachlaß seines Vaters.

A1 Diaries. Ca. 4 in.
    Appointment calendars with h. entries.
    Diary containing addresses.
    List of letters written and sent.

A3 Selbstporträt. 2 versions. T.c. with h. corr. 5p. and
      3p.
    Autobiographical notes. A. and T. with numerous h. corr.
      56p.
    "Als Ivan George Heilbut zu Beginn der zwanziger Jahre
    nach Berlin kam..." Untitled essay. T. with numerous
    corr. 2p.

B1,2 Ca. 2,500 L. 1940s-1970s, including L. to and from:
      Julius Bab, Bruno Frank, Reverend Frederick Forell,
      John Gassner, Manfred George, Emil Ludwig, Kurt Pin-
      thus, Gustav Regler, Hans Sahl, Albrecht Schaeffer,
      George N. Shuster, Ernst Waldinger, Franz Werfel,
      Kurt Wolff, Stefan Zweig.
      Additional 15 F. plus 7 in. of L. 1940s-1970s, includ-
      ing L. to and from: National Refugee Service, Deut-
      sche Bühnenverein, Ernst Reuter Gesellschaft, P.E.N.
      Club, Doubleday Publishers, Europäische Verlagsan-
      stalt, Walter Verlag, newspaper and magazine pub-
      lishers.

C1 1933. T. 250p.
    Der einsame Weg. T. 350p.
    Das falsche Dienen. T. and A. 350p. Notes. A. 10p.
      Synopsis of novel, drafts and sketches. 70p.
    Liebhaber des Lebens. T. 250p.
    Offene Gesellschaft. Numerous versions and copies.
    The Survivors/Die Überlebenen. Various versions. Ca.
      500p.
    Zugvögel/Birds of Passage. Various versions. Ca. 700p.

Miscellaneous loose p. and sections of novels. Ca. 1,500p.

C2 Enkel Jaakobs. Several versions. A. and T. 109p.
Eyolf. 2 c., 1 incomplete. 86p. and 75p.
Der Tod des Richters. A. with corr. 34p.
Weshalb. Ca. 30p.
Revanche/Marion. Ca. 150p.
Paul Ehrlich. Ca. 60p.
Fahre nach Salamis. Ca. 40p.
Schlagende Wetter. T. Ca. 25p.
Das würdige Leben. Ca. 50p.
Zwillinge. Ca. 200p.
Miscellaneous drama texts, acts, scenes. Ca. 1,000p.

C3 "Gedichte an die Etrusker." 1965. Ca. 50p.
"Neue Beiträge für Etrusker." Ca. 50p.
Untitled poems. Ca. 250p.
"Gedicht [aus Berlin]." Ca. 50p.
"Meine Wanderungen [aus Paris]." Ca. 25p.
Miscellaneous loose p. of poems. Ca. 1 1/2 in.

C4 Aphorisms.
Stories. Ca. 200p.

C6 Trompetensignale. Radio play. 40p.
Es ist nicht auf uns abgesehen. Radio play.
Untitled radio play. Ca. 35p.
Der Kampf um Shylock. Radio play. Also essay.

C7 Theater criticisms, opera, radio, etc. T. and A. Ca. 200p.
Over 5,000p. of essayistic work, including:
 "Erziehung durch Dichtung." Ca. 20p.
 "Deutsche Dichtung."
Miscellaneous essays on: Hermann Hesse, Friedrich Schiller, J. W. von Goethe, Stefan Zweig, Franz Werfel, Rainer Maria Rilke, Hermann Melville, Tennessee Williams, Thomas Wolfe, Carl Sandburg, Joseph Roth, Hugo von Hofmannsthal, Alfred Döblin, Friedrich Nietzsche, Heinrich Heine, William Shakespeare.

C9 Transcriptions of American folk songs. Ca. 200p.

D7 Newspaper and magazine cl. from American and German sources.

H3   Newspaper cl. German and English.

H4   Reviews of Heilbut's works. Ca. 20 cl.

I   Passport, financial documents, receipts, contracts,
      tax forms, bills, etc.
      Legal correspondence.

J   Photos.

L   Materials from Hunter College years. Ca. 30p.

O   Theater programs. 6 items.

State University of New York at Albany, Department of Germanic Languages and Literatures, 1400 Washington Avenue,
Albany, New York 12222.

STORM PUBLISHERS ARCHIVE

B1   2 L. to Alexander Gode von Aesch. 1950.

B3   7 L. from the League for Mutual Aid re: Heilbut. 1950.

C7   "Der Lebensneugierige. Der Lyriker Goethe." Lecture
      texts. 28p.

Immigration History Research Center of the University of
Minnesota, 826 Berry Street, St. Paul, Minnesota 55101.

AMERICAN COUNCIL FOR EMIGRÉS IN THE PROFESSIONS ARCHIVES

A3   Curriculum vitae, biographical sketches, recommenda-
      tions. 8p.

Mr. Hans Sahl, 800 West End Avenue, New York, N.Y. 10025.

B1   Several L. to Hans Sahl.

New York Public Library, Manuscript Division, Fifth Avenue
and 42nd Street, New York, N.Y. 10018.

EMERGENCY COMMITTEE IN AID OF DISPLACED FOREIGN SCHOLARS, 1933-1945

*   File compiled when assistance was granted. 1939-1944.

Mrs. Elisabeth M. Stoerk and Mrs. Susanne B. Hoeller, 288 Ocean Drive West, Stamford, Connecticut 06902.

FRIDERIKE ZWEIG ARCHIVE

B1   Several L. to Friderike Zweig.

Mrs. Peter M. Lindt, 949 West End Avenue, New York, N.Y. 10025.

B1   Small amount of correspondence with Peter M. Lindt.

C   Ms. submitted to Lindt for use on his radio program.

EDUARD HEIMANN

Economist, 1899-1967

Harvard University, Harvard Divinity School, Andover-Harvard
Theological Library, 45 Francis Avenue, Cambridge, Massachusetts 02138.

PAUL TILLICH COLLECTION

N1   19 L. to Paul Tillich. T. and A. 1956-1963.
      3 L.

B2   10 L. from Paul Tillich. T.cc. 1935-1963.

Immigration History Research Center of the University of
Minnesota, 826 Berry Street, St. Paul, Minnesota 55101.

AMERICAN COUNCIL FOR EMIGRÉS IN THE PROFESSIONS ARCHIVES

B1   1 L. to Curt Bondy. 1942.
      2 L.

B2   2 L. 1939.

C7   "Funeral Speech for Werner F. Bruck delivered by Edu-
      ard Heimann, June 1, 1945." 3p.

Yivo Institute, 1048 Fifth Avenue, New York, N.Y. 10028.

HORACE M. KALLEN PAPERS

B1,2 Individual items located in folders: 355-355A, 380,
      542, 559-560, 713, 942. 1934-1949.

Leo Baeck Institute, 129 East 73rd Street, New York, N.Y.
10021.

JULIE BRAUN-VOGELSTEIN COLLECTION

B1   Correspondence with Heinrich Braun.

State University of New York at Albany, Department of Ger-

manic Languages and Literatures, 1400 Washington Avenue, Albany, New York 12222.

KARL O. PAETEL COLLECTION

B1   6 L. to Karl O. Paetel. 1941-1946. (xerox)

Prof. Carl Landauer, 1317 Arch Street, Berkeley, California 94708.

B1,2 Correspondence with Carl Landauer.

University of Chicago, The Joseph Regenstein Library, 1100 East 57th Street, Chicago, Illinois 60637.

JAMES FRANCK PAPERS

B1,2 Correspondence between Heimann and James Franck.

JULIUS HELD

Art Historian, 1905-

Dr. Julius Held, 81 Monument Avenue, Old Bennington, Vermont
05201.

The materials in Dr. Held's possession consist of approximately 30 ft. of materials in addition to his personal library. They are at present inaccessible to the public.

*In Dr. Helds persönlichem Besitz befinden sich seine Privat-
bibliothek und etwa 9 m Archivmaterial. Beides ist zur Zeit
für die Öffentlichkeit unzugänglich.*

A1   Diary, begun with birth of oldest child, ended ca.
       1965.

A2   Notebooks of trips, especially to different museums.

B2   Correspondence, including L. from: Erika Tietze, Erwin
       Panofsky, J. P. Getty, Max Friedländer, P. Frankl,
       Ludwig Burckhardt.

C7   Ms. of book on Rubens. Incomplete.

C14   Several drawings and sketches by Held.

D7   Newspaper cl., offprints, etc. of most of Held's works.

F   Taped interview with Held, taken by Prof. Irene Jaffe.

H3,4   Reviews, critiques, and biographical statements about
       Held. Mostly cl.

I   Several documents.

J   More than 1,000 photos, primarily of works of art.
       Collection of photos for P. P. Rubens work.

K   Sizable art library with card catalog.

L   Numerous drawings by others, collected by Held over the
       years.
       Materials used in his work, including several micro-
       films.
       Materials on Grete Ring.
       Newspaper cl., etc., on famous personalities.

M   Memorabilia of Held and his family.

JULIUS HELD

Harvard University, Fogg Art Museum, Cambridge, Massachusetts
02138.

B1   Ca. 20 L. to Dr. Paul Sachs. 1933-1936.

New York Public Library, Manuscript Division, Fifth Avenue
and 42nd Street, New York, N.Y. 10018.

EMERGENCY COMMITTEE IN AID OF DISPLACED FOREIGN SCHOLARS,
1933-1945

*   File compiled, no assistance given. 1934-1938.

ERNST DAVID HELLINGER

Mathematician, 1883-1950

Northwestern University, Mathematics Library, Lunt Building,
Evanston, Illinois 60201.

The materials at Northwestern were assembled from the faculty
files of the Mathematics Department of the university. Ca.
6 in.

*Die Materialien in der Mathematics Library (etwa 1,80 m)
wurden aus den Akten des mathematischen Instituts der Universität zusammengestellt.*

B1,2   Correspondence concerning Hellinger's career at North-
        western University, including grant applications.

B3   1 L. from W. T. Reid to Max Dehn concerning Hellinger.
        1950.
        Invitations and responses to a dinner in honor of Hel-
        linger.

C7   "Notes on the History of Calculus with Implications
        for Our Teaching." Abstract.
        Notes on Greek Mathematics. Dated Jan. 1946.
        Notes on J. Gregory to the Math Club. 1940.
        Notes for a talk on history of math. May 1948.
        "History and Teaching of Mathematics." Seminar notes.
        1945-1946.

I   Documents concerning Hellinger's arrival in the U.S.,
        application for first citizenship papers. 1939.

Ms. Hanna H. Meissner, 176 East Stadium Avenue, West Lafayette, Indiana 47906.

Ms. Meissner is the sister of the late Dr. Hellinger.

*Frau Meissner ist die Schwester des verstorbenen Dr. Hellin-
ger.*

B1   "Private letters."

B1,2   Correspondence with Max Dehn concerning an article on
        James Gregory.

B2   2 L. from Max Born. 1925, 1926.

C7   Articles written in collaboration with Max Dehn:
      "Certain Mathematical Achievements of James Gregory."
         1943.
      "On James Gregory's Vera Quadratura."

C8   "Seminar on Quantentheory." Frankfurt, 1936. Notes. A.
         36p.
      Notes on quantentheory.
      Notes on dissertation.

I   Documents.

J   Photos of Hellinger.

New York University, Courant Institute of Mathematical Sciences, Library, 251 Mercer Street, New York, N.Y. 10012.

B1,2 File: "Ernst Hellinger." 1938-1947.

Harvard University, University Archives, Widener Library,
Cambridge, Massachusetts 02138.

RICHARD VON MISES COLLECTION

B1   1 L. to Richard von Mises. A. 1930.

Prof. W. T. Reid, Department of Mathematics, University of
Oklahoma, Norman, Oklahoma 73069.

D8   "Integralgleichungen und Gleichungen mit unendlichvie-
      len Unbekannten." With the designation "Author's
      copy."

New York Public Library, Manuscript Division, Fifth Avenue
and 42nd Street, New York, N.Y. 10018.

EMERGENCY COMMITTEE IN AID OF DISPLACED FOREIGN SCHOLARS,
1933-1945

*   File compiled when assistance was granted. 1933-1944.

PAUL HERTZ

Journalist, Socialist Politician, 1888-1961

Hoover Institution on War, Revolution and Peace, Stanford, California 94305.

The PAUL HERTZ PAPERS, 1920-1961 (microfilm HX276 H5 A3), consist of a microfilm collection of 64 reels. The original materials were given by Mrs. Paul Hertz to the Internationales Institut für Sozialgeschichte (Herengracht 262-266, Amsterdam, Holland). A complete description of the collection is available: Hermann W. Bott, Paul Hertz papers: table of contents. 2 vols. [Berlin, 1962].

Die PAUL HERTZ PAPERS, 1920-1961 (Mikrofilm HX276 H5 A3) ist eine Sammlung von 64 Mikrofilmspulen. Frau Hertz hat die Originalmaterialien dem Internationalen Institut für Sozialgeschichte (Herengracht 262-266, Amsterdam, Holland) überlassen. Es ist eine ausführliche Beschreibung der Sammlung erhältlich: Hermann W. Bott, Paul Hertz papers: table of contents. 2 Bände [Berlin, 1962].

Archive for History of Quantum Physics (locations in U.S.: Bancroft Library, University of California, Berkeley; American Philosophical Society, Philadelphia, Pennsylvania; American Institute of Physics, New York, N.Y.).

B1   3 L. to Alfred Landé. 1915-1924.
       13 L. to Niels Bohr. 1921-1922 and undated.

B2   9 L. from Niels Bohr. 1921-1922 and undated.

Leo Baeck Institute, 129 East 73rd Street, New York, N.Y. 10021.

GUSTAV STOLPER COLLECTION

B1,2   Correspondence with Gustav Stolper. 1938-1947. 18 L.

H3   Pamphlets on Paul Hertz.

State University of New York at Albany, Department of Ger-

manic Languages and Literatures, 1400 Washington Avenue, Albany, New York 12222.

KARL O. PAETEL COLLECTION

Bl   4 L. to Karl O. Paetel (xerox). 1951-1954.

Swarthmore College, Swarthmore, Pennsylvania 19081.

SWARTHMORE COLLEGE PEACE COLLECTION: WILLIAM F. SOLLMANN PAPERS

Bl,2 Correspondence with William F. Sollmann.

University of Chicago, The Joseph Regenstein Library, 1100 East 57th Street, Chicago, Illinois 60637.

JAMES FRANCK PAPERS

Bl,2 Correspondence between Hertz and James Franck.

State Historical Society of Wisconsin, 816 State Street, Madison, Wisconsin 53706.

TONI SENDER PAPERS

Bl,2 Correspondence between Paul and Hanna Hertz and Toni
      Sender. 1953, 1957-1960.

California Institute of Technology, Robert A. Millikan Library, Pasadena, California 91109.

THEODORE VON KARMAN CORRESPONDENCE

Bl   1 L. to Theodore von Karman. Undated.

New York Public Library, Manuscript Division, Fifth Avenue and 42nd Street, New York, N.Y. 10018.

PAUL HERTZ

EMERGENCY COMMITTEE IN AID OF DISPLACED FOREIGN SCHOLARS, 1933-1945

*   File compiled, no assistance given. 1933-1939.

Princeton University, Firestone Library, Princeton, New Jersey 08540.

THE PAPERS OF ALBERT EINSTEIN (1879-1955). For details concerning the use of this collection, see description under Albert Einstein.

THE PAPERS OF ALBERT EINSTEIN (1879-1955). Angaben über den Zugang zu der Sammlung finden sich unter "Albert Einstein."

B1,2   Unknown amount of correspondence between Einstein and Paul Hertz. 1910, 1915, 1922.

ERICH HERTZMANN

Musicologist, 1902-1963

Columbia University, Music Library, New York, N.Y. 10027.

The ERICH HERTZMANN COLLECTION, which consists of 339 file
folders of materials plus 59 microfilm reels, was donated to
the library from the estate of Hertzmann in 1963. Permission
to use the collection is obtainable from Mr. Thomas Watkins
(Music Librarian, Columbia University). All rights to the
materials remain with the widow of Erich Hertzmann.

*Die ERICH HERTZMANN COLLECTION, die aus 339 Aktenordnern und
59 Mikrofilmen besteht, war eine Schenkung an die Music Library aus dem Nachlaß von Erich Hertzmann im Jahre 1963.
Erlaubnis, die Sammlung einzusehen, erteilt: Mr. Thomas Watkins, Music Librarian, Columbia University. Alle Rechte
ruhen bei der Witwe von Erich Hertzmann.*

C7   Subject folders on numerous music topics and person-
       alities. Also student papers, course lecture notes,
       bibliographies, etc.

C13   Transcriptions by Hertzmann of compositions by: Att-
       wood, Beethoven, Bruckner, Haydn, Mozart, Willaert,
       and miscellaneous unclassified transcriptions.
       Sketchbooks of music Ms. and single Ms. from: Gesell-
       schaft der Musikfreunde, Vienna; Deutsche Staats-
       bibliothek, Berlin; Tübingen University Library;
       Koch Sammlung; Sammlung Bodmer, Zürich; National-
       bibliothek, Vienna; Moscow; Bibliothèque du Conser-
       vatoire, Paris; Deutsche Nationalbibliothek, Mar-
       burg; etc. Ca. 47 microfilm reels.
       Microfilm collection of Ms. by: Aosta, Attwood, Eit-
       ner, Haydn, Mendelssohn, Mozart, Petrucci, Schubert,
       Schumann. Ca. 12+ microfilm reels.

University of California, Santa Barbara, The Library, Santa
Barbara, California 93105.

K   Ca. 4,000 volumes from the personal music library of
       Erich Hertzmann.

Columbia University, Butler Library, New York, N.Y. 10027.

B1   1 L. to Daniel G. Mason. A. 1952. Also enclosure.

GERHARD HERZ

Musicologist, 1911-

Prof. Gerhard Herz, University of Louisville, School of
Music, Department of Music History, Louisville, Kentucky
40208.

Private collection: inaccessible. Dr. Herz intends to donate
his Bach collection to the University Music Library.

Unzugängliche Privatsammlung. Dr. Herz hat vor, seine Bach-
sammlung der University Music Library zu schenken.

A3   Bibliography.

B1,2   Correspondence with: Albert Schweitzer (15 L.), Edward
        Lowinsky (over 50 L.), Emmanuel Feuermann, W. W.
        Norton Publishers, Karl Geiringer, J. S. Bach schol-
        ars in East and West Germany. Also some c. of Herz's
        L.

C7   Several Ms. to critical articles.
        Lecture Ms. (e.g., American Musicological Society).
        Notes to lectures on 3" x 5" cards. 6 files.

D7   Offprint collection, primarily from 1965 on.

F   Ca. 25 recordings of popular lectures.
        Oral history interview (in the Archives of the Univer-
        sity of Louisville Music Library).

I   Documents.

J   Photos (personal collection). 1920-. Additional photos
        obtainable from the Louisville Courier-Journal (news-
        paper).

K   Music library, including a large photocopy collection
        of Bach Ms. (1/4 of Bach's extent Ms. work, 1/3 of
        Bach's vocal music).

New York Public Library, Manuscript Division, Fifth Avenue
and 42nd Street, New York, N.Y. 10018.

EMERGENCY COMMITTEE IN AID OF DISPLACED FOREIGN SCHOLARS,
1933-1945

*   File compiled when assistance was granted. 1937-1941.

<u>Prof. Hans Tischler</u>, 711 East First Street, Bloomington, Indiana 47401.

B1,2 Correspondence with Hans Tischler.

<u>Dr. Edward E. Lowinsky</u>, Prof. Emeritus, Department of Music, University of Chicago, Chicago, Illinois 60637.

B1   148 L. to Edward E. Lowinsky. 1947-1977.

B2   50 L. from Edward E. Lowinsky. 1947-1977.

ERNST EMIL HERZFELD

Archeologist, 1879-1948

Smithsonian Institution, Freer Gallery of Art, Washington, D.C. 20560.

The E. E. HERZFELD COLLECTION was established in 1946 as the result of a donation of materials by Herzfeld. Additional materials have since been added to the collection from donations by Mrs. Charlotte M. Bradford and Dr. George C. Miles. An unpublished detailed catalog of the collection has been prepared by Mr. Joseph Upton of the Freer Gallery.

Die E. E. HERZFELD COLLECTION beruht auf einer Schenkung von E. E. Herzfeld aus dem Jahre 1946. Seitdem ist diese Sammlung um Schenkungen von Mrs. Charlotte M. Bradford und Dr. George C. Miles erweitert worden. Mr. Joseph Upton von der Freer Gallery hat einen (unveröffentlichten) ausführlichen Katalog der Sammlung angefertigt.

A1   1 personal diary. 1897.

A2   Notebooks 1-5.
      131 notebooks in German, including sketches, tracings,
      blueprints, some photos, notes from sites of dig-
      gings. 1904-1957.
      35 sketchbooks in German, including photos of drawings,
      sites, maps, artifacts, notes, inscriptions, etc.
      Expeditions in Persia, Persepolis, Damascus, Spalato,
      etc. 1923-1930 and undated.

A3   8 travel journals. 1905-1928. A. and transcriptions.
      Also includes place name index.

B1   15 L. by Herzfeld. Professional correspondence.

B2   Large collection of L. to Herzfeld concerning publica-
      tion of Paikuli.

C8   Records of Samarra expeditions: listing of journals,
      notebooks, sketchbooks. Items are books, boxes,
      scrapbooks, fragments, sketches, with numbers and
      descriptions for each item or grouping of items.
      S-1 to S-31.

C14   Drawings and maps with catalog description of each.
      Folders numbered 1-1291, sometimes containing single
      items, sometimes several items.

       Paper squeezes of inscriptions with description of each
item and negative number if negative exists:
1) Arabic script, 1-61.
2) Middle Persian, 1-133.
3) Cuneiform, 1-125.

H5   Complete bibliography of publications by year. Reviews,
books, articles.

J   Photos from glass negatives, numbered 1-3850. Arranged
in 16 binders by categories: prehistoric pottery,
bronzes, stone, Persepolis, Sassanian monuments,
Syrian monuments, Persian architecture and land-
scapes, etc. Also 3 additional photo albums.
Photos from cut film that have been made into prints
and interfiled in photo file with similar subject
matter.
Photos (no negatives) of Samarra material. Total of
42 photo files with catalog of contents of each.

M,   List of archeological artifacts with detailed descrip-
N   tions of each compiled by Dr. Richard Ettinghausen.
Wood, stone, metal, pottery, glass, stucco, bone,
ivory, painted plaster, etc. H-1 through H-101 plus
several unnumbered artifacts.

Metropolitan Museum of Art, Department of Ancient Near-
Eastern Art, Fifth Avenue and 82nd Street, New York, N.Y.
10028.

The E. E. HERZFELD ARCHIVE was purchased in 1944. It has
been numbered and catalogued and a description of the collection published: Margaret Cool Root, "The Herzfeld Archive
of the Metropolitan Museum of Art," Metropolitan Museum
Journal, 11 (1976), 119-124.

*Das E. E. HERZFELD ARCHIVE wurde 1944 gekauft. Die Sammlung
ist numeriert und katalogisiert und eine Beschreibung findet
sich in folgender Veröffentlichung: Margaret Cool Root, "The
Herzfeld Archive of the Metropolitan Museum of Art," Metropolitan Museum Journal, 11 (1976), 119-124.*

A1   Diary. 1897.

A2   Notebooks, 1 with dried plant specimens.

B1,2 Ca. 20 L. from the early 1900s, with F. H. Weissbach,
        C. Uhlig.
        Correspondence relating to publishing.

C4   Short story. German. 10p.

C7   8 unpub. Ms.
        2 Ms. of pub. works.
        3 lecture Ms.

C14   Very large collection of Herzfeld's drawings and
        sketches of archeological sites, artifacts, sculp-
        tures.
        Sketchbooks, taken on travels of antiquarian interest.
        Notes and drawings, catalogued by Herzfeld according
        to period/place.
        Squeezes, 3-dimensional rubbings.

H4   Cl., book notices.

J   5 photo albums (labeled) from earliest trips to Middle
        East in first part of 20th century.

L   Maps, printed and hand-drawn. Some contour maps.

M   Postcards (unwritten and unsent).

Metropolitan Museum of Art, Department of Islamic Art, Fifth
Avenue and 82nd Street, New York, N.Y. 10028.

*   Unsorted materials.

Field Museum of Natural History, Roosevelt Road at Lake
Shore Drive, Chicago, Illinois 60605.

*   Collection of Iranian pottery (900 specimens - acces-
        sion no. A2360) purchased from E. E. Herzfeld in
        1945.

Smithsonian Institution Archives, Washington, D.C. 20560.

B1   4 L. to Smithsonian Institution. 1946.

ERNST EMIL HERZFELD

New York Public Library, Manuscript Division, Fifth Avenue
and 42nd Street, New York, N.Y. 10018.

EMERGENCY COMMITTEE IN AID TO DISPLACED FOREIGN SCHOLARS,
1933-1945

*   File compiled when assistance was granted. 1935-1938.

WIELAND HERZFELDE

Writer, Publisher, 1896-

<u>University of Southern California</u>, Lion Feuchtwanger Memorial Library, 520 Paseo Miramar, Pacific Palisades, California 90272.

B1   30 L. to Lion Feuchtwanger. 1942-1950.

B2   27 L. and 1 Tel. from Lion Feuchtwanger. 1942-1950.

<u>Southern Illinois University</u>, Morris Library, Department of Special Collections, Carbondale, Illinois 62901.

ERWIN PISCATOR PAPERS

B1   12 L. to Erwin Piscator. T. and A. 1936-1948.

B2   16 L. from Erwin Piscator. T.cc. and pc. 1936-1950.

<u>University of Texas</u>, Humanities Research Center, Manuscripts Collection, Box 7219, Austin, Texas 78712.

B1   3 L.

B2   3 L.

C   2 Ms.

<u>Yale University</u>, Beinecke Rare Book and Manuscript Library, New Haven, Connecticut 06520.

HERMANN BROCH ARCHIVE

B1   5 L. to Hermann Broch. 1944-1946.

B2   2 L. from Hermann Broch. 1944-1946.

<u>University of New Hampshire</u>, The Library, Department of Special Collections, Durham, New Hampshire 03824.

OSKAR MARIA GRAF COLLECTION

B1   2 L. to O. M. Graf. 1941, 1958.

State University of New York at Albany, Department of Germanic Languages and Literatures, 1400 Washington Avenue,
Albany, New York 12222.

KARL O. PAETEL COLLECTION

B1   2 L. to Karl O. Paetel. 1945. (xerox)

Dr. Gustave O. Arlt, 13220-C Admiralty Way, Marina del Rey,
California 90291.

FRANZ WERFEL ARCHIVE

B1   1 L. to Franz Werfel. 1942.

Archives of American Art, Fine Arts and Portrait Gallery
Building, Eighth and F Streets N.W., Smithsonian Institution,
Washington, D.C. 20560.

D7   "The Man Who Gave Me New Eyes." Essay on G. Grosz.
      1946.

PAUL HINDEMITH

Composer, 1895-1963

Yale University, School of Music, Stoeckel Hall, New Haven,
Connecticut 06520.

The PAUL HINDEMITH COLLECTION was begun in 1964, shortly
after the death of Hindemith. Materials were donated by
former colleagues, students and friends. Copies have also
been obtained of materials in the Hindemith Institute in
Frankfurt (primarily those pertaining to Hindemith's years
at Yale). The collection occupies two 4-drawer file cabinets in the Music Library, except for the more important
Ms. scores, which are housed in Yale's Beinecke Rare Book
and Manuscript Library.

*Man begann im Jahre 1964, kurz nach dem Tode Hindemiths, die
PAUL HINDEMITH COLLECTION zusammenzutragen. Ehemalige Kollegen, Studenten und Freunde steuerten Materialien bei. Im
übrigen wurden Kopien von Materialien des Hindemith Instituts in Frankfurt erworben (insbesondere solche, die sich
auf Hindemiths Jahre an der Yale University beziehen). Die
Sammlung nimmt 2 Aktenschränke mit je 4 Schubladen ein. Daneben sind besonders wichtige Partiturenhandschriften in
Yales Beinecke Rare Book and Manuscript Library untergebracht.*

B1   Ca. 130 L.
     Pc. of many important L. to publishers (Schott and
     Sons, Mainz). 1933-1940.

B3   Ca. 100 L. from Gertrude Hindemith.

C13 The Children's Crusade. 1939. Complete scenario for a
     ballet intended for use with his Symphonic Dances.
     Never performed. A.
     The Parable of the Blind. 1940. Complete scenario for
     a ballet, never set to music. A.
     Harmonie der Welt. Working T. of complete libretto for
     opera, with corr. and additions in Hindemith's hand.
     1957. A.

C13a Nine Songs for an American School Songbook. 1938. A.
     Third Organ Sonata. 1940. A.
     Theme with Four Variations (The Four Temperaments).
     Complete sketches for string orchestra and piano.
     1940.

La belle dame sans souci (Keats). For soprano and
 piano. 1942. A.
Sing On There in the Swamp (Whitman). For soprano and
 piano. 1943. A.
Recitative e Aria Ranatica. Unpub. song for bass voice
 and piano. 1944. A.
When Lilacs Last in the Dooryard Bloom'd. A Requiem
 for Those We Love. Full score for chorus, soloists,
 and orchestra. 1946. A.
Concerto for Clarinet and Orchestra. Commissioned by
 Benny Goodman. Full score. 1947. A.
Concerto for Horn and Orchestra. Full score. 1949. A.
Concerto for Trumpet and Bassoon. Complete sketches
 and full score. 1949. A.
Two Songs (Oscar Cox). For soprano or tenor and piano.
 1955.
Sonata for Solo Viola. Op. 31, No. 4. 1923. Score. pc.
 Another version. 1937. Score. pc.
Ludus tonalis. 1942. Complete sketches. pc.
Marienleben. Complete sketches for revision. 1936-1942.
 pc.
Craft of Musical Composition. Part II. Outline for re-
 vision (never completed). 1951. T. pc. Part III.
 Complete text. T. and A. pc. 1942-1949. Part IV.
 Complete text of first chap. T. pc. 1952?.
Traditional Harmony. First draft. T. 1942. pc.
Exercises for Advanced Students (became Part II of
 Traditional Harmony). Complete text. 1948. A. pc.
Elementary Training for Musicians. Pre-publication
 printing of first 6 chap. 1945. pc.
Several small compositions written as part of Hinde-
 mith's class work at Yale.

Cl3b Many arrangements of old music for use in his Colle-
 gium Music Concerts at Yale University. 1943-1953.
 A.

Dl3 Complete collection of pub. scores by Hindemith.

F Collection of Hindemith recordings, plus taped recordings of performances of several compositions not yet
 commercially recorded.

H3 Extensive bibliographical index (much of the material
 available in the Yale Music Library).

H3,   Extensive record of Hindemith's teaching activities at
L   Yale: details of his courses, names of students, etc.

H5   Complete chronological record (almost daily) of Hinde-
       mith's personal and professional life in the U.S.,
       compiled from his personal pocket diaries (Paul Hin-
       demith Institute, Frankfurt am Main, Germany).
       Covers the years 1940-1953 and 7 concert tours: 1937,
       1938, 1939, 1959, 1960, 1961, 1963.
       Considerable amount of biographical material unavail-
       able elsewhere, such as personal reminiscences writ-
       ten by his students, colleagues and friends at Yale.

L   Complete file of old music arranged by Hindemith for
       use in his Collegium Musicum Concerts at Yale.

Library of Congress, Reference Department, Music Division,
Independence Avenue and First Street S.E., Washington, D.C.
20540.

C13   "Art läßt nicht von Art." Ms. c. 1937.
       "Canon a tre." Ms. c. 1949.
       "Birthday canon for Mrs. Elizabeth Sprague Coolidge."
         Ms. c. 1949.
       ["Concerto, violoncello (1940)."] Concert. 1940.
         Score. c. 107p.
       "Frauenklage (Burggraf zu Regensburg)." Ms. c. 1937.
       "Hérodiade de Stéphane Mallarmé." Ms. 1944.
       "Konzertmusik für Klavier, Blechbläser und Harfen."
         A. pc. 1930.
       "Konzertstück für 2 alto Saxophone." Ms. 1933.
       "Landsknechtstrinklied." Ms. 1937.
       "Vier Lieder nach Gedichten von F. Hölderlin." Ms. c.
         1935.
       "Vom Hausregiment." Ms. c. 1937.

Princeton University, Firestone Library, Princeton, New Jersey 08540.

B1   18 L. to Oliver Strunk. 1937-1948.

C13a   "Sonate für Bratsche." Solo. 1937. A. 14p.

University of California, Los Angeles, Music Library, 405
Hilgard Avenue, Los Angeles, California 90024.

ERNST TOCH ARCHIVE

B1   7 L. to Ernst Toch.

University of Georgia, The University Libraries, Athens,
Georgia 30601.

OLIN DOWNES PAPERS

B1,2   7 L.

Indiana University, The University Libraries, Music Library,
Bloomington, Indiana 47401.

FRITZ BUSCH COLLECTION

C13   "Symphonic Metamorphosis of themes by C. M. von Weber,
      partially rewritten score and percussion part to
      accompany Associated Music Publishers edition."
      Undated.

Mr. Hans Sahl, 800 West End Avenue, New York, N.Y. 10025.

B1   Several L. to Hans Sahl.

University of Iowa, The University Libraries, Special Collections, Iowa City, Iowa 52240.

B1   1 L. to Earl E. Harper. 1947.

University of New Hampshire, The Library, Department of Special Collections, Durham, New Hampshire 03824.

OSKAR MARIA GRAF COLLECTION

B1   1 L. to O. M. Graf. 1945.

Metropolitan Opera Association, Inc., The Archives, Lincoln
Center Plaza, New York, N.Y. 10023.

H3   7 cl. 1955-1970.

University of Utah, Marriott Library, Western Americana
Department, Salt Lake City, Utah 84112.

PAPERS OF LEROY J. ROBERTSON

H4   Mathis der Maler. Thematic analysis by Hugo Leichten-
      tritt.

University of Pennsylvania, The Charles Patterson Van Pelt
Library, Philadelphia, Pennsylvania 19104.

ALMA MAHLER-WERFEL COLLECTION

B1   1 L. to Alma Mahler-Werfel. A. Undated.

HELMUT HIRSCH

Social Scientist, 1907-

State University of New York at Albany, Department of Germanic Languages and Literatures, 1400 Washington Avenue, Albany, New York 12222.

The HELMUT HIRSCH COLLECTION at SUNYA has been donated over a period of several years (1970s) by Prof. Hirsch (ca. 7 in.) and is a complementary collection to the HELMUT HIRSCH COLLECTION located at the Leo Baeck Institute in New York City. Both collections are still being added to periodically.

Die HELMUT HIRSCH COLLECTION at SUNYA ist der State University im Laufe mehrerer Jahre (in den 70ern) von Prof. Hirsch geschenkt worden; die Sammlung (etwa 18 cm) ergänzt die HELMUT HIRSCH COLLECTION im Leo Baeck Institute in New York City. Beide Sammlungen werden von Zeit zu Zeit erweitert.

A3   Complete bibliography of Hirsch's writings. T. 67p.

B1,2   Ca. 2,000 L., including L. to and from: Alfred Döblin, Ruth Fischer, Ossip Flechtheim, Karl Frank, Manfred George, Kurt Hiller, Max Horkheimer, A. Kantorowicz, R. M. W. Kempner, Thomas Mann, Heinz Pächter, Jacob Picard, Will Schaber, Hans Steinitz, Ludwig Wronkow, as well as numerous newspaper and magazine publishers.

C7   "Erinnerungen an Oberbürgermeister Ernst Reuter." T. pc. 4p.
       "New Saar Research." Review. Undated. 7p.

H3   1 cl. 1973.

L   B. F. Dolbin caricatures, copies.

N   Singer, Felix. "How to Get Art and Culture for Chicago."

Leo Baeck Institute, 129 East 73rd Street, New York, N.Y. 10021.

The HELMUT HIRSCH COLLECTION (AR 3150), consisting of over 15 archive boxes of materials, was donated to the Institute by Prof. Helmut Hirsch.

*Die HELMUT HIRSCH COLLECTION (AR 3150) umfaßt mehr als 15
Archivkartons Materialien, die dem Institut von Prof. Helmut
Hirsch geschenkt wurden.*

A3   Yankees from the Rhine. 161p.
       Lists of contents of Helmut Hirsch collections at:
       State University of New York at Albany;
       Schweizerische Sozialarchiv;
       University of Kansas;
       Marianne Tilgner (Düsseldorf);
       Tyska Institutionen (Stockholm).

B1,2   Correspondence with individuals, including: Frederick
       Forell, Paul and Rosi Fröhlich, Paul Harvey, Fried-
       rich Hirth, Alfred Kantorowicz, Karl Kautsky, Karl
       and Hedda Korsch, Prinz Hubertus zu Loewenstein,
       Siegfried Marck, Hans Rothfels, Desider Stern, Sieg-
       fried Thalheimer, Oswald Garrison Villard and fam-
       ily, Gerd Wollheim, and others.
       Correspondence with publishers, universities and col-
       leges, radio stations.

B3   Correspondence between Friedrich Engels and Eduard
       Bernstein, 1879-1895. Pc. and typed c. Originals in
       Institute for Marxism-Leninism-Moscow and Interna-
       tionaal Instituut voor Sociale Geschiednis. 174
       items. Ca. 9 in. (22 cm.).

C7   "Heine und Marx." Lecture. Heinrich Heine Gesellschaft
       and Volkshochschule (Düsseldorf), March 11, 1966.
       T. 22p.
       Notes on Karl Ludwig Bernays.
       "Karl Marx und die Bittschrift für die Gleichberechti-
       gung der Juden." T. 40p.
       "August Bebel - Mensch und Politiker." T. 24p.
       Radio scripts:
       "Interview mit Ferdinand Lassalle." T. 30p.
       "Der junge Moses Hess, sein Leben in Bonn, Köln und
       Wuppertal." Westdeutscher Rundfunk, Jan. 26, 1969.
       Mimeo. 33p.
       "Interview mit der Geschichte: Ferdinand Lassalle."
       By H. Hirsch and Jam Brede. Radio Bremen, July 17,
       1969. Mimeo. 29p.

C9   J. A. Hobson. Imperialism: A Study. German tr. done for

Kiepenheuer and Witsch. T. 438p.

D7   3 items.

I   C. of original documents concerning Moses Hess, Karl
      Ludwig Bernays, Jews in Rhineland (1843).

L   Various brochures, materials about Else Lasker-Schüler,
      Friedrich Engels.

Harvard University, Houghton Library, Cambridge, Massachusetts 02138.

OSWALD GARRISON VILLARD PAPERS

B1   38 L. to Oswald Garrison Villard. 1941-1949.

B2   20 L. from Oswald Garrison Villard. 1941-1949.

New York Public Library, Manuscript Division, Fifth Avenue
and 42nd Street, New York, N.Y. 10018.

EMERGENCY COMMITTEE IN AID OF DISPLACED FOREIGN SCHOLARS,
1933-1945

*   File compiled, no assistance given. 1934-1941.

JULIUS HIRSCH

Economist, 1882-1961

Mrs. Edith Hirsch, 400 East 56th Street, New York, N.Y.
10028.

Private collection (6 ft.): access permitted upon written
permission from Mrs. Hirsch.

*Privatsammlung (etwa 1,80 m). Zugang mit schriftlicher
Genehmigung von Frau Edith Hirsch.*

A1   Diaries, appointment calendars.

A3   Autobiography. Ca. 10p.
      Autobiography. 15p.

B1,2 Correspondence from the American years, including L.
         from: B. Baruch, A. Johnson, J. Schumpeter. Also
         copies of Hirsch's L.

C7   Several manuscripts.
      Manuscripts of lectures.
      Unpub. Ms. on Denmark. German and English. Ca. 150p.
      Unpub. article on Russia. German and English.

D7,   Collection of cl., including a collection of New York
H3   Times cl. about Julius and Edith Hirsch.

F   Tape recording.

H3   Articles on Hirsch, collected by Mrs. Hirsch for a
         book on his early years (civil service career).
         1922-.
      15p. summary of Julius Hirsch biography.

I   Documents: passports, award certificates, etc.

J   Photos dating from the 1930s.

K   Library of Hirsch's works.

Leo Baeck Institute, 129 East 73rd Street, New York, N.Y.
10021.

The JULIUS HIRSCH COLLECTION, ca. 3 in. of materials, was
donated to the Institute by his widow, Mrs. Edith J. Hirsch.

418

JULIUS HIRSCH

Die JULIUS HIRSCH COLLECTION, etwa 0,08 m Materialien, ist eine Schenkung seiner Witwe, Frau Edith J. Hirsch, an das Institute.

D7   Cl. and xerox c. of Hirsch's pub. writings. Late 1920s. Also microfilm of Hirsch's pub. writings of the 1920s. 500 frames.

American Philosophical Society, The Library, 105 South Fifth Street, Philadelphia, Pennsylvania 19106.

SIMON FLEXNER PAPERS

B1,2   Correspondence with Simon Flexner.

Harvard University, Baker Library, Graduate School of Business, Soldiers Field, Boston, Massachusetts 02163.

FRITZ REDLICH COLLECTION

B1   1 L. to Fritz Redlich. T. 1936.

New York Public Library, Manuscript Division, Fifth Avenue and 42nd Street, New York, N.Y. 10018.

EMERGENCY COMMITTEE IN AID OF DISPLACED FOREIGN SCHOLARS, 1933-1945

*   File compiled, no assistance given. 1934-1940.

HANS HOFMANN

Painter, 1880-1966

The Hans Hofmann estate is in the possession of Mrs. Hans Hofmann and the attorney for the estate is Mr. Robert S. Warshaw, 375 Park Avenue, New York, N.Y. The Project was unable to complete its contact with Mr. Warshaw before publication deadline.

Der Nachlaß von Hans Hofmann befindet sich im Besitz von Frau Hofmann, juristischer Nachlaßverwalter ist Herr Robert S. Warshaw, 375 Park Avenue, New York, N.Y. Es war nicht möglich, vor dem Veröffentlichungsdatum dieses Handbuchs mit Herrn Warshaw in Verbindung zu treten und genauere Auskünfte einzuholen.

University of California, Berkeley, University Art Museum, Berkeley, California 94720.

The HANS HOFMANN ARCHIVE, ca. 3 ft. of materials, has been assembled since 1965 from donations by Hans Hofmann, Sam Kootz, and from friends and students of Hofmann.

Das HANS HOFMANN ARCHIVE, etwa 0,90 m Materialien, ist seit 1965 aus Schenkungen von Hans Hofmann, Sam Kootz sowie Freunden und Studenten Hofmanns zusammengestellt worden.

B1   4+ L. Undated.

B3   Many L., primarily with museums and galleries concerning Hofmann's works.

C7   Lecture on abstract art. Feb. 1941.
       Lecture. Minneapolis [1930]. Also English tr.

C14   Class drawings in charcoal.

H1   Hans Hofmann by William C. Seitz. 2c.
       Hans Hofmann by Frederick S. Wight. 2c.

H3   Cl. from: Art Alliance Bulletin, Art Forum, San Diego, Arts Magazine.

H4   Programs of exhibitions/catalogs: Worth Ryder Gallery; Stedelijk Museum; Museo de Bellas Artes, Caracas; Galleria Civica d'Arte Moderna, Torino; Museum of

HANS HOFMANN

Modern Art; Wurttembergischer Kunstverein, Stuttgart;
Kootz Gallery (1950-1966); Stanford Art Museum;
University Art Museum, Berkeley; André Emmerich Gal-
lery; La Jolla Museum; Obelisk Gallery, Dayton Art
Institute.

I   Class announcements. Chouinard School of Art, 1931.

J   Photos of Hofmann and his works.
Photos of University of California Charter Day. Hofmann receives degree.
12 photos of Hofmann. 1962.
12 photos of Hofmann. Opening at Robert Motherwell.
1965.
Photos of Hofmann drawings on students' work.
Photos of Hofmann. 1940-1952.
Photos of Hofmann student drawings, Berkeley, 1930-
1931.

N   Notes of a student of Hofmann's lectures. 1930-1931.
5 drawings of student under Hofmann's instruction.
1932.

Archives of American Art, Smithsonian Institution, National
Collection of Fine Arts and National Portrait Gallery Build-
ing, Eighth and F Streets N.W., Washington, D.C. 20560.
(Microfilms of collections are available in each of the
branch locations: Boston, Massachusetts; New York, N.Y.;
Detroit, Michigan; San Francisco, California.)

PEGGY GUGGENHEIM PAPERS, FAY LASHER PAPERS, ANNE RYAN PAPERS,
HARRIS STEINBERG PAPERS, WHITNEY MUSEUM PAPERS, ADJA YUMKERS
PAPERS

B1   1 L. to Anne Ryan. 1953.

C7   9 lectures by Hofmann. T.
The Painter's Primer. Peggy Huck's tr. from the German,
as revised in 1948. T.

H3   Microfilm entitled "Clippings."
Microfilm entitled "Biography and Illustration."
Materials from Artists Files of the Whitney Museum of
American Art.
Bibliography.

H4   Catalog of first exhibit. March 7, 1944.

I   2 documents concerning Hofmann's work by Harris Stein-
         berg.
      "Exhibit announcements and catalogues, class schedules,
      school announcements."

J   Photo of Hofmann. Provincetown Studio, 1952.

N   Notes by student of Hofmann. 1948. 3p.

Mr. Hans Sahl, 800 West End Avenue, New York, N.Y. 10025.

B1   Several L. to Hans Sahl.

Museum of Modern Art, The Library, 11 West 53rd Street, New
York, N.Y. 10019.

HANS RICHTER ARCHIVE: Written permission to use the Archive
is required in advance of visits to the Museum.

*HANS RICHTER ARCHIVE: Vor Besuch des Archivs muß eine schrift-
liche Genehmigung eingeholt werden.*

B2   1 L. from Hans Richter. 1958.

HAJO HOLBORN

Historian, 1902-1969

The literary estate of Prof. Hajo Holborn passed into the
hands of his wife and daughter after his death. A collection of pamphlets and materials relating to the history of
the Weimar Constitution was subsequently donated to the Yale
University Library, Department of Manuscripts and Archives.
Of the personal papers of Prof. Holborn what remains are
mostly letters and manuscripts (ca. 1.5 file drawers) and
some further letters written to Louise Holborn during the
first several years of Prof. Holborn's residence in the U.S.
All of these have been deposited with Prof. Holborn's daughter, Hanna Holborn Gray, Provost at Yale University. The
papers are closed to research, and no plans for their disposition are available as of 1977.

Der literarische Nachlaß von Prof. Hajo Holborn gelangte
nach seinem Tode in den Besitz seiner Frau und seiner Toch-
ter. Aus diesen Materialien wurde eine Gruppe von Schrift-
stücken, die sich auf die Geschichte der Weimarer Verfassung
beziehen, zusammengestellt und der Yale University Library,
Department of Manuscripts and Archives, als Schenkung über-
lassen. Von den persönlichen Materialien blieben danach
hauptsächlich Briefe und Manuskripte übrig (etwa 1.5 Akten-
schrankfächer) sowie einige Briefe, die Prof. Holborn wäh-
rend der ersten Jahre seines Aufenthaltes in den Vereinigten
Staaten an Louise Holborn geschrieben hat. Alle diese Mate-
rialien befinden sich im Besitz von Prof. Holborns Tochter,
Hanna Holborn Gray, Provost an der Yale University. Diese
Materialien sind für Forschungszwecke nicht zugänglich, und
bis 1977 bestanden noch keine definitiven Pläne in Bezug auf
deren spätere Verwendung.

Yale University Library, Manuscripts and Archives Research
Room, 150 Sterling Memorial Library, New Haven, Connecticut
06520.

THE HOLBORN PAPERS (9 archive boxes) consist primarily of
materials relating to the history of the Weimar constitution. They were donated to the Yale University Library by
the family of Holborn.

THE HOLBORN PAPERS (9 Archivkartons) bestehen in erster
Linie aus Materialien, die sich auf die Geschichte der Wei-
marer Verfassung beziehen. Sie sind eine Schenkung der Fami-
lie Holborn an die Yale University Library.

B1,2   1 F. of correspondence, primarily concerning Holborn's
        book on Radowitz.

B2   1 L. from Meinecke.

B3   Copies of L. between Max Weber and Konrad Haussmann
        and Hugo Preuss. 1917-1918.

C7   Various Ms. for talks on Germany.
        "Die Entstehung der Weimarer Verfassung als national-
        politisches Problem." Ms. of lecture before the
        Deutsche Hochschule für Politik, Jan. 1931.
        "The Prussian and German School of Strategy."
        Article on 15th-16th century Humanism.
        "Gedanken über das Studium der Außenpolitik an den
        deutschen Hochschulen."
        "Umrisse der Weltpolitik 1890-1919."
        "Freihandel."
        "Vorgeschichte der Weimarer Verfassung: Räteherrschaft
        und Demokratie." Ms.
        "Max Weber und die deutsche Demokratie."
        "Max Weber."
        Ms. of minutes of the Fraktion of the DDP, 1919-1920.

D7   Copies of some of Holborn's early publications (pamph-
        lets and reprints of articles). Also reprints of
        articles by other historians.

I   Roll of microfilm containing various documents col-
        lected by Holborn for his research, most of them
        dealing with the Verfassungsausschuß of the Reichs-
        tag.

L   Additional printed documentary material on the Consti-
        tuent Assembly of 1919.
        Ca. 60 items, mostly pamphlets, some dealing with the
        Nazi period. 1 B.
        Mostly books and pamphlets on constitutional issues.
        1 B.
        Mostly pamphlets on the following topics (1 B.): consti-
        tutional reform, socialism, minorities, World War I,

424

reparations, Polish question, war guilt, disarma-
ment.
Samples of old paper (15th-16th centuries) with notes
(not by Holborn).
Pamphlets and contemporary newspapers of the postwar
period, Weimar Constitution, the Anschluß, the
Soldiers' and Workers' Councils, the Dolchstoßpro-
zeß of 1925. Also some on Hitler period. 2 B.
Materials on the beginnings of the Deutsche Demokra-
tische Partei, Constituent National Assembly. 1 B.
Substantial collection of Drucksachen und Ergebnis-
protokolle of the Staatenausschuß. 1919.
Some maps, especially 2 showing Germany's fortifica-
tions in 1918 and 1931.
Newspaper cl. on various topics: University affairs,
universities and politics, the corporate state
(Italy), constitutional policy (mostly 1932-1933),
history 1918-1933, miscellany (mostly 1918-1919,
1930-).
Class lists, lecture outlines, reading lists, students'
prospectuses and seminar papers.
Printed minutes to meetings.
Front matter and illustrations for Hutton book, Yale
Press.

M   Rare copy of Allgemeiner Kongreß der Arbeiter- und
       Soldatenräte Deutschlands vom 16.-21. Dez. 1918 -
       Stenographische Berichte.

N   von Oertzen, Etta. "The Co-operation of the Press in
       the Organization of Peace." Ms.
       von Hagen, Maximilian. Lengthy Aufzeichnung concerning
       reminiscences of Solf. Also numerous copies of L.
       from Solf papers.

New York Public Library, Manuscript Division, Fifth Avenue
and 42nd Street, New York, N.Y. 10018.

EMERGENCY COMMITTEE IN AID OF DISPLACED FOREIGN SCHOLARS,
1933-1945

*   File compiled when assistance was granted. 1934-1941.

<u>Prof. Alfred Vagts</u>, Sherman, Connecticut 06784.

B1   Several L. to Alfred Vagts.

<u>Dr. Hans Speier</u>, 167 Concord Avenue, Hartsdale, New York
10530.

B1   1 L. to Hans Speier. Undated.

ARNOLD HÖLLRIEGEL (RICHARD A. BERMANN)

Writer, 1883-1939

Dr. Clementine Zernik, 225-10 106th Avenue, Queens Village, New York 11429.

The following description of materials from the literary estate of Arnold Höllriegel was prepared by Mr. Will Schaber (New York, N.Y.). All rights to the materials in the collection are held by Dr. Clementine Zernik.

Die folgende Beschreibung der Materialien aus dem literarischen Nachlaß von Arnold Höllriegel wurde von Mr. Will Schaber (New York, N.Y.) erarbeitet. Alle Rechte in Bezug auf die Materialien der Sammlung ruhen bei Frau Dr. Clementine Zernik.

A3   Die Fahrt durch den Katarakt. Unpub. first part of a
      planned autobiography, leading up to the year 1918,
      and partial sketches of the rest of the work. A.
      (T. of Part I also at the Leo Baeck Institute, New
      York).

B2   Several hundred L. (no c. of Höllriegel's own L.).
      Primarily 1938-1939. Includes L. from: Elisabeth
      Bergner, Hermann Broch, Albert Ehrenstein, Albert
      Einstein, Douglas Fairbanks Jr., Prinz Hubertus zu
      Löwenstein, Thomas Mann, Leo Perutz, Oswald Garrison
      Villard, Joseph Wechsberg, Stefan Zweig.

C1   Das Mädchen von St. Helene. Novel. T.

C5   "Die Marseillaise. Skizze zu einem Film." T.
      "The Rope. A Film Synopsis." T.
      "Good Morning, Filipescu!" Short story, basis for a
      film script. T.

C7   Ms. and T. of many pub. articles.

C9   Matson, Norman H. Fleckers Magie. Tr. from the English
      by Arnold Höllriegel. T.

C11   Tusitala und der Tod. R. L. Stevenson's last years.
      Unpub. original German version of the book that
      appeared in 1939 in English as Home from the Sea. T.

D4,7 Hundreds of newspaper cl. from 1918-1938, the majority
      from the Berliner Tageblatt and the Tag (Vienna).

427

ARNOLD HÖLLRIEGEL (RICHARD A. BERMANN)

K   Several hundred books, the majority used as research
      material for Höllriegel's novels and travel reports.

Leo Baeck Institute, 129 East 73rd Street, New York, N.Y.
10021.

A3   Die Fahrt durch den Katarakt. Undated. T. 245p.

Yale University, Beinecke Rare Book and Manuscript Library,
New Haven, Connecticut 06520.

H5   Broch, Hermann. "Richard A. Bermann (Arnold Hoellrie-
      gel)." cc. 4p.

MAX HORKHEIMER

Social Scientist, 1895-1973

Harvard University, Houghton Library, Cambridge, Massachusetts 02138.

LEO LOWENTHAL COLLECTION (bMS Ger 185): accessible only with
the permission of Prof. Lowenthal (Department of Sociology,
University of California, Berkeley, California 94720).
Otherwise closed until Dec. 31, 1998.

*LEO LOWENTHAL COLLECTION (bMS Ger 185): zugänglich nur mit
persönlicher Erlaubnis von Prof. Leo Lowenthal (Department
of Sociology, University of California, Berkeley, California
94720). Im übrigen ist die Sammlung bis zum 31. Dez. 1998
gesperrt.*

B1   684 L. to Leo Lowenthal. 1933-1967.
       88 L. 1942-1955, including L. to: Theodor W. Adorno,
      Else Brunswik, Manfred George, Marie Jahoda, Paul
      Lazarsfeld, Herbert Marcuse, Paul W. Massing, Fried-
      rich Pollock, Max Rheinstein, Gerhart Seger, Paul
      Tillich.

B2   587 L. from Leo Lowenthal. 1934-1966. Some with enclo-
      sures.
       26 L. 1942-1953, including L. from: T. W. Adorno, Marie
      Jahoda, Paul Massing, Friedrich Pollock, Max Rhein-
      stein.

C7   9 essays. 1942-1953 and undated. T. 55p.

Joseph and Alice Maier, 991 Grace Terrace, Teaneck, New
Jersey 07666.

Files from the Institute for Social Research, Columbia University. Alice Maier was Horkheimer's assistant at the Institute.

*Akten aus dem Institute for Social Research, Columbia Univer-
sity. Alice Maier war Horkheimers Assistentin am Institut.*

B1,2 Correspondence between the Institute for Social Research
      and Alice Maier. 1934-.

429

H3 Obituaries. Cl.
    Memoranda of Institute for Social Research in U.S.

H5 Minutes of discussions between Horkheimer, P. Tillich,
    A. Lowe and F. Pollock.

J   Photos of Horkheimer, many "among the last ever made."

L   All brochures published by the Institute for Social
    Research in the U.S.

New York Public Library, Manuscript Division, Fifth Avenue
and 42nd Street, New York, N.Y. 10018.

ERICH FROMM PAPERS

B1,2 Correspondence between Horkheimer and Erich Fromm.
      1932-1943.

C7   Ms. of essay by Horkheimer.

Harvard University, Harvard Divinity School, Andover-Harvard
Theological Library, 45 Francis Avenue, Cambridge, Massachusetts 02138.

PAUL TILLICH COLLECTION

B1 1 6p. L. to Paul Tillich. T. 1942.
    3 L. to Paul Tillich. T. 1961-1965.

B2 1 L. from Paul Tillich. T.c. 1961.

B3 2 L. re: Horkheimer's loss of U.S. citizenship. 1956.

H4 Tillich, Paul. Review of Horkheimer's Vernunft und
    Selbsterhaltung. 1942. T. 9p.

Prof. Herbert Marcuse, Department of Philosophy, University
of California San Diego, La Jolla, California 92037

B1,2 Lengthy correspondence with Herbert Marcuse.

State University of New York at Albany, Department of Ger-

manic Languages and Literatures, 1400 Washington Avenue, Albany, New York 12222.

HELMUT HIRSCH COLLECTION

B1   2 L. to Helmut Hirsch. T. 1951-1952.

B2   4 L. from Helmut Hirsch. T. 1951-1954.

Library of Congress, Manuscript Division, Independence Avenue and First Street S.E., Washington, D.C. 20540.

PAPERS OF SIEGFRIED BERNFELD, BENJAMIN W. HUEBSCH PAPERS

B1   1 L. to Siegfried Bernfeld. 1951.
      1 L. to B. W. Huebsch. 1942. Also signed by Th. Mann,
      L. Feuchtwanger, B. Frank, E. M. Remarque, F. Werfel.

American Philosophical Society, The Library, 105 South Fifth Street, Philadelphia, Pennsylvania 19106.

L. C. DUNN PAPERS

B1,2 Correspondence in file marked: "Emergency Committee."

Indiana University, The University Libraries, The Lilly Library, Bloomington, Indiana 47401.

LEWIS BROWNE MSS., UPTON BEALL SINCLAIR MSS.

B1   1 L. ea. to Lewis Browne and Upton Sinclair. 1942.
      Also signed by Th. Mann, L. Feuchtwanger, B. Frank,
      E. M. Remarque, F. Werfel.

Yivo Institute, 1048 Fifth Avenue, New York, N.Y. 10028.

HORACE M. KALLEN PAPERS

B1,2 Individual item(s) in folder: 946.

<u>University of Southern California</u>, Lion Feuchtwanger Memorial Library, 520 Paseo Miramar, Pacific Palisades, California 90272.

B2   1 L. from Lion Feuchtwanger.

KAREN HORNEY

Psychoanalyst, 1885-1953

The descendants of Karen Horney have retained materials pertaining to Horney and her career. Some of these materials
are of a sensitive nature and as of 1977 there are no immediate plans to release them.

*Die Nachkommen von Karen Horney haben Materialien über Karen
Horney und ihre wissenschaftliche Laufbahn einbehalten.
Einige dieser Materialien sind vertrauliche Natur, und es
bestanden 1977 noch keine Pläne, diese Materialien freizugeben.*

<u>Columbia University</u>, Butler Library, New York, N.Y. 10027.

W. W. NORTON PAPERS

B1   Ca. 190 L. to W. W. Norton. T. and A. 1936-1952.

B2   Ca. 80 L. from W. W. Norton. 1936-1950.

B3   Ca. 80 L., many of the Karen Horney Foundation. 1936-
      1954.

H3   Cl. among correspondence, primarily from year of Hor-
      ney's death.

H4   Review, editorial suggestions, critique.

I   Vita, contracts, pamphlets, questionnaire.

<u>Dr. Jack Rubins</u>, 82-15 234th Street, Queens Village, New
York 11417.

The materials in Dr. Rubins' collection (2 archive boxes)
were assembled by Dr. Rubins personally, who is preparing a
biography of Karen Horney. The materials are closed for the
time being.

*Die Materialien in Dr. Rubins Sammlung (2 Archivkartons) wur-
den persönlich von Dr. Rubin, der eine Biographie über Karen
Horney vorbereitet, gesammelt. Die Materialien sind zur Zeit
nicht zugänglich.*

433

B1,2   20 L. to and from Horney. In German and English.
       Mostly pc. 1923-1927, 1950.

C7   Lecture notes. Chicago and New York: 1930-1932, 1945-
       1947, 1950. Ca. 1.5 in.
       Lecture notes, with h. corr. by Horney. [1945-1953].
       Miscellaneous loose sheets in Horney's hand. Undated.

C8   3 articles. T.

D8   Offprints of Horney articles over many years.

F   Tapes of Horney speaking. 5 volumes.

G   1 cl. 1946.

H3   Collection of cl. assembled by Rubins. 1940-1960.

I   Documents concerning the founding of Association for
       Advancement of Psychiatry. 1941.

J   Photo album.

N   Lecture notes by Horney students from seminars. 1945,
       1947 and earlier.

HEINRICH EDUARD JACOB

Writer, 1889-1967

Leo Baeck Institute, 129 East 73rd Street, New York, N.Y. 10021.

KURT KERSTEN COLLECTION and general archive files

B1   12 L. and 3 Ptc. to Kurt Kersten. 1949-1954.
       4 L. and 1 Ptc. to Lutz Weltmann. 1951-1956.
       1 L. and 1 Ptc. to Emil Ludwig (1939) and Hans Boehm
          (1927).

H3   "Heinrich Eduard Jacob." Publisher's pamphlet. 8p.
       3 cl. 1959-1967.

J   2 photos.

University of Southern California, Lion Feuchtwanger Memorial Library, 520 Paseo Miramar, Pacific Palisades, California 90272.

B1   3 L. to Lion Feuchtwanger. 1941-1947.

B2   3 L. from Lion Feuchtwanger. 1941-1947.

Mrs. Elisabeth M. Stoerk and Mrs. Susanne B. Hoeller, 288 Ocean Drive West, Stamford, Connecticut 06902.

FRIDERIKE ZWEIG ARCHIVE

B1   3 L. and 3 Ptc. to Friderike Zweig. 1951-1953.

H1   Bio-bibliographical publisher's advertisement. Double-
       day, Doran & Co.

State University of New York at Albany, Department of Germanic Languages and Literatures, 1400 Washington Avenue, Albany, New York 12222.

STORM PUBLISHERS ARCHIVE

B1   3 L. to Alexander Gode von Aesch. 1946-1947.

435

University of California, Los Angeles, Department of Special
Collections, 120 Lawrence Clark Powell Library, Los Angeles,
California 90024.

FRANZ WERFEL ARCHIVE

B1   2 L. to Franz Werfel. 1943.

B2   1 L. from Franz Werfel. 1943.

Columbia University, Butler Library, New York, N.Y. 10027.

B1   1 L. to N. M. Butler. T. 1944.

B2   1 L. from N. M. Butler. T.c. 1944.

University of Kansas, Kenneth Spencer Research Library,
Department of Special Collections, Lawrence, Kansas 66045.

HENRY SAGAN COLLECTION

B1   1 L.

University of Pennsylvania, The Charles Patterson Van Pelt
Library, Philadelphia, Pennsylvania 19104.

ALMA MAHLER-WERFEL COLLECTION

B1   2 L. to Alma Mahler-Werfel. 1944, 1945.
      1 L. to Franz Werfel. T. 1943.

New York Public Library, Manuscript Division, Fifth Avenue
and 42nd Street, New York, N.Y. 10018.

EMERGENCY COMMITTEE IN AID OF DISPLACED FOREIGN SCHOLARS,
1933-1945

*   File compiled, no assistance given. 1942-1944.

Mrs. Peter M. Lindt, 949 West End Avenue, New York, N.Y. 10025.

Bl   Small amount of correspondence with Peter M. Lindt.

C   Ms. submitted to Lindt for use on his radio program.

Mrs. Alice Loewy Kahler, 1 Evelyn Place, Princeton, New Jersey 08540.

ERICH VON KAHLER COLLECTION

Bl   1 L. to Erich von Kahler. 1954.

WERNER JAEGER

Classic Philologist, 1888-1961

Harvard University, Houghton Library, Cambridge, Massachusetts 02138.

The WERNER W. JAEGER PAPERS, ca. 10 ft. of materials, was
donated to the library by Jaeger's heirs in 1961. The collection is at present unsorted and uncatalogued and usage is
restricted. Jaeger's personal library, with the exception
of ca. 100 volumes that were retained by Houghton, was purchased by the Center for Hellenistic Studies in Washington,
D.C. (Harvard Institute).

*Die WERNER W. JAEGER PAPERS, etwa 3 m Material, sind eine
Schenkung der Erben Jaegers aus dem Jahre 1961. Die Sammlung
ist zur Zeit noch ungeordnet und nicht katalogisiert; der
Zugang ist beschränkt. Jaegers Privatbibliothek (abgesehen
von etwa 100 Bänden, welche die Houghton Library einbehalten
hat) wurde vom Center for Hellenistic Studies in Washington,
D.C. (Harvard Institute) käuflich erworben.*

B1,2   Small amount of correspondence from Jaeger's years in
       Germany, primarily with fellow philologists.

C7   Lecture notes. 1911-1912.
       Lecture notes from the years at Harvard.
       Ms. of many articles, primarily from Jaeger's years at
       Harvard.

K   Ca. 100 books from Jaeger's personal library.

GEORGE SARTON PAPERS, AUTOGRAPH FILE

B1   21 L. to Arthur Stanley Pease. 1939-1958 and undated.
       21 L. to George Sarton. 1939-1954.
       1 L. to [Edward Kennard] Rand. A. 1937.

B2   12 L. 1928-1952 and undated, including L. from: Hugo
       von Hofmannsthal, Arthur Stanley Pease, George Sar-
       ton.

C7   "Das Ziel des Lebens in der griechischen Ethik von den
       Sophisten bis Aristoteles."
       "Die Epiamos des Philippos von Opus."
       2 lecture texts. A. 1913.

Mrs. Werner Jaeger, 43 Bailey Road, Watertown, Massachusetts 02172.

B2   Selected (by Mrs. Jaeger) personal L. to Jaeger.

H3   Many cl. concerning Werner Jaeger and family.

LEOPOLD JESSNER
Writer, 1878-1945

Dr. Marta Mierendorff, 8633 West Knoll Drive, Hollywood, California 90069.

INSTITUT FÜR KUNSTSOZIOLOGIE: The several dozen items represented in the Institut's collection were assembled by Dr. Mierendorff.

INSTITUT FÜR KUNSTSOZIOLOGIE: Die mehreren Dutzend Nummern der Institutssammlung von und über Jessner wurden von Frau Dr. Mierendorff zusammengetragen.

B3   "France for Ever." Pc. of L. to Rudi Feld. 1943.

C7   "No East - No West: Judaism." Pc.

H3   "Jüdisches Ideal-Gemüt und Geblüt bei Leopold Jessner." Pc.
       "Erfassung führender Männer der Systemzeit." Pc.
       Miscellaneous materials pertaining to commemorative ceremonies in Jessner's honor in Los Angeles and Germany.

H4   William Tell. Cl. of reviews.

H5   Feuchtwanger, Lion. Pc. of "Festrede" for Jessner's 65th birthday in Los Angeles.
       Perry, Alfred. Transcript of memorial speech on Jessner.

J   Art pamphlet by Rudi Feld, with many photos, graphics, for William Tell. 16p.
       William Tell. Photos of scenes and actors.

M   "Max Reinhardt Memorial Committee." With mention of Jessner.

N   Dieterle, William. Ms. of radio speech introduction of the Continental Players.

O   William Tell. 4 programs. English and Hebrew.
       Program "France Forever." Jan. 16, 1943.
       "The Playgoers" for William Tell.

Yale University, Beinecke Rare Book and Manuscript Library, New Haven, Connecticut 06520.

B3   1 L. to Mrs. Leopold Jessner.

C2   4 drama Ms., with h. corr. and notations by Jessner.

C7,   11 articles by and concerning Jessner.
H3

O   1 F. of theater tickets.

State University of New York at Binghamton, Center for Modern Theater Research, Binghamton, New York 13901.

MAX REINHARDT ARCHIVE

B1   1 L. to Paul Rope. Undated.

Leo Baeck Institute, 129 East 73rd Street, New York, N.Y. 10021.

FRITZ MAUTHNER COLLECTION and general archive files

B1   1 L. ea. to Wolfgang Goetz (1920) and Fritz Mauthner
       (1919).

I   Membership card for Dr. Gustav Stresemann, Deutscher
       Bühnen-Klub. Berlin, 1923.

J   1 Photo of Jessner. Undated.

University of Pennsylvania, The Charles Patterson Van Pelt Library, Philadelphia, Pennsylvania 19104.

ALMA MAHLER-WERFEL COLLECTION

B1   6 L. and 1 Tel. to Alma Mahler-Werfel.

Southern Illinois University, Morris Library, Department of Special Collections, Carbondale, Illinois 62901.

ERWIN PISCATOR PAPERS

B1   1 L. to Erwin Piscator. T.cc. 1939.

B2   Draft of L. from Erwin Piscator. 1939.

University of Texas, Humanities Research Center, Manuscripts Collection, Box 7219, Austin, Texas 78712.

B1   4 L.

B2   4 L.

Mr. Hans Sahl, 800 West End Avenue, New York, N.Y. 10025.

B1   Several L. to Hans Sahl.

University of Southern California, Lion Feuchtwanger Memorial Library, 520 Paseo Miramar, Pacific Palisades, California 90272.

B2   1 L. from Lion Feuchtwanger.

FRITZ JOHN

Mathematician, 1910-

Dr. Fritz John, c/o New York University, Courant Institute of Mathematical Sciences, 251 Mercer Street, New York, N.Y. 10012.

Private collection: inaccessible. / *Unzugängliche Privat-sammlung.*

Al   Small diary.
Bl,2   Small amount of correspondence over many years.
D8   Offprints of all of John's publications.
H5   Complete bibliography of John's work.
K   Personal library that includes miscellaneous isolated periodical issues.

United States Army Missile Command, Headquarters, Redstone Scientific Information Center, Redstone Arsenal, Alabama 35809.

C8   "Technische Lieferbedingungen für exoxierte Teile."
            Aug. 1944. 28p.
        "Technische Lieferbedingungen für Oberflächenschutz."
            Oct. 1944. 4p.
        "Technische Lieferbedingungen für Steuerventil Pe 4."
            Nov. 10, 1944. 6p.
        "Technische Lieferbedingungen für verzinkte Teile."
            Aug. 1944. 2p.

New York University, Courant Institute of Mathematical Sciences, Library, 251 Mercer Street, New York, N.Y. 10012.

Bl,2   File: "Fritz John." 1951-1955.

New York Public Library, Manuscript Division, Fifth Avenue and 42nd Street, New York, N.Y. 10018.

EMERGENCY COMMITTEE IN AID OF DISPLACED FOREIGN SCHOLARS, 1933-1945

*   File compiled when assistance was granted. 1934-1944.

ERICH VON KAHLER

Philosopher, 1885-1970

Leo Baeck Institute, 129 East 73rd Street, New York, N.Y.
10021.

The ERICH KAHLER COLLECTION (AR 2141-2147, 3890, 3905, 4287,
4328) contains approximately 7 ft. of materials pertaining
not only to Erich Kahler, but to Antoinette Kahler, Josefine
Kahler, Alice Loewy Kahler, Hermann Broch, Friedrich Gundolf, and the Karl Kautsky family. The collection was
donated to the Institute in sections by Mrs. Kahler, widow
of Erich, and receives periodic additions. The Kahler-
Gundolf letters are, as of 1977, restricted by the estate of
Erich Kahler.

*Die ERICH KAHLER COLLECTION (AR 2141-2147, 3890, 3905, 4287,
4328) umfaßt etwa 2 m Materialien, die sich nicht nur auf
Erich Kahler beziehen, sondern auch auf Antoinette Kahler,
Josefine Kahler, Alice Loewy Kahler, Hermann Broch, Friedrich Gundolf sowie auf die Familie Karl Kautskys. Die Sammlung wurde dem Institute nach und nach von der Witwe Erich
Kahlers geschenkt und wird immer noch erweitert. Zumindest
bis 1977 war die Kahler-Gundolf-Korrespondenz nicht zugänglich.*

B1   4 L. 1941-1969.
      Thomas Mann - Erich von Kahler. Briefwechsel im Exil.
      Pub. by the Thomas Mann Gesellschaft. 68p.

B1,2 Correspondence between Erich Kahler and Friedrich
      Gundolf. 1910-1931. Over 250 L. (Restricted.)

B2   Correspondence, including L. from: Leo Baeck, Richard
      Beer-Hofmann (1 L., 1937), Martin Buber (20 L.,
      1912-1934), Efraim Frisch, Hans Kohn, Otto Loewi
      (4 L., 1946-1953), Hans Rosenfeld, Karl Wolfskehl
      (11 L., 1929-1946), Victor Zuckerkandl (1 L., un-
      dated).

B3   18 L. from Richard and Mirjam Beer-Hofmann to Antoi-
      nette Kahler. 1940-1945.
      64 L. between Hermann Broch and Antoinette Kahler.
      1941-1951 and undated.
      7 L. to Antoinette Kahler, including L. from: Thomas
      Mann, Albert Einstein.

5 L. to Susi Glaubach.
1 L. ea. from Richard Beer-Hofmann and Albert Einstein
to Hermann Broch.
9 L. to and from Alice Loewy Kahler, including 2 L.
from Richard Beer-Hofmann.
1 L. from Karl Wolfskehl to Kurt Wolff and 1 L. by
Wolff.

C7   Judaica. Essays and speeches. 192p. Includes:
"Die Juden in Europa." 60p.
"Die Juden im Abendland." 95p.
"Was ist Musik? Das Lebenswerk V[iktor] Z[uckerkandl]s."
23p.

D7   6 cl.

H3   4 cl.

H4   2 cl.

I   Invitation to lecture on Stefan George. Bayrische Akademie der Schönen Künste.
Hebrew marriage certificate for Erich Kahler and Josefine Sabotka.

J   Photomontage of Albert Einstein.
9 photos of Erich Kahler.
3 photos of Karl Wolfskehl.
1 photo ea. of Antoinette von Kahler, Eugen von Kahler,
Josefine Kahler, Alice Loewy Kahler, Hermann Broch,
Franz Werfel's mother.

L   Materials on personalities, including correspondence
about them, offprints, cl., photos. Includes: Paul
Celan, Otto Loewi, Franz Werfel, Karl Wolfskehl,
Kurt H. Wolff, Julius Bab, Richard Beer-Hofmann.
Cl. from newspapers, magazines, brochures concerning
Jews in W.W. I. 1939-1967. 46 items.
31 newspaper cl., etc. concerning: Paul Celan, Susi
Glaubach, Karl Kautsky, Franz Kobler, Otto Loewi,
Margarete Susman, Ernst Peter Pick, Karl Wolfskehl.

N   Kahler, Antoinette. "Kinderjahre." 88p.
Kahler, Alice Loewy. 1 poem.

Mrs. Alice Loewy Kahler, 1 Evelyn Place, Princeton, New

ERICH VON KAHLER

Jersey 08540.

The materials in Mrs. Kahler's possession are from the literary estate of Erich von Kahler. The listing below represents those materials that have been sorted and catalogued as of 1977. It is expected that the remaining materials from the estate will be sorted and catalogued by 1978. A detailed inventory of the collection is available from the State University of New York at Albany (Department of Germanic Languages and Literatures) or from Mrs. Kahler. Publication rights to all Kahler materials are retained by Mrs. Kahler.

Die Materialien im Besitz von Frau Kahler stammen aus dem Nachlaß von Erich von Kahler. Die Aufstellung (siehe unten) umfaßt die Materialien, die bisher (1977) geordnet und katalogisiert werden konnten. Es darf damit gerechnet werden, daß ein Verzeichnis der übrigen Bestände noch vor 1978 hergestellt werden kann. Eine detaillierte Aufstellung der Materialien ist von der State University of New York at Albany (Department of Germanic Languages and Literatures) oder von Frau Kahler erhältlich. Die Publikationsrechte ruhen bei Frau Kahler.

A1   Diaries (5). 1906-1913.

A2   10 notebooks, with numerous inserted p. 1910-1916.

A3   Bibliography of Kahler's writings on 4" x 6" index cards. Also bibliography of articles about Kahler.

B1   Ca. 60 L. 1940-1968. Includes L. to: Gottfried Bermann-Fischer, Hans A. Bethe, Elisabeth Mann Borgese, G. A. Borgese, Hermann Kasack, Hermann Kesten, Guido Kisch, Udo Rukser, Oskar Seidlin, Hans Staudinger, Kurt H. Wolff.

B2   Ca. 1,980 L. 1926-1968. Includes L. from: Günther Anders, Julius Bab, Richard Beer-Hofmann, Gottfried Bermann-Fischer, Hans A. Bethe, Elisabeth Mann Borgese, G. A. Borgese, Bernhard von Bothmer, Hermann Broch, Heinrich Brüning, Elias Canetti, Albert Einstein, James Franck, Erich Fromm, Curt Glaser, Willy Haas, Heinz Hartmann, Heinrich Eduard Jacob, Hermann Kasack, Hermann Kesten, Guido Kisch, Edward Lowinsky,

446

James H. Meisel, Karl O. Paetel, Erwin Panofsky, Wolfgang Pauli, Heinz Politzer, Hans Rosenfeld, Udo Rukser, Hans Sahl, Heinrich Schnitzler, Olga Schnitzler, Oskar Seidlin, Rudolf Serkin, Hans Speier, Richard Sterba, Erwin Straus, Albert Theile, Siegfried Trebitsch, Jean Starr Untermeyer, Ernst Waldinger, Bruno Walter, Kadidja Wedekind, Kurt and Helene Wolff, Kurt H. Wolff, Otto Zoff, Victor Zuckerkandl, Carl Zuckmayer.

B1,2 Correspondences with publishers, magazines, university presses, etc., including: American Scholar, Commentary, Cornell University Press, S. Fischer Verlag, Goverts Verlag, Koehler Verlag, Kohlhammer Verlag, Merkur, Pantheon Books, Princeton University Press, Rowohlt Verlag, Saturday Review of Literature, Social Research, Twice A Year. Ca. 385 items.
Correspondences with organizations, institutes, students, etc., including the Van Leer Foundation for the Advancement of Human Culture. Ca. 725 L. 1940-1967.
Recommendations. Ca. 150 L. by Kahler, ca. 100 L. to Kahler. Also numerous enclosures: forms, résumés, project outlines, etc.

B3 Ca. 175 condolence L. to Lily Kahler. 1970.
Miscellaneous correspondence concerning the Van Leer Foundation for the Advancement of Human Culture (including numerous L. to and from Polly Van Leer). 1965-1967. Ca. 65 L.

C4 "Short Story." Notes. 3p.

C7 Man the Measure. Early Ms., numerous notes, diagrams. Ca. 440p.
Menschheitsidee und Kulturgestaltung in Vergangenheit und Zukunft. Eine neue Art der Geschichtsbetrachtung. Ca. 650p.
The Germans. Primarily lecture notes used as a basis for book. Some duplicate sets.
Numerous folders containing notes (some lecture notes), including:
"Arbeiten aus den Kriegsjahren 1915-16. München."
"Juden."
"Herkunft und Sinn des modernen Romans."

"Verschiedene Entwürfe."
"Social and Intellectual Evolution of Germany."
"Alte Notizen zur Philosophie und Wissenschaft."
"Staat (Deutsche Werdensgeschichte)."
Numerous Ms. of essays, lectures, etc. including:
"A History of the Human Quality."
Critique of Broch's Tod des Vergil.
"Culture and Evolution."
"Debate on Freudianism."
"Denkschrift zur Begründung einer akademischen
   Brüderschaft."
"Forms and Features of Anti-Judaism."
"Fortdauer des Mythos/Indelibility of Myth."
"Germany and the Western World."
"Goethe lecture."
"Das Kunstwerk und die Geschichte."
"Lebensverwandlung des bürgerlichen Wesens."
"Das Symbol."
"The Transformation of Modern Fiction."
"Untergang und Übergang der epischen Kunstform."
"Urteil ohne Richter."
"Die Verinnerung des Erzählens."
"Das Wahre, das Gute und das Schöne."
"What are the Jews?"
"Die Zukunft des Romans."

D7   Offprints and cl. Ca. 2 ft. (0.6 m.).

H5   "Broch über Erich Kahler." Xerox c. of original Ms. in
     Beinecke Library, Yale University.
     "A Note on Erich Kahler's 'Forms and Features of Anti-
     Judaism'."

N   Manuscripts by other authors, including: Julius Bab,
     Hans A. Bethe, G. A. Borgese, Adelheid Eulenberg,
     Ernst Ginsberg, Michael Hamburger, Robert L. Hiller,
     Rudolf Pannwitz, Olga Schnitzler.

Yale University, Beinecke Rare Book and Manuscript Library,
New Haven, Connecticut 06520.

This portion of the HERMANN BROCH ARCHIVE, consisting of
approximately 300 items, was donated to Yale by Mrs. Alice
Loewy Kahler.

ERICH VON KAHLER

Dieser Teil des HERMANN BROCH ARCHIVE, der etwa 300 Nummern umfaßt, ist eine Schenkung von Frau Alice Loewy Kahler.

B1   3 L. to Hermann Broch. 1945-1948.
     Ca. 135 L. to individuals concerning Hermann Broch.
     1951-1971.

B1,2 Correspondence with Hermann Broch de Rothermann. 29 L.
     1952-1969.
     Correspondence with Daniel Brody and the Rhein Verlag.
     52 L. 1951-1954.

B2   19 sympathy L. upon death of Hermann Broch, including
     L. from: Hans Sahl, Ernst Waldinger. 1951.
     59 L. from Hermann Broch. 1940-1951.

B3   Recommendation L. from Hermann Broch to Guggenheim
     Foundation. Dated Christmas 1941. 9p.

H4   Broch, Hermann. "Geschichte als moralische Anthropo-
     logie (Erich Kahlers 'Scienza Nuova')." 1949. Early
     version. T. with h. corr. 11p.

H5   "Als Erich noch ein Knabe war (Der Zauber-Erich)."
     Written by Alice Kahler, edited by Hermann Broch.
     T. 1p.
     "Bin ich wirklich sechzig heute? (Erichs Schlaflied
     in der Badewanne)." Written by Alice Kahler, edited
     by Hermann Broch. T. 1p.

Princeton University, Firestone Library, Princeton, New Jersey 08540.

ERICH VON KAHLER ARCHIVE, THOMAS MANN COLLECTION, RARE BOOK COLLECTION

B1   1 L. to Katia Mann. c.

B2   24 L. from Katia Mann to Erich and Lily Kahler. c.
     9 L. from Erika Mann.
     58 L. from Thomas Mann. 1931-1955.

B1,2 Correspondence between Kahler and Aldous Huxley.
     Correspondence between Erich and Lily Kahler and Lewis
     Mumford.

C7   Kahler's typescripts of all his works in English,
      including:
      "Art and History."
      "Culture and Evolution."
      "The Forms of Form."
      "The Nature of the Symbol."
      "The Persistence of Myth."
      "The True, the Good and the Beautiful."
      "Varieties of the Unconscious."
      "What is Art?"
      Hermann Broch lecture given at Columbia University,
      1953. In German.

K   Thomas Mann books with dedications to Erich von Kahler.
      1934+.
      Albert Einstein books with dedications to Erich von
      Kahler.

THE PAPERS OF ALBERT EINSTEIN (1879-1955). For details
concerning the use of this collection, see description under
Albert Einstein.

*THE PAPERS OF ALBERT EINSTEIN (1879-1955). Angaben über den
Zugang zu der Sammlung finden sich unter "Albert Einstein."*

B1,2 Unknown amount of correspondence between Einstein and
      Kahler.

State University of New York at Albany, Department of Germanic Languages and Literatures, 1400 Washington Avenue,
Albany, New York 12222.

KARL O. PAETEL COLLECTION

B1   21 L. to Karl O. Paetel (xerox). 1944-1948, 1952.

Mrs. Gertrude Urzidil, 83-39 116th Street, Richmond Hill, New
York 11418.

JOHANNES URZIDIL COLLECTION

450

ERICH VON KAHLER

A3   Listing of Kahler's publications by Kahler. English
        and German.
        Biographical statement. Up to 1968.
        "Besondere Freundschaften, Beziehungen." List, with
        some explanations. A.

Bl   8 L. to Johannes Urzidil. T. and A. 1946-1965.

Barthold Fles Literary Agency, 507 Fifth Avenue, New York,
N.Y. 10016.

Bl   2 L. to Barthold Fles. 1939.

University of Texas, Humanities Research Center, Manuscripts
Collection, Box 7219, Austin, Texas 78712.

Bl   1 L.

Harvard University, Houghton Library, Cambridge, Massachusetts 02138.

RICHARD BEER-HOFMANN COLLECTION

B2   1 L. from Richard Beer-Hofmann. T.c. 1937.

Library of Congress, Manuscript Division, Independence Avenue
and First Street S.E., Washington, D.C. 20540.

LITERARY ESTATE OF HANNAH ARENDT (closed until 1980)

Bl,2   Unknown amount of materials.

University of Chicago, The Joseph Regenstein Library, 1100
East 57th Street, Chicago, Illinois 60637.

*   Materials concerning the Committee to Frame a World
        Constitution.

ERICH VON KAHLER

Immigration History Research Center of the University of
Minnesota, 826 Berry Street, St. Paul, Minnesota 55101.

AMERICAN COUNCIL FOR EMIGRÉS IN THE PROFESSIONS ARCHIVES

A3   Biographical statement. 2p.

ERICH ITOR KAHN

Pianist, 1905-1956

Mrs. Frida Kahn, 30 East End Avenue, Apt. 6F, New York, N.Y.
10028.

The materials in Mrs. Kahn's possession were assembled by
the Kahn family. A preliminary card cataloguing of the collection has been done.

*Die Materialien in Frau Kahns Besitz wurden von Familienmit-
gliedern zusammengetragen. Ein vorläufiger Kartenindex
wurde schon erstellt.*

B1,2   Correspondence with colleagues, friends, etc., for
        example with Erich Schmid. 1928-1955.

C13a   Ms. of compositions by Kahn. Also additional pc. of
        some compositions.

D13   Pub. compositions by Kahn.

E   Adaptations of Kahn's music.

F   Tapes, records of Kahn's performances.

H3   Newspaper cl.

J   Numerous photos.

K   Kahn's personal music library, including scores.

O   Numerous programs of performances.

American Composer's Alliance, 170 West 74th Street, New York,
N.Y. 10023.

The American Composer's Alliance collects copyist manuscripts
of compositions by its members, prepared either by the composer himself or by another. Kahn was a member of the American Composer's Alliance.

*Die American Composer's Alliance sammelt Kopistenmanuskripte
von Kompositionen ihrer Mitglieder, die entweder vom Komponisten selbst oder von einem anderen Komponisten erstellt werden. Kahn war Mitglied der Composer's Alliance.*

C13a   "3 x 6 Bagatellen." Copyist-Ms. 1935.

"6 Bagatelles." Op. 5. Copyist-Ms. 1938.
"3 Bagatelles." Op. 8. Copyist-Ms. 1938.
"Huit Inventions pour Piano." Copyist-Ms. 1937.
"Praeludien zur Nacht." Copyist-Ms. 1927.
"3 Pieces." Copyist-Ms. Undated.
"Reigen aus alt Wien." Copyist-Ms. 1931.
"Sonatina No. 3." Copyist-Ms. Before 1930.
"Les Symphonies Bretonnes." Copyist-Ms. 1940.
"Suite Concertante." Copyist-Ms. 1937. Orchestration
  completed by René Leibowitz. 1964.
"Spervogel." Copyist-Ms. Undated. Music for 10 instru-
  ments and soprano.

Library of Congress, Reference Department, Music Division,
Independence Avenue and First Street S.E., Washington, D.C.,
20540.

Cl3a   "Canon per modum speculi." 1945. A. 3p.

Mr. Hans Sahl, 800 West End Avenue, New York, N.Y. 10025.

Bl   Several L. to Hans Sahl.

OTTO KALLIR

Writer, Art Critic, 1894-

Dr. Otto Kallir, The Galerie St. Etienne, 24 West 57th Street, New York, N.Y. 10019.

The collection of materials in Dr. Kallir's possession was assembled by him over many years in the course of his work and is inaccessible at present.

Die Materialsammlung, die sich in Dr. Kallirs Besitz befindet, wurde im Laufe vieler Jahre zusammengestellt. Die Sammlung ist zur Zeit nicht zugänglich.

B1,2   Correspondence over many years.
       Correspondence with the Johannispresse. Also documents.

C7   Ms. of art books.
       Ms. of articles.
       Catalogs, written by Kallir (Klimt, Moses, etc.).

H3   Numerous cl.

H4   Several volumes of reviews of his works.

J   Photos of exhibitions.

L   Grandma Moses collection. Miscellaneous collection of
       materials over many years.

M   Memorabilia.

Harvard University, Houghton Library, Cambridge, Massachusetts 02138.

RICHARD BEER-HOFMANN COLLECTION

B1   14 L. to Richard Beer-Hofmann. 1921-1945 and undated.

University of Pennsylvania, The Charles Patterson Van Pelt Library, Philadelphia, Pennsylvania 19104.

ALMA MAHLER-WERFEL COLLECTION

B1   3 L. to Alma Mahler-Werfel. T. and A. 1942-1958.
       1 L. to Hans Guertler. T.cc. 1955.

I   1 "carte de visite."

State University of New York at Albany, Department of Germanic Languages and Literatures, 1400 Washington Avenue, Albany, New York 12222.

STORM PUBLISHERS ARCHIVE

B1   1 L. to Alexander Gode von Aesch. 1947.

B2   3 L. from Alexander Gode von Aesch. 1947-1948.

Mrs. Gertrude Urzidil, 83-39 116th Street, Richmond Hill, New York, N.Y. 11418.

JOHANNES URZIDIL COLLECTION

B1   1 L. to Johannes Urzidil. A. 1962.

Leo Baeck Institute, 129 East 73rd Street, New York, N.Y. 10021.

B1   1 L. to Fred Grubel. 1971.

University of Texas, Humanities Research Center, Manuscripts Collection, Box 7219, Austin, Texas 78712.

B1   1 L.

Mr. Fritz H. Landshoff, c/o Harry N. Abrams, Inc., Publishers, 110 East 59th Street, New York, N.Y. 10022.

B1,2   Correspondence between Kallir and Landshoff.

ERNEST KANITZ

Composer, 1894–

Dr. Ernest Kanitz, 6206 Murietta Avenue, Van Nuys, California 91401.

Dr. Kanitz has made plans for his materials to go to the University of Southern California after his death. Until that time, the materials will remain closed to the public.

Dr. Ernst Kanitz hat beschlossen, daß seine Materialien nach seinem Tode an die University of Southern California gehen sollen. Bis zu dem Zeitpunkt bleiben sie für die Öffentlichkeit unzugänglich.

B1,2   Correspondence over many years.

C   Ms. of Kanitz' literary works.

C13   Ms. of Kanitz' compositions: symphonies, concertos, etc. Much still unpublished.

H3   Newspaper cl.

K   Sizable music library.

L   Newspaper cl. on other composers, musicians.

Library of Congress, Reference Department, Music Division, Independence Avenue and First Street S.E., Washington, D.C. 20540.

C13a   "[Bläserspiele]. Serenade for 11 wind insruments [sic], piano and percussion." [1968]. A. pc. 47 leaves.
       "Cantata." 1961. Poem by Mynatt Breidenthal. 1964. A. pc. 28p.
       "[Concertino, piano, clarinet and strings.] Concertino for 5 players." 1964. A. pc. 20p.
       "[Concerto, bassoon]. Concerto." 1963. A. pc. 54p.
       "[Duo, violin and viola]. Duo." 1964. A. pc. 23p.
       "Moods, for chamber orchestra." 1966. A. pc. 35p.
       "Sinfonia seria." 1963. A. pc. 74p.
       "[Sonata, bassoon and piano.] Sonata." 1966. A. pc. 19p.
       "[Sonata, violin and piano, no. 2]. Second Sonata." 1965. A. pc. 20p.

ERNEST KANITZ

"[Sonata, violoncello.] Sonata." 1964. A. pc. 8p.
"Sonata breve, for violin, cello and piano." 1964. A.
pc. 27p.
"[Sonatina, viola and piano.] Sonatina." 1964. A. and
pc. 13p.
"[Symphony, no. 3.] Third Symphony (Sinfonia concertante for violin and cello)." 1967. A. pc. 67p.
"Tanz-Sonate. Dance Sonata, for 4 wind instruments and
piano." 1964. A. pc. 27p.
"Visiones in crepusculo: for flute, strings, piano and
women's chorus in unison." 1964. A. pc. 29p.

University of California, Los Angeles, Music Library, 405
Hilgard Avenue, Los Angeles, California 90024.

ERNST TOCH ARCHIVE

B1   1 L. to Ernst Toch.

New York Public Library, Manuscript Division, Fifth Avenue
and 42nd Street, New York, N.Y. 10018.

EMERGENCY COMMITTEE IN AID OF DISPLACED FOREIGN SCHOLARS,
1933-1945

*   File compiled when assistance was granted. 1937-1944.

ROBERT KANN

Historian, 1906-

Dr. Robert Kann, 143 Loomis Court, Princeton, New Jersey
08540.

Private collection: inaccessible. / *Unzugängliche Privatsammlung.*

A3   Bibliography of Kann's works.

B1,2   Small amounts of correspondence.

C7   Ms. of Kann's articles. T.
       Notes and rough drafts of articles.

D7   Nearly complete collection of offprints and cl.

D7,   Album of reviews by Kann of works of others, also
H4   reviews of Kann's works.

J   Photos.

K   Personal library.

New York Public Library, Manuscript Division, Fifth Avenue
and 42nd Street, New York, N.Y. 10018.

EMERGENCY COMMITTEE IN AID OF DISPLACED FOREIGN SCHOLARS,
1933-1945

*   File compiled, no assistance given. 1938-1944.

ALFRED KANTOROWICZ

Writer, 1899-

University of Southern California, Lion Feuchtwanger Memorial Library, 520 Paseo Miramar, Pacific Palisades, California 90272.

B1   33 L. to Lion Feuchtwanger. 1941-1957.

B2   37 L. and 1 Tel. from L. Feuchtwanger. 1941-1957.

University of Texas, Humanities Research Center, Manuscripts Collection, Box 7219, Austin, Texas 78712.

B1   23 L.

B2   15 L.

C   2 Ms.

Southern Illinois University, Morris Library, Department of Special Collections, Carbondale, Illinois 62901.

ERWIN PISCATOR PAPERS

B1   1 L. to Erwin Piscator. T. 1944.

B2   2 L. from Erwin Piscator. T.cc. 1941, 1948.

State University of New York at Albany, Department of Germanic Languages and Literatures, 1400 Washington Avenue, Albany, New York 12222.

KARL O. PAETEL COLLECTION, HELMUT HIRSCH COLLECTION

B1   6 L. to Karl O. Paetel (xerox). 1941-1942, 1957, 1970.
      1 L. to Helmut Hirsch. Pc. 1974.

University of Pennsylvania, The Charles Patterson Van Pelt Library, Philadelphia, Pennsylvania 19104.

ALMA MAHLER-WERFEL COLLECTION

460

ALFRED KANTOROWICZ

B1   2 L. to Franz Werfel. T. 1942-1944.

B2   1 L. and 1 draft of a L. from Franz Werfel. 1942, 1944.

Princeton University, Firestone Library, Princeton, New Jersey 08540.

THOMAS MANN COLLECTION

B2   Correspondence with Thomas Mann.

Leo Baeck Institute, 129 East 73rd Street, New York, N.Y. 10021.

D7   2 newspaper cl. of articles by Kantorowicz. 1958-1959.
        3p.

H4   Book notice. 2p. in print.

Yivo Institute, 1048 Fifth Avenue, New York, N.Y. 10028.

HORACE M. KALLEN PAPERS

B1,2 Individual items in folder no. 266.

University of California, Los Angeles, Department of Special Collections, 120 Lawrence Clark Powell Library, Los Angeles, California 90024.

FRANZ WERFEL ARCHIVE

B1   1 L. to Franz Werfel. 1942.

GINA KAUS

Writer, 1894-

New York Public Library at Lincoln Center, Library and Museum
of the Performing Arts, 111 Amsterdam Avenue, New York, N.Y.
10023.

EDMOND PAUKER COLLECTION

C2   It's in the Dictionary. A comedy in 3 acts by Gina Kaus
         and Andrew Solt. Tr. by Steven Vas. Hollywood, Cali-
         fornia: Playmarket, Inc., 1941. T.
       Luxury Liner. A play by Gina Kaus. Tr. by Margaret
         Goettel. Production rights Georg Marton, Vienna. T.cc.
         139p.
       The Man Who Knew Women. by Lee Walsch. Adapted from
         the drama Jean by Gina Kaus and Laslo Vadnai. T.
         178p.
       Mitsou. A comedy with Music. As suggested by Vicki Baum
         and Gina Kaus. Based on the novel by Colette. T.
         135p.
       Prison without Bars. By Peggy Barwell, based on a story
         by Gina Kaus. Mimeo. 129p.
         Sentenced for Life (Prison without Bars). Play in 8
         scenes by Gina Kaus. Based on an idea by Hilde Kova-
         loff. T. 73p.
       Die Stadt ist dunkel. Drama in zwölf Bildern von Gina
         Kaus und Ladislaus Fodor. T. 125p.
         The City Is Dark. A play in twelve scenes by Gina
         Kaus and Ladislaus Fodor. Ca. 1938. English tr. T.
         105p.
       Überfahrt. Ein Schauspiel in 15 Bildern von Gina Kaus.
         Production rights Georg Marton, Vienna. T. 130p.

Ms. Gina Kaus, 262 South Carmelina Avenue, Brentwood, California 94513.

Ms. Kaus still retains typescripts of some of her latest
works in her possession.

*Frau Kaus befindet sich noch im Besitz der maschinenschrift-
lichen Manuskripte ihrer letzten Werke.*

C1   Xanthippe oder Die Pest in Athen. Novel. T. 157p.

C5   The Red Danube. Screen play by Gina Kaus and Arthur
        Wimperis. Dated April 9, 1948. T.

Harvard University, Houghton Library, Cambridge, Massachusetts 02138.

C9   Simon, Neil. The Odd Couple. Tr. into German by Gina
        Kaus. Frankfurt, undated. T. 155p.

Yale University, Beinecke Rare Book and Manuscript Library,
New Haven, Connecticut 06520.

EDMOND PAUKER COLLECTION

I   Contracts:
        Jean
        Schrift an der Wand

Mrs. Elisabeth M. Stoerk and Mrs. Susanne B. Hoeller, 288
Ocean Drive West, Stamford, Connecticut 06902.

FRIDERIKE ZWEIG ARCHIVE

B1   L. to Friderike Zweig. 1944.

ROBERT MAX WASSILLI KEMPNER

Political Scientist, Lawyer, 1899-

Because of time limitations, the Project was unable to ascertain the existence or extent of papers still in the possession of Dr. R. M. W. Kempner (New York, N.Y.). The following represent various smaller amounts of materials located by the Project.

Zeitschwierigkeiten machten es unmöglich herauszufinden, ob und in welchem Umfang sich im Besitze von Dr. R. M. W. Kempner (New York, N.Y.) noch weitere Materialien befinden. Das Folgende stellt eine Aufzählung verschiedener anderer, kleinerer Materialsammlungen dar, die an anderen Orten ausfindig gemacht wurden.

Boston University, Mugar Memorial Library, 771 Commonwealth Avenue, Boston, Massachusetts 02215.

BELLA FROMM COLLECTION

B1   10 L. to Bella Fromm. 1941-1952 and 1967.

B2   6 L. from Bella Fromm. T.cc. 1941-1952.

University of New Hampshire, The Library, Department of Special Collections, Durham, New Hampshire 03824.

FRIEDRICH SALLY GROSSHUT COLLECTION

B1   10 L. to F. S. Grosshut. T. 1950-1965.

Leo Baeck Institute, 129 East 73rd Street, New York, N.Y. 10021.

KURT KERSTEN COLLECTION, KURT GROSSMANN COLLECTION, LEOPOLD SCHWARZSCHILD COLLECTION

B1   2 L. to Kurt Kersten. 1957.
      Correspondence with Kurt Grossmann.
      Correspondence with Leopold Schwarzschild. 1942-1949.

ROBERT MAX WASSILLI KEMPNER

Harvard University, Houghton Library, Cambridge, Massachusetts 02138.

Bl   6 L. to Lewis Stiles Gannett. 1935-1939.

Mrs. Gertrude Urzidil, 83-39 116th Street, Richmond Hill,
New York 11418.

JOHANNES URZIDIL COLLECTION

Bl   4 L. to Johannes Urzidil. T. and A. 1967.

State University of New York at Albany, Department of Germanic Languages and Literatures, 1400 Washington Avenue,
Albany, New York 12222.

HELMUT HIRSCH COLLECTION, KARL O. PAETEL COLLECTION

Bl   2 L. to Helmut Hirsch. 1972.
        3 L. to Karl O. Paetel (xerox). 1944, 1951.

Harvard University, Harvard Divinity School, Andover-Harvard
Theological Library, 45 Francis Avenue, Cambridge, Massachusetts 02138.

PAUL TILLICH COLLECTION

B2   2 L. from Paul Tillich. T.cc. 1959, 1962.

New York Public Library, Manuscript Division, Fifth Avenue
and 42nd Street, New York, N.Y. 10018.

EMERGENCY COMMITTEE IN AID OF DISPLACED FOREIGN SCHOLARS,
1933-1945

*   File compiled when assistance was granted. 1939-1943.

University of Chicago, The Joseph Regenstein Library, 1100

East 57th Street, Chicago, Illinois 60637.

EMIL GUMBEL PAPERS

B1,2   Correspondence between Gumbel and Kempner. 1940s.

KURT KERSTEN

Writer, 1891-1962

Leo Baeck Institute, 129 East 73rd Street, New York, N.Y.
10021.

The KURT KERSTEN COLLECTION was donated partially by Kurt
Kersten before his death, partially by Ms. Alice D. David
(stepdaughter) in 1966. The collection presently consists
of ca. 3 ft. of materials.

*Die KURT KERSTEN COLLECTION setzt sich zusammen aus einer
Schenkung, die Kurt Kersten selbst vor seinem Tode vorgenommen hat, und aus einer Schenkung von Frau Alice D. David,
seiner Stieftochter, aus dem Jahre 1966. Die Sammlung besteht zur Zeit aus etwa 0,90 m Materialien.*

A3   "Der Tod auf der Insel. Ein Westindisches Tagebuch."
      Undated. T. 139p. Also second copy.
      Curriculum vitae. Undated. 2p.
      Publications and books written by Dr. Phil. Kurt Ker-
      sten. 1p.
      Places of residence of Kurt Kersten. 1p.
      List of persons who guaranteed support of Kersten in
      the U.S. 1p.

B1   1 L. to Leo Baeck Institute concerning his Nachlaß.
      1961. 5p.

B2   743 L. and 43 Ptc. 1939-1961, including L. from: S.
      Aufhäuser, Julius Bab, Julius Deutsch, Alfred Döblin,
      John Dos Passos, Albert Ehrenstein, Lion Feuchtwan-
      ger, Leonhard Frank, René Fülöp-Miller, Claire Goll,
      Oskar Maria Graf, George Grosz, Emil Gumbel, Willy
      Haas, Theodor Heuss, Kurt Hiller, Heinrich Eduard
      Jacob, Erich Kaestner, Ossip Kalenter, Karl Kautsky,
      R. M. W. Kempner, Alfred Kerr, Hermann Kesten, Hil-
      degard Knef, Leo Lania, Emil Ludwig, Erika Mann,
      Thomas Mann, Ludwig Marcuse, Walter Mehring, H. L.
      Mencken, Martin Niemoeller, Emil Oprecht, Karl O.
      Paetel, Jacob Picard, Kurt Pinthus, Erwin Piscator,
      Ernst Reuter, Jules Romains, Ernst Rowohlt, Anna
      Seghers, Hans Siemsen, Upton Sinclair, Carl Spiecker,
      Dorothy Thompson, Fritz von Unruh, Veit Valentin,
      Thornton Wilder.

Correspondence with publishers. 1943-1961. 93 L.

C4,7   17 Ms. of essays, stories. All unpub. 1958 and undated.
T. 99p.

45 Ms. of essays, stories. All pub. 1950-1952 and undated. T. 381p.

D7   Newspaper cl. 1937-1961.

H3   Advertisement: "Kurt Kersten: Die Opposition der 'Ein-
samen'." 1p.

H5   "Record of Dr. Phil. Kurt Kersten." Written by stepdaughter Alice D. David. 1966. 3p.

J   Photo of Kersten.

L   Materials collection: "Breitscheid-Hilferding." Includes:

"Das Ende Rudolf Breitscheids und Rudolf Hilfer-
dings." 1957. T. 59p.

37 L. and 3 Ptc. of Tony Breitscheid. 1947-1957.

2 L. by Rose Hilferding. 1957-1958.

Miscellaneous correspondence on Breitscheid/Hilfer-
ding. 1951-1959. Ca. 50 items.

Newspaper cl. 1944-1957.

Materials collection: "G. Forster." Includes:

"Johannes von Müller und Georg Forster." Undated.
T. 4p.

"Von der Weltumseglung mit James Cook 1772-75."
Undated. T. 3p.

3 untitled Ms. 10p.

Dates, loose pages. 15p.

Correspondence and materials. 1948-1957. Ca. 70p.

Correspondence of Hans Hainebach. 55 L. and 5 Ptc.
1949-1957.

11 newspaper cl. (5 by Kersten). 1950-1957.

Miscellaneous materials collected by Kersten.

FRANZ JOURDAN FAMILIE COLLECTION, JACOB PICARD COLLECTION,
SALAMON DEMBITZER COLLECTION

B1   1 L. to Lucy Jourdan. 1961.

B1,2   Correspondence between Kersten and Jacob Picard.
Correspondence between Kersten and Salamon Dembitzer.

B2   1 L. from Lucy Jourdan. 1961.

D7   Newspaper cl. 1961. 2p.

H3   Memorial article. Newspaper cl. 1p.

J   Color photo of Kurt Kersten and Manfred George in
      photo album.

University of New Hampshire, The Library, Department of Special Collections, Durham, New Hampshire 03824.

OSKAR MARIA GRAF COLLECTION, FRIEDRICH SALLY GROSSHUT COL-
LECTION

B1   3 L. to O. M. Graf. 1960 and undated.

B3   Condolence L., including L. from: Jacob Javits, Peter
      M. Lindt, Theodor Heuss, O. M. Graf, E. Gumbel, Paul
      Mayer, Kurt Grossmann. 1962.

D7   Newspaper cl. from the 1950s and 1960s. Ca. 1.5 in.

H3   Newspaper cl. on the death of Kersten.

J   Several photos, including: photo with Manfred George
      in the Aufbau office.

State University of New York at Albany, Department of Germanic Languages and Literatures, 1400 Washington Avenue,
Albany, New York 12222.

KARL O. PAETEL COLLECTION

B1   30 L. to Karl O. Paetel. 1946-1962. (xerox)

University of Southern California, Lion Feuchtwanger Memorial
Library, 520 Paseo Miramar, Pacific Palisades, California
90272.

B1   8 L. to Lion Feuchtwanger. 1951-1958.

B2   7 L. from Lion Feuchtwanger. 1951-1958.

Immigration History Research Center of the University of
Minnesota, 826 Berry Street, St. Paul, Minnesota 55101.

AMERICAN COUNCIL FOR EMIGRÉS IN THE PROFESSIONS ARCHIVES

A3   Biographical questionnaire filled out by Kersten. 1p.

Mrs. Peter M. Lindt, 949 West End Avenue, New York, N.Y.
10025.

B1   Small amount of correspondence with Peter M. Lindt.

FRIEDRICH KESSLER

Professor of Law, 1901-

Dr. Friedrich Kessler, Boalt Hall, School of Law, University of California, Berkeley, California 94720.

Dr. Kessler's private collection is complete with the exception of a section of the "Casebook Library" (1,500-2,000 volumes) that was given partially to the Yale University Library, partially to the State University of New York at Stony Brook.

Dr. Friedrich Kesslers Privatsammlung ist vollständig geblieben bis auf einen Teil der "Casebook Library" (1500-2000 Bände), der zum einen Teil an die Yale University Library, zum anderen Teil an die State University of New York at Stony Brook ging.

B1,2   Correspondence, including L. to and from James Franck.

C7   Notes to lectures.

C8   Contracts: Cases and Materials. Ms. of second edition. "Casebook" on contracts.

D7   Published articles.

I   Documents of his career and personal life.

K   Casebook library.

L   Collection of clippings by colleagues, friends, others.

HERMANN KESTEN

Writer, 1900-

Mr. Kesten resides presently in Rome and maintains the most
substantial collection of his materials at his home there.
Materials located in the U.S. are primarily individual items
located in the collections of other emigrés or prominent
Americans.

*Hermann Kesten lebt zur Zeit in Rom und dort befindet sich
auch seine umfangreiche literarische Sammlung. Vereinzelte
Materialien finden sich in den U.S.A. in den Sammlungen
anderer Emigranten oder bekannter amerikanischer Persönlichkeiten.*

<u>Hoover Institution on War, Revolution and Peace</u>, Stanford,
California 94305.

FRANZ SCHOENBERNER COLLECTION

B1   47 L., 4 Ptc. and 1 Tel. to Franz Schoenberner. 1941-
      1953.

<u>Leo Baeck Institute</u>, 129 East 73rd Street, New York, N.Y.
10021.

KURT KERSTEN COLLECTION, GEORG HERMANN COLLECTION, LEOPOLD
SCHWARZSCHILD COLLECTION, JOSEPH BORNSTEIN COLLECTION and
general archive files

B1   16 L. to Kurt Kersten. 1942-1960.
      1 L. to Georg Hermann. T. 1933.
      1 L. to Leo Baeck Institute. T. 1962.
      1 L. to Joseph Bornstein. 1949.

B1,2 Correspondence with Leopold Schwarzschild. 1940-1941.

D7   5 cl.

H3   Cl. 1961-1965. 6p.

H4   Book notice: <u>Filialen des Parnaß</u>. Kindler Verlag. 4p.

<u>Mrs. Elisabeth M. Stoerk and Mrs. Susanne B. Hoeller</u>, 288

Ocean Drive West, Stamford, Connecticut 06902.

FRIDERIKE ZWEIG ARCHIVE

B1   16 L. and 4 Ptc. to Friderike Zweig. 1944-1970. Also
      L. filed under "Writers Service Center." 1944.
D4   "Oberst Kock." Story in _Aufbau_ (NY), July 1942.

University of New Hampshire, The Library, Department of
Special Collections, Durham, New Hampshire 03824.

FRIEDRICH SALLY GROSSHUT COLLECTION

B1   15 L. and Ptc. to F. S. Grosshut. T. and A. 1949-1963.
B2   1 L. from F. S. Grosshut. T.c. 1949.

Yale University, Beinecke Rare Book and Manuscript Library,
New Haven, Connecticut 06520.

HERMANN BROCH ARCHIVE

B1   3 L. to Hermann Broch. 1943.
B2   3 L. from Hermann Broch. 1943.

Library of Congress, Manuscript Division, Independence Avenue
and First Street S.E., Washington, D.C. 20540.

BENJAMIN W. HUEBSCH PAPERS

B1   3 L. to B. W. Huebsch. T. 1939-1945.
B2   2 L. from B. W. Huebsch. T.c. 1940, 1945.

University of Texas, Humanities Research Center, Manuscripts
Collection, Box 7219, Austin, Texas 78712.

B2   4 L.

Mrs. Gertrude Urzidil, 83-39 116th Street, Richmond Hill, New York 11418.

JOHANNES URZIDIL COLLECTION

B1   2 L. to Johannes Urzidil. T. 1961, 1962.

Harvard University, Harvard Divinity School, Andover-Harvard Theological Library, 45 Francis Avenue, Cambridge, Massachusetts 02138.

PAUL TILLICH COLLECTION

B1   1 L. to Paul Tillich. T. 1962.

B2   1 L. from Paul Tillich. T.c. 1962.

Columbia University, Butler Library, New York, N.Y. 10027.

B1   1 L. to B. W. Huebsch. T. 1960.

Mr. Hans Sahl, 800 West End Avenue, New York, N.Y. 10025.

B1   Several L. to Hans Sahl.

State University of New York at Albany, Department of Germanic Languages and Literatures, 1400 Washington Avenue, Albany, New York 12222.

KARL O. PAETEL COLLECTION

B1   2 L. to Karl O. Paetel. 1946.

Dr. Harold von Hofe, Department of German, University of Southern California, Los Angeles, California 90007.

LUDWIG MARCUSE PAPERS

B1,2 Correspondence with Ludwig Marcuse.

University of Pennsylvania, The Charles Patterson Van Pelt
Library, Philadelphia, Pennsylvania 19104.

ALMA MAHLER-WERFEL COLLECTION

Bl   2 L. to Franz Werfel. T. 1942.

Dr. Marta Mierendorff, 8633 West Knoll Drive, Hollywood,
California 90069.

SAMMLUNG WALTER WICCLAIR, WALTER WICCLAIR PRODUCTIONS

Bl   1 L. to Marta Mierendorff re: Stefan Zweig production.

Barthold Fles Literary Agency, 507 Fifth Avenue, New York,
N.Y. 10016.

Bl   2 L. to Barthold Fles. 1941, 1942.

Mr. Fritz H. Landshoff, c/o Harry N. Abrams, Inc., Publishers, 110 East 59th Street, New York, N.Y. 10022.

Bl,2 Correspondence between Kesten and Landshoff.

Mrs. Alice Loewy Kahler, 1 Evelyn Place, Princeton, New
Jersey 08540.

ERICH VON KAHLER COLLECTION

Bl   2 L. to Erich von Kahler. 1940 (xerox), 1964.

B2   1 L. from Erich von Kahler. 1963.

Prof. John M. Spalek, 23 Pheasant Lane, Delmar, New York
12054.

Bl,2 Correspondence with John M. Spalek concerning Ernst
       Toller.

OTTO KLEMPERER

Conductor, 1885-1973

Leo Baeck Institute, 129 East 73rd Street, New York, N.Y.
10021.

B1   2 L. 1926 and undated.

H3   1 article and 3 obituaries. 4 cl. 1956, 1973.

J   Photo of Klemperer. Berlin, 1938.
      5 photos of Klemperer. 1931-1965 and undated.
      1 photo with dedication to Max Kowalski. London, 1948.

O   Concert program. Berlin, undated.

Library of Congress, Reference Department, Music Division,
Independence Avenue and First Street S.E., Washington, D.C.
20540.

C13   "Merry-Valse and One-Step." Reproduced from copyist-Ms.
         for orchestra. 1963. 19p. and 14p.
      "Jean Philippe Rameau's Gavotte with six variations."
         Orchestration by O. Klemperer. 1968. 14 leaves.

University of Georgia, The University Libraries, Athens,
Georgia 30601.

OLIN DOWNES PAPERS

B1,2 Correspondence with Olin Downes. 11 L.

Columbia University, Butler Library, New York, N.Y. 10027.

ORAL HISTORY COLLECTION and general archive files

B1   1 L. to "John." T. 1958.

H5   Comments on Otto Klemperer in an interview with Roger
         Huntington Sessions. 1962. 309p. of interview in
         total.

University of California, Santa Barbara, The Library, Santa

Barbara, California 93105.

LOTTE LEHMANN COLLECTION

B1,2   Correspondence with Lotte Lehman.

University of California, Los Angeles, Music Library, 405
Hilgard Avenue, Los Angeles, California 90024.

ERNST TOCH ARCHIVE

B1   3 L. to Ernst Toch.

Mrs. Gertrude Urzidil, 83-39 116th Street, Richmond Hill,
New York 11418.

JOHANNES URZIDIL COLLECTION

B1   2 L. to Johannes Urzidil. T. 1968.

B2   1 L. from Johannes Urzidil. T.c. 1968.

Boston University, Mugar Memorial Library, 771 Commonwealth
Avenue, Boston, Massachusetts 02215.

JOSEPH SZIGETI PAPERS

B1   1 L. to Joseph Szigeti. T. 1966.

Academy of Motion Picture Arts and Sciences, Margaret Herrick
Library, 9038 Melrose Avenue, Hollywood, California 90069.

H3   Several newspaper cl., including one obituary.

University of Pennsylvania, The Charles Patterson Van Pelt
Library, Philadelphia, Pennsylvania 19104.

ALMA MAHLER-WERFEL COLLECTION

B1   6 L. and 1 Tel. to Alma Mahler-Werfel.

University of Chicago, The Joseph Regenstein Library, 1100
East 57th Street, Chicago, Illinois 60637.

JAMES FRANCK PAPERS

B1,2   Correspondence with James Franck.

Bruno Walter Memorial Foundation, c/o Miss Susie Danziger,
115 East 72nd Street, New York, N.Y. 10021.

B1,2   Correspondence with Bruno Walter.

HENRY KOERNER

Painter, 1915-

The Project was unable to contact Mr. Henry Koerner (Pittsburgh, Pennsylvania) or to obtain further information regarding Koerner materials of historic interest.

*Es war nicht möglich, Herrn Henry Koerner (Pittsburgh, Penn-
sylvania) persönlich zu erreichen bzw. weitere Auskünfte über
Koerner-Materialien von historischem Interesse zu erhalten.*

Syracuse University, The George Arents Research Library,
Syracuse, New York 13210.

The HENRY KOERNER PAPERS, 4 archive boxes of materials, were
donated to the library by Mr. Koerner in 1965.

*Die HENRY KOERNER PAPERS, 4 Archivkartons Materialien, sind
eine Schenkung von Henry Koerner an die Bibliothek aus dem
Jahre 1965.*

B1,2   Correspondence. 1955-1963, including L. to and from:
       Ben Shahn, Norman and Dorothy Chandler, Max Roden,
       Robert F. Kennedy, Nelson A. Rockefeller, Julie Har-
       ris.

C4,14 Four Stories in Paintings and Words. Typed texts and
       pencil drawings. Mock-up of book.

C7   Several Ms. on the subjects of art, the artist, seeing.
       Ms. text on the subject of art, written on oversize
           drawing paper.
       Text to a book on art.

C14   Pen and ink sketches (some oversize).
       Ca. 10 Office of War Information posters on the war
           effort.
       Original concepts to posters.
       Time Magazine covers painted by Koerner, including:
           Kennedy brothers, Paul Tillich, John Cheever, etc.
       Prints of Koerner paintings.

D14   Copy of Saroyan's Tracy's Tiger, illustrated by Koer-
           ner.
       C.B.S. calendar, illustrated by Koerner.

H3   Miscellaneous cl.

H4   Gallery exhibit poster, catalogs and announcements to
       exhibits.
       Cl. on Koerner's work.

J   Photos of Koerner's work, plus other miscellaneous
       photos.

WOLFGANG KÖHLER

Gestalt Psychologist, 1887-1959

<u>American Philosophical Society</u>, The Library, 105 South Fifth Street, Philadelphia, Pennsylvania 19106.

The major portion of the WOLFGANG KÖHLER PAPERS was donated to the American Philosophical Society by Mrs. Wolfgang Köhler in 1967. Additional materials were added to the collection as a result of donations by Dr. Mary Henle in 1968 and 1973, and by Mrs. Köhler in 1970.

Der größte Teil der WOLFGANG KÖHLER PAPERS ist eine Schenkung an die American Philosophical Society von Frau Köhler aus dem Jahre 1967. Spätere Schenkungen (von Dr. Mary Henle in den Jahren 1968 und 1973 sowie von Frau Köhler im Jahre 1970) erweiterten die Sammlung.

A2   16 research notebooks. 1914/1915-1959 and undated. Lecture notes, experimental data, records, etc.

A3   Autobiographical material. 10 items.

B1,2   Invitations. 283 L. 1954-1967.
Requests for articles. 59 L. 1956-1957.
142 L. concerning the article "Gespräche in Deutschland." 1933-1934.
Ca. 1,645 L. 1922-1967, including L. to and from: Rudolf Arnheim, Siegfried Bernfeld, Karl Bühler, Herbert Feigl, Richard Held, Kurt Lewin, J. Robert Oppenheimer, Erwin Panofsky, Max Planck, Hans Reichenbach, Hans Simons, Hans Wallach.

B2   Birthday greetings. 20 items. 1957-1967.

C7   "On Germany." T. 2 c.

C7,8   Notes for talks, lectures, seminars. 1 B. Includes notes on:
Brain physiology.
Cortical currents.
Gestalt psychology.
Gifford lecture series.
Hitchcock lectures and seminars.
Figural after-effects.
Langfeld lecture series.
Notes as president of A.P.A.
RNA, third dimension, thinking, perception.

Princeton lectures.
Swarthmore college lectures.
Manuscripts, drafts, notes. 1 B. includes:
Gifford lectures. Ms.
Langfeld lectures. Ms.
Lauenstein material. Ms., reprint, correspondence.
Kant lectures.
Texts of 88 lectures, speeches and papers delivered, including:
4 lectures on cortical currents (in cats, etc.).
11 lectures on Gestalt psychology, 1955-1967, 1970.
Gifford lectures. Series of 18 unpub. lectures.
Hitchcock lectures. Series of 4 lectures.
"Immigration of European Scientists" and "Wie hat die Einwanderung von Professoren und Ideen aus Europa die amerikanische Psychologie beeinflußt?"
Langfeld lectures. Series of 4 lectures. Princeton, 1966. 2 c.
Talk at NSSR on Wertheimer.

C8   "The time error in judgments of visual lengths." Ms., presumably written by Köhler.
Figural After-Effects. Ms. for book by Köhler and Wallach. 167p. Also shorter lecture version, and two other Ms. versions, one entitled: "Figural after-effects in the third dimension of visual space."

D7,8   Ca. 1,630 reprints of 20 different articles by Köhler.

H3   Newspaper cl.

H4   Reviews of Köhler's works.

I   Distinguished Scientific Contribution Award of American Psychological Association.
Membership certificates:
American Philosophical Society; National Academy of Sciences; Society of Sigma Xi; Società Italiana di psychologia scientifica; British Psychological Society; Deutsche Gesellschaft für Psychologie; Psi Chi National Honorary Society in Psychology; Association for the Study of Animal Behavior; American Academy of Arts and Sciences.
Honorary degrees, etc.:
Kenyon College; Albert-Ludwig University; University

of Pennsylvania; Swarthmore College; Freie Universität, Berlin; Westfälische Wilhelms-Universität; University of Upsala.
Grant materials:
Ford Foundation. 1959-1960.
National Science Foundation, no. 1725. 1956-1958
no. G5522. 1958-1962.
no. G18635. 1963.
no. GB-2497. 1964-1967.

J Photographs.

K Ca. 425 volumes, many by emigrés.

L Slide, used in lecturing.

M Gavel used as president of American Psychological Asso-
ciation.
M.I.T. nameplate in plastic.
Medals:
Howard Crosby Warren Medal of Society for Experimen-
tal Psychology.
Centennial Medal of Academy of Natural Sciences of
the U.S. 1963.
Wilhelm Max Wundt medal.

N Reports by assistants. 1 B. Including notes by: Pauline
A. Adams, John Ceroso, H. Crawford, Peggy Harding,
J. Nachmias, G. Theodore Talbot.
Müller, Ilse. "Versuche über phänomenal optische Un-
durchdringlichkeit."
Materials by: Adolf Ackermann, W. Brezinka, Sir Julian
Huxley.

L. C. DUNN PAPERS

B1,2 Correspondence with L. C. Dunn. Some L. in files of
"Emergency Committee in Aid of Displaced German
Scholars."

New York Public Library, Manuscript Division, Fifth Avenue
and 42nd Street, New York, N.Y. 10018.

MAX WERTHEIMER PAPERS

B1   1 L. to Max Wertheimer. 1929.

B2   1 L. from Max Wertheimer. 1929.

State University of New York at Albany, Department of Germanic Languages and Literatures, 1400 Washington Avenue, Albany, New York 12222.

KARL O. PAETEL COLLECTION

B1   2 L. to Karl O. Paetel (xerox). 1954, 1956.

Archives of the History of American Psychology, University of Akron, Akron, Ohio 44325.

B1   Individual L. by Wolfgang Köhler may be found in the collections of the various recipients. Names of individuals were unavailable at the time of publication.

HANS KOHN

Historian, 1891-1971

<u>Leo Baeck Institute</u>, 129 East 73rd Street, New York, N.Y. 10021.

HANS KOHN COLLECTION (AR 259 and uncatalogued). Ca. 3-5 ft. of materials from the estate of Hans Kohn (closed until 1991).

HANS KOHN COLLECTION (AR 259 und nicht Katalogisiertes). Etwa 0,90 - 1,50 m Materialien aus dem Nachlaß von Hans Kohn (unzugänglich bis 1991).

A3   Biographical sketch. 1960.

B1,2   Correspondence with the Freie Universität Berlin.
       1967-1968. 7p.

C7   <u>Heinrich Heine: the Man and the Myth</u>. 1958. 24p.

D7   3 cl. of articles by Kohn. 1962-1963.
      "Rethinking Recent German History." 1951. 21p.

H3,4   Cl. about Kohn, reviews of his works, death notices.
       1961-1971.

J   Photo. 1959.

PAUL AMANN COLLECTION, ERICH KAHLER COLLECTION, GEORG LAN-
DAUER COLLECTION, JACOB PICARD COLLECTION

B1,2   Correspondence with Paul Amann.
       Correspondence with Erich Kahler.
       Correspondence with Georg Landauer.
       Correspondence with Jacob Picard.

<u>Mrs. Gertrude Urzidil</u>, 83-39 116th Street, Richmond Hill, New York 11418.

JOHANNES URZIDIL COLLECTION

B1   78 L. to Johannes Urzidil. A. 1942-1969.
      1 L. to Wayne Andrews. T.c. 1958.

B2   3 L. from Johannes Urzidil. T.c. 1957-1964.

HANS KOHN

1 L. from Otto Pick. A. 1913.

<u>Harvard University</u>, Houghton Library, Cambridge, Massachusetts 02138.

RICHARD BEER-HOFMANN COLLECTION

B1 22 L. to Richard Beer-Hofmann. 1929-1945.

B2 1 L. from Oskar Seidlin. Undated.

<u>American Philosophical Society</u>, The Library, 105 South Fifth Street, Philadelphia, Pennsylvania 19106.

SIMON FLEXNER PAPERS

B1,2 Correspondence with Simon Flexner.

<u>Yivo Institute</u>, 1048 Fifth Avenue, New York, N.Y. 10028.

HORACE M. KALLEN PAPERS

B1,2 Individual items in folders: 423, 428, 745.

<u>Mr. Hans Sahl</u>, 800 West End Avenue, New York, N.Y. 10025.

B1 Several L. to Hans Sahl.

<u>Swarthmore College</u>, Swarthmore, Pennsyvlania 19081.

SWARTHMORE COLLEGE PEACE COLLECTION: ANNA MELISSA GRAVES CORRESPONDENCE

B1 6 L. to Anna Melissa Graves. 1928-1939.

<u>University of Pennsylvania</u>, The Charles Patterson Van Pelt Library, Philadelphia, Pennsylvania 19104.

HANS KOHN

ALMA MAHLER-WERFEL COLLECTION

81   2 L. to Alma Mahler-Werfel. 1944.

New York Public Library, Manuscript Division, Fifth Avenue
and 42nd Street, New York, N.Y. 10018.

EMERGENCY COMMITTEE IN AID OF DISPLACED FOREIGN SCHOLARS,
1933-1945

*   File compiled, no assistance given. 1933-1944.

Library of Congress, Manuscript Division, Independence Avenue
and First Street S.E., Washington, D.C. 20540.

PAPERS OF SIEGFRIED BERNFELD

1,2   Correspondence with Siegfried Bernfeld. 1920-1921.

Mrs. Alice Loewy Kahler, 1 Evelyn Place, Princeton, New
Jersey 08540.

ERICH VON KAHLER COLLECTION

97   1 offprint.

FREDERICK KOHNER

Screen Writer, Novelist, 1905-

Mr. Frederick Kohner, 12046 Coyne Street, Los Angeles, California 90049.

B2 32 L., including L. from: Ossip Dymov, Alfred Polgar, Joseph Roth, Anna Seghers, Stefan Zweig.

C1 The Skier. T.
  Visitor from Prague [Amanda]. T.

C2 Woman of My Life. Unpub. drama, based on the book by Ludwig Bemelmann.

Yale University, Beinecke Rare Book and Manuscript Library, New Haven, Connecticut 06520.

EDMOND PAUKER COLLECTION

B1 17 L. and 3 Tel. to Edmond Pauker. A. and T. 1956-1957.

B2 12 L. and 2 Tel. from Edmond Pauker. 1956-1957.
  1 L. from Eve Pauker. 1957.

I Contracts between Pauker and Kohner:
  The Bees and the Flowers.
  Stalinallee.
  Financial statements, box office receipts, royalties for Stalinallee. 1 F.
  Agent's correspondence, literary rights, etc. for Stalinallee. 1 F.

Museum of Modern Art, The Library, 11 West 53rd Street, New York, N.Y. 10019.

HANS RICHTER ARCHIVE: Written permission to use the Archive is required in advance of visits to the Museum.

HANS RICHTER ARCHIVE: Das Archiv darf nur mit vorheriger schriftlicher Genehmigung benutzt werden.

C5 Hier gibts keine Katharina. Film Ms. 1935-1935. Ca. 133p.

FREDERICK KOHNER

<u>Keine Zeit für Tränen</u>. Film Ms. 1934-1935. cc. 104p.

<u>Academy of Motion Picture Arts and Sciences</u>, Margaret Herrick Library, 9038 Melrose Avenue, Hollywood, California 90069.

H4   Reviews of <u>Gidget</u>. Newspaper and magazine cl.

ANNETTE KOLB

Writer, 1870-1967

Yale University, Beinecke Rare Book and Manuscript Library,
New Haven, Connecticut 06520.

KURT WOLFF ARCHIVE, HERMANN BROCH ARCHIVE

B1   1 L. to Hermann Broch. 1945.

B1,2 Correspondence with the Kurt Wolff Verlag. 50 L. 1913-
       1923.

Harvard University, Houghton Library, Cambridge, Massachusetts 02138.

RICHARD BEER-HOFMANN COLLECTION

B1   2 L. to Richard Beer-Hofmann. 1942-1944.

Mrs. Elisabeth M. Stoerk and Mrs. Susanne B. Hoeller, 288
Ocean Drive West, Stamford, Connecticut 06902.

FRIDERIKE ZWEIG ARCHIVE

B1   2 L. to Friderike Zweig. 1946 and undated.

University of California, Los Angeles, Department of Special
Collections, 120 Lawrence Clark Powell Library, Los Angeles,
California 90024.

FRANZ WERFEL ARCHIVE

B1   1 L. to Franz Werfel. [1942].

Leo Baeck Institute, 129 East 73rd Street, New York, N.Y.
10021.

B1   1 Ptc. to Dr. Lutz Weltmann. Undated.

ANNETTE KOLB

<u>University of Pennsylvania</u>, The Charles Patterson Van Pelt
Library, Philadelphia, Pennsylvania 19104.

ALMA MAHLER-WERFEL COLLECTION

31   1 L. to Alma Mahler-Werfel.

<u>Columbia University</u>, Butler Library, New York, N.Y. 10027.

VARIAN FRY PAPERS

31   2 L. to Varian Fry. 1941.

ERICH WOLFGANG KORNGOLD

Composer, 1897-1957

<u>Mr. Ernst Werner Korngold</u>, 9928 Toluca Lake Avenue, and <u>Mr.</u>
George Korngold, 9936 Toluca Lake Avenue, North Hollywood,
California 91602.

Ernst Werner and George Korngold are the sons and legal
heirs of Erich Wolfgang Korngold. With the exception of a
small amount of memorabilia in the possession of Ernst Werner Korngold, the majority of the materials from the estate
of Erich Korngold are presently with George Korngold, 9936
Toluca Lake Avenue.

*Ernst Werner und George Korngold sind als Söhne die Erben
von Erich Wolfgang Korngold. Ernst Werner Korngold besitzt
einige wenige Erinnerungsstücke an seinen Vater. Der Rest
des Materials aus dem Nachlaß von Erich Korngold befindet
sich zur Zeit noch im Besitz von George Korngold, 9936
Toluca Lake Avenue.*

Materials in the possession of Ernst Werner Korngold:

B2   Several L. from Hal Wallis and Jack Warner.

M   Memorabilia including: 1 academy award, certificates
       of nominations by the Motion Picture Academy, other
       certificates of awards, and a bronze bust of Erich
       Korngold by Anna Mahler.

Materials in the possession of George Korngold:

B1,2   Several L. to and from Korngold.

B3   Box of miscellaneous old L. and catalogs.

C13   "Acceleration Waltz." Score.
       "At Your Service." Miscellaneous sketches and ditto
          conductor parts; original piano score; complete
          orchestral material.
       "Baby Serenade." Parts II, III and IV. Piano Ms. Also
          orchestra score.
       "Cello Concerto." Opus 37. Score; vellums; part piano
          conductor and part sketch.
       "Child prodigy." 41 c.
       "Dance in Old Style." Orchestra parts.

"Fairy Tale Pictures" and "Sinfonietta." Orchestra
scores, in 1 volume.

"1st String Quartet," "Piano Quintet," "Suite for
String Quartet and Piano (left hand)," and various
sketches. All in 1 volume.

"Four gay little waltzes for piano." Original Ms. and
c.

"Four Songs (Shakespeare)." Opus 31. Bound c.

"The Great Waltz." Sketches; Ms.; piano originals of
"Like a Star" and "Duet"; book version and program
(1953).

"Hell Waltz from Orpheus." Various original piano
scores and orchestra scores. Also original score
with English lyrics (Ms.).

"I'm in Love with Vienna." Original piano score.

"Magic Fire." Sketches and arrangements.

"Military March." Set of parts.

"Much Ado About Nothing." Some score, some piano parts;
horn pipe, complete set of parts; orchestra score.

"Night in Venice," "Come to the Gondola." Vocal parts.

"O Nene."

"Ode to Goose Liver." Ms.

"Passover Psalm." Opus 30. Set of orchestra parts,
chorus parts and master vellums; Ms. with German
lyrics; original piano conductor Ms.; bound c.

"Piano concerto in C sharp." Opus 17. Orchestra score.

"Prayer." Opus 32. Parts; vellum; bound c.

"Primavera Ballet." Piano conductors.

"Radetzky March." Parts.

"Rübezahl." Parts for trio, miscellaneous parts for
Sinfonietta.

"Schauspiel. Overture." Opus 4.

"Sinfonietta." Complete orchestra score.

"The Snowman." Pantomime. Orchestra score.

"Sonata #1," "Don Quixote," "Sonata #2," and "Fairy
Tale Pictures."

"Sonata #3." For piano.

"Songs of Farewell." Orchestra score.

"Songs of the Clown." Opus 29. Bound c.

"Star Spangled Banner." Conductor and parts; another
set of parts.

"Straussiana." Original Ms. score.

"Suite." Opus 23. Violin #1 part only.

"Sursum Corda." Opus 13. Orchestra score.
"Sweet Melody of Night." Original Ms. score.
"Symphonic Serenade for Strings." Opus 39. Original
    sketches; orchestra score; complete set of parts;
    facsimile; copyist Ms.; negatives.
"Symphony in F sharp." Original sketches; last sketch-
    es; 3 facsimile c.; complete facsimile score;
    orchestra score; piano score; complete orchestral
    material.
"Theme and Variations." Original Ms. score.
"Trio," "Violin sonata," "Sextet." In 1 volume.
"12 Songs. Opus 14," "Four Songs of Farewell," "Three
    Songs for Middle Voice. Opus 18," "Prayer for Tenor,
    Soprano and Alto Voices. Opus 22," "Songs of the
    Clown. Opus 29," "Four Songs (Shakespeare). Opus 31,"
    "Three Songs for Soprano. Opus 22," "Five Songs.
    Opus 38," and various sketches.
"The Vampire (incidental music for a play)," "Three
    Songs (Eichendorff)," Two Songs: "Summer" and "A
    Little Loveletter." Orchestra scores.
"4 kleine Karikaturen für Klavier." Opus 19.
"Violin Concerto." Piano score.
"Wichtelmaennchen." For piano and violin.
"Women, Clowns and Songs." Ms. for Shakespeare Rein-
    hardt evening; "Dance in Old Style." Orchestra score.
    Also untitled number dedicated to Archduchess Maria.
"You Haunt My Heart." Original Ms. in English.
Several Offenbach arrangements.
Arrangements of Johann Strauss: "Russian Marches," and
    "Egyptian March."
Childhood compositions, sketches, homework. 1 F.
Fugues, choruses, etc. done as a child as homework.
Miscellaneous song Ms.
Sketches of 2 waltzes.
Some miscellaneous parts.
Opera scores:
    The Dead City. Orchestra score. 3 acts in 3 volumes.
        Also piano score.
    Helen Goes to Troy. Various original piano scores and
        orchestra scores. Original Ms. to: "Love at Last"
        and "What Will the Future Say?"
    Kathrin. English synopsis; libretto and synopsis;
        orchestra scores (Act I Scene 4, Act II Scenes 1-4);

set of string parts.

The Miracle of Heliane. Sketches and Ms.; orchestra score; piano score.

The Ring of Polykrates. Orchestra score.

Rosalinda. Sketches; set of parts; miscellaneous original scores; various parts; finale negative; script for television show.

Silent Serenade. German books and lyrics, piano score; orchestra score, German lyrics and some dialogue by Korngold; English lyrics; German libretto for Radio Vienna; complete set of parts; English book, Act II; pub. piano vocal score.

Violanta. Text book; orchestra score; piano score.

Film scores:

Adventures of Robin Hood. Original Ms.; miscellaneous piano conductors.

Anthony Adverse. Original Ms.

Another Dawn. Complete piano conductor.

Between Two Worlds. Piano conductor.

Captain Blood. Original Ms.

The Constant Nymph. Sketches; original Ms.; vellums and piano conductor for "Tomorrow"; complete piano conductor with original pencil notations.

Deception. Complete piano conductor; complete set of original scores.

Devotion. Original Ms.; 2 complete piano conductors.

Elizabeth and Essex. Incomplete and complete piano conductors.

Escape Me Never. Original Ms.; vellums for main theme; incomplete and complete piano conductors.

Give Us This Night. Original Ms.

Juarez. Original Ms.; complete piano conductor.

Kings Row. Sketches; original Ms.; miscellaneous c.; complete piano conductor.

Midsummer Night's Dream. Original Ms.

Of Human Bondage. Original Ms.; sketches and some piano conductors.

Sea Hawk. Sketches; "Ball Game"; miscellaneous c.; 2 complete piano conductors.

The Sea Wolf. Sketches; original Ms.; complete piano conductor.

Various sketches for pictures.

D13   Ca. 130 scores (including some duplicates) of Korngold's works.

H3,4   Wooden chest containing newspaper reviews and articles.

H4   Rosalinda. New York reviews. 1 F.

H4,
O   Miracle of Heliane. Reviews and programs. 1 F.

I   Bills, statements, income tax returns.
Box of old statements, etc.

J   Several old X-rays (Korngold).

J,
M   2 old briefcases containing old papers and pictures.

K   Ca. 350 scores (piano and orchestral), including: Bach, Bártok, Beethoven, Berlioz, Bittner, Bizet, Brahms, Chopin, Debussy, Dvořák, Gershwin, Gounod, Haydn, Hindemith, Křenek, Mahler, Mendelssohn, Mozart, Puccini, Rachmaninoff, Ravel, Rimsky-Korsakov, Rossini, Schnabel, Schoenberg, Schubert, Schumann, Shostakovich, Smetana, J. Strauss, R. Strauss, Stravinsky, Toch, Toscanini, Tschaikowsky, Verdi, Wagner, Weber, Zeisl.

L   Russian War Relief Program and reviews.

M   Guest book for Hoeselberg; folders and envelopes for memorial concert.
1 academy award.

N   Julius Korngold memoirs.

*   Miscellaneous microfilms.

Leo Baeck Institute, 129 East 73rd Street, New York, N.Y. 10021.

Several of the Erich Korngold items were deposited at the Institute by Wolfgang Brandes (Braunschweig), while others were purchased from various other sources (1958, 1966).

Mehrere Erich Korngold Nummern im Leo Baeck Institute wurden dem Institut von Wolfgang Brandes (Braunschweig) überlassen;

einige weitere Nummern kamen von anderen Besitzern (1958, 1966).

B1   1 L. to "Hochverehrter Herr Baron." A. 1917.

B3   6 L. by Julius Korngold concerning his son. 1910-1919.

C13   "Die tote Stadt." 4 measures. Musical scrapbook p. A. 1922. 4 measures. Musical scrapbook p. with accompanying text "Glück, das mir verblieb..." A. 1923. Another copy. A. 1924.
"Violanta." Beginning of prologue to the one-acter. Music Ms. with dedication to Prinz Friedrich Leopold von Preussen. 1915. A. 2p.
"Das Wunder der Heliane." 5 measures from the opera. Musical scrapbook p. with dedication. A. 1928.

J   Photo, with dedication to Eduard Elias. Ptc. A. Undated.

M   Original plaster bust of E. W. Korngold by Anna Mahler. E. W. Korngold death mask and plaster cast of hands at death.

O   Fledermaus. Program. Theater am Nollendorfplatz, 1929.

Burbank Public Library, 110 North Glenoaks Boulevard, Burbank, California 91502.

Warner Brothers Studio (Burbank, California) turned their archives over to Burbank Public Library after microfilming the orchestra scores for themselves.

Das Warner Brothers Studio (Burbank, California) hat sein Archiv der Burbank Public Library überlassen, nachdem es die Orchesterpartituren zum eigenen Gebrauch auf Mikrofilm aufgenommen hatte.

C13   Orchestra scores and parts to all of Korngold's films with Warner Brothers (6-8 films). Substantial amount of material.

State University of New York at Binghamton, Center for

Modern Theater Research, Binghamton, New York 13901.

MAX REINHARDT ARCHIVE

B1   1 L. to Lili Darvas. [1933].
       1 Tel. to Max Reinhardt. Undated.

B2   1 L. from Lili Darvas. Undated.

B3   2 L. from Max Reinhardt.

H3   3 cl.

J   La Belle Helene. Photo of production.

Mr. Jack Warner, Hollywood, California.

C13   Some original Ms. of motion picture scores.

Mr. Hal Wallis, Hollywood, California.

C13   Some original Ms. of motion picture scores.

Dr. Otto Neurath, 130 North Lacienda Boulevard, Los Angeles, California 90048.

C13   Original piano score Ms. of cello concerto, op. 37.

Library of Congress, Reference Department, Music Division, Independence Avenue and First Street S.E., Washington, D.C. 20540.

C13   "Another dawn, lyric by Al Dubin, music by E. W. Korngold." 4p. reproduction of Ms. Music Publisher's Holding Corp., c. 1937.

Mr. Lionel Newman, Twentieth Century-Fox Film Corporation, Music Department, 10201 West Pico Boulevard, P.O. Box 900, Los Angeles, California 90213.

ERICH WOLFGANG KORNGOLD

C13   Anthony Adverse. Partial Ms. of motion picture score
      (Reel 1).

University of Pennsylvania, The Charles Patterson Van Pelt
Library, Philadelphia, Pennsylvania 19104.

ALMA MAHLER-WERFEL COLLECTION

B1   1 L. to Igor Stravinsky. cc.
      3 L. and 2 Ptc. to Alma Mahler-Werfel.
H3   1 cl.

University of Southern California, Lion Feuchtwanger Memorial
Library, 520 Paseo Miramar, Pacific Palisades, California
90272.

B1   1 L. to Lion Feuchtwanger. Undated.

B2   1 L. from Lion Feuchtwanger. Undated.

University of California, Los Angeles, Music Library, 405
Hilgard Avenue, Los Angeles, California 90024.

ERNST TOCH ARCHIVE

B1   3 L. to Ernst Toch.

University of Georgia, The University Libraries, Athens,
Georgia 30601.

GUIDO ADLER PAPERS

B1   2 L.

Syracuse University, The George Arents Research Library,
Syracuse, New York 13210.

FRANZ WAXMAN PAPERS

B1   1 L. to Franz Waxman. 1951.

Academy of Motion Picture Arts and Sciences, Margaret Herrick
Library, 9038 Melrose Avenue, Hollywood, California 90069.

H3   Obituaries. Several cl.

J   Photo.

Metropolitan Opera Association, Inc., The Archives, Lincoln
Center Plaza, New York, N.Y. 10023.

H3   2 newspaper cl. 1957, 1960.

University of California at Riverside, Riverside, California
92302.

RAOUL AUERNHEIMER ARCHIVE

B2   3 L. from Raoul Auernheimer.

E   Stumme Serenade. Rough drafts of adaptation of Korn-
      gold's Singspiel by Raoul Auernheimer. T. 109p. Act
      II, Scene 3. A. 19p. Act III, Scene 6. T. English.
      20p.

JULIUS KORNGOLD

Music Critic, 1861-1945

Mr. George Korngold, 9936 Toluca Lake Boulevard, Los Angeles, California 91603; and Mr. Ernst Werner Korngold, 9928 Toluca Lake Boulevard, Los Angeles, California 91603.

Questions concerning the accessibility of the Julius Korngold materials should be directed to Mr. George Korngold. An inventory of the materials is available.

Fragen in Bezug auf den Zugang zu den Julius-Korngold-Materialien sollten an Herr George Korngold gerichtet werden. Ein Verzeichnis der Materialien ist erhältlich.

A1   Memoirs. Unpub.

B1,2 Correspondence from the American years.

C2   Play manuscripts.

C7   Printed but unpub. text of Korngold's last book.

H4   Reviews from American newspapers.

I   Documents: book contracts, etc.

Leo Baeck Institute, 129 East 73rd Street, New York, N.Y. 10021.

ERICH KORNGOLD COLLECTION

B1   25 L. from Julius Korngold to Max Kalbeck. [1902-1920].

University of Georgia, The University Libraries, Athens, Georgia 30601.

GUIDO ADLER PAPERS

B1,2 20 L.

University of Pennsylvania, The Charles Patterson Van Pelt Library, Philadelphia, Pennsylvania 19106.

JULIUS KORNGOLD

ALMA MAHLER-WERFEL COLLECTION

B1   1 L. to Alma Mahler-Werfel. Undated.

HENRY KOSTER

Producer, 1905-

Mr. Henry Koster, 1216 N. Lachman Lane, Pacific Palisades,
California 90272.

Private personal collection. Mr. Koster plans to eventually
donate his collection to the Archives of the Directors' Guild
in Los Angeles, California.

*Privatsammlung. Henry Koster hat vor, seine Sammlung den
Archives of the Director's Guild in Los Angeles, California,
zu vermachen.*

B1,2   Ca. 1 ft. (.3 m) of correspondence. A major portion of
       Koster's correspondence was lost in a flood in 1947.

C5   Ca. 30 shooting scripts (of the 50 films produced in
       the U.S.).

F   Prints of ca. 12 of Koster's early films (not including
       Die letzte Kompagnie).

H3   Collection of cl. (scrapbooks) from the 1920s - present.
       Ca. 3 ft. (1 m).

J   1 photo album containing childhood pictures as well as
       from later years.
       Collection of photos of actors and actresses with whom
       Koster worked.

K   Personal library:
       Ca. 200 books concerning the film.
       Several hundred misc. books.
       Small collection of magazines (including Life).

L   Casting directories.
       Harrison reports.

N   Ms. by others, including L. Marcuse (Plato) and Curt
       Goetz. Ca. 2 ft. (.7 m).

Academy of Motion Picture Arts and Sciences, Margaret Herrick
Library, 9038 Melrose Avenue, Hollywood, California 90069.

H3   Newspaper cl., obituaries, biographical statements. 1 F.

ERNST KŘENEK

Composer, Musicologist, 1900-

Dr. Ernst Křenek, 623 Chino Canyon Drive, Palm Springs,
California 92262.

The papers that Dr. Křenek accumulated in Europe before his
emigration in 1938 are now located in the City Library of
Vienna. All of Křenek's American (post-1938) papers are
still in Dr. Křenek's possession, although arrangements have
already been made for an Ernst Křenek Archive at the University of California, San Diego. The following is a description of the materials eventually to be deposited at the
University Archives.

*Die Schriftstücke, die Dr. Křenek vor seiner Emigration im
Jahre 1938 zusammengetragen hatte, sind in der Stadtbiblio-
thek von Wien aufbewahrt. Alles Material aus der Zeit nach
1938 befindet sich noch in Dr. Křeneks Besitz. Es sind jedoch schon Vorkehrungen für ein Ernst Křenek Archiv an der
University of California, San Diego, getroffen. Das Folgende
ist eine Beschreibung der Materialien, die später an die
Universitätsarchive gehen werden.*

A1   Diary/journal covering the years 1937 through mid-1942.

A3   C. of Křenek's autobiography to 1950. Original at
       Library of Congress. (Both copies restricted until
       15 years after the death of Dr. Křenek. / *Das Manu-
       skript darf erst 15 Jahre nach dem Tode von Křenek
       freigegeben werden.*)

B1,2   Correspondence over many years, mostly L. to Křenek.

C7   Ms. of a book.

C12   Film scripts, from Křenek's director/producer days.

C13   Music Ms.

C14   Sketches of stage layouts, scenes from operas.
       Paintings by Křenek.

J   Photos of performances, individuals.
       Photos of Křenek (in his home, etc.).

M   Memorabilia.

O   Programs, in 37 folders (by year).

ERNST KŘENEK

<u>Library of Congress</u>, Reference Department, Music Division, Independence Avenue and First Street S.E., Washington, D.C. 20540.

A3 Original Ms. of Křenek's autobiography to 1950. (Restricted until 15 years after Křenek's death. / *Das Manuskript darf erst 15 Jahre nach dem Tode von Křenek freigegeben werden.*)

C13 "Fivefold enfoldment." Op. 205. 1969. A. 24 leaves.
"George Washington Variations." 1950. A. 12 leaves.
"Die Jahreszeiten; vier kleine a-cappella Chöre nach Gedichten von Hölderlin." 1925. A. 7 leaves.
"Lamentatio Jeremiae Prophetae; Sekundum Breviarium Sacrosanctae Ecclesiae Romanae." Op. 93. 1941-1942. A. 39 leaves.
"Sieben leichte Stücke für Streichorchester." 1955. A. 8 leaves.
"Twenty miniatures." 1953-1954. A. 20 leaves.
"Missa, Duodecim tonorum." 1957. A. 26 leaves.
"Sechs Motetten nach Worten von Franz Kafka, für gemischten Chor a cappella." 1959. A. 33 leaves.
"Pallas Athene weint." 1955. A. 279 leaves.
"Eight piano pieces." 1946. A. 9 leaves.
"Five prayers for women's voices over the Pater Noster as cantus firmus, from the Litanie by John Donne: XV., XVI., XX., XXIII., XXVII." 1944. A. 7 leaves.
"Proprium Missae in Domenica tertia in Quadragesima." 1955. A. 7 leaves.
"Proprium Missae in festo SS. Innocentium, die XXVIII Decembris." Op. 89. 1940. A. 8 leaves.
"Seventh string quartet." Op. 96. A. 1944. 26 leaves.
"Two sacred songs. Zwei geistige Gesänge." 1952. A. 18 leaves.
"Sinfonietta (A Brasileira, The Brazilian) for string orchestra." 1952. A. 14 leaves.
"Sonata for harp." 1955. A. 7 leaves.
"Sonata." Op. 92. [1941]. A. with editor's additions. 7p.
"Third sonata." Op. 92, no. 4. 1942-1943. A. 14 leaves.
"Sonata no. 4." 1948. A. 17 leaves.
"Sonata for viola solo." Op. 92, no. 3. 1942. A. 3 leaves.

"Sonata for viola and piano." 1948. A. 12 leaves.
"Sonata for violin and piano." 1944-1945. A. 16 leaves.
"Sonatina." Op. 92, no. 26. 1942. A. 4 leaves.
"Suite for clarinet B ♭ and string orchestra." 1955. A.
   10 leaves.
"Suite for clarinet B ♭ and piano." 1955. A. 9 leaves.
"Suite for flute and string orchestra." 1954. A. 8
   leaves.
"Tarquin: drama with music, words by Emmet Lavery,
   music by E. Křenek." A. pc. 126p.
"Trio for violin, clarinet and piano." 1946. A. 13
   leaves.
"String trio." 1948-1949. A. 13 leaves.
"Twelve variations in three movements. 2d. rev. ver-
   sion (1940)." 1937-1940. A. 15 leaves.
"Veni Sanctificator." 1954. A. 2 leaves.

Prof. Russell G. Harris, Department of Music, Hamline University, St. Paul, Minnesota 55101.

B1   Ca. 80 L. to Russell G. Harris. 1940-1970.

Prof. John L. Stewart, Provost, John Muir College, University
of California, San Diego, La Jolla, California 92037.

Copies of the tapes in Prof. Stewart's possession have been
made (for preservation purposes only) and are deposited in
the University of California, San Diego, Křenek archives.
The tapes have not been made available for use by scholars
and researchers.

*Lediglich um die Erhaltung sicherzustellen, sind von den-
jenigen Tonbändern, die sich in Prof. Stewarts Besitz befinden, Kopien angefertigt und in den Křenek-Archiven der University of California, San Diego, aufbewahrt worden. Die
Tonbänder sind noch nicht für Forschungszwecke zugänglich.*

F   Tape recordings of ca. 40 hours of conversation be-
     tween Křenek and John Stewart concerning Křenek's
     career as a composer, the evolution of his ideas,
     his miscellaneous writings, and his musical works. /

ERNST KŘENEK

*Tonbandaufnahmen (etwa 40 Stunden insgesamt) einer
Unterhaltung zwischen John Stewart und Ernst Křenek
über Themen wie Křeneks Laufbahn als Komponist, seine
Entwicklung von Konzepten, seine verschiedenen
Schriften und musikalischen Werke.*

Mr. <u>Robert Holliday</u>, 390 Herschel Street, St. Paul, Minnesota 55104.

B1   Holliday, Robert. Ca. 20 L. 1942-1947.

F   "The Seasons." Ernst Křenek and the St. Paul Chamber
      Choir. Tape of live concert performance. Carlton
      College, Northfield, Minnesota, 1975.
      "Zur Erntezeit." Ernst Křenek and the St. Paul Chamber
      Choir.

Dr. <u>Edward E. Lowinsky</u>, Prof. Emeritus, Department of Music,
University of Chicago, Chicago, Illinois 60637.

B1   10 L. to Edward E. Lowinsky. 1947-1964.

B2   8 L. from Edward E. Lowinsky. 1947-1964.

<u>Bruno Walter Memorial Foundation</u>, c/o Miss Susie Danziger,
115 East 72nd Street, New York, N.Y. 10021.

B1,2 Correspondence with Bruno Walter.

<u>Roosevelt University</u>, The Library, 430 South Michigan Avenue,
Chicago, Illinois 60605.

C13   "Piano piece in eleven parts. Written for the 100th
      anniversary of, and dedicated to, Chicago Musical
      College." A. pc. 1967.

<u>University of Pennsylvania</u>, The Charles Patterson Van Pelt
Library, Philadelphia, Pennsylvania 19104.

ERNST KŘENEK

ALMA MAHLER-WERFEL COLLECTION

B1   9 L., 2 short L. and 2 Ptc. to Alma Mahler-Werfel.

B2   2 L. from Gustave Beer. T.cc. 1957.

New York Public Library, Manuscript Division, Fifth Avenue and 42nd Street, New York, N.Y. 10018.

EMERGENCY COMMITTEE IN AID OF DISPLACED FOREIGN SCHOLARS, 1933-1945

*   File compiled, no assistance given. 1938-1942.

New School for Social Research, Office of the Dean of the Graduate Faculty of Political and Social Science, 65 Fifth Avenue, New York, N.Y. 10003.

RECORDS OF THE UNIVERSITY IN EXILE, 1933-45

B1,2   3 L. 1938.

State of North Carolina, Department of Cultural Resources, Raleigh, North Carolina 27611.

BLACK MOUNTAIN COLLEGE ARCHIVES

I   [Faculty] file: "Ernst Křenek."
       [General] file: "Ernst Křenek."

Indiana University, The University Libraries, Music Library, Bloomington, Indiana 47401.

B1   1 L. to Dominique-René de Lerma.

University of California, Los Angeles, Music Library, 405 Hilgard Avenue, Los Angeles, California 90024.

ERNST TOCH ARCHIVE

B1   1 L. to Ernst Toch.

<u>University of Georgia</u>, The University Libraries, Athens, Georgia 30601.

OLIN DOWNES PAPERS

B1   1 L.

ERNST KRIS

Psychoanalyst, 1900-1957

Dr. Marianne Kris, 239 Central Park West, New York, N.Y.
10028.

Private collection from the estate of Ernst Kris.

Privatsammlung aus dem Nachlaß von Ernst Kris.

B1,2   Correspondence concerning psychoanalysis and art his-
       tory. Over 500 L. Ca. 1925-1957.

C7   Several Ms. of Kris' publications.

F   1 tape of Ernst Kris.

H4   Cl. of reviews.

I   Documents.

J   Photos. 1940s-1957.

K   Very large and comprehensive library (philosophy, art
       history, etc.).

Library of Congress, Manuscript Division, Independence Avenue
and First Street S.E., Washington, D.C. 20540.

PAPERS OF SIEGFRIED BERNFELD

B1,2   Correspondence between Ernst Kris and Siegfried Bern-
       feld.

C7   Research notes concerning Sigmund Freud.

Yivo Institute, 1048 Fifth Avenue, New York, N.Y. 10028.

HORACE M. KALLEN PAPERS

*   Materials in folders: 46, 560, 749, 894, 963. 1941-
       1950.

Columbia University, Butler Library, New York, N.Y. 10027.

ERNST KRIS

ORAL HISTORY COLLECTION

H5   Recollections about Ernst Kris, in interviews with
       Heinz Hartmann and Rudolph Maurice Loewenstein.

ALVIN KRONACHER

Writer, Theater Director, 1883-1951

State University of New York at Albany, Department of Germanic Languages and Literatures, 1400 Washington Avenue, Albany, New York 12222.

STORM PUBLISHERS ARCHIVE

B1   6 L. to Alexander Gode von Aesch. 1946-1950.

B2   6 L. from Alexander Gode von Aesch. 1946-1949.

B3   3 L. from Esther Kronacher to Alexander Gode von Aesch. 1951.
      Publisher's correspondence re: Kronacher's Fritz von Unruh book. Ca. 175 items.

C11   Fritz von Unruh. T. with some h. corr. 37p.

H4   Fritz von Unruh. 27 reviews (some duplicates).

Immigration History Research Center of the University of Minnesota, 826 Berry Street, St. Paul, Minnesota 55101.

AMERICAN COUNCIL FOR EMIGRÉS IN THE PROFESSIONS ARCHIVES

A3   Biographical statements, questionnaires, etc. 12p.

H3   Obituary.

University of Pennsylvania, The Charles Patterson Van Pelt Library, Philadelphia, Pennsylvania 19104.

ALMA MAHLER-WERFEL COLLECTION

B1   2 L. to Alma Mahler-Werfel.

New York Public Library, Manuscript Division, Fifth Avenue and 42nd Street, New York, N.Y. 10018.

EMERGENCY COMMITTEE IN AID OF DISPLACED FOREIGN SCHOLARS, 1933-1945

*   File compiled, no assistance given. 1941-1944.

STEPHAN KUTTNER

Historian of Canon Law, 1907-

Dr. Stephan Kuttner, Institute of Medieval Canon Law, Boalt Hall 450E, University of California, School of Law, Berkeley, California 94720.

Dr. Kuttner intends his private collection to eventually go to the Institute of Medieval Canon Law. Until that time, the materials will remain closed to the public.

Dr. Kuttner hat vor, seine Privatsammlung später einmal dem Institute of Medieval Canon Law zukommen zu lassen. Bis dahin ist das Material für die Öffentlichkeit unzugänglich.

B1,2   Correspondence from the years in Germany, Italy and the U.S. Ca. 1,500 L. Complete files of professional correspondence since 1930s.

C7   Incomplete collection of Ms. of articles and books. 1930s - present.

D7   Complete collection of offprints and cl. of Kuttner's writings.

I   Documents, including awards and honors received, degrees.

J   Numerous photos.

K   Dr. Kuttner has already donated a portion of his personal library to the Institute of Medieval Canon Law. The remainder of his personal library is still in his possession.

L   Card catalog and files concerning his legal studies. Press notices of the Institute. Offprints and cl. of works by others.

N   Several Ms. by other authors.

STEPHAN LACKNER

Writer, 1910-

Mr. Stephan Lackner, 601 El Bosque Road, Santa Barbara, California 93105.

Private collection. / *Privatsammlung.*

A1   Diaries and notes from early years.

B1,2   Lengthy correspondence with Max Beckmann.

C2   Junger Mann ohne Stammbaum. 1935. First version of Jan
        Heimatlos.
        Der Mensch ist kein Haustier. 1934. First version. A.
        Der Menschenfreund. Eine philosophische Komödie. [Etwa
        1940-1941]. T. 124p.
        Der Pfeifer von Hameln. Opera in one act. Text and
        music by Stephan Lackner. [1958]. A. 259p.
        Der Techniker und die Wasserfee. [1935-1967]. Lengthy,
        partially h. Ms.

C3   Unpub. poems. 1 F.

C4   "Der Sträfling von San Ysidro." Story. [1958]. A. 81p.

C7   "Thomas Mann äußert sich zu dieser Zeit." 1935. Unpub.
        statement (according to Thomas Mann's wishes) of a
        conversation between Lackner and Mann in Aug. 1935.
        The statement was written for Das Neue Tage-Buch.
        "Verdorbene Literatur." 1935. T. pc.

C8   "Edouard Manet und das Raumproblem." 1932. Unpub.
        seminar paper. T. 85p.

CARL LANDAUER

Economist, 1891-

Prof. Carl Landauer, 1317 Arch Street, Berkeley, California
94708.

Prof. Landauer has stipulated in his will that his personal
collection shall go to the Hoover Institution on War, Revolution and Peace, Stanford, California. Until that time,
the materials will remain closed to the public.

*Prof. Landauer hat in seinem Testament verfügt, daß seine
Privatsammlung an die Hoover Institution on War, Revolution
and Peace, Stanford, California, gehen soll. Bis zu diesem
Zeitpunkt sind die Materialien für die Öffentlichkeit unzugänglich.*

B1,2   Large volume of correspondence, dating in part back to
       the 1930s, with a large portion of the correspondence
       from the post-1945 period. Over 10 ft. Includes L.
       to and from: Eduard Heimann, Hans Reichenbach, Wil-
       liam Sollmann, Friedrich Stampfer, Hans Staudinger,
       Hans Vogel.

C7   Ms. of unpub. articles. (Prof. Landauer has discarded
       all Ms. of his books and other pub. works.)

D7   Offprints and cl. of his articles, nearly complete for
       the last 10-20 years. Less complete in the case of
       his reviews.

H3   Small no. of cl.

I   Documents.

J   Photos, individual and family.

K   Small personal library, mainly from recent years (many
       review copies).

L   Offprints and cl. of articles by others.
       Files of materials dealing with social movements. In-
       cludes documents and L.
       Lecture and seminar materials, including dittos, etc.

Leo Baeck Institute, 129 East 73rd Street, New York, N.Y.
10021; and The Research Foundation for Jewish Immigration,

515

CARL LANDAUER

570 Fifth Avenue, New York, N.Y. 10018.

The CARL LANDAUER COLLECTION at the Leo Baeck Institute, ca. 2.5 inches of materials, pertains to Landauer's association and communication with organizations dealing with Jewish refugees of the 1930s and 1940s. A duplicate set of materials is held by the Research Foundation for Jewish Immigration. Both sets are photocopies; the originals were returned to Dr. Landauer. Publication rights remain with Dr. Landauer and will pass to the Hoover Institution after his death.

Die CARL LANDAUER COLLECTION im Leo Baeck Institute, etwa 6 cm Materialien, beziehen sich auf Landauers Verbindungen zu und seinen Briefwechsel mit Organisationen, die sich in den 30er und 40er Jahren um jüdische Flüchtlinge kümmerten. Dieselben Materialien befinden sich auch im Besitz der Research Foundation for Jewish Immigration. In beiden Fällen handelt es sich um Kopien; die Originale gingen an Dr. Landauer zurück. Die Publikationsrechte ruhen bei Dr. Landauer und werden bei seinem Tode an die Hoover Institution übergehen.

Miscellaneous materials in other collections at the Leo Baeck Institute include:

D8   5 essays. Offprints. 1944-1955. 69p.

J   1 photo in photo album.

Harvard University, Harvard Divinity School, Andover-Harvard Theological Library, 45 Francis Avenue, Cambridge, Massachusetts 02138.

PAUL TILLICH CÒLLECTION

B1   1 L. to David Riesman. 1962.

State University of New York at Albany, Department of Germanic Languages and Literatures, 1400 Washington Avenue, Albany, New York 12222.

CARL LANDAUER

KARL O. PAETEL COLLECTION

Bl 2 L. to Karl O. Paetel. 1956. (xerox)

B2 1 L. from Karl O. Paetel. 1956. (xerox)

American Philosophical Society, The Library, 105 South Fifth
Street, Philadelphia, Pennsylvania 19106.

L. C. DUNN PAPERS: "American Committee for D. G. S."

I Detailed report of phone conversation on Landauer's
   appointment in California.

Yivo Institute, 1048 Fifth Avenue, New York, N.Y. 10028.

HORACE M. KALLEN PAPERS

Bl,2 Individual item(s) in folder no. 40. 1942.

New York Public Library, Manuscript Division, Fifth Avenue
and 42nd Street, New York, N.Y. 10018.

EMERGENCY COMMITTEE IN AID OF DISPLACED FOREIGN SCHOLARS,
1933-1945

* File compiled when assistance was granted. 1934-1942.

Mrs. Gertrude Lederer, 372 Central Park West, Apt. 3B, New
York, N.Y. 10024.

C7 Ms. by Landauer sent to Lederer on his 50th birthday.

FRITZ H. LANDSHOFF

Publisher, 1901-

Mr. Fritz H. Landshoff, c/o Harry N. Abrams, Inc., Publishers, 110 East 59th Street, New York, N.Y. 10022.

The Project was unable to get a complete listing of Mr. Landshoff's materials; however, they do include: correspondence from the American period (more than 25 years of professional correspondence with Abrams), among which correspondents such as Erika Mann, Hermann Kesten, Otto Kallir and other notable emigrés can be found. Mr. Landshoff's materials are not available to researchers and no plans for them are known as of 1977.

Es war nicht möglich, ein vollständiges Verzeichnis der Landshoff-Materialien zu erhalten; ein Teil davon ist jedoch sein Briefwechsel aus der amerikanischen Periode (über 25 Jahre berufliche Korrespondenz mit Abrams), worunter sich Briefe von und an Erika Mann, Hermann Kesten, Otto Kallir usw. befinden. Herr Landshoffs Materialien sind für Forschungszwecke nicht zugänglich, es sind auch keine derartigen Pläne für die Zukunft im Moment bekannt.

American Philosophical Society, The Library, 105 South Fifth Street, Philadelphia, Pennsylvania 19106.

FRANZ BOAS PAPERS

B1   1 L. to Franz Boas. 1939.

LEO LANIA (HERMAN LAZAR)

Writer, 1896-1961

Southern Illinois University, Morris Library, Department of
Special Collections, Carbondale, Illinois 62901.

ERWIN PISCATOR PAPERS

B1   19 L. to Erwin Piscator. A. and T. 1936-1947.

B2   16 L. from Erwin Piscator. cc. 1937-1947.

C2   "Scorro." Project. A. 2p.

C7   "Amerikanisches Zeit-Theater. Erwin Piscator insze-
      niert die Tragödie eines amerikanischen Diktators."
      Ca. Jan. 1948. T. with corr. 6p.
      "Das Ideentheater." June 1941. T. with commentary by
      Erwin Piscator and Lania. 6p.

C9   Hašek, Jaroslav. Schwejk. Notes to the drama by Hašek.
      A. and T. Ca. March/June 1937. 9p., 13p., 21p.
      Tolstoy, Leo N. War and Peace. Adaptation by J. W.
      Bienstock and Charles Martel. Ca. Aug. 1936 - Nov.
      1937. T. with commentary by Erwin Piscator and Leo
      Lania.
      Another version by Erwin Piscator and Alfred Neumann.
      First version. Ca. March - Aug. 1938. T. with commen-
      tary by Piscator, Neumann and Lania.

University of Southern California, Lion Feuchtwanger Memorial
Library, 520 Paseo Miramar, Pacific Palisades, California
90272.

B1   4 L. to Lion Feuchtwanger. 1941, 1952.

B2   5 L. from Lion Feuchtwanger. 1941, 1952-1956.

Leo Baeck Institute, 129 East 73rd Street, New York, N.Y.
10021.

KURT KERSTEN COLLECTION

B1   5 L. and 2 Ptc. to Kurt Kersten. 1947-1961.

519

LEO LANIA (HERMAN LAZAR)

Syracuse University, The George Arents Research Library,
Syracuse, New York 13210.

DOROTHY THOMPSON PAPERS

C7   "Why Hitler Lost the War." Original T.

State University of New York at Albany, Department of Germanic Languages and Literatures, 1400 Washington Ave.,
Albany, New York 12222.

KARL O. PAETEL COLLECTION

B1   1 L. to Karl O. Paetel (xerox). 1942.

University of Pennsylvania, The Charles Patterson Van Pelt
Library, Philadelphia, Pennsylvania 19104.

ALMA MAHLER-WERFEL COLLECTION

B1   3 L. to Alma Mahler-Werfel. 1941.

PAUL LAZARSFELD
Sociologist, 1901-1976

<u>Mrs. Paul Lazarsfeld</u>, 50 West 90th Street, New York, N.Y. 10025.

The survey of Dr. Lazarsfeld's papers is incomplete due to Dr. Lazarsfeld's death in 1976. The materials will be donated to Columbia University where they will become available for research.

Wegen des Todes von Dr. Lazarsfeld im Jahre 1976 mußte ein vollständiger Überblick über seine Materialien unvollständig bleiben. Die Materialien werden der Columbia University geschenkt und damit für Forschungszwecke zugänglich gemacht werden.

B1,2   Correspondence 1933-1935 (Rockefeller fellowship years), including correspondence with: Theodor W. Adorno, Charlotte Bühler. Some c. of Lazarsfeld's own L.
Miscellaneous correspondence, e.g., UNESCO.

D7   Complete collection of offprints.

J   Photos.

K   Personal library.

L   Classroom teaching materials.

<u>Columbia University</u>, Butler Library, New York, N.Y. 10027.

The PAUL FELIX LAZARSFELD PAPERS, which consist of some 8,100 items (90 archive boxes), were donated by Prof. Lazarsfeld in 1969.

Die PAUL FELIX LAZARSFELD PAPERS, die gut 8100 Nummern umfassen (90 Archivkartons), sind eine Schenkung von Prof. Lazarsfeld aus dem Jahre 1969.

L   Test questionnaires, analyses, notes, charts, respondent sheets, sorted and unsorted questionnaires. All materials related to preparation of the book <u>The Academic Mind</u>. Ca. 90% of the materials consist

of questionnaires that Lazarsfeld sent to academi-
cians.

ORAL HISTORY COLLECTION

H5   Recollections of Paul Lazarsfeld from an interview
      with Frank Stanton. 1968.

Boston University, Mugar Memorial Library, 771 Commonwealth
Avenue, Boston, Massachusetts 02215.

EUGENE BURDICK PAPERS, WILLIAM BENNETT LEWIS PAPERS

B1   6 L. to Eugene Burdick. T. 1957-1958.
      1 L. to William Bennett Lewis. T. 1946.
B2   1 L. from Eugene Burdick. T.cc. Undated.

Harvard University, Houghton Library, Cambridge, Massachusetts 02138.

LEO LOWENTHAL COLLECTION

B2   1 L. from T. W. Adorno. 1942.
      4 L. from Max Horkheimer. 1947-1951.
      2 L. from Friedrich Pollock. 1953.

University of Illinois at Urbana-Champaign, University Library, University Archives, Room 19, Urbana, Illinois 61801.

C7   "Problems facing a New Communications Research Cen-
      ter." Speech given at the University of Illinois,
      1948.

H3   Birthday celebration held for Lazarsfeld.

I   Law Forum. Tables, cost estimates, etc.

New York Public Library, Manuscript Division, Fifth Avenue
and 42nd Street, New York, N.Y. 10018.

ERICH FROMM PAPERS

B1,2   Correspondence with Erich Fromm.

EMIL LEDERER

Economist, 1882-1939

<u>Mrs. Gertrude Lederer</u>, 372 Central Park West, Apt. 3B, New York, N.Y. 10024.

Private collection from the estate of Emil Lederer: inaccessible.

Unzugängliche Privatsammlung aus dem Nachlaß von Emil Lederer.

B1,2   Personal correspondence. 1934-1939.

C14   Sketches by Lederer.

I   Documents.

J   Photos from the 1920s.

L   Pictures of Japan that were sent to Lederer upon the occasion of his 50th birthday.

N   Small collection of Ms. that were sent to Lederer upon his 50th birthday, including Ms. by: Carl Landauer, Adolf Lowe, Joseph Schumpeter, Hans Speier, Ludwig von Mises, Carl Zuckmayer, etc.

<u>Columbia University</u>, Butler Library, New York, N.Y. 10027.

B1   5 L. to W. C. Mitchell. 1926-1937.

<u>Yivo Institute</u>, 1048 Fifth Avenue, New York, N.Y. 10028.

HORACE M. KALLEN PAPERS

*   Miscellaneous materials pertaining to Graduate Faculty of the New School for Social Research, folders: 549-553. Further references to Lederer in folders: 236, 453, 455. 1934-1939.

<u>American Philosophical Society</u>, The Library, 105 South Fifth Street, Philadelphia, Pennsylvania 19106.

FRANZ BOAS PAPERS

EMIL LEDERER

Bl   3 L. to Franz Boas. 1923-1937.

New York Public Library, Manuscript Division, Fifth Avenue and 42nd Street, New York, N.Y. 10018.

EMERGENCY COMMITTEE IN AID OF DISPLACED FOREIGN SCHOLARS, 1933-1945

*   File compiled, no assistance given. 1934-1939.

Mr. Alfred Vagts, Sherman, Connecticut 06784.

Bl   Several L. to Alfred Vagts.

LOTTE LEHMANN

Opera Singer, 1888-1976

University of California, Santa Barbara, The Library, Santa
Barbara, California 93105.

The LOTTE LEHMANN COLLECTION, which presently consists of
approximately 25 ft. of materials and is being added to
periodically, was donated to the library by Ms. Lehmann in
1969. Inquiries concerning literary rights should be made
at the time the collection is being used.

*Die LOTTE LEHMANN COLLECTION, die z.Zt. etwa 7,5 m Materia-
lien umfaßt, allerdings ständig erweitert wird, ist im
wesentlichen eine Schenkung von Frau Lehmann aus dem Jahre
1969. Fragen in Bezug auf die literarischen Rechte werden
beantwortet, wenn man die Sammlung einsieht.*

A3   Memoirs Ms.

B1,2 Correspondences, including lengthy correspondences
         with Bruno Walter (complete) and Arturo Toscanini,
         as well as with Thomas Mann, Puccini, Richard
         Strauss, Otto Klemperer. Over 5 B.
      Correspondence from 80th birthday celebration.

C7   Ms. of lectures.
      Ms. of book.

F   Ca. 20 tapes.
      Motion picture of the life of Lotte Lehmann.
      Tape of dedication of Lotte Lehmann room, 1969.

G   Ms. of interviews.

H3   Ca. 26 scrapbooks of cl. on her career and life.

I   Documents, including many contracts.

J   Photos from many years, all with people, places,
         events, identified.
      Portrait sculpture of Mme. Lehmann by Gladys Lewis
         Bush. 1934.

M   Oil paintings.
      Tapestries.
      Glass work.
      Tiles.
      Objets d'art.

LOTTE LEHMANN

)   Opera programs. 1930-1963.

Metropolitan Opera Association, Inc., The Archives, Lincoln
Center Plaza, New York, N.Y. 10023.

31   5 L. to individuals at the Metropolitan. 1947-1966.

43   6 cl. in addition to numerous articles from Opera News,
     1937-1972.

[Contracts. 1933-1942.

University of Georgia, The University Libraries, Athens,
Georgia 30601.

OLIN DOWNES PAPERS

31,2   Correspondence with Olin Downes. 8 L.

Bruno Walter Memorial Foundation, c/o Miss Susie Danziger,
115 East 72nd Street, New York, N.Y. 10021.

31,2   Correspondence with Bruno Walter.

Museum of the City of New York, Fifth Avenue at 103rd Street,
New York, N.Y. 10029.

43   "Personality File" on Lotte Lehmann.

Syracuse University, The George Arents Research Library,
Syracuse, N.Y. 13210.

FRANZ WAXMAN PAPERS

31   1 L. to Franz Waxman. 1957.

State University of New York at Binghamton, Center for Modern
Theater Research, Binghamton, New York 13901.

LOTTE LEHMANN

MAX REINHARDT ARCHIVE

J   1 photo of Lotte Lehmann. 1936.

University of Pennsylvania, The Charles Patterson Van Pelt
Library, Philadelphia, Pennsylvania 19104.

ALMA MAHLER-WERFEL COLLECTION

Bl   2 L. to Alma Mahler-Werfel. 1944.

Mrs. Peter M. Lindt, 949 West End Avenue, New York, N.Y.
10025.

Bl   Small amount of correspondence with Peter M. Lindt.

C   Ms. submitted to Lindt for use on his radio program.

HUGO LEICHTENTRITT

Musicologist, 1874-1951

University of Utah, Marriott Library, Western Americana Department, Salt Lake City, Utah 84112.

The Leichtentritt materials in the PAPERS OF LEROY J. ROBERT-SON (1896-1971) came to the Library as a part of the ROBERT-SON PAPERS that were purchased in 1967. The music library of Dr. Leichtentritt was purchased by the library over the years 1948-1951.

Die Leichtentritt-Materialien in den PAPERS OF LEROY J. ROBERTSON (1896-1971) kamen 1967 durch Kauf als Teil der ROBERTSON PAPERS in den Besitz der Marriott Library. Die Musikalienbibliothek Dr. Leichtentritts wurde im Laufe der Jahre 1948-1951 käuflich erworben.

A3   Dr. Hugo Leichtentritt Autobiography. In 7 parts (6 F.):
        Book I: "Reminiscences of My Life."
        Book II: "Five Years in the United States of America, 1889-1894."
        Book III: "Music and Theatre in Boston in the Nineties."
        Book IV: "Back in Europe - London and Paris."
        Book V: "Back in Berlin."
        Book VI: missing.
        Book VII: "Berlin Intermezzo."

B1,2   Correspondence with LeRoy J. Robertson. 1933-1948. 1 F.

B3   Correspondence between LeRoy J. Robertson and Regina Buchwald concerning the estate of Leichtentritt and the Ms. of "History of the Motet." 1951-1963.

C7   Thematic analyses of compositions by other musicians (9 F.):
        Hector Berlioz. Symphonie Fantastique and Overture Benvenuto Cellini.
        Claude Debussy. La Mer and L'après-midi d'un faune.
        Paul Hindemith. Mathis der Maler.
        Felix Mendelssohn. Overture: Die Hebriden (Fingal's Cave). Op. 26.
        Albert Roussel. Symphony in G Minor. Op. 42.
        Richard Strauss. Till Eulenspiegels lustige Streiche. Op. 28, and Don Quixote. Op. 35.

529

D. Shostakovich. <u>First Symphony</u>. Op. 10, <u>Sixth Symphony</u>, and <u>Fifth Symphony</u>. Op. 47.
Carl Maria von Weber. <u>Overture Oberon</u>.
Ludwig van Beethoven. "Biography" and "Beethoven's Overtures."
"History of the Motet." T. 1 B.

H5   Short essay by LeRoy J. Robertson explaining his relationship to Leichtentritt.

K   Personal music library of Leichtentritt, consisting of:
Ca. 550 books and pamphlets.
Ca. 800 music scores.
Scrapbook with newspaper and magazine cl. on Leichtentritt.

O   Program of a lecture at Harvard University.

<u>Library of Congress</u>, Reference Department, Music Division, Independence Avenue and First Street S.E., Washington, D.C. 20540.

The HUGO LEICHTENTRITT PAPERS, ca. 10 ft. of materials, were donated to the Library of Congress from the estate of Hugo Leichtentritt. An incomplete listing of the collection was prepared by a group of music students from the University of Maryland.

Die HUGO LEICHTENTRITT PAPERS, etwa 3 m Materialien, sind eine Schenkung an die Library of Congress aus dem Nachlaß von Hugo Leichtentritt. Eine z.Zt. noch unvollständige Liste der Materialien in der Sammlung wurde von einer Gruppe Studenten der University of Maryland erarbeitet.

C7   Mss. of essays, critiques. Ca. 1,200p., including:
Analysis of Aaron Copland's Third Symphony. T. 1946. 22p.
"Claudio Monteverdi als Madrigalkomponist." A. Ca. 50p.
["Geschichte der Motette."] A. Ca. 400p.
"Music of the Nations (Music of Western Nations)." A. and T. Ca. 300p.
"Nationalism and Internationalism in Music." T. Ca. 50p.

"Die Nocturne [Chopin]." A. Ca. 150p.
"Richard Keiser in seinen Opern." A. Ca. 125p.

C13   Ca. 300 scores.

H3   6 volumes of cl. 1900- .

M   Memorabilia: pictures, award.

University of Georgia, The University Libraries, Athens, Georgia 30601.

OLIN DOWNES PAPERS

B1,2   Correspondence with Olin Downes. 54 L.

Leo Baeck Institute, 129 East 73rd Street, New York, N.Y. 10021.

A3   Curriculum vitae with photo. Printed. 2p.

H3   Obituaries. 4 cl. 1951.

J   3 photos:
Berlin 1923.
Cambridge 1939.
Age 71. 1945.
Photos from the publication: Harvard Graduates After 40 Years. Ca. 1934.

ERICH LEINSDORF

Conductor, 1912-

Because of scheduling difficulties, the Project was unable to complete its contact with Mr. Leinsdorf concerning the materials of historic interest in his possession.

Terminschwierigkeiten machten es unmöglich, weitere Auskünfte von Erich Leinsdorf über Materialien von historischem Interesse in seinem Besitz zu erlangen.

University of California, Los Angeles, Music Library, 405 Hilgard Avenue, Los Angeles, California 90024.

ERNST TOCH ARCHIVE

C13b   Toch, Ernst. "Jephta; a tragic symphony." Ca. 1964. With corrections by Erich Leinsdorf and the note to title: "A symphonic phantasy (5th symphony)."

University of Georgia, The University Libraries, Athens, Georgia 30601.

OLIN DOWNES PAPERS

B1,2   Correspondence with Olin Downes. 11 L.

Columbia University, Butler Library, New York, N.Y. 10027.

B1   7 L. 1948-1966.

Harvard University, Houghton Library, Cambridge, Massachusetts 02138.

AUTOGRAPH FILE

B1   2 L. to Howard Mumford Jones. 1967, 1968.

American Philosophical Society, The Library, 105 South Fifth

Street, Philadelphia, Pennsylvania 19106.

HANS T. CLARKE PAPERS

Bl   2 L. to Hans Clarke. 1940, 1951.

Metropolitan Opera Association, Inc., The Archives, Lincoln
Center Plaza, New York, N.Y. 10023.

H3   Cl. from Opera News. 1939-1969.

I   Contracts. 1937-1938.

Syracuse University, The George Arents Research Library,
Syracuse, New York 13210.

FRANZ WAXMAN PAPERS

Bl   1 L. to Franz Waxman. 1941.

WALTER J. LEVY

Economist, Oil Consultant, 1911-

Dr. Walter J. Levy, Room 3232, 30 Rockefeller Plaza, New York, N.Y. 10020.

The consulting firm of Dr. Levy maintains its own archive containing materials pertaining to the operations of the firm, as well as personal materials belonging to Dr. Levy. The materials are inaccessible to the public at present.

Das Beratungsbüro Levy besitzt ein eigenes Archiv mit Materialien über das Beratungsbüro und Materialien aus dem persönlichen Besitz von Dr. Walter Levy. Das Archiv ist zur Zeit für die Öffentlichkeit unzugänglich.

B1,2 Correspondence from the founding of the firm in 1949 to the present. Includes L. from famous personalities such as American presidents, heads of state, etc.

G Transcriptions of interviews for radio, television and the press.

I Documents, including minutes of various consulting jobs.

J Photos, both of Dr. Levy and of others connected with the firm.

K Dr. Levy's personal library. Ca. 10,000 volumes.

L Complete collection of newspaper cl. of the firm's (Dr. Levy's) activities.

M Memorabilia belonging to Dr. Levy.

N Manuscripts by third parties.

KURT LEWIN
Psychologist, 1890-1947

<u>Mrs. Gertrud Lewin</u>, 203 Lexington Avenue, Cambridge, Massachusetts 02138.

The ca. 2 ft. of materials in Mrs. Lewin's possession (widow of Dr. Lewin) are from the estate of Kurt Lewin.

Frau Gertrud Lewin, die Witwe von Kurt Lewin, besitzt etwa 0,60 m Materialien aus dem Nachlaß von Kurt Lewin.

B2   1 F. of selected correspondence entitled "famous people."

C7   Texts of lectures.
Notes, partially in stenography.

D7   Nearly complete collection of pub. writings. Offprints, cl.

K   Modest personal library.

<u>Yivo Institute</u>, 1048 Fifth Avenue, New York, N.Y. 10028.

HORACE M. KALLEN PAPERS

B1   70 L. and Tel. to Horace M. Kallen. 1934-1944.
4 L. 1935-1938.

B2   77 L. from Horace M. Kallen (mostly c.). 1933-1944.
11 L. from 1935-1936.

B3   104 L., memos, pertaining to Lewin. 1934-1944. Primarily correspondences of Horace M. Kallen.
Isolated references to Lewin in folders: 37, 64b, 508, 648, 672.

C7   "Tasks and Organizations of a Psychological Institute at the Hebrew University of Jerusalem." Undated. T.c. 7p.
"Psycho-Sociological Problems of Belonging to the Jewish Group." T.c. 20p.
"Research Problems for a Psychological Institute at the University of Jerusalem." Undated. T. 2c. 5p. and 10p.
"Psychological Research on Jewish Youth Adjustment and

535

Community Relations." Undated. T.c. 3p.

D7   "Education and Leadership." Reprint from <u>Areopagus</u>, Dec. 1934. 4p.

H5   2 biographical sketches plus an "item of information on K. Lewin."

<u>University of Iowa</u>, The University Libraries, Special Collections, Iowa City, Iowa 52240.

B1,2   Correspondences in faculty information folder. Possible materials also located in the University of Iowa President's Office Correspondence.

<u>American Philosophical Society</u>, The Library, 105 South Fifth Street, Philadelphia, Pennsylvania 19106.

WOLFGANG KÖHLER PAPERS

B1,2   Correspondence with Wolfgang Köhler. 6 L. 1929-1932.

<u>New York Public Library</u>, Manuscript Division, Fifth Avenue and 42nd Street, New York, N.Y. 10018.

MAX WERTHEIMER PAPERS, EMERGENCY COMMITTEE IN AID OF DISPLACED FOREIGN SCHOLARS, 1933-1945

B1   2 L. to Max Wertheimer. 1929.

*   File compiled by the Emergency Committee in Aid of Displaced Foreign Scholars when assistance was granted. 1933-1944.

<u>Duke University</u>, William R. Perkins Library, Manuscript Department, Durham, North Carolina 27706.

ROBERT LEE FLOWERS PAPERS

B1   1 L. to Robert Lee Flowers. 1942.

ERNST LEWY

Psychoanalyst, 1891-

Dr. Ernst Lewy, 1585 Manning Avenue, Los Angeles, California 90024.

Private collection: inaccessible. / *Unzugängliche Privatsammlung.*

B1,2 Short correspondence with Paul Federn.
      Short correspondence with David Rapaport.

C7   Ms. of articles and papers, from the time spent at the Menninger Clinic to the present.

D7   Reprints from prewar (Berlin) as well as postwar times.

K   Small library, containing some rare editions (Freud), editions of Frederick II, etc.

L   Materials collected by Lewy for "never written papers."

N   Collection of Ms. by David Rappaport, including:
      "The Conceptual Model of Psychoanalysis."
      "The Autonomy of the Ego."
      "Activity - Passivity."

American Philosophical Society, The Library, 105 South Fifth Street, Philadelphia, Pennsylvania 19106.

FRANZ BOAS PAPERS

B1   1 L. to Franz Boas. 1936.

537

PETER M. LINDT

Radio Broadcaster, Writer, 1908-1976

Mrs. Peter M. Lindt, 949 West End Avenue, New York, N.Y.
10025.

The materials in Mrs. Lindt's possession are from the estate
of her husband, Peter M. Lindt. With the exception of 1
package of materials that was lost in the course of the
Lindts' flight from Vienna via Switzerland to the U.S. (June
1938), the collection is complete. Manuscripts and printed
matter dating prior to 1938 illustrate Lindt's career in
Vienna, while those materials after Dec. 21, 1938 are a
result of Lindt's activities in the U.S.

*Die Materialien, die sich in Frau Lindts Besitz befinden,
stammen aus dem Nachlaß ihres Mannes. Die Sammlung ist
vollständig bis auf 1 Päckchen mit Materialien, das bei der
Flucht Lindts von Wien über die Schweiz in der Vereinigten
Staaten verlorenging (Juni 1938). Manuskripte und Gedrucktes aus der Zeit vor 1938 geben ein Bild von Lindts Laufbahn
in Wien, während die Materialien aus der Zeit nach dem 21.
Dez. 1938 seine Aktivitäten in den Vereinigten Staaten be-
leuchten.*

A2   Notebooks (ca. 15) with preliminary drafts, ideas,
     notes for broadcasts.

A3   Some autobiographical materials.

B1,2 Ca. 530 L. including correspondence with: Günther
     Anders, Raoul Auernheimer, Julius Bab, Vicki Baum,
     Ulrich Becher, Richard Beer-Hofmann, Hermann Broch,
     Ferdinand Bruckner, Martin Buber, Albert Einstein,
     Lion Feuchtwanger, Bruno Frank, René Fülöp-Miller,
     Manfred George, Alexander Gode von Aesch, Oskar
     Maria Graf, Ivan Heilbut, Heinrich Eduard Jacob,
     Kurt Kersten, Harold Kreuzberg, Lotte Lehmann,
     Alma Mahler-Werfel, Thomas Mann, L. Oberndorf, Karl
     O. Paetel, Hertha Pauli, Fritz Pentzoldt, Erwin
     Piscator, Alfred Polgar, Luise Rainer, Victor F.
     Ridder, Alexander Roda Roda, Max Roden, Franklin D.
     Roosevelt Jr., Hans Sahl, Franz Schoenberner, Irene
     Serkin, George N. Schuster, Paul Stefan, Wilhelm
     Sternfeld, Wolfgang Stresemann, Paul Tillich,

Friedrich Torberg, Ludwig Ullmann, Franz Ullstein,
Johannes Urzidil, Veit Valentin, Berthold Viertel,
Oswald Garrison Villard, Karl Vollmoeller, H. V.
Kaltenborn, Fritz von Unruh, Volkmar von Zuehlsdorf,
Kadidja Wedekind, Otto Zoff.

C1   Ms. of a novel. A.

C2   Ms. or T. of dramas, including:
        Die Ehe des François Beaupré.
        Salzburger Intermezzo.
        Das Leben spielt Komödie.
        From Heaven to Hell.
        To Die—Where?

C3   Ms. of 1 poem.

C4   74 Ms. and T.

C7   Ca. 800 broadcasts, timetables for broadcasts.
        Ms. of articles written for newspapers. T. and A.
        Texts of radio broadcasts on political and literary
            topics. 1942-1972 (10 years missing).
        Essay on Schopenhauer. T.

D4,7   Small collection of cl. from newspapers and magazines
            (overseas and U.S.).

D12   Several c. of Der Weltspiegel, edited by Lindt.

F   Records (6), mainly of interviews.
        Tapes (over 60) of Lindt reading poetry (Hesse, Wasser-
            mann), interviews, etc. Includes:
        "Vom Adel der menschlichen Vernunft."
        "Switzerland."
        Lindt's speech as new President of the Social Scien-
            tific Society. Oct. 1946.
        Lindt's speech before the "Schlaraffia" on German-
            American writers.
        Lindt's first broadcast on WEVD.
        Brotherhood Week, 1951.
        Radio interview of David Berger, Voice of America,
            with Peter M. Lindt.

G   Ca. 1/3 of Lindt's radio programs were interviews, the
            other 2/3 readings by Lindt.

H3   Hundreds of cl. from newspapers, magazines.

H4   Reviews mainly from: Aufbau, NY Staatszeitung.

I   Some documents.

J   Collection of photos.

K   Lindt's personal library of over 8,000 books (ca. 50%
       from the last 15 years; 20% in English) includes
       literature, politics, music, history, social science,
       art, etc.

L   Complete collection of materials on the Social Scien-
       tific Society of New York. 4 scrapbooks plus records.
       Also over 500 items of correspondence.

N   Ca. 2 in. of manuscripts by other authors, including:
       Richard Beer-Hofmann, Hermann Borchardt, Vera Crae-
       ner, Count Czernin, Lion Feuchtwanger, Bruno Frank,
       Prof. D. M. Gumpel, Ivan Heilbut, Heinrich Eduard
       Jacob, Hugo Jacobi, Hans Janowitz, R. Kaiser, Mascha
       Kaleko, Lotte Lehmann, Major Lessner, Emil Ludwig,
       Prinz Hubertus zu Loewenstein, Thomas Mann, L.
       Martin-Domke, Karin Michaelis, Alfred Polgar, Erich
       Maria Remarque, Marianne Rieser, Dr. Manfred Sackel,
       W. Sorel, Fritz von Unruh, Ernst Waldinger, Dr.
       Waxman, Dr. Weil, F. C. Weiskopf, Franz Werfel,
       Stefan Zweig.

State University of New York at Albany, Department of Germanic Languages and Literatures, 1400 Washington Avenue,
Albany, New York 12222.

KARL O. PAETEL COLLECTION, STORM PUBLISHERS ARCHIVE

B1   1 L. to Karl O. Paetel. 1956.
       6 L. and 1 Ptc. to Alexander Gode von Aesch. 1947-1950.

B2   7 L. from Alexander Gode von Aesch. 1947-1948.

D12   Welt-Spiegel, No. 11 (Sept. 1947). 1 c. of bulletin,
       ed. by Peter M. Lindt.

University of New Hampshire, The Library, Department of Special Collections, Durham, New Hampshire 03824.

PETER M. LINDT

FRIEDRICH SALLY GROSSHUT COLLECTION

B1   14 L. and 1 Ptc. to F. S. Grosshut. T. and A. 1950-
      1957.

University of California, Los Angeles, Department of Special
Collections, 120 Lawrence Clark Powell Library, Los Angeles,
California 90024.

FRANZ WERFEL ARCHIVE

B1   2 L. to Franz Werfel. 1943.

Harvard University, Houghton Library, Cambridge, Massachusetts 02138.

RICHARD BEER-HOFMANN COLLECTION, OSWALD GARRISON VILLARD
PAPERS

B1   1 L. ea. to Richard Beer-Hofmann (1943) and Oswald
      Garrison Villard (1948).

Library of Congress, Manuscript Division, Independence Avenue
and First Street S.E., Washington, D.C. 20540.

BENJAMIN W. HUEBSCH PAPERS

B1   1 L. to Benjamin W. Huebsch. 1943.

B2   1 L. from Benjamin W. Huebsch. 1943.

Leo Baeck Institute, 129 East 73rd Street, New York, N.Y.
10021.

JACOB PICARD COLLECTION

C9   Presentation of Jacob Picard's "Der Nachbar und der
      Garten," on WBNX by Peter M. Lindt. 3p.

541

FRITZ LIPMANN

Biochemist, 1899-

Dr. Fritz Lipmann, South Laboratory Building, Rockefeller
University, New York, N.Y. 10021.

Private collection: inaccessible. / *Unzugängliche Privatsammlung.*

A2	Ca. 3 ft. of notebooks of laboratory work by Lipmann and others. Undated. Early notebooks, pre-1933, in German and English. Ca. 1.5 ft.
A3	Bibliography of Lipmann's publications.
B1,2	Correspondences, from 1957 to present.
C7	Ms. of articles from 1957 to present. Ms. of full-length books.
D7	Numerous cl. and offprints.
F	Taped recordings of lectures by Lipmann. 1960s.
J	Numerous photos from all years.
L	12 cartons of offprints, cl. by others.
M	Prizes, medals, honors received. Nobel Prize album, including correspondence related to Nobel Prize.
N	Laboratory notebooks of Lipmann's co-workers and assistants.

Library of Congress, Manuscript Division, Independence Avenue
and First Street S.E., Washington, D.C. 20540.

A3	Wanderings of a Biochemist. 1 B. of rough drafts and materials.

American Philosophical Society, The Library, 105 South Fifth
Street, Philadelphia, Pennsylvania 19106.

HANS T. CLARKE PAPERS, SIMON FLEXNER PAPERS

B1,2   Correspondence with Hans T. Clarke.
        Correspondence with Simon Flexner.

<u>Smithsonian Institution</u>, Dibner Library, Washington, D.C.
20560.

MISCELLANEOUS COLLECTION

B1   2 L. Undated.

PRINZ HUBERTUS ZU LOEWENSTEIN

Statesman, 1906-

Harvard University, Houghton Library, Cambridge, Massachusetts 02138.

OSWALD GARRISON VILLARD PAPERS

B1   1 L. to Winston Churchill. 1945.
      1 L. to Cordell Hull (Secretary of State). 1944.
      181 L. to Oswald Garrison Villard. 1936, 1940-1949.
      4 L. to: John W. Davis, Joseph Dees, Mrs. Kimberly.
         1941-1949.

B2   72 L. from Oswald Garrison Villard.
      5 L.

B3   Correspondence between Oswald Garrison Villard and
         Prinzessin Helga zu Loewenstein. 21 L. 1941-1948.
      Correspondence between Oswald Garrison Villard and
         Volkmar von Zuehlsdorf, secretary of Loewenstein.
         17 L. 1941-1949.

D7   6 newspaper cl.

Columbia University, Butler Library, New York, N.Y. 10027.

NICHOLAS MURRAY BUTLER PAPERS

B1   165 L. to N. M. Butler. T. and A. 1936-1946.
      1 L. to Thomas Mann. T.c. 1936.

B2   106 L. from N. M. Butler. T.c. 1936-1946.
      1 L. from Thomas Mann. T.c. 1936.

C7   "The Future of Europe." Lecture. 1939. T. 19p.
      "Die deutsche Akademie in New York." T.c. 6p.
      "What Could a German Academy in America do to Preserve
         German Cultural Life?" T. 5p.
      "An Answer to Some Questions." T. 3p.
      Memorandum to N. M. Butler on American Guild for Ger-
         man Cultural Freedom. T. 11p.

I   By-laws of American Guild for German Cultural Freedom.
         Also minutes "Denkschrift."
      Biographical documents.

544

PRINZ HUBERTUS ZU LOEWENSTEIN

University of New Hampshire, The Library, Department of
Special Collections, Durham, New Hampshire 03824.

OSKAR MARIA GRAF COLLECTION

B1   8 L. to Oskar Maria Graf. 1938-1946.

B2   1 L. from Oskar Maria Graf. 1946.

University of Iowa, The University Libraries, Special Collection, Iowa City, Iowa 52240.

B1   6 L. to George Sylvester Viereck. 1957-1958.

State University of New York at Albany, Department of Germanic Languages and Literatures, 1400 Washington Avenue,
Albany, New York 12222.

KARL O. PAETEL COLLECTION

B1   7 L. to Karl O. Paetel (xerox). 1944-1947.

Library of Congress, Manuscript Division, Independence Avenue
and First Street S.E., Washington, D.C. 20540.

BENJAMIN W. HUEBSCH PAPERS

B1   1 L. to Benjamin W. Huebsch. T. 1940.

B2   1 L. from Benjamin W. Huebsch. T.c. 1940.

Yivo Institute, 1048 Fifth Avenue, New York, N.Y. 10028.

HORACE M. KALLEN PAPERS

B1,2 Individual items located in folder no. 25.

Mr. Hans Sahl, 800 West End Avenue, New York, N.Y. 10025.

PRINZ HUBERTUS ZU LOEWENSTEIN

B1   Several L. to Hans Sahl.

American Philosophical Society, The Library, 105 South Fifth
Street, Philadelphia, Pennsylvania 19106.

FRANZ BOAS PAPERS

B2   1 L. from Franz Boas. 1940.

University of Pennsylvania, The Charles Patterson Van Pelt
Library, Philadelphia, Pennsylvania 19104.

ALMA MAHLER-WERFEL COLLECTION

B2   1 L. from Hermann Borchardt. T. Undated.

Leo Baeck Institute, 129 East 73rd Street, New York, N.Y.
10021.

HELMUT HIRSCH COLLECTION

B1,2   Correspondence with Helmut Hirsch. 1940-1957, 1968.

Dr. Clementine Zernik, 225-10 106th Avenue, Queens Village,
New York 11429.

B1   Several L. to Arnold Höllriegel. 1938-1939.

Mrs. Peter M. Lindt, 949 West End Avenue, New York, N.Y.
10025.

C   Ms. submitted to Lindt for use on his radio program.

FRITZ W. LONDON

Physicist, 1900-1954

Duke University, William R. Perkins Library, Manuscript
Department, Durham, North Carolina 27706.

The FRITZ W. LONDON PAPERS, 31 volumes of materials plus
1971 individual items, were acquired by the library in 4
separate donations: from Mrs. Edith London, "Papers 1925-
1953" in 1954, and "Papers 1926-1954" in 1964; from the
American Institute of Physics, "Papers 1935-1948" in 1972;
and from Dr. Mattie Russell, Manuscript Department of Duke
University Library.

*Die FRITZ W. LONDON PAPERS, 31 Bände Materialien sowie 1971
Einzelnummern, sind der Bibliothek in 4 verschiedenen Schenkungen zugegangen: 1954 von Mrs. Edith London die "Papers
1925-1953" sowie 1964 die "Papers 1926-1954"; 1972 vom American Institute of Physics die "Papers 1935-1948"; und weiteres Material von Dr. Mattie Russell, Manuscript Department
of Duke University Library.*

B1   467 L., including 15 L. to 9 emigrés.

B2   31 L. from 10 emigrés.

C8   30 large format notebooks with mathematical calcula-
      tions, physics notes, solutions, etc. 1927-1942.
      Superfluids. Outline, drafts and proofs of first vol-
      ume. Ca. 400p. Drafts of second volume. T. Ca. 200p.
      Lecture notes. 1928-1947, including:
      "Die Quanten-mechanischen Grundgleichungen."
      "Elementare Theorie des periodischen Systems..."
      "Relativitätstheorie..."
      "Historical Development of Our Modern Concept of
        Molecular Physics."
      "Chemical Thermodynamics."
      "Electrodynamics."
      Course outlines.
      5 Ms. of articles. 1925-1928. Ca. 100p.
      Unpub. Ms. of a book. 1937. T. Ca. 280p.

C14   Ca. 5 drawings.

WILLIAM HANE WANNEMAKER PAPERS

B2   2 L. from W. H. Wannemaker. 1937, 1942.

I   Individual items in personnel file of W. H. Wannemaker.

Archive for History of Quantum Physics (locations in U.S.: Bancroft Library, University of California, Berkeley; American Philosophical Society, Philadelphia, Pennsylvania; American Institute of Physics, New York, N.Y.).

B1   11 L. to Alfred Landé. 1924-1927.
        6 L. to E. Schrödinger. 1926-1928.
        2 L. to E. C. Kemble. 1929-1930.
        1 L. to A. Sommerfeld. 1927.

B2   2 L. from E. Schrödinger. 1926.
        1 L. from E. C. Kemble. 1930.

American Institute of Physics, Niels Bohr Library, 335 East 45th Street, New York, N.Y. 10017.

FRITZ REICHE PAPERS and general archive files

B1   17 L. to Paul Zilsel. 1947-1954.

H5   Reiche, Fritz. Notes and calculations concerning London's "Die Zahl der Dispersionelektronen in der Undulationsmechanik." A. 10p.

New York Public Library, Manuscript Division, Fifth Avenue and 42nd Street, New York, N.Y. 10018.

EMERGENCY COMMITTEE IN AID OF DISPLACED FOREIGN SCHOLARS, 1933-1945.

*   File compiled, no assistance given. 1933-1936.

University of Chicago, The Joseph Regenstein Library, 1100 East 57th Street, Chicago, Illinois 60637.

JAMES FRANCK PAPERS

81,   L. of congratulations to James Franck on his 70th
       birthday. 1952. Accompanied by photo of London.

       2 group photos:
       Institute for Theoretical Physics. Copenhagen, 1935.
       Ninth Washington Conference on Theoretical Physics.
          Washington, Oct. 31 - Nov. 2, 1946.

STEFAN LORANT

Journalist, Publicist, 1901-

<u>Mr. Stefan Lorant</u>, West Mountain Road, Lenox, Massachusetts 02140.

Personal collection: over 60 ft.

Privatsammlung von über 18 m.

A1   Diaries from early years in Hungary.

A3   <u>I Was Hitler's Prisoner</u>. Ms.

B1   Very few c. of Lorant's own L.

B2   Correspondence. 1920-. Includes L. from: Harry Truman, John F. Kennedy, Conrad Veidt, Alfred Polgar and other emigrants.
Collection of L. from mothers of famous individuals (e.g., Noel Coward).

C5   Mss. of film scripts.

C7   Mss. to articles and speeches.

I   Numerous documents of all kinds.

J   Numerous photos.

L   Materials used by Lorant in his writing. Cl. from German and American sources.
Cl. collections on various topics.

ADOLF LOWE

Economist, 1893-

Prof. Adolf Lowe, 1125 Grand Concourse, The Bronx, New York 10452.

Private collection: inaccessible. / *Unzugängliche Privat-sammlung.*

B1,2	Correspondence with Ernst Bloch. 10 L. 1940s.
B2	Several L. from Paul Tillich.
C7	Notes from course lectures.
D7	Offprints of Lowe's writings.
H4	Reviews of Lowe's works.
J	Photos. 1915-.
K	Personal library, including literature, philosophy, theology, as well as economics.
M	Memorabilia.

Harvard University, Harvard Divinity School, Andover-Harvard Theological Library, 45 Francis Avenue, Cambridge, Massachusetts 02138.

PAUL TILLICH COLLECTION

B1	1 L. to Paul Tillich (draft). 1964.
B2	11 L. from Paul Tillich. 1956-1965.

Joseph and Alice Maier, 991 Grace Terrace, Teaneck, New Jersey 07666.

H5	Minutes of discussions between Adolf Lowe, Paul Tillich, Max Horkheimer and Friedrich Pollock.

Mrs. Gertrude Lederer, 372 Central Park West, Apt. 3B, New York, N.Y. 10024.

ADOLF LOWE

C7   Ms. sent to Lederer upon the event of his 50th birth-
      day (by Lowe).

New York Public Library, Manuscript Division, Fifth Avenue
and 42nd Street, New York, N.Y. 10018.

EMERGENCY COMMITTEE IN AID OF DISPLACED FOREIGN SCHOLARS,
1933-1945

*   File compiled, no assistance given. 1934-1943.

Yivo Institute, 1048 Fifth Avenue, New York, N.Y. 10028.

HORACE M. KALLEN PAPERS

*   Individual item(s) in folders: 559, 771, 1023.   1934.

Columbia University, Butler Library, New York, N.Y. 10027.

B1   1 L. to Wesley C. Mitchell. A. 1932.

LEO LOWENTHAL

Sociologist, 1900–

Prof. Leo Lowenthal, Department of Sociology, University of California, Berkeley, California 94720.

Prof. Lowenthal still retains the major portion of his collection (inaccessible to outside researchers). According to his will, the materials will go to Prof. Martin Jay, Department of History, University of California, Berkeley, California 94720.

Prof. Lowenthal befindet sich noch im Besitz eines großen Teils seiner Schriftensammlung; die Sammlung ist nicht zugänglich. Seinem Testament entsprechend werden die Materialien später an Prof. Martin Jay gehen (Department of History, University of California, Berkeley, California 94720).

B1,2 "Correspondence of historical importance." Ca. 3 ft.
Correspondence with Siegfried Kracauer.
Miscellaneous correspondence, including some prior to 1933 with Jaspers, Huber, etc.
Correspondence from student years with parents.
(Prof. Lowenthal also has xerox c. of all of the L. that he donated to Houghton Library, Harvard University.)

C7 Ms. of one book.
Ms. on sociology of literature.
Ms. of radio speeches.
Several Ms. of pub. works.
Ms. of articles from student years.

I Documents from the Institute for Social Research. 1949–1954.
Personal documents dating from very early years of career (1921 or 1922).

J Numerous photos. 1930–present.

K Personal library.

L Cl. concerning the Institute for Social Research in America.
"Confidential materials" concerning the Institute during the Geneva period.

N   Several Ms. of others.

Harvard University, Houghton Library, Cambridge, Massachusetts 02138.

The LEO LOWENTHAL COLLECTION (bMS Ger 185) was donated by
Dr. Leo Lowenthal in Aug. 1971. Use of the collection,
which consists of 7 boxes of materials, is restricted until
Dec. 31, 1998; however, written permission to use the collection may be obtained from Dr. Lowenthal (Department of
Sociology, University of California, Berkeley, California
94720).

*Die LEO LOWENTHAL COLLECTION (bMS Ger 185) ist eine Schenkung
von Prof. Lowenthal vom Aug. 1971. Bis zum 31. Dez. 1998 ist
der Zugang zu dieser Sammlung - 7 Kartons Materialien - beschränkt. Eine schriftliche Ausnahmegenehmigung kann jedoch
von Prof. Lowenthal eingeholt werden (Department of Sociology,
University of California, Berkeley, California 94720).*

B1   974 L. 1934-1968, among them L. to: Theodor W. Adorno
        (108), Max Horkheimer (587), Friedrich Pollock (261).

B2   1,274 L. 1933-1969, among them L. from: Theodor W.
        Adorno (138), Max Horkheimer (684), Friedrich Pol-
        lock (405).

B3   217 L., among them L. from: Adorno, Horkheimer, Her-
        bert Marcuse.

N   Adorno, Theodor W. 1 essay. 7p.
        Horkheimer, Max. 9 essays. 55p.
        Jahoda, Marie. Essays. 23p.
        Notebook of lectures by others. 1951.
        Miscellaneous untitled Ms. and T. 7 F.

Harvard University, Harvard Divinity School, Andover-Harvard
Theological Library, 45 Francis Avenue, Cambridge, Massachusetts 02138.

PAUL TILLICH COLLECTION

B1   14 L. and 1 Tel. to Paul and Hannah Tillich. 1955-1965.

B2   4 L. from Tillich. 1955-1962.

Harvard University, Baker Library, Graduate School of Business, Soldiers Field, Boston, Massachusetts 02163.

FRITZ REDLICH COLLECTION

B1   1 L. to Fritz Redlich. 1936.

Prof. Herbert Marcuse, Department of Philosophy, University of California, San Diego, La Jolla, California 92037.

B1,2   Correspondence with Herbert Marcuse.

EDWARD E. LOWINSKY

Musicologist, 1908-

Dr. Edward E. Lowinsky, Professor Emeritus, Department of
Music, University of Chicago, Chicago, Illinois 60637.

Private collection: over 60 ft.

Privatsammlung von etwa 20 m.

B1,2   Correspondence. 1935-1977. Thousands of L., including:
       Higinio Anglés. 14 L. (from Anglés), 16 replies (by
           Lowinsky). 1946-1969.
       Heinrich Besseler. 56 L., 50 replies. 1946-1969.
       Luigi Dallapiccolo. 26 L., 15 replies. 1950-1962.
       Hans T. David. 13 L., 21 replies. 1962-1967.
       Albert Einstein. 1 L. (A.), 2 replies. Also 1 sheet
           of mathematical calculations.
       Alfred Einstein. 104 L., 59 replies. 1941-1952.
       Donald J. Grout (extensive correspondence).
       William Heckscher (moderate correspondence).
       Gerhard Herz. 148 L., 50 replies. 1947-1977.
       H. W. Janson (extensive correspondence).
       Knud Jeppesen. 10 L., 15 replies. 1964-1972.
       Hugo Kauder. 22 L., 8 replies. 1946-1960.
       Ernst Křenek. 10 L., 8 replies. 1947-1964.
       Paul Oscar Kristeller. 75 L., 46 replies. 1943-1977.
       Erwin Panofsky. 92 L., 79 replies. 1943-1967.
       Nino Pirrotta. 102 L., 80 replies. 1953-1977.
       Gustave Reese (extensive correspondence).
       Curt Sachs. 5 L., 6 replies. 1948-1957.
       Albert Smijers. 13 L., 7 replies. 1947-1957.
       Igor Stravinsky. 5 L., 7 replies. 1950-1961. Also an
           autographed score.
       Oliver Strunk. 33 L., 25 replies. 1947-1977.
       Geneviève Thibault (Mme H. de Chambure) (moderate
           correspondence).
       Charles van den Borren. 104 L., 59 replies. 1935-
           1965.
       Emanuel Winternitz. 14 L., 11 replies. 1954-1977.

C7   Ms. of unpub. works.
       Ms. of lectures at Black Mountain College and else-
       where.

EDWARD E. LOWINSKY

D7   Nearly complete offprint collection.

H3,4 Numerous cl., reviews (in xerox).

I   Documents.

J   Photos, from childhood years to present.

K   Large library (with rare books).
Runs of journals (music, Renaissance studies).

L   Classroom teaching materials (primarily from Queens
College).
Scrapbook about the Second Black Mountain College
Music Institute (cl., programs). Also some materials
on the first Institute.
Materials used by Lowinsky in his work, including
scores, records, musical Ms., etc. 10 file cabinet
drawers.

M   Memorabilia: drawing of Einstein, notes from Alfred
Einstein.

N   Ms. of a Baroque lecture by Erwin Panofsky.

Prof. Gerhard Herz, University of Louisville, School of
Music, Department of Music History, Louisville, Kentucky
40208.

B1   Correspondence with Gerhard Herz. Over 50 L.

State of North Carolina, Department of Cultural Resources,
Raleigh, North Carolina 27611.

BLACK MOUNTAIN COLLEGE ARCHIVES

*   Faculty file: "Edward E. and Gretel Lowinsky."
General file: "Summer Music Institute 1945-. Edward
Lowinsky."

J   Portrait of Lowinsky.

Harvard University, Houghton Library, Cambridge, Massachusetts 02138.

EDWARD E. LOWINSKY

LYONEL FEININGER COLLECTION

B1   12 L. to Lyonel and Julia Feininger. 1913-1947.

Prof. Hans Tischler, 711 East First Street, Bloomington, Indiana 47401.

B1,2 Correspondence with Hans Tischler.

New York Public Library, Manuscript Division, Fifth Avenue and 42nd Street, New York, N.Y. 10018.

EMERGENCY COMMITTEE IN AID OF DISPLACED FOREIGN SCHOLARS, 1933-1945

*   File compiled when assistance was granted. 1941-1944.

University of Georgia, The University Libraries, Athens, Georgia 30601.

OLIN DOWNES PAPERS

B1   2 L.

Mrs. Alice Loewy Kahler, 1 Evelyn Place, Princeton, New Jersey 08540.

ERICH VON KAHLER COLLECTION

B1   11 L. to Erich von Kahler. 1945-1960.

EMIL LUDWIG

Writer, 1881-1948

The major collection of Emil Ludwig materials remains, as of
1977, with Ludwig's son, Mr. Gordon Ludwig (Via Piscone 24,
CH-6616 Losone, Switzerland), who intends to donate the
materials to the Landesbibliothek, Berne, Switzerland. This
collection consists of stenographic diaries, some manuscripts and fragments of manuscripts, documents, several
privately printed Emil Ludwig editions, clippings, notes and
various other personal materials.

*Die Hauptsammlung von Emil-Ludwig-Materialien befindet sich
zum jetzigen Zeitpunkt (1977) in den Händen von Emil Ludwigs
Sohn, Gordon Ludwig, Via Piscone 24, CH 6616 Losone, Schweiz).
Herr Ludwig hat vor, diese Materialien der Landesbibliothek
in Bern zu schenken. Die Sammlung besteht aus in Kurzschrift
geschriebenen Tagebüchern, einigen Manuskripten sowie Manu-
skriptfragmenten, Dokumenten, verschiedenen Privatdrucken
von Emil-Ludwig-Ausgaben, Zeitungsausschnitten, Notizen und
sonstigen persönlichen Materialien.*

Leo Baeck Institute, 129 East 73rd Street, New York, N.Y.
10021.

GEORG HERMANN COLLECTION, KURT KERSTEN COLLECTION, FRITZ
MAUTHNER COLLECTION, WALTER VON MOLO COLLECTION

B1   9 L. 1911-1943, including L. to: Kurt Kersten, Georg
       Hermann.
       4 L. and 6 Ptc. to Fritz Mauthner. 1913-1921.

B2   1 L. ea. from: Raoul Auernheimer (1938), Heinrich
       Eduard Jacob (1939), Hermann Keyserling (1919),
       Bernard Shaw (1948).

C3   8-line poem on verso of Ptc. Suvrettina, Jan. 1931.

C10   "Die Farben meines Landes." Essay for a protest meet-
       ing against Hitler in New York under Prinz Hubertus
       zu Loewenstein. New York, 1943. A. 2p.

H3   1 obituary.

H5   "Der elfte August 1950." A. 1928. 3p.
       Landsberger, Franz. "Emil Ludwig. Eine Jugenderinne-
       rung." T. 4p.

I   Files of Berlin secret police. Confiscation of per-
     sonal belongings and rescinding of confiscation.
     T. pc. 1933-1934. 20p.

J   Photo of Ludwig with dedication. 1903.
     Photo of Ludwig and Bernard Shaw. Undated.

Franklin D. Roosevelt Library, Hyde Park, New York 12538.

FRANKLIN D. ROOSEVELT COLLECTION, HENRY WALLACE COLLECTION

B1   3 L. to Franklin D. Roosevelt. 1937-1944.
     2 L. to Vice President Wallace. 1943.
     4 L. 1937-1943.

B2   16 L., including L. from: Eleanor and Franklin D.
     Roosevelt.

B3   7 L., including L. from: Franklin D. Roosevelt.

C7   "Private Memorandum Concerning the Treatment of the
     Germans." T. 5p.

University of Pennsylvania, The Charles Patterson Van Pelt
Library, Philadelphia, Pennsylvania 19104.

ALMA MAHLER-WERFEL COLLECTION

B1   22 L., 1 Ptc. and 1 condolence L. to Alma Mahler-
     Werfel. 1910-1945.

H3   1 cl.

Princeton University, Firestone Library, Princeton, New Jersey 08540.

BARROWS MUSSY COLLECTION

C9   Mediterranean (Das Mittelmeer). English tr. with corr.
     and additions. Some German p. Ca. 600p.

THE PAPERS OF ALBERT EINSTEIN (1879-1955). For details

concerning the use of this collection, see description under Albert Einstein.

THE PAPERS OF ALBERT EINSTEIN (1879-1955). Angaben über den Zugang zu der Sammlung finden sich unter "Albert Einstein."

B1,2   Unknown amount of correspondence between Einstein and Ludwig.

Library of Congress, Manuscript Division, Independence Avenue and First Street S.E., Washington, D.C. 20540.

BENJAMIN W. HUEBSCH PAPERS

B1   11 L. to Benjamin W. Huebsch.

University of Texas, Humanities Research Center, Manuscripts Collection, Box 7219, Austin, Texas 78712.

B1   8 L.
B2   2 L.
I   1 document.

Columbia University, Butler Library, New York, N.Y. 10027.

B1   2 L. and 1 Ptc. 1928, 1930, 1942.
C7   Comment on The Seed Beneath the Snow by Ignazio Silone. 1942. T. 1p.
        "Das Haupt der Spanischen Regierung." Undated. T. 13p. English tr. 11p.

Indiana University, The University Libraries, The Lilly Library, Bloomington, Indiana 47401.

UPTON BEALL SINCLAIR MSS.

B1   10 L. 1935-1944, including 9 L. to Upton Sinclair.

Hoover Institution on War, Revolution and Peace, Stanford, California 94305.

FRANZ SCHOENBERNER COLLECTION

B1   Reply to Franz Schoenberner's open L. "How to Treat Inflated Mr. Ludwig?"

B2   Schoenberner, Franz. "How to Treat Inflated Mr. Ludwig?" Dec. 1943.

Harvard University, Houghton Library, Cambridge, Massachusetts 02138.

RICHARD BEER-HOFMANN COLLECTION, OSWALD GARRISON VILLARD PAPERS

B1   5 L. to Richard Beer-Hofmann. 1941-1944 and undated.
     2 L. to Oswald Garrison Villard. 1937-1940.

B2   2 L. from Oswald Garrison Villard. 1932-1938.

University of Iowa, The University Libraries, Special Collections, Iowa City, Iowa 52240.

B1   6 L. to George Sylvester Viereck. 1928 and undated.

University of California at Riverside, Riverside, California 92502.

RAOUL AUERNHEIMER ARCHIVE

B1   6 L. to Raoul Auernheimer. 1940-1943.

University of Southern California, Lion Feuchtwanger Memorial Library, 520 Paseo Miramar, Pacific Palisades, California 90272.

B1   3 L. to Lion Feuchtwanger. 1942-1943.

B2   1 L. from Lion Feuchtwanger. 1942.

Mrs. Elisabeth M. Stoerk and Mrs. Susanne B. Hoeller, 288
Ocean Drive West, Stamford, Connecticut 06902.

FRIDERIKE ZWEIG ARCHIVE

B1   1 L. and 1 Tel. to Friderike Zweig. 1942, 1943.
B2   2 L. from Friderike Zweig. 1942.
        4 L. from Stefan Zweig.

Yale University, Beinecke Rare Book and Manuscript Library,
New Haven, Connecticut 06520.

HERMANN BROCH ARCHIVE

B1   1 L. to Hermann Broch. 1947.
B2   1 L. from Hermann Broch. 1947.

Dr. Gustave O. Arlt, 13220-C Admiralty Way, Marina del Rey,
California 90291.

FRANZ WERFEL ARCHIVE

B1   2 L. to Franz Werfel. 1942.

Yivo Institute, 1048 Fifth Avenue, New York, N.Y. 10028.

HORACE M. KALLEN PAPERS

B1,2   Individual items in folder no. 780.

Mr. Francis Heilbut, 328 West 96th Street, New York, N.Y.
10025.

IVAN HEILBUT PAPERS

B2   Draft of a L. from Ivan Heilbut. A. 1942.

<u>Mrs. Peter M. Lindt</u>, 949 West End Avenue, New York, N.Y.
10025.

C   Ms. submitted to Peter M. Lindt for use on his radio
      program.

JOACHIM MAASS

Writer, 1901-1972

State University of New York at Albany, Department of Germanic Languages and Literatures, 1400 Washington Avenue, Albany, New York 12222.

The following is a description of the literary estate of Joachim Maass. The original materials were deposited at the Deutsches Literaturarchiv, Marbach am Neckar, by Prof. and Mrs. Harry Pfund in 1977. Photocopies of the originals are located at the State University of New York at Albany (JOACHIM MAASS COLLECTION). Researchers may be allowed access to the xeroxed materials at the State University of New York at Albany; however, publication of any novel, novella, essay or book review in toto or the publication of revisions or early versions of any of the materials shall be subject to permission by the Deutsches Literaturarchiv.

Das Folgende stellt eine Beschreibung des literarischen Nachlasses von Joachim Maass dar. Die Originalmaterialien wurden 1977 von Prof. Harry Pfund und seiner Frau dem Deutschen Literaturarchiv, Marbach am Neckar, übergeben. Photokopien dieser Originalmaterialien befinden sich in der State University of New York at Albany (JOACHIM MAASS COLLECTION). Für Forschungszwecke kann Zugang zu diesen abgelichteten Materialien gewährt werden. Die Veröffentlichung jeglicher Novelle, jedes Romans oder Essays oder von Buchkritiker in toto oder die Veröffentlichung von Revisionen früherer Versionen irgendwelcher Teile von Maass' literarischen Materialien bedarf der Erlaubnis des Deutschen Literaturarchivs, Marbach am Neckar.

B1,2   Correspondence with the Kurt Desch Verlag concerning
I   Maass' works. Also contracts.

C1   Carl Schurz. T.cc. with h. corr. 104p.
     "Senator, Innenminister und 'Mugwump'-Fuehrer. [Carl
       Schurz]." T. with numerous h. corr. 36p.
     "Schurz." Partial English Ms. T.cc. with h. corr.
       p. 105-158.
     "Schurz in Deutschland." A. 62p.
     "The Lawmaker. Adventures ... of Carl Schurz." A. 45p.
     "Deutsche Schule 1918. Ein Romankapitel." p. 1-7, 21-26,
       34-39.

<u>Gouffé</u>. A. 90p.
<u>Roman de la Roncière</u>. T. with h. corr. 114p.
"Roman - 2. Band." T.cc. 39p.
<u>La Roncière und Marie Morell</u>. T.cc. 90p. Notes. 12p.
<u>Thomas und Maria</u>. "Erste Fassung." T. 52p.
<u>The Times Collapse</u>. T. with h. corr. 42p.
"True Story?" T.cc. 132p.
<u>Zwischen den Zeiten/Astride the Times</u>. A. and T. Ca.
  150p.
  "Notizen zu Band II 'Zwischen den Zeiten.' Neue Fas-
  sung." A. Ca. 75p.
Untitled Ms. English. T.cc. 147p.

C2   "The Case of Lieutenant de la Roncière. A Television
      Play by Joachim Maass." Translated by Holger Hagen.
      T.cc. 43p.
      <u>Heinrich der Vierte. Tragödie in 2 Teilen (22 Bilder)</u>.
        T. 103p.
      "Die Zwillingsbrüder (Arbeitstitel). Komödie in vier
      Akten." T.cc. 126p.

C3   "Die enge Pforte." Collection of poems. T.cc. Ca. 65p.
      "Frühe handschriftliche Gedichte." Ca. 50p.
      "Gesänge vom guten Geschick." Poems. T. 85p.
      "Handgeschriebene Gedichte." A. and T. 34p.
      "Neue Gedichte." T. 22p. Loose pages. 15p.
      "Vers und Prosa." 4p.
      "Vom lusitanischen Parnaß. Nachdichtungen jüngerer
      portugiesischer Lyrik." 18p.
      Poems. T. 25p.
      Poems. T.cc. Some duplicates. Ca. 150p.

C3,4 "Kleine handschriftliche Arbeiten/handschriftliche
      Gedichte." A. Ca. 100p.

C4   <u>Anjuta oder Die Schule der Armut. I. Teil eines Er-</u>
        <u>zählungsbuchs 'Junge Leute.'</u> T.cc. 48p.
      "Ein Schulmorgen." T. 6p.
      "Das Erwachen." T.cc. 4p.
      "Das Frauenbüchlein. Briefe und Gedichte in Prosa."
      T.cc. 45p.
      "Die Hand des Herrn, oder: Der böse Blick." With the
      note: "Begonnen am 14. Oktober 1946." A. Ca. 95p.
      "Der böse Blick. Eine Erzählung." T. with h. corr.
        36p.

Notes and loose p. T. 13p.
"Die Liebe der Bohème. Eine Erzählung." T.cc. with h.
   corr. 29p.
"The Snow of Nebraska." English tr. T.cc. 2c. 28p. ea.
"Zwarte Nevel." Dutch translation. Mimeo. 50p.

C4,7   Miscellanous short texts. T. Ca. 300p.
        Ms. of short published articles, stories. T. Ca. 200p.

C7   "Imaginierter Toast zu Carl Zuckmayers 50. Geburtstag
        am 27. Dezember 1946." T. and cc. 2c. 8p. ea.
        "Friedo Lampe." T. with h. corr. 6p.
        "Leben, Sterben und Unsterblichkeit Rainer Maria Ril-
        kes. Ein Vortrag." Mount Holyoke College, Nov. 25,
        1940; Haverford College, March 26, 1941; University
        of Pennsylvania, March 25, 1942. T. 25p. plus sev-
        eral Rilke poems.
        "Meetings with Thomas Mann." Incomplete c.
        Lecture notes. 1957. In 3 small (4" x 6") notebooks.
        Haverford lectures. Spring 1957; Spring 1959; Spring
        1961.
        Lectures for the course "Problems of Re-education in
        Post War Germahy." Notes to 8 lectures.
        "Der sechzigjährige Martin Beheim-Schwarzbach." T.cc.
        5p.
        "Thomas Mann. Geschichte einer Liebe im Geiste." T.cc.
        28p. In German.
        "Thomas Mann. An Essay." English tr. T. with h.
        corr. 28p.
        "Vorwort" and "Schlußwort" to an unidentified work.
        T.cc. 12p., 4p.

D4,7   Ca. 20 cl.

D7   "Beiträge fürs Hamburger Freundesblatt." 3 notebooks
        of cl. 1927-1936.
        "Beiträge für die Vossische Zeitung." Notebook of cl.
        1927-1932.
        "Tagebuch-Notiz zu August Strindbergs hundertstem
        Geburtstag am 22. Januar 1949." Offprint (2).

F   2 tapes.

H3,4   Ca. 15 cl.

I   Birth certificate, certificates, letter of award

(Literaturpreis). 12 items.

J   Photos (ca. 20) and caricatures of Maass.
      Photo of Maass' parents.

M   Literaturpreis des Jahres 1961. Bayerische Akademie
      der Schönen Künste.
      Medal in blue box.

KARL O. PAETEL COLLECTION

B1   1 L. to Karl O. Paetel (xerox). 1945.

Harry and Marie Pfund, 624 Overhill Road, Ardmore, Pennsylvania 19003.

Private collection. / *Privatsammlung.*

C1   Das magische Jahr. Ms. A.
      Complete T. version. 356p.
      Part of an earlier version. T. 210p.

C7   "Kriterien der Dichtung." Presented to Harry and Marie
      Pfund, Christmas 1942. Preliminary sketch to Die
      Geheimwissenschaft der Literatur (1949). Written on
      both sides of loose-leaf notebook paper (8.5" x 5.5").
      37p.

University of Pennsylvania, The Charles Patterson Van Pelt Library, Philadelphia, Pennsylvania 19104.

ALMA MAHLER-WERFEL COLLECTION

B1   4 L. to Alma Mahler-Werfel. A. 1945-1949.

Mrs. Elisabeth M. Stoerk and Mrs. Susanne B. Hoeller, 288 Ocean Drive West, Stamford, Connecticut 06902.

FRIDERIKE ZWEIG ARCHIVE

B1   2 L. to Friderike Zweig. 1947.

Mrs. Gertrude Urzidil, 83-39 116th Street, Richmond Hill,
New York 11418.

JOHANNES URZIDIL COLLECTION

B1   2 L. to Johannes Urzidil. T. 1955, 1961.
B2   2 L. from Johannes Urzidil. T.c. 1955, 1961.

Mrs. Alice Loewy Kahler, 1 Evelyn Place, Princeton, New Jersey 08540.

ERICH VON KAHLER COLLECTION

B1   1 L. to Erich von Kahler. 1945.

FRITZ MACHLUP

Economist, 1902-

Prof. Fritz Machlup, 279 Ridgeview Road, Princeton, New Jersey 08540.

Private collection: inaccessible. / *Unzugängliche Privatsammlung.*

A1   Diaries, appointment calendars.

A3   Complete bibliography of all publications.

B1,2 Ca. 25 ft. of correspondence. 1933-present, including L. to and from many other emigrés.

C7   Ms. of unpub. works. Ca. 4 essays.

D7   Offprints of ca. 80 articles.

H4   Several F. of reviews and critiques of Machlup's writings.

K   Personal library.

L   Cl. collection.

ALMA MAHLER-WERFEL

Writer, 1879-1964

University of Pennsylvania, The Charles Patterson Van Pelt
Library, Philadelphia, Pennsylvania 19104.

The ALMA MAHLER-WERFEL ARCHIVE, consisting of 47 boxes of
materials (including over 5,000 L.) plus additional bound
Ms., was received by the University of Pennsylvania in Feb.
1968. All publication rights to the materials are held by
Anna Mahler, daughter of Alma. Although the collection
remains as yet uncatalogued, a catalog of the collection is
presently being prepared for publication by Dr. Glyns Waldman of the University of Pennsylvania German Department.
The following is a description of the Alma Mahler-Werfel
materials in the collection. For a more complete description of the Franz Werfel materials, see under Franz Werfel.

*Das ALMA MAHLER-WERFEL ARCHIVE, das aus 47 Kartons (einschl.
über 5000 Briefe) sowie zusätzlichen gebundenen Manuskripten
besteht, wurde der University of Pennsylvania im Feb. 1968
überlassen. Alle Publikationsrechte ruhen bei Anna Mahler,
der Tochter Alma Mahler-Werfels. Die Sammlung ist z.Zt.
noch nicht katalogisiert, es wird aber von Dr. Glyns Waldman
vom German Department der University of Pennsylvania ein
Katalog zur Veröffentlichung erarbeitet. Es folgt eine Beschreibung der Alma Mahler-Werfel Materialien dieser Sammlung. Eine genauere Beschreibung der Franz Werfel Materialien findet sich unter "Franz Werfel."*

A1   Diaries, 1898-1902. Nos. 4-25, with numerous inserts
      (L., Ptc., drawings, music, poems). 3 B.
      Diaries, 1902-1940s. T. with h. notes. 377p.
      Diary, 1961. Loose-leaf notebook.

A2   Latin notebook.

A3   Ein Leben mit Gustav Mahler. T. with h. corr. Ca. 500p.
      Mein Leben. T. with h. corr. Ca. 500p. Notes. 6p.
      "Lecture Tour in Saxony." Tr. by Gustave Arlt for
      Mein Leben. T. 3p. Also 3 cl.

B1,2 Over 5,000 L., including many L. to and from Franz
      Werfel. Included in the L. by Alma are L. to: T. W.
      Adorno, Gottfried Bermann-Fischer, Walter Gropius,
      Felix Guggenheim, Willy Haas, Benjamin Huebsch,

Franz Kafka, Hertha Pauli, Arnold and Gertrud Schoenberg, Fritz von Unruh, Bruno Walter, Franz Waxman, Kurt Weill, Thornton Wilder, Kurt Wolff, Friderike Zweig.
Drafts of L. by Alma, addressee unknown. Ca. 150p.
C. of L. to and from Gustav Mahler. 1880-1892. p. 20-90. Also English tr. of L. Includes L. to and from: Alma, A. Schoenberg.
Included in the L. to Alma are L. from: T. W. Adorno, Raoul Auernheimer, Julius Bab, Alban Berg, Gottfried Bermann-Fischer, Hermann Borchardt, Hermann Broch, Fritz Busch, Richard Coudenhove-Kalergi, Franz Csokor, Marlene Dietrich, Alfred Döblin, Carl Ebert, Albert Ehrenstein, Paul Elbogen, Lion Feuchtwanger, Frederick Forell, René Fülöp-Miller, Manfred George, Oskar Maria Graf, Walter Gropius, Hans Habe, Kurt Hellmer, Paul Hindemith, Artur Holde, H. E. Jacob, Hans Janowitz, Leopold Jessner, Otto Kallir, Otto Klemperer, Hans Kohn, Annette Kolb, Erich Korngold, Julius Korngold, Ernst Křenek, Alvin Kronacher, Leo Lania, Robert Lantz, Lotte Lehmann, Lotte Lenya, Ernst Lothar, Emil Ludwig, Joachim Maass, Golo Mann, Heinrich Mann, Klaus Mann, Thomas Mann, Ludwig Marcuse, Fritzi Massary, Hans Natonek, Paul Nettl, Alfred Neumann, Robert Neumann, John M. Oesterreicher, Hertha Pauli, Robert Pick, Kurt Pinthus, Erwin Piscator, Hermann Rauschning, Max Reinhardt, Erich Maria Remarque, Curt Riess, Arnold Schoenberg, Gerhart H. Seger, William Steinberg, Ernst Toch, Ernst Toller, Friedrich Torberg, Ludwig Ullmann, Johannes Urzidil, Veit Valentin, Berthold Viertel, Fritz von Unruh, Odo von Württemberg, Bruno Walter, Hans Wilhelm, Emanuel Winternitz, Kurt Wolff, Paul Zech, Guido Zernatto, Otto Zoff, Carl Zuckmayer, Friderike Zweig, Stefan Zweig.
L. from Franz Werfel (including xerox c. of many of the L. from the Franz Werfel Archive, University of California, Los Angeles):
1920-1934, 1944-1945. Xerox c. and cc. Ca. 475p.
1918-1945. T. with h. corr. 292p.
1918. Cc. and xerox. Ca. 100p.
1919. Cc. and xerox. Ca. 100p.
4 L. Undated. A. 10p.

12 L. Xerox c. and cc. 44p.
"Meine Freunde." C. of L. from: Julius Bittner, Max
  Burckhard, Richard and Isi Dehmel, Herbert Eulenberg,
  Gerhart Hauptmann, Friedrich Hirth, Paul Kammerer,
  Otto Klemperer, Josef Labor, Josef Olbrich, Arthur
  Schnitzler, Franz Schrecker, Josef Strzygowski, Ju-
  lius Tandler, Heinrich Tessenow, Erika Tietze (in-
  cluding poems), Hugo von Hofmannsthal. 280p. (1 B.)
71 condolence L. and Tel. 1945.
C. of L. to Alma from Oskar Kokoschka (with commen-
  tary). Ca. 300p.
C. of L. to Alma from: Schoenberg, Weber, Richard
  Strauss and L. Karpath. 1906-1920. 153p.
"Briefe von Hans Pfitzner an Alma Maria Mahler." 154p.

B3   Mahler, Gustav. Tel. from: Burckhard, Gustave Charpen-
  tier, Gerhart Hauptmann, Thomas Mann, Richard
  Strauss.
Correspondences of Morton and Albine Werfel.
Cc. of L. from Werfel and Hofmannsthal to Marie von
  Thurn und Taxis. 4p.
L. re Alma's book, Mein Leben.

C1   Der schimmernde Weg. T.cc. with h. corr. Bound. 614p.

C7   "Alma Mahler-Werfel's Vortrag in Wien am 12. Okt. 47."
  2 cc. 3p. ea.
"Mozart." T. with h. corr. 14p.
"Nachwort" to Werfel's Jeremias. Draft. T.
"Plaidoyer." A. 2p.
"Die vierte Symphonie." Re: Gustav Mahler. Cc. with
  extensive h. corr. 1p. Biographical sketch. Cc. 4p.
Personal notes, drafts, etc. Ca. 150p.

C13   Der Erkennende. Composition with text by Franz Werfel.
  49p.

D13   Fünf Lieder. Printed c. of lyrics and music. 19p.

H3   Miscellaneous cl.

H4   Ein Leben mit Gustav Mahler. Several cl. and reviews.
Mein Leben. Cl. and critical notes.
[Aschkenasy]. "Notizen zu den Memoiren der Alma Maria."
  Undated. T. 6p.

H5   5 short essays. 11p.

I   Lists of possessions in Austria, cl. concerning prop-
erty in Austria. Also related correspondence and
drafts of Alma's L. 30p.
Index of Nachlaß of Carl Moll-Eberstaller. T. and cc.
8p. ea.
Various documents concerning the estate of Franz Werfel.
Gustav Mahler's passport, signature cut out. 1907.
Passports, birth certificates, safe conduct papers,
naturalization papers, other identification papers
for Alma and Franz.
Contracts concerning Gustav Mahler. 6p.
List of royalties for Alma Mahler-Werfel.

J   Snapshots of Alma and Franz Werfel.
Snapshots and formal portraits of Franz Werfel alone.
Snapshots and formal portraits of Alma alone.
Mahler-Werfel houses.
Photos of friends.
Formal portraits of Mahler alone, photos of busts, his
mother.
Snapshot of Schindler with others in studio, photos of
statue.
Album of photos and souvenir Ptc. from Palestine. An-
other album compiled by A. A. Bedikian of photos and
scenes in and around Musa Dagh. Sundry photos not
from Middle East.

L   Collection of materials on the refugee problem, includ-
ing 2 short Werfel Ms.
Collection of materials on religion, including some
Werfel Ms.

M   Gustav Mahler memorabilia. 11 cl., programs, auction
list, list of works, notes.
Schindler memorabilia. 1 Ms., 1 program.
1 B. of sundry Mahler and Werfel "cartes de visites."
Franz Werfel memorabilia, including ca. 15 cl., programs, etc. Also 2 citations.
Miscellaneous memorabilia: cl., cards, programs, etc.

N   C. of Franz Werfel's poems in Alma's hand. A. Ca. 20p.
Auernheimer, Raoul. 1 poem.
Becher, J. R. 1 poem. Undated. T. 1p.
Borchardt, Hermann. "Germany Speaking." 4p.
Conrat-Tietze, Erika. Essay on Mahler. 10p.

Csokor, Franz T. "Das große Wolfslied." Undated. 1p.
"Die Heldenreizerin." About Alma.
"Kalypso." 1942. T. 48p.
Greiner, Leo. Ms.-composition. 3p. Printed composition with notes. 11p.
Klarmann, Adolf. "Franz Werfel und die Bühne." Undated. 7p.
"Franz Werfel." For Collier's Encyclopedia. 1947. 2p.
Lester, Conrad H. "Das Reich des Achilles." Mimeo, with dedication to Alma. 1955. 62p.
Lipiner, Siegfried. Adam. Drama. A.
Malipiero. Torneo Notturno. Ms. A. 26p.
Newlin, Dika. 2 poems in honor of Werfel. 10p.
Redfern, Cecil A. Mimeo. tr. of Mahler's "Lieder," with dedication to Alma. 16p. 3c.
Schoenberg, Arnold. "Über Gustav Mahler." 1911. 27p.
Schueck, Karl. "Illuminated Isle." Dedicated to Alma. 63p.
Specht, Richard. Franz Werfel. Versuche einer Zeitspiegelung. A. 216p.
Thom, Andreas. Das Fräulein. Drama in 4 acts. 65p.
Werfel, Franz. Numerous Ms. of novels, dramas, stories, poems, and essays. Complete description may be found under Werfel.
Wiener, Karl. Ms.-composition dedicated to Alma. 24p.
Wilder, Thornton. "The Drunken Sisters." Cc. with dedication to Alma. 13p.
Zemlinsky, Alexander. "Ahnung Beatrikens." Composition. 3p.

University of California, Los Angeles, Department of Special Collections, 120 Lawrence Clark Powell Library, Los Angeles, California 90024.

FRANZ WERFEL ARCHIVE

82   264 L. and 36 Tel. from Franz Werfel. A. 1918-1945.

Dr. Gustave O. Arlt, 13220-C Admiralty Way, Marina del Rey, California 90291.

FRANZ WERFEL ARCHIVE

B2   Several L., including L. from Irene O. Hay (Unitarian
      Service Committee) and Paul Zsolnay Verlag.

Yale University, Beinecke Rare Book and Manuscript Library,
New Haven, Connecticut 06520.

KURT WOLFF ARCHIVE, EDMOND PAUKER COLLECTION

B1,2 Correspondence between Alma Mahler-Werfel and the Kurt
      Wolff Verlag. 1917-1922. 25 L.

B2   4 L. from Edmond Pauker. 1954.

I   Contract. Ca. 1919/1920. c.
      Embezzled Heaven. Contracts, film rights. 1954.

Library of Congress, Manuscript Division, Independence Avenue
and First Street S.E., Washington, D.C. 20540.

BENJAMIN W. HUEBSCH PAPERS

B1   22 L. and 7 Tel. to B. W. Huebsch. T. and A. 1934-1946
      and undated.

B2   7 L. from B. W. Huebsch. T.cc. 1943-1945.

Columbia University, Butler Library, New York, N.Y. 10027.

B1   9 L. to Harry and Bernardine Kielty Scherman. 1936-
      1945.

University of Texas, Humanities Research Center, Manuscripts
Collection, Box 7219, Austin, Texas 78712.

B1   7 L.

B2   4 L.

I   1 document.

Mrs. Elisabeth M. Stoerk and Mrs. Susanne B. Hoeller, 288 Ocean Drive West, Stamford, Connecticut 06902.

FRIDERIKE ZWEIG ARCHIVE

B1   6 L. and 1 Ptc. to Friderike Zweig. 1942-1950 and
      undated.

Harvard University, Houghton Library, Cambridge, Massachusetts 02138.

RICHARD BEER-HOFMANN COLLECTION, LYONEL FEININGER COLLECTION

B1   2 L. to Richard Beer-Hofmann. 1934.
      1 L. to Lyonel Feininger. A. 1922.

Leo Baeck Institute, 129 East 73rd Street, New York, N.Y. 10021.

B1   2 L. to [Friderike Zweig]. A. 1949 and undated.
H4   Mein Leben. 1 review. 1960.
I   Death notice. 1960.

University of California at Riverside, Riverside, California 92502.

RAOUL AUERNHEIMER ARCHIVE

B1   2 L. to Raoul Auernheimer. 1942-1944.

Southern Illinois University, Morris Library, Department of Special Collections, Carbondale, Illinois 62901.

ERWIN PISCATOR PAPERS

B1   2 L. to Erwin Piscator. A. 1940, 1942.

Indiana University, The University Libraries, The Lilly Library, Bloomington, Indiana 47401.

UPTON BEALL SINCLAIR MSS.

Bl   1 L. and 1 Tel. to Upton Sinclair. 1945.

Mrs. Gertrude Urzidil, 83-39 116th Street, Richmond Hill, New York 11418.

JOHANNES URZIDIL COLLECTION

Bl   1 L. to Johannes Urzidil. A. 1942.

J   1 late photo of Alma Mahler-Werfel.

Syracuse University, The George Arents Research Library, Syracuse, New York 13210.

FRANZ WAXMAN PAPERS

Bl   Several L. to Franz Waxman. 1948-1960.

Mrs. Peter M. Lindt, 949 West End Avenue, New York, N.Y. 10025.

Bl   Small amount of correspondence with Peter M. Lindt.

ERIKA MANN

Writer, 1905-1969

University of Southern California, Lion Feuchtwanger Memorial
Library, 520 Paseo Miramar, Pacific Palisades, California
90272.

B1   5 L. to Lion Feuchtwanger. 1950-1958.

B2   10 L. from Lion Feuchtwanger. 1950-1958.

University of New Hampshire, The Library, Department of Special Collections, Durham, New Hampshire 03824.

OSKAR MARIA GRAF COLLECTION, FRIEDRICH SALLY GROSSHUT COLLEC-
TION

B1   1 L. to Oskar Maria Graf. 1938.
      12 L. to Friedrich Sally Grosshut. T. and A. 1949-1966.

B2   1 L. from F. S. Grosshut. T.c. 1949.

Leo Baeck Institute, 129 East 73rd Street, New York, N.Y.
10021.

LEOPOLD SCHWARZSCHILD COLLECTION, KURT KERSTEN COLLECTION

B1   6 L. to Kurt Kersten. 1939-1949.

B1,2 Correspondence with Leopold Schwarzschild. 1940-1942.

Boston University, Mugar Memorial Library, 771 Commonwealth
Avenue, Boston, Massachusetts 02215.

HANS HABE COLLECTION

B1   1 L. to "R. H." Undated.

C7   Comments by Erika Mann concerning an essay by Thomas
      Mann. Also T. of essay, with verification by Erika
      Mann. Dated Dec. 20, 1961. Pc.

Southern Illinois University, Morris Library, Department of

ERIKA MANN

Special Collections, Carbondale, Illinois 62901.

ERWIN PISCATOR PAPERS

B1   1 L. to Erwin Piscator. 1939.
B2   1 L. from Erwin Piscator. 1940.

Mills College, Library, Oakland, California 94613.

B1   3 L. to Albert Maurice Bender. 1939-1940.

Library of Congress, Manuscript Division, Independence Avenue
and First Street S.E., Washington, D.C. 20540.

REINHOLD NIEBUHR PAPERS

B1   1 L. to Reinhold Niebuhr. T. 1941.
B2   1 L. from Reinhold Niebuhr. T.c. 1941.

University of Texas, Humanities Research Center, Manuscripts
Collection, Box 7219, Austin, Texas 78712.

B1   2 L.

Mr. Hans Sahl, 800 West End Avenue, New York, N.Y. 10025.

B1   Several L. to Hans Sahl.

Mrs. Elisabeth M. Stoerk and Mrs. Susanne B. Hoeller, 288
Ocean Drive West, Stamford, Connecticut 06902.

FRIDERIKE ZWEIG ARCHIVE

B1   1 L. to Friderike Zweig. 1942.

Columbia University, Butler Library, New York, N.Y. 10027.

31   1 L. to Mrs. James Lees Laidlaw. T. 1939.

Princeton University, Firestone Library, Princeton, New Jersey 08540.

LOUIS FISCHER PAPERS

31   1 L. to Louis Fischer. 1941.

Dr. Harold von Hofe, Department of German, University of Southern California, Los Angeles, California 90007.

LUDWIG MARCUSE PALERS

31,2   Correspondence with Ludwig Marcuse.

Barthold Fles Literary Agency, 507 Fifth Avenue, New York, N.Y. 10016.

31   3 L. to Barthold Fles. 1937-1938.

32   6 L. from Barthold Fles. 1937-1938.

Mr. Fritz H. Landshoff, c/o Harry N. Abrams, Inc., Publishers, 110 East 57th Street, New York, N.Y. 10022.

31,2   Correspondence with Fritz H. Landshoff.

HEINRICH MANN

Writer, 1872-1950

The HEINRICH-MANN-ARCHIV was founded in 1963 at the Deutsche Akademie der Künste in Berlin. Heinrich Mann materials in the U.S. are primarily individual items located in the collections of other emigrés or prominent Americans.

Das HEINRICH-MANN-ARCHIV der Deutschen Akademie der Künste in Berlin wurde 1963 gegründet. Heinrich Mann Materialien in den Vereinigten Staaten sind in erster Linie Einzelnummern in den Sammlungen anderer Emigranten oder berühmter amerikanischen Persönlichkeiten.

University of Southern California, Lion Feuchtwanger Memorial Library, 520 Paseo Miramar, Pacific Palisades, California 90272.

B1   18 L. and 2 Tel. to Lion Feuchtwanger. 1937-1949.

B2   24 L. and 2 Tel. from Lion Feuchtwanger. 1925-1949.

C1   Die Jugend des Königs Heinrich IV and Die Vollendung des Königs Heinrich IV. Complete Ms. A.

University of New Hampshire, The Library, Department of Special Collections, Durham, New Hampshire 03824.

OSKAR MARIA GRAF COLLECTION, FRIEDRICH SALLY GROSSHUT COLLECTION

B1   5 L. to Oskar Maria Graf. 1936-1943.

B2   1 L. from Oskar Maria Graf. 1943.

H5   Grosshut, F. S. Essay on Heinrich Mann.

Princeton University, Firestone Library, Princeton, New Jersey 08540.

THOMAS MANN ARCHIVE, BARROWS MUSSY COLLECTION

B1   5 L. to Agnes Speyer-Ulmann. 1911-1912.

HEINRICH MANN

C11   Report on Lidice. Tr. by Mussy.

University of Texas, Humanities Research Center, Manuscripts
Collection, Box 7219, Austin, Texas 78712.

B1   4 L.
B2   1 L.

Yale University, Beinecke Rare Book and Manuscript Library,
New Haven, Connecticut 06520.

KURT WOLFF ARCHIVE

B1   1 L. and 1 Ptc. to Kurt Wolff. A. 1916-1917.

Mrs. Liselotte Stein, 115-25 Metropolitan Avenue, Kew Gardens, New York 11418.

FRED STEIN PAPERS

J   Photos of Heinrich Mann.

Yale University Library, Manuscripts and Archives Research
Room, 150 Sterling Memorial Library, New Haven, Connecticut
06520.

DECISION: A REVIEW OF FREE CULTURE.   CORRESPONDENCE AND
PAPERS OF KLAUS MANN

B1   1 L. to Klaus Mann. 1940.
C   Ms. of article written for Decision magazine.

Dr. Harold von Hofe, Department of German, University of
Southern California, Los Angeles, California 90007.

LUDWIG MARCUSE PAPERS

583

HEINRICH MANN

B1,2   Correspondence with Ludwig Marcuse.

<u>Southern Illinois University</u>, Morris Library, Department of Special Collections, Carbondale, Illinois 62901.

ERWIN PISCATOR PAPERS

B1   1 L. to Erwin Piscator. A. 1941.

B2   1 L. from Erwin Piscator. T.c. 1937.

<u>Mrs. Elisabeth M. Stoerk and Mrs. Susanne B. Hoeller</u>, 288 Ocean Drive West, Stamford, Connecticut 06902.

FRIDERIKE ZWEIG ARCHIVE

B1   L. to Friderike Zweig, filed under "Writers Service Center." 1944.

<u>University of California at Riverside</u>, Riverside, California 92502.

RAOUL AUERNHEIMER ARCHIVE

B1   1 L. to Raoul Auernheimer. 1943.

<u>Hoover Institution on War, Revolution and Peace</u>, Stanford, California 94305.

FRANZ SCHOENBERNER COLLECTION

B1   1 L. to Franz Schoenberner. 1941.

<u>American Philosophical Society</u>, The Library, 105 South Fifth Street, Philadelphia, Pennsylvania 19106.

FRANZ BOAS PAPERS

B1   1 L. to Franz Boas. 1938.

HEINRICH MANN

Yivo Institute, 1048 Fifth Avenue, New York, N.Y. 10028.

HORACE M. KALLEN PAPERS

B1,2   Individual items in folder no. 266. 1934.

University of Pennsylvania, The Charles Patterson Van Pelt
Library, Philadelphia, Pennsylvania 19104.

ALMA MAHLER-WERFEL COLLECTION

B1   1 L. to Alma Mahler-Werfel. 1945.

KLAUS MANN

Writer, 1906-1949

, Manuscripts and Archives Research
Room, 150 Sterling Memorial Library, New Haven, Connecticut
06520.

DECISION: A REVIEW OF FREE CULTURE. CORRESPONDENCE AND PAPERS
OF KLAUS MANN. The Decision magazine papers, 2 archive boxes
(200 items), were purchased from Klaus Mann on Aug. 7, 1942.
A microfilm of the collection is obtainable from the Yale
University Library.

*DECISION: A REVIEW OF FREE CULTURE. CORRESPONDENCE AND PAPERS
OF KLAUS MANN. Diese Materialien, 2 Archivkartons (200 Nummern), wurden am 7. Aug. 1942 von Klaus Mann gekauft. Ein
Mikrofilm der Sammlung ist von der Yale University Library
erhältlich.*

B1   1 L. to Mr. Duell. 1941.
      1 L. to Archibald MacLeish. 1942.
      1 L. to Meyer Weisgal. 1941.

B2   62 L. 1940-1942 and undated, including L. from: Louis
      Adamic, Max Ascoli, Marc Chagall, Albert Einstein,
      Bruno Frank, André Gide, Aldous Huxley, Christopher
      Isherwood, Archibald MacLeish, Heinrich Mann, Thomas
      Mann, Frederick Prokosch, Ezra Pound, Kerker Quinn,
      Robert Sherwood, Stephen Spender, Dorothy Thompson,
      H. W. van Loon, H. G. Wells, Stefan Zweig.

B3   1 L. from Stephen Vincent Benet. Undated.
      1 L.

C7   Editorials written for Decision magazine, including:
      "The Present Greatness of Walt Whitman."
      "What is Wrong About the Anti-Nazi Films."

D12   Galley proofs of the April 1941 issue of Decision.

I   Important legal documents concerning Decision magazine,
      including: certificate of incorporation, official
      audits, contracts and proxy votes.

L   News cl., prospectuses, photos of art works for the
      magazine.

N   Drafts of poems and articles by: Auden, Sir Julian

Huxley, Heinrich Mann, Muriel Rukeyser, Williams, Stefan Zweig, etc.

Yale University, Beinecke Rare Book and Manuscript Library, New Haven, Connecticut 06520.

B1   1 L. to Alfred Stieglitz.

C7   "The Other Germany." 229p.

University of New Hampshire, The Library, Department of Special Collections, Durham, New Hampshire 03824.

OSKAR MARIA GRAF COLLECTION, FRIEDRICH SALLY GROSSHUT COLLECTION

B1   11 L. to Oskar Maria Graf. 1933-1939.
     1 L. to Georg Jacobi. T. 1949.

B2   1 L. from Georg Jacobi. T. 1949.

Barthold Fles Literary Agency, 507 Fifth Avenue, New York, N.Y. 10016.

B1   13 L. to Barthold Fles. 1937-1939, 1945 and undated.

B2   11 L. from Barthold Fles. 1937-1942.

University of Texas, Humanities Research Center, Manuscripts Collection, Box 7219, Austin, Texas 78712.

B1   10 L.

B2   3 L.

I   1 document.

Columbia University, Butler Library, New York, N.Y. 10027.

B1   7 L. to Justin O'Brien. T. 1941.

1 L. to Beatrice Wolff. T. 1939.
1 L. to Leonore Marshall. T. 1941.

Mills College Library, Oakland, California 94613.

B1   7 L. to Albert Maurice Bender. 1935, 1939-1940.

Indiana University, The University Libraries, The Lilly
Library, Bloomington, Indiana 47401.

UPTON BEALL SINCLAIR MSS.

B1   7 L. to Upton Sinclair. 1941-1948 and undated.

Southern Illinois University, Morris Library, Department of
Special Collections, Carbondale, Illinois 62901.

ERWIN PISCATOR PAPERS

B1   2 L. to Erwin Piscator. T. 1939-1940.

B2   1 L. from Erwin Piscator. T.c. 1940.

Leo Baeck Institute, 129 East 73rd Street, New York, N.Y.
10021.

LEOPOLD SCHWARZSCHILD COLLECTION, F. S. GROSSHUT COLLECTION

B3   Correspondence concerning Klaus Mann/Leopold Schwarz-
       schild affair (Schwarzschild's accusation that K.
       Mann was a Communist agent).

H5   Grosshut, F. S. "Der Fall Klaus Mann." 5p.

Dr. Harold von Hofe, Department of German, University of
Southern California, Los Angeles, California 90007.

LUDWIG MARCUSE PAPERS

KLAUS MANN

B1,2   Correspondence with Ludwig Marcuse.

University of Illinois at Urbana-Champaign, University Library, University Archives, Room 19, Urbana, Illinois 61801.

KERKER QUINN PAPERS

B1   Several L. to Kerker Quinn.

Dr. Gustave O. Arlt, 13220-C Admiralty Way, Marina del Rey, California 90291.

FRANZ WERFEL ARCHIVE

B1   1 L. to Franz Werfel. 1940.
B2   1 L. from Franz Werfel. 1941.

Hoover Institution on War, Peace and Revolution, Stanford, California 94305.

FRANZ SCHOENBERNER COLLECTION

B1   1 L. to Franz Schoenberner.

Library of Congress, Manuscript Division, Independence Avenue and First Street S.E., Washington, D.C. 20540.

BENJAMIN W. HUEBSCH PAPERS

B2   1 L. from Benjamin W. Huebsch. T.c. 1945.

University of Pennsylvania, The Charles Patterson Van Pelt Library, Philadelphia, Pennsylvania 19104.

ALMA MAHLER-WERFEL COLLECTION

B1   3 L. (including 1 condolence L.) to Alma Mahler-Werfel. 1937-1945.
H3   1 cl.

589

THOMAS MANN

Writer, 1875-1955

Princeton University, Firestone Library, Princeton, New Jersey 08540.

Thomas Mann manuscripts are held in several different collections. To assist in locating specific pieces, checklists of these collections are available. Manuscripts are accessible to qualified researchers, either in the original or in photocopy at the discretion of the Library. Permission to quote or publish must be the object of a particular request. The collections consisting primarily of original Mann materials are: THOMAS MANN COLLECTION, CAROLINE NEWTON COLLECTION OF THOMAS MANN. Collections that contain material relating to Thomas Mann are: MOLLY SHENSTONE PAPERS RELATING TO THOMAS MANN, CAROLINE NEWTON COLLECTION. Other Mann manuscripts and letters exist as parts of various other correspondence or groups of papers. The following is a summary of the Library's holdings as prepared by Ms. Kim Hunter of Princeton University.

Thomas Mann Manuskripte befinden sich in mehreren verschiedenen Sammlungen. Um bestimmte Einzelstücke zu lokalisieren, sind Listen dieser Sammlungen erhältlich. Manuskripte sind für qualifizierte Forscher entweder im Original oder als Photokopie nach freiem Ermessen der Bibliothek zugänglich. Es ist ein besonderer Antrag erforderlich, wenn man Teile dieser Manuskripte zitieren oder veröffentlichen will. Die THOMAS MANN COLLECTION und die CAROLINE NEWTON COLLECTION OF THOMAS MANN enthalten hauptsächlich Originalmanuskripte; die MOLLY SHENSTONE PAPERS RELATING TO THOMAS MANN und die CAROLINE NEWTON COLLECTION enthalten Materialien, die sich auf Thomas Mann beziehen. Andere Thomas Mann Manuskripte und Briefe sind Teil verschiedener anderer Korrespondenzen und Sammlungen. Es folgt eine Zusammenfassung der Bibliotheksbestände, wie sie von Frau Kim Hunter von der Princeton University erarbeitet wurde.

A3   Untitled biographical lecture Ms. T. with corr. English. 34p.
      Biographical notes.

B1   Ca. 755 L., including L. to: Paul Bekker, Felix Bertaux (64), Julian P. Boyd, Anna Brenner, Whit

Burnett, Richard G. Casey, Joseph Chapiro, Nikolaus Cossmann (22), Edward Cushing, George B. de Huszar, J. R. Bueno de la Torre, Harold W. Dodds, Arthur Eloesser, Fritz Endres, Edward Engel, Ludwig Ewers, Hans Feist, Mrs. Hedwig Fischer, Samuel Fischer, Alexander M. Frey (63), Christian Gauss, Ernst Hanhart, Rudolf Heidler, Harvey W. Hewett-Thayer, Karl Hoenn, Henry Holt, Arthur Huebscher, Arnold Eugene Jenny, Charles H. Jordan, Antoinette von Kahler, Erich von Kahler (58), Alfred Kantorowicz, Robert Klein, Max Krell, John H. H. Lyon, Nelly Mann, Viktor Mann, Frank Jewett Mather Jr., Hans Muehlenstein, Charles Neider (50 + 4 L. from Mann's secretary), Caroline Newton (62), Walter H. Perl, George M. Priest, Paul Raché, Hans Reisiger, George M. Richter (67), Gigi Richter, David Riesman, Carl F. Riter, Robert K. Root, Roger Senhouse, Ronald Gregor Smith, Agnes Speyer-Ulmann (18), Hudson Strode, G. S. Viereck, Ludwig von Hofmann, Hans von Huelsen (102), Hans von Weber, Wolfgang von Weber, Bruno Walter.

B2   L. to Mann from: Whit Burnett, "Colonial Descend," Nikolaus Cossmann, Harold W. Dodds, Alexander M. Frey, Christian Gauss, Henry Holt, Hermann Keyserling, Frank Jewett Mather Jr., Hans von Huelsen, Charles Neider.

B3   Charles Neider correspondence relating to his "On the Stature of Thomas Mann," from many authors. Also correspondence of Neider and Katia, Klaus, and Monica Mann.

C1   Die Betrogene (The Black Swan). Ms. A. German text. 91p.
Der Erwählte (The Holy Sinner). Page proofs (bound). German text.
Lotte in Weimar (The Beloved Returns). Proof sheets. German text. 16p.

C7   Convocation, delivered after receiving honorary degree. Princeton University, May 18, 1939. German text. A. 7p.
"Bemerkungen zu einem Kapitel aus 'Buddenbrooks'." T. with author's corr. (signed). 5p. T.c. with corr. 7p. Both with German text.

"My Relation to Psychoanalysis." T. with corr. English
  text. 2p.
"Richard Wagner und der Ring des Nibelungen." A. Ger-
  man text. 35p.
Royal Highness preface. T.c. English text. 5p.
"The Masters of Buddenbrooks." T.c. Fragment. 1p.
"Mr. X is speaking of the so called Fifth Column . . ."
  A. English text. 1p.
Letter to editorial board of the Stockholm Svenska
  Dagbladet. T. German text, signed. 13p.
Letter to the editor of the Süddeutschen Monatshefte.
  German text. T. with author's corr. 6p. and galley
  proofs.
Lectures:
  "From Childhood Play to 'Death in Venice'." T. with
    author's corr. English text. 19p.
  Untitled (on Magic Mountain). 2 versions, both in
    German. T. and T.c. with corr. 17p. T.c. with
    author's corr. 16p.
Radio broadcasts:
  Radio broadcast to Britain. Dec. 18, 1940. T.c.
    German text. 4p.
  Radio broadcast to Norway, Dec. 31, 1940. T.c. Eng-
    lish text. 3p.
  "Es jaehrt sich der Tag der Zerstoerung . . ." April
    6, 1942 (to Germany through BBC). T.c. (signed).
    German text. 3p.
  "America talks to Australia . . ." Feb. 2, 1943. A.
    German text. 3p.
Statement, 1939, made on the occasion of an interview
  with Albert Hubbell shortly after the German occupa-
  tion of Austria. English text. T. 3p.
"Die Lager." Statement, with confirming text on a tele-
  gram. German text. T.cc. with h. corr. 3p.

D7,   Printed material (by and about Mann).
H3   Cl. 10 items.

J   Pencil sketch of Mann by J. J. Muller, signed by Mann
       and dated by him. 1938.
       12 photos of Mann.

M   Souvenirs.

THE PAPERS OF ALBERT EINSTEIN (1879-1955). For details
concerning the use of this collection, see description under
Albert Einstein.

*THE PAPERS OF ALBERT EINSTEIN (1879-1955). Angaben über den
Zugang zu der Sammlung finden sich unter "Albert Einstein."*

B1,2   Unknown amount of correspondence between Einstein and
         Thomas Mann.

<u>Yale University</u>, Beinecke Rare Book and Manuscript Library,
New Haven, Connecticut 06520.

The THOMAS MANN COLLECTION was established in 1938 by a gift
from Joseph W. Angell, Jr. and has been supplemented by
gifts from Thomas Mann, Mrs. Patricia Lowe Pitzele (daughter
of Mrs. Helen Tracy Lowe-Porter) and others, and by the purchase of Mrs. H. T. Lowe-Porter's collection in 1969.

*Die THOMAS MANN COLLECTION wurde im Jahre 1938 mit einer
Schenkung von Joseph W. Angell, Jr. begründet und ist seitdem erweitert worden durch Schenkungen von Thomas Mann
selbst, von Frau Patricia Lowe Pitzele (der Tochter von Frau
Helen Tracy Lowe-Porter) u.a. sowie durch den Kauf der Sammlung von Frau H. T. Lowe-Porter im Jahre 1969.*

A1   Diary pages. Original German version. T. with h. corr.
         14p.

B1   "Brief an Hermann Grafen Keyserling." A. 22p.
         1 L. to editor of <u>New York Times</u>. T.c. Feb. 4, 1951.
         1 L. to editor of <u>PM</u>. T.c. June 29, 1945.
         1 L. to Mr. Hudson. Undated. A. 3p.
         1 L. to <u>Kopenhagener Zeitung</u>. Undated. A. 3p.
         119 L. and 2 Ptc. to Mrs. Helen Tracy Lowe-Porter.
            A. and T. 1924-1952.
         1 L. to "Rotarlan." 1930. A. 9p.
         1 L. to Dr. Seipel. Undated. A. 4p.
         1 L. to Warsaw P.E.N. Club. Undated. A. 4p.

B2   "Brief aus Feldafing." June 11, 1922. A. 9p.
         "Brief aus München." Sept. 15, 1921. A. 12p.
         4 L. and 1 partial L. from Mrs. Helen Tracy Lowe-Porter.

A. and T.c. 1948-1951.

B3   35 L. including L. by: Helen Tracy Lowe-Porter, Katia Mann, Erwin Panofsky.

C1   Buddenbrooks. Notes. A. 1p.
Doktor Faustus. German version. T. with h. corr. 952p.
"Doktor Faustus in process of translation." Original English tr. T. with corr. by translator. Ca. 1,500p. Final English tr. T. with h. corr. by translator. 731p. Notes. 5p.
Der Erwählte. T. with h. corr. 344p. English version. T. 347p.
Das Gesetz/The Tables of the Law. Original English tr. T. with h. corr. by translator. 90p.
Joseph, der Ernährer. Original German version. T. with numerous h. corr. 512p. Also copy. 512p.
Joseph, the Provider. Final English version. T. with h. corr. by translator and author. 606p.
Der vertauschten Köpfe. Original German version. T.cc. 112p.
The Transposed Heads. Final English tr. T.cc. with h. corr. by translator. 91p. Notes. 1p.
Der Zauberberg. First drafts of 3 different parts. A. 71p. (Restricted.)

C4   "Little Grandma." Original German version. T. with h. corr. 10p.
"Meerfahrt mit Don Quixote"/"Sea-voyage with Don Quixote." Draft of English tr., plus several p. of another version. 73p.
"Der Tod in Venedig." Notes. A. 1p.

C7   "Achtung, Europa!"/"Europe, Beware." Final English tr. T. with numerous h. corr. by translator. 17p.
"Address, Book and Author Luncheon, New York, 9 November, 1938." English tr. T. with numerous h. corr. 8p.
"Anna Karenina." T.cc. 25p.
Speech, given at book market. A. 4p.
English tr. of 3 untitled speeches. T. 4p. T. with h. corr. 7p. T.cc. with h. corr. by translator. May 3, 1936. 33p.
2 untitled German speech texts. T. with h. corr. 8p. T. with h. corr. 11p.

Untitled speech with notation "In England". English
  tr. T. with h. notes by translator. 1p.
"Deutsche Hörer." Original German version of chap.
  "Weihnacht". T. with h. corr. 4p. Original German
  version of chap. "1. Mai 1944". T.
  "Listen, Germany!" Original English tr. of chap.
  "Christmas". T. with h. corr. by translator. 4p.
"Dieser Friede." T.cc. with numerous h. corr. 19p.
Essay on Frans Masereel. A. 6p.
Essay on Goethe's Werther. Original English tr. T.
  with h. corr. and notes. 23p.
Essay on Lessing. Notes. A. 16p.
Essays of Three Decades. Original English tr. T. with
  numerous h. corr. by translator. Ca. 500p.
"Freud und die Zukunft." Original German. T. with h.
  corr. 27p.
  "Freud and the Future." Original English tr. T. with
  h. corr. by translator and notes by author. 26p.
["Gedenkrede an Rathenau"]. A. 9p.
"Gegen die falsche Revolution." Original German. T.
  with h. corr. by author. 6p.
"Goethe." Original German. T. with h. corr. 10p.
"Goethe und Tolstoi." Notes. A. 100p.
"In Memoriam Hugo von Hofmannsthal." A. 7p.
"Kosmopolitismus." A. 9p.
"Der Krieg und die Zukunft." Original German. T. with
  h. corr. 20p.
"Kultur und Sozialismus." A. 14p.
"Lecture on 'Der Zauberberg'." Original English tr. T.
  with h. corr. by translator. 17p.
"Leiden und Größe Richard Wagners." Original German.
  T. with h. corr. 36p.
"Lübeck als geistige Lebensform." A. 26p.
"Maß und Wert." Original German. T. with h. corr. 17p.
"Max Liebermann zum achtzigsten Geburtstag." A. 4p.
"Niemoeller." Original German. T. 8p. Notes. 1p. with
  corr. by H. T. Lowe-Porter.
Notes to Alfred Jeremias' Handbuch der Altorientali-
  schen Geisteskultur, which Mann used in writing his
  Joseph und seine Brüder. A. 4p.
Notes to an untitled essay. A. 5p.
Swarthmore Chapter, Phi Beta Kappa speech. English tr.
  1940. T. 5p.

"Rede, gehalten beim Festessen des P.E.N.-Klubs in
Warschau." A. 7p.
"Rede, gehalten zum Festessen für Ambassador Del Vayo."
English tr. [1940]. T. with h. corr. by translator.
4p.
"Rede über Nietzsche." A. 6p.
Review of André Gide's Si le grain ne meurt——. A. 12p.
"Roosevelt." Incomplete draft of English tr. 5p.
"Schopenhauer." English tr. Mimeo. 32p.
Untitled sketches. A. 11p. A. 7p.
"This Man is My Brother." English tr. A.
"Über die Kunst des Romans." Original German. T. with
h. corr. 18p.
"Über den Film." A. 5p.
"Über Goethes Faust." Original German. T. with h. corr.
45p.
"Goethe's Faust." Original English tr. T. with h.
corr. 60p.
"Ueber The Holy Sinner." T. German and English ver-
sions. 5p. ea.
"Unordnung und frühes Leid." Introduction. A. 3p.
"Vom Geist der Medizin." A. 7p.
"Vom zukünftigen Sieg der Demokratie." Fragment. T.cc.
5p.
Introductions to:
Taped version (for the blind) of Buddenbrooks. Eng-
lish tr. by H. T. Lowe-Porter. T.cc. 3p.
Erika Mann's School for Barbarians. German. T.cc. 5p.
English tr. T.cc. 5p.
Erika and Klaus Mann's Escape to Life. Original Eng-
lish tr. T. 2p.
Hermann Ungar's Colberts Reise. A. 7p.
"Vorwort zu Joseph Conrads Roman 'Der Geheimagent'."
A. 16p.
Order of the Day. "Working sheets." T. 5p. Original
German version. T. with h. corr. 14p. Also 24p.
by H. T. Lowe-Porter.
Royal Highness. English tr. T.cc. with h. corr. by
H. T. Lowe-Porter. 9p.
"What I Believe." English tr. T. and cc. with h. corr.
by translator. 18p.
"Zu Masaryk's Gedächtnis." German version. T.cc. with
h. corr. 5p.

"In Memory of Masaryk." Original English tr. T. with
h. corr. by translator. 6p.
"Zum 60. Geburtstag Ricarda Huchs." A. 6p.

C11   Short biography of Mann's mother. A. 4p.

D7   "An Appeal to Reason." Proofs of English tr.
5 German magazines.
31 English magazines and special issues.
Several hundred newspaper and magazine cl. English.

D10   9 political essays.

E   4 tr. (not English).

H1   Publications on Thomas Mann. 6 items.

H3   Newspaper cl. and special issues. 11 items.
1 F. of newspaper and magazine cl.

H5   Gauss, Christian. Speech given at honorary dinner for
Thomas Mann. 1945. T. 5p.
Jonas, Klaus. Bibliography of Thomas Mann's works.
Rough draft. T.cc. 2p.

N   Lowe-Porter, Helen Tracy. "The Thought and the Deed."

KURT WOLFF ARCHIVE, HERMANN BROCH ARCHIVE, ERNST CASSIRER
MSS. DEPOSIT

B1   6 L. to Hermann Broch. 1945-1951.

B1,2   Correspondence with the Kurt Wolff Verlag. 6 L. 1922-
1936.

H5   Cassirer, Ernst. "Thomas Mann." Notes and drafts. A.
German. "Thomas Mann's Picture of Goethe." Ms. in
German.

Harvard University, Houghton Library, Cambridge, Massachusetts 02138.

RICHARD BEER-HOFMANN COLLECTION, GEORGE SARTON PAPERS,
SCHWEIZER COLLECTION OF GERMAN AUTOGRAPHS, OSWALD GARRISON
VILLARD PAPERS, AUTOGRAPH FILE

B1   1 L. to Richard Beer-Hofmann. 1920.
       7 L. to Henry C. Hatfield. 1947-1951.
       3 L. to George Sarton. 1940-1946.
       1 L. to Oswald Garrison Villard. 1934.
      10 L. 1910-1954. A. and T.

B2   1 L. from George Sarton. 1946.
       2 L. from Oswald Garrison Villard. 1933-1934.

C4   "Meerfahrt mit Don Quixote." A. 70p.

C7   ["Dieser Krieg"]. A. pc. 58p.
      ["Das Ende"]. A. pc. 9p.
      ["Praise of America"]. A. pc. 5p.
      "Vortrag, gehalten in der Vereinigung 'Kadimah'." 1937.
      A. 13p. Another copy. T. 16p.

J   Portrait. Reproduction of photo. Inscribed to Hugo
      Heller.

Library of Congress, Manuscript Division, Independence Avenue
and First Street S.E., Washington, D.C. 20540.

PAPERS OF SIEGFRIED BERNFELD, BENJAMIN W. HUEBSCH PAPERS,
FRANCES ICKES PAPERS, BINGHAM R. NIEBUHR PAPERS and general
archive files

B1   5 L. to Benjamin W. Huebsch. 1933-1948.
       3 L. to Archibald MacLeish. 1940-1949.
       1 L. to Charles Scribner's Sons. 1948.
       1 L. to Paul Zsolnay Verlag. 1933.

B1,2 Correspondence with Reinhold Niebuhr.
      Correspondence with Frances Ickes. Closed.

B2   3 L. from Benjamin W. Huebsch. T.cc. 1940-1948.

C4   "Das Gesetz." 1944. A. 93p.

C7   "Joseph and his brethren." Speech, given at Library
      of Congress, Nov. 17, 1942. T. with h. additions.
      23p.
      "Nietzsche in the light of contemporary events."
      Speech, given at Library of Congress, April 29, 1947.
      T. with h. corr. and additions. 56p.

"The war and the future." Speech, given at Library of
Congress, Oct. 13, 1943. T. with h. additions. 24p.
Research and background notes on Sigmund Freud by
Thomas Mann and Siegfried Bernfeld.

Leo Baeck Institute, 129 East 73rd Street, New York, N.Y.
10021.

JULIUS BAB COLLECTION, WLADIMIR G. ELIASBERG COLLECTION,
GEORG HERMANN COLLECTION, ERICH KAHLER COLLECTION, KURT
KERSTEN COLLECTION, JACOB PICARD COLLECTION, VICTOR POLZER
COLLECTION, KURT GROSSMANN COLLECTION, EFRAIM FRISCH AR-
CHIVES and general archive files

31   2 L. to Julius Bab. A. and pc. 1918, 1927.
        Transcription of L. to Wladimir G. Eliasberg. 1950.
        2 L. to Efraim Frisch. A. pc. 1921.
        2 L. and 2 Ptc. to Georg Hermann. A. 1914, 1930, 1936.
        3 L. to Antoinette Kahler. A. 1940-1947.
        1 L. to Kurt Kersten. 1955.
        1 Ptc. to Jacob Picard. A. 1937.
        3 L. to Victor Polzer. Pc. and 1 transcription. 1938-
        1940 and undated.
        "Vom Geist der Medizin." Open letter to editor of
        Deutsche Medizinische Wochenschrift. 1925. 7p.
        6 L. 1925-1947.

31,2   Thomas Mann - Erich von Kahler. Briefwechsel im Exil.
        Zürich, 1970. 68p. in print.
        Correspondence with Kurt Grossmann.

32   3 L. 1925, 1946.

33   3 L. from Katia Mann to Kurt Kersten. 1940, 1955.
        1 L. from Katia Mann to Leo Baeck Institute. A. 1968.
        3 L. from Hedwig Pringsheim (mother-in-law of Th.
        Mann) to Fritz Mauthner and 1 draft by Mauthner.
        1901-1919.
        Correspondence between Prof. Alfred Vagts, Dr. H.
        Krausnik, Golo Mann and Prof. A. E. Zucker. 16 L.
        1963-1964.

D7   1 cl. and 1 offprint.

H3   12 cl. and 1 special issue on Mann.

H5   Articles on Mann. T.cc. 1962-1968. 9p.

J   Photo of Mann with Hans Reisinger.

Indiana University, The University Libraries, The Lilly
Library, Bloomington, Indiana 47401.

ARTHUR FISHER BENTLEY MSS., LEWIS BROWNE MSS., CYRIL CLEMENS
MSS., JACK HIRSCHMANN MSS., DAVID HERBERT LAWRENCE MSS.,
LUDWIG LEWISOHN MSS., UPTON BEALL SINCLAIR MSS., VIKING PRESS
MSS., ORLO WILLIAMS MSS.

B1   1 L. ea. to Lewis Browne and Upton Sinclair. 1942.
        Signed also by Lion Feuchtwanger, Bruno Frank, Max
        Horkheimer, Erich Maria Remarque, Franz Werfel.
      5 L. and 1 Ptc. to Ludwig Lewisohn. 1927-1931.
      22 L., Tel. and Ptc. to Upton Sinclair. 1936-1946 and
        undated.
      1 L. ea. to Cyril Clemens, Herbert Mar-Cluyton, Warren
        Allen Smith.

B2   1 L. from Upton Sinclair. T.cc. 1941.

B3   2 L. from T. S. Eliot. 1927.
      1 L. from Ernest Hemingway. 1953.
      1 L. from D. H. Lawrence. 1929.

New York Public Library, Manuscript Division, Fifth Avenue
and 42nd Street, New York, N.Y. 10018.

EMERGENCY COMMITTEE IN AID OF DISPLACED FOREIGN SCHOLARS,
A. A. KNOPF ARCHIVE, THEO FELDMAN PAPERS and general archive
files

B1   1 L. to Theo Feldman. A. 1946.

C1   The Beloved Returns. T.
      Joseph und seine Brüder. T.c. 1933-1934.

C7   "Der zukünftige Sieg der Demokratie." Lecture. c. 1937.
        42p.

THOMAS MANN

H4   Collection of reviews.
*   File compiled by the Emergency Committee. 1933-1944.

Colby College, Rare Books and Manuscripts, Waterville, Maine
04901.

B1   12 L. and 2 Ptc. to John Eastman Jr. Also h. dedica-
       tion to Eastman. 60p.
C7   "Vom Buch der Bücher und Joseph." A.

Columbia University, Butler Library, New York, N.Y. 10027.

NICHOLAS MURRAY BUTLER PAPERS, ORAL HISTORY COLLECTION

B1   1 L. to Prinz Hubertus zu Loewenstein. T.c. 1936.
       1 Tel. to N. M. Butler. 1931.
       4 L. to Bishop Francis J. McConnell. T. 1939-1940.
       13 L. 1930-1949.
B2   1 L. from N. M. Butler. T.c. 1931.
       1 L. from Prinz Hubertus zu Loewenstein. T.c. 1936.
C7   Speech on Del Vayo. New York, 1937. T.cc. 4p.
H5   Recollections of Thomas Mann in an interview with
       Alfred Knopf. 1961.

University of New Hampshire, The Library, Department of Special Collections, Durham, New Hampshire 03824.

OSKAR MARIA GRAF COLLECTION, FRIEDRICH SALLY GROSSHUT COL-
LECTION

B1   1 L. and 2 Ptc. to F. S. Grosshut. T. and A. 1936-1950.
       19 L. to O. M. Graf. 1938-1955.
B2   7 L. to O. M. Graf. 1942-1955.

Syracuse University, The George Arents Research Library,
Syracuse, New York 13210.

FRANZ WAXMAN PAPERS, DOROTHY THOMPSON PAPERS

B1   1 L. to Franz Waxman. 1945.
      17 L. to Dorothy Thompson. 1937-1941.

C7   "Manifesto to the Civilized World." T.cc.
      "Richard Wagner and the Ring of the Nibelung." T.
      "To the Civilized World."

University of Southern California, Lion Feuchtwanger Memorial
Library, 520 Paseo Miramar, Pacific Palisades, California
90272.

B1   14 L. and 1 Tel. to Lion Feuchtwanger. 1940-1954.

B2   16 L. and 2 Tel. from Lion Feuchtwanger. 1940-1954.

Ms. Edna Anderson, 16016 San Ysidro Place, Pacific Palisades,
California 90272.

B1   12 L. to Edna Anderson. 1939-1954.

Barthold Fles Literary Agency, 507 Fifth Avenue, New York,
N.Y. 10016.

B1   8 L. to Barthold Fles. 1939-1941.

B2   11 L. from Barthold Fles. 1937-1942.

Rabbi Bernhard N. Cohn, 90 Riverside Drive, New York, N.Y.
10024.

EMIL BERNHARD PAPERS

B1   5 L. to Emil Bernhard. A. 1942-1946.
      4 L. to Grete Cohn (wife of Bernhard). 1950-1951.

Mills College, Library, Oakland, California 94613.

B1   10 L. to Albert Maurice Bender. 1938-1940.

C7   "Politik und Kultur." With the comment "Weihnachten
      1939". A. 11p.

University of California at Riverside, Riverside, California
92502.

RAOUL AUERNHEIMER ARCHIVE

B1   13 L. to Raoul Auernheimer (10 on microfilm). 1938-
      1945.

University of Minnesota, University Libraries, Social Welfare
History Archives, Minneapolis, Minnesota 55455.

SURVEY ASSOCIATES PAPERS

B1,2 Correspondence with Survey Associates. 10 L. 1939-1941.
C7   Transcription of speech. Ca. 1939-1941. Mimeo.
F   "The Problems of Freedom." Tape recording of speech.
      Feb. 15, 1940.

American Academy of Arts and Letters/National Institute of
Arts and Letters, 633 West 155th Street, New York, N.Y.
10032.

A3   Ms. of biographical sketch.

B1,2 Correspondence with the American Academy of Arts and
      Letters.

H3   Wilder, Thornton. Tribute to Thomas Mann, given at a
      special meeting of the Academy, May 23, 1956.

Boston University, Mugar Memorial Library, 771 Commonwealth
Avenue, Boston, Massachusetts 02215.

MEYER LEVIN PAPERS, ROBERT LEWIS SHAYON PAPERS, HANS HABE
COLLECTION

603

B1   1 L. ea. to Meyer Levin (1950) and W. C. Peebles
(1935).
1 Tel. to Robert Lewis Shayon. 1946.

B2   1 L. from Harlow Shapley. T. 1946.

C7   Unpub. essay. Christmas gift from the Mann family to
Hans Habe. 1961. A. pc. 2p. Accompanied by comments
and verification by Erika Mann on the essay, dated
Dec. 20, 1961. Pc.

University of Pennsylvania, The Charles Patterson Van Pelt
Library, Philadelphia, Pennsylvania 19104.

ALMA MAHLER-WERFEL COLLECTION

B1   3 L. and 1 Tel. to Alma Mahler-Werfel. 1947-1948.

B2   2 L. from Arnold Schoenberg. 1948. Also cl.
1 L. from Annemarie Burchard. T.cc. 1948.

D7   Obituary for Franz Werfel.

F   Recording by Franz Werfel re: relationship between
Schoenberg and Thomas Mann.

State University of New York at Albany, Department of Germanic Languages and Literatures, 1400 Washington Avenue,
Albany, New York 12222.

STORM PUBLISHERS ARCHIVE, HELMUT HIRSCH COLLECTION, JOACHIM
MAASS COLLECTION

B1   3 L. to Alexander Gode von Aesch. 1946-1951.
Transcription of L. to Dr. Weinberg. Undated.
1 L. to Helmut Hirsch. pc. 1946.

B2   1 L. from Alexander Gode von Aesch. 1946.

H5   Maass, Joachim. "Meeting with Thomas Mann." Incomplete
c.
"Thomas Mann. Geschichte einer Liebe im Geiste."
T.cc. 28p. In German.
"Thomas Mann. An Essay." English tr. with h. corr.
28p.

Mrs. Gertrude Urzidil, 83-39 116th Street, Richmond Hill, New York 11418.

JOHANNES URZIDIL COLLECTION

B1   4 L. to Johannes Urzidil. T. and A. 1941-1948.

Immigration History Research Center of the University of Minnesota, 826 Berry Street, St. Paul, Minnesota 55101.

AMERICAN COUNCIL FOR EMIGRÉS IN THE PROFESSIONS ARCHIVES

B1   1 L. to Mrs. Henry Canby. 1946.
     1 L. to Leland Rex Robinson. 1945. c.
     1 L. to Else Staudinger. 1945.
B2   1 L. from Else Staudinger. 1945.

American Philosophical Society, The Library, 105 South Fifth Street, Philadelphia, Pennsylvania 19106.

FRANZ BOAS PAPERS

B1   1 L. to Franz Boas. 1940.
B2   2 L. from Franz Boas. 1938.

Buffalo and Erie County Public Library, Lafayette Square, Buffalo, New York 14203.

B1   1 L. to Mark van Doren. 1945.
C7   "Rede auf Alvin Johnson." Speech on the occasion of the 70th birthday of Alvin Johnson. New York, 1944. A. 6p.

Cornell University, John M. Olin Library, Department of Manuscripts and University Archives, Ithaca, New York 14850.

B1   1 L. to "Blanche." 1948.

THOMAS MANN

1 L. to Imre Domonkos. 1934.

University of Iowa, The University Libraries, Special Collections, Iowa City, Iowa 52240.

B1   1 L. to George Sylvester Viereck. 1930.
      1 L. to Erich Funke. 1945.

Mrs. Lotte Lenya Weill-Detwiler, 404 East 55th Street, New York, N.Y. 10022.

B1   Correspondence between Thomas Mann and family and Kurt Weill.

Harvard University, Harvard Divinity School, Andover-Harvard Theological Library, 45 Francis Avenue, Cambridge, Massachusetts 02138.

PAUL TILLICH COLLECTION

B1   2 L. to Paul Tillich. A. and T. 1934, 1939.

B2   1 L. from Paul Tillich. T.c. 1943.

Southern Illinois University, Morris Library, Department of Special Collections, Carbondale, Illinois 62901.

ERWIN PISCATOR PAPERS

B1   1 L. to Erwin Piscator. 1939. pc.

B2   3 drafts of L. from Erwin Piscator. 1938-1939.

Academy of Motion Picture Arts and Sciences, Margaret Herrick Library, 9038 Melrose Avenue, Hollywood, California 90069.

H3   11 newspaper and magazine cl.

'ivo Institute, 1048 Fifth Avenue, New York, N.Y. 10028.

IORACE M. KALLEN PAPERS

1,2 Individual items located in folders: 284, 901. 1949-1950.

Jniversity of California, Santa Barbara, The Library, Santa Barbara, California 93105.

.OTTE LEHMANN COLLECTION

1,2 Correspondence with Lotte Lehmann.

Bruno Walter Memorial Foundation, c/o Miss Susie Danziger, .15 East 72nd Street, New York, N.Y. 10021.

1,2 Correspondence between Thomas Mann and Bruno Walter.

California Institute of Technology, Robert A. Millikan Library, Pasadena, California 91109.

1,2 Item(s) in 1 F. 1938.

Ir. Hans Sahl, 800 West End Avenue, New York, N.Y. 10025.

1 Several L. to Hans Sahl.

Ioover Institution on War, Revolution and Peace, Stanford, California 94305.

KARL BOROMAEUS FRANK COLLECTION

1,2 Correspondence with Karl Frank.

Jniversity of California, Los Angeles, Music Library, 405 Iilgard Avenue, Los Angeles, California 90024.

ERNST TOCH ARCHIVE

B1   Several L. to Ernst Toch.

Mrs. Elisabeth M. Stoerk and Mrs. Susanne B. Hoeller, 288
Ocean Drive West, Stamford, Connecticut 06902.

FRIDERIKE ZWEIG ARCHIVE

B1   2 L. to Friderike Zweig. T.cc. 1942, 1949.

University of Illinois at Urbana-Champaign, University Library, University Archives, Room 19, Urbana, Illinois 61801.

KERKER QUINN PAPERS

B1   L. to Kerker Quinn.

Oberlin College Library, Oberlin, Ohio 44074.

B1   1 card to the University. 1p.

Minnesota Historical Society, 690 Cedar Street, St. Paul,
Minnesota 55101.

JAMES GRAY PAPERS

B1   1 L. to James Gray. 1947.

Duke University, William R. Perkins Library, Manuscript
Department, Durham, North Carolina 27706.

BENNET HARRIS BRANSCOMB PAPERS

B1   1 L. to Bennett Harris Branscomb. 1940.

Yale University Library, Manuscripts and Archives Research

Room, 150 Sterling Memorial Library, New Haven, Connecticut 06520.

DECISION: A REVIEW OF FREE CULTURE. CORRESPONDENCE AND PAPERS OF KLAUS MANN

B1   1 L. and 1 Tel. to Klaus Mann. 1941.

Dr. Harold von Hofe, Department of German, University of Southern California, Los Angeles, California 90007.

LUDWIG MARCUSE PAPERS

B1,2   Correspondence between Ludwig Marcuse and Thomas and Katia Mann.

Dr. Friedrich J. Hacker, The Hacker Clinic, 160 Lasky Drive, Beverly Hills, California 90212.

B1,2   Correspondence between Friedrich Hacker and Thomas Mann and family.

Mrs. Liselotte Stein, 115-25 Metropolitan Avenue, Kew Gardens, New York 11418.

FRED STEIN PAPERS

J   Photos of Thomas Mann.

Prof. Kurt H. Wolff, 58 Lombard Street, Newton, Massachusetts 02158.

B1,2   Correspondence with Kurt H. Wolff.

University of Chicago, The Joseph Regenstein Library, 1100 East 57th Street, Chicago, Illinois 60637.

JAMES FRANCK PAPERS and general archive files

B1,2   Correspondence with James Franck.
Correspondence related to the Committee to Frame a
World Constitution. 1 F.

Mr. Stephan Lackner, 601 El Bosque Road, Santa Barbara, California 93105.

H5   Lackner, Stephan. "Thomas Mann äußert sich zu dieser
Zeit." 1935. Unpub. statement (after Th. Mann's
wishes) of a conversation between Lackner and Mann
in Aug. 1935. The statement was written for Das
Neue Tage-Buch.

Dr. Hans Speier, 167 Concord Avenue, Hartsdale, New York
10530.

B1   1 L. concerning Hans Speier.

Profs. Gertrud and Walter Weisskopf, Sharon Park Drive,
Menlo Park, California 94025.

B1   1 L.

Dr. Clementine Zernik, 225-10 106th Avenue, Queens Village,
New York 11429.

B1   L. to Arnold Höllriegel. 1938-1939.

Mrs. Peter M. Lindt, 949 West End Avenue, New York, N.Y.
10025.

B1   Small amount of correspondence with Peter M. Lindt.

C   Ms. submitted to Lindt for use on his radio program.

Mrs. Alice Loewy Kahler, 1 Evelyn Place, Princeton, New Jersey 08540.

ERICH VON KAHLER COLLECTION

5   Kahler, Erich von. "Motif and Motive. The Origins of
       Thomas Mann's 'Doctor Faustus'." Lecture. Princeton
       University, 1960. T. with h. corr. 27p.

HERBERT MARCUSE

Philosopher, 1898-

Prof. Herbert Marcuse, Department of Philosophy, University
of California San Diego, La Jolla, California 92037.

Private collection: inaccessible. / *Unzugängliche Privatsammlung.*

B1,2   Business correspondence concerning the Institute for
       Social Research, primarily from the New York period.
       Also c. of the Joseph Maier materials in New York
       City.
       Correspondence with individuals, including lengthy cor-
       respondences with: T. W. Adorno (until 1969), Max
       Horkheimer, Leo Lowenthal, Franz Neumann (small
       amount), Friedrich Pollock.
       Very few c. of L. by Marcuse, except in the case of
       business matters (publications, etc.).

C7   Ms. and notes to lectures and seminars.
       "Nachruf an Adorno." T. 4p.

D7,   Numerous cl. as well as substantial collection of off-
H3   prints of his articles.

H4   Files of reviews of Marcuse's works.

I   Documents.

J   Numerous photos, many of which were used in his biogra-
       phy (Rowohlt).

K   Personal library.

L   Materials used for lectures and seminars (since ca.
       1960).
       Miscellaneous offprints and cl.

Harvard University, Harvard Divinity School, Andover-Harvard
Theological Library, 45 Francis Avenue, Cambridge, Massachusetts 02138.

PAUL TILLICH COLLECTION

B1   1 L. ea. to Paul and Hannah Tillich. 1960, 1965.

B2   2 L. from Paul Tillich. T. 1960.

C7   Remarks at the meeting of the Members of the Social
       Studies Association. Also minutes. [1958]. 40p.

Harvard University, Houghton Library, Cambridge, Massachusetts 02138.

LEO LOWENTHAL COLLECTION

B2   6 L. from Leo Lowenthal. 1946-1951.

Leo Baeck Institute, 129 East 73rd Street, New York, N.Y.
10021.

J   3 photos of Herbert Marcuse. Frankfurt am Main, 1966.

New York Public Library, Manuscript Division, Fifth Avenue
and 42nd Street, New York, N.Y. 10018.

EMERGENCY COMMITTEE IN AID OF DISPLACED FOREIGN SCHOLARS,
1933-1945

*   File compiled when assistance was granted. 1939-1944.

Mrs. Alice Loewy Kahler, 1 Evelyn Place, Princeton, New
Jersey 08540.

ERICH VON KAHLER COLLECTION

B1   1 L. to Erich von Kahler. 1965.

B2   1 L. from Erich von Kahler. 1965.

LUDWIG MARCUSE

Writer, 1894-1971

Dr. Harold von Hofe, Department of German, University of
Southern California, Los Angeles, California 90007.

The LUDWIG MARCUSE PAPERS in Dr. von Hofe's possession re-
sulted partially from gifts from Marcuse and from Gerhard
Szczesny (literary co-executor with von Hofe), partially
from von Hofe's own correspondence with Marcuse, and partially from photocopies of Marcuse letters in private collections of others. Many of the more important letters have
been edited and published in: Harold von Hofe, Briefe von
und an Ludwig Marcuse (Zürich: Diogenes, 1975). 400p.

*Die LUDWIG MARCUSE PAPERS im Besitz von Professor von Hofe
sind aus folgenden Quellen entstanden: Schenkungen von Ludwig Marcuse und von Gerhard Szczesny (zusammen mit von Hofe
literarischer Nachlaßverwalter), Hofes eigene Korrespondenz
mit Marcuse, Photokopien von Marcuse-Briefen in anderen
Privatsammlungen. Viele der bedeutenderen Briefe sind veröffentlicht worden: Harold von Hofe, Briefe von und an Ludwig
Marcuse (Zürich: Diogenes, 1975), 400p.*

A1 Diaries, also containing some rough drafts and aphor-
    isms.

B1 Lengthy correspondence with Harold von Hofe. Ca. 450p.

B1,2 Numerous L. to and from Marcuse, including L. to and
    from: Alfred and Erna Döblin, Bruno Frank, Erich
    Kästner, Hermann Kesten, Erika Mann, Heinrich Mann,
    Klaus Mann, Thomas and Katia Mann, Fritzi Massary,
    Alfred Neumann, Robert Neumann, Kurt Pinthus, Joseph
    Roth, Bruno Walter, Stefan Zweig.

C7 Ms. of articles by Marcuse.

H4 Reviews from German, Swiss and Austrian newspapers.

I   Documents concerning Marcuse's emigration.

J   Photos.

Leo Baeck Institute, 129 East 73rd Street, New York, N.Y.
10021.

KURT KERSTEN COLLECTION, KURT HIRSCHFELD COLLECTION, LEOPOLD
SCHWARZSCHILD COLLECTION and general archive files

B1   52 L. and 1 Ptc. to Kurt Kersten. 1946-1950.
        Marcuse's reply to "Questionnaire about the Theatre."
        1 L. and 1 Ptc. to Dr. Lutz Weltmann. T. 1954, 1959.
        Correspondence with Leopold Schwarzschild.
D7   8 cl. 1960-1964.

University of Southern California, Lion Feuchtwanger Memorial
Library, 520 Paseo Miramar, Pacific Palisades, California
90272.

B1   4 L. to Lion Feuchtwanger. 1937.
B2   2 L. from Lion Feuchtwanger. 1937.

University of New Hampshire, The Library, Department of Special Collections, Durham, New Hampshire 03824.

OSKAR MARIA GRAF COLLECTION, FRIEDRICH SALLY GROSSHUT COL-
LECTION

B1   1 L. to Oskar Maria Graf. 1954.
        2 L. to Friedrich Sally Grosshut. 1953-1954.

University of Pennsylvania, The Charles Patterson Van Pelt
Library, Philadelphia, Pennsylvania 19104.

ALMA MAHLER-WERFEL COLLECTION

B1   2 L. and 2 Tel. to Alma Mahler-Werfel. 1943 and un-
        dated.

New York Public Library, Manuscript Division, Fifth Avenue
and 42nd Street, New York, N.Y. 10018.

EMERGENCY COMMITTEE IN AID OF DISPLACED FOREIGN SCHOLARS,
1933-1945

LUDWIG MARCUSE

*   File compiled, no assistance given. 1942-1944.

<u>Yivo Institute</u>, 1048 Fifth Avenue, New York, N.Y. 10028.

UNITED SERVICE FOR NEW AMERICANS ARCHIVE

I   Immigration documents. File no. 3246.

<u>Southern Illinois University</u>, Morris Library, Department of
Special Collections, Carbondale, Illinois 62901.

ERWIN PISCATOR PAPERS

B1   1 L. to Erwin Piscator. T. 1963.

B2   1 L. from Erwin Piscator. T.cc. 1963.

<u>Mr. Hans Sahl</u>, 800 West End Avenue, New York, N.Y. 10025.

B1   Several L. to Hans Sahl.

<u>Harvard University</u>, Harvard Divinity School, Andover-Harvard
Theological Library, 45 Francis Avenue, Cambridge, Massachusetts 02138.

PAUL TILLICH COLLECTION

B1   1 L. to Paul Tillich. T. 1960.

<u>University of Texas</u>, Humanities Research Center, Manuscripts
Collection, Box 7219, Austin, Texas 78712.

B1   1 L.

<u>Mr. Henry Koster</u>, 1216 N. Lachman Lane, Pacific Palisades,
California 90272.

C7   Ms. of Marcuse's <u>Plato</u>.

<u>Barthold Fles Literary Agency</u>, 507 Fifth Avenue, New York,
N.Y. 10016.

B1   1 L. to Barthold Fles. 1940.

MARIA GOEPPERT MAYER

Physicist, 1906-

University of California San Diego, Mandeville Library,
Department of Special Collections, La Jolla, California
92037.

The MARIA MAYER COLLECTION, 2 archive boxes of materials,
was given to the University in 1972.

*Die MARIA MAYER COLLECTION, bestehend aus zwei Archivkartons
mit Materialien, wurde der Universität im Jahre 1972 überlassen.*

A3,   Documentation concerning trips taken by Maria Mayer.
I

B1,2   Ca. 510 L. with individuals (including E. Teller, E.
       Wigner, H. Jensen), organizations and institutions.

C7,8   Scientific and mathematical notes.
       Lecture notes.

C8   Ca. 60 Ms. of articles.

D8   Offprints of works by Maria Mayer.

H3   Cl. about Maria Mayer.

I   Documents concerning the career of Maria Mayer.

J   Photos.

L   Miscellaneous offprints, cl.

M   Memorabilia.

Prof. Joseph E. Mayer, Prof. Emeritus of Chemistry, University of California San Diego, La Jolla, California 92037.

A3   Written account of the Mayers' trip across the U.S.,
       addressed to Max Born.

B1   L. written to Joseph Mayer from Germany in the 1930s.

B2   Born, Max. Ca. 70p. of L. to and from Joseph and Maria
       Mayer. [1920-1937].

I   Documents: old passports, etc.

M   Memorabilia: Nobel medal, silver replica of Nobel
      medal, certificates in frames, etc.

Archive for History of Quantum Physics (locations in U.S.:
Bancroft Library, University of California, Berkeley; American Philosophical Society, Philadelphia, Pennsylvania; American Institute of Physics, New York, N.Y.).

C7   Interview by Maria Mayer of James Franck and Herta
      Sponer. Transcript. 1962. 115p.

C8   Notes taken from Max Born's lecture "Kinetische Gas-
      theorie." Göttingen, 1928. 128p.

G   Transcript of one interview session. 1962. 9p.

Duke University, William R. Perkins Library, Manuscript
Department, Durham, North Carolina 27706.

FRITZ WOLFGANG LONDON PAPERS

B2   3 L. from Fritz London. cc. 1952.

University of Chicago, The Joseph Regenstein Library, 1100
East 57th Street, Chicago, Illinois 60637.

JAMES FRANCK PAPERS

B1,2   Correspondence between Maria Mayer and James Franck.

B1,   L. of congratulations to Franck on his 70th birthday.
J   1952. Accompanied by photo of Maria and Joseph E.
        Mayer.

J   Group photo. Franck Memorial Symposium. Chicago, 1966.

WALTER MEHRING

Poet, Writer, 1896-

Walter Mehring is living, as of 1977, in Switzerland, where,
the Project assumes, he retains materials of historical interest regarding his career.

*Walter Mehring lebt z.Zt. (1977) in der Schweiz, wo er ver-
mutlich Materialien über seine Laufbahn, die von historischem Interesse sind, aufbewahrt.*

Southern Illinois University, Morris Library, Department of
Special Collections, Carbondale, Illinois 62901.

ERWIN PISCATOR PAPERS

B1   8 L. and 1 Tel. to Erwin Piscator. 1937-1963.

B2   10 L. from Erwin Piscator. T.cc. 1937-1963.

C2   Rally of Hope. Various versions, presumably by Mehring.
       T. with commentary by Piscator and Chouteau Dyer.
       4 F.

D2   Rally of Hope. 4 scriptbooks.

Columbia University, Butler Library, New York, N.Y. 10027.

VARIAN FRY PAPERS

B1   7 L. to Varian Fry. 1941-1944.

B2   4 L. from Varian Fry. 1941-1944.

Leo Baeck Institute, 129 East 73rd Street, New York, N.Y.
10021.

KURT KERSTEN COLLECTION and general archive files

B1   3 L. to Kurt Kersten. 1956 and undated.

H3   1 cl. 1961.

J   Photo of Mehring in photo album.

WALTER MEHRING

O   Program for a lecture by Mehring. 1961. 4p.

Yale University, Beinecke Rare Book and Manuscript Library, New Haven, Connecticut 06520.

KURT WOLFF ARCHIVE

B1   3 L. to the Kurt Wolff Verlag. 1921-1922.

B2   2 L. from the Kurt Wolff Verlag. 1921-1922.

State University of New York at Albany, Department of Germanic Languages and Literatures, 1400 Washington Avenue, Albany, New York 12222.

KARL O. PAETEL COLLECTION

B1   2 L. to Karl O. Paetel (xerox). 1945, 1952.

Library of Congress, Manuscript Division, Independence Avenue and First Street S.E., Washington, D.C. 20540.

J. ROBERT OPPENHEIMER PAPERS

B2   1 L. from J. Robert Oppenheimer. T.c. 1949.

Mr. Hans Sahl, 800 West End Avenue, New York, N.Y. 10025.

B1   Several L. to Hans Sahl.

University of Southern California, Lion Feuchtwanger Memorial Library, 520 Paseo Miramar, Pacific Palisades, California 90272.

B1   1 L. to Lion Feuchtwanger. 1949.

B2   1 L. from Lion Feuchtwanger. 1949.

WALTER MEHRING

<u>Mrs. Gertrude Urzidil</u>, 83-39 116th Street, Richmond Hill, New York 11418.

JOHANNES URZIDIL COLLECTION

B1   1 L. to Johannes Urzidil. A. 1968.

<u>University of Texas</u>, Humanities Research Center, Manuscripts Collection, Box 7219, Austin, Texas 78712.

B1   1 L.

<u>Museum of Modern Art</u>, The Library, 11 West 53rd Street, New York, N.Y. 10019.

HANS RICHTER ARCHIVE: written permission to use the Archive is required in advance of visits to the Museum.

HANS RICHTER ARCHIVE: Vor Besuch des Archivs muß eine schriftliche Genehmigung eingeholt werden.

B1   2 L. to Hans Richter. 1959 and undated.

B2   1 L. from Hans Richter. Undated.

<u>Princeton University</u>, Firestone Library, Princeton, New Jersey 08540.

THE PAPERS OF ALBERT EINSTEIN (1879-1955). For details concerning the use of this collection, see description under Albert Einstein.

THE PAPERS OF ALBERT EINSTEIN (1879-1955). Angaben über den Zugang zu der Sammlung finden sich unter "Albert Einstein."

B1,2 Unknown amount of correspondence between Einstein and Mehring.

<u>Mr. E. B. Ashton</u>, 102 Woodhull Road, Huntington, New York 11743.

B1   Correspondence with Hertha Pauli.

<u>Prof. John M. Spalek</u>, 23 Pheasant Lane, Delmar, New York 12054.

B1,2 Correspondence with John M. Spalek concerning Ernst Toller.

ERICH MENDELSOHN

Architect, 1887-1953

The rather substantial archive of architect Erich Mendelsohn, surveyed by the Editor in 1974, has now been transferred to the Staatliche Museen deutscher Kulturbesitz, Abteilung: Kunstbibliothek, c/o Prof. E. Berckenhagen, Jebenstraße 2, 1 Berlin 12, West Germany. The widow of Erich Mendelsohn, Mrs. Louise Mendelsohn of San Francisco, made the decision for the transfer. A preliminary inventory of these archives is available through the Editor.

Das ziemlich umfangreiche Archiv des Architekten Erich Mendelsohn (so wie es 1974 von uns aufgenommen wurde) ist jetzt an die Staatliche Museen deutscher Kulturbesitz, Abteilung Kunstbibliothek, c/o Prof. Dr. E. Berckenhagen, Jebenstraße 2, 1 Berlin 12, BRD, übergegangen. Die Witwe Erich Mendelsohns, Frau Louise Mendelsohn (San Franzisko), entschied sich für diese Übergabe. Ein vorläufiges Verzeichnis dieses Archivs ist von uns erhältlich.

University of Illinois at Chicago Circle, Department of Architecture and Art, Chicago, Illinois 60680.

B1,2   Correspondence. 1947-1950.

Harvard University, Houghton Library, Cambridge, Massachusetts 02138.

LYONEL FEININGER COLLECTION and autograph files

B1   2 L. to Lyonel Feininger. 1921-1930.
       2 L. to Sir William Rothenstein. 1936-1937.

Library of Congress, Manuscript Division, Independence Avenue and First Street S.E., Washington, D.C. 20540.

BENJAMIN W. HUEBSCH, PAPERS OF LUDWIG MIES VAN DER ROHE

B1   2 L. to B. W. Huebsch. A. 1926-1942.

B1,2   Correspondence with Ludwig Mies van der Rohe. 1949-1955.

B2   1 L. from B. W. Huebsch. T.c. 1942.

Leo Baeck Institute, 129 East 73rd Street, New York, N.Y.
10021.

H3   1 cl. 1959.

J   1 framed photo. Ca. 1930.

KARL MENGER

Mathematician, 1902-

<u>Prof. Karl Menger</u>, 5506 North Wayne Avenue, Chicago, Illinois 60640.

Prof. Menger has designated that his entire collection be willed to a colleague upon his death. Until that time, the materials will remain closed to the public.

Prof. Menger hat bestimmt, daß seine Materialsammlung bei seinem Tode vollständig einem Kollegen zukommt. Bis zu dem Zeitpunkt sind die Materialien für die Öffentlichkeit nicht zugänglich.

C7	Ms. of shorter prose writings. Ms. of unpub. work on the history of the Vienna Circle. Ca. 200p.
C7, L	Limited amount of seminar materials.
D7	Collection of offprints of Menger's publications.
F	Several tapes of talks, lectures, given by Menger.
I	Miscellaneous documents.
K	Mathematics library. Also philosophy annex to library.
L	Offprints of colleagues, arranged alphabetically. Up until 1922-1923.

<u>Library of Congress</u>, Manuscript Division, Independence Avenue and First Street S.E., Washington, D.C. 20540.

OSWALD VEBLEN PAPERS

B1	21 L. to Oswald Veblen. A. and T. 1930-1939 and undated.
B2	13 L. from Oswald Veblen. T.c. 1930-1938.
B3	1 L. 1934.

<u>New York University</u>, Courant Institute of Mathematical Sciences, Library, 251 Mercer Street, New York, N.Y. 10012.

KARL MENGER

B1,2   File: "Karl Menger." 1938-1944.

American Philosophical Society, The Library, 105 South Fifth
Street, Philadelphia, Pennsylvania 19106.

WARREN STURGIS MCCULLOCH PAPERS

B1,2   Correspondence between Menger and W. S. McCulloch.

Northwestern University, Mathematics Department, Evanston,
Illinois 60201.

B1   1 L. to H. T. Davis. 1949.

California Institute of Technology, Robert A. Millikan
Library, Pasadena, California 91109.

THEODORE VON KARMAN CORRESPONDENCE

B1,2   Correspondence with Theodore von Karman. 1938-1943.
       1 F.

Princeton University, Firestone Library, Princeton, New
Jersey 08540.

THE PAPERS OF ALBERT EINSTEIN (1879-1955). For details
concerning the use of this collection, see details under
Albert Einstein.

*THE PAPERS OF ALBERT EINSTEIN (1879-1955). Angaben über
den Zugang zu der Sammlung finden sich unter "Albert Einstein."*

B1,2   Unknown amount of correspondence between Albert Ein-
       stein and Karl Menger. 1953.

LUDWIG MIES VAN DER ROHE

Architect, 1886-1969

Museum of Modern Art, Department of Architecture and Design,
11 West 53rd Street, New York, N.Y. 10019.

The MIES VAN DER ROHE ARCHIVE, consisting of ca. 15,000
items, was founded in 1968. The Museum of Modern Art received with the Mies van der Rohe bequest in 1969 nearly all
of the extant drawings and documents of the architect. Permission to use the materials is required in advance of any
visit to the Museum.

*Das MIES VAN DER ROHE ARCHIVE besteht aus etwa 15.000 Num-
mern. Nach der Gründung des Archivs im Jahre 1968 wurde dem
Museum of Modern Art im Jahre 1969 der gesamte Nachlaß Mies
van der Rohes übergeben, der auch seine Zeichnungen und Dokumente einschließt. Die Erlaubnis zur Benutzung der Materialien muß im voraus vom Museum of Modern Art eingeholt werden.*

B1   Non-personal job correspondence. 12 B. from the German
     period and complete files after 1938.

C14 Of the total number of items, two-thirds are drawings,
     ca. one-third prints. For the pre-1938 period,
     three-quarters are drawings, over half by Mies' own
     hand. For the post-1938 period, the ratio of draw-
     ings and prints is about equal with the percentage
     of drawings by Mies' own hand declining toward the
     later years.

F   Recorded conversations with Mies.
     Conversations/interviews made for film productions.
     Footage from television films on Mies, including the
     Krumgold Project.

H1   Both the Archive and the Museum of Modern Art library
     have books on architecture and Mies. The Archive
     will continue to acquire all work published on Mies.

H5   Interviews with friends and associates (tapes and
     notes), mostly made in Germany.

I   Bibliography: the Archive is preparing an ongoing
     bibliography for Mies.
     Miscellaneous documentary materials, obtained largely

through personal contact or German institutional
exchange.

J   Original photos of Mies' work from the pre-1938, as
well as post-1938 periods. Also copy prints.

HANS RICHTER ARCHIVE: Written permission to use the Archive
is required in advance of visits to the Museum.

*HANS RICHTER ARCHIVE: Das Archiv darf nur mit schriftlicher
Genehmigung aufgesucht werden.*

B1   2 Tel. to Hans Richter. 1958, 1966.

B2   1 L. from Hans Richter. 1966.

O   Program to a Mies van der Rohe exhibition. 1947.

Library of Congress, Manuscript Division, Independence Avenue
and First Street S.E., Washington, D.C. 20540.

The PAPERS OF LUDWIG MIES VAN DER ROHE at the Library consist of approximately 22,000 items or ca. 27 shelf ft. of
materials. They were received by the Library of Congress in
1971 and 1973 as a bequest from Mies van der Rohe. With the
exception of some photographs, which have been transferred
to the Prints and Photographs Division, the materials are
located in the Manuscript Division of the Library. Information on the collection is available in the form of a detailed
24-page inventory of the collection, which was prepared by
Ms. Mary M. Wolfskill in 1974. Permission to use the materials is obtainable from the Library of Congress.

*Die PAPERS OF LUDWIG MIES VAN DER ROHE in der Library of Con-
gress bestehen aus ca. 22.000 Nummern, d.h. etwa 8 m Material.
Sie sind ein Vermächtnis Mies van der Rohes an die Library of
Congress aus den Jahren 1971 und 1973. Die Materialien befinden sich in der Manuscript Division der Bibliothek (mit
Ausnahme einiger Photographien, die an die Prints and Photographs Division gingen). Es ist ein 24seitiger Index zu der
Sammlung erhältlich, der im Jahre 1974 von Frau Mary M. Wolfskill erarbeitet wurde. Erlaubnis, die Materialien zu be-*

LUDWIG MIES VAN DER ROHE

nutzen, erteilt die Library of Congress.

A1   Appointment calendars. 1 B.

B1,2 Early correspondence. 1921-1940 and undated. Primarily
      in German. 3.5 B.
      Late correspondence. 1930-1969 and undated, including
      correspondence with: Edward Kennedy, Jacqueline Ken-
      nedy, John F. Kennedy, Robert Kennedy. 3 B.

B1,2   General office files. 1923-1969 and undated, including
I,   L., cl., blueprints, patents, photos, printed matter
L   and miscellaneous items, arranged alphabetically by
          subject or correspondent. Among the correspondents
          represented are: Josef and Anni Albers, Willy Brandt,
          Will Grohmann, Walter Gropius, Theodor Heuss, Hans
          Huth, Lyndon B. Johnson, Paul Klee, Charles Le Cor-
          busier, Erich Mendelsohn, Richard Neutra, Richard
          Nixon, Pablo Picasso, Hans Richter, Edward Durell
          Stone, Konrad Wachsmann, Frank Lloyd Wright. 54 B.

C7,   Speeches and articles by and about Mies. 1 B. Includes
H3   Mies' writings on: Walter Gropius, Charles Le Cor-
          busier, Walter Peterhans, Frank Lloyd Wright.

H3,4 Biographical material, including cl. 1937-1969. Also
      biographical and various other materials concerning
      Mies' work located throughout the general office
      files.
      Death notices and obituaries.

I   Miscellaneous documents: naturalization papers, pass-
      port and visas, licenses, honors, memberships,
      financial papers.
      Numerous documents located in correspondence files,
      including 3 B. of patents.

<u>University of Illinois at Chicago Circle</u>, The Library, Box
8198, Chicago, Illinois 60680.

The MIES VAN DER ROHE LIBRARY, which is housed in the Rare
Book Room of the Library, was purchased from the estate of
Mies van der Rohe in 1971. Use of the library is restricted
to the premises of the University.

LUDWIG MIES VAN DER ROHE

Die MIES VAN DER ROHE LIBRARY, die sich im Rare Book Room
der Bibliothek der University of Illinois befindet, wurde
1971 aus dem Nachlaß von Mies van der Rohe erworben. Es
handelt sich um eine reine Präsenzbibliothek.

K   The collection consists of ca. 900-1,000 books, pam-
        phlets, and some scattered single issues of various
        journals.

INSTITUTE OF DESIGN RECORDS, 1927-1970

C7   Address on the Institute of Design, together with
        Walter Gropius and Serge Chermayeff. April 1950.

Archives of American Art, Smithsonian Institution, National
Collection of Fine Arts and National Portrait Gallery Build-
ing, Eighth and F Streets N.W., Washington, D.C. 20560.
(Microfilms of collections are available in each of the
branch locations: Boston, Massachusetts; New York, N.Y.;
Detroit, Michigan; San Francisco, California.)

J   75 photos by Hugo Weber and photographer Harry Calla-
        han. 1961-1964.

Massachusetts Institute of Technology, Rotch Library, Cambridge, Massachusetts 02139.

C14   16 blueprints of the Illinois Institute of Technology,
        Chicago, Illinois, 1946.

RUDOLF MINKOWSKI

Astronomer, 1895-1976

<u>Mrs. Rudolf Minkowski</u>, 1011 Siler Place, Berkeley, California 94705.

The following materials from the estate of Rudolf Minkowski (inaccessible to researchers) are in the possession of his widow. The papers will go to Bancroft Library, University of California, Berkeley. Further materials (primarily offprints) may be found at the former office of Dr. Minkowski (Department of Astronomy, University of California, Berkeley).

Die folgenden Materialien aus dem Nachlaß von Rudolf Minkowski befinden sich im Besitz seiner Witwe und sind zur Zeit für Forschungszwecke unzugänglich. Die Materialien werden später der Bancroft Library, University of California, Berkeley, zukommen. Weiteres Material, hauptsächlich Sonderdrucke, befindet sich in dem früheren Büro Professor Minkowskis (Department of Astronomy, University of California, Berkeley).

A1   Appointment calendars from many years showing important dates, appointments and meetings.

B1,2   Several L. among the Ms. 1945-.

C7,8   Astronomy Ms. of various types, including: scientific notes, records of scientific meetings, charts, graphs, etc. 1945-.

D8   Offprints of articles by Minkowski.

H3   Cl. and articles on Minkowski. Also articles in which Minkowski is mentioned.

I   Documents, including passports, immigration papers, etc.

J   Photos of Minkowski and family.
        Photos of colleagues, meetings.
        Slides from trips taken by Minkowski.

K   Science and classics library. Also some old music scores (opera).
        Astrophysical periodicals, including: <u>Astrophysical Journal</u>, <u>Katalog der astronomischen Gesellschaft</u>, etc.

L   Offprints and cl. of articles by others, collected by

RUDOLF MINKOWSKI

Minkowski, some dating back to 1900. Ca. 2 ft.

M   Memorabilia, awards.

New York Public Library, Manuscript Division, Fifth Avenue and 42nd Street, New York, N.Y. 10018.

EMERGENCY COMMITTEE IN AID OF DISPLACED FOREIGN SCHOLARS, 1933-1945

*   File compiled when assistance was granted. 1934-1942.

University of Chicago, The Joseph Regenstein Library, 1100 East 57th Street, Chicago, Illinois 60637.

JAMES FRANCK PAPERS

B1,2   Correspondence with James Franck.

CARL MISCH

Writer, 1896-1965

<u>State University of New York at Albany</u>, Department of Germanic Languages and Literatures, 1400 Washington Avenue, Albany, New York 12222.

The CARL MISCH PAPERS, ca. 5 inches of materials, were donated by Mrs. Carl Misch in 1973.

Die CARL MISCH PAPERS, etwa 0,12 m Materialien, sind eine Schenkung von Frau Misch aus dem Jahre 1973.

B1   7 L. 1946-1962, including L. to: F. C. Weiskopf.

B2   40 L. 1942-1965, including L. from: Siegfried Marck, Ernst Erich Noth, Max Osborn, Kurt Schwerin, Paul Tillich, Walter Victor.

C7   "Ossietzky zum 25. Todestag." Lecture for a memorial celebration of the Presseverband, Berlin. May 4, 1963. T. 12p.
        "Deutschlands Schicksal." Lecture. 1946. T. 29p.
        "Berlin." Lecture. Undated. T. 18p.
        "This is Paris Today. Report of an Eyewitness." Undated. T.c. 22p.
        "Geschichte des deutschen Zeitungswesens." 1962. T. 16p.
        "Lieber tot als Refugié." Report. 1948. A. 1p.
        "Veit Valentin." Speech in his memory for a memorial celebration in New York. Feb. 28, 1947. T. and cc. 23p. ea.
        "The Downfall of the Weimar Republic." Lecture. 1954. T. 19p.

H3   "No time to weep." Newspaper cl. 1961.

<u>New York Public Library</u>, Manuscript Division, Fifth Avenue and 42nd Street, New York, N.Y. 10018.

EMERGENCY COMMITTEE IN AID OF DISPLACED FOREIGN SCHOLARS, 1933-1945

*   File compiled, no assistance given. 1940-1944.

634

CARL MISCH

Boston University, Mugar Memorial Library, 771 Commonwealth
Avenue, Boston, Massachusetts 02215.

BELLA FROMM COLLECTION

B1   L. to Bella Fromm.

LUDWIG VON MISES

Economist, 1881-1973

Mrs. Margrit von Mises, 777 West End Avenue, New York, N.Y.
10025.

The LUDWIG VON MISES COLLECTION, ca. 60 shelf feet of mate-
rials from the Nachlaß of von Mises, has been partially
catalogued (4 cartons of cl.). The collection was used by
Mrs. von Mises in the writing of her autobiography: My
Years with Ludwig von Mises (New Rochelle, New York:
Arlington House, 1977).

*Die LUDWIG VON MISES COLLECTION, etwa 18 m Materialien aus
dem Nachlaß von Mises', ist z.T. katalogisiert (4 Kartons
mit Zeitungsausschnitten). Die Sammlung wurde von Frau von
Mises bei der Erarbeitung ihrer Autobiographie benutzt: My
Years with Ludwig von Mises (New Rochelle, New York: Arlington House, 1977).*

B1,2   Correspondence with colleagues (von Hayek, etc.), with
       industry, with friends.

C7   Ms. of pub. and unpub. writings. Ca. 600 F. containing
       fragments, notes, and Ms., including Ms. of all
       books.

D7,   Extremely large collection of pub. materials (cl.,
L   pamphlets, offprints, etc.) spanning more than 50
       years. Ca. 50 cartons.

K   Inventory listing of books in library of von Mises.
       The library itself was sold.

M   Memorabilia, including honors received, etc.

Hillsdale College, Mossey Learning Resources Center, Hillsdale, Michigan 49242.

The personal library of Ludwig von Mises was purchased from
his widow shortly after his death (Oct. 1973).

*Hillsdale College hat die Privatbibliothek Ludwig von Mises'
kurz nach seinem Tode im Okt. 1973 von seiner Witwe gekauft.*

K   Personal library of Ludwig von Mises:
     Ca. 3,000 books, primarily on economics, also poli-
     tical science, philosophy, religion, literature.
     Ca. 1,500 pamphlets and brochures.
     Ca. 1,000 offprints.

Kephart Communications, Inc., 410 First Street Southeast,
Washington, D.C. 20003.

AUDIO FORUM

G   "Why Socialism Always Fails." 86 min. tape by L. von
     Mises. Available from Audio Forum, $10.95.

Mrs. Gertrude Lederer, 372 Central Park West, Apt. 3B, New
York, N.Y. 10024.

C7   Manuscript by Ludwig von Mises.

RICHARD VON MISES

Mathematician, 1883-1953

Harvard University, University Archives, Widener Library,
Cambridge, Massachusetts 02138.

The RICHARD VON MISES COLLECTION (HUG 4574.x), which consists
of more than 58 archive boxes of materials, is the result of
3 separate donations. The major portion of the collection
(38 archive B.) was donated by Mrs. Hilda von Mises, widow
of Richard, over the period 1965-1967. In 1973, the stepdaughter of von Mises, Mrs. Robert Buka, donated another 20
archive B. of materials to the Archives. Additional materials were also donated in 1973 by the American Institute of
Physics.

*Die RICHARD VON MISES COLLECTION (HUG 4574.x), die mehr als
58 Archivkartons Materialien umfaßt, ist aus 3 verschiedenen
Schenkungen entstanden. Der Hauptteil der Sammlung (38
Archivkartons) ist eine Schenkung von Frau Hilda von Mises,
der Witwe von Richard von Mises, aus dem Zeitraum von 1965 -
1967. 1973 hat die Stieftochter von Mises', Frau Buka,
weitere Materalen (20 Archivkartons) den University Archives
überlassen. Das restliche Material ist eine Schenkung des
American Institute of Physics aus dem Jahre 1973.*

A1   14 diaries (private and professional), in shorthand.
      1903-1952 with some gaps.

A2   1 notebook entitled "Arbeiten-Verzeichnis-Separats
      [sic] früherer Arbeiten."

A3   "Biographical material." Correspondence regarding
      faculty minutes on the life of von Mises, auto-
      biographical items, bibliographical references.
      Résumés and lists of publications. 1939.
      List of publications. 1940.
      Notes, booklists in German.
      Partial list of books bought by von Mises since 1906.
      A.
      "1933 verkaufte Bücher." List. T.
      "Verzeichnis der an die Istanbuler Ingenieurschule
      abgegebenen Zeitschriften und Bücher." List. T.
      "List of Periodicals which Mises sold in 1953." T. 2c.
      List of people to whom Mises sent reprints.

RICHARD VON MISES

Small Harvard address book.

B1   Ca. 205 L. 1934-1953, including L. to: Brauer, Hermann
Broch, Rudolf Carnap, Richard Courant, K. O. Fried-
richs, Philipp Frank, Kurt Jacoby, Willy Prager,
Leo Spitzer, Hermann Weyl.
L. and Ptc. to mother of Richard von Mises.
Miscellaneous personal L. 1951-1952.
Miscellaneous correspondence. 1899-1953.

B1,2 "Theory of Flight" correspondence. Concerns progress
of Ms. and publication arrangements.
"Personal 1949-1951." Correspondence with colleagues,
including Leo Spitzer. Ca. 500 L. (1 archive B.).
"Kleines Lehrbuch des Positivismus." Correspondence
with libraries, publishers, public institutions and
individuals. 1946-1951. Ca. 4 in. (10 cm.).
"Navy Projects." June 1944 - Jan. 1949. 5 F.
"Navy Contracts." Feb. 1, 1949 - Aug. 31, 1951. 5 F.
United States Naval Ordnance Laboratory. Correspondence.
July 1, 1948 - Jan. 31, 1949. Ca. 2 in. (5 cm.).
United States National Advisory Committee for Aeronau-
tics (NACA). Projects and contracts correspondence.
Feb. 1, 1949 - Aug. 31, 1951. Ca. 7 in. (17 cm.).
"School. Harvard." 1948-1953. 1 B.
"International Union, National and International Con-
gresses." Feb. 1, 1950 - Jan. 31, 1953. 2 in. (5 cm.).
University correspondence. 1940-1948. Includes many cl.
and offprints. 2 B.
Correspondence re: food packages sent to friends and
former students in Europe. 1946-1949, 1951.
Correspondence and documentation of Mises' service
time with the k.u.k. Luftfahrttruppen, concerning
the 3-motor airplane. Includes many documents 1916-
1918. Ca. 2 in. (5 cm.).
"Herbst 1945." Some correspondence. Primarily class
lists, pub. materials, agendas, receipts, etc.
"Frühling 1946." Primarily university correspondence,
including L. from Kurt Jacoby.
"Herbst 1946." Ca. 200 L., including L. from Kurt
Jacoby.
"Frühling 1947." Ca. 200 L.
"Herbst 1947." Ca. 200 L., including L. from: Kurt
Jacoby, Emil Gumbel, Rudolf Carnap.

639

B2   71 L. 1919-1952, including L. from: Erich Auerbach, Siegfried Bernfeld, A. Brauer, Hermann Broch, Egon Brunswik, Rudolf Carnap, Richard Courant, Albert Einstein, Philipp Frank, K. O. Friedrichs, E. J. Gumbel, Ernst Hellinger, Edward Hitschmann, Kurt Jacoby, Karl Löwith, Otto Meyerhof, Otto Neugebauer, William Prager, Hans Rademacher, Leo Spitzer, Hermann Weyl, Otto Zoff.

L. and Ptc. from Hannah Szasz. 1919-1952.

67 L. from "Gelehrte außer Mathematikern und Physikern." [18--]-1950, including L. from: Otto Meyerhof, F. Hartung, Anna Freud, E. R. Curtius.

42 L. and Ptc. from F. Klein. A. 1909-1911.

Ca. 500 L. 1903-1920, including L. from: Richard Courant, Albert Einstein, and professors from universities such as Brünn, Karlsruhe, Hamburg, Aachen, Prag.

Ca. 680 L. (German, English, French, Turkish). 1921-1934, including 50th birthday greetings and documentation concerning von Mises' giving up of his university position in Germany.

Ca. 550 L., Ptc. and Tel. 1934-1944, including L. from: Hilda Geiringer (later wife of von Mises), 60th birthday greetings.

84 L. 1945-1953.

B3   Correspondence between Hilda Geiringer and publishers, universities, and individuals concerning von Mises commemorative publication. 1952-1954. Ca. 7 in. (17.5 cm.).

Numerous third-party L. from all years.

C7   Lecture notebooks. 1893-1952. 1 B.

"Vorträge über Fluglehre." 1899-1937.

"Vorlesungen über Festigkeitslehre." 1899-1937.

"Mss. of writings."

"Miscellaneous Manuscripts."

"Aufgabe aus der angewandten Mathematik." Notes. 1927. T.

"Vorträge und Reden." Notes on many technical subjects.

"On a Textbook of Positivism." Lecture to the International Congress for the Unity of Sciences Movement. 1939. T.

"Attitude of School Philosophy toward Language." Undated. T.

RICHARD VON MISES

"Aperçu historique." T. 2c.

C8   Kleines Lehrbuch des Positivismus/Small Textbook on
       Positivism. English tr. by Isaac Rosenfeld. 1941.
       First section only.
    "Notes to Positivism." T. Several c.
    German text. T.c.
    Selecta. The Selected Papers of Richard von Mises. Ms.
       of papers pub. posthumously.
    "Älteres MS: Compressibility Effects in Theory of
       Flight."
    "Analysis of Population."
    "As[ymptomatic] Distribution of Quantities."
    "Aufgabe aus der mathematischen Statistik."
    "Bayes' Problem Modified." [1938]. A.
    "Darstellende Geometrie." 1920-1921.
    "Differential Expression of the Second Order." Notes
       and calculations.
    "Drawings to Thickness of a Steady Shockwave." Graphs.
    "Einführung in die Raumgittertheorie." T. and A.
    "Das Element zweiter Ordnung einer optischen Strahlen-
       Kongruenz."
    "Falling Bomb Correction for High Speed." Notes.
    "Figuren und Zahlentafeln z. Hydromechanik." 1 F.
    "Figuren zu Mises, Hydromechanik II." 1 F.
    "Fluglehre." 2 paperbound c. plus blueprints.
    "Mises' Fluglehre." Data and technical illustrations.
    "Motoren-Rechnung, 1912-13." 1 F.
    "New Approach to the Three-Dimensional Wing Theory."
       1945. T.
    "Note on the Numerical Solution of the Equation $\Delta U=0$."
       T.
    "Notes on Probability and Statistics." Undated. A.
    "Notions générales [on probability]." Undated. A.
    "Notizen zu Theory of Flight." Extensive calculations
       on aerodynamic theory.
    "On Network Methods in Conformal Mapping." T. and A.
       1949.
    "On Some Topics in the Fundamentals of Flow Theory."
       1951. 15p.
    "On Statistical Functions."
    "On the Asymptomatic Distribution of Differentiable
       Statistical Functions." Undated. T.

641

"Operational Units." Memorandum. 6c.
"Propeller-jet Airplane." Notes, calculations and Ms.
   on slipstream airplane.
"Quelques inégalités pour les moments de distributions
   discontinues." T. and A. 3 Ms.
"Regulator-Reibungs-Theorie." Includes drawings,
   graphs, calculations.
"Schub-Kurbelgetriebe." Includes notes on kinematics.
"Supplementary Notes by Herzberger." 1945. T. and A.
"Technische Mechanik (Kinematik)." 1922. A.
"Theorie der Tragfläche." Undated. A.
"Three Remarks on the Theory of the Ideal Plastic Body."
   1948. T. 3 incomplete c.
"Untersuchung der Eigenwert-Probleme von $\Delta U+\lambda$, or $\Delta U=0$."
   Undated. T.
"Vorlesungen über Festigkeitslehre." Technische Hoch-
   schule. Dresden, 1919. 2c.
"Vorwort zur dritten Auflage." Draft to preface for
   Wahrscheinlichkeit, Statistik und Wahrheit. 1949.
"Zu Bd. II der Hydromechanik." 1 F.
"2 Bd. der Hydromechanik." 1915. A.
"Die Ψ-Reihe." Function analysis. Notes. A.
"Hans Reichenbach. The Theory of Probability." Undated.
   T. and A.
Several short texts, presumably by von Mises (among the
   correspondence files), including:
"Flugzeug. Theoretische Grundlagen." 6p.
"Bemerkung zum Spar-Los-System." 2p.
"Bemerkungen zur Errichtung eines Instituts für an-
   gewandte Mathematik." 8p.
Also mathematical texts, reports, reviews of scien-
   tific writings, offprints, etc.
Article on Quarterly of Applied Mathematics. Undated.
   T. and proofs.
Blueprints, data, drawings and photo of airplane con-
   figuration. Ca. 1917.
Data, drawings, graphs concerning flight endurance
   tests. Ca. 1915.
Drawings, graphs on flight mechanics, wing theory.
   Undated.
Drawings, graphs, stencils on flight mechanics. Un-
   dated.
Mathematical problems with solutions (apparently used

for instructional purposes). French. 1930s. T. and A. Ms. on fluid flow, probability, positivism. A. Notebook and sheets of unidentified data and calculations. Notes and calculations on wing theory. Undated. Notes on plasticity and stability. Statistical analysis of atomic weights. Unpub. Ms., notes, letters (some used for Selecta).

C9 "Übersetzung des Auszuges a) aus dem Code des assurances, b) aus Théorie Mathématique des Assurances." T.

D7 "A Declaration of the Council for a Democratic Germany." With Paul Tillich. 1944. 6p.
"Buchbesprechungen und kleine Beiträge in Zeitschrift für Angewandte Mechanik und Mathematik."
"Buchbesprechungen und kleine Beiträge in verschiedenen Zeitschriften und Büchern."
Book reviews by von Mises in Science, May 1940 and Jan. 1944.

D8 "Zur Frage der Bewertung von Flugleistungen bei Wettbewerben," in Zeitschrift für Flugtechnik und Motorluftschiffahrt. 1914.
Article on probability in Forschungen und Fortschritte. 1931. 7c.
Page proofs of "Introduction" to Small Textbook of Positivism.
"Publications: books with inserted notes and corrections."
"Reprints: processed notes and publications."

H2 Publications about R. v. Mises.

H3 Cl., broadsides, printed items concerning von Mises.

H4 Reviews of von Mises' works.
"Besprechungen der eigenen Bücher."

I Documents located among the correspondence (Boxes 1, 2, 3, 4, 11): identification cards, credentials, passport, programs, invitations 1903-1920, financial documents, minutes of meetings, protest L., agenda for meetings, recommendations, membership cards, receipts, résumés of various individuals, diploma, contracts, etc.

"Verschiedene Gutachten." T. German, English, French.
"Steuern 1941-43." Tax records.
Notebooks of references to works by von Mises (with
   appended notes, possibly of distribution of re-
   prints).
Hilda Geiringer résumés. French and English. 1938.
"II Staatsprüfung. Bericht. 1905: von Mises' report
   for the Staats-Prüfung-Commission für das Maschinen-
   baufach [Mechanical Engineering Trade] an der k.u.k.
   Technische Hochschule in Wien."
Book lists for various purposes.
"Notes on Ph.D. Candidates." Ca. 1920-1933.

J   Photographs of drawings on hydrodynamics of a turbine
       airplane engine.
    Photographs labeled "Zur Geometr. Optik."
    "Photographs" and "Photos of R.v.M."
    "Autographed photo album of friends in the Café Central,
       Vienna, Dec. 1928."
    Unidentified photos.
    2 photos located in the correspondence files. 1915.

K   "Catalogue of Scientific Library - Richard von Mises."

L   Cl., broadsides, other miscellaneous printed items
       concerning Hilda Geiringer.
    Notebook of pencil data and notations on airplane per-
       formance. Photograph collection of early airplanes
       and zeppelins.
    "Verdichtungsstöße - Compression Waves." Diverse notes,
       drawings and reprints of articles by P. W. Bridgman
       (1942) and M. S. Uberoi and L. S. G. Kovasznay (1953).
    Pc. of documents relating to Joseph Popper.
    Reprints of articles by others. 1926, 1931.

M   "Medal."
    Unused picture postcards.
    "Diverse." Includes programs from 1870s meetings of
       Chemiker Kneipe and Ingenieur-Kneipe, folios of stu-
       dent songs from 1870s, German newspapers and maga-
       zines (1903-1934), pamphlets, book advertisements.
    "Den Gästen zur Jahrhundertfeier der Technischen Hoch-
       schule Dresden." 1925. Booklet of plates of German
       cities and landscapes.

RICHARD VON MISES

List of 51 people and menu for dinner held in honor
of von Mises. 1953.

N   "Diplom Arbeit." Thesis of father of R. v. Mises. 1874.
     Notebook on "Fachpsychologie" (not by von Mises).
     Notes by Hilda Geiringer von Mises.
     Articles by: F. Behrend, Stefan Bergmann, Uttam Chand,
     Dr. G. Frege, Hilda Geiringer, A. Gottstein, Shigeo
     Kase, M. G. Kendall, Rufus Oldenberger, George Pólya,
     K. Reach, H. Schelling, A. Stodola, Alfred Tauber,
     Gerhard Tintner, H. S. Tsien.
     Unidentified articles by colleagues.

O   Program: "The Ceremonies in Honor of Winston Spencer
     Churchill." 1943.

Dr. G. S. Ludford, Thurston Hall, Cornell University, Ithaca,
New York 14853.

The materials in Dr. Ludford's possession were given to him
by Hilda Geiringer von Mises.

Die Materialien in Dr. Ludfords Besitz sind ein Geschenk von
Hilda Geiringer von Mises.

A2   Scientific notebooks:
     Nos. 1-50. 1911-1926. Bound by von Mises. 20p. ea.
       Ca. 1,000p. in total.
     Nos. 51-104. 1926-1945. Ca. 1,000p.
     Loose pages. 1945-1949. Ca. 200p.
     Looseleaf notebook. 1950-1951. Ca. 150p.

B3   Correspondence between Dr. Ludford and Hilda Geiringer
     concerning book on von Mises. 1956-1959.

J   3 photo albums: family, colleagues, and work projects.
     1950s.

University of Maryland, Engineering and Physical Sciences
Library, College Park, Maryland 20742.

The RICHARD VON MISES LIBRARY was purchased from the von
Mises family in 1955.

645

RICHARD VON MISES

Die University of Maryland hat die RICHARD VON MISES LIBRARY
im Jahre 1955 von der Familie von Mises gekauft.

K   Ca. 1,100 books and magazines from the private library
      of Richard von Mises.
      217 cartons of offprints and reprints, some with anno-
      tations by von Mises.

California Institute of Technology, Robert A. Millikan
Library, Pasadena, California 91109.

THEODORE VON KARMAN CORRESPONDENCE

B1,2   Correspondence with Theodore von Karman. 1920-1952. 3 F.

Harvard University, Houghton Library, Cambridge, Massachusetts 02138.

GEORGE SARTON PAPERS, RICHARD BEER-HOFMANN COLLECTION

B1   1 L. to George Sarton. 1952.

B2   1 L. from George Sarton. 1952.
       Several L. from Richard Beer-Hofmann.

New York University, Courant Institute of Mathematical Sciences, Library, 251 Mercer Street, New York, N.Y. 10012.

B3   File: "Hilde von Mises." 1943-1955.

Princeton University, Firestone Library, Princeton, New
Jersey 08540.

THE PAPERS OF ALBERT EINSTEIN (1879-1955). For details concerning the use of this collection, see description under
Albert Einstein.

THE PAPERS OF ALBERT EINSTEIN (1879-1955). Angaben über den
Zugang zu der Sammlung finden sich unter "Albert Einstein."

31,2 Unknown amount of correspondence between von Mises
      and Einstein. 1919, 1920.

LÁSZLÓ MOHOLY-NAGY

Painter, 1895-1946

University of Illinois at Chicago Circle, The Library, Box
8198, Chicago, Illinois 60680.

The INSTITUTE OF DESIGN RECORDS, 1927-1970, comprise approximately 3.5 ft. of materials. The Moholy-Nagy materials in
the collection are from his years as Director of the Institute of Design, 1937-1946.

*Die INSTITUTE OF DESIGN RECORDS, 1927-1970, enthalten etwa
1 m Material von und über Moholy-Nagy. Das Material dieser
Sammlung stammt aus seinen Jahren als Direktor des Institute
of Design, 1937-1946.*

B1   Correspondence. 1940-1946, including L. to: Donald
       Fairchild, Walter A. Jessup, Oscar Mayer, Walter
       Paepcke, Crombie Taylor.
       Correspondence to the Chicago Historical Society. 1943.

B2   Correspondence. 1940-1946, including L. from: Julian S.
       Huxley, George Fred Keck, Walter Paepcke.

C7   Articles by Moholy-Nagy. Nov. 1943 - March 1947.
       Texts of lectures. 1930s and 1940s.

C8   Book of New Artists. Film negatives. Undated.

H3   Newspaper and magazine cl. Aug. 1937 - June 1969.
       Obituaries.

Archives of American Art, Smithsonian Institution, National
Collection of Fine Arts and National Portrait Gallery Build-
ing, Eighth and F Streets N.W., Washington, D.C. 20560.
(Microfilms of collections are available in each of the
branch locations: Boston, Massachusetts; New York, N.Y.;
Detroit, Michigan; San Francisco, California.)

KURT SELIGMANN PAPERS, HUGO WEBER PAPERS, and general archive
files

B1   Correspondence. 1920s and later.

B1,2   Correspondence with James Edward Davies. Undated.

B2   1 L. from the Ruth White Gallery.

H3   Cl., press notices of 1967-1970 retrospective.

H4   Review of Experiment in Totality by R. J. Wolff.

J   Photos of Moholy-Nagy and family.
      Several photos of Moholy-Nagy among the Hugo Weber
      Papers.

Columbia University, Butler Library, New York, N.Y. 10027.

B1   3 L. to W. W. Norton. T. and A. 1939.
      3 L. to Oscar Jaszi. T. 1941-1943.

Harvard University, Houghton Library, Cambridge, Massachusetts 02138.

B1   1 L. to E. E. Cummings. 1944.

Yale University Library, Manuscripts and Archives Research
Room, 150 Sterling Memorial Library, New Haven, Connecticut
06520.

JOSEF ALBERS PAPERS

B1   2 L. to Josef Albers. A. and T. 1937-1938.
B3   3 L. concerning Moholy-Nagy. Ca. 1937-1938.

Harvard University, Harvard Divinity School, Andover-Harvard
Theological Library, 45 Francis Avenue, Cambridge, Massachusetts 02138.

PAUL TILLICH COLLECTION

B2   1 L. from Paul Tillich. T.c. 1962.

Yivo Institute, 1048 Fifth Avenue, New York, N.Y. 10028.

HORACE M. KALLEN PAPERS

B1,2   Individual item(s) in folder no. 982.

SIBYL MOHOLY-NAGY

Historian of Architecture, 1903-1971

Archives of American Art, Smithsonian Institution, National Collection of Fine Arts and National Portrait Gallery Building, Eighth and F Streets N.W., Washington, D.C. 20560. (Microfilms of collections are available in each of the branch locations: Boston, Massachusetts; New York, N.Y.; Detroit, Michigan; San Francisco, California.)

The microfilming of the SIBYL MOHOLY-NAGY COLLECTION, 7 archive cartons of materials from the years 1918-1971, was made possible by Ms. Hattula M. Hug in 1971 (microfilm 944-949). The original materials as well as all rights to the collection were retained by Ms. Hug, Zähringerplatz 11, CH-8001, Zürich, Switzerland.

Im Jahre 1971 ermöglichte Frau Hattula M. Hug die Herstellung von Mikrofilmen der SIBYL MOHOLY-NAGY COLLECTION, die aus 7 Archivkartons mit Materialien aus den Jahren 1918 - 1971 besteht (microfilm 944 - 949). Die Originalmaterialien sowie alle Rechte befinden sich bei Frau Hug, Zähringerplatz 11, CH 8001 Zürich, Switzerland.

A1   Diaries, 1918-1945, 1947-1959. Includes 1 diary on South American trip, 1959.

B1,2   Correspondence.

C7   Manuscripts, notes to her books.
Lecture notes.
Lecture manuscripts.

D7   Offprints and cl. of her writings.

J   Family and childhood photos, as well as several from films in Berlin (1924-1931).

M   Medals from the American Institute of the Arts.

JAMES E. DAVIES COLLECTION, KATHERINE KUH COLLECTION, ROBERT JAY WOLFF COLLECTION (N69-73, 406-442)

B1,2   Correspondence (Davies).
25 L. 1945-1949, 1968 (Wolff).

J   Photos (Kuh).

University of Illinois at Chicago Circle, The Library, Box
8198, Chicago, Illinois 60680.

INSTITUTE OF DESIGN RECORDS, 1927-1970

B1,2   Correspondence between Sibyl and Lászlo Moholy-Nagy
        and: Donald Fairchild, Walter A. Jessup, Oscar
        Mayer, Walter Paepcke, Crombie Taylor. 1940-1955.

B2   1 L. from Walter P. Paepcke. 1952. Restricted.

University of Illinois at Chicago Circle, Department of
Architecture and Art, Chicago, Illinois 60680.

B1,2   Correspondence. 1950-1953.

Columbia University, Butler Library, New York, N.Y. 10027.

B1   1 L. ea. to Oscar Jaszi (1946) and Storen B. Lunt
        (1955).

FERENC MOLNAR

Screen Writer, Dramatist, 1878-1952

Yale University, Beinecke Rare Book and Manuscript Library,
New Haven, Connecticut 06520.

The large collection of Molnar materials is a part of the
EDMOND PAUKER COLLECTION, which has been deposited at Yale
by Mr. John Pauker.

*Die große Sammlung von Molnar Materialien ist Teil der EDMOND
PAUKER COLLECTION, die der Yale University von Herr John
Pauker übergeben wurde.*

A3   "The Peculiar Relationship of the Artist and His
        Model." Unpub. article. T. 9p.
     "The Producing Manager Requests the Author to Make a
        Few Infinitesimal, Insignificant Changes in His
        Latest Play." Short autobiographical drama. T. 6p.
     "Props. 4. From a Playwright's Notebook." T. 4p.
     "We Plan a Supper Party for Our Artist Friends or The
        Most Complicated Chess Game of My Life." Short auto-
        biographical drama. T. 6p.

B1   2 Ptc. and 2 short notes to Edmond Pauker. A. 1951 and
        undated.
     1 L. to Crown Publishers. T. 1951.

B2   4 L. from: Dramatists Guild, Franz Horch, Billy Rose,
        Viking Press. 1940s.
     23 L. from Edmond Pauker and 1 L. from Eve Pauker.
        1940s.

C1   Autumn Journey. T. and cc. 2c. 186p. ea. Short synop-
        sis. T. and cc. 3c. 2p. ea.
     The Derelict Boat. T. 90p.
        "Story of a Derelict Boat." English synopsis. T. and
        cc. 4c. 4p. ea.
     Eva. Novel. T. 90p. Also English synopsis. T. and cc.
        5c. 5p. ea.
     Fall, Caesar. Synopsis. 1942. T. and cc. 2c. 35p. ea.
     My Life is Wind. Hungarian text. T. with corr. 143p.
        English tr. by E. Rice. T. 169p.
     The Piping Cherub. Tr. by G. Halasz. T. 185p.

C2   Blue Danube. 1941. T. 134p.

The Boys of Paul Street. Synopsis. T. and cc. 2c. 8p.
   ea.
The Cab. T. 5p.
Carnival. T. 107p.
The Coal Pilferers. Prose synopsis, probably not by
   Molnar. A. 15p.
A Dada Rosszul Mesél. Hungarian text. T. 6p.
Delicate Story/A Cukrászné. English text. T. 124p.
   Hungarian text. T. 110p. Also notes, outlines, rough
   drafts in Hungarian. 1 volume.
Delilah/Delila. English text. Copyright 1937. T. and
   cc. 3c. 94p. ea. Hungarian text. T. 24p. Short table
   of contents in Hungarian. T. 4p.
The Dentist. English tr., probably not by Molnar. A.
   5p.
Department of Scandals. T. 5p.
The Double Eraser. English tr., probably not by Molnar.
   A. 5p.
Duel with the Great Tenor. T. 5p.
The Emperor/A Császár. English text. 1947, copyright
   1942. T. and cc. 3c. 67p. ea. Introduction. T. 16p.
   Notes, first drafts, in Hungarian. 1 volume.
Empress. Synopsis. T. 21p. English drafts. T. and cc.
   3c. 18p. ea.
Game of Hearts. "Version July 1947." Copyright 1946.
   T. and cc. 2c. 163p. ea. "Version 1948." T. and cc.
   3c. 120p. ea.
Girl from Trieste. T. 32p.
The Gold Watch Chain. English tr., probably not by Mol-
   nar. A. 6p.
A Gray Hat with Olivegreen Ribbon. Short drama. T. 6p.
Große Liebe/Great Love. "Lese-Exemplar." German ver-
   sion. T. 116p. English version. T. and cc. 2c. 109p.
   ea. Second English version. T. and cc. 4c. 101p. ea.
Harmonie/Harmony. German version. T. 97p. English ver-
   sion. T. and cc. 2c. 106p. ea.
The Hat Pin. Prose synopsis. T. 5p.
Homok-Satonyok. Prose synopsis. T. 4p.
A Husband Who Would Like to Be Jealous. T. 6p.
An Inventor. T. 5p.
Joe the Poor Boy. English tr., probably not by Molnar.
   A. 4p.
The Key of the Third Drawer. Prose synopsis, probably

not by Molnar. A. 7p.
The King's Maid. "First version." 1940. T. 2c. 70p.
  ea. 8 different later versions. T. and cc. In total
  1,096p.
Miracle in the Mountains. T. 95p. "Rough translation."
  T. 95p.
Miss Q Wants to Marry. T. 5p.
More than Woman? Less than Man? T. 8p.
The Most Dangerous Woman. Draft of a drama. T. 4p.
  Second draft. T. 6p.
Never Only Now. Draft of a drama. T. and cc. 2c. 3p.
  ea.
Noah's Ark. T. and cc. 5c. 127p. ea.
Nuptial Song. 1944. Hungarian text. T. 103p. English
  text. T. 126p.
  "Wedding Song." Synopsis. T. 6p.
  "Music." Synopsis. T. 5p.
Olympia. Tr. by S. Howard. 1928. T. 91p.
...Or Not to Be. English version. T. and cc. 5c. 66p.
  ea. Another version. T. 101p. Another version. T.
  and cc. 3c. 111p. ea. Hungarian version. T. 66p.
  Another version. T. and cc. 2c. 81p. ea.
The Pastry Baker's Wife. T. 72p.
Pete. Tr., probably not by Molnar. A. 5p.
Pit-a-pet/Szivdobogás. Hungarian text. T. 144p. First
  drafts, notes, outlines, in Hungarian. 1 volume.
Portrait of an Actor. 1949. Based on "Marsal." T. 40p.
  Another version with stage directions. 39p.
The Refuge (Comedy in Two Acts). T. 88p.
Sandy. English tr., probably not by Molnar. A. 7p.
Scenario of a Comedy in 3 Acts. English synopsis. 1941.
  T. 11p.
The Silk Cocoon. Tr., probably not by Molnar. A. 6p.
The Smile of a Woman. A Comedy. T. 2c. 54p. ea.
  Hungarian version. T. 56p. Hungarian synopsis. T. 38p.
Somebody. Also entitled Arthur. Dated 1947, copyright
  1932. Copyright of English version 1946. T. and cc.
  3c. 121p. ea. Later version dated 1951. T. and cc.
  2c. 122p. ea. Original tr. from the Hungarian. T.
  107p.
  Jemand. Prose synopsis. 1931. T. 11p.
Street and Number. T. 4p.
Tale of the Wolf. Synopsis for TV program. T. 26p.

<u>The Wolf</u>. Synopsis. T. 18p.
<u>There is a Play Tonight</u>. T. and cc. 2c. 132p. ea.
"Version 1940." T. and cc. 2c. 146p. ea.
<u>Die Theaterhexe</u>. Copyright 1928. German text. T. 10p.
<u>The Violet</u>. T. 39p.
<u>Waxworks</u>. 1948 version. T. and cc. 2c. 99p. ea. Vienna
    version, with stage directions. 1949. Tr. by A.
    Richman. T. and cc. with corr. by Molnar. 3c. 99p.
    ea.
<u>The Wedding/Hochzeit</u>. English version. T. and cc.
    2c. 35p. ea. German text. T. 37p.
<u>Wedding Day/Esküvö</u>. Outlines, notes, first drafts, in
    Hungarian. 1 volume. "Rough translation, first ver-
    sion." 1945. T. and cc. 2c. 91p. ea.
<u>Yvonne</u>. Synopsis. T. and cc. 2c. 32p. ea.
Untitled drama. Several drafts of different acts and
    scenes. T. and A. Ca. 120p.
"Andor." Synopsis. German text. T. 7p.
"Baron March." Synopsis. English text. T. and cc. 4c.
"Bill Duval." Short story. English text. T. 48p.
"The Blue+Eyed Lady [in the Show Window]." Ca. 1940.
    T. and cc. 2c. 27p. ea. 2c. 28p. ea.
"Borromeo." Synopsis with dialog. T. 9p.
"Children at War." English draft. T. and cc. 4c. 7p.
    ea. Synopsis. T. and cc. 2c. 9p. ea.
"Children in War (Children of Kiev)." Synopsis. T. 8p.
"Cosmopolitan Theater. Molnar Synopses." 1p. synopses,
    mostly stories, including: "The Merciless Mrs. Roy,"
    "The Smile of a Woman," "Eva," "Children at War,"
    "Story for a Film," "The Greedy City," "The Derelict
    Boat," "Autumn Journey," "Prisoners," "Jewels for
    Milady," "The Empress," "Girl of My Dreams," "Wax-
    works," "Untitled Story A," "Untitled Story B,"
    "Nuptial Song," "Noah's Ark," "The Sands Run Out,"
    "The Emperor," "Harmony," "There is a Play Tonight,"
    "Stella," "The King's Maid," "Miracle in the Moun-
    tains," "Baron Marcius," "The Piping Cherub," "Or
    Not to Be."
"Disquiet Night." T. and cc. 3c. 5p. ea. Hungarian
    offprint, with corr. 5p.
"The Gambler." English tr., probably not by Molnar.
    A. 31p.

"Girl of My Dreams." Short story. Hungarian text. 1941.
T. 2c. 32p. ea. English text. T. and cc. 2c. 37p.
ea.
"Jewels." Short story. Hungarian text. T. 24p.
"Mademoiselle Jourfix." English synopsis. T. 2c. 4p.
ea.
"Material for a Story." English text. T. 25p.
"The miraculous stroke - a modern legend." English tr.,
probably not by Molnar. A. 5p.
"The Musical Angel." English synopsis. T. and cc. 5c.
7p. ea.
"Outline of a Story about 20 Little French Children at
War." English draft. T. 9p.
"Princess Olga at the Funeral." English tr., probably
not by Molnar. A. 9p.
"Soldier Story." Short story. English text. T. 9p.
Hungarian text. T. 9p. "Material for a soldier
story." English text. T. 9p.
"Stella, Material for a story." T. and cc. 3c. 25p. ea.
"Story II." Hungarian text. T. 25p. English text. T.
and cc. 4c. 26p. ea.
"Story III." English text. T. and cc. 3c. 26p. ea.
"Two Boys and a Girl." Short story. Hungarian text.
T. 3p.
"Vanity Fair." Designated "A". Hungarian text. T. 5p.
Another version marked "B". Hungarian text. T. 5p.
"Wasser kommt aus den Bergen." Synopsis of a story.
T. 5p.
Untitled story. Draft. English text. T. 7p.

C5   Love Makes Me Sick. English adaptation of Pasternak's
Daddy is a Wolf. T. 197p. Another copy, dated 1945.
Story III. 1927. Synopsis of a film story. T. 26p.
Hungarian text. 1921. T. 25p.
Untitled film story. Synopsis. T. 46p.

C7   Short explanation of "A Tale of the Wolf." 1950. T.
and cc. 2c. 1p. ea.
"Wer war Delila?" Discussion in dialog form. Mimeo. 3p.

C12 The Good Fairy. "Acting version 1951." Roll book. T.
162p.

D2   Offprints and printed versions of:
Carnival. Tr. by Melville Baker. First performance

1924. 2c. 44p. ea.
Delila. Lustspiel in 3 Akten. 88p.
Fashions for Men. Tr. by B. Glazer. First perform-
ance 1922. 2c. 61p. ea.
The Lawyer. Tr. by G. Halasz. 50p.
Liliom. Script book.
Marshal. English version. 2c. 25p. ea.
Still Life. Tr. by S. Greenburger. 2c. 12p. ea.
The Swan. Tr. by B. Glazer. First performance 1923.
57p.
Theater. English tr. by L. Rittenburg. First per-
formance 1921. 2c. 19p. and 20p.
The Violet. 25p.
The Witch. Tr. by S. Greenburger. 5p.

E   Adaptations of Molnar dramas:
The Devil. Adaptation by Oliver Herford. 1908. 42p.
The Glass Slipper. Adaptation by P. Moeller. 1925.
2c. 51p. ea.
The Good Fairy. Adaptation and tr. by J. Hinton.
T. 108p.
The Guardsman. Tr. by Colbron-Bartsch. Adaptation
by Moeller. 2c. 37p. ea.
Heaven and Earthly Love. Adaptation by Edna St.
Vincent Millay. 2c. 49p. ea.
Mima. Adaptation by D. Belasco of The Red Mill. 68p.
The Play's the Thing. Adaptation by P. G. Wodehouse.
87p.
The White Cloud. Adaptation. T. 106p.
Adaptation of the novel:
Die Jungens von der Paulstraße. Adaptation by Alex-
ander Hevesi. 1936. German text. Mimeo. 105p.

H3   1 cl. French.

H5   Halasz, George. "Ferenc Molnar: The Man Behind the
Monocle." T. 144p.
List of stories and sketches by Molnar. T. and cc. 3c.
1p. ea.
Nadas, Sandor. "A few famous sayings of Ferenc Molnar."
1940. A. and cc. 2c. 2p. ea.
"Budapest: the town whose modern literature was born
in a café." T. and cc. 4c. 5p. ea.
Hungarian essay on Molnar. T. 4p.

I   Financial documents: cash box receipts, royalties, etc.
      Delicate Story. 1951-1957. 1 F.
      The Good Fairy. 1950-1957. 1 F.
      ...Or Not to Be. 1953-1955. 3 F.
      The Play's the Thing. 1933-1949. 1 F. 1951-1954. 2 F.
      Ca. 60 contracts from the 1930s, 1940s, and 1950s,
      dealing primarily with the English dramas.
      Additional 29 F. with contracts.

K   36 books from Molnar's library, primarily tr. of his
      works.

Academy of Motion Picture Arts and Sciences, Margaret Herrick
Library, 9038 Melrose Avenue, Hollywood, California 90069.

C5   Film scripts (closed to the public):
      Breath of Scandal. 1960. 4 F.
      Olympia. Short synopsis.
      The Swan. 1925.

H3   Newspaper and magazine cl., including 2 "Profiles"
      from the New Yorker.

State University of New York at Binghamton, Center for Modern Theater Research, Binghamton, New York 13901.

MAX REINHARDT ARCHIVE

D2   Harmonie. Original promptbook.

J   Production photos:
      Fasching. 1 photo. 1917.
      Liliom. 1 photo from the Theater am Kurfurstendamm.
        Undated.
      Olympia. 5 photos.
      Riviera. 1 photo. 1925.

O   Riviera. 1 program.

University of Utah, Marriott Library, Western Americana
Department, Salt Lake City, Utah 84112.

FERENC MOLNAR

PAPERS OF LEROY J. ROBERTSON

31,2   Correspondence with LeRoy J. Robertson.

Museum of the City of New York, Fifth Avenue at 103rd Street,
New York, N.Y. 10029.

43   "Personality File."

Mrs. Elisabeth M. Stoerk and Mrs. Susanne B. Hoeller, 288
Ocean Drive West, Stamford, Connecticut 06902.

FRIDERIKE ZWEIG ARCHIVE

31   L. to Friderike Zweig filed under "Writers Service
      Center." 1945.

Southern Illinois University, Morris Library, Department of
Special Collections, Carbondale, Illinois 62901.

ERWIN PISCATOR PAPERS

B2   1 draft of a L. and c. of a L. from Erwin Piscator.
      1946, 1948.

Dartmouth College, Baker Memorial Library, Hanover, New
Hampshire 03755.

RENÉ FÜLÖP-MILLER PAPERS

H4   "Stories for Two." Review by René Fülöp-Miller. T. 3p.

Leo Baeck Institute, 129 East 73rd Street, New York, N.Y.
10021.

OTTO FANTL COLLECTION, FOTOS A-Z

I   Signature of Molnar in album. Dated Karlsbad 1936.

J   Photo from newspaper.

Harvard University, Houghton Library, Cambridge, Massachusetts 02138.

I   Inscription. Budapest, Dec. 15, 1909. A. 1p.

OSKAR MORGENSTERN

Economist, 1902-1977

<u>Dr. Oskar Morgenstern</u>, 94 Library Place, Princeton, New
Jersey 08540.

Private collection: inaccessible. / *Unzugängliche Privat-*
sammlung.

B1,2	Extremely large amounts of correspondence over many years.
C7	Some Ms. of articles and essays.
D7	Newspaper and magazine cl. of Morgenstern's writings.
F	Tape recordings of Morgenstern. Film of Morgenstern.
K	2,000-volume personal library.
L	Materials collected and used by Morgenstern in his work.

<u>Columbia University</u>, Butler Library, New York, N.Y. 10027.

B1   3 L. to Wesley C. Mitchell. T. 1936-1946.

<u>Mrs. Alice Loewy Kahler</u>, 1 Evelyn Place, Princeton, New
Jersey 08540.

ERICH VON KAHLER COLLECTION

B1   1 Ptc. to Erich von Kahler. Undated.

HANS JOACHIM MORGENTHAU

Political Scientist, 1904-

Prof. Hans Joachim Morgenthau, 19 East 80th Street, New York, N.Y. 10023.

Dr. Morgenthau intends to donate his private personal collection (over 30 ft.) to the Library of Congress. Details concerning the donation may be obtained from Mr. Nathan Einhorn (Exchange and Gifts Division, Library of Congress).

Professor Morgenthau beabsichtigt, seine Privatsammlung (über 9 m Materialien) der Library of Congress zu vermachen. Auskünfte über die beabsichtigte Schenkung erteilt Mr. Nathan Einhorn (Exchange and Gifts Division, Library of Congress).

A3   Appointment calendars. (Dr. Morgenthau plans to write his autobiography with the help of the calendars.)

B1,2 Correspondence 1937-present. Includes L. to and from: D. Acheson, W. Lippmann, etc.

C7   Ms. of all of Morgenthau's articles and books.

D7   Complete collection of offprints and cl. of all of Morgenthau's writings. Also c. of his longer works (books).

F   Tape recordings of lectures.
      Tape recording of an interview. Chicago, 1966.

H3   Newspaper and periodical cl. about Morgenthau (1937-present).

H4   Reviews of Morgenthau's works.

H5   Ms. of dissertations and theses on Morgenthau.

I   Documents (passports, etc.).

J   Photos over many years.

K   Personal library (political science, philosophy, etc.).

M   Honors received.

Library of Congress, Manuscript Division, Independence Avenue and First Street S.E., Washington, D.C. 20540.

REINHOLD NIEBUHR PAPERS, J. ROBERT OPPENHEIMER PAPERS,
LAWRENCE SPIVAK PAPERS, HANNAH ARENDT PAPERS

B1   1 L. to Reinhold Niebuhr. T. 1955.
       1 L. to New York Times. T. 1954.
       3 L. to J. R. Oppenheimer. T. 1954-1955.

B1,2   Unknown amount of correspondence with Hannah Arendt.

B2   2 L. from J. R. Oppenheimer. T. 1954-1955.

B3   Several L. to Lawrence Spivak concerning Morgenthau's
       appearance on "Meet the Press." 1965.

C7   The Moral Standards of the Social Scientist. Unpub.
       1953. T.c. 7p.

Columbia University, Butler Library, New York, N.Y. 10027.

B1   2 L. to Lindsay Roberts. T. 1960, 1967.
       13 L. to Peter Jacobsohn. T. and A. 1964.

C11   "The crossroad papers; a look into the American future."
       1964. T. with corr. and editorial marks. 323p.

Princeton University, Firestone Library, Princeton, New
Jersey 08540.

LOUIS FISCHER PAPERS

B1   3 L. to Louis Fischer. 1962-1965.

University of Notre Dame, Archives, Box 513, Notre Dame,
Indiana 46556.

FREDERICK P. KENKEL PAPERS

B1   1 L. to F. P. Kenkel. 1938.

New York Public Library, Manuscript Division, Fifth Avenue
and 42nd Street, New York, N.Y. 10018.

EMERGENCY COMMITTEE IN AID OF DISPLACED FOREIGN SCHOLARS, 1933-1945

*   File compiled when assistance was granted. 1933-1942.

NORBERT MUHLEN

Journalist, Author, 1909-

Dr. Norbert Muhlen, 315 West 106th Street, New York, N.Y. 10025.

The papers, materials and books of Norbert Muhlen have been acquired in the course of his professional career as correspondent to several newspapers and magazines and as political author. To the extent that he kept the materials, all of them are from the period after his arrival in the U.S. on Sept. 12, 1940. The papers are still being used by Dr. Muhlen professionally; however, he is willing to answer written inquiries concerning his materials.

Die Materialien von Norbert Muhlen wurden von ihm während seiner Laufbahn als Korrespondent mehrerer Zeitungen und Zeitschriften und als politischer Autor gesammelt. Soweit er die Materialien aufbewahrt hat, stammen sie alle aus der Zeit nach seiner Ankunft in den Vereinigten Staaten am 12. Sept. 1940. Dr. Muhlen benutzt seine Materialien noch selber, ist jedoch bereit, schriftliche Fragen zu beantworten.

A1   Appointment books. 1953+.

A2   Notebooks beginning with the early 1950s. The note-
      books are the results of note-taking on trips and
      interviews with individuals.

A3   Ms. of the autobiography that Muhlen is writing, as
      of 1977.

B1,2 Ca. 12-15 ft. of correspondence, ca. 1945-. Primarily
      L. to Muhlen since carbons of Muhlen's own L. were
      made only where it was important for legal reasons.
      Mainly professional correspondence with non-exiles,
      both political figures and journalists.

C7   T. of essays from the 1970s. (Earlier T. have all been
      discarded.)

C11   T. of Muhlen's recent books (6).

D7   Complete collection of cl. of Muhlen's writings from
      various newspapers dating back to 1945. Ca. 8,000
      items plus duplicates of syndicated articles.

G   Cl. of interviews in German newspapers.
Transcripts of interviews, mainly on German radio and
     television.

H3   Cl. from books and newspapers.

H4   Several hundred cl. of reviews of Muhlen's recent
     works.

I   Several awards, including the Bundesverdienstkreuz.

J   Large collection of photos, dating from 1950.

K   Library of ca. 4,000 books, primarily politics and
history but also including psychology and theology.
Also substantial or complete runs of the periodicals
Monat, Hochland, Time Magazine, Modern Age and Spiegel.

L   Collections of cl. on various subjects.
Script of the interview at the Institut für Zeitge-
     schichte about Konrad Heiden with Muhlen's notations.

State University of New York at Albany, Department of Germanic Languages and Literatures, 1400 Washington Avenue,
Albany, New York 12222.

KARL O. PAETEL COLLECTION

B1   2 L. to Karl O. Paetel (xerox). 1943.

PAUL NETTL

Musicologist, 1899-1972

<u>Indiana University</u>, The University Libraries, Music Library,
Bloomington, Indiana 47401.

The PAUL NETTL COLLECTION, which consists of approximately
160 file folders of materials (1 large file cabinet), was
donated to the Library in 1973 by Dr. Bruno Nettl, son of
Paul Nettl. The collection is arranged alphabetically by
either subject or individual name and contains such types
of materials as: manuscripts and proofs of articles and
longer works by Nettl, newspaper cl., notes, correspondences, programs, etc. The collection may be used for research
by all patrons of the Music Library.

*Die PAUL NETTL COLLECTION, die aus annähernd 160 Ordnern mit
Materialien besteht (1 großer Aktenschrank), ist eine Schenkung von Dr. Bruno Nettl aus dem Jahre 1973. Dr. Bruno
Nettl ist der Sohn von Paul Nettl. Die Sammlung ist alpha-
betisch nach Schlagwörtern und nach Namen geordnet und umfaßt folgende Arten von Materialien: Manuskripte, Fahnen
kürzerer und längerer Veröffentlichungen von Nettl, Zeitungsausschnitte, Notizen, Briefwechsel, Programme usw. Benutzer
der Music Library dürfen die Sammlung für Forschungszwecke
benutzen.*

<u>State University of New York at Albany</u>, Department of Ger-
manic Languages and Literatures, 1400 Washington Avenue,
Albany, New York 12222.

STORM PUBLISHERS ARCHIVE

B1	39 L. to Alexander Gode von Aesch. 1947-1968.
B2	21 L. from Alexander Gode von Aesch. 1946-1968.
	1 L. from Friderike Jacobi. 1948.
B3	Correspondence between Trudy Nettl and Alexander Gode
	von Aesch. 1947. 3 L.
	Publisher's correspondence. 4 L.
C8	<u>Das Veilchen. Geschichte eines Liedes</u>. T. with h. corr.
	22p. Also proofs.

Das Veilchen——The Violet. The History of a Song.
2 different English versions. T. with h. corr.
25p. and 29p.

H4   Das Veilchen. 15 reviews.

University of Georgia, The University Libraries, Athens,
Georgia 30601.

GUIDO ADLER PAPERS

B1,2 Correspondence between Nettl and Guido Adler. 68 L.

Prof. Bruno Nettl, College of Fine and Applied Arts, School
of Music, University of Illinois at Urbana-Champaign,
Urbana, Illinois 61801.

Bruno Nettl is the son of Paul Nettl.

J   Family photos.

M   Memorabilia, including some papers and materials.

Mrs. Elisabeth M. Stoerk and Mrs. Susanne B. Hoeller, 288
Ocean Drive West, Stamford, Connecticut 06902.

FRIDERIKE ZWEIG ARCHIVE

B1   12 L. to Friderike Zweig. 1948-1962. Also L. filed
      under "Writers Service Center." 1944.

University of Texas, Humanities Research Center, Manuscripts
Collection, Box 7219, Austin, Texas 78712.

B1   5 L.

B2   6 L.

University of Illinois at Urbana-Champaign, Music Libraries,
Urbana, Illinois 61801.

B1   5 L. to Thor Wood.

B2   3 L. from Thor Wood.

Bruno Walter Memorial Foundation, c/o Miss Susie Danziger,
115 East 72nd Street, New York, N.Y. 10021.

B1,2 Correspondence with Bruno Walter.

Metropolitan Opera Association, Inc., The Archives, Lincoln
Center Plaza, New York, N.Y. 10023.

H3   Cl. from Opera News. 1941-1960.

University of Pennsylvania, The Charles Patterson Van Pelt
Library, Philadelphia, Pennsylvania 19104.

ALMA MAHLER-WERFEL COLLECTION

B1   3 L. and 1 Ptc. to Alma Mahler-Werfel. 1956-1964.

H3   1 cl.

New York Public Library, Manuscript Division, Fifth Avenue
and 42nd Street, New York, N.Y. 10018.

EMERGENCY COMMITTEE IN AID OF DISPLACED FOREIGN SCHOLARS,
1933-1945

*   File compiled when assistance was granted. 1939-1944.

OTTO NEUGEBAUER

Historian of Mathematics, 1899-

Materials concerning the career and life of Dr. Otto Neugebauer consist primarily of individual items found in collections of other prominent individuals. Dr. Neugebauer (Department of History of Mathematics, Brown University, Providence, Rhode Island 02912) has systematically destroyed any
materials that could be used for biographical purposes and
intends that any additional materials that are left at the
time of his death also be destroyed.

*Materialien, die den privaten und beruflichen Werdegang Dr.
Otto Neugebauers betreffen, existieren in erster Linie als
Einzelstücke in den Sammlungen anderer bekannter Persönlichkeiten. Prof. Neugebauer (Department of History of Mathematics, Brown University, Providence, Rhode Island 02912)
hat systematisch alles Material vernichtet, das für biographische Zwecke benutzt werden könnte, und er möchte, daß
alles eventuell nach seinem Tode sich noch findende Material
ebenfalls vernichtet wird.*

Library of Congress, Manuscript Division, Independence Avenue
and First Street S.E., Washington, D.C. 20540.

OSWALD VEBLEN PAPERS, J. ROBERT OPPENHEIMER PAPERS

B1   1 L. to W. Blaschke. T.c. 1938.
      2 L. to J. Robert Oppenheimer. A. 1954.
      35 L. and 2 Ptc. to Oswald Veblen. 1932-1948.

B2   1 L. from J. Robert Oppenheimer. T.c. 1954.
      2 L. from F. Springer. T.c. 1938.
      18 L. from Oswald Veblen. T.c. 1932-1945.

B3   29 L. 1938.

C8   "On the Planetary Theory of Copernicus." Undated. T.
      22p.

H3   Biographical sketch. 1938. 3p.

Harvard University, Houghton Library, Cambridge, Massachusetts 02138.

OTTO NEUGEBAUER

GEORGE SARTON PAPERS

B1   36 L. to George Sarton. 1933-1956.

New York University, Courant Institute of Mathematical Sciences, Library, 251 Mercer Street, New York, N.Y. 10012.

B1,2   File "Otto Neugebauer." 1938-1953.

Harvard University, University Archives, Widener Library, Cambridge, Massachusetts 02138.

RICHARD VON MISES COLLECTION

B1   1 L. to Richard von Mises. T. 1941.

Mrs. Richard Courant, 142 Carlton Road, New Rochelle, New York 10804.

B1,2   Correspondence between Neugebauer and Richard Courant, primarily 1932.

California Institute of Technology, Robert A. Millikan Library, Pasadena, California 91109.

THEODORE VON KARMAN CORRESPONDENCE

B1,2   Correspondence with Theodore von Karman. 1932-1933.
        1 F.

New York Public Library, Manuscript Division, Fifth Avenue and 42nd Street, New York, N.Y. 10018.

EMERGENCY COMMITTEE IN AID OF DISPLACED FOREIGN SCHOLARS, 1933-1945

*   File compiled when assistance was granted. 1934-1944.

671

OTTO NEUGEBAUER

University of Chicago, The Joseph Regenstein Library, 1100
East 57th Street, Chicago, Illinois 60637.

JAMES FRANCK PAPERS

B1,2   Correspondence with James Franck.

New School for Social Research, Office of the Dean of the
Graduate Faculty of Political and Social Science, 65 Fifth
Avenue, New York, N.Y. 10003.

RECORDS OF THE UNIVERSITY IN EXILE, 1933-45

A3   Curriculum vitae.

B1   1 L.

ALFRED NEUMANN

Writer, 1895-1952

<u>Southern Illinois University</u>, Morris Library, Department of
Special Collections, Carbondale, Illinois 62901.

ERWIN PISCATOR PAPERS

B1   48 L. and 2 Tel. to Erwin Piscator. T., A. and cc.
        1938-1950.

B2   29 L. and 2 drafts of L. from Erwin Piscator. 1939-
        1945.

C9   Tolstoy, Leo N. <u>War and Peace</u>. Adaptation by Alfred
        Neumann and Erwin Piscator. First version. Ca. March
        - Aug. 15, 1938. T. with commentary by Piscator,
        Neumann and Leo Lania. 5 F. Adaptation by Erwin Pis-
        cator and Alfred Neumann. Second version. Aug. 16,
        1938 - March 9, 1939. T. with commentary by Piscator
        and Neumann. 4 F.
        Adaptation by Erwin Piscator and Alfred Neumann,
        with Maurice Kurtz and Harold L. Anderson. Third
        version. Ca. Dec. 1941 - April 1942. T. with commen-
        tary by Piscator, Neumann, Kurtz and Anderson. 13 F.

<u>Academy of Motion Picture Arts and Sciences</u>, Margaret Herrick
Library, 9038 Melrose Avenue, Hollywood, California 90069.

C5   2 film scripts (closed to the public):
        <u>The Patriot</u>. 1928.
        <u>Paying the Piper</u>. 1921.

<u>University of Texas</u>, Humanities Research Center, Manuscripts
Collection, Box 7219, Austin, Texas 78712.

B1   1 L. to A. A. Knopf. 1929.

B2   1 L.

C   3 B. of Ms.

H3   Newspaper cl.

J   Photos of Neumann.

ALFRED NEUMANN

Dr. Harold von Hofe, Department of German, University of Southern California, Los Angeles, California 90007.

LUDWIG MARCUSE PAPERS

B1,2 Correspondence between Alfred Neumann and Ludwig Marcuse.

University of Pennsylvania, The Charles Patterson Van Pelt Library, Philadelphia, Pennsylvania 19104.

ALMA MAHLER-WERFEL COLLECTION

B1   10 L. to Alma Mahler-Werfel. 1946-1952.

Bruno Walter Memorial Foundation, c/o Miss Susie Danziger, 115 East 72nd Street, New York, N.Y. 10021.

B1,2 Correspondence with Bruno Walter.

University of New Hampshire, The Library, Department of Special Collections, Durham, New Hampshire 03824.

OSKAR MARIA GRAF COLLECTION, FRIEDRICH SALLY GROSSHUT COLLECTION

B1   1 L. to Oskar Maria Graf. 1950.
      1 L. to F. S. Grosshut. T. 1949.

New York Public Library, Manuscript Division, Fifth Avenue and 42nd Street, New York, N.Y. 10018.

THEO FELDMAN PAPERS

B1   2 Ptc. and 1 L. to Theo Feldman. T. and A. 1937.

Leo Baeck Institute, 129 East 73rd Street, New York, N.Y. 10021.

ALFRED NEUMANN

F. S. GROSSHUT COLLECTION

H5   Grosshut, F. S. "Wiedersehen mit Alfred Neumann."
       Undated. 3p.

ADOLF LEO OPPENHEIM

Assyriologist, 1904-1974

Mrs. Adolf Leo Oppenheim, 946 Creston Road, Berkeley, California 94708.

The materials in Mrs. Oppenheim's possession are from the estate of her husband and are inaccessible to the public.

Die Materialien in Frau Oppenheimers Besitz stammen aus dem Nachlaß ihres Mannes und sind zur Zeit für die Öffentlichkeit nicht zugänglich.

B1,2   Correspondence between Oppenheim and his wife. 1939-1940. Ca. 3 in.
L. of testimony relating to Oppenheim's internment and his attempts to get out.

C7,8   Microfiche of articles written by Oppenheim in many varied journals over a period of many years.

D7,8   Individually bound offprints of Oppenheim's earliest articles. 14 items.
A few offprints of Oppenheim's later writings.

I   Documents.

J   Photographs of Oppenheim at functions, meetings, publication festivities.

K   Long runs of periodicals.
Books from Oppenheim's personal library, unannotated.

L   Collection of newspaper cl.

M   Memorabilia.

Prof. Erika Reiner, c/o Oriental Institute, and **The Oriental Institute**, University of Chicago, 1155 East 58th Street, Chicago, Illinois 60637.

All materials are from the estate of Oppenheim.

Alle Materialien stammen aus dem Nachlaß von Oppenheim.

B1,2   Correspondence dealing with business matters of the Oriental Institute (property of the Institute).

C7   Ms. of pub. works.
        Ms. that were discarded (never pub.). Some as much as
        30 years old. Includes some lecture Ms. Ca. 6 in.

D7   Nearly complete collection of offprints of Oppenheim's
        publications.

K   Books from Oppenheim's personal library, annotated by
        Oppenheim.

New York Public Library, Manuscript Division, Fifth Avenue
and 42nd Street, New York, N.Y. 10018.

EMERGENCY COMMITTEE IN AID OF DISPLACED FOREIGN SCHOLARS,
1933-1945

*   File compiled when assistance was granted. 1941-1944.

KARL O. PAETEL

Writer, 1906-1975

State University of New York at Albany, Department of Germanic Languages and Literatures, 1400 Washington Avenue, Albany, New York 12222.

The materials of Karl O. Paetel were acquired in 1975-1976 by the State University of New York Library. The KARL O. PAETEL COLLECTION contains all the manuscripts of Paetel, a substantial part of his correspondence (a major part on xerox), an extensive collection of newspaper clippings on a number of subjects and other materials collected by Paetel systematically in the course of his work. The largest units of materials within the collection aside from manuscripts and letters are materials pertaining to the Youth Movement, Ernst Jünger, German resistance, refugee question, and Exile.

The largest part of Paetel's correspondence (mainly letters to him) was transferred to the Archiv der Deutschen Jugendbewegung at Burg Ludwigstein. Ludwigstein also received a collection of periodicals of the Youth Movement and miscellaneous other related materials.

A detailed list of the collection is being prepared by the State University of New York at Albany, Department of Germanic Languages and Literatures and will be available upon request. Publication rights remain with Mrs. Elisabeth Paetel.

Die Materialien aus dem Nachlaß von Karl O. Paetel werden im Laufe von 1975-1976 von der State University of New York at Albany Library übernommen. Die KARL O. PAETEL COLLECTION enthält sämtliche erhaltenen Manuskripte von Paetel, einen Teil seiner Korrespondenz (überwiegend Xeroxkopien), eine umfangreiche Sammlung von Zeitungsausschnitten zu verschiedenen Themen und andere Materialien, die Paetel systematisch im Laufe seiner schriftstellerischen Tätigkeit gesammelt hat. Die wichtigsten Teile der Sammlung, abgesehen von den Manuskripten und Briefen, sind die Materialien zur Jugendbewegung, über Ernst Jünger, Widerstand, Flüchtlingsprobleme, und Exil.

Der größte Teil der Paetel-Korrespondenz (hauptsächlich Briefe an ihm) wurde an das Archiv der Deutschen Jugendbewegung, Burg Ludwigstein, überführt. Ludwigstein hat ferner eine Sammlung von Jugendbewegung-Zeitschriften erhalten,

KARL O. PAETEL

sowie andere Materialien, die mit der Jugendbewegung zu tun haben.

Eine detaillierte Aufstellung der Paetel-Materialien ist in Vorbereitung und wird von der State University of New York at Albany, Department of Germanic Languages and Literatures, erhältlich sein. Die Publikationsrechte ruhen bei Frau Elisabeth Paetel.

A1   Diary pages. April 1 - July 20, 1949. Ca. 50p.

A3   Several T. of an autobiographical nature, concerning
     various periods in Paetel's life. Ca. 100p.
     Ein Deutsches Tagebuch. Pc. Ca. 300p. (Original at
     Ludwigstein.)
     Reise ohne Uhrzeit. Pc. of final original version.
     (Original at Ludwigstein.) Ca. 275p. Additional
     corrected and uncorrected carbon versions. Ca. 1,500p.

B1,2 Ca. 2,200 L. with individuals, primarily pc. of origi-
     nals (at Ludwigstein). 1940-1972. Includes: T. W.
     Adorno, Gertrude Albrechtova, Günther Anders, Stefan
     Andres, Hannah Arendt, Siegfried Aufhäuser, Julius
     Bab, Max Barth, Vicki Baum, Arnold Bergsträsser,
     Curt Bondy, Elisabeth Mann Borgese, Willy Brandt,
     Joseph Buttinger, Pablo Casals, Julius Epstein,
     Barthold Fles, Friedrich W. Forell, Karl Frank, Paul
     Froelich, Bella Fromm, Varian Fry, Manfred George,
     Oskar Maria Graf, Kurt Grossmann, Emil J. Gumbel,
     Waldemar Gurian, Arkadij Gurland, Walter Hammer,
     Walter Hasenclever, Henry Hatfield, Konrad Heiden,
     Eduard Heimann, Ferdinand A. Hermens, Paul Hertz,
     Wieland Herzfelde, Pablo Hesslein, Dietrich von
     Hildebrand, Kurt Hiller, Artur Holde, Franz J. Horch,
     Richard Huelsenbeck, Alvin Johnson, Marie Juchacz,
     Ernst Jünger, Erich von Kahler, Ossip Kalenter,
     Alfred Kantorowicz, Joseph Kaskell, Erich Kästner,
     Rudolf Katz, Robert M. W. Kempner, Kurt Kersten,
     Hermann Kesten, Henry Kissinger, Wolfgang Köhler,
     Karl Kraus, J. F. M. Lampel, Carl Landauer, Leo
     Lania, Adolf Leschnitzer, Peter M. Lindt, Prinz
     Hubertus zu Loewenstein, Louis P. Lochner, Joseph
     Luitpold (Stern), Joachim Maass, Valeriu Marcu,
     Walter Meckauer, Walter Mehring, Norbert Muhlen,
     Alfred Neumeyer, Ernst Erich Noth, John Oesterreicher,

Emil Oprecht, Heinz Pächter, Hertha Pauli, Rudolf
Pechel, Jacob Picard, Kurt Pinthus, Erwin Piscator,
Heinz Pol, Hermann Rauschning, Gustav Regler, Walter
Reuter, Curt Riess, Hans Rothfels, Hans Sahl, Will
Schaber, Rudolf Schick, Willi Schlamm, Arnold Schoen-
berg, Geschwister-Scholl (Stiftung), Gerhart Seger,
Toni Sender, George N. Schuster, Otto von Simson,
Kurt Singer, Walter Sokel, Wilhelm Sollmann, Hans
Speier, Hans Staudinger, Fritz Sternberg, Wilhelm
Sternfeld, Hans Steinitz, Otto Strasser, Frank
Thiess, Paul Tillich, Gottfried R. Treviranus,
Johannes Urzidil, Alfred Vagts, Walther Victor, Karl
Viëtor, Werner Vordtriede, Ernst Waldinger, F. C.
Weiskopf, Karl August Wittfogel, Arnold Wolfers,
Erich Wollenberg, Paul Zech, Otto Zoff, Carl Zuck-
mayer.

Also L. from publishers, newspapers, etc. including:
Books Abroad, Aufbau (NY), Argentinisches Tageblatt,
New Yorker Staats-Zeitung und Herold, Deutscher
Press-Klub, etc.

Deutsche Blätter correspondence (Udo Rukser, Albert
Theile). Ca. 200 L. 1946.

65th birthday correspondence. 1971. Pc. Ca. 50p.

Aufrecht zwischen den Stühlen correspondence, concerning a Festschrift for Paetel's 50th birthday, 1956.
Ca. 50p.

"Offizielle Briefe." 1940-1944. 239p. (Pc. sent to
Ludwigstein.)

L. to Paetel concerning his arrival in U.S. Aug. - Nov.
1940. (Pc. sent to Ludwigstein.)

C3   Originals and xeroxes of a few poems.

C4   Unter'm Fragezeichen. Geschichten und Aphorismen. 6
      stories. T.
      Wuuzi der Tyrann. T.

C6   40 radio scripts. 1954-1963.

C7   Manuscripts of books. Over 3,000p. including:
      Das Bild vom Menschen in der deutschen Jugendführung;
      Deutsche Jugend Gestern, Heute und Morgen;
      Das dritte Reich und seine Gegner;
      Ernst Jünger. Eine Biografie;
      Versuchung oder Chance?

Manuscripts of short essays. Ca. 2 ft. on youth, radi-
calism, black movements, German problems, authors
(American and German), American politics.
Reviews. Ca. 3 in.
Unsorted manuscripts. Ca. 2 ft.
Essays by Paetel tr. into English. Ca. 1 in.

D7 Complete collection of cl. and offprints by Paetel
(reviews, articles, etc.). Over 1,000 items, either
original or xerox. Index available.

D12 Materials to magazines published by Paetel:
Das junge Volk;
Die Kommenden;
Die Linke Front;
Wille zum Reich;
Die sozialistische Nation.

F Tape by Artur Grosse for Paetel's 60th birthday, in
Germany.
Tape by K. O. Paetel, spoken for Heinz Gollong.

H1 Aufrecht zwischen den Stühlen. Festschrift.
Don Quichotte en Miniatur. Printer's copy.

I Documents (and other materials) concerning: Paetel's
entry into the U.S.; reparation (ca. 100p.); naturalization (ca. 40p.).

J Photo collection.

L Card catalog consisting of Paetel's working bibliogra-
phy on different subjects (ca. 12 ft.).
Miscellaneous cl. on German and American political
questions and various authors. Ca. 8 ft.
Mimeographed periodicals, mainly German postwar, 1945-
1950. Ca. 4 ft.
Large collections of materials concerning:
Youth Movement. (Ca. 250 books, pamphlets, periodicals; ca. 1,000 cl.).
German Resistance. (Ca. 200 books, pamphlets; ca.
1,000 cl.).
Ernst Jünger. (Ca. 80 editions by Jünger, books
about Jünger; ca. 1,000 cl., photos and L.).
Refugee Problem 1945-. (Cl., correspondence, pam-
phlets, documents. Ca. 4 ft.).

KARL O. PAETEL

Smaller collections of materials concerning:
Council for a Democratic Germany;
Deutsche Blätter;
Deutschsprachiges Forum;
German Press Club;
Gesprächsfetzen;
Nationalkomittee Freies Deutschland.

Long Island University, C. W. Post Center, B. Davis Schwartz
Memorial Library, Greenvale, New York 11548.

L   Books and periodical issues dealing with the Beat Gen-
     eration:
     Ca. 200 books and periodical issues;
     Ca. 300 cl.

Mrs. Alice Loewy Kahler, 1 Evelyn Place, Princeton, New Jersey 08540.

ERICH VON KAHLER COLLECTION

Bl   4 L. to Erich von Kahler. 1945, 1949 and undated.

New York Public Library, Manuscript Division, Fifth Avenue
and 42nd Street, New York, N.Y. 10018.

EMERGENCY COMMITTEE IN AID OF DISPLACED FOREIGN SCHOLARS,
1933-1945

*   File compiled when assistance was granted. 1944.

University of Chicago, The Joseph Regenstein Library, 1100
East 57th Street, Chicago, Illinois 60637.

EMIL GUMBEL PAPERS

Bl,2 Correspondence between Emil Gumbel and Karl O. Paetel.
      1940s.

682

Mr. Joseph Kaskell, 410 Riverside Drive, New York, N.Y. 10025.

B2   3 L. from Udo Rukser. 1943, 1947.
      1 L. from Albert Theile. 1943.

Leo Baeck Institute, 129 East 73rd Street, New York, N.Y. 10021.

JACOB PICARD COLLECTION, KURT KERSTEN COLLECTION

B1   1 L. to Kurt Kersten. 1954.

B1,2 Correspondence with Jacob Picard.

Mrs. Gertrude Urzidil, 83-39 116th Street, Richmond Hill, New York 11418.

JOHANNES URZIDIL COLLECTION

B1   1 short note to Johannes Urzidil. A. 1951.

Mrs. Peter M. Lindt, 949 West End Avenue, New York, N.Y. 10025.

B1   Small amount of correspondence with Peter M. Lindt.

Mrs. Elisabeth Paetel, 68-49 Burns Street, Forest Hills, New York 11375.

J   Collection of photos (ca. 200).

Prof. Joseph Buttinger, R.R. 1, Box 264, Pennington, New Jersey 08534.

B1,2 Extensive correspondence with Joseph Buttinger.

ERWIN PANOFSKY

Art Historian, 1892-1968

DORA PANOFSKY

Art Historian, 1885-1966

Mrs. Gerda Panofsky, 97 Brattle Road, Princeton, New Jersey 08540.

The materials in Mrs. Panofsky's possession are from the estate of Erwin Panofsky. The materials, primarily concerning Erwin Panofsky, will remain inaccessible to the public for the present time.

Die Materialien im Besitz von Mrs. Panofsky stammen aus dem Nachlaß von Erwin Panofsky. Sie beziehen sich in erster Linie auf Erwin Panofsky und sind im Moment nicht zugänglich.

B1,2   Ca. 15,000 L. to and from E. Panofsky. 1920s-1960s, including some c. of L. by Panofsky from his years at the Institute for Advanced Studies (1935+). Primarily correspondence with friends and colleagues.

C7   Ms. and rough drafts of books, articles and lectures (several still unpub.). Several 1,000p.

D7   Complete collection of offprints by Panofsky.

H3   Articles on E. Panofsky's lectures, visits, etc.

H4   Reviews of book by E. Panofsky.

I   Numerous documents.

J   Art historical photos used for books and articles, some for anticipated future research.
Several personal photos.

K   Art library, including periodicals. Divided into two sections, those kept by Mrs. Panofsky and those given to the Institute for Advanced Studies.

L   Many offprints of articles by others.

Harvard University, Fogg Art Museum, Cambridge, Massachusetts 02138.

ERWIN PANOFSKY / DORA PANOFSKY

B1,2 Correspondence with Paul Sachs. Ca. 60 items. 1926-
     1947.

Library of Congress, Manuscript Division, Independence Avenue
and First Street S.E., Washington, D.C. 20540.

OSWALD VEBLEN PAPERS, J. ROBERT OPPENHEIMER PAPERS

B1   7 L., 1 Tel. and 1 Ptc. to Oswald Veblen. T. and A.
     1936-1954.
     4 L. to J. Robert Oppenheimer. T. and A. 1958-1966.
B2   1 L. from J. Robert Oppenheimer. T.c. 1963.

Princeton University, Firestone Library, Princeton, New Jersey 08540.

B1   1 L. to Booth Tarkington. T.c. 1944.
B2   25 L. from Booth Tarkington. Originals and microfilm.
     1936-1946.
C7   "Humanitas Tarkingtoniana." Article on Booth Tarking-
     ton. 1946.

Harvard University, Houghton Library, Cambridge, Massachusetts 02138.

GEORGE SARTON PAPERS

B1   3 L. to George Sarton. 1947-1955.

American Philosophical Society, The Library, 105 South Fifth
Street, Philadelphia, Pennsylvania 19106.

WOLFGANG KÖHLER PAPERS, FRANZ BOAS PAPERS

B1   1 L. to Wolfgang Köhler. 1959.
B2   1 L. from Franz Boas. 1935.

Columbia University, Butler Library, New York, N.Y. 10027.

Bl   1 L. to Stafford Bryant Jr. T. 1963.

Yale University, Beinecke Rare Book and Manuscript Library,
New Haven, Connecticut 06520.

THOMAS MANN COLLECTION

Bl   1 L. to Alfred A. Knopf. T.cc. 1940.

Dr. Julius Held, 81 Monument Avenue, Old Bennington, Vermont
05201.

Bl   Several L. to Julius Held.

New York Public Library, Manuscript Division, Fifth Avenue
and 42nd Street, New York, N.Y. 10018.

EMERGENCY COMMITTEE IN AID OF DISPLACED FOREIGN SCHOLARS,
1933-1945

*   File compiled, no assistance given. 1934-1944.

Dr. Edward E. Lowinsky, Professor Emeritus, Department of
Music, University of Chicago, Chicago, Illinois 60637.

Bl   92 L. to Edward E. Lowinsky. 1943-1967.

B2   79 L. from Edward E. Lowinsky. 1943-1967.

C7   Ms. of a Baroque lecture by Erwin Panofsky.

Mrs. Alice Loewy Kahler, 1 Evelyn Place, Princeton, New
Jersey 08540.

ERICH VON KAHLER COLLECTION

Bl   1 L. to Erich von Kahler. 1965.

HERTHA PAULI

Writer, 1909-1973

<u>Mr. E. B. Ashton</u>, 102 Woodhull Road, Huntington, New York 11743.

The main collection of Hertha Pauli papers and materials is located at her former home in the possession of her husband, E[rnst] B[asch] Ashton. With the exception of 1 unfinished manuscript of a novel that Hertha Pauli brought with her when she came to the U.S., all the materials are from her years in this country. The entire collection was accumulated in the course of her professional work and is in relatively good order, having been sorted by Mr. Ashton. It is expected that the German papers will go to the Institut für Neuere Österreichische Literatur in Vienna and a xerox copy of the German materials will be placed at the State University of New York at Albany, which is also expected to receive her papers in English.

Die größte Sammlung von Hertha-Pauli-Materialien befindet sich im Besitz ihres Mannes, E. B. Ashton. Mit Ausnahme eines unvollendeten Romanmanuskripts, das Hertha Pauli mitbrachte, als sie in die Vereinigten Staaten emigrierte, stammen alle Materialien aus der Zeit ihres Aufenthaltes in diesem Lande. Die Sammlung wurde im Laufe ihres Berufslebens zusammengetragen; sie ist von Herrn Ashton geordnet worden und befindet sich in recht gutem Zustand. Wahrscheinlich werden die Materialien in deutscher Sprache an das Institut für Neuere Österreichische Literatur in Wien gehen. Photokopien dieser Materialien sowie ihre englischsprachigen Materialien werden der State University of New York at Albany zukommen.

A1   A number of appointment books, not a systematic collection.

A2   Several h. notebooks, which usually contain notes that she took when she did research in a library.

A3   Autobiographical sketches, generally replies to questionnaires from publishers, publicity or reference works (WHO'S WHO, Kürschner, etc.).
      <u>Break of Time</u>. Outlines, drafts and edited T. of English version of Pauli's last work, an account of her

first two years in exile. (German T. with Paul
Zsolnay Verlag, Vienna.)

B1,2   Business correspondence (filed in binders) with publishers, agents, research sources, etc. Typed, filed
by book titles and in chronological order. Also contains carbons of almost all of Pauli's business L.
since 1950.
Private correspondence (filed in envelopes), mainly
h., no carbons of Pauli's L.

B1   4 L., 1 Ptc. to Franz Theodor Csokor. France, 1939-
1940. (Returned to Pauli 25 years later, having been
printed with some changes in Csokor's Zeuge einer
Zeit; originals now with K. H. Danner, Universität
des Saarlandes, for planned exhibit on "Exile Literature in France."

B2   Over 100 L. from Franz Theodor Csokor, since 1948.
Ca. 50 L. from Walter Mehring, since his return to
Europe in 1953.
Also L. from: Eleanor Roosevelt, Albert Einstein, etc.

C1   Jugend nachher. Materials. (T. probably with Paul
Zsolnay Verlag; since Pauli always typed, there are
virtually no h. Ms. of her works.)
Partial drafts of 2 novels, never finished.

C2   Jugend vor Gericht. Dramatization of Jugend nachher. T.
Play commissioned by Young People's Theater, New York,
1953. T.

C3   Poems from the 1930s, reconstructed from memory in
1970-1972, posthumously pub. in Zürich, 1975. A.

C4   Some T. of, and voluminous materials for, her 19 pub.
juvenile works (filed by book title). A few outlines
and drafts of juvenile works she did not finish, or
for which she cancelled contracts.

C5   T. revision commissioned by Paul Muni of Alfred Neumann's screen play based on Pauli's Nobel biography,
on which Muni had an option. Film was never produced.

C6   T. of radio plays for Young People's Theater (broadcast by WNYC, 1947), for Voice of America, German

Unit (1951), and for series of book reviews broadcast over RIAS, Berlin in 1960s.

C7   T. of number of articles for Commentary, Aufbau, New
Yorker Staats-Zeitung und Herold, and other periodicals, of book reports for publishers, etc.

C9   Sponsel, Heinz. Tr. of 2 juvenile works by Pauli.

C11 T. drafts and voluminous materials for Pauli's biogra-
phies and monographs. Incomplete materials for:
Alfred Nobel. 1942.
I Lift My Lamp. 1948.
Complete materials for:
Bertha von Suttner story (rewritten 4 times: 1937,
1945, 1955, 1957).
Her Name Was Sojourner Truth. 1962.
The Secret of Sarajevo. 1965 (German version, 1966).
Der Riß der Zeit. 1970 (English version, 1972).

C14 Drawings by Fritz Kredel and other illustrators of
Pauli's juvenile works.

D   Mr. Ashton possesses at least 1 c. of every book written by Pauli, of every tr. of her books, and of
every newspaper or magazine in which anything of
hers, or about her, was ever originally printed or
reprinted.

E   Condensations in Reader's Digest and some 15 of its
international editions, in Catholic Digest, Topix,
Ambos Mundos, Revue, Praline and other American and
German magazines.

F   16 tapes of interviews and readings by Pauli (2 in English).

G   Some c. of her interviews in the press.

H3,4 Nearly complete collection of cl. about Pauli and her
works.

I   Czech passport, documents pertaining to her obtaining
her U.S. citizenship.
Contracts (in correspondence notebooks). Complete collection.

J   Collection of photos, also from before 1940.

K   Library assembled by Pauli and E. B. Ashton. 1,500-
2,000 volumes.

M   Awards, including: Das Silberne Ehrenzeichen für Ver-
dienste um die Republik Oesterreich.
Many items in her home.

N   Neumann, Alfred. Film script of the Nobel book.

Mrs. Elisabeth M. Stoerk and Mrs. Susanne B. Hoeller, 288
Ocean Drive West, Stamford, Connecticut 06902.

FRIDERIKE ZWEIG ARCHIVE

B1   20 L., 1 Tel. and 1 Ptc. to Friderike Zweig. 1942-1970.

B2   2 L. from Friderike Zweig. 1944 and undated.
1 L. from Stillman & Stillman.

B3   1 L.

H3   1 cl.

H5   1 curriculum vitae.

Austrian American Federation, 55 West 42nd Street, New York,
N.Y. 10036.

C1   Jugend Nachher. Dated Sept. 17, 1958. Wien: Paul Zsolnay Verlag, 1959. T.cc. with some corr. 280p.
Two Trumpeters of Vienna. Illustrations and cover sheet
by Emil Weiss. Garden City, N.Y.: Doubleday [1961].
T. with h. and typed corr. on nearly every page. 195p.

State University of New York at Albany, Department of Germanic Languages and Literatures, 1400 Washington Avenue,
Albany, New York 12222.

KARL O. PAETEL COLLECTION

B1   2 L. to Karl O. Paetel (xerox). 1940s.

<u>Library of Congress</u>, Manuscript Division, Independence Avenue and First Street S.E., Washington, D.C. 20540.

J. ROBERT OPPENHEIMER PAPERS

B1   1 L. to J. Robert Oppenheimer. T. 1949.

B2   2 L. from J. Robert Oppenheimer. T.c. 1949.

<u>University of Pennsylvania</u>, The Charles Patterson Van Pelt Library, Philadelphia, Pennsylvania 19104.

ALMA MAHLER-WERFEL COLLECTION

B1   2 L. to Alma Mahler-Werfel. 1957-1958.

B2   Draft of a L. from Alma Mahler-Werfel.

<u>Mrs. Peter M. Lindt</u>, 949 West End Avenue, New York, N.Y. 10025.

B1   Small amount of correspondence with Peter M. Lindt.

WOLFGANG PAULI

Physicist, 1900-

Mrs. Franca Pauli, widow of Wolfgang, still retains in her possession original correspondence of her husband at her home in Switzerland. The materials have been microfilmed and are available on film at the American Philosophical Society.

Frau Franca Pauli, die Witwe Wolfgang Paulis, befindet sich noch im Besitz der Originalkorrespondenz ihres Mannes. Die Materialien sind auf Mikrofilm aufgenommen worden und sind als solche bei der American Philosophical Society erhältlich.

American Philosophical Society, The Library, 105 South Fifth Street, Philadelphia, Pennsylvania 19106.

SIMON FLEXNER PAPERS, JAMES B. MURPHY PAPERS, NIELS BOHR CORRESPONDENCE

B1   12 L., including L. to: Albert Einstein.
       61 L. to Niels Bohr. 1924-1956.

B1,2   Correspondence with Simon Flexner.
       Correspondence with James B. Murphy.

B2   78 L. from Niels Bohr.

Archive for History of Quantum Physics (locations in U.S.: Bancroft Library, University of California, Berkeley; American Philosophical Society, Philadelphia, Pennsylvania; American Institute of Physics, New York, N.Y.).

B1   63 L., including L. from: George Gamow (1), Hans Gei-
       ger (1), Walther Gerlach (1), S. A. Goudsmit (4),
       W. Heisenberg (1), Pascual Jordan (1), H. A. Kramers
       (3), Ralph Kronig (8), Alfred Landé (24), Lise
       Meitner (1), Adelbert Rubinowicz (2), Erwin Schrö-
       dinger (2), A. G. Shenstone (1), Arnold Sommerfeld
       (6), V. F. Weisskopf (3), Gregor Wentzel (4).
       5 L. to Niels Bohr. 1922.

B1,2   Correspondence with Werner Heisenberg. 1922-1950. Ca.
       525p.

692

WOLFGANG PAULI

B2 2 L. from Niels Bohr. 1922.
1 L. ea. from: S. A. Goudsmit (1931), Rudolf Peierls
(1933), Erwin Schrödinger (1926), A. Sommerfeld
(1949).

C8 "Formulierung der Quantenelektrodynamik..." Draft.
[1932]. 8p.
"Beiträge zur Theorie der Elektronen und Positronen."
Draft. Undated. 9p.
"The Foundations of Quantum Theory." Notes of a lecture taken by M. H. L. Pryce. Undated. 11p.
Recollections of Fermi Statistics, of the Introduction
of the Neutrino in 1930-1931, and of the Rome Congress 1931. 1956. 10p.

Library of Congress, Manuscript Division, Independence Avenue
and First Street S.E., Washington, D.C. 20540.

J. ROBERT OPPENHEIMER PAPERS

A3 "Comment on Heisenberg's Radio Advertisement." [1958].
1p.
"Top Secret." 1950. 1p.

B1 17 L. and 2 Tel. to J. Robert Oppenheimer. T. and A.
1943-1954 and undated.
2 L.

B2 5 L. and 2 Ptc. from J. Robert Oppenheimer. 1943-1957.
1 L. from C. N. Yang and T. D. Lee. T.c. 1957.

H5 Anonymous funeral speech.

California Institute of Technology, Robert A. Millikan Library, Pasadena, California 91109.

PAUL S. EPSTEIN PAPERS, MAX DELBRÜCK CORRESPONDENCE and
general archive files

B1 4 L. to Paul Epstein. 1922-1943.
2 L. to Weigle. 1958.
11. L. to Max Delbrück. 1945-1962.

693

B1,2   Individual item(s) in folder. 1931.

B2   1 L. from Max Delbrück. 1945.

B3   1 L. from H. Weyl to Epstein re: Pauli.

University of Chicago, The Joseph Regenstein Library, 1100
East 57th Street, Chicago, Illinois 60637.

JAMES FRANCK PAPERS

B1,2   Lengthy correspondence between Pauli and James Franck.
       1944-1959.
       L. of congratulations to Franck on his 70th birthday.
       1952. Accompanied by photo of Pauli.

J   Group photo. Institute for Theoretical Physics. Copen-
       hagen, 1935.

Franklin Institute, The Library, Philadelphia, Pennsylvania
19103.

B1   3 L. to the Franklin Institute.

I   Certificate of Pauli's receipt of the Institute's
       "Franklin Medal." 1952.

Princeton University, Firestone Library, Princeton, New Jersey 08540.

THE PAPERS OF ALBERT EINSTEIN (1879-1955). For details concerning the use of the collection, see description under
Albert Einstein.

*THE PAPERS OF ALBERT EINSTEIN (1879-1955). Angaben über den
Zugang zu der Sammlung finden sich unter "Albert Einstein."*

B1,2   Unknown amount of correspondence between Albert Ein-
       stein and Wolfgang Pauli. 1923-1949.

University of California, Berkeley, The Bancroft Library,

Berkeley, California 94720.

E. O. LAWRENCE PAPERS

B1   3 L. to E. O. Lawrence. 1945, 1956.

Columbia University, Butler Library, New York, N.Y. 10027.

ORAL HISTORY COLLECTION

H5   Recollections of Wolfgang Pauli in an interview with
      Isidor Isaac Rabi.

Smithsonian Institution, Dibner Library, Washington, D.C.
20560.

D8   7 reprints of articles by Pauli. 1913-1927.

Duke University, William R. Perkins Library, Manuscript
Department, Durham, North Carolina 27706.

FRITZ WOLFGANG LONDON PAPERS

B1   1 L. to F. W. London. A. 1945.

Mrs. Maria Reichenbach, 456 Puerto Del Mar, Pacific Palisades,
California 90272.

B1   Several L. to Hans Reichenbach.

Mrs. Alice Loewy Kahler, 1 Evelyn Place, Princeton, New Jersey 08540.

ERICH VON KAHLER COLLECTION

B1   8 L., 4 Ptc. to Erich and Lily von Kahler. 1949-1958.
B2   1 L. from Kurt Wolff. 1950.

B3   2 cards, 3 L. to Erich von Kahler from Franca Pauli.
       1959-1966.
       1 L. from Kahler to Franca Pauli. 1962.

YELLA PESSL-SOBOTKA

Harpsichordist, 1906-

Mrs. Yella Pessl-Sobotka, 101 Franklin Street, Greenfield, Massachusetts 01301, and Mrs. Margrit Cartwright, Box 240, Mt. Hermon, Massachusetts 01354.

Private collections: accessible with permission of Mrs. Sobotka or her sister, Mrs. Cartwright (over 30 ft.).

Privatsammlung (über 9 m): zugänglich mit Erlaubnis von Frau Sobotka oder ihrer Schwester, Frau Cartwright.

A2	Notebooks.
B1,2	Correspondence, including L. to famous musicians, composers, etc. (Bruno Walter).
F	Records. Tape of Nucleonic Rocks.
H3	Newspaper and magazine cl., arranged in albums. Ca. 1926-.
I	Miscellaneous documents.
J	Photos.
K	Personal library.
L	Music manuscripts to operas (e.g., Nucleonic Rocks).
O	Programs to concerts.

University of Georgia, The University Libraries, Athens, Georgia 30601.

OLIN DOWNES PAPERS

B1,2   Correspondence with Olin Downes. 17 L.

JACOB PICARD

Writer, 1883-1967

<u>Leo Baeck Institute</u>, 129 East 73rd Street, New York, N.Y.
10021.

The JACOB PICARD COLLECTION was donated to the Institute in
1969 by Mrs. R. von Dijk-Picard, daughter of Jacob, in ac-
cordance with his will. The collection, which has been initially sorted and catalogued (AR 6016-6024), consists of
approximately 14 shelf feet of materials.

*Die JACOB PICARD COLLECTION ist eine Schenkung von Frau R.
von Dijk-Picard (einer Tochter von Jacob Picard) aus dem
Jahre 1969. Die Schenkung erfolgte gemäß den Bestimmungen
des Testaments. Die Sammlung ist vorläufig geordnet und
katalogisiert (AR 6016-6024) und besteht aus etwa 4,20 m
Materialien.*

A1   14 diaries. 1906-1950.
      Account books. 1909, 1919, 1919-1924.

A3   "Autobiography I & II." A. and T.
      "Erinnerungen eigenen Lebens." German. 6 versions.
      "Sommererlebnis 1911." German. 7p.
      Curriculum vitae. 4 versions.

B1,2 Correspondence, including L. to and from: Alexander
      Abusch, Paul Amann, Stefan Andres, Julius Bab, Leo
      Baeck, Max Barth, Gertrud Chodziesner (Kolmar),
      Albert Ehrenstein, Alfred Einstein, Manfred George,
      Francis Golffing, Oskar Maria Graf, Willy Haas, Her-
      mann Hesse, Theodor Heuss, Franz Horch, Walter Jens,
      Mascha Kaleko, Ossip Kalenter, Kurt Kersten, Hans
      Kohn, Ludwig Lewisohn, Thomas Mann, Otto Meyerhoff,
      Hans Nathan, Ernst Erich Noth, Karl Otto Paetel, Pem,
      Kurt Pinthus, Paul Raabe, Nelly Sachs, Selfhelp, Karl
      Viëtor, Ernst Waldinger, Arnold Wolfers, Stefan Zweig.
      Correspondence with brothers and sisters and close
      relatives. 1919-1958.
      Correspondence with daughter Renate. 1929-1958, includ-
      ing correspondence concerning her emigration.
      Correspondence during World War I with family (mother,
      brothers and sisters, relatives and friends). 1914-
      1918.

Correspondence concerning emigration and naturalization.

B2   Congratulatory notes upon 70th birthday.
Congratulatory notes upon 75th birthday.
Congratulatory notes upon 80th birthday.

B3   Family correspondences. 1882-1939.
Business correspondence of parents and grandparents of
Picard with the Schweizerische Unionbank, Schweizeri-
sche Volksbank. 1892-1911.

C3   "Erschütterung. Gedichte." 1920.
"Gedichte." Undated.
"Heimkehr. Ausgewählte Gedichte." Incomplete. 112p.
plus copies.

C4   "Am Tag von Serajewo oder Wie es für mich begann." 6p.
"Letztes Idyll am Tag von Serajewo." 6p.
"Apostles of Discord." German. 3p.
"Begegnung." 2 versions. 1p. and 3p.
"Der Bruder"/"The Brother." German and 2 English ver-
sions. 17p., 19p. and 21p.
"Das Bureau." 1912. 3p.
"The Burial." English. 8p.
"The Call." 2 versions. 2p. ea.
"Ein Gang nur." 1959. 1p.
"Ende, Anfang und Erinnerung." 2 versions. 5p. ea.
"Erkenntnisse." 4p.
"Eva und der holländische Liqueur." 4p.
"Der Falke." 1936. 4p.
"Fastnacht in der kleinen Stadt." 4p.
"Der Fisch." German and 2 English versions. 10p., 8p.
11p.
"The Forest." 8p.
"The Fox." 2 versions. 5p.
"Das Gewitter und der Abend." 2 versions, German. 3p.,
4p.
"Haß." 6p.
"Hoax." 3p.
"Joselmanns schwerste Stunde." German and English. 30p.,
32p., 21p.
"Landmann Hal." 1920. 6p.
"Das Lotterielos." German and English. 4p., 12p.
"The Martyrdom of General Porter." English.
"The Case of Fitz John Porter." German.

"Max Liebermann und der junge jüdische Maler." German and English.

"The Monument." English. 10p.

"Der Nachbar und der Garten." German and English. Also Introduction by Peter Lindt, radio station WBNX.

"Parnes erhält eine Lehre." German, English and French versions. 4p., 7p., 5p.

"Raphael und Recha." German and English. 46p., 52p.

"The Sin." 3p.

"Späte Entlohnung." 1962. 1p.

"Das Steinbeil." 1937. 4p.

"Der Untersee." 3p.

"Die Vergeltung." German and English. 13p., 22p.

"The Victim. The Marked Man." 30p.

"Wie ich Hölderlin entdeckte. Ein Knabenerlebnis von einst." 2 versions. 36p., 32p.

"Winterfeldzug." 2 c. 7p. ea.

"Wir sind Utopia." German and English. 15p., 16p.

"The Wooer." 11p.

"Das Zeitungsblatt." 2 versions.

"Zurs." 3p.

"Zwei Boote am Morgen." 3p.

"Zwei Dörfer. Novelle." 2 versions.

"Zwei gelbe Männer." 3p.

"Zwei Mütter. Die Gütige, eine Novelle." German and English. 8p., 7p.

Untitled Ms. 5p., 15p., 8p., 11p.

C7   "Abschied von Albert Ehrenstein." 2p.

"Alfred Mombert 70 Jahre alt." 3p.

"Alfred Mombert zum 15. Todestag." 2 versions. 9p., 10p.

"Die alte Lehre." German. Südwestfunk Studio Freiburg. 4p.

"Anhang zum Lift für Julius Bab und eigentlicher Lift zum 70. Geburtstag." 3p.

"Arendts Eichmann." German. 1p.

"Die Atombombe wird von niemandem in einem zukünftigen Kriege benützt werden." 1949. 4p. plus notes by M. George.

Auerbach, Berthold. Essay for Auerbach's 150th birthday, notes.

"Aus einer Selbstcharakterisierung der jüdischen Erzählungen." 1p.

"Ausstellung Gustav Wolf." 1p.
"Ben Hur, Lew Wallace und der Amerikanische Bürger-
krieg." German. Different versions.
"Bodensee." German. 9p.
"Bodenseebuch 1960: Die Konstanzer Proklamation von
1848." German. Offprint.
"Der Dichter Ernst Waldinger." 2p.
"Dichtung in Deutschland seit 1933. Exposé zu dem Vor-
trag." 4p.
"Ein Licht auf Ernst Jünger." 2p.
"Erinnerung an der Rheinischen Hausfreund, zum 125.
Todestag von Johann Peter Hebel." 9p.
"Ernst Blass zum 20. Todestag." 8p.
"Der erste Verleger in Deutschland." 1946. 3p.
"Finally 'J'accuse' in Germany or 'The Voice of the
Other Germany'." 3 versions. 18p., 12p., 13p.
"The French and the German General Staff in 1940." 15p.
"Gertrud Chodziesner." Afterword. 2 versions. 2p. ea.
"Julius Bab in Amerika." 2 versions, German. 5p., 6p.
"Der Lift." 1939. 4p. plus copies.
"Methoden der Verhetzung." 1941. English and German.
8p., 6p.
"Die Möglichkeit jüdischer Dichtung in der Diaspora."
German and English versions. 3p., 6p.
"Münchener Karneval vor dem 1. Krieg." 6p.
"Naphtali Hirz Wesseley." German. 4p.
"Non-Nazi Literature in Nazi-Germany." English. 15p.,
16p. Incomplete German version. 3p.
"Otto Hirsch." 1941. German and English. 3p., 7p.
"The Poet Mascha Kaleko." 1p.
"Poetical Re-creation." English and German. 6p., 8p.
"Prelude." 6p.
"Quaker-Erlebnis." German and English. 6p., 8p.
"Rückkehr der Juden nach Deutschland." German and 2
English versions. 7p., 6p., 9p.
"Die Schuld an der Niederlage der Verbündeten im Som-
mer 1940." 1941. 6p.
"Sind die Juden ein Wandervolk?" German, English and
Bremer-Rundfunk versions. 7p., 8p., 10p.
"Stefan Andres. Fünfzig Jahre." 20p.
"Stefan George, eine Nachdichtung." 6p.
"Trauer um Felix Warburg." 3p.
"Van Gogh und Delacroix." 1938. 4p.

"Was Democracy Unknown in Germany?" 10p.

"Wildhagen." German. 3p.

"Wird die Atombombe in Zukunft benützt werden?" 1945.
5p.

"You Can't Manufacture Generals." 1941. English and
German. 9p., 5p.

"Zum 125. Geburtstag von Franz Sigel." German. 12p.

C9 Rothstein, James. "Die Künstler." Words by Jacob
Picard.

C11 Franz Sigel. Biographie. German. Vol. II, p. 205-329;
Vol. III, p. 330-422; Vol. IV, p. 423-580. Another
incomplete version. 600p. Outlines and rough drafts.
Franz Sigel. Biography. Incomplete English version.
600p. Additional c. of first 3 volumes. Also notations by translator. 5p.
Bibliographies for biography of Franz Sigel. Several c.
"A Few Words about the Biography of Franz Sigel." 2p.
plus copies.

D3 "Gedichte, 1909-1961." Pub. in various newspapers.

D4 Cl. of stories that appeared under the pseudonyms J. P.
Wangen and Jakob Badner. 25 cl.

D4,7 Newspaper cl. 1908-1964. 167 cl.

H4 Cl. concerning Picard's writings.

I Divorce decree.
Personal and family documents. 25 items.

J Photo of Julius Bab on 80th birthday.
Photo of Siegfried Guggenheim.
Family photos, photos of friends.
Photos of Wangen, Konstanz, Synagogue Wangen, etc.
Photos of Jacob Picard.
2 photo albums.
Photos of daughter Renate.
Photo of Heine.
Photos of pictures, etc.

L Materials for Franz Sigel Biography. Cl., notes by
Picard, notebooks.
Newspaper cl. on Gertrud Kolmar [Gertrud Chodziesner].
Senf. Student newspaper, Constance. Undated.

N   Andres, Stefan. "Gedichte." 1945.
       Articles, poems, etc. by: Eugen Horner, Neter Deganiah,
       Stefan Andres, Ludwig Lewisohn, Marianne Rein, Mala
       Moyes, Dora Edinger, Alfred Mombert, Gertrud Kolmar.

KURT KERSTEN COLLECTION, JULIUS BAB COLLECTION, PAUL AMANN
COLLECTION, ILSE BLUMENTHAL-WEISS COLLECTION

Bl   6 L. and 2 Ptc. to Kurt Kersten. 1952-1959.
       1 Ptc. to Julius Bab. 1956.
       9 L.

Bl,2   Correspondence with Paul Amann.

C3   1 poem text.

C7   1 essay text.

New York Public Library, Manuscript Division, Fifth Avenue
and 42nd Street, New York, N.Y. 10018.

EMERGENCY COMMITTEE IN AID OF DISPLACED FOREIGN SCHOLARS,
1933-1945

*   File compiled, no assistance given. 1943.

Immigration History Research Center of the University of
Minnesota, 826 Berry Street, St. Paul, Minnesota 55101.

AMERICAN COUNCIL FOR EMIGRÉS IN THE PROFESSIONS ARCHIVES

A3   Curriculum vitae, questionnaires, etc. 7p.

Bl   2 L. to Else Staudinger. 1943, 1945. Also outline of
       proposed Franz Sigel biography.

B3   5 L. 1943-1945, including L. from: Else Staudinger,
       Karl Viëtor.

H4   Excerpts of reviews of the collection of stories, Der
       Gezeichnete. 1p.

I   Receipt for $600 donation for Picard.

State University of New York at Albany, Department of Germanic Languages and Literatures, 1400 Washington Avenue, Albany, New York 12222.

HELMUT HIRSCH COLLECTION, KARL O. PAETEL COLLECTION

B1   1 L. to Helmut Hirsch. 1951.
       12 L. to Karl O. Paetel (xerox). 1950-1964.
B2   1 L. from Karl O. Paetel (xerox). 1963.

Mrs. Gertrude Urzidil, 83-39 116th Street, Richmond Hill, New York, N.Y. 11418.

JOHANNES URZIDIL COLLECTION

B1   2 L. and 2 Ptc. to Johannes Urzidil. A. 1958-1963.
J   Photo postcard. 1958.

University of New Hampshire, The Library, Department of Special Collections, Durham, New Hampshire 03824.

OSKAR MARIA GRAF COLLECTION

B1   1 L. to Oskar Maria Graf. 1954.

GERHARD PIERS

Psychoanalyst, 1908-

MARIA PIERS

Psychoanalyst, 1911-

Dr. Maria Piers, c/o Erikson Institute for Early Education,
1525 East 53rd Street, Chicago, Illinois 60637.

The materials located at the Erikson Institute belong to
Drs. Maria and Gerhard Piers, as well as to the Institute.
A majority of the materials are from the Piers' private col-
lections and are inaccessible to the public.

*Die Materialien im Erikson Institute gehören sowohl Dr.
Maria und Dr. Gerhard Piers als auch dem Institut. Der
Hauptteil der Materialien stammt aus Piers-Privatsammlungen
und ist für die Öffentlichkeit nicht zugänglich.*

B   Correspondence of the Institute over the past 10 years.

B1,2   Correspondence concerning a task force for a political
           campaign.
           Lengthy correspondence with Erik Erikson, primarily
           during recent years.
           Lengthy correspondence with René Spitz, primarily over
           the past few years.
           Correspondence with Anna Freud.
           Correspondence with Edward Teller.
           Inherited Arnold Schoenberg correspondence.

C7   Ms. of books and articles by Maria Piers.
           Ms. of unpub. writings of Gerhard Piers.

D7   Offprints of writings by Gerhard and Maria Piers.

G   Six-hour interview between Maria Piers and René Spitz.
           Numerous interviews for TV, film, taped, on subjects
           such as: psychoanalysis, adolescence, etc.

I   Documents, including genealogical documents.

J   Photo file of the Institute, including photos of the
           Piers.
           Private photo collection of the Piers from various
           places and times.

K   Personal libraries of Gerhard and Maria Piers.

L   Offprints of writings of René Spitz.
      Materials concerning the Institute.

N   Erikson, Erik. <u>Identity, Youth and Crisis</u>. Ms.
      <u>Young Man Luther</u>. Ms.
      Ms. of writings of others.

<u>Reiss-Davis Child Study Center</u>, 9760 West Pico Boulevard,
Los Angeles, California 90035.

F   Taped lectures of Maria Piers.

<u>Dr. Friedrich J. Hacker</u>, The Hacker Clinic, 160 Lasky Drive,
Beverly Hills, California 90212.

B1,2   Correspondence between Hacker and Gerhard and Maria
       Piers.

KURT PINTHUS

Critic, Historian of Literature, 1886-1975

Leo Baeck Institute, 129 East 73rd Street, New York, N.Y. 10021.

KURT KERSTEN COLLECTION, JACOB PICARD COLLECTION

B1	5 L. and 5 Ptc. to Kurt Kersten. 1946-1959.
B1,2	Correspondence with Jacob Picard.
D7	1 cl. 1963.

Southern Illinois University, Morris Library, Department of Special Collections, Carbondale, Illinois 62901.

ERWIN PISCATOR PAPERS

B1	3 L. to Erwin Piscator. A. and T. 1940-1941, 1963.
B2	2 L. from Erwin Piscator. T.cc. 1941.

University of New Hampshire, The Library, Department of Special Collections, Durham, New Hampshire 03824.

OSKAR MARIA GRAF COLLECTION

B1	1 L. to Max Kolmsperger. 1962.
	1 L. to Oskar Maria Graf. 1962.

State University of New York at Albany, Department of Germanic Languages and Literatures, 1400 Washington Avenue, Albany, New York 12222.

KARL O. PAETEL COLLECTION

B1	3 L. to Karl O. Paetel (xerox). 1961-1966.
B2	1 L. from Karl O. Paetel (xerox). 1961.

Mrs. Gertrude Urzidil, 83-39 116th Street, Richmond Hill, New York 11418.

707

KURT PINTHUS

JOHANNES URZIDIL COLLECTION

B1   2 L. and 1 Ptc. to Johannes Urzidil. T. and A. 1941,
      1962 and undated.

University of Pennsylvania, The Charles Patterson Van Pelt
Library, Philadelphia, Pennsylvania 19104.

ALMA MAHLER-WERFEL COLLECTION

B1   3 L., 2 Ptc. to Alma Mahler-Werfel. 1941-1961.
C14   Drawing of Franz Werfel.

University of Southern California, Lion Feuchtwanger Memorial
Library, 520 Paseo Miramar, Pacific Palisades, California
90272.

B1   1 L. to Lion Feuchtwanger. 1950.
B2   1 L. from Lion Feuchtwanger. 1950.

Dr. Harold von Hofe, Department of German, University of
Southern California, Los Angeles, California 90007.

LUDWIG MARCUSE PAPERS

B1,2 Correspondence with Ludwig Marcuse.

New York Public Library, Manuscript Division, Fifth Avenue
and 42nd Street, New York, N.Y. 10018.

EMERGENCY COMMITTEE IN AID OF DISPLACED FOREIGN SCHOLARS,
1933-1945

*   File compiled when assistance was granted. 1939-1944.

Barthold Fles Literary Agency, 507 Fifth Avenue, New York,
N.Y. 10016.

B1   2 L. to Barthold Fles. 1941.

Mr. Hans Sahl, 800 West End Avenue, New York, N.Y. 10025.

B1   Several L. to Hans Sahl.

Dr. Gustave O. Arlt, 13220-C Admiralty Way, Marina del Rey, California 90291.

FRANZ WERFEL ARCHIVE

B1   1 L. to Franz Werfel. 1942.

Immigration History Research Center of the University of Minnesota, 826 Berry Street, St. Paul, Minnesota 55101.

AMERICAN COUNCIL FOR EMIGRÉS IN THE PROFESSIONS ARCHIVES

B2   1 L. from Mrs. Henry Seidel Canby. 1944.

Mr. Francis Heilbut, 328 West 96th Street, New York, N.Y. 10025.

IVAN HEILBUT PAPERS

B2   1 L. from Ivan Heilbut. 1943.

ERWIN PISCATOR

Theater Director, 1893-1966

Southern Illinois University, Morris Library, Department of
Special Collections, Carbondale, Illinois 62901.

The ERWIN PISCATOR PAPERS (Collection 31) consist of over
195 archive boxes or approximately 57.60 cubic feet of materials. The collection was officially donated to the Library
on June 24, 1971 by Dr. Maria Piscator, widow of Erwin. The
major portion of the collection was stored until April 1969
in the summer home of Maria Piscator, Stony Brook, N.Y. A
smaller portion was located in the Piscator home, 17 East
76th Street, New York. Because the papers were stored in
the cellar of the Piscator home for many years, some of the
correspondence is in rather fragile condition. The major
portion of the materials, however, is in good condition. A
detailed inventory as well as a detailed card index of the
collection have been prepared by Dr. Jürgen Stein, who worked
with the materials from April 1970 to Aug. 1972. The information represented in the following report was supplied by
Dr. Stein as a result of his work with the collection. With
the exception of the correspondence between Erwin and Maria
Piscator, which is restricted, all materials in the collection are open to researchers and scholars.

*Die ERWIN PISCATOR PAPERS (Collection 31) umfassen mehr als
195 Archivkartons (annähernd 1,60 m³ Materialien). Die Sammlung wurde offiziell am 24. Juni 1971 der Morris Library von
Dr. Maria Piscator, der Witwe Erwin Piscators, als Schenkung
übergeben. Der größte Teil der Sammlung war bis April 1969
im Sommerhaus von Maria Piscator in Stony Brook, N.Y., gela-
gert. Eine kleinere Menge befand sich im New Yorker Wohnung
(17 East 76th Street). Wegen der Lagerung der Materialien in
Kellerräumen ist ein Teil des Briefwechsels ziemlich brüchig
geworden. Der größte Teil der Materialien befindet sich jedoch in gutem Zustand. Ein ausführliches Inventar sowie ein
genauer Kartenindex der Sammlung wurde von Dr. Jürgen Stein
in der Zeit von April 1970 bis Aug. 1972 erarbeitet. Die
nachfolgenden Informationen stammen von Dr. Stein. Mit Ausnahme des Briefwechsels zwischen Erwin und Maria Piscator,
der nur beschränkt zugänglich ist, können alle Materialien
der Sammlung für Forschungszwecke benutzt werden.*

A1   "Tagebuch der Reise Erwin Piscators nach Spanien."

ERWIN PISCATOR

1936. A. 2p.
Diary pages and notes. Ca. 1940. A. 36p.
Diary. Jan. - March 1945. A. 97p.
Diaries. 1945 and 1949. A. 44p.
Loose diary pages. 1946. A. 22p.
Diary pages. Oct. - Nov. 1948. A. 30p.
Diary pages. 1949. A. 21p.
Diary pages and notes. Ca. 1950. A. 11p.
Diaries, written in Starnberg Hospital. March 1966.
Transcriptions by Aleida Montijn. T. 21p.
Diary pages. Transcriptions. Undated.
Appointment calendars. 1938, 1943, 1965-1966. Commentary by Piscator and Chouteau Dyer.

A2   Notes. 1936-1939. A. 30p.
Notes. Jan. - Nov. 1937. A. 71p.
Notes. 1940-1942. A. 31p.
Notes. 1943. A. 44p.
Notes. 1944-1948. A. 38p.
Notes. 1949. A. 17p.
Notes. 1960s. A. 13p.
Notes on Bertolt Brecht and the Epic Theater. A. 14p.
Notes on the Freie Volksbühne, Berlin. Ca. 1963-1964.
A. 23p.

B1   Ca. 25,000 L. to and from Erwin Piscator. 1936-1966,
including L. to: Theodor W. Adorno, Julius Bab,
Albert Bassermann, Simone de Beauvoir, Ulrich Becher,
Harry Belafonte, Elisabeth Bergner, Marlon Brando,
Willy Brandt, Bertolt Brecht, Willi Bredel, Felix
Bressart, Max Brod, Ferdinand Bruckner, Pearl S.
Buck, Charles Chaplin, Noel Coward, Ernst Deutsch,
William Dieterle, Theodore Dreiser, Albert Einstein,
Hanns Eisler, Lion Feuchtwanger, Barthold Fles,
Bruno Frank, John Gassner, Norman Bel Geddes, André
Gide, Iwan Goll, Mordecai Gorelik, Alexander Granach,
Walter Gropius, George Grosz, Moss Hart, Elisabeth
Hauptmann, Konrad Heiden, Theresa Helburn, Ernest
Hemingway, Wieland Herzfelde, Stefan Heym, Rolf
Hochhuth, Oskar Homolka, Hans Jaray, Leopold Jessner,
Alvin Johnson, Alfred Kantorowicz, Elia Kazan, Alfred
A. Knopf, Arthur Koestler, Oskar Kokoschka, Fritz
Kortner, Fritz Lang, Leo Lania, Charles Laughton,
Lotte Lenya, Sinclair Lewis, Erika Mann, Golo Mann,
Heinrich Mann, Klaus Mann, Thomas Mann, Ludwig

711

Marcuse, Walter Mehring, Arthur Miller, Leo Mittler,
Ferenc Molnar, Paul Muni, Alfred Neumann, Reinhold
Niebuhr, Louis Nizer, Clifford Odets, Sir Laurence
Olivier, P.E.M., Kurt Pinthus, Otto Preminger, Luise
Rainer, Gustav Regler, Hans José Rehfisch, Max Rein-
hardt, Erich Maria Remarque, Alexander Roda Roda,
Jules Romains, Fritz Rotter, Hans Sahl, William Sa-
royan, Jean-Paul Sartre, Anna Seghers, Upton Sinclair,
Rod Steiger, Lee Strasberg, Erich von Stroheim,
Helene Thimig, Dorothy Thompson, Paul Tillich, Ernst
Toller, Alexsey Tolstoy, Ludwig Ullmann, Fritz von
Unruh, Robert Penn Warren, Helene Weigel, Kurt Weill,
Orson Welles, Franz Werfel, Thornton Wilder, Tennes-
see Williams, Friedrich Wolf, Paul Zech, Carl Zuck-
mayer.

B2   Also L. from: Theodor W. Adorno, Günther Anders,
Raoul Auernheimer, Julius Bab, Albert Bassermann,
Ulrich Becher, Elisabeth Bergner, Willy Brandt, Ber-
tolt Brecht, Willi Bredel, Max Brod, Ferdinand Bruck-
ner, Pearl S. Buck, Franz Theodor Csokor, Kurt Desch,
Ernst Deutsch, William Dieterle, Theodor Dreiser,
Albert Einstein, Hanns Eisler, Lion Feuchtwanger,
Bruno Frank, John Gassner, Norman Bel Geddes, André
Gide, Iwan Goll, Mordecai Gorelik, Oskar Maria Graf,
Alexander Granach, Walter Gropius, George Grosz,
Moss Hart, Elisabeth Hauptmann, Theresa Helburn,
Kurt Hellmer, Wieland Herzfelde, Stefan Heym, Rolf
Hochhuth, Herbert Ihering, Hans Jaray, Leopold Jess-
ner, Alvin Johnson, Alfred Kantorowicz, Sidney Kauf-
man, Arthur Koestler, Paul Kohner, Fritz Kortner,
Leo Lania, Lotte Lenya, Rudolf Leonhard, Sinclair
Lewis, Ernst Lothar, David Luschnat, Erika Mann,
Heinrich Mann, Klaus Mann, Thomas Mann, Walter Meh-
ring, Leo Mittler, Alfred Neumann, Reinhold Niebuhr,
Louis Nizer, Clifford Odets, Laurence Olivier, P.E.M.,
Kurt Pinthus, Theodor Plievier, Alfred Polgar, Otto
Preminger, Gustav Regler, Hans José Rehfisch, Max
Reinhardt, Jules Romains, Hans Sahl, William Saroyan,
Jean-Paul Sartre, Heinrich Schnitzler, Anna Seghers,
Upton Sinclair, Lee Strasberg, Helene Thimig, Doro-
thy Thompson, Paul Tillich, Ernst Toller, Alexsey
Tolstoy, Ludwig Ullmann, Fritz von Unruh, Berthold

Viertel, Robert Penn Warren, Helene Weigel, Kurt Weill, Alma Mahler-Werfel, Franz Werfel, Thornton Wilder, Tennessee Williams, Friedrich Wolf, Carl Zuckmayer.

C2   Circle of Wisdom. Fragment. June 1943. A. 11p.
      Eva Braun - Drama. Ca. Nov. 1945. A. and T. 3p.
      Hitler's Gang. Presumably written by Piscator.
      Liebe ohne Paß. Dated Jan. 14, 1936. T. with corr.
      Presumably written by Piscator. 4p.
      Rally of Hope. Fragments. A. and T. with commentary by
      Erwin Piscator and Chouteau Dyer. 2 F. Notes. A. 24p.
      Various other versions, presumably written by Walter
      Mehring with commentary by Erwin Piscator and Chou-
      teau Dyer. 4 F.
      Toulon, oder die 16 Tage. Ca. 1942. A. 13p.

C3   Poetry and prose. A. and T. 27p.

C7   Erwin Piscator - Schriften 2. Aufsätze, Reden, Ge-
      spräche. T. with h. corr. 500p.
      "Objective Acting." T. 27p. Corr. by Maria Piscator
      and John Gassner. T. 12p.
      "Der Schrei nach der Kunst / The Cry for Art. Ten
      Years of European Theatre." A. 26p.
      "Some Remarks and Suggestions Concerning the Re-Organi-
      zation of the German Theater." Written in collabora-
      tion with Berthold Viertel. 1947-1948. T. with h.
      corr. by Piscator. Pc. 6p.
      "The Theatre Around the World." 1939. T. 21p.
      "The Theater of the Future." 1938-1939. T. 9p.
      Drafts to various works. 1936-1938. Ca. 30p.
      Publications of the Dramatic Workshop and Studio Thea-
      tre. 1939-1940. A. 45p.
      Texts of 14 speeches. 1936-1948. Ca. 225p.
      Untitled Ms. 1939. A. 19p.

C9   Goethe, Johann Wolfgang von. Faust. A. 21p.
      Mayer, Edwin Justus. Sunrise in My Pocket. Adaptation
      by Piscator with commentary by Piscator, Chouteau
      Dyer, John Gassner. Different scenes. A. and T. 1 B.
      Tolstoy, Alexsey and P. Shchegolev. Rasputin, die
      Romanovs, der Krieg und das Volk, das gegen sie auf-
      stand. Adaptation, presumably by Piscator and co-
      workers. T.

Tolstoy, Leo N. War and Peace. Adaptation by Erwin
Piscator and Alfred Neumann. First version. Ca.
March - Aug. 15, 1938. T. with commentary by Pisca-
tor, Neumann and Leo Lania. 5 F.
Second version. Aug. 16, 1938 - March 9, 1939. T.
with commentary by Piscator and Neumann. 4 F.
Third version. Co-workers Maurice Kurtz and Harold
L. Anderson. Ca. Dec. 1941 - April 1942. T. with
commentary by Piscator, Neumann, Kurtz and Anderson.
13 F.

C12 94 B. of scripts, roll books, author's notes, lighting
and prop books, etc. of works performed by the Dra-
matic Workshop, including:
Aeschylus. Agamemnon.
Aristophanes. Lysistrata.
Calderón de la Barca. Great Theatre of the World.
Wolfgang Borchardt. Outside the Door.
Bertolt Brecht. The Horatians and the Curiatians;
The Private Life of the Master Race; The Rise of
Arturo Ui; The Threepenny Opera.
Ferdinand Bruckner. Chaff; The Criminals.
Georg Büchner. Leonce and Lena.
Albert Camus. The Stranger.
Lewis Carroll. Alice in Wonderland.
Miguel de Cervantes. Numantia.
Anton P. Chekhov. A Marriage Proposal; The Sea Gull.
Noel Coward. Blithe Spirit; Fumed Oak; Hay Fever;
Private Lives; Red Peppers; Tonight at 8:30.
Theodore Dreiser. An American Tragedy.
Friedrich Dürrenmatt. Night Talk with a Contemptible
Visitor.
Alexander Dumas. The Lady of the Camellias.
Everyman.
Max Frisch. House in Berlin.
John Galsworthy. Escape.
André Gide. The Trial.
Johann Wolfgang von Goethe. Iphigenia in Tauris.
Gerhart Hauptmann. Hannele's Way to Heaven.
Ben Hecht. The Terrorist.
Rolf Hochhuth. The Deputy.
Henrik Ibsen. Peer Gynt.
Eugene Ionesco. The Chairs.

Erich Kästner. Emil and the Detectives.
Georg Kaiser. The Coral; Gas I; Gas II.
Garson Kanin. Born Yesterday.
George S. Kaufman. If Men Played Cards as Women Do;
  Of Thee I Sing.
Jerome Kern. The Doughgirls.
Joseph Kesselring. Arsenic and Old Lace.
Fritz Kortner. The World Unseen.
D. H. Lawrence. Lady Chatterly's Lover.
Gotthold E. Lessing. The Jews; Nathan the Wise.
Christopher Marlowe. Doctor Faustus.
Guy de Maupassant. The Olive Grove.
Edna St. Vincent Millay. Aria Da Capo.
Arthur Miller. All My Sons; Death of a Salesman.
Molière. The Imaginary Invalid.
Ferenc Molnar. Liliom.
Clifford Odets. Waiting for Lefty.
Eugene O'Neill. Desire Under the Elms; The Long Voy-
  age Home; Mourning Becomes Electra.
Luigi Pirandello. Tonight We Improvise.
Jean Racine. Esther.
Hans José Rehfisch. My Sister, My Spouse; Revolt of
  the Virgins.
Romain Rolland. Robespierre.
Jules Romains. Give the Earth a Little Longer.
William Saroyan. Don't Go Away Mad; Hello Out There;
  The Incurables; Jim Dandy; Subway Circus; Time of
  Your Life.
Jean-Paul Sartre. The Flies; The Unburied Dead.
William Shakespeare. King Lear; Macbeth; Midsummer
  Night's Dream; Romeo and Juliet; The Taming of the
  Shrew; Twelfth Night.
George Bernard Shaw. Androcles and the Lion; The
  Devil's Disciple; The Millionairess; Saint Joan.
Upton Sinclair. A Giant's Strength.
Sophocles. Antigone.
John Steinbeck. Of Mice and Men.
Carl Sternheim. Mask of Virtue.
August Strindberg. The Bridal Crown; The First Warn-
  ing.
Dorothy Thompson and Fritz Kortner. Spell Your Name.
James Thurber and Elliott Nugent. The Male Animal.
Leo Tolstoy. War and Peace.

Mark Twain. <u>Tom Sawyer, Ballad of the Mississippi</u>.
Fritz von Unruh. <u>The End Is Not Yet</u>.
Lope de Vega. <u>Sleep Well</u>.
Robert Penn Warren. <u>All the King's Men</u>.
Oscar Wilde. <u>The Importance of Being Earnest</u>; <u>Lady Windermere's Fan</u>.
Thornton Wilder. <u>Our Town</u>.
Tennessee Williams. <u>Battle of Angels</u>; <u>The Lady of the Larkspur Lotion</u>; <u>Mooney's Kids Don't Cry</u>; <u>A Streetcar Named Desire</u>; <u>Summer and Smoke</u>; <u>This Property Is Condemned</u>; <u>Twenty-Seven Wagons Full of Cotton</u>.
Friedrich Wolf. <u>Beaumarchais oder Die Geburt des Figaro</u>.
Phillip Yordan. <u>Any Day Now</u>.

D7   Newspaper and magazine cl. 1 F.

F   4 records: "Barry Gray Show," "Hochhuth und der Stell-
      vertreter," "Tilla Durieux - Erzähltes Leben," "Vom
      Essener Theater."
      2 tapes: "Barry Gray Show."
      Filmed interview with Piscator by Sender Freies Berlin.
      Ca. 7 minutes.

G   Radio interview. Jan. 21, 1947. T. 9p.
      Radio interview with Saul Colin. 1949. T. 18p.

H3   Piscator's career during the 1920s and 1930s. 1 F.
      Piscator's activities in Barcelona (Dec. 1936) and
        Bruxelles, Amsterdam (April 1937). 1 F.
      Piscator's years in Paris. 1936-1938. 1 F.
      Materials concerning the Mexico project. 1938-1939.
        1 F. Jan. 1939. 1 F.
      Erwin and Maria Piscator's arrival in the U.S. Jan.
        1939. 1 F.
      Erwin and Maria Piscator's activities in Washington,
        D.C. 1940. 1 F.
      Erwin and Maria Piscator's activities during 1940. 1 F.
      Erwin and Maria Piscator's activities, 1941-1949. 1 F.
      Erwin and Maria Piscator's activities, 1950-1951. 1 F.
      Erwin Piscator's activities in the 1950s and 1960s.
        1 F.
      Erwin Piscator's burial. April 6, 1966. 1 F.
      Memorial speeches for Piscator. 1 F.

ERWIN PISCATOR

Obituaries. 1 F.
Lieutier, Odette. "The Theater in New York: Erwin Pis-
cator and the Dramatic Workshop." T. with corr. 8p.
Sahl, Hans. "Gedenkblatt für Erwin Piscator." T. with
corr. 5p.
H5   Askin, Leon. Memorial speech at Memorial Dinner for
Erwin Piscator. Actors Studio, Hollywood, April 3,
1966. T. with corr. 6p.
Cabello, Virgilio. "Notiert zum 70. Geburtstag Erwin
Piscators." Jan. 1964. T. 11p.
Lania, Leo. "Amerikanisches Zeit-Theater. Erwin Pisca-
tor inszeniert die Tragödie eines amerikanischen
Diktators." T. 6p.
"Die Versuchsbühne. Eine Komposition in 15 Zeichnungen
nach Ideen und Inszenierungen Erwin Piscators; kon-
struiert von Julius Richter." Berlin 1959. Dedicated
to Piscator, signed. A. 11p.
I   Address books. 1933-1965. 7 items.
Deutsche Akademie der Darstellenden Künste, Frankfurt.
Ca. 15 items (in correspondence files). 1962-1965.
Dramatic Workshop:
Financial reports, account books. 1938-1959. 7 items.
Journals, cash journals, general ledgers. 1950-1960.
10 items.
Bills, receipts, invoices. 1 B.
Gains and losses. Cost estimates, inventories, state-
ments of accounts. 1934-1963. 20 F.
Cash box receipts. 1941-1960. 4 F.
Class and performance schedules. 1940-1968. 6 F.
Guest and membership lists. 1940-1968. 1 B.
Contracts, minutes, agenda. Ca. 140 items (in cor-
respondence files). 1932-1966.
Educational records: registration figures, question-
naires, etc. 1940-1963. 1 B.; attendance records,
educational requirements. 1942-1964. 1 B.; gradua-
tion statistics. 1945-1950. 2 F.
Exams, recommendations, etc. 1945-1950. 1 B.
Statistical reports by Paul Ransom. 1948. 1 F.
Advertising files. 1930-1970. 9 B.
Audience attendance records. Yearly reports. 1942-
1951. 5 F.
Guest books. 1940-1967. 5 items.

717

Floor plan of stage of Rooftop Theater.
New School for Social Research:
  List of theater books in library. 1941. 1 F.
  Contracts, minutes of faculty meetings, etc. Ca. 25
    items. 1942-1966.

J   Erwin Piscator:
  Childhood photos. Dillenburg, Marburg.
  Photos of artistic endeavors in 1920s and 1930s.
  Piscator's American years. 1 F.
  Photos from 1950s.
  Photos from 1960s.
  Apartment in Berlin, Bingerstraße 34. 1960s.
  X-rays. 1963-1965.
  Burial. Berlin-Zehlendorf, April 6, 1966.
Relatives and friends of Piscator. 5 F.
Maria Piscator. 5 F.
Dramatic Workshop:
  Performances of the Dramatic Workshop. 5 B.
  Unidentified performances. 4 F.
  Children's Theater. 1 F.
  Receptions at the DW. 1 F.
  Class photos, rehearsals. 1940-1948. 7 F.
  Graduation ceremonies. May 28, 1948. 1 F.
  Photos of lectures, discussion groups. 1 F.
  Miscellaneous photos: individuals, performances. 4 F.
  Miscellaneous slides, most unidentifiable. 1 F.
Dramatic Workshop Players:
  Sayville Playhouse. Sayville, New York, Summer 1944.
  Chapel Theatre. Great Neck, New York, Summer 1945.
  Intervale Stadium Summer Theater. Lake Placid, New
    York, July 30, 1949.
Epic Theater Exhibit at Piscator Institute, 39 West
  54th Street, New York, Jan. 19, 1960. 5 F.
Freie Volksbühne, Berlin. 1960s. 1 F.
New School for Social Research, Dramatic Workshop,
  Studio Theatre. 1 F.

L   Blätter der freien Volksbühne Berlin. Publication of
  the Volkstheater, Berlin. 1 F.
Miscellaneous articles by German emigrés. 1 F.
Costume designs for performances of the Dramatic Workshop.

Materials concerning the faculty and alumni of the
Dramatic Workshop. 1 F.
New School for Social Research. 1 F.
"Pem's Privat-Berichte." Some with comments by Pis-
cator. 1 F.
Scrapbook: The New York Repertory Group, Inc.; The
Dramatic Workshop; The Dramatic Workshop and Tech-
nical Institute.
Miscellaneous newspaper and magazine cl., with com-
ments and underlinings by Piscator. 2 F.
Advertisements for performances of the Dramatic Work-
shop. 2 B., 5 F.
Miscellaneous advertising materials concerning perform-
ances at:
Sayville Playhouse, Sayville, New York, Summer 1944.
1 F.
Chapel Theatre. Great Neck, New York, Summer 1946
and 1947. 1 F.
Tanglewood Theatre and Martha's Vineyard. Falmouth,
Massachusetts, Summer 1948. 1 F.
Adirondack Festival of Arts, High School Auditorium
and Intervale Stadium. Lake Placid, New York,
Summer 1949. 1 F.
Newspaper advertisements. 1940s-1960s. 1 F.
Newspaper advertisements of the Senior Dramatic Work-
shop under the direction of Saul Colin. 1960s. 1 F.

M   2 death masks of Piscator.

N   Csokor, Franz Theodor. "Dem Boden gleich." 44p.; "Der
Stern und das Tier." 6p.; "Tangenten zum Tod." 97p.
Forter, Adolphe. "Wirklichkeit und Abstrahierung
Film." T. with corr. 8p.
Gassner, John. "The Director" and untitled Ms. T. with
corr. 1949. 10p.
Kerz, Leo. "Projekt." June 4, 1965. T. 18p.
Lania, Leo. "Das Ideentheater." June 1941. T. 6p.
Marshall, Herbert. "The Roles of Ira Aldridge" and
"The Art of Ira Aldridge." Ca. 1970. T. pc. 44p., 18p.
Memoirs of Bertha Zuckerkandl. Ca. 1930-1937. T. and
A. 314p.
Piscator, Maria. Novels. 1,876p. Stories and short
prose. 115p. Essayistic. 56p. Lecture notes. 16 note-
books, 6 F. and 287p. Seminar papers, dissertation.

998p. Adaptations of works of others. 698p. Mono-
graph. 26 F. and 962p. Fragmentary scenes. 1 F.
Rehfisch, Hans José. "A Short History of Woman." T.
with corr. 1947. 39p.
Sahl, Hans. "To the Editor of the New York Times." T.
3p.
Thompson, Dorothy. "The Theater in War Time." Tran-
script of lecture. Jan. 29, 1942. T. with corr. 26p.
Wendriner, Henry. "Theatre of Tomorrow" and "Mörder
unter uns." Ca. 1948. T. and A. 5p., 3p.
Zuckmayer, Carl. "Aufruf zum Leben." T. with corr. 4p.
Articles and seminar papers of students of Dramatic
Workshop. 1945-1948, 1964. 14 F.
Miscellaneous Ms. concerning Frank G. Deutsch, first
husband of Maria Piscator. 1930s. A. and T.
"Nathan the Wise" Symposium. Feb. 21, 1944. Lecture
texts. 7p.
"The Role of the Post-War Theatre" Symposium. Oct.
8-9, 1947. Lecture texts. T. 19p.
Lectures. 175p.
Untitled and titled Ms. by unknown authors. 3 F.

O   Miscellaneous posters of Piscator performances. 1 F.
Programs in which former students or faculty members
of the Dramatic Workshop were named.
Programs, playbills from German theater in the U.S.
1 F.
Programs and playbills from Piscator performances. 1 F.
Programs, playbills from German performances. 1 F.
Playbills with comments by Piscator. 1 F.

University of Texas, Humanities Research Center, Hoblitzelle
Theater Arts Library, Box 7219, Austin, Texas 78712.

B1   3 notes to John Gassner. T., in German.
C7   "Technique, an Artistic Necessity." Speech for Modern
Theater. T.
Cc. of 4 articles for newspaper, 1 definitely by Pisca-
tor, 3 presumably by Piscator.

University of Texas, Humanities Research Center, Manuscripts

ERWIN PISCATOR

Collection, Box 7219, Austin, Texas 78712.

B1   1 L.
I   Miscellaneous documents.

Leo Baeck Institute, 129 East 73rd Street, New York, N.Y.
10021.
KURT HIRSCHFELD COLLECTION, KURT KERSTEN COLLECTION, VERA
RUBIN COLLECTION

B1   1 L. to Kurt Kersten. 1946.
B1,2 Correspondence with Kurt Hirschfeld.
O   Programs and data on 3 Piscator productions prior to
      1933.

University of New Hampshire, The Library, Department of
Special Collections, Durham, New Hampshire 03824.

FRIEDRICH SALLY GROSSHUT COLLECTION

B1   3 L. to F. S. Grosshut. T. 1950-1951.

Mrs. Elisabeth M. Stoerk and Mrs. Susanne B. Hoeller, 288
Ocean Drive West, Stamford, Connecticut 06902.

FRIDERIKE ZWEIG ARCHIVE

B1   2 L. to Friderike Zweig. 1947, 1951.

State University of New York at Albany, Department of Germanic Languages and Literatures, 1400 Washington Avenue,
Albany, New York 12222.

KARL O. PAETEL COLLECTION

B1   2 L. to Karl O. Paetel (xerox). 1940s.

Museum of the City of New York, Fifth Avenue at 103rd Street, New York, N.Y. 10029.

H3   "Personality File" on Erwin Piscator.

Mr. Hans Sahl, 800 West End Avenue, New York, N.Y. 10025.

B1   Several L. to Hans Sahl.

Yivo Institute, 1048 Fifth Avenue, New York, N.Y. 10028.

HORACE M. KALLEN PAPERS

B1,2 Individual items in folder no. 548. 1940-1948.

Columbia University, Butler Library, New York, N.Y. 10027.

B1   1 L. to Isidor Schneider. T. 1946.

Harvard University, Harvard Divinity School, Andover-Harvard Theological Library, 45 Francis Avenue, Cambridge, Massachusetts 02138.

PAUL TILLICH COLLECTION

B1   1 L. to Paul Tillich. A. 1965.

University of Southern California, Lion Feuchtwanger Memorial Library, 520 Paseo Miramar, Pacific Palisades, California 90272.

B1   1 L. to Lion Feuchtwanger. 1947.

Immigration History Research Center of the University of Minnesota, 826 Berry Street, St. Paul, Minnesota 55101.

AMERICAN COUNCIL FOR EMIGRÉS IN THE PROFESSIONS ARCHIVES

B2   1 L. from Alvin Johnson. 1941.

ERWIN PISCATOR

Academy of Motion Picture Arts and Sciences, Margaret Herrick Library, 9038 Melrose Avenue, Hollywood, California 90069.

H3   Obituaries.

State University of New York at Binghamton, Center for Modern Theater Research, Binghamton, New York 13901.

MAX REINHARDT ARCHIVE

B1   1 L. to Paul Rose. Undated.

Mrs. Liselotte Stein, 115-25 Metropolitan Avenue, Kew Gardens, New York 11418.

FRED STEIN PAPERS

J   Photos of Erwin Piscator.

University of Pennsylvania, The Charles Patterson Van Pelt Library, Philadelphia, Pennsylvania 19104.

ALMA MAHLER-WERFEL COLLECTION

B1   3 L. to Alma Mahler-Werfel. A. and T. 1943-1945.

Dr. Marta Mierendorff, 8633 West Knoll Drive, Hollywood, California 90069.

SAMMLUNG WALTER WICCLAIR, WALTER WICCLAIR PRODUCTIONS

J   Photo of Erwin Piscator and Walter Wicclair. 1962.

Mrs. Peter M. Lindt, 949 West End Avenue, New York, N.Y. 10025.

B1   Small amount of correspondence with Peter M. Lindt.

MARIA LEY PISCATOR

Writer, Director, 1907?-

Because of time limitations, the Project was unable to interview Mrs. Piscator (New York, N.Y.) to ascertain the
existence of further materials of historical interest in
her possession.

*Aus zeitlichen Gründen war es unmöglich, Frau Piscator (New
York, N.Y.) persönlich zu befragen, ob und welche weiteren
Materialien von historischem Interesse sich noch in ihrem
Besitz befinden.*

Southern Illinois University, Morris Library, Department of
Special Collections, Carbondale, Illinois 62901.

ERWIN PISCATOR PAPERS: Collection 31. For complete description of the collection, see Erwin Piscator.

A1   Appointment calendars. 1956-1963.

A3   Notes concerning the dancing career of Maria Piscator.
     1 F.

C1   April in Warsaw. Ca. 1960. T. 69p.
     The Death of Erato. Prototype for a novel. Ca. 1963-
     1968. T. 25p.
     Enroll My Heart. Fragments, single chap., different
     versions, character descriptions. Ca. 1958-1960. T.
     Ca. 575p. Final version. T. with corr. 351p.
     Fire in the Stone (also entitled: The Man Who Liveth
     the Longest). Drafts, fragments, single chap., etc.
     Ca. 1961-1962. T. Ca. 400p.
     Grace Benett sucht das Leben. With the comment "My
     first novel - 1927." T. with some corr. 145p.
     The Portrait. Prototype of a novel. Fragment. Ca.
     1957-1958. A. and T. with corr. by Erwin Piscator.
     20p.
     The Sting of the Bee. Synopsis, different versions,
     drafts. Ca. 1950. T. 161p.
     Untitled prototype for a book on the Fugger family.
     Ca. 1956-1959. Fragment. A. and T. 35p., 95p.

C2   The Adventures of Danny Doubt and Tommy Trust. Written
     together with Molla Pascal. Dec. 1944. T. with corr.
     24p.

724

Aux Environs de l'Amour. Comedy one-acter. Ca. 1931.
T. with corr. 45p.
Le Chien Dangereux. Comedy written under the pseudonym
of Claude Viennet with Gaston Bergame. Ca. 1932-1934.
T. with corr. 161p., 66p.
Beware of Dogs. Incomplete English tr. Ca. 1955.
La Dame de Florence. Fragments. 1936. A. and T.
Fanny Elssler. Scenario. 1937. T. with corr. 83p.
The Flight of Erato. Fragments. Ca. 1957-1958. A. and
T. 14 F.
Fumée Bleue. Incomplete scenario. Ca. 1932. T. 57p.
Genève. Incomplete scenario. Written together with
Gaston Biasini. Ca. 1930-1932. T. 43p.
The Giant of Flanders. Drama in 3 acts. Fragments,
English and German versions. A. and T. with commen-
tary by Maria and Erwin Piscator. Ca. 1936-1937. 5 F.
The Governor. Drama in 3 acts. 1957. T. Revised ver-
sion. 1962. A. and T. with commentary by Maria and
Erwin Piscator.
Inside Stories of Famous Women. 1939. A. and T. with
corr. 2 F.
Lendemains. One-acter. Ca. 1931-1934. T. with corr.
31p.
Luther. T. with commentary. 7p.
The Metamorphosis. Drama in 3 acts. Completed 1964.
T. with commentary. 19 F.
Nichka ou La Comédie du Success (also entitled: Trois
Gares and Passages à Neveau). Ca. 1929. T. with
commentary. 4 F.
Par Dessus les Frontières. Scenario. Fragments. Writ-
ten with Gaston Biasini. Ca. 1930. T.
Pilate. Fragments. Ca. Summer 1957 - Sept. 1962. A.
and T.
Pinkie and the Fairies. Presumably by Maria Piscator.
Ca. 1953. T.
La Poupée de Dieu. Fragments. Presumably by Maria Pis-
cator. Jan. 1931. T.
Showdown. Drama in 3 acts. T. with commentary. 20p.
Der Spiegel. Scenario, presumbly by Maria Piscator.
Ca. 1930. T. with corr.
The Stallions. Drama in 2 acts. Fragments, different
scenes. Written with John Carlino. Ca. 1963. A. and
T. 8 F.

The Stranger. A dance epic. Ca. 1937. T. 11p.

Tanzhaus. Exposé. Ca. 1932. A. 3p.

Truculor. Comedy in 3 acts, written by Maria Piscator
under the pseudonym of Claude Viennet with Gaston
Biasini. Ca. 1930. T.

Une Tragédie Bourgeoise. Exposé. Ca. 1929. A. 17p.

Voice of Reason. Ca. 1962. A. 24p.

C4   "Anne Dacier." Fragment. Ca. 1928-1934. T. 14p.

"Captain Jimmy." Ca. 1933. T. 29p.

"Destinées." Ca. 1931. T. 20p.

"L'Esprit de la Rue." Jan. 1937. T. with corr. 17p.

"Lot's Wife." A. and T. 14p. Pub. New York: Bobbs-
Merrill, 1954.

"The Parting of the Ways." Ca. 1967. T. 10p.

"The Tower of Babel." Ca. 1944. T. 11p.
Fragmentary scenes. A. and T. 1 F.

C5   Eine einzige Liebe. Film exposé. Ca. 1931. T. 10p.

C7   "Education through the Drama." 1950s. T. 19p.

"Epic Theatre." Ca. 1962. T. with commentary by Maria
Piscator. 4p.

"The Future Lies in Our Children." Feb. 1950. T. 3p.

"Molière à la Comedia del'Arte." Ca. 1951-1952. T. 8p.

"Notes on the Masters of the Revels." 1950s. T. 22p.
16 notebooks, various topics.

Lecture notes, etc. A. and T. 6 F.

Lecture notes. Ca. 1948. A. 14p. April 1952. A. 7p.
Spring 1959. T. 114p. Ca. Dec. 1961. T. 7p. March 9,
1962. T. with commentary. 24p. April 11, 1966. T.
18p.

Transcriptions of lectures from tapes. March 10 - May
5, 1962. T. 93p.

"Le Ballet et l'Opéra vers 1830." Seminar paper. Ca.
1935-1936. T. 70p.

"Le Ballet Jeunes France." Seminar paper. Ca. 1935-
1936. T. 16p.

"La Canaille au Théâtre au XVIII Siècle." Diploma
d'Études Universitaires. Ca. 1934. T. 224p.

"Le Gueux chez Victor Hugo." Dissertation. T. 273p.

"H.-R. Lenormand." Seminar paper. 1936. T. 194p.

"Histoire de l'Art." Ca. 1932-1934. A., T. with corr.,
T. 8p., 10p., 69p.

Personality Dynamics, Inc. Theatre School Project.
   Ca. Aug. 1959. A. and T. 45p.
"Schiller on the Moral Utility of Aesthetic Manners."
   Preliminary work to Ph.D. study at Columbia Univer-
   sity, New York. Ca. 1951-1953. T. 89p.

C9   Dreiser, Theodore. American Tragedy. Revised and with
        notes by Maria Piscator. Scriptbook.
     Gide, André and Jean-Louis Barrault. The Trial. Adap-
        tation by Maria Piscator. May 3, 1965. T. with com-
        mentary. 4 F.
     Hašek, Jaroslav. Schwejk. French tr. by Maria Pisca-
        tor. Ca. 1937-1938. T. with commentary.
     Kinoshita, Junji. Twilight Crane. Adaptation by Maria
        Piscator. Dec. 1959. T. with commentary.
     Klabund. Circle of Chalk. Script book. Adaptation of
        drama.
     Memoirs of Bertha Zuckerkandl. Tr. by Maria Piscator.
        Ca. 1930-1937. A. and T. 662p.
     Tolstoy, Alexsey and P. Shchegolev. Rasputin, die
        Romanovs, der Krieg und das Volk, das gegen sie auf-
        stand. Tr., presumably by Maria Piscator. Ca. 1938.
     Wildgans, Anton. "Rede über Österreich." Tr. by Maria
        Piscator. Ca. 1930-1932. T. 36p.

C11 The Piscator Experiment. The Political Theatre. Vari-
        ous versions, single pages, parts. 1967. A. and T.
        26 F. Final version. T. 962p.

C12 Tribute to Erwin Piscator.

D2   The Giant of Flanders. German and French versions.
        Scripts. 2 F.
     The Governor. 1957.
     The Metamorphosis. Script. 4 F.
     The Stallions. Written with Lewis John Carlino.

D9   Gide, André and Jean-Louis Barrault. The Trial. Adap-
        tation by Maria Piscator. 4 scripts.

H3   Maria Piscator's dance career and student years at the
        Sorbonne. 1920s and 1930s. 1 F.
     Erwin and Maria Piscator's arrival in the U.S. Jan.
        1939. 1 F.
     Erwin and Maria Piscator's activities in Washington.
        1940. 1 F.

727

Erwin and Maria Piscator's activities in 1940. 1 F.
Erwin and Maria Piscator's activities, 1941-1949. 1 F.
Erwin and Maria Piscator's activities, 1950-1951. 1 F.
Erwin and Maria Piscator's activities, 1950s and 1960s.
1 F.

J   Maria Piscator's childhood years and dance career.
1920s.
Maria Piscator in the 1930s.
Maria Piscator in the 1940s.
Maria Piscator in the 1950s.
Maria Piscator in the 1960s.

L   Advertisements and materials on performances of the
Dramatic Workshop. 1950-1964. 1 F.

University of Texas, Humanities Research Center, Hoblitzelle
Theater Arts Library, Box 7219, Austin, Texas 78712.

B1   8 L., 2 Christmas cards, 1 Tel., 1 invitation to a
performance, and 2 notes to John and Molly Gassner
concerning the burial of Erwin Piscator.

Yivo Institute, 1048 Fifth Avenue, New York, N.Y. 10028.

HORACE M. KALLEN PAPERS

B1,2   Individual items in folder no. 992. 1945-1951.

Harvard University, Harvard Divinity School, Andover-Harvard
Theological Library, 45 Francis Avenue, Cambridge, Massachusetts 02138.

PAUL TILLICH COLLECTION

B1   1 L. to Paul Tillich. T. 1965.

PAUL AMADEUS PISK

Composer, 1893–

<u>Prof. Paul Pisk</u>, 2724 Westshire Boulevard, Los Angeles, California 90068.

Private personal collection: inaccessible to researchers at present. Prof. Pisk intends to donate his personal music library to Washington University. The remainder of his collection will go to the Moldenhauer Archives in Spokane, Washington. The materials are to remain inaccessible to researchers and scholars until that time.

Privatsammlung, z.Zt. für Forscher nicht zugänglich. Prof. Pisk hat vor, seine private Musikaliensammlung der Washington University zukommen zu lassen. Der Rest seiner Sammlung wird an die Moldenhauer Archives in Spokane, Washington, gehen. Die Materialien werden bis zu diesem Zeitpunkt unzugänglich bleiben.

C13a Recent compositions by Pisk (master sheets with the American Composer's Alliance, New York).

C14 Sketches.

F Records.
Quite a few tapes.

H3, Cl. about Pisk and others.
L

I All documents concerning personal and professional life.

J Photos of Pisk.

K Music library.

M Memorabilia.

<u>University of Texas</u>, Barker Texas Historical Center, Austin, Texas 78712.

The 10 archive boxes of materials that comprise the PAUL AMADEUS PISK PAPERS were donated to the library by Dr. Paul Pisk.

PAUL AMADEUS PISK

Die PAUL AMADEUS PISK PAPERS umfassen etwa 10 Archivkartons Materialien; sie sind eine Schenkung von Dr. Paul Pisk.

C13a Opus 1: "Overture." 2 scores. 1914.
Opus 2: "2 Frauenchöre." 1918.
Opus 3: "Vier Klavierstücke: Piano solo." Pub. sheet music.
Opus 4: "4 Orchesterlieder." 1920.
Opus 5: "1. Sonate für Violine und Klavier." 1921.
Opus 6: "Sänge eines fahrenden Spielmanns (I, II, and III)." Sheet music.
Opus 7: "Sechs Konzertstücke." Sheet music.
Opus 8: "1. Streichquartett." Sheet music.
Opus 9: "Drei Gesänge für mittlere Stimme mit Streichquartett-Begleitung." 1921.
Opus 10: "Partita für Orchester." 2 scores. 1924.
Opus 11: "Kleine Suite für Klavier." 2 scores. 1922, 1932.
Opus 12: "Vier geistlichen Gesänge für eine mittlere Singstimme mit Orgel." 1922.
Opus 13: "Phantasie für Klarinette und Klavier." 1925.
Opus 14: "Der Tod: Solokantata." 2 scores. 1923, 1934.
Opus 15: "Ein Sommer." 1924.
Opus 16a/I-III: "Sonate für Violoncello allein," "Sonate für Violine allein," "Sonate für Bratsche allein." 1926.
Opus 17: "Zweite Suite für Klavier." 1927.
Opus 17a: "Music for Violin, Clarinet, Cello, Bassoon." 1926.
Opus 18: "Trio für Oboe, Clarinette (B), und Fagott." 1926.
Opus 19: "Drei Männerchöre, a capella." 1927.
Opus 20: "Konzertarie (nach Childe Harold von Lord Byron), für Sopran (Koloraturstimme) und Orchester." 1927.
Opus 21: "Drei Psalmen, für Baritonstimme und Orchester." 1928/1929.
Opus 22: "II. Sonate für Violine und Klavier." 1927.
Opus 23a: "Drei Lieder für hohe Stimme und Klavier." 1927.
Opus 23b: "Der abnehmende Mond." 1928.
Opus 23c: "Zwischendeck, für tiefe Stimme." 2 scores. 1930.

PAUL AMADEUS PISK

Opus 24: "Tanzfolge für Klavier." 1930.
Opus 25: "Schattenseite: ein Monodram." 1930/1931.
Opus 26: "Lieder, nach Gedichten von Alfons Paquet."
   2 scores. 1931.
Opus 27: "Rondo Suite für Violine und Klavier." 1932.
Opus 28: "Campanella." 1938.
Opus 29: "Vier Kinder-Verwirr-Lieder." 1932.
Opus 30: "Trio for Violin, Cello and Piano." 1933/1935.
Opus 31: "Music for Orchestra (Divertimento)." 1930/
   1936.
Opus 32: "Balletmusik für Klavier." 1934.
Opus 33: "Moresca-Figures." 1934.
Opus 34: "Arie der 'Donna Clara' aus Lenaus 'Don Juan'."
   2 scores. 1934.
Opus 35/I-II: "5 Lieder nach Texten von Gustav Falke,"
   "5 Lieder nach Texten von Rudolf List." 1935.
Opus 36: "Drei Sätze für Viola und Klavier." 1936.
   Revised 1952.
Opus 37a: "Herbstzeitlosen." 1935.
Opus 37b: "Fünf kleine Duette." 1936.
Opus 37b[sic]: "Trois aphorismes." 1927.
Opus 38: "Drei Sonette." 1936/1938.
Opus 39: "Skizzen für Klavier." 1936.
Opus 40: "Steichermusik." 1936.
Opus 41: "6 Choral Preludes (6 Choralvorspiele für
   Orgel)." 1938.
Opus 42: "Six Songs." 1938/1939.
Opus 43: "Sonata for Violin and Piano." 1938/1939.
Opus 44: "Four Beasts Characterized." 1938.
Opus 45/1-2: "The LIV Psalm for male chorus a capella,"
   "The XXX Psalm for male chorus a capella." 1935/40,
   1952.
Opus 46: "Sonata for Organ." 1940.
Opus 47: "Lover's Lament." 1940.
Opus 48/I-VI: "Twilight," "I Saw a Stable," "A Grace,"
   "Rondel: The Wanderer," "A White Blossom," "Drums."
   1939-1940.
Opus 49: "Sonatina 'Death Valley' for Piano." 1942.
Opus 50: "Passacaglia." Orchestra score and piano re-
   duction. 1944.
Opus 51: "Requiem for Gerald." 1943.
Opus 52: "The Voice of the Prophet." 1944.
Opus 53a: "Little Woodwind Music." 1943/1945.

Opus 53b: "Cortege for Brass Choir." 1945.
Opus 54/1-6: "Easter Dawning," "Red Apples," "Last Camelot," "Bare Trees," "The Mountain Road," "Silver Sails."
Opus 55: "Bucolic Suite for String Orchestra." 2 scores. 1946.
Opus 56: "Prelude: Adagio and Canzone for Organ." 1946.
Opus 57: "Variations and Fugue on an American Theme." 1946.
Opus 58: "A Toccata of Galuppi's." 1947.
Opus 59: "Sonata for Clarinet (B-flat) and Piano." 1947.
Opus 60: "Suite for Oboe and Piano." 1947.
Opus 61: "Introduction and Rondo for Flute and Piano." 1948.
Opus 62: "Four Songs." 1948.
Opus 63: "Adagio and Fugue for Piano." 1954.
Opus 64: "Suite for Organ." 1949.
Opus 65: "Five Two-Part Studies on Permutations of Semitone Progressions for Piano." 1949.
Opus 66: "Sonata Based upon Sesquitone Progressions for Piano."
Opus 67: "Three Chorusses [sic] for S.A.T.B." 1950.
Opus 68: "Suite for Flute Solo." 1950.
Opus 69: "Six Songs." 1944-1950.
Opus 70/I: "Intermezzo for Clarinet and Piano." 1949.
Opus 70/II: "Elegy and Scherzino for Woodwind Quartet." 1951.
Opus 71/I-IV: "Daisies for Women's Chorus," "Sweet Spring. Chorus for Male Voices and Piano," "Chimes," "The Homecoming of the Sheep." 1950-1951.
Opus 72: "Quartet." 1951. Also piano reduction.
Opus 73: "Choral fantasy in 'When I Survey the Wondrous Cross'." 1951.
Opus 74a: "Rondo Scherzoso for Piano." 1951.
Opus 74, no. 2: "Essay for Piano Solo." 1952.
Opus 75: "Four Songs." 1951.
Opus 76: "Daniel's Vision." 1952.
Opus 77: "Sonata for Horn and Piano." 1953.
Opus 78: "Three Sea Poems." 1952.
Opus 79: "Prelude, Fugue and Hymn for Organ Solo." 1952.
Opus 80: "Duet for 2 Flutes." 1953.

Opus 81: "Sunset 1952."
Opus 82: "Sonata for Flute and Piano." 1954.
Opus 83: "Prayer to Mary." 1954.
Opus 84: "Canzona for Small Chamber Orchestra." 1954.
Opus 85: "Suite for 2 Woodwinds and Piano." 1954/1955.
Movement II. 1949.
Opus 86: "Eclogue for Violin and Piano." 1955-1956/57.
Opus 87/I-II: "Pastorale for Organ," "Aria Variata for
Organ," "Capriccio."
Opus 88: "Trial of Life." 2 scores. 1956.
Opus 89: "The Prophecy of Zechariah." 1957.
Opus 90: "Three Ceremonial Rites." 1957-1958. Piano
reduction and orchestral score.
Opus 91/I-IV: "Visitant," "The Difference," "The
Wind," "Thanksgiving." 1957.
Opus 92: "Improvisation on an American Folk Melody."
1957.
Opus 93: "Elegy for String Orchestra." 1958.
Opus 94: "Sonatina in E. 1954."
Opus 95: "Trio for Violin, Viola, Cello." 1958.
Opus 96: "Quintet for Flute, Oboe, Clarinet, Bassoon
and Horn." 1958.
Opus 97/I-IV: "Two Wisdoms," "The Spirit of God,"
"Lamentation," "Salomon's Prayer." 1959.
Opus 97a: "Moses Speaks." 1960.
Opus 98: "Sonnet." 1960.
Opus 99: "God's Omnipotence." 1960.
Opus 100: "Trio for Oboe, Clarinet, Bassoon." 1960.
Opus 101: "Nine Songs." 1960.
Opus 105a: "Song from Shakespeare's 'Much Ado About
Nothing'." Undated.
Opus 105b: "Prayer." Undated.
Opus 106: "Duo for Clarinet and Bassoon."
Opus 107: "For Gail Delente: 13 Variations on an Eight-
Bar Theme."
Opus 108: "In Memoriam Carl Sandburg."
Opus 109: "Perpetuum Mobile for Organ."
Opus 110/1: "He Wishes for the Cloths of Heaven."
Opus 110/a: "Two Goethe Songs."
Opus 111: "Four Miniatures for Piano."
Opus 112: "Second Suite for Flute Solo."
Opus 113: "Four Duets for 2 Equal Instruments."
Eight untitled melodies.

733

"Der Tag der Republik." 1932.
"Stunde der Erinnerung." Undated.
"Der Stein im Brot." 1926.
"Das römische Glas." 1927.
"Auf Gold." 1926.
"Es wird alles gut." 1936.
"Das gefährliche Wort." 1936.
"Der Schimmer auf der Wimper." 1927.
"Phantasy on 'Trotzlied' by Josef Seyfried." 1961/62.
"Arbeitersage." 1927.
"Trio." Op. 30. 1933/35.
"Die neue Stadt." 1927.
"Kleine Musik um Karl Marx." 1933.
"Sonate für Klavier."
"My Pretty Little Pink." 1944.
"Suite on American Folksongs for Small Orchestra."
  1942-1944.
Arrangement of arias by Haydn. 1931.
"Salute to Don Juan." 1961.
"'I tell thee, Charmion!'." 1956.
"Gesang vom Rundfunk." 1929.
"Baroque Chamber Concerto: Eccles Valentini." 1953.
"Rococo Suite: Five Dances by Marin Marais." 1953.
"Zehn Variationen über einen Walzer von Beethoven."
  1933.
"6 Variations on an Old Trumpet-Hymn-Tune." 1942.
"Shanty Boy: A Fantasy on an American Ballad Tune."
  1940.
"Ballad for Viola Sextet." 1958.
"Amusement à la Suisse." 1935.
"So war's einmal." 1931.
"6 Folksongs." 1927.
"Arrangement of Old Austrian Folk Dances." 1938.
"Phantasy on a Mexican Folksong." 1941.
"Dance from the (Rio Grande) Valley." 1956.
"Dance of the Engines." 1945/1950.
"Suite for 4 clarinets (B)."
"Caribbeana: Dance for Harpsichord." 1939.
"Four American Folksongs." 1953/1956.
"Honey Take Me Back." 1953/1956.
"A Prayer."
"Feet." 1941.
"Five Piece Set for Piano." 1945.

PAUL AMADEUS PISK

"Prayer." 1941.
"Nocturnal Interlude: for Piano." 1957.
"Salve Regina (Gregorian Chant)." 1950.
"Adagio and Rondo Concertante for 2 accordions and
orchestra (with loose Ms. sketches for Adagio and
Rondo Concertante for 2 accordions and orchestra)."
1961/62.
Gallus Jacobus. 6 masses of G. J. taken from a book
printed by Georg Negrinus, 1580.
Youthful works and sketches: "l. Fuge, 3-stimmig,"
"3. Fuge, 3-stimmig," "4. Fuge, 4-stimmig," "Fuge:
IV," "Fuge 5," "9 Variationen über ein Thema von
J. S. Bach für Pianoforte solo."

Washington University Libraries, Gaylord Music Library, St.
Louis, Missouri 63130.

THE PISK COLLECTION, ca. 3 ft. of materials, was donated to
the library by Dr. Pisk in 1972.

*THE PISK COLLECTION, etwa 0,90 m Materialien, ist eine
Schenkung von Dr. Pisk aus dem Jahre 1972.*

C13a Original Ms.:
"Daisies (Bliss Carman)." Op. 71. 1950. 6p.
"Drei Männerchöre." Op. 19. 1927. 13p.
"A Forest Song (Alfred Noyes)." Op. 67, no. 1 2 ver-
sions. 6p. ea.
"Fünf Lieder (Gustav Falke)." Op. 35/I. 1935.
"Gesang von Rundfunk." Words by Heinrich Infeld.
Aug. 12, 1929. 2 versions. 21p., 35p.
"Der große Regenmacher. Szenische Ballade in 1 Auf-
zug." Words by Josef Luitpold. Adapted for stage
by Max Brand. Dec. 20, 1927. 2 versions. 23p., 29p.
"Meadow-saffrons." 1956. Pisk's tr. of "Herbstzeit-
losen." 1935. 3p.
"Kerker (Harmonium)."
"Intermezzo for w.w. and piano." Op. 70/I. Oct. 28,
1949. 4p.
"Lieder nach Gedichten von Alfons Paquet." Op. 26.
1931. 12p.

735

"Psalm 48." 2 c.
"Schattenseite - Monodrama in one act (Alfons
Paquet)." Op. 25. 1930/31. 65p.
"Sechs Volkslieder für Singstimme u. kleines Orche-
ster." 1927.
"Sonata for Violin and Piano." Rondo finale. 1921.
14p.
"Slow Song." 2p.
"String Music." Op. 40. 1936.
"Sunset, a cycle of three poems by Emily Dickinson
for four-part women's chorus a capella." Op. 81.
1954. 6p.
"Suite on American folksongs." Piano solo. 1942. 2 c.
13p. ea. For small orchestra. Aug. 15, 1944. 51p.
"March." 3p. "I Ride an Old Paint." 1942. 3p.
"Thy God Reigneth." 1946.
Photocopies of original Ms.:
"Prayer for Peace. Anthem for mixed chorus, soprano
and baritone solo with organ accompaniment."
"Duet for Two Flutes (or Other Equal Instruments)."
Op. 80.
"The Prophecy of Zechariah." Op. 89. 3 c. 10p. ea.
"Quartet for 2 Trumpets, Horn and Trombone." Op. 72.
1951. 2 c.
"Two Sonnets (Shakespeare) N. VIII and LV." Aug. 26,
1964.
"Trio for Violin, Viola, Cello." Op. 95. 1958. 13p.
"Arabesque for Oboe and Piano." Op. 102, no. 1.
"Composer's Facsimile Edition, c1964."
"Caribbeana. Dance for Harpsichord." 1939.
"Dialogue for Clarinet and Piano." 2p.
Copyist-Ms. and photocopies of copyist-Ms.:
"Kleine Musik um Karl Marx." Lyrics by Josef Luit-
pold. 1933.
"Passacaglia für das Pleyel-Moor Duplexklavier in A
moll."
"Shanty-boy. A Fantasy on an American Ballad Tune."
6p.
"6 Variations on an Old Trumpet-Hymn Tune." 1940.
"Suite on American Folk Songs: 3. March." 6p.
"Marcia Finale." Op. 17. 4p.
"Vier Kinder-Verwirr-Lieder." Words by Joachim Rin-
gelnatz. Op. 29. 9p.

PAUL AMADEUS PISK

"Zwei Frauenchöre mit Orchester." Op. 2. 1918.
"Die Gondol." Text by Goethe. 6 c. 2p. ea.
"Choral Prelude for Organ: O Lord, I Acted Badly
(Ach Herr, ich habe mißgehandelt)." Op. 41, no. 6
1938. 5p.
"Choral Prelude for Organ: Hast Thou Hidden Thy face,
Jesus (Hast Du denn, Jesu, Dein Antlitz gänzlich
verborgen?)." Op. 41, no. 2. 1938. 2 c. 4p. ea.
"Four Duets for Equal Instruments." After 1960. 9p.
6 c.
"Four Miniatures for Piano." After 1960. 6 c. 9p. ea.
"Song from Shakespeare's 'Much Ado about Nothing'."
Undated. 4 c. 5p. ea.
"Sonata for Violin Solo." Op. 16, no. 2.1925. 16p.
"A Kiss." From: "Six Songs: 4. Rose Leaves 1, 2, 3."
Op. 69, no. 4. 1950. 2p.
"Perpetuum Mobile." Score. 27p.
"Processional for Organ." After 1960. 2 c. 4p. ea.
"Regenbogen." Text by Goethe. After 1960. 6 c. 2p.
ea.
"Variations and Fugue on an American Theme; for
violin and cello." Op. 57. 1946. 8p.
"Two Sonnets - Shakespeare LV and VIII." Aug. 22,
1964. 2 c. 11p. ea.
"Second Suite for Flute Alone." After 1960. 6 c. 5p.
ea.
"The Trail of Life. Cantata for soprano and baritone
solos, narrator, chorus and orchestra." Op. 88.
1956. 45p.
"13 Variations on an Eight-bar Theme, for piano."
Op. 107. St. Louis, undated. 3 c. 7p. ea.
"God's Omnipotence." Op. 99. 1960. 8p.

C13b   Hummel, Johann Nepomuk. "Amusement à la Suisse."
Adapted and arranged for string quartet by Paul Pisk.
1935. 8p.

D13a   73 scores, all signed by Pisk.

Library of Congress, Reference Department, Music Division,
Independence Avenue and First Street S.E., Washington, D.C.
20540.

The Pisk materials at the Library of Congress were donated by Dr. Paul A. Pisk, with the exception of 6 manuscripts that were transferred from the Pisk Collection at Washington University (St. Louis) at the request of Dr. Pisk.

Die Pisk Materialien der Library of Congress sind eine Schenkung von Dr. Paul A. Pisk - mit Ausnahme von 6 Manuskripten, die entsprechend dem Wunsch von Dr. Pisk von der Pisk Collection der Washington University in St. Louis an die Library of Congress übergeben wurden.

B1,2   Correspondence, up to 1972. (Selected by Dr. Pisk.)

C13a   <u>Ein Sommer</u>. 15 Lieder. Op. 15. Songs.
        <u>Campanella</u>. Cantata. Op. 28.
        <u>Donna Clara</u>. Aria. (Lenau. Don Juan). Op. 34.
        <u>Herbstzeitlosen</u>. Op. 37a. Score and parts for Alt-
           stimme, clarinet and bass clarinet.
        <u>Drei Sonette</u>. (E. Geibel). For baritone and string
           quartet.
        <u>Der große Regenmacher</u>. Scenic ballad.
        <u>Passacaglia</u>. 1958. Reproduced from holograph. 53p.
        <u>Sonata</u>. Op. 59. Reproduced from holograph. 20p.

H3   Collection of cl.

<u>Moldenhauer Archives</u>, 1011 Comstock Court, Spokane, Washington 99203.

The materials at the Moldenhauer Archives were donated by Dr. Paul Pisk.

Die Materialien der Moldenhauer Archives sind eine Schenkung von Dr. Paul Pisk.

B1,2   Small amount of correspondence.

C13   Copies of manuscripts at other locations.

H3   Publicity materials on Pisk. Also some cl.

O   Programs.

<u>American Composer's Alliance</u>, 170 West 74th Street, New York,

PAUL AMADEUS PISK

N.Y. 10023.

Examination copies of many of Pisk's compositions are on
file with the American Composer's Alliance. Some are available for purchase from the Composer's Facsimile Edition.

*Kopien von vielen Kompositionen Pisks befinden sich bei der
American Composer's Alliance und können dort eingesehen werden. Einige können bei der Composer's Facsimile Edition
käuflich erworben werden.*

<u>University of Georgia</u>, The University Libraries, Athens,
Georgia 30601.

GUIDO ADLER PAPERS

B1,2   Correspondence with Guido Adler. 25 L.

<u>Mrs. Elisabeth M. Stoerk and Mrs. Susanne B. Hoeller</u>, 288
Ocean Drive West, Stamford, Connecticut 06902.

FRIDERIKE ZWEIG ARCHIVE

B1   2 L. to Friderike Zweig. 1944, 1954.

<u>Dr. Eric Werner</u>, 900 West 190th Street, New York, N.Y. 10040.

B1,2   Correspondence between Paul Pisk and Eric Werner.

ALFRED POLGAR

Writer, 1873-1955

No substantial amount of literary materials exists, either
with the family or elsewhere. Only the following smaller
pieces are known.

*Weder die Familie Polgars noch sonst irgendjemand besitzt
eine größere Menge literarischen Materials von Alfred Polgar.
Es sind nur folgende kleine Einzelstücke bekannt.*

Mr. Frederick Kohner, 12046 Coyne Street, Los Angeles, California 90049.

B1   21 L. to Frederick Kohner.

Yale University, Beinecke Rare Book and Manuscript Library,
New Haven, Connecticut 06520.

HERMANN BROCH ARCHIVE, KURT WOLFF ARCHIVE

B1   2 L. to Hermann Broch. 1945-1949.
       1 Ptc. to Kurt Wolff. A. 1917.

H4   Kleine Zeit. Review by Hermann Broch. T. 1p.

H5   Broch, Hermann. "Der Theaterkritiker Polgar." 1920.
       T. 5p. Another version. T. 4p.

Mrs. Elisabeth M. Stoerk and Mrs. Susanne B. Hoeller, 288
Ocean Drive West, Stamford, Connecticut 06902.

FRIDERIKE ZWEIG ARCHIVE

B1   1 L. and 1 Ptc. to Friderike Zweig. 1942.

B3   4 L. from Liesl Polgar to Friderike Zweig. Undated.

Leo Baeck Institute, 129 East 73rd Street, New York, N.Y.
10021.

JULIUS BAB COLLECTION, LEOPOLD SCHWARZSCHILD COLLECTION,

ALFRED POLGAR

JOSEPH BORNSTEIN COLLECTION

B1   5 L. to Joseph Bornstein. 1949-1952.
      2 L. to Julius Bab. 1927.

B1,2 Correspondence with Leopold Schwarzschild. 1942-1949.

New York Public Library, Manuscript Division, Fifth Avenue
and 42nd Street, New York, N.Y. 10018.

THEO FELDMAN PAPERS

B1   2 L. to Theo Feldman. A. 1946.

Mr. Hans Sahl, 800 West End Avenue, New York, N.Y. 10025.

B1   Several L. to Hans Sahl.

University of Wyoming, Archive of Contemporary History, The
Library, Box 3334, Laramie, Wyoming 82071.

ALFRED FARAU COLLECTION

B5   Farau, Alfred. "Alfred Polgar" and "Polgar zum 80.
      Geburtstag." Lectures.

California Institute of Technology, Robert A. Millikan Library, Pasadena, California 91109.

THEODORE VON KARMAN CORRESPONDENCE

B1   1 L. to Theodore von Karman. 1944.

Bruno Walter Memorial Foundation, c/o Miss Susie Danziger,
115 East 72nd Street, New York, N.Y. 10021.

B1,2 Correspondence with Bruno Walter.

741

<u>Mr. Stefan Lorant</u>, West Mountain Road, Lenox, Massachusetts
01240.

B1,2   Correspondence with Stefan Lorant.

<u>Southern Illinois University</u>, Morris Library, Department of
Special Collections, Carbondale, Illinois 62901.

ERWIN PISCATOR PAPERS

B1   Several L. to Erwin Piscator.

<u>Mr. Erik G. Ell</u>, 500-A East 87th Street, New York, N.Y.
10028.

M   Memorabilia.

<u>Mrs. Peter M. Lindt</u>, 949 West End Avenue, New York, N.Y.
10025.

B1   Small amount of correspondence with Peter M. Lindt.

C   Ms. submitted to Lindt for use on his radio program.

FRIEDRICH POLLOCK

Social Scientist, 1894-1970

Harvard University, Houghton Library, Cambridge, Massachusetts 02138.

LEO LOWENTHAL COLLECTION and general files. The materials in the Lowenthal Collection are closed until Dec. 31, 1998. Permission to use the materials may be obtained from Prof. Leo Lowenthal (Department of Sociology, University of California, Berkeley, California 94720).

LEO LOWENTHAL COLLECTION und allgemeine Ordner. Die Materialien in der Lowenthal-Sammlung sind bis zum 31. Dez. 1998 nicht zugänglich. Erlaubnis, die Materialien zu benutzen, kann von Prof. Leo Lowenthal (Department of Sociology, University of California, Berkeley, California 94720) eingeholt werden.

31   61 L. 1937-1957, including L. to: T. W. Adorno, Max Horkheimer, Paul Lazarsfeld, Alice H. Maier, Paul W. Massing.
        405 L. to Leo Lowenthal. 1935-1969.
        1 L. to Arcadij Gurland.

32   262 L. from Leo Lowenthal. 1935-1968.
        16 L., including L. from: T. W. Adorno, Max Horkheimer, Alice H. Maier.

Columbia University, Butler Library, New York, N.Y. 10027.

C11   **Spinoza.** Ms. pub. in "Great Lives" series, 1935. 210p.

Joseph and Alice Maier, 991 Grace Terrace, Teaneck, New Jersey 07666.

J5   Minutes of discussions between F. Pollock, Adolf Lowe, M. Horkheimer and Paul Tillich.

Yivo Institute, 1048 Fifth Avenue, New York, N.Y. 10028.

HORACE M. KALLEN PAPERS

FRIEDRICH POLLOCK

B1,2   Individual item(s) in folders: 225, 252, 946, 993.
        1944-1945.

Harvard University, Harvard Divinity School, Andover-Harvard
Theological Library, 45 Francis Avenue, Cambridge, Massachusetts 02138.

PAUL TILLICH COLLECTION

B1   4 L. to Paul Tillich. T.cc. 1958-1965.

B2   1 L. from Paul Tillich. T.c. 1964.

Prof. Herbert Marcuse, Department of Philosophy, University
of California San Diego, La Jolla, California 92037.

B1,2   Correspondence between Pollock and Herbert Marcuse.

University of Chicago, The Joseph Regenstein Library, 1100
East 57th Street, Chicago, Illinois 60637.

EMIL GUMBEL PAPERS

B1,2   Correspondence between Gumbel and Pollock. 1940s.

OTTO RANK

Psychoanalyst, 1884-1939

Columbia University, Butler Library, New York, N.Y. 10027.
The OTTO RANK COLLECTION, which consists of 556 items, was a
gift of Dr. Jessie Taft (widow of Otto Rank) and Mrs. Pierre
Simon, 1957.

*Die OTTO RANK COLLECTION, die aus 556 Nummern besteht, ist
eine Schenkung von Frau Dr. Jessie Taft, der Witwe von Otto
Rank, und von Frau Simon aus dem Jahre 1957.*

A1   Early diaries.

A2   Early notebooks.
       Philosophy notes from student years.

A3   Analysis of his own writings, 1906-1939. Ca. 1940.

B1   6 L. 1920-1922 to: Karl Abraham, Abraham Brill, Ernest
       Jones, Theodor Reik.

B1,2   Early correspondence.
       Miscellaneous L. 1909-1926. 2 F.
       Correspondence with Sigmund Freud. 1907-1924. 74 L.,
         mostly with Freud. Several L. from: Lou Andreas,
         Hanns Sachs, Karl Abraham, Anna Freud, Ernest Jones.
       Correspondence with Sigmund Freud concerning Rank's
         works: Trauma of Birth, Technik der Psychologie,
         Genetic Psychology. 1924-1926.
       "Journal correspondence" with Hiller, E. Jones. 1920.
         143 L.
       "Rundbriefe." 163 L. from Rank, Jones, Sachs, Eitingon,
         Abraham, Ferenczi, Freud. 1970, 1920-1921.
       Doppelgänger-correspondence with Beatrice Taussig,
         Helma Briffault, Louise Brink. 1920s.

B2   5 L. to Rank. 1919-[1923].

C1   Fragments of a novel.

C2   Fragments of a drama.

C3   Early poetry.

C7   Early articles.
       Foreword to 1914 edition of Freud's Traumdeutung.
       "Practical Bearing of Psychoanalysis." German Ms. and
         English T. of 4 speeches.

745

Speech. N.Y. Neurological Society, May 1924.
Speech. N.Y. Psychoanalytic Society, May 29, 1924.
"The Trauma of Birth." Lecture. American Psychoana-
lytic Association, June 1924.
Lecture. National Conference of Social Work, Mental
Hygiene Division, June 1924.
Notes to 4 seminars. N.Y. Psychoanalytic Society, Jan.
1925.
Lecture. Conference on Parental Education, Nov. 2,
1927.
Notes to lecture. College of Physicians and Surgeons,
Philadelphia, 1928.
"The Psychological Approach to Personal Problems."
Lecture. Stenography with corr. by Rank. Yale Univer-
sity, Feb. 2, 1929.
Lecture. Student organization, New York School of
Social Work, Nov. 1935.
"Activity and Passivity in Social Work." Lecture.
April 1935. A. and T.
Notes to a lecture given in Minneapolis.
"Mark Twain and Humor." Notes.
Notes to a course at the Graduate School of Jewish
Social Work, 1935.
"Symbols of Government." Notes to a course. Pennsyl-
vania School of Social Work, 1938.
Publicity work for the "Centre psychologique" of the
Sorbonne.
Report on Sorbonne summer session. 1934.
Opening speech for the "Centre psychologique" of the
Sorbonne.

C8   Beyond Psychology. Early notes.
      Der Künstler. 1906. Original Ms., corr. and later
      versions.
      Miscellaneous unpub. articles on money, sexuality,
      homosexuality. 1906.
      Ein Traum der selbst deutet. 1910. Ms. and English tr.
      Die Lohengrin Sage. Dissertation. 1911.
      The Trauma of Birth. Early draft, everything crossed
      out. 46p. Page proofs, notes and early writing. 1 F.
      Complete h. Ms. 1 F. Envelope with notes and cl.
      Outline of a planned book to be written by members of
      Rank's New York Seminar.

746

Art and Artist. German. T. 2 c.

Homer. Psychologische Beiträge zur Entstehungsgeschich-
te des Volksepos. 3 F. with Ms. and articles pub. in
Imago in 1917. Also unpub. materials on Macaulay's
Lays of Ancient Rome, Shakespeare's Macbeth, the
Nibelungenlied, Beowulf, etc.

Psychoanalytische Beiträge. Chap. XII: "Mythus und
Märchen."

Analysis of a dream, presumably from Freud's Traumdeutung.

Der Doppelgänger. Pub. in Imago, 1914. Ms., notes,
final bound version with corr., several newspaper cl.

Don Juan Gestalt. Ms., proofs, typed English tr. Ca.
1922-1924.

Eine Neurosenanalyse in Träumen. Ms. 1924. 2 F.

Sexualität und Schuldgefühl/Perversion and Neurosis.
English tr. of chap.: "Psychic Potency." 1 F.

Genetic Psychology. Written 1926. 8 F. in total. First
part: foreword (German and English), chap. outline,
Ms. of chap.: "Genesis of Genitality." Second part:
German Ms. Third part: German Ms., English T., French
T. Also proofs of first 2 parts. 1 B.

Entwicklungsziele der Psychoanalyse. Written 1924 with
S. Ferenczi. A. and T.

Technik der Psychoanalyse. First volume: sketches and
complete German Ms. Second volume: Die analytische
Reaktion. T. Third volume: Die Analyse des Analyti-
kers. Proofs.

Seelenglaube und Psychoanalyse. 1930. German and French
versions.

Das Inzest-Motiv in Dichtung und Sage. T., typed corr.
and notes to 1912 edition. Outline of French tr. Ms.
of 1926 edition. 1 B.

"Die beiden Angstpole." Article pub. May 1931 in Action
et Pensée.

Modern Education. Ms. of several chap.

07 Pamphlet with 2 lecture texts: "Character Formation"
and "The Task of Education." 1928.

08 Der Mythus der Geburt des Helden. 1909. Incomplete
proofs.

"Development of the Emotional Life." Advance printing
of Rank's paper for First International Congress of

Mental Hygiene. Washington, May 1930. Also 10-minute summary of speech.

H3   Announcements of lectures. 1926-1929.
Announcements of lectures. Paris 1934.
Bailey, Pearce. "Theory and Therapy." Pamphlet on the psychology of Rank.
Announcements of courses. Pennsylvania School of Social Work, 1935-1937.

H4   Cl. of reviews and critiques, which Rank used for an analysis of his writings.
Das Inzest-Motiv in Dichtung und Sage. Reviews. 1 F.

H5   Notebook with dates, title, names of persons in regard to Rank's first four New York lectures.

I   Application for stipend. Ca. 1910.
Library card. 1910.

K   17 books by Rank and 4 books by others. German and English.

L   "Freud Vorlesungen." Notebook.
Art and Artist. Cl. and illustrations for the book.
Dreams of a patient, probably used as material for the book Neurosenanalyse in Träumen.
"Traumdeutung." Research materials and dream interpretations. 2 F.
Das Inzest-Motiv in Dichtung und Sage. Cl. and notes. 1912.
Materials from period of Rank's army service in Poland. 1916-1918. 3 F.

O   Program of First International Congress of Mental Hygiene. Washington, May 1930.

ORAL HISTORY COLLECTION

H5   Recollections of Rank in interviews with Abram Kardiner (1963) and Theodor Reik (1965).

Dr. Helene Rank Veltfort, 215 North San Mateo Drive, San Mateo, California 94401.

Dr. Veltfort is the daughter of the late Otto Rank.

J   Photos of Rank.

K   Rank's personal collection of his own pub. works in German.

M   Memorabilia, including Rank's desk, etc.

Boston University, Mugar Memorial Library, 771 Commonwealth Avenue, Boston, Massachusetts 02215.

BELLA FROMM COLLECTION

B1   Several L. to Bella Fromm.

Library of Congress, Manuscript Division, Independence Avenue and First Street S.E., Washington, D.C. 20540.

PAPERS OF SIEGFRIED BERNFELD

B1,2   Correspondence with Siegfried Bernfeld. 1914-1937. Includes notes on Rank's writings.

FRITZ REDLICH

Economist, 1892-

<u>Harvard University</u>, Baker 'Library, Graduate School of Business, Soldiers Field, Boston, Massachusetts 02163.

The FRITZ REDLICH COLLECTION, which consists of approximately 3 archive boxes of materials, was deposited by Dr. Redlich in 1968. Since that time the collection has been periodically enlarged by donations of further materials by Dr. Redlich. The materials are to remain closed until 5 years after Dr. Redlich's death, while publication rights are restricted until 25 years after the death of Redlich.

Die FRITZ REDLICH COLLECTION, etwa 3 Archivkartons Materialien, wurde 1968 von Dr. Redlich übergeben. Seit der Zeit ist die Sammlung periodisch durch weitere Schenkungen Dr. Redlichs erweitert worden. Die Materialien sollen erst 5 Jahre nach seinem Tode zugänglich gemacht werden, können jedoch erst 25 Jahre nach dem Zeitpunkt des Todes von Dr. Redlich veröffentlicht werden.

A1   Diary. Italy 1906.
     Diaries. 1910-1935 with some gaps. 26 volumes.

A2   Scrapbook. Ca. 1937-1964, 1964-.
     Scrapbook. 70th birthday.

A3   School "yearbooks."
     "About trip to Porto Rico 1955." T. 5p.
     "Report on trip to Knoxville and Washington, 1952."
        T. 5p.

B1   96 L. 1936-1974, including L. to: Dietrich Gerhard,
        Henry Kissinger, Alfred Vagts.
     Correspondence concerning <u>Der Unternehmer</u>. 1946-1963.
     Correspondence concerning book on banking. First edition, 1942-1948. Second edition, 1964-1966.
     Correspondence concerning Redlich's will. Undated.
     Early letters. 1909-1910.
     Correspondence re: Immigration, Notgemeinschaft deutscher Wissenschaftler im Ausland. 1934-.
     "Essays on American Economic History" (Eric Bollmann).
        1942-1944. Ca. 15 L.
     "Riersma-Lane Book of Readings." 1948-1952. Ca. 25 L.

"German Military Enterprises 1962-1966." Primarily publisher's correspondence. Ca. 40 L.
"George S. Coe Papers (Coe Family and National Archives) 1946." Ca. 6 L.
"Gift of Library to Harvard." 1947. Ca. 10 L.
"Tulane - Rice Visits, 1964." Ca. 6 L.
"Langdon - Cheves Papers." 1964-1965. Ca. 25 L.
"Report on summer scholars, Baker Library, 1938." 2 L.

B1,2 Correspondence with publishers. 1943-1973.
Family correspondence. 1914-1918. 8 volumes.
Correspondence with Frieda Wunderlich (New School for Social Research). Ca. 20 L. 1933-1937.
Miscellaneous correspondence, labeled by subject. 1936-1950. Ca. 180 L.

B2 897 L. 1914-1973, including L. from: Gerhard Colm, Dietrich Gerhard, Julius Hirsch, Edward M. Kennedy, Henry Kissinger, Leo Lowenthal, Gerhard Masur, David Riesman, Joseph Schumpeter, Hans Speier, Hans Staudinger, Alfred Vagts.
Family L. and papers: father, mother, sisters, nephews.
Letters from childhood friends. 1956-.
"Comment on Redlich's writings, 1964." 4 L.
"80th birthday, April 7, 1972, letters of congratulation." Ca. 15 L.

B3 42 L., including 3 recommendations for citizenship.

C3 Early poems.

C4 Fairy tales by Redlich.

C7 Paper on salt mining. 1906.
"Talk, Tulane-Rice, 1964." T. with h. corr. Ca. 30p.
"Institute, Univ. of Vermont, 1966, lectures and notes." Primarily notes. 5p.
"Talk, WGBH, Nov. 1970 re German exhibit in Kress." Ms. Ca. 12p.
3 book reviews.
"Notes of 3 German Generations." 1934. A. 6p. Also transcription and explanation.
"Comparative Company History." 1962. T.c. 8p.
"Projected note on the supercargo." 1969. T.c. 3p.
"Ausschaltung des Handels." Ca. 1920s.

Untitled Ms. 1935.
"European Nobility and Economic Development." 1952-
1953. T.c. 19p.

H4   Reviews of Redlich's writings.

I   Complete list of Redlich's publications. 10p.
School records, military records, ration books from
WWI, curriculum vitae.
Diplomas: Nürnberg, 1960; Berlin, 1967.
Sample exam. Mercer University.
"German Relief 1944-1954, incl. clothing shipment."

J   Several photos among the correspondence.
Photos of Redlich and his family.
2 photo albums: 1 with pictures of Redlich, 1 of
family and friends.

L   "Mercer University Heresy Trial 1939." Essay and cl.
1 F.
"Housing. Processed materials re 1949-1950." 1 F.

M   University of Berlin Songs. 1910.
Nazi postal markings.

N   Bentin, Ludwig. "Commentary on German Economic History." Sealed until 1986.
Verses about Redlich.

Hoover Institution on War, Revolution and Peace, Stanford,
California 94305.

FRITZ REDLICH PAPERS

B1,2 Correspondence between Fritz Redlich and Wilhelm Gehl-
hoff. Restricted until Jan. 1, 1978. 1928-1958. Over
150 L.

B2   Ca. 30 L. 1930-1970. Mostly from the 1940s, Germany and
Italy.

**Immigration History Research Center of the University of
Minnesota**, 826 Berry Street, St. Paul, Minnesota 55101.

FRITZ REDLICH

AMERICAN COUNCIL FOR EMIGRÉS IN THE PROFESSIONS ARCHIVES

A3   Curriculum vitae and autobiographical statements. 18p.
B1   9 L. 1936-1948, including L. to Alvin Johnson.
B2   10 L. 1936-1948, including L. from Alvin Johnson.
B3   23 L. 1936-1948.

Prof. Alfred Vagts, Sherman, Connecticut 06784.

B1   Several L. to Alfred Vagts.

Yivo Institute, 1048 Fifth Avenue, New York, N.Y. 10028.

HORACE M. KALLEN PAPERS

B1,2   Individual item(s) in folder no. 343.

Columbia University, Butler Library, New York, N.Y. 10027.

B1   1 L. to Wesley Mitchell. A. 1934.

Harvard University, Harvard Divinity School, Andover-Harvard
Theological Library, 45 Francis Avenue, Cambridge, Massachusetts 02138.

PAUL TILLICH COLLECTION

B2   1 L. from Paul Tillich. T.c. 1962.

New York Public Library, Manuscript Division, Fifth Avenue
and 42nd Street, New York, N.Y. 10018.

EMERGENCY COMMITTEE IN AID OF DISPLACED FOREIGN SCHOLARS,
1933-1945

*   File compiled, no assistance given. 1940-1943.

WILHELM REICH

Psychoanalyst, 1897-1957

<u>Mrs. Mary Higgins</u>, Wilhelm Reich Infant Trust Fund, 382
Burns Street, Forest Hills, New York 11375.

The literary estate of Wilhelm Reich, known as the WILHELM
REICH ARCHIVE, is closed to researchers until 50 years after
the date of Reich's death. Until that time it will remain
totally uncatalogued and undescribed. The entire collection
will then go to the Francis A. Countway Library of Medicine,
Harvard University, 10 Shattuck Street, Cambridge, Massachusetts 02115.

*Der literarische Nachlaß von Wilhelm Reich (das WILHELM REICH
ARCHIVE) wird erst 50 Jahre nach dem Zeitpunkt seines Todes
zugänglich gemacht werden. Bis dahin bleiben die Materialien
unsortiert. Die Sammlung wird dann vollständig an die Francis A. Countway Library of Medicine, Harvard University, 10
Shattuck Street, Cambridge, Massachusetts 02115, gehen.*

<u>New York Public Library</u>, Manuscript Division, Fifth Avenue
and 42nd Street, New York, N.Y. 10018.

ERICH FROMM PAPERS

Bl,2 Correspondence between Erich Fromm and Wilhelm Reich.

FRITZ REICHE

Physicist, 1883-1969

American Institute of Physics, Niels Bohr Library, 335 East
45th Street, New York, N.Y. 10017.

The FRITZ REICHE PAPERS, which consist of 12 boxes of materials, were deposited at the Institute during 1971 by
Reiche's widow, Bertha, and son, Hans. Copies of all papers
written or published papers are with Mr. Hans Reiche, 22
Chapleau Avenue, Ottawa, Ontario, Canada.

Die FRITZ REICHE PAPERS, 12 Kartons Materialien, wurden im
Laufe des Jahres 1971 von Fritz Reiches Witwe, Bertha Reiche,
und von seinem Sohn, Hans Reiche, dem Institut übergeben.
Alle Publikationen sowie Kopien aller sonstigen Schriften
befinden sich im Besitz von Hans Reiche, 22 Chapleau Avenue,
Ottawa, Ontario, Canada.

B1	1 L. to H. F. Ludloff. 1932. A. 8p.
B2	43 L. 1911-1968, including L. from: M. Born, A. Ein-stein, W. Ericson, J. Franck, F. Haber, Alexander Kolin, H. F. Ludloff, O. Lummer, L. Natanson, M. Planck, E. Schrödinger.
B3	2 L. from A. Kolin to Hutchinson. 1953.
	1 L. from A. Einstein to F. Haber. Ca. 1920-1921.
	1 Tel. from O. Hahn and L. Meitner to R. Ladenberg. 1928.
C8	Notes and calculations by Reiche concerning work by Alexander Kolin. 300p. Also 2 reprints by Kolin.

"Electromagnetic Velometry II - Elimination of the
Effects of Induced Currents in Explorations of the
Velocity Distribution in Axially Symmetrical Flow."
cc. 15p. Written with Alexander Kolin.
Notes and calculations by Reiche concerning the work of
H. F. Ludloff. Ca. 57p. Also 3 reprints by Ludloff.
Notes and calculations on work of other scientists,
in German:
G. Krutow. 1919. A. 15p.
"Referat über Weizsäcker und Saunter-Heitler in
Prager Kolloquium." 1934. A. 19p.
"Schwarz - Die Gauss'sche Hypergeometrische Reihe."
1935. A. 24p.
F. London. "Die Zahl der Dispersionselektronen in

der Undulationsmechanik." A. 10p.
"Theoretical Physics - Different Problems." A. 20p.
"Bethe and Weizäcker - Nuclear Physics." A. Ca. 250p.
"Different explanations, evaluations, Einstein's
  equations, etc." A. Ca. 75p.
"Diverses - (Tests for Atomic Physics, etc.) - Laue
  Diagrame." A. Ca. 200p.
Lecture notes and notebooks, in German:
"Analytische Mechanik mit Übungsaufgaben." 1919-1929.
  Ca. 400p.
"Elektrizität I." 1921-1931. Ca. 300p.
"Klassische Physik. I. Mechanik und Wärme. II. Elek-
  trodynamik und Optik. III. Relativitätstheorie."
  Breslau University, 1921-1932. 400p.
"Optik (Elektrizität III)." 1922-1931. 245p.
"Kinetische Gastheorie. Statische Mechanik." 1922-
  1929. Ca. 350p.
"Höhere Probleme der Quantentheorie." 1923. Ca. 240p.
"Prager Vorlesung." Ca. 1934-1935. 598p.
"Quantentheorie." Undated. Ca. 1,200p.
"Thermodynamik." Undated. 366p.
"Hydrodynamik. Elastizität." Undated. 509p.
"II Atomphysik. Kap. IV. Atomphysik der Materie. Kap.
  V. Atomphysik der Elektrizität. Kap. VI. Der Elek-
  trische Aufbau der Atome. Kap. VII. Das Eingreifen
  der Quantentheorie. Kap. VIII. Die Atomtheorie von
  Niels Bohr." pp. 389-863.
"Übungsaufgaben für die Vorlesungen in Breslau." Ca.
  342p.
2 lectures presented at Breslau University. Untitled.
  T. 20p.
Lecture notes, problems, calculations, and examina-
tions, in English:
"Physics 52/62 - Mechanics - Synge and Griffith."
  NYU, 1951-1952. Ca. 600p.
"Physics 65 - Elasticity, Sound, Hydrodynamics."
  NYU, 1954. Ca. 200p.
"Physics 52/62 - Mechanics (Keith R. Symon - Mechan-
  ics)." NYU, 1955-1956. Ca. 600p.
"Vector: Analysis and Algebra." Undated. pp. 1-571,
  600-697.
Propagations of Plane Electromagnetic Waves Through a
Conducting Uniformly Moving Substance. Notes, first

draft, second draft. Unfinished at the time of Reiche's death. Ca. 2,300p. in all.

D8   20 reprints by Reiche (some co-authored).

H5   Reiche, Hans. Biographical sketch of Fritz Reiche.

N   Senftleben, Hermann. "Über die Zahl der Emissionszentren der in Flammen leuchtenden Metalldämpfe und die Beziehungen dieser Zahl zur Helligkeit der ausgesandten Spektrallinien." Ph.D. thesis. Breslau, 1915. A. Also 1p. of notes by Reiche.

University of Chicago, The Joseph Regenstein Library, 1100 East 57th Street, Chicago, Illinois 60637.

JAMES FRANCK PAPERS

B1,2   Correspondence between James Franck and Fritz Reiche. Correspondence with Robert L. Platzman, concerning Platzman's The Selected Papers of James Franck.

C8   "Über Helium und Parhelium." Written together with James Franck. A. 5p.

J   Institute for Theoretical Physics. Group photo. Copenhagen, 1935.

HANS REICHENBACH

Philosopher of Science, 1891-1953

Mrs. Maria Reichenbach, 456 Puerto Del Mar, Pacific Palisades, California 90272.

The papers of Hans Reichenbach consist of ca. 30 ft. of materials.

Die Materialien von Hans Reichenbach umfassen etwa 9 m.

A3   Memoirs of Maria Reichenbach.
Autobiographical statements of Hans Reichenbach.

B1,2   Correspondence, organized by years and alphabetically within years. 1919-1953. Includes correspondence with: Rudolf Carnap, Albert Einstein (ca. 20 L. 1919-1940), Carl Gustav Hempel, Wolfgang Pauli. Also copies of Reichenbach's L.

C7   Ms. of Reichenbach's books, including: Quantenmechanik, Direction of Time.
Unpublished manuscripts.
Notes to lectures.
Work notes and manuscripts to unpublished works.

D7   Cl. and reprints of all Reichenbach's writings. 1911-.

H4   Reviews of all of Reichenbach's works.

I   Documents: school certificates, invitations, etc.

J   Photos.

L   Albert Einstein reprints.
Rudolf Carnap reprints.

Ms. Elizabeth Austin, 4173 Stowe Way, Sacramento, California 95825.

J   Family photo album, containing early photos of Hans and Maria Reichenbach.

Princeton University, Firestone Library, Princeton, New Jersey 08540.

ALBERT EINSTEIN COLLECTION

B1,2 Duplicates of correspondence between Einstein and Reichenbach in possession of Mrs. Maria Reichenbach.

<u>Prof. Carl Landauer</u>, 1317 Arch Street, Berkeley, California 94708.

B1,2 Correspondence between Carl Landauer and Hans Reichenbach.

<u>University of Chicago</u>, The Joseph Regenstein Library, 1100 East 57th Street, Chicago, Illinois 60637.

JAMES FRANCK PAPERS

B1,2 Correspondence between James Franck and Hans Reichenbach.

<u>California Institute of Technology</u>, Robert A. Millikan Library, Pasadena, California 91109.

* 1 F. of items. 1933.

<u>American Philosophical Society</u>, The Library, 105 South Fifth Street, Philadelphia, Pennsylvania 19106.

WOLFGANG KÖHLER PAPERS

B1,2 Correspondence between Wolfgang Köhler and Hans Reichenbach. 1930-1931.

<u>University of Minnesota</u>, University Libraries, University Archives, Minneapolis, Minnesota 55455.

GEORGE P. CONGER PAPERS

B1 2 L. to George P. Conger. 1939-1940.

Duke University, William R. Perkins Library, Manuscript Department, Durham, North Carolina 27706.

FRITZ WOLFGANG LONDON PAPERS

B1   1 L. to F. W. London. 1930.

University of Southern California, Lion Feuchtwanger Memorial Library, 520 Paseo Miramar, Pacific Palisades, California 90272.

B2   1 L. from Lion Feuchtwanger. 1947.

University of California, Los Angeles, Department of Special Collections, 120 Lawrence Clark Powell Library, Los Angeles, California 90024.

THE CARNAP PAPERS

H4   Carnap, Rudolf. Hans Reichenbach: Review of Reichenbach, Axiomatik 1924.

THEODOR REIK

Psychoanalyst, 1888-1969

Dr. Murray Sherman, 350 Central Park West, New York, N.Y. 10024.

Dr. Sherman is writing a biography of Theodor Reik, to be completed ca. 1978.

Dr. Sherman arbeitet z.Zt. an einer Biographie über Theodor Reik, die etwa 1978 fertiggestellt sein soll.

B1,2   Correspondence between Reik and Murray Sherman.
D7   Sizable number of reprints of Reik's writings.
F   2 or 3 tapes of Reik.

Columbia University, Butler Library, New York, N.Y. 10027.

W. W. NORTON PAPERS, ORAL HISTORY COLLECTION

A3   Memoir by Theodor Reik. 2 microfiches (4 in. x 6 in.). Available for purchase.

B1   2 L. to W. W. Norton and Co. T. 1950.

B2   1 L. from Otto Rank. 1922.

G   Interviews: Recollections of Otto Rank and Hanns Sachs; analysis with Dr. Karl Abraham; founding of National Association for Allied Psychoanalysts. 1965. Transcript. 99p. Permission required for use.

Harvard University, Houghton Library, Cambridge, Massachusetts 02138.

RICHARD BEER-HOFMANN COLLECTION, SCHWEIZER AUTOGRAPH COLLECTION

B1   31 L. to Richard Beer-Hofmann. 1912-1945.

B2   9 L. from Arthur Schnitzler. 1912-1918.

Library of Congress, Manuscript Division, Independence Avenue and First Street S.E., Washington, D.C. 20540.

PAPERS OF SIEGFRIED BERNFELD

B1,2 Correspondence with Siegfried Bernfeld. 1918-1944. Correspondence with Sigmund Freud. 1912-1938. c.

I   Minutes, in Reik's hand, of the Lehr-Institut of the Wiener Psychoanalytischer Verein. 1918-1920.

American Academy of Psychotherapists, Fair Lawn, New Jersey 07410.

F   Taped interview with Theodor Reik.

New York Public Library, Manuscript Division, Fifth Avenue and 42nd Street, New York, N.Y. 10018.

EMERGENCY COMMITTEE IN AID OF DISPLACED FOREIGN SCHOLARS, 1933-1945

*   File compiled, no assistance given. 1938-1941.

MAX REINHARDT

Stage Director, 1873-1943

State University of New York at Binghamton, Center for Modern Theater Research, Binghamton, New York 13901.

The MAX REINHARDT ARCHIVE, consisting of ca. 500,000 items (including copies, duplicates), was begun in 1966 and is being continually enlarged by further gifts and purchases. A substantial portion of the collection was received from Gottfried Reinhardt and Helene Thimig. Although the majority of the materials are legally owned either by the State University of New York, the S.U.N.Y. Binghamton Foundation, or the Max Reinhardt Foundation, other materials in the collection are on perpetual loan to the Archive, with ownership still held by the original donors. Restrictions on the use of the collection vary from no restraints at all to totally inaccessible until some stipulated later date.

The individual items in the collection have been only partially catalogued (ca. 8,000 of the 500,000 itmes). The following cursory description attempts only to indicate the types of materials that are represented in the collection.

Das MAX REINHARDT ARCHIVE, das etwa 500.000 Nummern (einschl. Kopien und Duplikate) umfaßt, wurde 1966 begonnen und wird ständig durch Schenkungen oder Käufe erweitert. Ein wesentlicher Bestandteil stammt von Gottfried Reinhardt und Helene Thimig. Der größte Teil der Materialien ist legaler Besitz der State University of New York, der S.U.N.Y. Binghamton Foundation oder der Max Reinhardt Foundation; einige der Materialien sind jedoch Dauerleihgaben an das Archiv und somit noch im Besitz der Spender. Was den Zugang zu den Materialien betrifft, so sind einige völlig frei zugänglich, andere sind bis zu einem jeweils festgesetzten Zeitpunkt gesperrt.

Die einzelnen Nummern der Sammlung sind z.Zt. nur teilweise katalogisiert (etwa 8000 der 500.000 Nummern). Die folgende grobe Aufstellung will nur die Arten der Materialien aufzeigen, die in der Sammlung vorhanden sind.

I. Catalogued materials. Ca. 8,000 items on individual index cards, grouped under the following subject headings:

   1. Plays. Ca. 125 titles (printed matter, photos,

promptbooks, cl.).
2. Plays Not Directed by Reinhardt.
3. Unidentified Plays.
4. Actors. Ca. 400 names (mostly photos).
5. Actors Not Under Reinhardt's Direction.
6. Unidentified Actors.
7. Playwrights (cross-references to authors of category 1).
8. Max Reinhardt. 71 photos, 17 theses, and 1 book on Reinhardt.
9. Max Reinhardt Actor. 34 photos (1896-1907 and undated), 9 xeroxes, cl.
10. Max Reinhardt Director. Photos, criticisms, pc. of articles.
11. Reinhardt Sketches, Caricatures.
12. Articles/Printed Material. Ca. 175 items including obituaries, some scripts. Mostly articles about Reinhardt (cl.), several by Reinhardt.
13. Letters, Telegrams, Legal Documents. Ca. 60 L. to and from Reinhardt, 7 documents, articles, obituaries, third party L.
14. Criticisms. Ca. 75 newspaper cl. (critiques) of various plays, a few photos and L.
15. Max Reinhardt's Residences. Ca. 100 photos.
16. Composers. Printed matter, photos, ca. 50 L.
17. Lyricists. 2 items.
18. Architects. 2 items.
19. Conductors. Ca. 50 items.
20. Directors Other Than Reinhardt (cross-references to directors who appear in other categories). Includes: J. Bab, B. Brecht, W. Dieterle, C. Goetz, L. Jessner, B. Viertel.
21. Designers. Includes G. Grosz.
22. Designers Not Working with Reinhardt.
23. Unidentified Scene Designs.
24. Producers and Stage Managers.
25. Administrative Assistants and Business Associates.
26. Directors and Administrative Assistants Not Connected with Reinhardt.
27. [Lists of the] Reinhardt Family. Miscellaneous materials on the family.
28. Recordings, Slides, Tapes, Microfilm.
29. Artists. Ca. 30 items, primarily photos and drawings.

30. Correspondence: Publishers and Writers to MR. 7 L.
    1903-1925 and undated.
31. Authors and Editors of Books on File; Other Writers.
    Primarily photos and printed articles.
32. Students and Their Theses.
33. Persons Not of the Theater.
34. Unidentified Persons.
35. Books, Catalogs, Programs, Posters, Magazines,
    Floor Plans. Ca. 150 items.
36. Various Programs, Other Than Reinhardt Directed
    Plays.
37. Guest Performances at S.U.N.Y. Binghamton—Original
    Promptbooks.

II. Uncatalogued materials. Over 450,000 items, including:

1. Over 1,000 L., dating back to early 1900s. Includes
   L. by Bertolt Held, Hugo von Hofmannsthal, Karl
   Vollmoeller, etc.
2. Cl.
3. Programs.
4. Photos.
5. Documents, including numerous contracts.
6. Ca. 1,000 playscripts of Reinhardt productions,
   some original T.
7. Max Reinhardt personal library.
8. Large scenic designs collection.

Among the individuals represented in the Reinhardt
    Archive are: Julius Bab, Albert Bassermann, Richard
    Beer-Hofmann, Elisabeth Bergner, Bertolt Brecht,
    William Dieterle, Lion Feuchtwanger, George Grosz,
    Friedrich Holländer, Oscar Homolka, Leopold Jessner,
    Lotte Lenya, Erwin Piscator, Otto Preminger, John
    Reich, Berthold Viertel, Fritz von Unruh, Kurt
    Weill, Franz Werfel.

III. Additional materials located at the Center for Modern
     Theater Research: Selected portions of the WILDGANS
     COLLECTION (Director of the Burgtheater), on microfilm.
     Primarily materials relating to negotiations between
     Reinhardt and the Burgtheater. Ca. 200p.

MAX REINHARDT

*Weitere Materialien befinden sich im Center for Modern
Theater Research: Ausgewählte Teile der WILDGANS COL-
LECTION (Leiter des Burgtheaters) auf Mikrofilm. Es
handelt sich hauptsächlich um Materialien über Verhand-
lungen zwischen Reinhardt und dem Burgtheater; etwa
200 Seiten.*

University of Kansas, Kenneth Spencer Research Library,
Department of Special Collections, Lawrence, Kansas 66045.

The MAX REINHARDT WORKSHOP COLLECTION (Ms. 10), ca. 18 folders of materials, was donated to the library ca. 1960 by Ms.
Adah Clarke, student of the Max Reinhardt Workshop in 1939.

*Die MAX REINHARDT WORKSHOP COLLECTION (MS. 10), etwa 18 Mappen
mit Materialien, ist eine Schenkung (etwa 1960) von Frau Adah
Clarke, einer Studentin am Max Reinhardt Workshop im Jahre
1939.*

C12   Roll books of performances of the Workshop, including:
       At Your Service.
       Six Characters in Search of an Author.
       Daughters of Atreus.
       Radio program. Orson Welles Campbell Playhouse, 1939.
       2 film scripts and 1 TV program script.

H5   Materials from Reinhardt's obituary program. Wilshire
       Ebell Theatre, Hollywood, California, Dec. 15, 1943.

J   Photos of Reinhardt and others.
       Photos of productions:
       At Your Service.
       Six Characters in Search of an Author.
       Daughters of Atreus.

L   Course notes (Adah Clarke): Radio Production Class,
       Motion Picture Class, Production and Acting (taught
       by William Dieterle), Speech Class, Stage Lighting
       Class.
       Miscellaneous materials concerning productions, in-
       cluding:
       Wilder's Happy Journey.
       Booth's The Women.

The Barretts of Wimpole Street.
Nanette Fabares' Madame Guillotine.
Radio version of Ben Hur.
Noel Coward's Hands Across the Sea.
Sister Beatrice.
Two Many Husbands.
Merrily We Roll Along.

O Miscellaneous programs of productions.

University of Texas, Humanities Research Center, Manuscripts
Collection, Box 7219, Austin, Texas 78712.

B1 2 L.

B2 3 L.

C9 A Midsummer Night's Dream. T. with deletions, etc. for
  the planned Reinhardt version of the play.

C12 Macbeth. Production notes.

C12, A Midsummer Night's Dream. Winson Classic Edition used
J, by Reinhardt for Hollywood Bowl Production (1934),
L, containing all cues, cuts, etc. Also prompter's copy.
O   7 photos of different performances. 1934.
   8 miscellaneous items. 1934.
   4 programs. 1934.

University of Pennsylvania, The Charles Patterson Van Pelt
Library, Philadelphia, Pennsylvania 19104.

ALMA MAHLER-WERFEL COLLECTION

B1 4 L. and 5 Tel. to Alma Mahler-Werfel. 1941-1943.

Harvard University, Houghton Library, Cambridge, Massachusetts 02138.

RICHARD BEER-HOFMANN COLLECTION and general archive files

B1 37 L. to Richard Beer-Hofmann. 1904-1933 and undated.

2 L. to Sir John Martin Harvey. 1921.

B2   1 L. from U.S. Dept. of State. 1938.

Museum of the City of New York, Fifth Avenue at 103rd Street, New York, N.Y. 10029.

H3   Materials in the Museum's "Personality File" and "Over-size File."

L   Production files for Reinhardt productions, including:
      The Miracle.
      Merchant of Venice.
      Merchant of Yonkers.
      Captive.
      Redemption.
      Sons and Soldiers.
      Saint Joan.
      Servant of Two Masters.

Southern Illinois University, Morris Library, Department of Special Collections, Carbondale, Illinois 62901.

ERWIN PISCATOR PAPERS

B1   1 Tel. and 1 L. (pc.) to Erwin Piscator. 1938-1939.

B2   4 L. from Erwin Piscator. T.cc. 1938-1940.

Academy of Motion Picture Arts and Sciences, Margaret Herrick Library, 9038 Melrose Avenue, Hollywood, California 90069.

H3   Newspaper and magazine cl. on Reinhardt.

J   2 photos of Reinhardt.

State Historical Society of Wisconsin, 816 State Street, Madison, Wisconsin 53706.

LOUIS P. LOCHNER PAPERS

MAX REINHARDT

G   Report by Lochner on 2 interviews with Reinhardt. Nov.
        10, 1925 and [Nov.] 1926. T.cc. 7p.

Bruno Walter Memorial Foundation, c/o Miss Susie Danziger,
115 East 72nd Street, New York, N.Y. 10021.

B1,2 Correspondence with Bruno Walter.

University of Texas, Humanities Research Center, Hoblitzelle
Theater Arts Library, Box 7219, Austin, Texas 78712.

B1   1 signed printed invitation.

J   1 photo.

Dr. Gustave O. Arlt, 13220-C Admiralty Way, Marina del Rey,
California 90291.

FRANZ WERFEL ARCHIVE

B1   1 L. to the Paul Zsolnay Verlag, 1934.

Library of Congress, Manuscript Division, Independence Avenue
and First Street S.E., Washington, D.C. 20540.

BENJAMIN W. HUEBSCH PAPERS

B1   1 L. to B. W. Huebsch. 1957. T.

Cornell University, John M. Olin Library, Department of Rare
Books, Ithaca, New York, 14850.

B1   1 L. to George Jean Nathan. 1923.

American Philosophical Society, The Library, 105 South Fifth
Street, Philadelphia, Pennsylvania 19106.

MAX REINHARDT

FRANZ BOAS PAPERS

B2   2 L. from Franz Boas. 1910.

<u>Leo Baeck Institute</u>, 129 East 73rd Street, New York, N.Y.
10021.

MAXIMILIAN HARDEN COLLECTION, VERA RUBIN COLLECTION, FRANZ
WERFEL COLLECTION

B2   1 Tel. from Franz Werfel. 1929.

B3   Correspondence revealing Maximilian Harden's relation-
       ship with the Max Reinhardt Circle.

O   Programs, data on 48 Reinhardt productions prior to
       1933.

WALTER REISCH

Screen Writer, 1903-

Mr. Walter Reisch, 420 Amapola Lane, Los Angeles, California
90024.

Mr. Reisch has a nearly complete collection of materials concerning his life and career after 1933. All older manuscripts, correspondences, etc. were lost during his flight
from Nazi Germany.

*Herr Walter Reisch besitzt eine nahezu vollständige Sammlung
von Materialien über seinen privaten und beruflichen Werdegang nach 1933. Alles frühere Material, z.B. Manuskripte
und Briefwechsel, ist bei seiner Flucht vor dem national-
sozialistischen Regime verlorengegangen.*

A1   Detailed diaries. 1933 to the present

B1,2 Business correspondence, some going back to England and
      European periods. Ca. 25% destroyed or lost.
      Private correspondence.

C5   Ms. of 75% of the film scripts written by Reisch during
      his career, including unfilmed texts such as:
      Boutique.
      Demaskierung.
      Footprints in the Sand.
      The Great St. Bernard.
      Der Hochzeitsmarsch von Felix Mendelssohn.

G   Transcripts of taped interviews that Reisch gave to
      the American Film Institute. Ca. 20 hours.

H4   Reviews of all movies. Cl.

I   Documentary materials, passports, awards.
      All contracts.

J   Photos of Reisch.

K   Reisch's personal literary library. German and Ameri-
      can authors.

M   Memorabilia.

University of Texas, Humanities Research Center, Manuscripts
Collection, Box 7219, Austin, Texas 78712.

B2   2 L.

ERICH MARIA REMARQUE
Novelist, 1898-1970

The major portion of Remarque's estate is located with his widow, Paulette Goddard, in the Remarque villa in Porto Ronco near Ascona, Switzerland. The materials remain unsorted and uncatalogued.

Der größte Teil des Nachlasses von Erich Maria Remarque befindet sich in Händen seiner Witwe, Paulette Goddard, in der Remarque-Villa in Porto Ronco bei Ascona, Switzerland. Die Materialien sind weder katalogisiert noch sortiert.

Indiana University, The University Library, The Lilly Library, Bloomington, Indiana 47401.

APPLETON-CENTURY MSS., LEWIS BROWNE MSS., UPTON BEALL SINCLAIR MSS.

B1   1 L. ea. to Upton Sinclair and Lewis Browne. 1942.
      Signed also by Lion Feuchtwanger, Bruno Frank, Max Horkheimer, Thomas Mann, Franz Werfel.
      2 L.
B2   1 L. from W. M. Schuster. 1946.
B3   1 L. from Thomas Mann to Lewis Browne. 1942.
I   Receipt for $7,500. Dated Dec. 30, 1946.
      Spark of Life. 2 contracts.

Harcourt Brace Jovanovich, Inc., 757 Third Avenue, New York, N.Y. 10017.

B1   56 L. to Denver Lindley. 1952-1957.
      1 L. to "the chief corrector." 1963.
B2   39 L. from Denver Lindley. 1952-1957.
      4 L. 1960-1963.
H4   Collection of reviews of works by Remarque pub. by Harcourt Brace.

Mr. Sam Salz, 7 East 76th Street, New York, N.Y. 10021.

B1,2   Correspondence between Salz and Remarque.

C1   Liebe Deinen Nächsten. A. and T. with numerous corr.
by Remarque. 433p.
Die Nacht von Lisbon. Mimeo. c. with remark "Unveröf-
fentlichtes Manuskript. Eins von zehn Exemplaren.
Nr. 2. Copyright 1961." Signed by Remarque, July 22,
1962. 324p.
The Night of Lisbon. Tr. by Ralph Manheim. Uncor-
rected. Signed by Remarque, March 1964. T. 311p.

Mr. Otto Klement, 9772 Olympic Boulevard, Beverly Hills,
California 90213.

B1,2   Correspondence between Remarque and Otto Klement.

University of Pennsylvania, The Charles Patterson Van Pelt
Library, Philadelphia, Pennsylvania 19104.

ALMA MAHLER-WERFEL COLLECTION

B1   12 L., 2 Tel. and 1 Ptc. to Alma Mahler-Werfel. 1941-
1945.

Boston University, Mugar Memorial Library, 771 Commonwealth
Avenue, Boston, Massachusetts 02215.

HANS HABE COLLECTION

B1   2 L. to Hans Habe. A. 1968 and undated.
1 L. to Miss Southman. A. 1966.

Universal Studios, Universal Central Files Department, 100
Universal City Plaza, Universal City, California 91608.

C5   A Time to Love and a Time to Die. Microfilm of film
script.

ERICH MARIA REMARQUE

Library of Congress, Manuscript Division, Independence Avenue and First Street S.E., Washington, D.C. 20540.

BENJAMIN W. HUEBSCH PAPERS

B1   1 L. to B. W. Huebsch. A. 1946. Also signed by Lion Feuchtwanger, Bruno Frank, Thomas Mann, Max Horkheimer, Franz Werfel. 1942.

University of New Hampshire, The Library, Department of Special Collections, Durham, New Hampshire 03824.

OSKAR MARIA GRAF COLLECTION

B1   1 L. to Oskar Maria Graf. 1963.

B2   1 L. from Oskar Maria Graf. 1964.

Mr. Hans Sahl, 800 West End Avenue, New York, N.Y. 10025.

B1   1 L. to Hans Sahl. 1962.

Academy of Motion Picture Arts and Sciences, Margaret Herrick Library, 9038 Melrose Avenue, Hollywood, California 90069.

H3   Newspaper cl., including obituaries.

Southern Illinois University, Morris Library, Department of Special Collections, Carbondale, Illinois 62901.

ERWIN PISCATOR PAPERS

B2   1 L. from Erwin Piscator. T.cc. 1940.

Syracuse University, The George Arents Research Library, Syracuse, New York 13210.

DOROTHY THOMPSON PAPERS

B2   1 L. from Dorothy Thompson. Undated.

ERICH MARIA REMARQUE

<u>Mrs. Peter M. Lindt</u>, 949 West End Avenue, New York, N.Y.
10025.

C   Ms. submitted to Lindt for use on his radio program.

MAX RHEINSTEIN

Lawyer, 1899-

University of Chicago, The Joseph Regenstein Library, 1100
East 57th Street, Chicago, Illinois 60637.

The MAX RHEINSTEIN PAPERS, 70 archive boxes plus 552 offprints and newspapers, were donated to the library by Max
Rheinstein in 1973.

*Die MAX RHEINSTEIN PAPERS, 70 Archivkartons sowie 552 Son-
derdrucke und Zeitungen, sind eine Schenkung von Max Rheinstein aus dem Jahre 1973.*

A2   Notebooks from student years. 1917-1924. 5 F.

A3   Materials from student years. 1907-1917, 1911-1918.
      3 F.
      Student lecture notes and certificates. University of
      Munich, 1920-1922. 1 F.

B1,2 Correspondence. 1910-1918. 2 F.
      Correspondence. 1933-1935. 1 F.
      Correspondence, arranged alphabetically and chrono-
      logically. 1947-1969. 30 1/2 B.
      "Committee Correspondence and Conferences 1950s,
      1960s." 5 1/2 B.
      "Visiting Professors and foreign students." Univ. of
      Chicago, 1959. 2 F.
      Correspondence with Ernst Rabel. 1 F.
      Letters from Germany 1946-1947. 1 F.
      Correspondence. Japan, 1961. 2 F.
      Correspondence. Taiwan, Korea, India, 1961. 1 F.
      "Rheinstein personal" correspondence. 1 F.

C7   Reviews from the 1930s. University of Chicago. 3 F.
      Lectures. Chicago, 1944. 1 F.
      Drafts to articles, lectures, reviews from the 1950s.
      2 B.
      Lecture materials. Univ. of Chicago, 1972. 1 F.
      Lecture materials. Luxembourg, 1959. 1 F.
      Lectures. Japan, 1961. 1 F.
      Encyclopaedia Britannica articles. 1960. 2 F.
      Drafts of journal articles, lecture notes, book re-
      views, 1950s. Ca. 1 1/2 B.
      Research and lecture notes. 1907-1944. Ca. 4 B.

C7,   Manuscripts, lecture notes, reference materials, 1950s
L   Univ. of Chicago course materials. Ca. 6 1/2 B.

C8   French law. 3 B.
Notes and Ms. to the following cases and topics:
"Deportation Case. 1950." 1 F.
Legal consultation. 1 F.
"Testimony in Colisimo Case 1954-1955" and "Colisimo
Case 1954-1955." 3 F.
"Abele Estate 1943-1953." 1 F.
"Wasserman Estate 1962." 2 F.
"Insurance Claim 1960." 1 F.
"Federal Security Agency Consultation." 1 F.
"James Foster Foundation Consultation." 1 F.
"Family Law Inquiry." 2 F.

D7,8 Reprints, some with comments in margin.

I   Doctoral exams. Univ. of Chicago, 1938.
German government bonds. 1 F.
Papers from work in legal division, U.S. military gov-
ernment of Germany. 1946-1947. 3 F.
Stocks.
Ford Foundation Grant. 1957-1958.
Applications to Comparative Law Center, Univ. of Chi-
cago, 1950.
Comparative Law: Budgets, Minutes, Records. 1950-1957.
2 F.
Comparative Law Conference. 1966. 2 F.
Strasbourg conference on comparative law. Undated.
Foreign Law Program, U.S., 1959-1962. 10 F.
Univ. of Chicago Law School. 1963-1966. 1 F.
Budget information for Comparative Law and Comparative
Law Programs, U.S. 1958-1964. 1 F.

L   Death notice. 1912.
Ray School newspaper. 1936.
Syllabus. Univ. of Chicago.
Conferences for the study of international and compara-
tive law. 3 F.
Société Jean Bodin.
Printed estate planning materials. 1946-1955. 3 F.
Univ. of Chicago course materials. 1942. 1 F.
Univ. of Chicago course materials. 1940-1959. 1 B.
Univ. of Chicago course materials on marriage and

divorce. 1938-1939. 3 F.
Course materials, lecture notes. 1935-1951. Conferences 1961-1962. Ca. 3 B.
Course materials, lecture notes and student papers. 1943-1968. 4 B.
Newspaper cl. 1929-1930, 1933-1935. 4 F.
Student Problem Book 1967. 3c.
Annual Message of Clayton F. Smith, president of Cook County Board of Commissioners. 1937.
Comparative Studies in Society and History. 1 F.
Reference collection on the subjects of international and comparative law and family law. Ca. 1927-1958. Several hundred items.
Offprints and journals containing articles by friends and colleagues of Rheinstein.

M   Table cloth.
New York City souvenirs.
Italy souvenirs.
Japan souvenirs.

N   Manuscript of a Univ. of Chicago student. 1960.
Student papers, Univ. of Chicago. 1960.
3 Ms.

JAMES FRANCK PAPERS

B1,2   Correspondence with James Franck.

New York Public Library, Manuscript Division, Fifth Avenue and 42nd Street, New York, N.Y. 10018.

EMERGENCY COMMITTEE IN AID OF DISPLACED FOREIGN SCHOLARS, 1933-1945

*   File compiled when assistance was granted. 1934-1943.

Harvard University, Houghton Library, Cambridge, Massachusetts 02138.

LEO LOWENTHAL COLLECTION

B1   1 L. to Max Horkheimer. T.c. 1953.
B2   1 L. from Max Horkheimer. T.c. 1953.

HANS RICHTER

Filmmaker, 1888-1976

<u>Museum of Modern Art</u>, The Library, 11 West 53rd Street, New
York, N.Y. 10019.

The HANS RICHTER ARCHIVE, 54 volumes of inventoried materials, was donated to the Museum Library by Hans Richter in
1969. Written permission to use the Archive is required in
advance of visits to the Museum. Dates covered: 1929-1969.

*Das HANS RICHTER ARCHIVE, 54 Bände inventarisierten Mate-
rials, aus der Zeit von 1929 bis 1969, ist eine Schenkung
von Hans Richter aus dem Jahre 1969. Das Archiv darf nur
mit vorheriger schriftlicher Genehmigung benutzt werden.*

B1,2   Personal correspondence. Ca. 300 L. 1940-1970, includ-
        ing L. to and from: J. Albers, R. Arnheim, E. Auer-
        bach, M. Ernst, G. Grosz, H. Hofmann, R. Huelsenbeck,
        S. Kracauer, W. Mehring, Ludwig Mies van der Rohe,
        H. Sahl.
        Business correspondence, including ca. 75 L. by Rich-
        ter. 1935-1966.

C5   <u>8 x 8</u>. Original script, production schedule. Ca. 200p.
        Also miscellaneous materials (analysis, publicity,
        script, contracts, correspondence, memorabilia).
        1950s.
        <u>Passionate Pastime</u>. Original script and sketches.
        1957. Ca. 70p.
        <u>Dadascope</u>. Notes. 1958. Ca. 15p.
        <u>Hier gibts keine Katharina</u>. 1934-1935. Ca. 133p.
        <u>Keine Zeit für Tränen</u>. 1934-1935. cc. 104p.
        <u>Die Lüge des Münchhausen</u>. 1938-1939. History of story,
        outline, first version, synopsis.
        <u>Les Mensonges du Baron de Crac / Le Peroquet du Baron
        de Crac</u>. Plan for film and scenario. Notes and re-
        lated materials. 1938-1939. Ca. 200p.
        <u>The Minotaur</u>. Script. 1952. A. Ca. 100p. Also related
        materials (notes, correspondence, typed Ms.). Ca.
        150p.
        <u>Dreams That Money Can Buy</u>. Script, notes, titles.
        1947. Ca. 200p.
        <u>Komödie um eine Schallplatte</u>. 1934. 20p.
        <u>The Stock Exchange</u>. 1938. English. 8p. French. 5p.
        <u>Edouard the Noble Beggar</u>.

The Movies Take a Holiday. 1944. Another version with
the title: 30 Years of Avant-Garde.
Synopses and short descriptions (1p. ea.):
Everything Turns. 1929.
Europe-Radio. 1930.
From Lightning to Television. 1935.
A Small World in the Dark. 1938.
Haus im Glück. 1939.
2 film proposals: one on problem of the races, one
on women.
Untitled script for a film on tyranny and democracy.

C7   "How to train documentary film people." T. 5p.
Texts to proposed projects. T. and A. 110p. Includes
topics such as: Movement in modern art, experiment-
ing in color film, art and personalities in Central
Europe after World War I.
Ms. of 52 articles, primarily on film subjects. 1946-
1960 and undated. T. and A. Ca. 400p.
"Dada Profiles." 1961. T. with corr. Ca. 60p. for book.
Dada Kunst und Anti-Kunst. 1964. T. and A. Parts 1 and
2. Ca. 200p. Parts 3-8. Ca. 200p. for book.
Der Kampf um den Film. T. 2 versions. Ca. 300p. ea.
Also working draft (xerox c. of same version) for
book.

D7   35 xeroxed articles from cl. 1952-1969.

F   3 tapes. Southbury, Connecticut, Aug. 1970.

H3   61 xeroxes of articles on Richter. 1930-1969.

H4   Catalogs to one-man shows. 1946-1971. Ca. 30.
Catalogs to group shows. 1936-1968. Ca. 32.
Announcements, cl., brochures, etc. to films. Ca. 300
items.

J,   Materials to films, primarily visual, including nega-
L   tives, photos, transparencies. Ca. 600 items:
Rhythmus 21. 1921.
Bauen und Wohnen. 1927.
Metal. 1931-1933.
Conquest of the Air. 1937.
Dadascope.
Passionate Pastime.
Dreams That Money Can Buy.
8 x 8.

K   Miscellaneous periodicals.

L   Cl. and xeroxes of cl. Ca. 150 items.
Materials for catalog to Goethe Institute exhibit:
"Dada 1916-1966." Also texts for essay. Ca. 50p.
Documentary materials on war, weapons, defense, history, American culture. 1941-1942. Includes cl.
Material for women in democracy film. Project of
Women's Centennial Congress: Women Fight for America.
1940-1942. Includes text and cl.

N   Seghers, Anna. Der sogenannte Rendel. Story. Ca. 1940.
cc. 26p. Also cl. of serialization in National-
Zeitung (Basel).

O   Announcements, programs. 1940-1968. Ca. 200 items.

American Philosophical Society, The Library, 105 South Fifth
Street, Philadelphia, Pennsylvania 19106.

WOLFGANG KÖHLER PAPERS

B1   2 L. to Wolfgang Köhler. 1931 and undated.

Library of Congress, Manuscript Division, Independence Avenue
and First Street S.E., Washington, D.C. 20540.

PAPERS OF LUDWIG MIES VAN DER ROHE

B1,2 Correspondence between Hans Richter and Ludwig Mies van
der Rohe. 1946-1947.

RUDOLF ROCKER

Political Activist, Author, 1873-1958

Brandeis University, Goldfarb Library, Special Collections, Waltham, Massachusetts 02154.

The Rudolf Rocker materials at Brandeis are part of the GONZALES MALO PAPERS, which were donated by Malo's widow in April 1970. Permission to use the materials must be obtained from Mrs. Carmen Aldacoa de Gonzáles Malo (through Mr. Victor Berch of the Goldfarb Library).

Die Rudolf Rocker Materialien in der Brandeis University sind ein Teil der GONZALES MALO PAPERS, einer Schenkung von Malos Witwe vom April 1970. Die Materialien sind mit Erlaubnis von Frau Carmen Aldacoa de Gonzáles Malo zugänglich. (Die Erlaubnis ist über Herrn Victor Berch von der Goldfarb Library einzuholen.)

B1	33 L. 1945-1958, including 12 L. to Gonzáles Malo.
B2	42 L. 1946-1958, including 19 L. from Gonzáles Malo.
B3	Ca. 15 L. 1950s.
B2,3	L. to and about Rocker, some clippings. 1946-. Ca. 1/2 in.
H3	Ca. 20 cl. at the death of Rocker, mostly Spanish. Malo, J. Gonzáles. Text on Rocker. 1958. Spanish. 4p. "Noticias biográficas del Movimiento Obrero." 1957. c. 2p.

Harvard University, Houghton Library, Cambridge, Massachusetts 02138.

A3	"Milly Witkop Rocker." Autobiographical essay. 1948. T. 8p.
B1	58 L. to Joseph Ishill. 1922-1957. 12 L. 1926-1944, including 1 L. to George Sarton.
H5	Goldman, Emma. "Rudolf Rocker on the occasion of his 50th birthday." Tr. by Rose Freeman-Ishill. 1923. 18p. Souchy, Augustin. "Rudolf Rocker." Undated. T. 15p.

3 different bibliographies of Rocker's works. 69p.,
    76p., 7p.

Yivo Institute, 1048 Fifth Avenue, New York, N.Y. 10028.

HORACE M. KALLEN PAPERS

B1,2   Individual item(s) in folder no. 996.

New York University, Tamiment Library, 70 Washington Square
South, New York, N.Y. 10012.

H3   Folder of biographical items on Rocker. 5 items.

J   Ink drawing of Rocker by his son Fermin Rocker.

EUGEN ROSENSTOCK-HUESSY

Philosopher, 1888-1973

Mrs. Freya von Moltke, Hopson Road, Norwich, Vermont 05055.

The materials in Mrs. von Moltke's possession, ca. 30 ft. of materials plus the personal library of Rosenstock-Huessy, are from the estate of Rosenstock-Huessy. Literary rights to the materials are held by Mrs. von Moltke and Dr. Hans Rosenstock-Huessy, Jericho, Vermont, son of Eugen. Mrs. von Moltke is in the process of organizing the materials in the collection.

Die Materialien in Mrs. von Moltke's Besitz, etwa 9 m Materialien sowie die Privatbibliothek von Rosenstock-Huessy, stammen aus dem Nachlaß von Rosenstock-Huessy. Die literarischen Rechte ruhen bei Mrs. von Moltke und bei seinem Sohn, Dr. Hans Rosenstock-Huessy, Jericho, Vermont. Mrs. von Moltke ist im Begriff, die Materialien der Sammlung zu ordnen.

B2 Correspondence over many years. Over 2,000 L., primarily to Rosenstock-Huessy, including L. from: E. Hermann, A. Bergsträsser, etc.

C7 Numerous Ms.

J Photos.

K Personal library of Rosenstock-Huessy.

L Materials used in his work.

Dartmouth College, Baker Memorial Library, Hanover, New Hampshire 03755.

The materials in the EUGEN ROSENSTOCK-HUESSY COLLECTION were donated to the library by Rosenstock-Huessy over the course of many years up to the time of his death.

Die Materialien in der EUGEN ROSENSTOCK-HUESSY COLLECTION wurden der Bibliothek im Laufe vieler Jahre von Erich Rosenstock-Huessy selbst geschenkt.

B1 1 L. 1950.

C7   "Buddha, Lao-tzu, Abraham, Jesus. A Diagnosis of Edu-
      cation and Redirection." Dartmouth, 1939. Pc.
      "A Classic and a Founder. I. The Scientific Grammar of
      Michael Faraday's Diaries. II. The Tripartition in
      the Life of Theophrastus Paracelsus." Dartmouth,
      1937. Pc. 73p.
      "Eastern and Western Christendom." Dartmouth, 194?. c.
      18p.
      "Europe and Christ." Tr. from German by Robert G.
      Heath. 1918. c. 57p.
      "Metabolism of Science." Hanover, New Hampshire, un-
      dated. c. 25p.
      "Modern Man's Disintegration and the Egyptian Ka."
      Introduction and 4 parts. Hanover, New Hampshire,
      undated. c. 12p.
      "The Multiformity of Man; ecodynamics of a mechanized
      world; a course in the philosophy of modern society."
      Hanover, New Hampshire, 1936. c. 58p.
      "The Next Homer." Hanover, New Hampshire, 1944. c. 22p.
      "The Penetration of the Cross. Abraham, Jesus, Lao-tzu,
      Buddha. I. The Cross of Reality. II. The Redirection
      of the Mind." Hanover, New Hampshire, undated. c.
      Ca. 35p.
      "Reformation Sunday." Sermon delivered at Methodist
      Church, Morrisville, Vermont. 1957. 4p.
      "The Soul of William James, Jan. 11, 1842 - Jan. 11,
      1942." Hanover, New Hampshire, 1942. c. 22p.
      "Sozialer Dienst der Universität und ihrer Studenten."
      Undated. Original Ms. 3p.
      "Student and University Service to the Community." Un-
      dated. 10p.
      "Time bettering days." [Hanover, New Hampshire], 1954.
      c. 23p.
      "360 + 5 and the year as period. I. The ten-month year
      in ancient Rome. II. The Latin year. III. The Sopdit
      year. IV. Survey." [Hanover, New Hampshire]. c. 14p.
      "Supertime, or the correspondence of society investiga-
      tions in the fields of biography, time, politics and
      education." [Hanover, New Hampshire], undated. c. 40p.

F   Lectures. Comparative Religion. 1954-1955. 24 reels.
      Ca. 36 hours.
      Lectures. The History of Greek Philosophy. 1956-1957.
      13 reels. Ca. 20 hours.

Lectures. The Circulation of Thought. 1954. 13 reels.
Ca. 20 hours.
Lectures. The Cross of Reality. 1953-1954. 12 reels.
Ca. 18 hours.
Lectures. The Christian Era. 1954. 13 reels. Ca. 20
hours.
The Santa Monica Church Talks, St.-Augustine-by-the-
Sea, Santa Monica. 1962. 3 reels.
"Make Bold to be Ashamed: On Freedom, Growth and Self-
Knowledge" and "Mass Media's New Methodism." Record.
1954.

H3   Several cl.

H4   Review of R. H.'s Out of Revolution by Alexander Mei-
keljohn. 15p.

H5   Bibliography. 1957. 5p.

L   Alumni folder. Miscellaneous offprints, cl., photos,
documents, etc. pertaining to Hans Rosenstock-Huessy.
File on Camp William James (boys' camp), with which
Rosenstock-Huessy was associated in 1940s. Includes
correspondence, cl., etc.

K   Numerous editions and offprints of Rosenstock-Huessy's
works.

Syracuse University, The George Arents Research Library,
Syracuse, New York 13210.

DOROTHY THOMPSON PAPERS

B1   32 L. to Dorothy Thompson. 1944-1957.

B3   1 L. 1957.

C7   "A Soldier in the Larger Sense." Mimeo.
"A Surrender to Whom." Mimeo.

University of California, Santa Barbara, The Library, Santa
Barbara, California 93105.

F   "Gold Goods Government or the Massacre." Tape. 1965.

"The Two Defectors: Adam Smith and Karl Marx." Tape.
1965.
"The Report on Measures by J. Q. Adams Had Its Promise
for the Planet." Tape. 1965.
"The Old Economy of Salvation." Tape. 1965.

Harvard University, Harvard Divinity School, Andover-Harvard
Theological Library, 45 Francis Avenue, Cambridge, Massachusetts 02138.

PAUL TILLICH COLLECTION

B1   2 L. to Paul Tillich. 1961.

B2   3 L. from Paul Tillich. 1935-1951.

University of Chicago, The Joseph Regenstein Library, 1100
East 57th Street, Chicago, Illinois 60637.

JAMES FRANCK PAPERS

B1,2 Correspondence with James Franck.

HANS SAHL

Writer, 1902-

<u>Mr. Hans Sahl</u>, 800 West End Avenue, New York, N.Y. 10025.

Private collection: ca. 15 ft. / *Privatsammlung: etwa 4,50 m.*

A1   Diaries. 1933+.

B1   "Letters to Lotte." 1934-1940.

B1,2 Correspondence, including L. to and from: W. H. Auden,
      E. Bergner, H. Böll, H. Broch, F. Bruckner, M.
      Chagall, B. F. Dolbin, J. Dos Passos, H. M. Enzens-
      berger, M. Ernst, R. Fischer, B. Frank, M. Frisch,
      V. Fry, M. George, E. Ginsberg, C. Glaser, I. Goll,
      A. Granach, G. Grass, G. Grosz, G. Gründgens, I.
      Heilbut, P. Hindemith, K. Hirschfeld, H. Hofmann,
      K. Jaspers, L. Jessner, E. I. Kahn, E. Kalser, G.
      Kaufmann, H. Kesten, A. Koestler, H. Kohn, O. Ko-
      koschka, F. Lang, L. Lenya, L. Lindtberg, J. Lip-
      chitz, Prinz H. zu Löwenstein, E. Mann, Th. Mann,
      L. Marcuse, F. Masereel, W. Mehring, L. Meidner,
      G. C. Menotti, T. Otto, K. Pinthus, E. Piscator, A.
      Polgar, G. Regler, E. M. Remarque, E. Reuter, H. W.
      Richter, T. Roethke, A. Schaeffer, R. Schweizer, G.
      Seger, H. Siemsen, I. Silone, W. Speyer, L. Steckel,
      P. Tillich, F. von Unruh, J. Urzidil, H. Weichmann,
      F. C. Weiskopf, T. Wilder, E. Wilson, K. Wolff, O.
      Zoff, C. Zuckmayer, S. Zweig.

C1   <u>Die Wenigen und die Vielen</u>. Ms. of novel.

C2   <u>Jemand. Ein weltliches Oratorio</u>.

C3   <u>Die hellen Nächte</u>.
      Numerous poems from many years.

C4   Stories, including:
      "Die Perle."
      "Der Besuch."
      "Der Schmied von Zollikon."

C6   "Furlough from Death." Radio play. 1942. Signed by cast
      members. German and English.

C7   Ms. of essays, feuilletons.

C9   Tr. of works by T. Wilder, T. Williams, A. Miller,

789

A. Kopit, J. Osborne.

C11 George Grosz.

D7 Reviews, articles, written after 1933 (mostly cl.)
from: Süddeutsche Zeitung, Züricher Zeitung, Die
Welt, Der Monat, Aufbau (NY), Staatszeitung, Deutsche Blätter, Das neue Tagebuch, Prager Mittag, Die
neue Weltbühne, Pariser Tageszeitung, Karl Schoß
Gesellschaft, New Leader, Politics, Protestant,
Commonweal, Common Sense, etc.

I Alien Registration pass.
Travel permits.
War ration book.

K Back issues of Das Tagebuch, Das neue Tagebuch, Die
Neue Weltbühne, etc.

L Collections of materials:
George Grosz. Correspondence.
Thornton Wilder. Original Ms., text corrections,
correspondence.
Schauspielhaus Zürich. Correspondence with K. Hirsch-
feld, E. Ginsberg, etc.
Emergency Rescue Committee. Memoranda, correspond-
ence, reports, biographies, programs, etc.
Theodor Roethke. Correspondence, memoranda, printed
items.
Council for a Democratic Germany. Correspondence, cl.
Duggan Committee.
American Guild for German Cultural Freedom.
American Friends of German Freedom.
International Study Center.
Committee on Educational Reconstruction (in Germany).
American Committee for Emigré Scholars, Writers and
Artists.

N 2 caricatures of H. Sahl. 1940.

O Program: American Academy of Arts and Letters. Auto-
graphed by Marilyn Monroe and Arthur Miller. 1959.

Southern Illinois University, Morris Library, Department of
Special Collections, Carbondale, Illinois 62901.

HANS SAHL

ERWIN PISCATOR PAPERS

B1   22 L. to Erwin Piscator. A. and T. 1939-1967.

B2   12 L. from Erwin Piscator. T.cc. 1939-1962.

C7   "Gedenkblatt für Erwin Piscator." Pub. in Tribute to
     Erwin Piscator. New York, June 4, 1967. T. with corr.
     5p.
     "To the Editor of the New York Times." Article concern-
     ing performance of War and Peace. May 28, 1942. T.
     3p.

Yale University, Beinecke Rare Book and Manuscript Library,
New Haven, Connecticut 06520.

HERMANN BROCH ARCHIVE

B1   29 L. to Hermann Broch. 1943-1950.
     1 L. to Erich von Kahler. 1951.

B2   8 L. from Hermann Broch. 1943-1950.

Harvard University, Houghton Library, Cambridge, Massachusetts 02138.

OSWALD GARRISON VILLARD PAPERS and general archive files

B1   3 L. to O. G. Villard. 1941-1944.

B2   1 L. from O. G. Villard. 1941.

C4   "Die hellen Nächte." Written in concentration camp,
     France, and New York. 1939-1942. A. 65p.

State University of New York at Albany, Department of Germanic Languages and Literatures, 1400 Washington Avenue,
Albany, New York 12222.

KARL O. PAETEL COLLECTION

B1   9 L. to K. O. Paetel (xerox). 1942-1943, undated, 1960.

New York Public Library, Manuscript Division, Fifth Avenue
and 42nd Street, New York, N.Y. 10018.

EMERGENCY COMMITTEE IN AID OF DISPLACED FOREIGN SCHOLARS,
1933-1945

*   File compiled when assistance was granted. 1938-1944.

Mrs. Elisabeth M. Stoerk and Mrs. Susanne B. Hoeller, 288
Ocean Drive West, Stamford, Connecticut 06902.

FRIDERIKE ZWEIG ARCHIVE

B1   1 L. to Friderike Zweig. 1942.

B2   1 L. from Friderike Zweig. c. 1941.

Harvard University, Harvard Divinity School, Andover-Harvard
Theological Library, 45 Francis Avenue, Cambridge, Massachusetts 02138.

PAUL TILLICH COLLECTION

B1   1 L. to Paul Tillich. A. 1965.

Mrs. Liselotte Stein, 115-25 Metropolitan Avenue, Kew Gardens, New York 11418.

FRED STEIN PAPERS

J   Photos of Hans Sahl.

Museum of Modern Art, The Library, 11 West 53rd Street, New
York, N.Y. 10019.

HANS RICHTER ARCHIVE: Written permission to use the Archive
is required in advance of visits to the Museum.

*HANS RICHTER ARCHIVE: Vor Besuch des Archivs muß eine schrift-
liche Genehmigung eingeholt werden.*

B1   1 L. to Hans Richter. 1958.

Barthold Fles Literary Agency, 507 Fifth Avenue, New York,
N.Y. 10016.

B1   1 L. to Barthold Fles. 1937.

Mrs. Peter M. Lindt, 949 West End Avenue, New York, N.Y.
10025.

B1   Small amount of correspondence with Peter M. Lindt.

Mrs. Alice Loewy Kahler, 1 Evelyn Place, Princeton, New
Jersey 08540.

ERICH VON KAHLER COLLECTION

B1   3 L. to Erich von Kahler. 1941, 1944, 1952.

ARNOLD SCHOENBERG

Composer, 1874-1951

Arnold Schoenberg Institute, University of Southern California, School of Performing Arts, University Park, Los Angeles,
California 90007.

The ARNOLD SCHOENBERG COLLECTION of the Arnold Schoenberg
Institute consists of ca. 6,000 pages of manuscript by
Schoenberg, the personal library of Schoenberg (ca. 2,000
volumes), memorabilia, photos, etc. The collection, which
is virtually complete with the exception of the correspondence of Schoenberg, was donated by Schoenberg's heirs in
1969. The correspondence is in the process of being photocopied. Upon completion the copies will be added to the
collection.

*Die ARNOLD SCHOENBERG COLLECTION des Arnold Schoenberg In-
stitute besteht aus etwa 6000 Manuskriptseiten von Schoenberg, seiner Privatbibliothek (etwa 2000 Bände), Andenken,
Photographien usw.. Die Sammlung, vollständig bis auf
Schoenbergs Korrespondenz, ist eine Schenkung der Erben
Schoenbergs aus dem Jahre 1969. Die Korrespondenz wird
z.Zt. photokopiert; wenn das geschehen ist, werden die Photokopien der Sammlung hinzugefügt.*

A1   Notebooks and calendars, including some diaries, agen-
        das, address books, engagement calendars.

A3   Indices. Lists made by Schoenberg.
        Biographical Ms. from early up to later years.

A3,   Poems, texts, fragments and sketches. Over 50 items,
C3,4,7 including aphorisms, autobiographical materials,
        ethnic essays, essays on other composers, etc.

C7   Ms. of all of Schoenberg's theoretical works, includ-
        ing drafts of completed textbooks:
        Harmonielehre/Theory of Harmony.
        Models for Beginners in Composition.
        Structural Functions of Harmony.
        Fundamentals of Musical Composition.
        Die Lehre vom Kontrapunkt.
        Ms. other than music, including:
        Totentanz der Prinzipien.
        Die Schildbürger.

Aberglaube.

C13a Scores of published works, including nearly complete
collection of original Ms. and sketches of compositions, including: ·
"Pelleas und Melisande. Symphonic Poem." Op. 5. 95p.
plus later corr.
"First Chamber Symphony." Op. 9 in E major. Nearly
complete version in 2 sketchbooks and 59p. Ms.
"Second String Quarter in F sharp minor." Op. 10.
"Three Piano Pieces." Op. 11. First draft.
"Erwartung (Expectation). Monodrama." Op. 17. First
draft. A. Also piano reduction prepared by Schoen-
berg.
"Gurrelieder." A. with numerous corr., compositional
changes, additions and completions. 68p.
"Die glückliche Hand (The Hand of Fate). Drama with
Music." Op. 18. Sketches for text and music, 2
typed c. of text with h. corr.
"Die Jakobsleiter (Jacob's Ladder)." A. 22p.
"Serenade." Op. 24. First draft.
"Piano Suite." Op. 25. First draft of 4 of 6 move-
ments.
"Four Pieces for Mixed Chorus." Op. 27. First draft.
A.
"Variations for Orchestra." Op. 31. A. 30p.
"Von heute auf morgen (From Today till Tomorrow)."
Op. 32. 1-act opera. A. 72p.
"Moses and Aaron. Opera in Three Acts." Complete
text, music for first 2 acts, sketches of music
for third act. Over 200p. plus numerous drafts and
sketches.
"Concerto for Violin and Orchestra." Op. 36. Over
40p.
"Kol Nidre." Op. 39. First complete draft. A. 11p.
Fair copy. A. 19p. Plus 10 sketch-sheets.
"Concerto for Piano and Orchestra." Op. 42. A. 46p.
plus 23p. of sketches.
Scores of all unpub. works, including 15 completed
works, 59 unfinished works and 13 miscellaneous
pieces.
5 musical sketchbooks. Ca. 100-150 p. ea.
Loose "sketches."

"Tone rows and miscellaneous music."

H3   C. and pc. of articles and music by and about Schoenberg.

I   Biographical documents.

J   Photos, portraits.

K   Printed music. Annotated.
Printed music. Unmarked.
Printed music, not by Schoenberg. Annotated by Schoenberg.
Librettos.
Printed music, not by Schoenberg. Unmarked.
Printed books. Unmarked (includes world literature as well as music).
Printed books. Annotated by Schoenberg.
Completed magazines. Unmarked. Generally important in 20th-century German and modern music, many rare.
Magazine articles. Annotated.
Magazine articles. Unmarked.

L   "The Verein Musical Club." Documents, reports, etc.
"Portfolios, Maps, Exhibition Catalogues, Art Books."
"Teaching materials (with musical scores)."

M   Musical instruments.
Birthday memorabilia.
Self-made objects (wood, machines, paintings, objects, gadgets).

N   Arrangements for "Verein" in various hands, including Ms. of other composers.
Music written to honor Schoenberg.

O   Posters, handbills, newspaper cl.

North Texas State University, Denton, Texas 76203.

Photocopies of Schoenberg manuscripts from the ARNOLD SCHOENBERG ARCHIVE are also located at North Texas State University.

In der North Texas State University befinden sich ebenfalls Photokopien von Schoenberg-Manuskripten aus dem ARNOLD

ARNOLD SCHOENBERG

Library of Congress, Reference Department, Music Division,
Independence Avenue and First Street S.E., Washington, D.C.
20540.

The manuscripts in the library's collection were donated by
Schoenberg prior to the time of his death. All publication
rights remain with the family of Schoenberg. Permission to
use the collection is obtainable from Mr. Lawrence Schoenberg, 1221 Bienvenedo Avenue, Pacific Palisades, California
90272.

Die Manuskripte in der Library of Congress sind eine Schen-
kung, die Schoenberg selbst vor seinem Tode vorgenommen hat.
Alle Rechte der Veröffentlichung ruhen bei der Familie Schoen-
bergs. Erlaubnis, die Sammlung einzusehen, erteilt Herr Law-
rence Schoenberg, 1221 Bienvenedo Avenue, Pacific Palisades,
California 90272.

C13a "III. Streichquartett." Op. 30. 1927. A. 36 leaves. 2c.
"IV. Streichquartett." Op. 37. 1936. A. 54p. 2c.
"A survivor from Warsaw. For narrator, men's choir and
orchestra." Op. 46. [1947]. 20p. Composer's Ms.
"Alla marcia." For piano. A. pc. 1 leaf.
"Die glückliche Hand. Drama mit Musik." Op. 18. [1923].
Composer's Ms. with explanatory L. by Schoenberg.
27p.
"Gurre-Lieder, von Jens Peter Jacobson (Deutsch von
Robert Franz Arnold) für Soli, Chor und Orchester."
A. pc. Music by Schoenberg.
["Introduction to the four Quartets. 1936?]. 4 leaves.
"Drei kleine Orchesterstücke." [1910]. A. pc. 5 leaves.
"Kol nidre." Op. 39. 1967. 29p. Reproduced from compo-
ser's Ms.
"Pierrot lûnair." 1912. For narrator, flute, piano (+
piccolo), clarinet (+ bass clarinet), violin (+
viola), + violoncello. A. 42p.
"Presto." For string quarter. 1974. Reproduced from
holograph.
"Streichquartett." 1905. A. 55p.
"II. Quartett für 2 Violinen, Viola und Violoncello."

1907-1908. A. 45p.
["Serenade, op. 24"]. 1921. A. 45p.
"Verklärte Nacht, von Richard Dehmel. Für sechs Streich-
instrumente." 1899. A. 39p.
"Von heute auf morgen. Oper in einem Akt." 1930. A.,
part pc. 164p.

C13b Bach, Johann Sebastian. "Schmücke dich o liebe Seele."
Adaptation by Schoenberg. 1922. 14p.
Schubert, Franz Peter. "Ständchen." Adapted by Schoen-
berg. A. pc. Pub. 1974.
"Die Winterreise. Der Lindenbaum." Adaptation. A.pc.
Tuma, Franz. "Partita a tre (con violino obligato)."
Adaptation. A. 10 leaves.
"Partita à tre." Adaptation. A. 6 leaves.
"Partita à 3." Adaptation. A. 7 leaves.
"Sinfonia a 4tro." Adaptation. A. 8 leaves.
"Sinfonia a 4tro." Adaptation. A. 6 leaves.
Zepler, Bogumil. "Mädchenreigen. Frauen-Terzett."
Adaptation. A. 31p.

University of Pennsylvania, The Charles Patterson Van Pelt
Library, Philadelphia, Pennsylvania 19104.

ALMA MAHLER-WERFEL COLLECTION

B1   1 L. ea. to: Olin Downes, W. Kandinsky, Deems Taylor,
Friedrich Torberg.
2 L. to Thomas Mann. 1948. Also cl.
22 L. and 10 Ptc. to Alma Mahler-Werfel. 1904-1955.

B1,2 C. of L. between Thomas Mann and Gustav Mahler. Also
English tr. of L.

B2   1 L. to Franz Werfel. 1943.

B3   L. from Gertrud Schoenberg to Alma Mahler-Werfel. 24p.

C7   "Arnold Schoenberg über Gustav Mahler." T.cc. 27p.

F   Recording by Franz Werfel re: relationship between
Schoenberg and Thomas Mann.

H3   Several cl.

J   1 photo.

ARNOLD SCHOENBERG

University of California, Los Angeles, Music Library, 405
Hilgard Avenue, Los Angeles, California 90024.

ERNST TOCH ARCHIVE and general archive files

B1   17 L. to the UCLA Music Department.
        8 L. to Ernst Toch.

C13a "Mailied." A.

J   2 photos, signed.

M   Schoenberg memorabilia.

Erikson Institute for Early Education, 1525 East 53rd Street,
Chicago, Illinois 60637.

Private collection of Gerhard and Maria Piers.

Privatsammlung von Gerhard und Maria Piers.

B1,2 Correspondence between Schoenberg and parents of Ger-
       hard Piers.

University of Georgia, The University Libraries, Athens,
Georgia 30601.

GUIDO ADLER PAPERS, OLIN DOWNES PAPERS

B1,2 Correspondence with Guido Adler. 38 L.
       Correspondence with Olin Downes. 4 L.

Leo Baeck Institute, 129 East 73rd Street, New York, N.Y.
10021.

MAX KOWALSKI COLLECTION

B1   11 L. to Max Kowalski (originals and facsimiles).
       1933-1934, 1948-1949.

H3   Articles and music with Schoenberg's dedications.

I   Papers in law case of Schoenberg vs. Frankfurt Opera
       House. 1930.

Columbia University, Butler Library, New York, N.Y. 10027.

B1   18 L. 1938, 1939, 1948, including 15 L. to W. W. Norton
       & Co.

University of Chicago, The Joseph Regenstein Library, 1100
East 57th Street, Chicago, Illinois 60637.

ELINOR CASTLE NEF PAPERS, JOHN U. NEF JR. PAPERS, and archival biographical files

B1   4 L. to John U. Nef, Jr. 1946-1947. (Permission of Mr.
       Nef required.)
       3 L. to Elinor C. Nef. 1946, [1947].
       4 L. 1946 and undated.

Princeton University, Firestone Library, Princeton, New
Jersey 08540.

THE PAPERS OF ALBERT EINSTEIN (1879-1955). For restrictions
governing the use of this collection, see description under
Albert Einstein.

*THE PAPERS OF ALBERT EINSTEIN (1879-1955). Nähere Angaben,
den Zugang zu dieser Sammlung betreffend, finden sich unter:
Albert Einstein.*

B1,2   Unknown amount of correspondence.

Harvard University, Houghton Library, Cambridge, Massachusetts 02138.

C13b   "Rosen aus dem Süden: Walzer von Johann Strauss op.
       388 für Kammerorchester gesetzt." Arrangement made
       for performance at Verein für musikalische Privat-
       aufführungen. Unpub. A. May 17, 1921. 18p.

Mrs. Elisabeth M. Stoerk and Mrs. Susanne B. Hoeller, 288 Ocean Drive West, Stamford, Connecticut 06902.

FRIDERIKE ZWEIG ARCHIVE

B1   2 L. to Friderike Zweig. 1951.

Yivo Institute, 1048 Fifth Avenue, New York, N.Y. 10028.

HORACE M. KALLEN PAPERS

B1,2 Individual item(s) located in folder no. 841.

Syracuse University, The George Arents Research Library, Syracuse, New York 13210.

FRANZ WAXMAN PAPERS

B1   1 L. to Franz Waxman. Undated.

State University of New York at Albany, Department of Germanic Languages and Literatures, 1400 Washington Avenue, Albany, New York 12222.

KARL O. PAETEL COLLECTION

B1   1 L. to Karl O. Paetel (xerox). 1959.

University of Utah, Marriott Library, Western Americana Department, Salt Lake City, Utah 84112.

PAPERS OF LEROY J. ROBERTSON

M   Signature of Arnold Schoenberg.

FRANZ SCHOENBERNER

Writer, 1892-1970

Hoover Institution on War, Revolution and Peace, Stanford,
California 94305.

The FRANZ SCHOENBERNER COLLECTION, 4 archive boxes of materials, was purchased by Hoover in 1972.

*Die FRANZ SCHOENBERNER COLLECTION, 4 Archivkartons Materia-
lien, wurde 1972 vom Hoover Institut gekauft.*

A3   "Family portraits." Biographical notes, photos, dia-
     ries, school documents, etc.
     Confessions of a European Intellectual. 1946. Ms.
     The Inside Story of an Outsider. 1949.

B1   "An Answer to Arthur Koestler's Challenge to Knights
     in Rusty Armor." Open L. to The New Republic and the
     New York Times.
     Open L. to Emil Ludwig. "How to Treat Inflated Mr.
     Ludwig?" 1943.
     4 L.

B1,2 Correspondence. 1899-1970, including L. to and from:
     Albert Einstein, Hermann Kesten, D. H. Lawrence,
     Mechthilde Lichnowsky, Golo Mann, Heinrich Mann,
     Klaus Mann, Reinhold Niebuhr, Gustav Regler, Jules
     Romains, René Schickele, Upton Sinclair, Kurt H.
     Wolff, Otto Zoff, Stefan Zweig. 1.5 B.

B2   Emil Ludwig's reply to Schoenberner's "How to Treat
     Inflated Dr. Ludwig?" L.

C1   "Life and Death of 'Simplicissimus'." Plan for a book.

C7   "The German Language Shall Never Perish from the
     Earth." Lecture. German and English.
     "The Dilemma of Modern Liberalism." German and English.
     "The Adventure of Reading Goethe's Novel 'Wilhelm
     Meister's Apprenticeship'." English and German.
     Article for L'Age Nouveau. Jan. 1939. German.
     "Beware of False Prophets." English and German.
     "Haben die Deutschen Humor?" German.
     "Faith and Skepticism." English and German.
     "German Literature in Exile." German and English.

"Why Intellectuals are Treasonable." German and English.
"Stefan Zweig and We." German and English.
"Facts and Opinions." German and English.
"Goethe Revival." English.
"Roman und Film im Kampf gegen Rassenvorurteile."
   German.
"Innocents from Abroad." English.
"The Paradox of Katherine Anne Porter." English.
"Speaking of German Literature." English.
"What's the Matter with France?" German.
"North Africa - A Test Case." English
"Begegnung mit D. H. Lawrence." German.
"A propos of Blasphemy." German and English.
"Das Nibelungenlied." German.
"Dokumente amerikanischer Demokratie." German.
"Die deutschen Zeitschriften des Departments of the
   Army." German.
"Georges Bernanos: 'Nous autres Français'." German.
"Lektüre für die Hitler-Jugend." German.
"Mes heures avec Leon Souguenet." French.
Schoenberner's assessments of 34 books by German au-
   thors for American publishers, including:
   Peter Bamm. An den Küsten des Lichts.
   Werner Bergengruen. Das Feuerzeichen.
   Willi Heinrich. The Cross of Iron.
   Wolfgang Koeppen. Tauben im Gras.
   Mechthilde Lichnowsky. Kindheit.
   Luise Rinser. Mitte des Lebens.
   Friedrich Torberg. Die zweite Begegnung.
C7,   Typescripts and cl. of reviews, including:
D7   Lilly Abegg. Ostasien denkt anders.
       H. Boeschenstein. The German Novel, 1939-1944.
       Berthold Bierman. Goethe's World as seen in his let-
          ters and memoirs.
       Sigmund Freud. Leonardo da Vinci, a psychoanalytical
          study.
       John Hersey. The Wall.
       Albert Guerard. Education of a Humanist.
       Willi Heinrich. Cross of Iron.
       Richard Kaufmann. Der Himmel zahlt keine Zinsen.
       Hermann Kesten. Ferdinand and Isabella.

Ernst Kreuder. Die Unauffindbaren.
Anna Mahler. Gustav Mahler.
Harry T. Moore. D. H. Lawrence's letters to Bertrand
 Russell.
Ludwig Lewisohn. Goethe, the Story of a Man.
Pandit S. S. Nehru. Gandhi, sein Leben und Werk.
Max Pribilla. Deutsche Schicksalsfrage.
Wilhelm Roepke. The Solution of the German Problem.
Albert Schweitzer. Goethe, Four Studies. Also 3 addi-
 tional books by Schweitzer and 3 about him.
Vercors. Three Short Novels.
Coulton Waugh. The Comics.
Hermann J. Weigand. Goethe: Wisdom and Experience.
Ernst von Salomon. Die Geächteten.

H4   Reviews and critiques of books and other works by
      Schoenberner.

I   Certificates, affidavits, identification cards, etc.

State University of New York at Albany, Department of Germanic Languages and Literatures, 1400 Washington Avenue,
Albany, New York 12222.

The State University of New York purchased the FRANZ SCHOEN-
BERNER COLLECTION, a xerox copy of the materials located at
the Hoover Institution, from Mr. Stephan Congrat-Butler in
1976.

*Die State University of New York kaufte die FRANZ SCHOEN-
BERNER COLLECTION von Mr. Stephan Congrat-Butler im Jahre
1976. Die Sammlung besteht aus Photokopien der Materialien,
die sich in der Hoover Institution befinden.*

Immigration History Research Center of the University of
Minnesota, 826 Berry Street, St. Paul, Minnesota 55101.

AMERICAN COUNCIL FOR EMIGRÉS IN THE PROFESSIONS ARCHIVES

A3   Curriculum vitae, progress reports, questionnaires.
      9p.

B1   20 L. 1945-1967, including L. to: Mrs. Henry Canby,
       Otto Zoff.

B2   16 L. 1945-1967.

B3   Correspondence of Mrs. Ellie Nerac-Schoenberner. 7 L.
       1946-1948. Also curriculum vitae. 2p.
       16 L. 1946-1966.

H3   2 cl.

I   6 receipts. 1953-1967.
       1 memorandum. 1965.

Yivo Institute, 1048 Fifth Avenue, New York, N.Y. 10028.

HORACE M. KALLEN PAPERS

B1,2   Individual item(s) in folder no. 982.

Mrs. Elisabeth M. Stoerk and Mrs. Susanne B. Hoeller, 288
Ocean Drive West, Stamford, Connecticut 06902.

FRIDERIKE ZWEIG ARCHIVE

B1   2 L. to Friderike Zweig. 1946.

Mrs. Peter M. Lindt, 949 West End Avenue, New York, N.Y.
10025.

B1   Small amount of correspondence with Peter M. Lindt.

JOSEPH SCHUMPETER

Economist, 1883-1950

<u>Harvard University</u>, University Archives, Widener Library, Cambridge, Massachusetts 02138.

The papers of Joseph Schumpeter are located in 4 places at Harvard University: the University Archives, the Houghton Library (to be transferred to the University Archives), Kress Library (Harvard Business School), and with Prof. Arthur Smithies (Economics Department). The materials have not been catalogued and no description of the papers is available as of 1977.

Joseph Schumpeter Materialien befinden sich an folgenden verschiedenen Orten der Harvard University: in den University Archives, der Houghton Library (diese Materialien sollen den University Archives eingegliedert werden), in der Kress Library (Harvard Business School) und bei Prof. Arthur Smithies (Economics Department). Die Materialien sind nicht katalogisiert und 1977 war noch keine Beschreibung der Materialien erhältlich.

<u>Harvard University</u>, Houghton Library, Cambridge, Massachusetts 02138.

GEORGE SARTON PAPERS

B1   2 L. to George Sarton. 1928.

<u>Mrs. Edith Hirsch</u>, 400 East 56th Street, New York, N.Y. 10028.

B1,2   Correspondence between Julius Hirsch and Joseph Schumpeter.

<u>Mrs. Gertrude Lederer</u>, 372 Central Park West, Apt. 3B, New York, N.Y. 10024.

C7   Manuscript.

LEOPOLD SCHWARZSCHILD

Writer, 1891-1950

Leo Baeck Institute, 129 East 73rd Street, New York, N.Y.
10021.

The LEOPOLD SCHWARZSCHILD COLLECTION, ca. 4.5 ft. of materials, was donated in 1956 by Schwarzschild's widow, Mrs.
Valerie Schwarzschild.

*Die LEOPOLD SCHWARZSCHILD COLLECTION, etwa 1,50 m Materia-
lien, ist eine Schenkung von Schwarzschilds Witwe, Frau
Valerie Schwarzschild, aus dem Jahre 1956.*

A3   Biography of Schwarzschild. 2c. 3p. ea.
        Many versions of autobiographical sketch. 5p.
        Curriculum vitae.

B1,2   Correspondence. 1940-1949, including L. to and from:
        Bruno Frank, Robert Kempner, Hermann Kesten, Erika
        Mann, Golo Mann, Klaus Mann, Ludwig Marcuse, Alfred
        Polgar Curt Riess, Friedrich Torberg, Franz Wer-
        fel, Carl Zuckmayer.
        Family correspondence. 1942-1949.
        Correspondence with publishers and magazines. 1947-
        1949.
        Correspondence with H. G. Wells concerning contro-
        versy over Schwarzschild's World in Trance.

C7,   Numerous Ms. of articles and speeches (also fragments).
C10   T. and A.
        Weekly articles written by "Argus." Nov. 23, 1942 -
        Feb. 18, 1945.
        Texts of 59 daily broadcasts to Germany by Schwarz-
        schild on the world situation. German T., some with
        English versions. Jan. 6, 1942 - May 8, 1942.

C11   Der Rote Preuße. Biography of Karl Marx. 4 notebooks.
        German T. 552p. Preface, notes, fragments, epilog,
        outlines. Also radio program script based on book.
        Gog and Magog, the Nazi-Bolshevik Twins. Written ca.
        1940-1941. Never published. T. 212p. and introduc-
        tion.
        Binder containing T. with h. corr. 369p.
        Notebook containing "Zehn Jahre nach den schwärze-
        sten Tag." 1949. 2 c. T. 52p.

807

World in Trance. German version. T. 584p. Notes,
chronology. Original German Ms. T. and A. 783p.
Chap. IV: "The first appeasements."
Primer of the Coming World. Complete original German
T. 363p. Also German T. with h. corr. p. 6-363.
English T. 303p.

H4   Reviews of Der Rote Preuße. Cl. 1954-1955.
Scrapbook of cl. of reviews of World in Trance and
Primer of the Coming World. 1942-1945.

I   Contracts for Der Rote Preuße.

J   Photos.

JOSEPH BORNSTEIN COLLECTION

B1   1 L. to Joseph Bornstein. 1949.

New York Public Library, Manuscript Division, Fifth Avenue
and 42nd Street, New York, N.Y. 10018.

C11   Primer of the Coming World. T. and proofs. 302p.

Indiana University, The University Libraries, The Lilly
Library, Bloomington, Indiana 47401.

MAX EASTMAN MSS.

E   "The Real Karl Marx." Adaptation by Max Eastman. Ca.
1951. Draft and proofs.

Yivo Institute, 1048 Fifth Avenue, New York, N.Y. 10028.

HORACE M. KALLEN PAPERS

B1,2 Individual item(s) in folder no. 240. 1934.

MARTIN SCHWARZSCHILD
Astronomer, 1912-

Dr. Martin Schwarzschild, 12 Ober Road, Princeton, New Jersey 08540.

Private collection: inaccessible. / *Unzugängliche Privatsammlung.*

B1,2   Nominal amount of correspondence from the 1930s and early 1940s. Primarily recommendations, etc.

C7,8   Because Dr. Schwarzschild has dictated the texts of his works over the past 20 years, there are few original Ms. in the collection.

University of California, Los Alamos Scientific Laboratory, P.O. Box 1663, Los Alamos, New Mexico 87544.

DIRECTOR'S PERSONNEL FILE

B1   1 L. 1958.

B2   4 L. 1958-1959.

B3   3 L. 1959.

I   Document reporting work done at site other than Los Alamos.

Smithsonian Institution Archives, Washington, D.C. 20560.

B1   2 L. 1962.

GERHART SEGER

Political Scientist, 1896-1967

Immigration History Research Center of the University of
Minnesota, 826 Berry Street, St. Paul, Minnesota 55101.

AMERICAN COUNCIL FOR EMIGRÉS IN THE PROFESSIONS ARCHIVES

A3   Biographical statement, questionnaires, progress
        reports. 17p.

B1   10 L. 1938-1953, including L. to: Alvin Johnson, Toni
        Stolper.

B2   5 L. 1938-1953.

B3   9 L. 1950. Primarily concerning recommendations for
        Seger.

D7   Cl. 7p.

Swarthmore College, Swarthmore, Pennsylvania 19081.

SWARTHMORE COLLEGE PEACE COLLECTION: WILLIAM F. SOLLMANN
PAPERS

B1,2   Correspondence between Gerhart Seger and William
        Sollmann.

State Historical Society of Wisconsin, 816 State Street,
Madison, Wisconsin 53706.

TONI SENDER PAPERS

B1,2   Correspondence with Toni Sender. 1946, 1952-1953.

University of Pennsylvania, The Charles Patterson Van Pelt
Library, Philadelphia, Pennsylvania 19104.

ALMA MAHLER-WERFEL COLLECTION

B1   1 L. and 1 note to Alma Mahler-Werfel. 1942 and un-
        dated.

B2   1 L. from Franz Werfel. 1942.

810

Columbia University, Butler Library, New York, N.Y. 10027.

N. M. BUTLER PAPERS

B1   1 L. to N. M. Butler. 1938.

B2   1 L. from N. M. Butler. 1938.

Yivo Institute, 1048 Fifth Avenue, New York, N.Y. 10028.

HORACE M. KALLEN PAPERS

B1,2   Individual item(s) in folder no. 352. 1938.

Mr. Hans Sahl, 800 West End Avenue, New York, N.Y. 10025.

B1   Several L. to Hans Sahl.

State University of New York at Albany, Department of Germanic Languages and Literatures, 1400 Washington Avenue, Albany, New York 12222.

KARL O. PAETEL COLLECTION

B1   1 L. to Karl O. Paetel (xerox). 1958.

B3   1 L. from family of Gerhart Seger. 1967.

Minnesota Historical Society, 690 Cedar Street, St. Paul, Minnesota 55101.

HOWARD YOLAN WILLIAMS PAPERS

B1   1 L. to Howard Yolan Williams. 1937.

Boston University, Mugar Memorial Library, 771 Commonwealth Avenue, Boston, Massachusetts 02215.

BELLA FROMM COLLECTION

B1   1 L. to Bella Fromm. 1944.

Harvard University, Houghton Library, Cambridge, Massachusetts 02138.

LEO LOWENTHAL COLLECTION

B2   1 L. from Max Horkheimer. 1944.

University of Minnesota, University Libraries, Social Welfare History Archives, Minneapolis, Minnesota 55455.

SURVEY ASSOCIATES PAPERS

B3   2 L. 1947.

KURT SELIGMANN

Painter, 1900-1962

Archives of American Art, Smithsonian Institution, National
Collection of Fine Arts and National Portrait Gallery Build-
ing, Eighth and F Streets N.W., Washington, D.C. 20560.
(Microfilms of collections are available in each of the
branch locations: Boston, Massachusetts; New York, N.Y.;
Detroit, Michigan; San Francisco, California.)

KURT SELIGMANN PAPERS, 1936-1968 (from the Ruth White Gallery), HENRY C. PEARSON PAPERS and individual items. The
KURT SELIGMANN PAPERS comprise 1 microfilm reel.

*KURT SELIGMANN PAPERS, 1936-1968 (aus der Ruth White Gal-
lery), HENRY C. PEARSON PAPERS sowie Einzelnummern finden
sich in den Archives of American Art. Die KURT SELIGMANN
PAPERS bestehen aus einer vollen Mikrofilmspule.*

B1   14 L. to the Ruth White Gallery. T. and A. 1956-1961.
        1 L. to Samuel Rosen. T. 1961.

B2   67 L. from the Ruth White Gallery. T.c. 1956-1962.

B3   Ca. 350 L. concerning Seligmann, mostly between the
        Ruth White Gallery and various museums and individ-
        uals.

C7   "Dissertation on Whether I Have a Philosophy on Paint-
        ing or Even on Art in General."

C14   Sketches of Henry C. Pearson.

H3   Ca. 50 cl. 1960-1968.
        "Clippings and Reproductions." 6 microfilm frames.

I   Biographical data, press releases, notes about Selig-
        mann paintings, listings of paintings, designs for
        brochures, invoices, catalogs, announcements, repro-
        ductions, etc.

I   *Biographische Daten, Presseauszüge, Notizen über Selig-
        manns Bilder, Bilderlisten, Entwürfe für Broschüren,
        Rechnungen, Kataloge, Ankündigungen, Reproduktionen
        usw.*

J   Photo reproductions of works.

M   Memorabilia.

<u>Columbia University</u>, Butler Library, New York, N.Y. 10027.

PANTHEON BOOKS COLLECTION and general archive files

B1   Ca. 22 L. to Kurt Wolff. T. and A. 1951-1958.
      6 L.

B2   Ca. 40 L. from Kurt Wolff. T. and A. c. 1950-1958.

B3   Cal 40 L. concerning Seligmann's works pub. by Pantheon.
      Ca. 1950-1958. T. Also some enclosures, documents.

<u>American Philosophical Society</u>, The Library, 105 South Fifth
Street, Philadelphia, Pennsylvania 19106.

FRANZ BOAS PAPERS

B1   1 L. to Franz Boas. 1940.

TONI SENDER

Economist, 1888-1964

State Historical Society of Wisconsin, 816 State Street,
Madison, Wisconsin 53706.

The TONI SENDER PAPERS, which consist of 15 boxes of materials, primarily cover the years from her arrival in the
U.S. (Dec. 1935) to her death (July 1964). The collection
was donated by Mr. Leo Holz (New York) on Dec. 22, 1964 and
Aug. 9, 1965.

*Die TONI SENDER PAPERS, 15 Kartons Materialien, umfassen
hauptsächlich die Zeit von ihrer Ankunft in den Vereinigten
Staaten (Dez. 1935) bis zu ihrem Tode (Juli 1964). Die Sammlung ist eine Schenkung von Herrn Leo Holz (New York) vom 22.
Dez. 1964 und 9. Aug. 1965.*

Al   Diaries. June 1937 - Aug. 1940. 3 volumes.

A2   Miscellaneous notebooks. 13 volumes.

A3   Autobiography of a German Rebel. 2 rough drafts of Ms.
        plus 2 sketches under the title "The Torch Still
        Flames."

Bl,2   Correspondence 1934-1964. 3 B. Includes correspondence
        with: Siegfried Aufhäuser, Albert C. Grzesinski,
        Hanna and Paul Hertz, Gerhart Seger, William F.
        Sollmann, Hedwig Wachenheim.

Bl,2   Correspondence, memoranda, and reports for the United
C7   Nations Relief and Rehabilitation Administration.
        1944-1946. 2 B.

C7   Reports on U.N. activities. 1947-1956.
        Reports on labor.
        Speeches and broadcasts.
        Miscellaneous articles by Sender.

H3   Miscellaneous biographical materials on Sender, includ-
        ing numerous cl.

L   Notes, miscellaneous. 4 B.

N   Miscellaneous articles by other authors.

Swarthmore College, Swarthmore, Pennsylvania 19081.

815

SWARTHMORE PEACE COLLECTION: WILLIAM F. SOLLMANN PAPERS

B1,2   Correspondence with William F. Sollmann.

Duke University, William R. Perkins Library, Manuscript Department, Durham, North Carolina 27706.

SOCIALIST PARTY OF AMERICA PAPERS

B1   2 L. to M. de Haan. 1935.
B2   3 L. from M. de Haan. 1935.
     1 L. ea. from: Anna Caples (1936) and P. Heller (1949).

State University of New York at Albany, Department of Germanic Languages and Literatures, 1400 Washington Avenue, Albany, New York 12222.

KARL O. PAETEL COLLECTION

B1   2 L. to Karl O. Paetel (xerox). 1942.

American Philosophical Society, The Library, 105 South Fifth Street, Philadelphia, Pennsylvania 19106.

FRANZ BOAS PAPERS

B1   2 L. to Franz Boas.

Barthold Fles Literary Agency, 507 Fifth Avenue, New York, N.Y. 10016.

B1   1 L. to Barthold Fles. 1941.

CARL L. SIEGEL

Mathematician, 1896-

Library of Congress, Manuscript Division, Independence Avenue
and First Street S.E., Washington, D.C. 20540.

OSWALD VEBLEN PAPERS

B1   24 L., 6 Ptc. and 1 Tel. to Oswald Veblen. T. and A.
       1935-1960.
       4 L., including 1 L. to Richard Courant. T.c. 1939.
B2   24 L. and 1 Tel. from Oswald Veblen. T.c. 1938-1960.
       7 L., including 4 L. from Richard Courant. 1946.
B3   32 L., including 6 L. from Richard Courant.
I   Memo from Oswald Veblen: "Memo on steps to take re
       C.L.S."

New York University, Courant Institute of Mathematical Sciences, Library, 251 Mercer Street, New York, N.Y. 10012.

B1,2 2 files entitled "C. L. Siegel" and "Carl Siegel."
      1943-1957.

New York Public Library, Manuscript Division, Fifth Avenue
and 42nd Street, New York, N.Y. 10018.

EMERGENCY COMMITTEE IN AID OF DISPLACED FOREIGN SCHOLARS,
1933-1945

*   File compiled when assistance was granted. 1935-1943.

ERNST SIMMEL

Psychoanalyst, 1882-1947

<u>Los Angeles Institute of Psychoanalysis</u>, 344 North Bedford
Drive, Beverly Hills, California 90210.

ERNST SIMMEL PAPERS: ca. 1 1/2 ft. of materials.

Die ERNST SIMMEL PAPERS umfassen etwa 0,50 m Materialien.

B1,2   Small amount of correspondence, including L. from S.
      Freud.

C7,8   "Der Coitus Interruptus und sein Gegenstück der Coitus
      Prolongatus. (Ein Beitrag zur Psychopathogenese des
      Präventivverkehrs)." Abstract. T.
      "Criminal Neurosis and Masturbation Complex." Notes.
      Undated. T.
      "Neurotic Criminality and Lust Murder." 1939. T. 47p.
      "Psychoanalysis and Civilization." 1940. T. 42p.
      "Psychoanalyse. Die klinischen Möglichkeiten." Lecture.
      1927. T.
      "Repression, Regression and Organic Disease." Lecture.
      1940. T. 90p.
      "Über die Psychogenese von Organstörungen und ihre
      psychoanalytische Behandlung." English tr. T.
      "War and Crime, Thoughts on (Violence)." 1941. T. 24p.
      "Addiction: zum Problem von Zwang und Sucht." English
      tr. 1930. T. p. 112-126.
      "Ausbildung des Psychotherapeuten vom Standpunkt der
      Psychoanalyse." English tr. 1931. T.
      "Case of the Baker's Apprentice." Undated. T.
      "Ego Defense Mechanisms with the Help of the Id." 1940.
      T. 6p.
      "Kann man an der Analyse sterben?" 1926. T.
      "Psychological Radio Offensive Against Germany from a
      Psychoanalytical Viewpoint." Undated. T.
      "Spielleidenschaft." German text. 1920. T.
      "Über die Bedeutung des 'Psychischen Traumas' für die
      Entstehung und Heilung von Kriegsneurosen." 1919. T.
      Also rough English version. A.

<u>Prof. Edward C. Simmel</u>, Department of Psychology, Miami Uni-
versity, Oxford, Ohio 45056.

Prof. Edward Simmel is the son of Ernst Simmel and has retained certain personal materials from his father's papers. These materials will remain closed to the public.

Prof. Edward Simmel, der Sohn Ernst Simmels, hat verschiedenes Material persönlicherer Natur behalten. Dieses bleibt für die Öffentlichkeit unzugänglich.

B1,2   Personal correspondence files. 1935-1947.

California Institute of Technology, Robert A. Millikan Library, Pasadena, California 91109.

PAUL S. EPSTEIN PAPERS

B1,2   Miscellaneous items of correspondence.

Dr. Friedrich J. Hacker, The Hacker Clinic, 160 Lasky Drive, Beverly Hills, California 90212.

B1,2   Correspondence between Hacker and Simmel.

Library of Congress, Manuscript Division, Independence Avenue and First Street S.E., Washington, D.C. 20540.

PAPERS OF SIEGFRIED BERNFELD

B1,2   Correspondence with Siegfried Bernfeld. 1936-1942, 1950.
         Correspondence with Sigmund Freud. 1927-1935. c.

HANS SIMONS

Political Scientist, 1893-1972

<u>Library of Congress</u>, Manuscript Division, Independence Avenue
and First Street S.E., Washington, D.C. 20540.

FELIX FRANKFURTER PAPERS, BENJAMIN W. HUEBSCH PAPERS

B1   11 L. to Felix Frankfurter. T. 1942-1959.
      1 L. to Benjamin W. Huebsch. T. 1950.
      1 L. to the <u>New York Times Book Review</u>. T. 1953.
B2   15 L. from Felix Frankfurter. T.c. 1942-1959.

<u>Yivo Institute</u>, 1048 Fifth Avenue, New York, N.Y. 10028.

HORACE M. KALLEN PAPERS

B1,2 Individual correspondence items and references to
      Simons in folders: 20A, 261, 341, 538, 539, 540,
      640, 657, 846, 701, 902, 903, 907, 908, 912, 942,
      957, 1011, 1012. 1935-1942.

I   Miscellaneous materials pertaining to Graduate Faculty
      of New School for Social Research: minutes, memos,
      etc. 14 F.

<u>American Philosophical Society</u>, The Library, 105 South Fifth
Street, Philadelphia, Pennsylvania 19106.

WOLFGANG KÖHLER PAPERS

B1   4 L. to Wolfgang Köhler. 1928-1931.

<u>Boston University</u>, Mugar Memorial Library, 771 Commonwealth
Avenue, Boston, Massachusetts 02215.

BELLA FROMM COLLECTION

B1   Several L. to Bella Fromm.

HANS SIMONS

<u>Princeton University</u>, Firestone Library, Princeton, New Jersey 08540.

LOUIS FISCHER PAPERS

B1   1 L. to Louis Fischer. 1959.

<u>Harvard University</u>, Harvard Divinity School, Andover-Harvard Theological Library, 45 Francis Avenue, Cambridge, Massachusetts 02138.

PAUL TILLICH COLLECTION

B2   1 L. from Paul Tillich. T.c. 1956.

CURT SIODMAK

Writer, 1902-

<u>Boston University</u>, Mugar Memorial Library, 771 Commonwealth Avenue, Boston, Massachusetts 02215.

The CURT SIODMAK COLLECTION, 9 archive boxes of materials plus 22 books, was donated by Siodmak in installments from 1969 to 1971. Siodmak still maintains a major part of his manuscripts and other materials.

Die CURT SIODMAK COLLECTION, 9 Archivkartons Materialien sowie 22 Bücher, wurden der Mugar Memorial Library nach und nach in der Zeit von 1969 bis 1971 überlassen. Siodmak befindet sich noch im Besitz des größten Teils seiner Manuskripte und anderer Materialien.

A3   Curriculum vitae. T. 3p.

B1   18 L. 1966-1971, primarily to publishers and literary
        agents.

B2   43 L.
        12 L. from publishers and literary agents.

C1   <u>Hauser's Memory</u>. T. with h. corr. 2 c. 346p. ea. T.
        with h. corr. 101p. Cc., with the comment "I.M.U."
        2 c. 103p. ea. 4 pc. with h. corr. 344p, 346p., 251p.,
        173p.
        Also various partial versions. T. with corr. 192p.
        Notes. A. and T. 12p. Synopses. T. 2 c. 3p., 13p.
        <u>The Third Ear</u>. T. pc. 319p. Various other versions and
        partial versions. Ca. 2,500p. Early draft. T. 12p.
        Pc. of proofs.

D1   <u>Donovan's Brain</u>. 13 editions in 7 languages.
        <u>F.P. 1 Does Not Reply</u>. English edition.
        <u>For Kings Only</u>. English edition.
        <u>Hauser's Memory</u>. 7 editions in 3 languages.

D7   "Epistles to the Germans," <u>Story</u> (Spring 1948), p. 94-
        116.

H4   <u>Hauser's Memory</u>. 13 reviews. pc. 1968-1969.

L   <u>Hauser's Memory</u>. Background materials. Aug. 1965 - Feb.
        1966. 13 items.
        <u>The Third Ear</u>. 1 cl.

Academy of Motion Picture Arts and Sciences, Margaret Herrick
Library, 9038 Melrose Avenue, Hollywood, California 90069.

H3   3 newspaper cl.

WILLIAM F. SOLLMANN

Political Scientist, 1881-1951

Swarthmore College, Swarthmore, Pennsylvania 19081.

The WILLIAM F. SOLLMANN PAPERS (DG 45) in THE SWARTHMORE
COLLEGE PEACE COLLECTION were received from Mrs. William
Sollmann, Elfrieda Sollmann (daughter of William) and Herta
Kraus in February 1951. Literary rights to the materials,
which are contained in 17 archive boxes (approximately 8
shelf ft.), are held by Elfrieda Sollmann (Guatemala, Guatemala).

*Die WILLIAM F. SOLLMANN PAPERS (DG 45) in der SWARTHMORE
PEACE COLLECTION wurden dem Swarthmore College im Februar
1951 von Sollmanns Frau, von seiner Tochter (Frau Elfrieda
Sollmann) und von Frau Herta Kraus überlassen. Die literarischen Rechte des Materials (17 Archivkartons, etwa 2,40
m) ruhen bei Elfrieda Sollmann (Guatemala, Guatemala).*

A3   Curriculum vitae, outline of major events in Soll-
       mann's public career.

B1,2   Correspondence with Konrad Adenauer, Heinrich Bruening
       (50 L.), Max Sievers, Otto Strasser (56 L.). Also L.
       relating to the return of the ex-Crown Prince to
       Germany, 1932.
       General correspondence. 7 B., including L. to and
       from: Brockdorff-Rantzau, Otto Buchwitz, Groener,
       Paul Hertz, Rudolf Katz, Philipp Scheidemann, Ger-
       hart Seger, Toni Sender, Kurt Singer, Sinzheimer.
       Arranged chronologically: 1901, 1903, 1909-1924;
       1925-1933; 1934-1936; 1936-1939; 1940-1942; 1943-
       1945; 1946-1950 and undated.
       Special dossier on the Versailles Treaty correspond-
       ence.
       Correspondence on lecture engagements by Sollmann,
       1938-1944.

C7   Reports on Germany. 1949, 1950.

C7,   English T., including lectures, drafts of articles and
C10   reports. Ca. 750p. Includes:
       "The Rise of Present Day Germany."
       "Is European War Inevitable?"
       "Germany's Youth Speaks Up."
       German T., dating from 1910. Ca. 700p. Includes:

824

WILLIAM F. SOLLMANN

"Die interparlamentarische Union - ein Weltparlament."
"Die Arbeiterjugend und Staat."
"Hitler und sein Stab - Notorische Verbrecher!"
"Amerikanische Reise." 1925.
"Freundeswort aus Amerika an die Deutschen."

D7,   Printed articles: editorial, magazine, pamphlet, news-
D10   paper. 4 B. Arranged chronologically: 1908-1926;
       1927-1933; 1934-1939; 1940-1950 and undated.

H3   Publicity about Sollmann. Newspaper and magazine arti-
       cles, cl. and cartoons. 2 B. Arranged chronologi-
       cally: 1911-1937; 1938-1950 and undated.
       Memorials on the death of Sollmann. 1951.
       Published inventory of the W. F. Sollmann materials in
       Cologne, Federal Republic of Germany, Historical
       Archives.

L   List of anti-Nazi leaders in Germany.

Prof. Carl Landauer, 1317 Arch Street, Berkeley, California
94708.

B1,2   Correspondence between Sollmann and Carl Landauer.

State Historical Society of Wisconsin, 816 State Street,
Madison, Wisconsin 53706.

TONI SENDER PAPERS

B1,2   Correspondence with Toni Sender. 1942, 1946, 1950.

State University of New York at Albany, Department of Germanic Languages and Literatures, 1400 Washington Avenue,
Albany, New York 12222.

KARL O. PAETEL COLLECTION

B1,2   Transcript of correspondence between Sollmann and Pae-
       tel. Ca. 10p. (xerox).

WILLIAM F. SOLLMANN

<u>Yivo Institute</u>, 1048 Fifth Avenue, New York, N.Y. 10028.

HORACE M. KALLEN PAPERS

B1,2   Individual item(s) in folders: 316, 849. 1936-1940.

HANS SPEIER

Sociologist, 1905–

Dr. Hans Speier, 167 Concord Avenue, Hartsdale, New York 10530.

Dr. Speier has expressed the intention to donate his materials to the State University of New York at Albany. Until that time the materials will remain at the home of Dr. Speier and are inaccessible to researchers.

Dr. Speier hat der Absicht Ausdruck verliehen, seine Materialien der State University of New York at Albany zu schenken. Bis zu dem Zeitpunkt bleiben die Materialien in seinen Händen und sind für Forschungszwecke nicht zugänglich.

A3   Small amount of autobiographical writings. ·
     Bibliography of Speier's writings.

B1   Large collection of L. written by Speier (primarily to
     wife) during his trip to Germany. 1949-1952.

B1,2 Correspondence, some dating to 1920s. Nearly complete
     files since 1933, including L. from: H. Gerth, H.
     Holborn, A. Johnson, S. Kracauer, T. Mann, Kurt
     Riezler, L. Strauss, F. von Unruh.

B3   Collection of L. concerning Speier, including L. by:
     Willy Brandt, Arnold Brecht, Hans Staudinger, etc.

C7   Notes, some Ms. of unpub. works, dating back to stu-
     dent years.

C7, Ms., primarily from unpub. works:
C10   Ms. of writings on propaganda of fascism and related
       topics.
       Interviews by Speier of German generals and politi-
       cians after World War II. Ca. 1950.
       Ms. from Speier's years with Rand Corporation.
       Literary Ms., including some tr.

D7   Nearly complete collection of offprints and books.

F   Several tapes and records of lectures and interviews.

H3   Cl. on lectures by Speier, about Speier in general.

H4   Reviews of Speier's works.

I   Documents dating prior to 1933 as well as later.

J   Photos.

K   Personal library.

L   Materials on the subject of propaganda.

State University of New York at Albany, Department of Germanic Languages and Literatures, 1400 Washington Avenue, Albany, New York 12222.

STORM PUBLISHERS ARCHIVE, KARL O. PAETEL COLLECTION

B1   5 L. to Alexander Gode von Aesch. 1940-1947.
     1 L. to Rudolf Schick. 1946.
     1 L. to Fritz von Unruh. 1947.
     1 L. to Karl O. Paetel (xerox). 1947.

B2   8 L. from Alexander Gode von Aesch. 1946-1947.

Yivo Institute, 1048 Fifth Avenue, New York, N.Y. 10028.

HORACE M. KALLEN PAPERS

B1,2   Individual item(s) in folder no. 850.

I   Miscellaneous materials pertaining to Graduate Faculty
      of New School for Social Research: meetings, memos,
      etc. F. 549-555. 1934-1942.

Mrs. Gertrude Lederer, 372 Central Park West, Apt. 3B, New York, N.Y. 10024.

C7   Manuscript by Speier.

Immigration History Research Center of the University of Minnesota, 826 Berry Street, St. Paul, Minnesota 55101.

AMERICAN COUNCIL FOR EMIGRÉS IN THE PROFESSIONS ARCHIVES

Bl   1 L. to Werner Richter. 1946.

Harvard University, Baker Library, Graduate School of Business, Soldiers Field, Boston, Massachusetts 02163.

FRITZ REDLICH COLLECTION

Bl   1 L. to Fritz Redlich. T. 1938.

Harvard University, Harvard Divinity School, Andover-Harvard Theological Library, 45 Francis Avenue, Cambridge, Massachusetts 02138.

PAUL TILLICH COLLECTION

Bl   1 L. to Paul Tillich. A. 1944.

Mrs. Alice Loewy Kahler, 1 Evelyn Place, Princeton, New Jersey 08540.

ERICH VON KAHLER COLLECTION

Bl   3 L. to Erich von Kahler. 1939-1940.

WILHELM SPEYER
Writer, 1887-1952

<u>Mr. Gerard W. Speyer</u>, 117 Overlook Road, Hastings-on-Hudson, New York 10706.

Gerard Speyer is the nephew of Wilhelm Speyer and heir to his papers. However, information concerning the collection may be obtained from Mr. Günther Speyer, brother of Gerard, 160 East 84th Street, New York, N.Y. 10028.

Gerard Speyer ist der Neffe von Wilhelm Speyer und Erbe seiner literarischen Materials. Auskünfte über die Materialien können jedoch auch von Herrn Günther Speyer (ein Bruder Gerards), 160 East 84th Street, New York, N.Y. 10028, eingeholt werden.

A2   "Allgemeines Notizbuch (Skizzen, Pläne) Teil I." Contains notes and preliminary sketches to <u>Senorita Maria Teresa</u>, <u>Das Glück der Andernachs</u>, and a list of themes for later works. A. 106p.

A3   Travel report. Trip from England to France in Sept. 1938. Undated. T. 2p.
"Rückkehr nach München." T. 2p.

B1   122 L. to Gerard W. Speyer. 1932-1949.

B2   1 L. from Herr Schwetje. 1948.

C1   <u>Das Glück der Andernachs</u>. Prologue and first 3 chap. Dated March 2, 1939. A. 261p. Another version of prologue and first 3 chap. T. with comment "Begonnen: 14. XI, 39." 118p.

C4   "Be on Your Way, Dear" ("Geh zu, mein Liebster").
Story in English. T. 6p.
"Bemerkung zu Ariane." Undated. T. 8p.
"Ein großer Tag in seinem Leben." Story. Undated. T. 13p.
"Eine Nacht lang Hausbesitzer." Story. Undated. T. 6p.
"Das faule Mädchen" ("Lazy Lass"). Undated. T. 19p.
"Melody of Life." Original story by Wilhelm Speyer and Paul Frank. Undated. T. 26p.
"One Minute to Five. A Boy Scout Story." Dated May 17, 1941. T. 32p.
"Shake Well Before Using." Story. Undated. T. 11p.
"Treatment." Story in English. Undated. T. 57p.

WILHELM SPEYER

Untitled short story. Undated. T. 6p.
Untitled story about a Polish family. Undated. T. 61p.

C5 Dr. Palland. Screen story. Undated. T. 54p.
Film script without title or first page. T. 24p.
Der Mann mit der weißen Krawatte. Film Novelle. Un-
dated. T. 2 c. 41p. ea.
Maria Teresa and the Bear. English version of Senorita
Maria Teresa. Undated. T. 77p.
Das vierundzwanzigste Kapitel. Film novella. 1937. T.
34p.

C7 "Amerikanisches Wüstenland." Undated, after 1949. T.
6p.
"German Frenzy." Dated Feb. 6, 1945. T. 3p.
"Hier spricht ein Hochschullehrer aus den Vereinigten
Staaten." Undated, ca. 1945. T. 4p.
"Kleine US-Tugenden." Undated, ca. 1949. T. 6p.
"Selbstschutz der Kinder in US." Undated, after 1949.
T. 5p.
"To the German People." Dated March 30, 1945. T. 3p.
Untitled statement of Speyer's stand on Germany. 1p.

D4 3 newspaper cl.

Immigration History Research Center of the University of
Minnesota, 826 Berry Street, St. Paul, Minnesota 55101

AMERICAN COUNCIL FOR EMIGRÉS IN THE PROFESSIONS ARCHIVES

A3 Autobiographical statement, curriculum vitae. 8p. with
recommendations.

B1 3 L. to Else Staudinger. 1946-1948.

B2 4 L. from Else Staudinger. 1946-1948.

B3 9 L. 1946-1948, including L. by: Thomas Mann, Franz
Horch, Martin Gumpert.

New York Public Library at Lincoln Center, Library and
Museum of the Performing Arts, 111 Amsterdam Avenue, New
York, N.Y. 10023.

C5   Portland House. Film script. Copyright Georg Marton.
       T. 51p.

Paul Kohner, Inc., 9169 Sunset Boulevard, Hollywood, California 90068.

C5   Maria Teresa and the Bear. T. 77p.

Mr. Hans Sahl, 800 West End Avenue, New York, N.Y. 10025.

B1   Several L. to Hans Sahl.

University of Southern California, Lion Feuchtwanger Memorial
Library, 520 Paseo Miramar, Pacific Palisades, California
90272.

B1   1 L. to Lion Feuchtwanger. 1942.

RENÉ SPITZ

Psychoanalyst, 1887-1974

The RENÉ SPITZ ARCHIVES, a direct legacy of Dr. Spitz, is
being organized at the University of Colorado Medical School.
In addition, there will be a special RENÉ SPITZ FILM AR-
CHIVES, containing both published films and many of the new
materials that formed the basis for his early research. Dr.
Spitz's professional library is also being catalogued and
made available to scholars. Dr. David Metcalf will publish
the last book on which he and Dr. Spitz were collaborating
at the time of Dr. Spitz's death. Indications to the Project
are that there is relatively little material in German in
the Archives, and relatively little correspondence. The
Project was unable to contact the Spitz heirs at this time.

Die RENÉ SPITZ ARCHIVES, ein Vermächtnis von Dr. Spitz, wer-
den z.Zt. an der Medical School der University of Colorado
geordnet. Zusätzlich baut man spezielle RENÉ SPITZ FILM
ARCHIVES auf, in denen sowohl schon veröffentlichte Filme
als auch neue Materialien, die die Grundlage seiner frühen
Forschungen bildeten, enthalten sind. Die Arbeitsbibliothek
von Dr. Spitz wird ebenfalls katalogisiert und steht dann für
Forschungszwecke zur Verfügung. Dr. David Metcalf bereitet
die Herausgabe des Bandes vor, an dem er mit Dr. Spitz bis
zu dessen Tod zusammenarbeitete. Es scheint, daß sich in
den Archives verhältnismäßig wenig Materialien in Deutsch
sowie verhältnismäßig wenig Korrespondenz befindet. Die
Erben von Dr. Spitz konnten nicht erreicht werden.

Erikson Institute for Early Education, 1525 East 53rd Street,
Chicago, Illinois 60637.

Private collection of Gerhard and Maria Piers.

Privatsammlung von Gerhard und Maria Piers.

B1,2   Lengthy correspondence between Spitz and Gerhard and
       Maria Piers, primarily from the 1970s.

D7   Offprints of Spitz's writings.

G   6-hour TV interview with Maria Piers.

Columbia University, Butler Library, New York, N.Y. 10027.

ORAL HISTORY COLLECTION

G   Interview with René Spitz. 1965. 104p. transcript.

Library of Congress, Manuscript Division, Independence Avenue
and First Street S.E., Washington, D.C. 20540.

THE PAPERS OF SIEGFRIED BERNFELD, MAXWELL GITELSON PAPERS

B1,2 Correspondence between Bernfeld and Spitz. 1934-1939.
      Correspondence between Gitelson and Spitz.

Dr. Martin Grotjahn, 416 North Bedford Drive, Beverly Hills,
California 90210.

B1,2 Correspondence between Grotjahn and Spitz.

HERTA SPONER

Chemist, 1895-1968

Dr. Harold P. Stephenson, Prof. of Physics, Pfeiffer College, Misenheimer, North Carolina 28109.

The ca. 75 ft. of materials in Dr. Stephenson's possession are from the papers of Herta Sponer. Dr. Stephenson is a former student of Herta Sponer.

Die Materialien im Besitz von Dr. Stephenson (etwa 23 m) stammen aus der Sammlung von Herta Sponer. Dr. Stephenson ist ein Schüler von Herta Sponer.

B1,2 Correspondence. 1953-1963. Professional, business, and personal L., as well as correspondences with students.

C7   Lecture notes.

C7,8 Notes left over from writing articles. Technical reports.

D7,8 Hundreds of reprints and offprints, dating from as early as 1913. Textbooks.

J   Hundreds of spectroscopic plates, with interpretations, covering Sponer's years at Duke.

L   Professional magazines, etc.

N   Copies of all theses and dissertations supervised by Sponer while at Duke.

University of Chicago, The Joseph Regenstein Library, 1100 East 57th Street, Chicago, Illinois 60637.

JAMES FRANCK PAPERS

B1,2 2 F. of correspondence, including L. to James Franck. Correspondence with Robert Platzman concerning Platzman's editing of The Selected Papers of James Franck.

B2   Condolence L. upon the death of James Franck.

C8   "Remarks on Photosynthesis in Relation to Energy

Supply on Earth." Written with James Franck. T.c. 20p. T.c. with corr. by Franck and Sponer. 12p. A. 2p. Miscellaneous odd c.
"Remarks on Radiationless Transitions in Complex Molecules." Written with James Franck. Notes. A. 10p. T. with h. notes. 5p.
Notes on fluorescence. A. 1p.
Miscellaneous notes. A. 6p.

I Marriage certificate to James Franck. North Carolina, June 29, 1946.

J Herta Sponer's photo album. Göttingen, 1920-1933. Includes photos of Franck, Sponer, colleagues and friends. 55 photos with captions.
Group photos (with James Franck and others). 1920s (4), 1966 (1).

Duke University, William R. Perkins Library, Manuscript Department, Durham, North Carolina 27706.

FRITZ WOLFGANG LONDON PAPERS, ROBERT LEE FLOWERS PAPERS, WILLIAM PRESTON FEW PAPERS, WILLIAM HANE WANNAMAKER PAPERS

B1 6 L. 1935-1948, including L. to: F. W. London, Robert Lee Flowers, William Few, W. H. Wannamaker.

B2 42 L. 1934-1937.

I Personnel files. 1945.

Archive for History of Quantum Physics (locations in U.S.: Bancroft Library, University of California, Berkeley; American Philosophical Society, Philadelphia, Pennsylvania; American Institute of Physics, New York, N.Y.).

G Interview conducted by T. S. Kuhn and Maria Goeppert Mayer with James Franck and Herta Sponer. 1962. Transcript. 115p.

Lawrence Livermore Laboratory, P.O. Box 808, Livermore, California 94550.

B1,2   Correspondence between Herta Sponer and Edward Teller.

California Institute of Technology, Robert A. Millikan Library, Pasadena, California 91109.

B1,2   Individual item(s) in 1 F.   1926.

HANS STAUB

Physicist, 1908-

University of California, Los Alamos Scientific Laboratory,
P.O. Box 1663, Los Alamos, New Mexico 87544.

DIRECTOR'S PERSONNEL FILES, LIBRARY SERVICES GROUP COLLEC-
TIONS. The notebooks as well as a number of the documents
are closed to the public.

*Materialien finden sich in den DIRECTOR'S PERSONNEL FILES
und den LIBRARY SERVICES GROUP COLLECTIONS. Die Notizbücher
sowie eine Anzahl der Dokumente sind für die Öffentlichkeit
nicht zugänglich.*

B1 12 L. and 1 Tel. 1946-1969.

B2 14 L. 1946-1969.

B3 13 L. 1946-1948, 1968.

C8 23 notebooks (one with Felix Bloch) from work done at
    Los Alamos.

I   Consultant's agreement, drawn up by Staub. 1946.
    2 patents.
    Los Alamos Scientific Laboratory records. 1948-1949.
    2 items.
    27 documents reporting work done at Los Alamos Scien-
    tific Laboratory.
    6 documents reporting work done at locations other
    than Los Alamos.
    Interoffice memos, directives, etc. pertaining to
    Staub's activities at Los Alamos. 1949. 5 items.

HANS STAUDINGER

Economist, 1899-

Because of time limitations, the Project was unable to ascertain the existence or extent of papers still in the possession of Dr. Hans Staudinger (New York, N.Y.). The following represent various smaller amounts of materials located by the Project.

Zeitschwierigkeiten machten es unmöglich herauszufinden, ob und in welchem Umfang sich im Besitze von Dr. Hans Staudinger (New York, N.Y.) noch weitere Materialien befinden. Das Folgende stellt eine Aufzählung verschiedener anderer, kleinerer Materialsammlungen dar, die an anderen Orten ausfindig gemacht wurden.

Yivo Institute, 1048 Fifth Avenue, New York, N.Y. 10028.

HORACE M. KALLEN PAPERS

*   Miscellaneous materials pertaining to Graduate Faculty of New School: memos, meetings, correspondences, etc. 1937-1952. Folders: 552-560.
    Further references to Staudinger in folders: 226A, 330, 355, 537, 540, 543, 544, 645, 703, 1015, 1045.

University of Minnesota, University Libraries, Social Welfare History Archives, Minneapolis, Minnesota 55455.

SURVEY ASSOCIATES PAPERS

31,2   Correspondence with Survey Associates. 8 L. 1941-1945.

New School for Social Research, Office of the Dean of the Graduate Faculty of Political and Social Science, 65 Fifth Avenue, New York, N.Y. 10003.

RECORDS OF THE UNIVERSITY IN EXILE, 1933-45

*   File containing 5 items: curriculum vitae, 2 L., etc.

HANS STAUDINGER

Columbia University, Butler Library, New York, N.Y. 10027.

PANTHEON BOOKS COLLECTION

B1   2 L. to Pantheon Publishers. T. 1947.

State University of New York at Albany, Department of Germanic Languages and Literatures, 1400 Washington Avenue, Albany, New York 12222.

KARL O. PAETEL COLLECTION

B1   1 L. to Karl O. Paetel (xerox). 1962.
B2   3 L. from Karl O. Paetel (xerox). 1962.

Mrs. Alice Loewy Kahler, 1 Evelyn Place, Princeton, New Jersey 08540.

ERICH VON KAHLER COLLECTION

B1   1 L. to Kyrill Schabert (Pantheon Books). 1948.
B2   1 L. from Erich von Kahler. 1948.

Prof. Carl Landauer, 1317 Arch Street, Berkeley, California 94708.

B1,2 Correspondence with Carl Landauer.

University of Illinois at Urbana-Champaign, University Library, University Archives, Room 19, Urbana, Illinois 61801.

ROGER ADAMS PAPERS

B1   1 L. to Roger Adams. 1927.

Harvard University, Baker Library, Graduate School of Business, Soldiers Field, Boston, Massachusetts 02163.

FRITZ REDLICH COLLECTION

B1   1 L. to Fritz Redlich. 1941.

American Philosophical Society, The Library, 105 South Fifth Street, Philadelphia, Pennsylvania 19106.

WOLFGANG KÖHLER PAPERS

B2   1 L. from Wolfgang Köhler. 1959.

FRED STEIN

Photographer, 1909-1967

<u>Mrs. Liselotte Stein</u>, 115-25 Metropolitan Avenue, Kew Gardens, New York 11418.

The collection of photos and other materials was accumulated by Fred Stein in the course of his professional work as a photographer. The collection dates from 1934 when the Steins left Germany for Paris. The copyright to all materials is retained by Mrs. Liselotte Stein, who is willing to answer inquiries concerning the papers and photos in her possession.

Der Nachlaß Fred Steins, der aus Photoarbeiten und anderen dazugehörigen Materialien besteht, stammt aus seiner Tätigkeit als Photograph in Frankreich und in den U.S.A. Die Materialien gehen bis auf das Jahr 1934 zurück, als Fred und Liselotte Stein Deutschland verlassen mußten und nach Paris übersiedelten. Das Copyright zu sämtlichen Arbeiten ruht bei Frau Stein. Sie ist bereit, Auskünfte über die Sammlung zu geben.

Al   Diary (reading list only).

B1,2   Business correspondence (6 notebooks). Over 2,000p.

B,   Scrapbook with documentary materials, letters.
I

C7,   Collection of reviews by and about Stein.
H4

F   Film on Fred Stein.

J   Collection of Stein's work, including book jackets by
       him.
      Prints of photos (ca. 25 ft. in cartons). Also an
       alphabetical listing of photos in the collection.
      Card file of negatives.
      Rough prints (20 notebooks).

K   Several hundred books, many by people Stein had photo-
       graphed, others on political science, law. Also 5
       books by Stein.

M   Guestbook.
      Scrapbook of unusual names.
      Scrapbooks: ca. 10 with pictures, cl., on France, Paris,
       Belgium, Fifth Avenue, children's photos, originals
       to <u>Mehr Licht</u>.

WILLIAM STEINBERG

Conductor, 1899-

Mr. Steinberg retired from the Pittsburgh Symphony Orchestra in 1976 and resides in Atherton, California.

William Steinberg, ehemaliger Dirigent des Pittsburgh Symphony Orchesters, lebt seit 1976 in Atherton in Kalifornien im Ruhestand.

University of Pittsburgh, Hillman Library, 4200 Forbes Avenue, Pittsburgh, Pennsylvania 15260.

The WILLIAM STEINBERG PAPERS, consisting of approximately 2,000 items, were donated by William Steinberg in 1976. A portion of the collection (pre-1914 scores) will remain closed until 1978.

Die WILLIAM STEINBERG PAPERS, etwa 2000 Nummern, sind eine Schenkung von William Steinberg aus dem Jahre 1976. Ein Teil der Sammlung (Partituren aus der Zeit vor 1914) ist bis 1978 nicht zugänglich.

J   169 photos of Steinberg.

K   Ca. 1,000 books, including many signed copies (2/3 literary or trade books on music).
816 music scores.

M   8 medallion awards.
One stone sculpture.
2 silver presentation bowls.
6 framed items.
Miscellaneous memorabilia.
Arnold Schoenberg and Richard Wagner autographs.

Syracuse University, The George Arents Research Library, Syracuse, New York 13210.

FRANZ WAXMAN PAPERS

B1   Correspondence with Franz Waxman. 1949-1961.

University of California, Los Angeles, Music Library, 405
Hilgard Avenue, Los Angeles, California 90024.

ERNST TOCH ARCHIVE

B1   6 L. to Ernst Toch.

F   2 tapes of Steinberg conducting Toch compositions:
      "Big Ben."
      "Symphony no. 3, op. 75."

University of Pennsylvania, The Charles Patterson Van Pelt
Library, Philadelphia, Pennsylvania 19104.

ALMA MAHLER-WERFEL COLLECTION

B1   3 L. and 1 note to Alma Mahler-Werfel. 1948-1954 and
      undated.

Metropolitan Opera Association, Inc., The Archives, Lincoln
Center Plaza, New York, N.Y. 10023.

H3   2 cl. from Opera News, 1962-1963.

I   Contracts, 1964-1965.

Columbia University, Butler Library, New York, N.Y. 10027.

B1   2 L. to Nicolai Berezowsky. T. 1950.

Museum of the City of New York, Fifth Avenue at 103rd Street,
New York, N.Y. 10029.

H3   "Personality File" on Steinberg.

Bruno Walter Memorial Foundation, c/o Miss Susie Danziger,
115 East 72nd Street, New York, N.Y. 10021.

B1,2 Correspondence with Bruno Walter.

KURT STEINER

Lawyer, Political Scientist, 1912-

<u>Prof. Kurt Steiner</u>, Department of Political Science, Stanford University, Stanford, California 94305.

The case files in Dr. Steiner's private possession are from his activities as Special Assistant to the Chief of Council, International Prosecution Section, GHQ, SCAP in proceedings of the International Military Tribunal for the Far East, and from his activities as prosecutor against General Hiroshi Tamura, Chief of POW Information and Management Bureau in the Japanese Ministry of War (10/29/48 - 2/9/49). The memoranda, checknotes, speeches and other materials are from his activities as Deputy Chief and Chief of Civil Affairs and Civil Liberties Branch, Legislation and Justice Division, Legal Section, SCAP.

Die Prozeßakten in Dr. Steiners Privatbesitz stammen aus der Zeit seiner Beschäftigung als Special Assistant to the Chief of Council, International Prosecution Section, GHQ, SCAP in den Verfahren der International Military Tribunal for the Far East, und aus seiner Zeit als Ankläger gegen General Hiroshi Tamura, Leiter der Kriegsgefangenen- und Management-Abteilung im Japanischen Kriegsministerium (29. Okt. 1948 - 9. Feb. 1949). Die Memoranden, Notizen, Ansprachemanuskripte usw. stammen aus seiner Zeit als Deputy Chief and Chief of Civil Affairs and Civil Liberties Branch, Legislation and Justice Division, Legal Section, SCAP.

B2   Correspondence, including L. from: Albert Ehrenzweig, Takeyoshi Kawashima, Alfred C. Oppler, George F. Rohrlich. Ca. 1.5 in. (A major portion of Dr. Steiner's correspondence was discarded at the time of his move to a new office at Stanford University.)

C7,8 Ms. of essays, books, speeches.
      Memoranda and checknotes concerning drafts of bills to the Government Section, GHQ, Supreme Commander for the Allied Powers.

H3   Newspaper cl., primarily concerning Steiner's activities in Japan.

I   Certificates, documents.

L   Japan, 1945-1951. Ca. 16 in. of materials.
        Case files:
          International Military Tribunal for the Far East.
            18 vols.
          Proceedings against General Tamura. 2 vols.

O   Several human rights posters. 1949-1950.

CURT STERN

Geneticist, 1902-1974

Although Curt Stern materials do exist, there has been no decision as to their disposition.

Zwar existieren Curt-Stern-Materialien, doch ist über deren Verbleib noch keine Entscheidung getroffen worden.

Indiana University, The University Libraries, The Lilly Library, Bloomington, Indiana 47401.

HERMANN JOSEPH MULLER MSS.

B1   39 L. to Hermann Joseph Muller. 1929-1947.
        3 L. 1930, 1932, 1946.

B2   77 L., including 75 L. from Hermann Joseph Muller.
        1926-1949.

University of Missouri, Library, Western Historical Manuscript Collection/State Historical Society Manuscripts, Columbia, Missouri 65201.

L. J. STADLER PAPERS

A3   List of publications of Curt Stern. 3p.

B1   1 L. 1949.
        4 L. to L. J. Stadler. 1933-1945.

B2   3 L. 1945, 1951.

C8   "Gene and Character." 2p.

American Philosophical Society, The Library, 105 South Fifth Street, Philadelphia, Pennsylvania 19106.

MAX BERGMANN PAPERS, ALBERT F. BLAKESLEE PAPERS, CHARLES B. DAVENPORT PAPERS, MILISLAV DEMEREC PAPERS, L. C. DUNN PAPERS, WARREN H. LEWIS PAPERS.

B1,2   Correspondence with Albert F. Blakeslee. 6 L. 1931-
        1949.

847

Correspondence with Charles Davenport.
Correspondence with Milislav Demerec.
Correspondence with L. C. Dunn in "Amercan [sic] Committee for Displaced German Scholars" file. [1934-1935]. Also additional correspondence. Ca. 25 L. 1928-1970.
Correspondence with Warren H. Lewis.

Bl,2   Individual F. compiled by Max Bergmann entitled "Curt
I   Stern."

University of California, Los Alamos Scientific Laboratory, P.O. Box 1663, Los Alamos, New Mexico 87544.

I   13 documents reporting work done at locations other than Los Alamos.

JOSEF LUITPOLD (STERN)
Writer, 1886-1966

Mrs. Elisabeth M. Stoerk and Mrs. Susanne B. Hoeller, 288
Ocean Drive West, Stamford, Connecticut 06902.

FRIDERIKE ZWEIG ARCHIVE

B1   26 L. and 6 Ptc. to Friderike Zweig. 1939-1941, 1943-
      1947, 1964.

B2   1 L. from Friderike Zweig. Undated.

B3   1 L.

H1   Program-brochure entitled: Josef Luitpold Stern zum
      80. Geburtstag.

University of New Hampshire, The Library, Department of Special Collections, Durham, New Hampshire 03824.

OSKAR MARIA GRAF COLLECTION

B1   5 L. to Oskar Maria Graf. 1963-1965.

B2   1 L. from Oskar Maria Graf. 1966.

Washington University Libraries, Gaylord Music Library, St.
Louis, Missouri 63130.

THE PISK COLLECTION

C3   "Der große Regenmacher. Szenische Ballade in 1 Auf-
      zug." Words by Josef Luitpold Stern. Adapted for the
      stage by Max Brand. Music by Paul A. Pisk. Dec. 20,
      1927. 23p. Another version. 29p.

State University of New York at Albany, Department of Germanic Languages and Literatures, 1400 Washington Avenue,
Albany, New York 12222.

KARL O. PAETEL COLLECTION

B1   1 L. to Karl O. Paetel (xerox). 1946.

Columbia University, Butler Library, New York, N.Y. 10027.

VARIAN FRY PAPERS

I   2 documents mentioning Stern.

OTTO STERN

Physicist, 1888-1969

The Project's attempts to locate the materials from the
estate of Otto Stern were unsuccessful.

*Es war nicht möglich, die Materialien aus dem Nachlaß von
Otto Stern zu lokalisieren.*

University of California, Berkeley, The Bancroft Library,
Berkeley, California 94720.

E. O. LAWRENCE PAPERS, GILBERT N. LEWIS PAPERS

B1   19 L. and 2 Tel. to E. O. Lawrence. 1931-1944.

B1,2   Item(s) of correspondence. 1928-1942.

University of Chicago, The Joseph Regenstein Library, 1100
East 57th Street, Chicago, Illinois 60637.

JAMES FRANCK PAPERS

B1   L. of congratulations to James Franck on Franck's 70th
        birthday. 1952.

B1,2   Lengthy correspondence between Stern and James Franck.
        1933-1963.

J   Group photo. Institute for Theoretical Physics. Chi-
        cago, 1935.

California Institute of Technology, Robert A. Millikan
Library, Pasadena, California 91109.

PAUL S. EPSTEIN PAPERS

B1,2   Correspondence with P. S. Epstein.
        "Miscellaneous correspondence."

American Philosophical Society, The Library, 105 South Fifth
Street, Philadelphia, Pennsylvania 19106.

851

OTTO STERN

NIELS BOHR CORRESPONDENCE

B1   5 L. to Niels Bohr. 1946-1947.

Archive for History of Quantum Physics (locations in U.S.: Bancroft Library, University of California, Berkeley; American Philosophical Society, Philadelphia, Pennsylvania; American Institute of Physics, New York, N.Y.).

B2   1 L. from Walther Gerlach. 1924.
       2 L. from Alfred Landé. 1919, 1923.

G   2 unrecorded interviews. Notes. 8p. 1962, 1963.
       Notes on miscellaneous conversations.

Duke University, William R. Perkins Library, Manuscript Department, Durham, North Carolina 27706.

FRITZ WOLFGANG LONDON PAPERS

B2   1 L. from F. W. London. 1931.

New York Public Library, Manuscript Division, Fifth Avenue and 42nd Street, New York, N.Y. 10018.

EMERGENCY COMMITTEE IN AID OF DISPLACED FOREIGN SCHOLARS, 1933-1945

*   File compiled, no assistance given. 1933-1938.

Princeton University, Firestone Library, Princeton, New Jersey 08540.

THE PAPERS OF ALBERT EINSTEIN (1879-1955). For details concerning the use of this collection, see description under Albert Einstein.

THE PAPERS OF ALBERT EINSTEIN (1879-1955). Angaben über den Zugang zu der Sammlung finden sich unter "Albert Einstein."

B1,2   Unknown amount of correspondence between Einstein and Stern.

<u>New York University</u>, Courant Institute of Mathematical Sciences, Library, 251 Mercer Street, New York, N.Y. 10012.

*   General file on Otto Stern. 1940-1944.

HELENE STOECKER

Political Figure, 1869-1943

Swarthmore College, Swarthmore, Pennsylvania 19081.

The HELENE STOECKER PAPERS (DG 35) in the SWARTHMORE COLLEGE
PEACE COLLECTION consist of 9 archive boxes of materials
donated by friends (Mrs. Ellen Brinton, April 1952) and from
the estate of Dr. Stoecker.

*Die HELENE STOECKER PAPERS (DG 35) in der SWARTHMORE COLLEGE
PEACE COLLECTION umfassen 9 Archivkartons Materialien, die
z.T. von Freunden (Frau Ellen Brinton, April 1952) und z.T.
aus dem Nachlaß von Frau Dr. Stoecker stammen.*

A1,3 Autobiographical materials. T. and A. Ca. 700p. In-
     cludes:
     "Lebensabriß I. 1896-1913."
     "Lebensabriß II. 1869-1914."
     "Kriegstagebuch. 1914-1918."
     "Lebensabriß I. 1914-1940."
     "Material for Autobiography."

A3   Account of journey from Sweden, via Russia and Japan,
     to U.S.A.

B1,2 Correspondence. 1930-1943, including: Gertrude Baer,
     Max Barth, Ruth G. Colby, Ludwig Quidde, Rosika
     Schwimmer.
     Ca. 200 L., including:
     Personal L. 1913-1926.
     Miscellaneous correspondence during residence in
     Sweden. 1939-1940.
     Personal L. from friends in Vienna. 1937-1941.

B3   Correspondence about Stoecker. 1940-1944.

C7   Miscellaneous notes.
     Speech in Philadelphia. 1942.

C7,   German Ms., including many on women and women's rights.
C10   1930s. Ca. 550p.

D7,   Newspaper and magazine articles, cl.
D10

H3   Printed and typed publicity about Stoecker. 1 B.

HELENE STOECKER

I   Travel documents.

J   Photos.

L   Lists of leading German pacifists outside Germany.
Books and pamphlets.

M   Address books of various people.

Hoover Institution on War, Revolution and Peace, Stanford, California 94305.

HELENE STOECKER COLLECTION: 1 F.

B1,2   Correspondence between Helene Stoecker and the following individuals: Imogene Bellquist, Alice Park, Ludwig Quidde, and the Verlag der Neuen Generation, Berlin-Nikolassee, Germany.

Harvard University, Houghton Library, Cambridge, Massachusetts 02138.

OSWALD GARRISON VILLARD PAPERS and general archive files

B1   4 L. and 1 Tel. to Joseph Ishill. 1928-1929.
        3 L. to O. G. Villard. 1942-1943.

B2   2 L. from O. G. Villard. 1942-1943.

C7   "Havelock Ellis and Sexual Reform." German. T. 15p.

University of Texas, Humanities Research Center, Manuscripts Collection, Box 7219, Austin, Texas 78712.

B1   5 L.

B2   6 L.

American Philosophical Society, The Library, 105 South Fifth Street, Philadelphia, Pennsylvania 19106.

FRANZ BOAS PAPERS

B1   2 L. to Franz Boas. 1925.

GUSTAV STOLPER

Economist, 1888-1947

The bulk of the literary estate of Gustav Stolper was donated by his widow, Mrs. Toni Stolper (43 Cross Street, Dundes, Ontario L9H 2R5, Canada), to the Deutsches Bundesarchiv in Koblenz, West Germany, shortly after Stolper's death in 1947. Mrs. Stolper, author of a biography on her husband, <u>Ein Leben in Brennpunkten unserer Zeit, Wien, Berlin, New York - Gustav Stolper 1888-1947</u> (Tübingen: Rainer Wunderlich Verlag, 1960), has retained some materials of a personal nature (personal correspondence, fragments of diaries) that are not as yet open to scholars.

Der Hauptteil des literarischen Nachlasses von Gustav Stolper ist als Schenkung von Frau Toni Stolper (43 Cross Street, Dundes, Ontario L9H 2R5, Canada), der Witwe Gustav Stolpers, nach seinem Tode 1947 an das Deutsche Bundesarchiv (Koblenz, West Germany) gegangen. Frau Stolper, Verfasserin einer Biographie über ihren Mann - <u>Ein Leben in Brennpunkten unserer Zeit, Wien, Berlin, New York - Gustav Stolper 1888-1947</u> (Tübingen: Rainer Wunderlich Verlag, 1960) -, hat einige Materialien persönlicher Natur, wie privaten Briefwechsel und Teile von Tagebüchern, behalten. Diese Materialien sind noch nicht für Forschungszwecke zugänglich.

<u>University of California, Los Angeles</u>, Music Library, 405 Hilgard Avenue, Los Angeles, California 90024.

ERNST TOCH ARCHIVE

B1,2   Correspondence between Stolper and Ernst Toch. 1902-1947. Ca. 500 L.

<u>Leo Baeck Institute</u>, 129 East 73rd Street, New York, N.Y. 10021.

GUSTAV STOLPER COLLECTION: 32 items, donated in 1966 by Toni Stolper.

GUSTAV STOLPER COLLECTION: 32 Nummern - eine Schenkung von Toni Stolper aus dem Jahre 1966.

GUSTAV STOLPER

B1,2   Correspondence with Paul Hertz. 1938-1947. 18 L.
       Correspondence with Heinrich Bruening. 1940-1947. 7 L.

B3   Correspondence between Toni Stolper and the Leo Baeck
       Institute; 1 L. from Hans Schaeffer to Toni Stolper.

J   Photos.

L   Pamphlets on Paul Hertz.

Harvard University, Houghton Library, Cambridge, Massachusetts 02138.

OSWALD GARRISON VILLARD PAPERS

B1   3 L. to O. G. Villard. 1933-1939.

B2   4 L. from O. G. Villard. 1933-1939.

Yivo Institute, 1048 Fifth Avenue, New York, N.Y. 10028.

HORACE M. KALLEN PAPERS

B1,2   Individual item(s) in folder no. 856. 1934.

University of Chicago, The Joseph Regenstein Library, 1100
East 57th Street, Chicago, Illinois 60637.

JAMES FRANCK PAPERS

B1,2   Correspondence with James Franck.

OTTO STRASSER

Political Scientist, 1897-1974

The largest collection of correspondence of the late Dr.
Otto Strasser concerning his years in exile in Canada is
located at the Institut für Zeitgeschichte (8000 München 19,
Leonrodstraße 46b) where it is cared for by his widow, Mrs.
Hilde-Renate Strasser. A second important collection of
Strasser materials is housed in the Historical Division,
Department of External Affairs, Lester B. Pearson Building
(125 Sussex Drive, Ottawa, Ontario K1A 0G2, Canada). Prof.
Clause R. Owen (84 Centre Street, P.O. Box 176, Niagara-on-
the Lake, Ontario L0S 1J0, Canada) also possesses an exten-
sive Strasser collection consisting of articles by and about
Strasser, books and pamphlets, and a large amount of docu-
mentation on Strasser's life and career.

Die größte Briefwechsel-Sammlung von Dr. Otto Strasser aus
der Zeit seiner Exiljahre in Kanada befindet sich im Insti-
tut für Zeitgeschichte (Leonrodstraße 46b, 8000 München 19).
Sie wird von seiner Witwe, Frau Hilde-Renate Strasser, be-
treut. Eine weitere wichtige Sammlung von Strasser-Materia-
lien befindet sich bei: Historical Division, Department of
External Affairs, Lester B. Pearson Building (125 Sussex
Drive, Ottawa, Ontario K1A 0G2, Canada). Prof. Claude R.
Owen (84 Centre Street, P.O. Box 176, Niagara-on-the-Lake,
Ontario L0S 1JO, Canada) besitzt ebenfalls eine umfangreiche
Strasser-Sammlung, bestehend aus Artikeln von und über
Strasser, Büchern, Broschüren und einer größeren Menge doku-
mentarischen Materials über Strassers privaten und berufli-
chen Werdegang.

<u>Swarthmore College</u>, Swarthmore, Pennsylvania 19081.

SWARTHMORE COLLEGE PEACE COLLECTION: WILLIAM F. SOLLMANN
PAPERS

B1   42 L. to Wilhelm Sollman. 1936-1946 and undated.
      1 L. ea. to H. Bruening (1941) and Max Sievers (1936).

B2   12 L. from Wilhelm Sollman. 1936-1943.

H5   Memo of visit by Strasser to Paris. 1936. 6p.
      Statement on Strasser. 1941.

OTTO STRASSER

L   "Lagebericht Mitte April 1940." Memo concerning Hit-
     ler's attack on Denmark and Norway. 2p.
     "Freies Deutschland Bewegung." Memo. Undated. 2p.
     Also statement of purpose and planning. Undated. 2p.

U. S. General Services Administration, National Archives and
Records Service, Washington, D.C. 20408.

RECORDS OF THE GERMAN FOREIGN MINISTRY - Microfilm T120;
Microfilm T580

I   Records concerning Otto Strasser and "Die Schwarze
     Front." Sections of 7 microfilm reels.

Leo Baeck Institute, 129 East 73rd Street, New York, N.Y.
10021.

KURT GROSSMANN COLLECTION

B1,2 Correspondence with Kurt Grossmann.

Harvard University, Houghton Library, Cambridge, Massachusetts 02138.

B1   1 L. to Alexander Woollcott. 1941.

State University of New York at Albany, Department of Germanic Languages and Literatures, 1400 Washington Avenue,
Albany, New York 12222.

KARL O. PAETEL COLLECTION

B2   2 L. from Karl O. Paetel. 1961, 1965. Xerox.

H3   Cl., pamphlets and brochures assembled by Karl O. Pae-
     tel.

LEO SZILARD

Physicist, 1898-1964

Dr. Gertrud Weiss-Szilard, 8038 El Paseo Grande, La Jolla, California 92037.

Dr. Gertrud Weiss-Szilard is the widow of Leo Szilard. The ca. 24 ft. of materials from the estate of Szilard are at present being stored at the University of California, La Jolla. Dr. Weiss-Szilard and Dr. Bernard T. Feld are in the process of preparing a second volume of Szilard papers containing manuscripts and correspondence that will be ready for publication after 1976. The first volume contains Szilard's scientific writings: Bernard T. Feld and G. Weiss-Szilard (eds.), The Collected Works of Leo Szilard: Scientific Papers (Cambridge, Massachusetts: MIT Press, 1972). The materials in the collection will remain closed to the public until such time as they are officially deposited at a public archive or repository.

Frau Dr. Gertrud Weiss-Szilard ist die Witwe von Leo Szilard. Die etwa 7,20 m Materialien aus dem Nachlaß von Leo Szilard sind gegenwärtig in der University of California, La Jolla, aufbewahrt. Frau Dr. Weiss-Szilard und Dr. Bernard T. Feld sind im Begriff, einen zweiten Band mit Schriften Szilards für die Publikation vorzubereiten. Dieser Band mit Manuskripttexten und Korrespondenz wird nicht vor 1977 erscheinen. Der erste Band enthält Szilards wissenschaftliche Schriften: Bernard T. Feld und G. Weiss-Szilard (Hg.), The Collected Works of Leo Szilard: Scientific Papers (Cambridge, Massachusetts: MIT Press, 1972). Die Materialien der Sammlung werden so lange nicht zugänglich sein, bis sie endgültig in einem Archiv oder einem anderen Aufbewahrungsort untergebracht sein werden.

Al   Diaries, appointment calendars.

A2   Notebooks.

Bl,2   Correspondence. 1930s-1960s. Including L. to and from: Albert Einstein, J. F. Kennedy, L. B. Johnson, Henry Kissinger.

C7,   Articles by and about Szilard.
H3

C8   Scientific Ms. Complete texts and rough drafts.

C8,   Newspaper and magazine cl. by Szilard and others.
L

F   Tapes by Szilard. Also transcripts of tapes.

I   Memoranda.

J   Photos.

L   Materials used by Szilard in his work.

University of California, Los Alamos Scientific Laboratory,
P. O. Box 1663, Los Alamos, New Mexico 87544.

DIRECTOR'S PERSONNEL FILES, collections of the LIBRARY SER-
VICES GROUP

*DIRECTOR'S PERSONNEL FILES, Sammlungen der LIBRARY SERVICES
GROUP*

B1   1 L. to President John F. Kennedy. 1961. pc.
       11 L. 1958-1964.

B2   6 L. 1958-1963.

B3   4 L. concerning Szilard's activities at Los Alamos
       Scientific Laboratory.

C7   "Is Los Alamos capable of taking up molecular biology?"
       Report addressed to Norris Bradbury. Dated Jan. 20,
       1959. 2c. 5p. ea.

I   "Atoms for Peace Awards, Inc." 2 items.
       1 patent.
       Miscellaneous documents concerning Szilard's work at
       Los Alamos. 7 items.
       51 documents reporting work done at locations other
       than Los Alamos.

N   2 reports. 5p., 10p.

Indiana University, The University Libraries, The Lilly Library, Bloomington, Indiana 47401.

HERMANN JOSEPH MULLER MSS.

B1   16 L. to H. J. Muller. 1950-1963.

B2   16 L. from H. J. Muller. 1950-1963.

B3   Correspondence between Gertrud Weiss-Szilard and Hermann Muller. 1960-1964.
      3 L.

Library of Congress, Manuscript Division, Independence Avenue and First Street S.E., Washington, D.C. 20540.

J. ROBERT OPPENHEIMER PAPERS

B1   13 L. and 1 Tel. to J. Robert Oppenheimer. T. and A. 1945-1963.
      Open L. to the President of the United States. T.c. 1945.

B1,2 Correspondence between Szilard and others concerning a Citizen's Committee. 1950.

B2   9 L. and 1 Tel. from J. Robert Oppenheimer. 1945-1963.
      1 L. from Edward Teller. T.c. 1945.
      1 L. from E. Creutz. T.c. 1945.

C7   "Can We Have International Control of Atomic Energy?" Lecture. 1949. T.c. 15p.
      "The Diary of Dr. Davis." 1948. T.c. Ca. 30p.
      "Atomic Bombs and the Postwar Position of the United States in the World." 1945. T.c. 14p.

American Institute of Physics, Niels Bohr Library, 335 East 45th Street, New York, N.Y. 10017.

NIELS BOHR CORRESPONDENCE, PICTORIAL FILE

B1   3 L. to Niels Bohr. Microfilm. 1933-1947.
      1 L. to J. A. Wheeler. Microfilm. 1939.

B2   1 L. from Niels Bohr. 1936.

F   Film footage in "The World of Enrico Fermi."

J Photos, individual and group.

Columbia University, Butler Library, New York, N.Y. 10027.

ORAL HISTORY COLLECTION and general archive files

A3 "Development of Chain Reaction." Undated. c. 12p.

B1 8 L. 1947-1960.

H5 Recollections of Leo Szilard in an interview with
    Kenneth Tompkins Bainbridge. 1960.

Duke University, William R. Perkins Library, Manuscript
Department, Durham, North Carolina 27706.

FRITZ WOLFGANG LONDON PAPERS, FRANZ BOAS PAPERS

B1 6 L., including 1 L. ea. to: Franz Boas and F. W.
    London. 1930-1933.

B2 3 L. 1933.

University of California, Berkeley, The Bancroft Library,
Berkeley, California 94720.

E. O. LAWRENCE PAPERS

B1 4 L., 2 Tel. and 1 memo to E. O. Lawrence. 1940, 1945.

U.S. Atomic Energy Commission, Division of Classification,
Data Index System, Washington, D.C. 20545.

I Patent. "Device for Effecting a Nuclear Chain Reac-
   tion." Chicago Operations Office, April 27, 1943.
   Draft of patent. "Basic Lattice Case." Univ. of Chicago,
   Metallurgical Labs, April 20, 1943.

Princeton University, Firestone Library, Princeton, New Jersey 08540.

LEO SZILARD

THE PAPERS OF ALBERT EINSTEIN (1879-1955). For details concerning the use of the collection, see description under Albert Einstein.

THE PAPERS OF ALBERT EINSTEIN(1879-1955). Angaben über den Zugang zu der Sammlung finden sich unter "Albert Einstein."

B1,2   Unknown amount of correspondence between Einstein and Szilard. 1926-1954.

I   File concerning opinions relating to patents about which Einstein was consulted.

Syracuse University, The George Arents Research Library, Syracuse, New York 13210.

MIKE WALLACE COLLECTION

F   Interview.

University of Missouri, Library, Western Historical Manuscript Collection/State Historical Society Manuscripts, Columbia, Missouri 65201.

L. J. STADLER PAPERS

B2   1 Tel. from Shipley. Pc.

New York Public Library, Manuscript Division, Fifth Avenue and 42nd Street, New York, N.Y. 10018.

EMERGENCY COMMITTEE IN AID OF DISPLACED FOREIGN SCHOLARS, 1933-1945

*   File compiled, no assistance given. 1933-1940.

University of Chicago, The Joseph Regenstein Library, 1100 East 57th Street, Chicago, Illinois 60637.

JAMES FRANCK PAPERS

B1,2   Correspondence with James Franck.

J   Group photo. Ninth Washington Conference on Theoreti-
       cal Physics. Washington, Oct. 31 - Nov. 2, 1946.

Prof. Eugene P. Wigner, 8 Ober Road, Princeton, New Jersey
08540.

B1,2   Correspondence between Wigner and Szilard.

EDWARD TELLER

Physicist, 1908-

Dr. Edward Teller, 943 Casanueva Place, Palo Alto, California 94302.

Private personal collection: at present inaccessible. Some of the materials have already been transferred to the Hoover Institution on War, Revolution and Peace and the Lawrence Livermore Laboratory.

Privatsammlung, z.Zt. noch unzugänglich. Einige der Materialien sind bereits weitergeleitet worden an die Hoover Institution on War, Revolution and Peace und an das Lawrence Livermore Laboratory.

B1,2 Correspondence, 1953-1976 (the years at Lawrence Livermore Laboratory), located at Livermore.

F   Tape recordings of Edward Teller.

J   Photos dating from the 1930s.

Lawrence Livermore Laboratory, P. O. Box 808, Livermore, California 94550.

Private collection of Dr. Edward Teller and the Lawrence Livermore Laboratory: inaccessible at the present time.

Privatsammlung von Dr. Edward Teller und dem Lawrence Livermore Laboratory, z.Zt. nicht zugänglich.

A3   Complete bibliography of Teller's writings.

B1,2 Correspondence from the years 1953-1976, including L. from: Hertha Sponer, Eugene Wigner, etc.

D8   Offprints and cl. of all of Teller's publications, including several from his years at Los Alamos.

F   Tape recordings of Edward Teller.

H3   Clippings. 1953-present.

I   Documents.

J   Photos over the course of many years.

866

EDWARD TELLER

M   Memorabilia: awards, etc.

Hoover Institution on War, Revolution and Peace, Stanford, California 94305.

EDWARD TELLER PAPERS: 7 Ms. boxes, 9 oversized boxes, 1 package of materials (1940-1975).

EDWARD TELLER PAPERS: 7 Manuskriptkartons, 9 übergroße Kartons, 1 Bündel Materialien von 1940 bis 1975.

B1,2   Correspondence.

C7,8   Articles, speech texts, reports, lectures.

D7,8   Collection of newspaper cl.
H3

F   Films.

J   Photos.

M   Honors received.

University of California San Diego, Mandeville Library, Department of Special Collections, La Jolla, California 92037.

MARIA GOEPPERT MAYER COLLECTION

B1,2   Ca. 130 L. to and from Maria Mayer. 1948-1953 and un-
        dated.

D8   3 articles by Teller.

Library of Congress, Manuscript Division, Independence Avenue and First Street S.E., Washington, D.C. 20540.

J. ROBERT OPPENHEIMER PAPERS, E. V. MURPHEE PAPERS, LAURENCE SPIVAK PAPERS

B1   15 L. to J. Robert Oppenheimer. 1942-1963 and undated.
        1 L. to Leo Szilard. T.c. 1945.

867

3 L. 1950.

B2 4 L. and 1 Tel. from J. Robert Oppenheimer. 1942-1963.
1 L. from E. V. Murphee. T.c. 1957.

B3 Several L. to Lawrence Spivak concerning Teller's TV
appearance on "Meet the Press." 1958, 1960, 1963.

C3 "There are mesons π, there are mesons μ..." Poem or
song by Teller. Undated. T.c. 1p.

University of Chicago, The Joseph Regenstein Library, 1100
East 57th Street, Chicago, Illinois 60637.

JAMES FRANCK PAPERS

A3 Untitled Ms. beginning with "One third of a century
ago I arrived in Göttingen as a quite newly-baked
physicist." T. 2p.

B1 L. of congratulations to Franck on his 70th birthday.
1952.

B1,2 Lengthy correspondence between James Franck and Edward
Teller. 1935-1957.
Correspondence with Robert Platzman concerning Platz-
man's edition of The Selected Papers of James Franck.

C8 "Migration and Photochemical Action of Excitation
Energy in Crystals." Written with James Franck.
Notes. A. 15p.

J Group photos:
Institute for Theoretical Physics. Copenhagen, 1935.
Ninth Washington Conference on Theoretical Physics.
Washington, Oct. 31 - Nov. 2, 1946.
Franck Memorial Symposium. Chicago, 1966. 3 photos.

American Institute of Physics, Niels Bohr Library, 335 East
45th Street, New York, N.Y. 10017.

F Tapes made by Stanley Blomberg in preparation for the
biography: Energy and Conflict: Life and Times of
Edward Teller.

EDWARD TELLER

University of California, Berkeley, The Bancroft Library,
Berkeley, California 94720.

E. O. LAWRENCE PAPERS

B1   24 L. and 3 Tel. to E. O. Lawrence. 1945-1958.
H3   Newspaper cl. 1957-1959.
I   3 memos. 1950, 1955, 1958.

Duke University, William R. Perkins Library, Manuscript
Department, Durham, North Carolina 27706.

FRITZ WOLFGANG LONDON PAPERS, WILLIAM PRESTON FEW PAPERS

B1   4 L. to Fritz London. 1934, 1938.
      1 L. ea. to William Preston Few and William Hane
      Wannemaker.
B2   1 L. from Fritz London. T.c. 1935.
      2 L. from William Preston Few. 1937.

U.S. Atomic Energy Commission, Division of Classification,
Data Index System, Washington, D.C. 20545.

A2   Technical notebook. Argonne National Laboratory, 1951.
B1,2 Correspondence. Argonne National Laboratory, 1951.

University of California, Santa Barbara, The Library, Santa
Barbara, California 93105.

F   "Three Revolutions in Physics." Part I, II. 2 tapes.

Columbia University, Butler Library, New York, N.Y. 10027.

ORAL HISTORY COLLECTION

G   Recollections of Edward Teller in an interview with
      Norman Ramsey. 1960.

EDWARD TELLER

<u>New York University</u>, Courant Institute of Mathematical Sciences, Library, 251 Mercer Street, New York, N.Y. 10012.

B1,2   2 files: "Edward Teller." 1952-1960.

<u>American Philosophical Society</u>, The Library, 105 South Fifth Street, Philadelphia, Pennsylvania 19106.

WARREN STURGIS MCCULLOCH PAPERS

B1,2   Correspondence with W. S. McCulloch.

<u>California Institute of Technology</u>, Robert A. Millikan Library, Pasadena, California 91109.

THEODORE VON KARMAN CORRESPONDENCE

B1,2   Correspondence between Edward and Mici Teller and
        Theodore von Karman. 1941-1962. 1 F.

<u>New York Public Library</u>, Manuscript Division, Fifth Avenue and 42nd Street New York, N.Y. 10018.

EMERGENCY COMMITTEE IN AID OF DISPLACED FOREIGN SCHOLARS, 1933-1945

*   File compiled, no assistance given. 1933-1939.

<u>Erikson Institute for Early Education</u>, 1525 East 53rd Street, Chicago, Illinois 60637.

Private collection of Gerhard and Maria Piers.

Privatsammlung von Gerhard und Maria Piers.

B1,2   Correspondence with Gerhard and Maria Piers.

<u>Smithsonian Institution</u>, Dibner Library, Washington, D.C. 20560.

MISCELLANEOUS COLLECTION

31   1 Ptc. Undated.

PAUL TILLICH

Theologian, 1886-1965

Harvard University, Harvard Divinity School, Andover-Harvard
Theological Library, 45 Francis Avenue, Cambridge, Massachusetts 02138.

The PAUL TILLICH COLLECTION was donated to the Andover-
Harvard Library by Mrs. Hannah Tillich, widow of Paul, in
1965. The collection consists of ca. 125 archive boxes of
materials as well as a personal library comprising approximately 25 shelf ft. The collection is open (mostly) to
scholars; permission to quote is required from the executor
of Tillich's estate, Mr. Robert C. Kimball, Starr King School
for Religious Leadership, 2441 Le Conte Avenue, Berkeley,
California 94709. Only 12 boxes are still restricted.

*Die PAUL TILLICH COLLECTION ist eine Schenkung an die
Andover-Harvard Library von Frau Hannah Tillich, der Witwe
Paul Tillichs, aus dem Jahre 1965. Die Sammlung besteht
etwa aus 125 Archivkartons Materialien sowie einer Privat-
bibliothek von etwa 7,50 m Umfang. Die Sammlung ist für
Forschungszwecke hauptsächlich zugänglich. Will man aus der
Sammlung zitieren, so ist die Erlaubnis des Testamentsvoll-
streckers dazu erforderlich: Mr. Robert C. Kimball, Starr
King School for Religious Leadership, 2441 Le Conte Avenue,
Berkeley, California 94709. Nur 12 Kartons der Sammlung
sind im Moment noch nicht zugänglich.*

A2   54 notebooks. English, unpub. Union Theological Semi-
      nary, 1930s. Including such subjects as: History
      of Philosophy, Philosophy of Existence, Philosophy
      of Religion, History of Theology, History of Dogma,
      The Doctrine of Man, Systematic Theology, Philoso-
      phy of History, Protestant Theology in the 19th
      Century.
      40 cloth binders containing notes. German, unpub. Ca.
      2,000p. Including such topics as: Christentum und
      Sozialismus, Persönlichkeit und Masse, Religion und
      Kultur, Religion und Erneuerung, Formkräfte der
      abendländischen Geistesgeschichte, die religiöse
      Erneuerung des Sozialismus, das Unbedingte und die
      Geschichte, Mythos und Metaphysik, die ökonomische
      Geschichtsauffassung, Hegel und die Erfassung des

Göttlichen, Rechtfertigung und Zweifel, Kirche und
Kultur, das Dämonische in Natur und Geschichte,
Zwang und Freiheit im sozialen Leben, der junge
Hegel und das Schicksal Deutschlands, Logos und
Mythos der Technik, die Geisteslage der Gegenwart,
die Idee in der Offenbarung, die Staatslehre Augu-
stins.
155 notebooks. German, unpub. 1905-. Various topics,
including: die deutsche Klassik, Schelling, Hegel,
Husserl, Metaphysik, Encyclopaedie, Apologetik, Dog-
matik, altes und neues Testament, Philosophie.

A3   "Timetables." Time plans for trips, lectures, etc.
Calendar p. from various years. 1955-.
Notes from a trip to Germany. A. 1948.
"Autobiographical Reflections." 1952. T.
Unpub. travel reports. English. 1960, 1964. A., T. and
mimeo. Includes:
"Informal Report on Lecture Trip to Japan." 114p.
"Report About my Trip to Israel." 41p.

B1   Ca. 700 L. 1936-1965, including L. to: T. W. Adorno,
Günther Anders, Hannah Arendt, Ernst Bloch, Julie
Braun-Vogelstein, Gerhard Colm, T. S. Eliot, John
Kenneth Galbraith, Manfred George, Eduard Heimann,
Max Horkheimer, Ernst Kantorowicz, R. M. W. Kempner,
Hermann Kesten, Henry Kissinger, Leo Lowenthal,
Adolf Lowe, Archibald MacLeish, Thomas Mann, Herbert
Marcuse, Sibyl Moholy-Nagy, Reinhold Niebuhr, Pastor
Martin Niemoeller, Norman Vincent Peale, Richard
Plant, Friedrich Pollock, Fritz Redlich, David Ries-
man, Eugen Rosenstock-Huessy, Hans Simons, Arnold
Wolfers, Kurt Wolff.
"Brief an das Kuratorium." A. 1910.
6 "Rundbriefe an Freunde." 1948-1951, 1962. Mimeo.
"Informationsblatt an Freunde." 1959. Mimeo.
10 open L. to "Friends." 1946-1964. A., T. and mimeo.

B1,2 Numerous additional L., primarily to and from various
institutions, publishers, universities, Christian
organizations, newspapers, students, etc. 21 archive
B.
"Recommendations." 1950s and 1960s. Ca. 500 items.
Correspondence between Tillich and Robert Kimball

(literary executor). T. and A. 1961-1962. Ca. 1 in.

B2   Ca. 2,000 L. to Tillich. 1943-1965, including L. from: T. W. Adorno, Günther Anders, Hannah Arendt, Ernst Bloch, Julie Braun-Vogelstein, Heinrich Bruening, T. S. Eliot, Erich Fromm, John Kenneth Galbraith, Manfred George, Walter Gropius, Eduard Heimann, Max Horkheimer, J. F. Kennedy, Hermann Kesten, Maria Ley-Piscator, Adolf Lowe, Leo Lowenthal, Karl Löwith, Archibald MacLeish, Thomas Mann, Siegfried Marck, Herbert Marcuse, Ludwig Marcuse, Margaret Mead, Reinhold Niebuhr, Norman Vincent Peale, Erwin Piscator, Friedrich Pollock, Werner Richter, David Riesman, Eugen Rosenstock-Huessy, Hans Sahl, Hans Speier, Kurt Wolff.
"Fragliche Korrespondenz." 1960s. Ca. 3 in.
"Fan letters." 1/2 B.

B3   Ca. 500 L. to and from Tillich's various secretaries, many on behalf of Tillich.
Ca. 400 L., including 143 condolence L. to Hannah Tillich.

C7   Unpub. lectures in English on the following topics:
Luther. Undated. A. 113p.
Humanities - Self Interpretation of Man. 1961-1962. A. 200p.
World religions. 1958-1964 and undated. A. 160p.
Theology. 1948-1963 and undated. A., T. and mimeo. 633p.
Symbolism. 1946, 1952, 1960-1961 and undated. A., T. and mimeo. 235p.
Society. 1955-1958 and undated. A. and T. 83p.
Religion and science. 1960-1964 and undated. A. 61p.
Religious socialism. Undated. A. and mimeo. 33p.
Religion and politics. 1938, 1953, 1964 and undated. A. 320p.
Religious resurgence. 1937, 1956-1957 and undated. A. and T. 129p.
Depth psychology. 1955-1958 and undated. A., T., mimeo. and cc. 275p.
Psychology of the self. 1957-1960 and undated. A. and T. 67p.
Protestantism. 1938, 1963 and undated. A. and T. 169p.

Politics. 1944-1946, 1962 and undated. A. 209p.
Religion and culture. 1959-1963 and undated. A. 95p.
Philosophy of religion. 1951, 1955-1957, 1960-1961
and undated. A., T. and cc. 83p.
Philosophy. 1954-1959 and undated. A. and T. 110p.
Individuality. Undated. A. and T. 43p.
Life. 1958-1962 and undated. A., T. and mimeo. 81p.
Judaism. 1955, 1959 and undated. A. and T. 47p.
The Interpretation of history. 1936-1938, 1956 and
undated. A. and T. 357p.
Germany. Undated. A. and T. 134p.
Existentialism. 1957-1963 and undated. A., T. and
mimeo. 207p.
Ethics. 1943, 1952-1964 and undated. A., T. and
mimeo. 284p.
Pedagogy. 1957-1961 and undated. A. and T. 122p.
"Doctrine of Man." 1935, 1956-1962 and undated. A.,
T. and mimeo. 652p.
Art. 1945-1965 and undated. A., T. and mimeo. 530p.
44 pub. lectures on various topics. 1940-1961. T., A.
and mimeo.
"Vorträge I." 16 lectures. 1922-1955:
1. "Vorträge vor 1933."
2. "Veröffentlichte Vorträge vor und nach 1933."
3. "Committee on Germany (1941-1945)."
"Vorträge II." 31 lectures. 1936-1961:
1. "Die Lehre vom Menschen."
2. "Geschichtsdeutung."
3. "Religionsphilosophie."
4. "Gesellschaft."
5. "Theologie."
"Vorlesungen vor 1933." 10 lectures:
1. "Seminare."
2. "Geschichtsphilosophische Vorlesungen."
3. "Hegel."
4. "Sozialpädagogische Vorlesungen."
5. "Begriff und Methode der Theodizee."
"Vorlesungen nach 1933." 55 lectures:
1. "Lehre vom Menschen."
2. "Existentialismus, Leben."
3. "Philosophie, Theologie."
4. "Geschichtsphilosophie, Religionsphilosophie."
5. "Amerika, Weltlage, Weltreligion."

"Philosophy and Theology." Inaugural speech. 1941.
Mimeo.
Wedding sermon for René and Mary Tillich. 1959. T.
with h. corr. 6p. plus 2 c.
2 sermons: "Lukas," "Jesaja." 1954, 1958.
6 addresses. 1930-1958. T. and A.
Sermons for weddings, deaths, christenings. English,
unpub. 1947-1964 and undated. A. 129p.
Discussions:
June 27, 1931. Participants: Blum, Brunner, Dibe-
lius, Frick, Horkheimer, Mannheim, Mennicke,
Pollock, Riezler, Schafft, von Soden, Tillich,
Adorno, Frl. Zarncke. T.
"Utopie und Eschatologie." Evangelische Akademie,
Berlin, June 5, 1961. T.
"Theologisch-systematischer Fragenkreis." Missions-
akademie der Universität Hamburg, 1961.
"Tillich-Kreis." Hofgeismar, 1961. T.
Cases. Hamburger Psychoanalytisches Institut.
"Bemerkungen zu Vernunft und Selbsterhaltung." Review
of book by Horkheimer. 1942. 9p.
Colloquia and seminars. English, unpub. 1965 and un-
dated. A. 129p.
Theology seminar notes. English, unpub. 1952. A. 45p.
Meetings. Notes, outlines. 1957-1960. A., T., cc.,
mimeo. 79p.
Discussions. Notes, outlines. 1956, 1960. A., mimeo.
and cc. 37p.
25 reviews and critiques, including discussions of
works by: Karl Barth, Reinhold Niebuhr, Jacques
Maritain, Arthur Koestler, Erich Fromm, Margaret
Mead, Karl Mannheim, Gustav Radbruch, Max Horkheimer, Hans Speier.
58 pub. articles, various themes. 1908-1963. T. and A.
8 unpub. articles. 1912-193-. T. and A.
Unpub. English essays. Undated. A., T., mimeo. and cc.
68p.
15 essays, various themes. Outlines, rough drafts.
[1940-1950]. T. and A. Ca. 100p.
Introduction to second volume of Gesammelte Werke.
1961-1962.
Introduction to The Protestant Era. 1957.
Short statements. English, unpub. 1955, 1960-1961. A.,

T. and cc. 15p.
13 original prayers. English, unpub. 1950-1954 and
  undated. T., A., mimeo., and cc. 17p.
12 short prose works: sermons, answers to articles,
  etc. 1940s-1960s.
Longer prose works:
Biblical Religion and the Search for Ultimate Real-
  ity. 1955. A.
The History of Christian Thought. 1968.
Perspectives in 19th and 20th Century Protestant
  Theology. 1967.
My Search for Absolutes. 1967.
The Future of Religions. 1966.
The Eternal Now. 1963.
The New Being. 1955.
Dynamics of Faith. 1957. A. 271p.
The Shaking of the Foundations. 1948.
Ultimate Concern. 1965.
Morality and Beyond. 1963.
Courage to Be. 1950-1952.
Love, Power and Justice. 1954.
Theology of Culture. 1959.
Religion und Weltpolitik. 1939.
Das System der religiösen Erkenntnis. Undated.
Systematic Theology. 3 volumes.
Christianity and the Encounter of the World Reli-
  gions. 1961-1962.
Der Begriff des Übernatürlichen, sein dialektischer
  Charakter und das Prinzip der Identität, darge-
  stellt an der supranaturalistischen Theologie von
  Schleiermacher. T. 1915.
Die christliche Gewißheit und der historische Jesus.
  Table of contents. A. 192-.

F Tape recordings of Tillich's class lectures:
   "Systematic Theology." 1955-1956. 22 reels.
   "Schelling and Hegel." 1958. 4 reels.
   "Protestant Theology in the Nineteenth and Twentieth
     Centuries." 1963. 8 reels.
   Tapes of Tillich's guest lectures, sermons, talks.
   1956-1965. 26 reels.

I Documents and materials from the Harvard Divinity
   School years: lecture announcements, ideas for

seminar papers, student lists, notices, lecture
plans, offprints, etc. 4 in.
"Finanzielles 1957/1958," "Finanzielles 1959/1960,"
"Finanzielles 1962/1963," "Finanzielles 1965/1966."
2 B.
5 recommendations written by Tillich for: Hannah
Arendt, Dr. Laurence Farmer, Erich Fromm, Elisabeth
Hellersberg, Winifred Saha.
Documents concerning Tillich's father.
Miscellaneous documentary materials. 1 F.

J   Photos of Tillich from World War I to his death. Also
several baby pictures.

K   Tillich's personal library. 25 ft.

M   Memorabilia: material for art lectures, honorary
degrees, Peace Prize, student notebooks, birthday
materials, World War I photo album, engraving, gifts
to Paul Tillich, etc.

Leo Baeck Institute, 129 East 73rd Street, New York, N.Y.
10021.

KURT GROSSMANN COLLECTION, JULIE BRAUN-VOGELSTEIN COLLECTION

B1   44 L. to Kurt Grossmann.

B1,2 Unknown amount of correspondence with Julie Braun-
Vogelstein.

Boston University, Mugar Memorial Library, 771 Commonwealth
Avenue, Boston, Massachusetts 02215.

EDGAR BRIGHTMAN PAPERS, MARTIN LUTHER KING PAPERS

B1   4 L. to Edgar Brightman. A. and T. 1935-1940.
1 L. to Martin Luther King. T. 1954.

C7   Lecture. Episcopal Theological School. T.

Syracuse University, The George Arents Research Library,

Syracuse, New York 13210.

DOROTHY THOMPSON PAPERS, HENRY KOERNER PAPERS

B1   3 L. to Dorothy Thompson. 1943-1945.

B2   1 L. from Dorothy Thompson. 1943.

C7   Questionnaire on Nazi Germany.

J   Time Magazine cover of Tillich, painted by Henry Koer-
      ner.

Southern Illinois University, Morris Library, Department of
Special Collections, Carbondale, Illinois 62901.

ERWIN PISCATOR PAPERS

B1   3 L. to Erwin Piscator. T. 1944.

B2   2 L. from Erwin Piscator. T.cc. 1939, 1965.

Joseph and Alice Maier, 991 Grace Terrace, Teaneck, New
Jersey 07666.

H5   Minutes of discussions between Paul Tillich, Max
      Horkheimer, A. Lowe and F. Pollock.

University of California, Santa Barbara, The Library, Santa
Barbara, California 93105.

F   7 tapes including:
      "Religion and Politics."
      "Religion and the Visual Arts."
      "Religion, Science and Philosophy."
      "Is Theology Obsolete?"
      "Meaning of Religion and Culture."

Yale University Library, Manuscripts and Archives Research
Room, 150 Sterling Memorial Library, New Haven, Connecticut
06520.

PAUL TILLICH

ARNOLD WOLFERS PAPERS

B1,2 Correspondence with Arnold Wolfers. 1923-1963.

Mrs. Elisabeth M. Stoerk and Mrs. Susanne B. Hoeller, 288
Ocean Drive West, Stamford, Connecticut 06902.

FRIDERIKE ZWEIG ARCHIVE

B1,2 Correspondence with Friderike Zweig re: Council for a
      Democratic Germany. June-July 1944.

University of Texas, Humanities Research Center, Manuscripts
Collection, Box 7219, Austin, Texas 78712.

B1   3 L.

Mr. Hans Sahl, 800 West End Avenue, New York, N.Y. 10025.

B1   Several L. to Hans Sahl.

Library of Congress, Manuscript Division, Independence Avenue
and First Street S.E., Washington, D.C. 20540.

BINGHAM R. NIEBUHR PAPERS, HANNAH ARENDT PAPERS

B1   1 L. to Reinhold Niebuhr. T. 1931.
B1,2 Correspondence with Hannah Arendt.

University of Illinois at Urbana-Champaign, University Library, University Archives, Room 19, Urbana, Illinois 61801.

C7   "Faith, Doubt and Our Intellectual Climate." Lecture.

American Philosophical Society, The Library, 105 South Fifth
Street, Philadelphia, Pennsylvania 19106.

PAUL TILLICH

FRANZ BOAS PAPERS

B1   1 L. to Franz Boas. 1934.

B2   1 L. from Franz Boas. 1940.

Yivo Institute, 1048 Fifth Avenue, New York, N.Y. 10028.

HORACE M. KALLEN PAPERS

B1,2   Individual items in folders: 237, 353, 863, 1021.

Prof. Adolf Lowe, 1125 Grand Concourse, The Bronx, New York 10452.

B1   Several L. to Adolf Lowe.

Columbia University, Butler Library, New York, N.Y. 10027.

B1   1 L. to Dorothy Norman. T. 1946.

New York Public Library, Manuscript Division, Fifth Avenue and 42nd Street, New York, N.Y. 10018.

EMERGENCY COMMITTEE IN AID OF DISPLACED FOREIGN SCHOLARS, 1933-1945

*   File compiled when assistance was granted. 1933-1944.

State University of New York at Albany, Department of Germanic Languages and Literatures, 1400 Washington Avenue, Albany, New York 12222.

CARL MISCH COLLECTION, KARL O. PAETEL COLLECTION

B1   1 L. to Carl Misch. T. 1959.

B2   1 L. from Karl O. Paetel (xerox). 1961.

PAUL TILLICH

Immigration History Research Center of the University of
Minnesota, 826 Berry Street, St. Paul, Minnesota 55101.

AMERICAN COUNCIL FOR EMIGRÉS IN THE PROFESSIONS ARCHIVES

B1   L. of recommendation for Karl Löwith. c.

Harvard University, Houghton Library, Cambridge, Massachusetts 02138.

RICHARD BEER-HOFMANN COLLECTION

B2   1 L. from Max Horkheimer. 1942.

Long Island Historical Society, 128 Pierrepont Street,
Brooklyn, New York 11201.

H3   1 pub. article.

Mrs. Liselotte Stein, 115-25 Metropolitan Avenue, Kew Gardens, New York 11418.

FRED STEIN PAPERS

J   Photos of Paul Tillich.

Mrs. Peter M. Lindt, 949 West End Avenue, New York, N.Y.
10025.

B1   Small amount of correspondence with Peter M. Lindt.

HANS TISCHLER

Musicologist, 1915-

Prof. Hans Tischler, 711 East First Street, Bloomington, Indiana 47401.

Materials of historical interest from Prof. Tischler's private collection will be donated to the State University of New York at Albany.

Materialien von historischem Interesse aus der Privatsammlung von Prof. Tischler werden der State University of New York at Albany zukommen.

A2 Lecture notes, studies.

A3 Records of professional and international meetings.
  Records of talks given (where and when).
  Bibliography.

B2 Correspondence from the 1950s-1970s. Ca. 350 L.,
  including L. from: Willi Apel, Gerhard Herz, E.
  Lowinsky, H. Nathan, C. Sachs, E. Werner.

C7 Vienna dissertation.
  Few Ms. to articles (late 1960s, 1970s).
  Ms. to current books.

C13 Unpub. musical compositions from Vienna days.

D7 Complete set of offprints. Ca. 7 in. (17.5 cm.)

I Citizenship papers, army papers, passports, diplomas,
  etc.

J Photos, early years to 1970s.

K Music library, mostly Mahler and medieval.

M Memorabilia.

O Programs to concerts, operas (from Vienna days).
  Programs to talks given.

Roosevelt University, The Library, 430 South Michigan Avenue, Chicago, Illinois 60605.

C7 Theory and its Application; a syllabus for the first

semester of integrated music study at Roosevelt College. Vorbereitet von H. Tischler und M. v. Silvius. 1949. c. 115p.
Works (5 Präludien; Fugen für 2 Flügel; Romanze für Horn und Klavier; Sechs Lieder). c. 64p.

Yivo Institute, 1048 Fifth Avenue, New York, N.Y. 10028.

HORACE M. KALLEN PAPERS

*   Miscellaneous item(s) in folder no. 1023. 1945.

ERNST TOCH

Composer, 1887-1964

<u>University of California, Los Angeles</u>, Music Library, 405
Hilgard Avenue, Los Angeles, California 90024.

The TOCH ARCHIVE, ca. 45 ft. of materials, is a result of
purchases as well as gifts from Lilly Toch, widow of Ernst,
in 1966 and in later years.

*Das TOCH ARCHIVE, etwa 13,50 m Materialien, ist sowohl aus
Käufen wie auch aus Schenkungen von Lilly Toch, der Witwe
Ernst Tochs, seit 1966 entstanden.*

A1   Appointment calendars. 1948+.

B1   Correspondence labeled "Toch to others," including
        many L. to conductors. 1960-1965. 3 B.

B1,2 Correspondence. 1906-1945. 10 B.
       Correspondence. 1945-1960s. 5 B.
       Correspondence. Undated. 1 B.
       Correspondence from the 1950s. Completely unsorted in
         cartons.
       Correspondence pertaining to the war years and emigra-
         tion.
       Miscellaneous unsorted correspondence.
       Correspondence between Gustav Stolper and Ernst Toch.
        Ca. 500 L. 1902-.

B2   Among the numerous L. are L. from: Alban Berg, Bertolt
        Brecht, Aaron Copland, Alfred Einstein, Karl Geirin-
        ger, Paul Hindemith, Ernst Kanitz, Otto Klemperer,
        Erich Korngold, Serge Koussevitzky, Ernst Křenek,
        Fritz Mahler, Thomas Mann, Hans Pfitzner, Artur
        Schnabel, Arnold Schoenberg, William Steinberg, Leo-
        pold Stokowski, George Szell, Bruno Walter, Kurt Weill.

B3   Correspondence between Lilly Toch and her mother.

C7   Lecture notes. Accompanied by notes of Toch's lectures
        by Ren Weschler, grandson of Toch.

C13a Original h. Ms. of compositions:
       "Bunte Suite for orchestra, op. 48."
       "Circus Overture."
       "3 Originalstücke für das elektrische Welte-Mignon-
        Klavier."

"Gesprochene Musik" (including "Fuge aus der Geo-
graphie").
"Kammersymphonie für zehn Soloinstrumente."
"Der Kinder Neujahrstraum."
"Klavierstücke, op. 78 (Diversions und Sonatinetta)."
"Kleine Overture." Fragment.
"Komödie für Orchestra." Fragment.
"Sonata for violin and piano, op. 44."
"Song of Myself."
"Spitzwegs Serenade, op. 25."
"Suite, the Idle Stroller."
"Valse for mixed speaking chorus."
2 untitled fragments.
Musical accompaniments to stage productions.
Musical accompaniments to films:
Ladies in Retirement.
Address Unknown.
None Shall Escape.
Musical accompaniments to radio plays.
Musical sketches. 1 F.
Miscellaneous music Ms. 2.5 ft.
Pc. of Toch compositions:
"An mein Vaterland; Symphonie für großes Orchester,
Orgel, Sopran-Solo und Chor. Klavier-Auszug und
Text."
"Begegnung."
"Big Ben. Variation phantasy on the Westminster
Chimes." Op. 62. 1934.
"Bunte Suite; für Orchester." Op. 48. 64 leaves.
["Burlesken"]. Op. 31. 1923. Microfilm.
"Cantata of the bitter herbs." Op. 65. [1938].
["Capriccet"]. "5 Klavierstücke, Capriccetti." Op. 36.
[1925]. 9 leaves.
["Concerto"]. "Klavierkonzert." Op. 38. 1926. 154
leaves.
["Concerto, violoncello and orchestra, op. 35"].
"Konzert für Violoncello und Kammerorchester." Op.
35. 1924. 150 leaves.
["Diversions, piano, op. 78a"]. "Manuskript der Kla-
vierstücke, incl. Sonatinetta." Op. 78. [1956].
8 leaves.
["Divertimenti, op. 37"]. "2 Divertimenti, op. 37,
Nr. 1 für Violine und Violoncell. Nr. 2 für

Violine und Bratsche." 1925. 19 leaves.
"Egon und Emile. Kein Familiendrama von Christian
Morgenstern." Op. 46. [1928]. 23 leaves. Another
version. 34 leaves.
"Epilogue." Ca. 1961. 12p.
"Der Fächer." [1930]. Text by Ferdinand Lion. 351
leaves. ["Der Fächer. Overture"]. "Ouvertüre zur
Oper 'Der Fächer'." [193-]. 17 leaves.
"Fanal, für gr. Orchester und Orgel." Op. 45. 1928.
32 leaves.
"Fünfmal zehn Etüden für Klavier; op. 55, 56, 57,
58, 59." [1931].
"Hyperion; a dramatic prelude." Op. 71. 1947. 70
leaves.
["In Spitzwegs Art"]. "Serenade für zwei Violinen und
Bratsche." [ca. 1917]. 16p. plus 3 parts.
"Intermezzo." [1960?]. 12 leaves.
["Jephta"]. "5th Symphony. Op. 89." [1963]. 48p.
["Kammersymphonie"]. "Chamber Symphony [for 10 solo
instruments] parts."
"Kleine Theater-Suite; op. 54." [1931]. 78 leaves.
"Kleinstadtbilder, op. 49 [Echoes from a small town.
14 leichte Stücke - 14 easy pieces]." Mannheim,
1929. 23 leaves.
"Komödie für Orchester [in einem Satz]. Op. 42."
1927. 66 leaves.
["Das letzte Märchen"]. "The last tale; opera in one
act. Libretto by Melchior Lengyel." Santa Monica,
Calif., Aug. 28, 1962. 173p. Another version. 61
leaves.
["Lieder, op. 41. No. 1, Der Abend"]. "Der Abend
(R. M. Rilke)." 1927. 3 leaves.
["Lieder, op. 41. No. 2, Heilige"]. "Heilige (R. M.
Rilke)." 1927. 3 leaves.
"Musik für Orchester und eine Baritonstimme [nach Wor-
ten von Rainer Maria Rilke]. Op. 60. [1932]. 24
leaves.
["Nocturne, orchestra"]. "Notturno [Op. 77]." 1953.
23 leaves. 2 c.
"Pastorale (Quintett für Flöte, Oboe, Klarinette,
Fagott u. Horn) aus der Musik in den 'Bacchantin-
nen' des Euripides." 12 leaves.
"Phantoms, op. 81." [1957]. 15 leaves.

["Pieces, wood-winds, 2 horns and percussion, op.
83"]. "Five pieces for wind instruments and percussion, op. 83." [1959]. 42 leaves.
["Pinocchio. Overture"]. "Pinocchio; a merry overture." 1935. 44 leaves.
"Die Prinzessin auf der Erbse. Op. 43." 1927. 77
leaves. Another version. 44 leaves.
"Punch and Judy." Incomplete. 1964. 5 leaves.
["Quartet, strings, no. 14"]. "Quartet no. 14, op.
89." [1964?]. 5 leaves.
["Quartet, strings, op. 15"]. "Streichquartett. G-
dur. Op. 15." [1905?]. 27 leaves.
["Quartet, strings, op. 28"]. "Streichquartett auf
den Namen 'Bass'." Op. 28. 1921 [1922]. 46 leaves.
Another version. [1931].
["Quartet, strings, op. 34"]. "Streichquartett, op.
34." [1924]. 41 leaves.
["Quartet, wood-winds and viola, op. 98"]. "Quartet
for oboe, clarinet, bassoon and viola. Op. 98."
[Santa Monica, 1964]. 7p.
"Short story." [Op. 82? 196?]. 8p.
["Sinfonietta, band, op. 97"]. "Symphonietta for
wind-instruments and percussion. Op. 97." [Santa
Monica, 1964]. 20p.
["Sonata, piano, 4 hands, op. 87"]. "Sonata for
piano, 4 hands." [1962]. 8 leaves.
["Sonata, violin and piano, op. 21"]. "Sonata for
violin and piano." 1912. 41p.
["Sonata, violin and piano, op. 44"]. "Sonate für
Violine und Klavier, op. 44." 1928. 31 leaves.
["Sonata, violoncello and piano"]. "Sonate für Cello
und Klavier, op. 50." Mannheim, 1929.
["Sonatinetta, flute, clarinet and bassoon, op. 84"].
"Sonatinetta, for flute, clarinet and bassoon."
[1959]. 9 leaves. 2c.
"Song of myself, from 'Leaves of Grass' by Walt Whit-
man, for mixed chorus a capella." [1961?]. 4 leaves.
"Stammbuchverse. Für Klavier zu 2 Händen. Op. 13."
[1905?]. 15 leaves.
["Stücke, orchestra, op. 33"]. "5 Stücke für Kammer-
orchester, op. 33." [1924]. 38 leaves.
["Stücke, piano, op. 32, no. 2-3"]. "Klavierstücke.
Aus op. 32, 'Remember,' The merry Billy Gral."

1924. 4 leaves.
["Symphony, no. 1, op. 72"]. "Erste Symphonie, op.
72." 1950. 182 leaves.
["Symphony, no. 2, op. 73"]. "Zweite Symphonie, op.
73." 1951. 154 leaves.
["Symphony, no. 4, op. 80"]. "Symphonie Nr. 4, op.
80." [ca. 1957]. 47p.
["Symphony, no. 6, op. 93"]. "Sixth Symphony." 1963.
42 leaves.
["Symphony, no. 7, op. 95."]. "Seventh Symphony, op.
95." [1964]. 49p.
["Symphony, piano and orchestra, op. 61"]. "Symphony
for piano and orchestra (2d piano concerto) Op.
61." [1932]. 148 leaves.
"Tanz- und Spielstücke, op. 40." [1927]. 24 leaves.
"Thema mit Variationen über 'Muss i denn zum Städle
hinaus'. Schwäbisches Volkslied." [1964]. 15
leaves.
"Three Pantomimes for Orchestra." Op. 92, 94. 1963-
1964.
"Vanity of vanities, all is vanity [op. 79]. Eccle-
siastes I." [1954].
["Das Wasser, op. 53"]. "Das Wasser, op. 53 [Kantate
nach Worten von Alfred Döblin für Tenor, Bariton,
Sprecher und Chor mit Instrumenten, Flöte, Trom-
pete, Violinen, Violoncelli, Kontrabaß und Schlagzeug. 1930]." 29 leaves.

C13b   Mozart, Wolfgang Amadeus. "Variationen über Unser dum-
mer Pöbel meint, piano, K. 455." Arrangement by Toch.
[1953]. 24 leaves. Pc. and microfilm.

D8   Melodielehre. Ein Beitrag zur Musiktheorie. Berlin:
M. Hesse [1923]. 182p.
The shaping forces in music. An inquiry into harmony,
melody, counterpoint, form. N.Y.: Criterion Music
Corp. [1948]. 245p.

D13a   7 scores, with annotations by Toch.
Ca. 175 scores, unannotated.

F   Ca. 40 tapes of performances of Toch compositions.
Tapes of Toch compositions, with Toch at piano:
"Ideas, op. 69. Kleinstadtbilder, op. 49."
"Quintet, piano and strings, op. 64."

G   Oral history interviews with Lilly Toch, 1971-1972.
20 separate interviews, including one with Ernst
Toch. 850p.

H3   Newspaper cl. 3 B.
3 publications of the Toch Archive concerning the
archive.

H4   Newspaper cl. Critiques, arranged by Opus no. 2 ft.

I   Nearly complete collection of Toch's contracts, passports, other documents.

J   Photos of Toch at University of California, Los Angeles, and at home.

K   Toch's private music library, including both books and
scores.

M   Death mask and other memorabilia.
Address books.
Diary of Lilly Toch's mother's escape from Europe,
notes from 1920s.
Paintings of Lilly Toch's family.

O   Toch programs. 1920-.

Library of Congress, Reference Department, Music Division,
Independence Avenue and First Street S.E., Washington, D.C.
20540.

C13a   "An mein Vaterland: Symphonie in drei Sätzen." 1912-
1913. A. 285p.
"Peter Pan: a fairy tale for orchestra in 3 parts."
Op. 76. 195-. 47 leaves.
"Quartet for Oboe, clarinet, bassoon and viola." Op.
98. 1964. A. pc. 7p.
"Quintet for piano, 2 vls, vla, cello." Op. 64. 1938.
A. 61p.
"Trio for violin, viola and cello." Op. 63. 1938. A.
38p.

University of Pennsylvania, The Charles Patterson Van Pelt
Library, Philadelphia, Pennsylvania 19104.

ERNST TOCH

ALMA MAHLER-WERFEL COLLECTION

B1   23 L. and 2 Ptc. to Alma Mahler-Werfel. 1948-1963.

Academy of Motion Picture Arts and Sciences, Margaret Herrick
Library, 9038 Melrose Avenue, Hollywood, California 90069.

H5   Several Toch biographies.
J   2 photos of Toch.
O   Programs of Toch performances.

Yivo Institute, 1048 Fifth Avenue, New York, N.Y. 10028.

HORACE M. KALLEN PAPERS

B1,2   Individual items in folders: 62, 65, 622-623, 841,
       864, 1023. 1933-1951.

Syracuse University, The George Arents Research Library,
Syracuse, New York 13210.

FRANZ WAXMAN PAPERS

B1   1 L. to Franz Waxman. 1960.

University of Southern California, Lion Feuchtwanger Memorial
Library, 520 Paseo Miramar, Pacific Palisades, California
90272.

B1   1 L. to Lion Feuchtwanger. 1947.

Metropolitan Opera Association, Inc., The Archives, Lincoln
Center Plaza, New York, N.Y. 10023.

H3   2 newspaper cl. 1962, 1965.

ERNST TOLLER

Dramatist, 1893-1939

Yale University Library, Manuscripts and Archives Research
Room, 150 Sterling Memorial Library, New Haven, Connecticut
06520.

The ERNST TOLLER COLLECTION consists of 8 archive boxes of
materials. After the death of Toller, the materials were
acquired by Sidney Kaufman, who with the aid of Dr. S. R.
Shapiro, New York, donated the materials to the Yale University Library. The collection was augmented in 1977 by the
purchase of about 150 German editions and translations of
Toller's works, as well as copies of secondary literature,
from Prof. John M. Spalek. Publication rights to all Toller
materials are held by Mr. Sidney Kaufman, Performance Guar-
antees, 100 West 57th Street, New York, N.Y. 10019.

*Die ERNST TOLLER COLLECTION umfaßt 8 Archivkartons. Nach
dem Tode Tollers wurden die Materialien von Sidney Kaufman
erworben, der sie durch Vermittlung von Dr. S. R. Shapiro
an die Yale University Library als Schenkung übergab. Die
Yale University Library hat im Jahre 1977 etwa 150 deutsche
Ausgaben sowie Übersetzungen der Werke Tollers und Sekundärliteratur von Prof. John M. Spalek käuflich erworben. Die
Publikationsrechte ruhen bei Sidney Kaufman.*

B1   53 L. 1935-1939, including L. to: Bennett Cerf, Sidney
        Kaufman, F. D. Roosevelt.

B2   Over 100 L. to Toller, the majority in reference to
        the Spanish Refugee action.

C2   Blind Man's Buff. Notes and sections of dialog, in
        English and German. A. 36p.
        Draw the Fires! An Historical Play. Texts consists of
        loose p. cut out of the volume Seven Plays, with
        numerous h. corr. Additional notes to production.
        20p. Score by Hanns Eisler. Second version. Ca. 1935.
        T. 80p. Third version. Ca. 1938. T. 76p.
        Nie wieder Friede! Komödie von Ernst Toller. Ca. 1936.
        German. T. with some corr. 62p.
        Pastor Hall. Schauspiel von Ernst Toller. Early ver-
        sion. German. T. 104p. Later German version. Copy-
        right 1938. T. 105p.

Pastor Hall. Play in Three Acts. Undated. T. and cc.
3c. 78p. ea. Another English version. Copyright
1938. T. 75p.

C4   "Art and Life (From My Notebook)." Aphorisms. Before
Sept. 1935. T. and cc. 2c. 6p. ea.
"Begegnung auf der Landstraße." Short story. Undated.
First version. T. with numerous corr. and cc. 7p.
ea. Second version. T. and cc. 3c. 5p. ea.
"Meeting on the Road." English version. T. 2c. 5p. ea.
"Begegnung in Barcelona." Short story. [Fall 1938]. T.
6p. Second version. T. with h. corr. and cc. 5p. ea.
Third version. T. and cc. 4c. 5p. ea.
"The fire squad. An episode of the German War." Short
story. [1936]. T. 5p.
"From My Notebook. Political Aphorisms." Undated. T.
and cc. 3p. Second version. T. 3p.
"Grabbed by the Tail." Short story. [Before Aug. 1935].
4c. T. and cc. 5p. ea.
"The Interrogatory." Short story. [Before Feb. 1936].
T. with corr. 2p. 2 other versions. T. 3p. ea.
"Marriage in Morocco." Short story. Undated. T. 7p.
Another version. T. 7p.
"Resurrected from Death." Short story. Undated. T. 2p.
"Der Tod einer Mutter." Short story. [1939]. T. with
corr. 5p. Second version. T. and cc. with corr. 4c.
5p. ea.
"The Death of a Mother." English version. T. and cc.
5p. ea.
"Tradition and Ideology: Incidents from Life." Sketch-
es. Undated. T. with corr. 2p. Second version. cc.
2c. 2p. ea.
"The Victor of Kertsch." Short story. Undated. T. and
cc. 4p. ea.
"You have all heard the story of 'The Appointment in
Samarra'..." Untitled short story. T. and A. 1p.

C5   Der Weg nach Indien. Das Epos vom Suezkanal. Ca. 1936.
A. and T. with numerous corr. 132p.

C7   Essays (some with several c. or different versions):
"Alea jacta est, sagt der alte Römer..."/"The Meaning
of the André Trial." 20p.
"Appell"/"Appeal." 18p.

"Carl vom Stein." 15p.
"Cultural Consequences of the Reichstag Fire." 8p.
"Extra." 2p.
"Flamencos." 4p.
"Forget Europe." 3p.
"Help for Starving in Spain. Ernst Toller Explains His
    Non-Partisan Plan. To the New York Herald Tribune."
    2p.
"I saw Hitler." 30p.
"Interview with the Swedish Kronprinz Gustav Adolf
    Ulriksdal." 10p.
"Kein Volk ist ein Volk von Engeln." 5p.
"Letter from Prison." 4p.
"Man and the Masses: The Problem of Peace." 50p.
"The Modern Writer and the Future of Europe." 30p.
"Prisoner's Letters to Children." 2p.
"Proposals." 10p.
"Results." 10p.
"The Sexual Life of Prisoners." 18p.
"Sind wir verantwortlich für unsere Zeit?" 52p.
"Spain waits for you." 18p.
"Spanische Arbeiter"/"The Spanish Laborer." 18p.
"Spanish Help Action. Memo by Ernst Toller." 13p.
"Syndicalism in Spain." 19p.
"Das Versagen des Pazifismus in Deutschland." 8p.
"Warning."
"Was denken junge Offiziere in Nazideutschland?" 8p.
"What means this liberty?" 18p.
"Whither are we going?"/"Where are we going?" 18p.
"Worldly Requiem. Choral Work." 19p.
15 untitled essays and fragments of essays. 162p.
Lectures and speeches (some with several c. or versions):
    "Aufruf zum Jahrestag der Revolution von 1918." 16p.
    "The Failure of Pacifism in Germany." 35p.
    "Intellectual Dishonesty." 14p.
    "Madrid—Washington." 14p.
    "Projet pour la conférence." 9p.
    "Radio Speech (auspices Anti-Nazi League) Sept. 16,
        1937." 13p.
    "Short Remarks on European Theatres." 11p.
    "Speech Made at Madison Square Garden November 21st,
        1938." 14p.

ERNST TOLLER

"Warnung an England." 10p.
"The Word. Opening Speech on the International Writ-
    ers Conference in London, June 19, 1936. London,
    Friends House." 6p.
"20. Jahrestag des Krieges." 10p.
14 untitled lectures and speeches. 174p.

H3   Ca. 90 newspaper cl. concerning Toller's role in the
      relief program for Spain.

H4   Ca. 100 cl. of reviews of Toller's plays, including:
      Draw the Fires!
      Blind Man's Buff.
      No More Peace!

J   Hoppla! wir leben. 6 photos of Leipzig, Altes Theater,
      production.
      No More Peace! 18 photos of different performances.
      25 individual photos of Toller.
      25 group photos of Toller and others.

L   Relief program for Spain. 1 F.
      Swiss newspaper cl. concerning a legal case.
      Art in the Third Reich. Cl. from American newspapers.

Yale University, Beinecke Rare Book and Manuscript Library,
New Haven, Connecticut 06520.

PALMER SCHREIBER COLLECTION, THEATER GUILD COLLECTION, HARRY
WEINBERGER COLLECTION

B1   34 L. and Ptc. 1919-1937, including L. to: Nichols
      Dudley, Theresa Helburn, Annemarie von Puttkammer,
      Harry Weinberger, Kurt Wolff and the Kurt Wolff
      Verlag.

B2   5 L. from Harry Weinberger. 1936-1937.

B3   Correspondence of Harry Weinberger, Toller's lawyer.
      11 L.

C12   Man and the Masses (Masse Mensch) in Seven Scenes by
      Ernst Toller. 2 prompt books. 112p., 88p.

I   Contract between Toller and his lawyer, Harry Weinber-
      ger. Dated Nov. 5, 1936. T. 1p.

ERNST TOLLER

J   Photo ptc.
      Masse Mensch. 11 photos of Theatre Guild production.

Prof. John M. Spalek, 23 Pheasant Lane, Delmar, New York
12054.

The following collection of Toller materials (mainly Xerox
copies) was assembled by Dr. Spalek primarily during the
course of his work on: Ernst Toller and His Critics. A Bibliography (Charlottesville: The University Press of Virginia,
1968; reprinted: New York: Haskell House, 1973). The collection has been augmented by additional materials since the
publication of the bibliography in 1968.

*Die folgende Sammlung von Toller-Materialien wurde von Dr.
Spalek zusammengestellt, während er an seinem Werk Ernst
Toller and His Critics. A Bibliography (Charlottesville: The
University Press of Virginia, 1968; nachgedruckt: New York:
Haskell House, 1973) arbeitete. Die Sammlung besteht zum
größten Teil aus Xeroxkopien und wird ständig erweitert.*

B1   20 L. and 2 Ptc. to Mirko Kus-Nikolayev (xerox). 1931-
        1936.
      6 L. to Grete Turnovsky-Pinner (xerox). 1918-1923.
      2 L. to Anne Cohn-Schönblum (xerox). 1939.

B2   15 L. from Mirko Kus-Nikolayev (xerox). 1931-1936.

B1,2 Collection of ca. 1,000p. (xerox) of the materials in
C7   the possession of Dr. Harold Hurwitz (Berlin): 2
      loose-leaf notebooks with correspondence (mainly to
      Toller); Justiz (T. with corr. by Toller. 147p.);
      drafts and T.c. of articles and autobiographical
      items.

B3   Collection of L. about Toller, mostly to John M. Spa-
      lek from: Kurt F. Adler, Josef Breitenbach, Tankred
      Dorst, Leonie Frank-Landsberg, Alfred Frankenstein,
      Christiane Grautoff-Toller, Ruth Hellberg, Hugh Hunt,
      Graham Hutton, Denis Johnston, Rudolf Jonas, Hermann
      Kesten, Ilse Klapper-Burroughs, F. H. Landshoff,
      Walter Mehring, Kitty Neumann, Martin Sobotker,
      Armin T. Wegner, Rebecca West.

C2 The Night Is Far Spent. Original title of Pastor Hall.
    T. 76p.

C3 "Das Buch der Berge und der Meere lesend." Poem. Tr.
    from the Chinese. A. 2p.

D3 Poems from newspapers and magazines, mostly xerox c.
    Ca. 60 poems in German and 35 tr. in 11 languages.

D4 Stories, excerpts from dramas. Newspaper and magazine
    cl., mostly xerox. Ca. 45 items in German, 40 tr. in
    11 languages.

D7 Essays, speeches, etc. Newspaper and magazine articles,
    mostly xerox. Ca. 200 items in German, 110 tr. in 12
    languages.
    Publications of provisional revolutionary central
    council of Bavaria, signed by Ernst Toller. April
    1919. Newspaper and magazine articles, mostly xerox.
    Ca. 25 items.

H1 20 books or dissertations on Toller and his works.

H2 Ca. 35 articles on Toller and the Bavarian Revolution.
    Ca. 120 articles on Toller in German, ca. 120 articles
    in 11 different languages. Mostly xerox c.

H3 Newspaper and magazine articles, mostly pc.:
    Ca. 180 articles, mostly German, on Toller and the
      Bavarian Revolution.
    Ca. 100 articles concerning Toller's Spanish Relief
      program.
    Biographical essays and obituaries. Ca. 300 in Ger-
      man, 175 in English, and 120 in 14 other languages.

H4 Reviews and critiques, mostly pc. of newspaper and
    magazine articles:
    Ausgewählte Schriften. 7 items.
    Bilder aus der großen französischen Revolution. 9
      items.
    Die blinde Göttin. Ca. 20 items.
    Blind Man's Buff. Ca. 50 items.
    Bourgeois bleibt Bourgeois. 7 items.
    Briefe aus dem Gefängnis. 11 items.
    Die deutsche Revolution. 1 item.
    Eine Jugend in Deutschland. 7 items.
    Der entfesselte Wotan. Ca. 65 items.
    Erwachen (Massenfestspiel). 5 items.

Feuer aus den Kesseln! Ca. 75 items.
Gedichte der Gefangenen. 5 items.
Hinkemann. Ca. 130 items in German, 30 items in Russian, 140 items in 11 other languages.
Hoppla, wir leben! Ca. 125 items in German, 50 items in French, 50 items in Russian, 50 items in 6 other languages.
Justiz. 11 items.
Krieg und Frieden. 5 items.
Die Maschinenstürmer. Ca. 40 items in German, 30 items in English, 25 items in 5 other languages.
Masse Mensch. Ca. 70 items in German, 200 items in English, and 70 items in 11 other languages.
Nationalsozialismus. 1 item.
No More Peace! Ca. 30 items.
Pastor Hall. Ca. 75 items, mostly in German or English.
Prosa, Briefe, Dramen, Gedichte. Ca. 40 items.
Quer Durch. 12 items in 4 languages.
Die Rache des verhöhnten Liebhabers. 18 items.
Das Schwalbenbuch. 16 items.
Seven Plays. 8 items in English.
Tag des Proletariats and Requiem den gemordeten Brüder. 8 items in German.
Vormorgen. 3 items in German.
Die Wandlung. Ca. 90 items.
Wunder in Amerika. 11 items.

J   Photo collection.

O   Posters and playbills.

Hoover Institution on War, Revolution and Peace, Stanford, California 94305.

HOOVER INSTITUTION MICROFILM COLLECTION: NSDAP-HAUPTARCHIV. The original materials are located at the Bundesarchiv in Koblenz, West Germany.

HOOVER INSTITUTION MICROFILM COLLECTION: NSDAP-HAUPTARCHIV. Die Originalmaterialien befinden sich im Bundesarchiv in Koblenz, BRD.

A3   Autobiographical statement by Toller made to the
      authorities after his arrest. Dated June 4, 1919.
      T. 13p.

B1   1 L. to Rechtsanwalt Dr. Apfel. T.cc. 1927.
      15 L. to Max Hölz. T.cc. 1927-1928.

B2   1 L. from Dr. Apfel. T. 1927.
      28 L. from Max Hölz. A. and T. 1926-1928.
      1 L. from Traute Hölz. T. 1928.

I   Receipt for RM 100.- for the Max Hölz Fund. Dated June
      13, 1927.
      Contract form to Toller's banker. Dated July 14, 1927.

Columbia University, Butler Library, New York, N.Y. 10027.

SPANISH REFUGEE COLLECTION, MARIA M. MELONEY COLLECTION

B1   17 L. 1934-1938, including 10 L. and 1 Ptc. to Maria
      Meloney.

B2   10 L. 1938.

B3   3 L. 1935-1938.

C7   "Spanish Help Action. Memo by Ernst Toller." T. 13p.
      "The Twentieth Anniversary of the War." T. with sev-
      eral h. corr. 13p.

Leo Baeck Institute, 129 East 73rd Street, New York, N.Y.
10021.

ERNST TOLLER PAPERS, 1917-1938 (Ms. 70-1614) - 46 items.
Other Toller materials may be found in the JOHANNA MEYER
COLLECTION and the KURT GROSSMANN COLLECTION.

ERNST TOLLER PAPERS, 1917-1938 (Ms. 70-1614) - 46 Nummern.
Andere Toller Materialien befinden sich in der JOHANNA MEYER
COLLECTION und in der KURT GROSSMANN COLLECTION.

B1,2 Correspondence with Fritz Joss. 1937-1938.
      Correspondence between Toller and Kurt Grossmann.
      1 L. from Toller to Joseph Roth. Undated.

H3   Article on literature in the 1920s. 1966.
        1 cl. by Ludwig Marcuse.
        Newspaper cl. Ca. 30p.

I   Pc. of police files on Toller. 1,038p.
        Warrant for arrest of Toller, with photo. 1919.

J   1 photo, framed.
        1 photo in photo album.
        1 drawing. 1917. pc.

O   Programs:
        Hinkemann. 1924.
        Hoppla! wir leben. 1927.

Harvard University, Houghton Library, Cambridge, Massachusetts 02138.

OSWALD GARRISON VILLARD PAPERS and general archive files.

B1   7 L. 1934-1937, including L. to: Horace Reynolds, Sir
        William Rothenstein, Oswald Garrison Villard.

B2   1 L. from Oswald Garrison Villard.

C6   Berlin, letzte Ausgabe. Hörspiel. Undated, ca. 1924-
        1927. Mimeo. 53p.

University of Texas, Humanities Research Center, Manuscripts Collection, Box 7219, Austin, Texas 78712.

HERMON OULD COLLECTION. Permission to use the materials must be obtained from Mr. David Carver, General Secretary of the International PEN-Club.

HERMON OULD COLLECTION. Erlaubnis, die Materialien zu benutzen, muß von Mr. David Carter, General Secretary of the International PEN-Club, eingeholt werden.

B1   10 L. and 2 Ptc. to Hermon Ould. T. and A. 1933-1936.
        2 L. 1933.

B2   15 L. from Hermon Ould. T.cc. 1933-1938.

B3   1 L. from Lotte Israel-Toller to Hermon Ould. T. 1932.

Indiana University, The University Libraries, The Lilly
Library, Bloomington, Indiana 47401.

LEWIS BROWNE MSS., UPTON BEALL SINCLAIR MSS.

B1   2 L. to Lewis Browne. 1937-1938.
      11 L. to Upton Sinclair. 1929-1937.
      "Offener Brief an Herrn Goebbels." Undated. T. 2p.
      1 Ptc. to Farrar & Rinehart. T. 1931.

U.S. General Services Administration, National Archives and
Records Service, Washington, D.C. 20408.

NA Microcopy No. T 84, Item No. EAP 116/125, Record Group
No. 242/1048, Roll No. 410, Frames 281-348.

I   Police files: Toller's high treason trial, 1919, and
      Toller's activities after 1933. H. notes by Toller,
      reports and cl. 67p.

Library of Congress, Manuscript Division, Independence Avenue
and First Street S.E., Washington, D.C. 20540.

H3   Ca. 100 newspaper and magazine cl. on Toller.

I   Files of Munich Polizeidirektion, No. 1997. 1 F.
      Police and case files. 1919. Includes witness state-
      ments, minutes, etc. Ca. 200p.

New York Public Library at Lincoln Center, Library and Museum
of the Performing Arts, 111 Amsterdam Avenue, New York, N.Y.
10023.

HALLIE FLANAGAN COLLECTION

C12   Man and the Masses. Prompter's script. T. with h. corr.
      Ca. 110p.

901

J   Masse Mensch. 25 photos of Theatre Guild production.
      No More Peace! 5 photos of Federal Theatre production,
        Roslyn, New York.

University of Cincinnati, University Libraries, Cincinnati,
Ohio 45221.

The Ms. was purchased by the library on Dec. 8, 1953.

C2   Bloody Laughter. Tr. of Hinkemann. Undated. T.cc. with
        h. corr. 108p.

University of California, Los Angeles, Department of Special
Collections, 120 Lawrence Clark Powell Library, Los Angeles,
California 90024.

The materials were donated to the library by Jerome D. Ross
in Dec. 1968.

*Diese Materialien sind eine Schenkung von Jerome D. Ross vom
Dez. 1968.*

B1   1 L. to Dr. Volkmar von Zühlsdorf.

C2   Pastor Hall. Early version. A. with numerous corr. 88p.
        Also 9p. with Toller's h. corr.

Mr. Sidney Kaufman, 14 Fairway Close, Forest Hills, New York
11375.

C5   Heavenly Sinner. Written together with Sidney Kaufman
        for Metro-Goldwyn-Mayer. Los Angeles, 1937. Never
        filmed.

Dr. Ralph Greenson, 902 Franklin Street, Santa Monica, California 90406.

B1   8 L. to Greenson. A. and T. 1937-1938.

ERNST TOLLER

<u>New York Public Library</u>, Manuscript Division, Fifth Avenue
and 42nd Street, New York, N.Y. 10018.

A3   <u>Look through the Bars (Letters from Prison)</u>. Proofs.

C7   "An appeal from the young workers of Germany. To the
      young people of all lands." 1918. T. pc. 4p.

<u>Southern Illinois University</u>, Morris Library, Department of
Special Collections, Carbondale, Illinois 62901.

ERWIN PISCATOR PAPERS

B1   3 L. to Erwin Piscator. A. and T. 1936-1937.

B2   4 L. from Erwin Piscator. T.cc. 1936-1937.

<u>Dr. Frank Borchardt</u>, German Department, Duke University,
Durham, North Carolina 27706.

HERMANN BORCHARDT PAPERS

E   Documents re: Borchardt's case against Ernst Toller in
      connection with the drama <u>Pastor Hall</u>. Also corres-
      pondence concerning the case, to and from Toller's
      lawyers.

<u>University of New Hampshire</u>, The Library, Department of Spe-
cial Collections, Durham, New Hampshire 03824.

OSKAR MARIA GRAF COLLECTION

C7   Speech. 2c. 4p. ea.

<u>University of Illinois at Urbana-Champaign</u>, University Li-
brary, University Archives, Room 19, Urbana, Illinois 61801.

H. G. WELLS COLLECTION

B1   3 L. to H. G. Wells. A. and T. 1933, 1938.

Princeton University, Firestone Library, Princeton, New Jersey 08540.

THE PAPERS OF ALBERT EINSTEIN (1879-1955). For details concerning the use of this collection, see description under Albert Einstein.

THE PAPERS OF ALBERT EINSTEIN (1879-1955). Angaben über den Zugang zu der Sammlung finden sich unter "Albert Einstein."

B1,2   Unknown amount of correspondence between Toller and Einstein.

Mr. William Denis Johnston, Head, Theater Department, Smith College, Northampton, Massachusetts 01060.

B1   3 L. to Denis Johnston. T. 1937.

Yivo Institute, 1048 Fifth Avenue, New York, N.Y. 10028.

HORACE M. KALLEN PAPERS

B2   1 L. from M. Weichert. Undated.

H3   1 cl.

J   Hinkemann. Photo of Maurice Schwartz as Hinkemann.

American Philosophical Society, The Library, 105 South Fifth Street, Philadelphia, Pennsylvania 19106.

FRANZ BOAS PAPERS

B1   1 L. to Franz Boas. 1938.

B2   1 L. from Franz Boas. 1938.

Mrs. Liselotte Stein, 115-25 Metropolitan Avenue, Kew Gardens, New York 11418.

ERNST TOLLER

FRED STEIN PAPERS

J   Photos of Ernst Toller.

University of Pennsylvania, The Charles Patterson Van Pelt
Library, Philadelphia; Pennsylvania 19104.

ALMA MAHLER-WERFEL COLLECTION

Bl   2 L. to Alma Mahler-Werfel. T. and cc. 1927.

Barthold Fles Literary Agency, 507 Fifth Avenue, New York,
N.Y. 10016.

Bl   1 L. to Barthold Fles. 1936.

LUDWIG ULLMANN

Writer, 1886-1959

Immigration History Research Center of the University of
Minnesota, 826 Berry Street, St. Paul, Minnesota 55101.

AMERICAN COUNCIL FOR EMIGRÉS IN THE PROFESSIONS ARCHIVES

A3 Questionnaires, curriculum vitae, progress reports. 9p.
  "Statement about the progress of my work." Sept. 5,
  1945. 2p.

B1 49 L. to Mrs. Henry Canby. 1944-1950.
  11 L. to Otto Zoff. 1948-1951.
  14 L.

B2 34 L. 1944-1951, 1958, including L. from: Mrs. Henry
  Canby, Else Staudinger, Otto Zoff.

B3 29 L. 1944-1951, 1958-1959, including L. to and from:
  Franz Horch, Ernst Lothar, Thomas Mann, Kurt Pinthus.
  4 L. from Irene Ullmann. 1948, 1958-1959.

C7 The Great History of the Theatre. Synopsis. 2 versions.
  3p., 2p. Notes. 5p.

H5 Unsigned statement about progress of Ullmann's work.

University of Texas, Humanities Research Center, Manuscripts
Collection, Box 7219, Austin, Texas 78712.

B1 17 L.
B2 22 L.

Mrs. Elisabeth M. Stoerk and Mrs. Susanne B. Hoeller, 288
Ocean Drive West, Stamford, Connecticut 06902.

FRIDERIKE ZWEIG ARCHIVE

B1 13 L. and 4 Ptc. to Friderike Zweig. 1943-1957.

H5 File on Ullmann in Friderike Zweig's Lives and Outlines files.

LUDWIG ULLMANN

<u>Southern Illinois University</u>, Morris Library, Department of
Special Collections, Carbondale, Illinois 62901.

ERWIN PISCATOR PAPERS

B1   11 L. to Erwin Piscator. A. and T. 1942-1951.
B2   6 L. from Erwin Piscator. T.cc. 1947-1948.

<u>University of California, Los Angeles</u>, Department of Special
Collections, 120 Lawrence Clark Powell Library, Los Angeles,
California 90024.

FRANZ WERFEL ARCHIVE

B1   8 L. to Franz Werfel. 1942-1945.

<u>University of California at Riverside</u>, Riverside, California
92502.

RAOUL AUERNHEIMER ARCHIVE

B1   1 L. to Raoul Auernheimer. 1946.

<u>Harvard University</u>, Houghton Library, Cambridge, Massachu-
setts 02138.

RICHARD BEER-HOFMANN COLLECTION

B1   3 L. to Richard Beer-Hofmann. 1943-1944.

<u>University of Pennsylvania</u>, The Charles Patterson Van Pelt
Library, Philadelphia, Pennsylvania 19104.

ALMA MAHLER-WERFEL COLLECTION

B1   8 L. to Alma Mahler-Werfel. T. 1942-1948.
C7   Notes. cc. 2p.

<u>New York Public Library</u>, Manuscript Division, Fifth Avenue
and 42nd Street, New York, N.Y. 10018.

EMERGENCY COMMITTEE IN AID OF DISPLACED FOREIGN SCHOLARS,
1933-1945

*   File compiled when assistance was granted. 1942-1944.

<u>Mrs. Peter M. Lindt</u>, 949 West End Avenue, New York, N.Y.
10025.

Bl   Small amount of correspondence with Peter M. Lindt.

FRITZ VON UNRUH

Writer, 1885-1970

A major collection of Unruh materials, consisting of numerous personal letters, as well as early manuscripts of Der nie verlor, has been retained by Unruh's brother, Kurt von Unruh, 8495 Roching/Opf., Postfach 86, West Germany. The remainder of Unruh's literary estate was deposited at the Deutsches Literaturarchiv, Marbach am Neckar, West Germany.

Der Hauptteil der Unruh-Materialien - zahlreiche persönliche Briefe sowie frühe Manuskripte von Der nie verlor - befinden sich noch im Besitz des Bruders, Kurt von Unruh, 8495 Roching/Opf., Postfach 86, BRD. Der übrige literarische Nachlaß befindet sich im Deutschen Literaturarchiv, Marbach am Neckar, BRD.

State University of New York at Albany, Department of Germanic Languages and Literatures, 1400 Washington Avenue, Albany, New York 12222.

STORM PUBLISHERS ARCHIVE

A3   Self portrait. T.

B1   85 L., Ptc. and 1 Tel. to Alexander Gode von Aesch.
     1945-1966.
     1 L. ea. to Johanna Gode and Bernard Jasmand.

B2   32 L. including L. from Robert L. Crowell, Alexander
     Gode von Aesch, George N. Shuster.

B3   Correspondence concerning a cocktail party in honor of
     Unruh.
     11 L. from and 1 L. to Friederike Unruh.
     Publisher's correspondence concerning The End is Not
     Yet. 63 L.

C1   The End is Not Yet. Prose fragments, foreword and
     chap. IV. T. 2c.

C2   Am offenen Meer. Drama von Fritz von Unruh. A. with
     many h. corr. 41p.
     Der nie verlor/The End is Not Yet. Various acts and
     scenes. T. with some h. corr. Ca. 500p. Prose version, partly dramatized. T. with some h. corr. Ca.

150p. Outline of acts and scenes. A. Ca. 30p. Prose
synopsis of drama. T. and cc. 2c. 56p. Drama version
in 8 scenes. T. with h. corr. 2c. 95p. ea.
Flora und die sieben Mondflieger. Ein Spiel von Fritz
von Unruh. T. with few h. corr. iii, 49p.
Untitled piece in 3 acts. T. 10p.
The Unknown Lover. Draft. A. Ca. 60p. Several newspaper cl. Heavily corrected version. A. and T. 125p.
Version in 3 acts. Cc. with h. corr. on nearly every
page. 127p.

C3   Poems, notes. A. and T. 10 items.

C7   "Friede auf Erden." T. 23p. Also English tr.
"Rede an die Deutschen." Essay. T. with many h. corr.
38p. Also English tr.
"Vorwort an den Leser." Incomplete. 11p.

H3   Newspaper and magazine cl. 12 items.

H4   The End is Not Yet. Cost estimates, tables, etc. Ca.
30 items. Advertising materials, some biographical
materials. Ca. 125 items.

Yale University, Beinecke Rare Book and Manuscript Library,
New Haven, Connecticut 06520.

KURT WOLFF ARCHIVE, EDMOND PAUKER COLLECTION

B1   89 L., 18 Ptc., 9 Tel. to the Kurt Wolff Verlag. 1916-
1929.

B2   Ca. 20 L. from the Kurt Wolff Verlag. 1916-1929.
L. to Unruh from: Maximilian Harden, Gerhart Hauptmann,
Felix Holländer, Erich Reiss.

B3   Correspondence between Friederike Ergas and the Kurt
Wolff Verlag. 28 L. (22 signed also by Unruh).
1 L. from Kurt Albrecht von Unruh to the Kurt Wolff
Verlag.
2 L. from unknown authors (also signed by Unruh).

I   Receipt signed by Unruh.
Financial records.
Phaea. Contracts between Edmond Pauker and Unruh.

J   2 newspaper photos of Unruh.

L   Invitation to first performance of Ein Geschlecht.
June 16, 1918.
List of theaters at which Ein Geschlecht and Platz
were performed.

N   Announcement of Unruh's Ein Geschlecht. A.

Mrs. Elisabeth M. Stoerk and Mrs. Susanne B. Hoeller, 288
Ocean Drive West, Stamford, Connecticut 06902.

FRIDERIKE ZWEIG ARCHIVE

31   1 L. and 4 Ptc. to Friderike Zweig. 1951-1952. Also
L. filed under "Writers Service Center."

33   2 L. from Friederike von Unruh to Friderike Zweig.
Undated, 1946.

35   "The Tragic Fate of Fritz von Unruh." Essay. T.

Southern Illinois University, Morris Library, Department of
Special Collections, Carbondale, Illinois 62901.

ERWIN PISCATOR PAPERS

31   13 L. to Erwin Piscator. A. and T. 1943-1963.

32   9 L. from Erwin Piscator. T.cc. 1943-1963.

C   The End is Not Yet. Adaptation of novel by Erwin Piscator. A. 9p. Also 1 p. by Unruh. A.

J   1 photo of Unruh.

Mrs. Gertrude Urzidil, 83-39 116th Street, Richmond Hill,
New York 11418.

JOHANNES URZIDIL COLLECTION

31   23 L., 4 Ptc. and 1 Tel. to Johannes Urzidil. 1947-
1967 and undated. T. and A.

B2   1 L. from Johannes Urzidil. T.cc. 1957.

State University of New York at Binghamton, Center for Modern Theater Research, Binghamton, New York 13901.

MAX REINHARDT ARCHIVE

D2   Original promptbooks:
      Offiziere.
      Phaea.

J   Geschlecht. 1 scene design, 2 sketches (photos). Berlin, 1918.
      Offiziere. 1911. 6 drawings for scenes.
      Napoleon. 2 photos of scene designs.
      Phaea. 3 photos. Berlin, 1930.

Syracuse University, The George Arents Research Library, Syracuse, New York 13210.

DOROTHY THOMPSON PAPERS

B1   28 L. to Dorothy Thompson. 1946-1960.

University of Pennsylvania, The Charles Patterson Van Pelt Library, Philadelphia, Pennsylvania 19104.

ALMA MAHLER-WERFEL COLLECTION

B1   24 L., 9 Ptc. and 2 Tel. to Alma Mahler-Werfel. 1919-1945 and undated.
      1 L. ea. to: Heinrich Bitsch and Kurt Wolff.

B2   Draft of a L. from Alma Mahler-Werfel.

Leo Baeck Institute, 129 East 73rd Street, New York, N.Y. 10021.

JULIUS BAB COLLECTION, KURT KERSTEN COLLECTION

B1   1 Ptc. to Julius Bab. 1944.
      6 L. and 3 Ptc. to Kurt Kersten. 1943-1969.

University of New Hampshire, The Library, Department of Special Collections, Durham, New Hampshire 03824.

OSKAR MARIA GRAF COLLECTION

B1   2 L. to O. M. Graf. 1949, 1955.
B2   1 L. from O. M. Graf. 1949.

Mr. Hans Sahl, 800 West End Avenue, New York, N.Y. 10025.

B1   Several L. to Hans Sahl.

Princeton University, Firestone Library, Princeton, New Jersey 08540.

THE PAPERS OF ALBERT EINSTEIN (1879-1955). For details concerning the use of this collection, see description under Albert Einstein.

THE PAPERS OF ALBERT EINSTEIN (1879-1955). Angaben über den Zugang zu der Sammlung finden sich unter "Albert Einstein."

B1,2 Unknown amount of correspondence between Einstein and Fritz von Unruh.

Harvard University, Houghton Library, Cambridge, Massachusetts 02138.

H4   Gerhard, Hans. "Gedanken zu Unruhs Drama Stürme." Gießen, 1929. T. 43p.

Dr. Gustave O. Arlt, 13220-C Admiralty Way, Marina del Rey, California 90291.

FRANZ WERFEL ARCHIVE

B1   1 L. to Franz Werfel. Undated.

Indiana University, The University Libraries, The Lilly
Library, Bloomington, Indiana 47401.

MAX EASTMAN MSS.

B3   1 L. from Re Soupault to Max Eastman concerning Unruh.
        1950.

Dr. Hans Speier, 167 Concord Avenue, Hartsdale, New York
10530.

B1   Several L. to Hans Speier.

Swarthmore College, Swarthmore, Pennsylvania 19081.

SWARTHMORE COLLEGE PEACE COLLECTION

D7   "Rede an die Deutschen."
        "Europa Erwache."

Dr. Marta Mierendorff, 8633 West Knoll Drive, Hollywood,
California 90069.

SAMMLUNG WALTER WICCLAIR, WALTER WICCLAIR PRODUCTIONS

B1   1 L. to Marta Mierendorff re: Stefan Zweig production.

Mrs. Peter M. Lindt, 949 West End Avenue, New York, N.Y.
10025.

B1   Small amount of correspondence with Peter M. Lindt.

C7   Ms. submitted to Lindt for use on his radio program.

JOHANNES URZIDIL

Writer, 1896-1970

Mrs. Gertrude Urzidil, 83-39 116th Street, Richmond Hill, New York 11418.

JOHANNES URZIDIL COLLECTION.: Mrs. Gertrude Urzidil, widow of Johannes, still retains the largest single collection of materials by and about her late husband in her home in New York City. The nearly 30 ft. of materials, located in her apartment, were collected by the author and his wife, primarily since their arrival in the United States in 1941. The collection remains in its original order with no attempt having been made to sort or index the materials until the time of this report. The literary estate of Johannes Urzidil will eventually be deposited at the Leo Baeck Institute.

JOHANNES URZIDIL COLLECTION: Frau Gertrude Urzidil, die Witwe des Schriftstellers, befindet sich noch im Besitz der größten Sammlung von Materialien von und über ihren verstorbenen Mann. Die etwa 9 m Materialien in ihrer Wohnung wurden von Johannes Urzidil und seiner Frau zur Hauptsache seit ihrer Ankunft in den Vereinigten Staaten im Jahre 1941 zusammengetragen. Die Materialien befinden sich noch in ihrer ursprünglichen Anordnung, und 1977 existierte noch kein Index. Der literarische Nachlaß von Johannes Urzidil soll später einmal an das Leo Baeck Institute gehen.

A1   Diaries, calendars, notes on works. 1939-1969.

A2   Musenalmanach 1911. Notebook with drawings, short entries, on literary topics. Ca. 50p.

A3   "Briefe von Petr Bezruc." 1963. 4p. "Autobiographien." Outline. 4p.

B1   459 L. (mostly c.), 1929-1969, among them L. to: Ilse Blumenthal-Weiss, Heinrich Böll, Max Brod, René Fülöp-Miller, Claire Goll, Iwan Goll, Hermann Kasack, Otto Klemperer, Hans Kohn, Joachim Maass, Heinz Politzer, Peter Suhrkamp, Dorothy Thompson, Fritz von Unruh, Jean Starr Untermeyer, Theodor Ziolkowski, Carl Zuckmayer, Friderike Zweig. "Literarische Korrespondenz mit Einzelpersonen." 15 in. "Redaktionen von Zeitschriften und Zeitungen." 10 in. "U.S. offizielle Stellen." 1 in.

"Verlagskorrespondenz." (Artemis, Merkur, etc.). 15 in.

"Verschiedene Institute mit literarischen Interessen." 10 in.

"Vorträge, öffentliche und Radiosendungen in U.S.A. und Europa." 10 in.

B2   2,746 L., 1926-1929, among them L. from: Raoul Auernheimer, Julius Bab, Arnold Bergstrasser, Ilse Blumenthal-Weiss, Hermann Broch, Philipp Frank, René Fülöp-Miller, Manfred George, Claire Goll, Iwan Goll, Erich von Kahler, Mascha Kaleko, Ossip Kalenter, Otto Kallir, R. M. W. Kempner, Hermann Kesten, Otto Klemperer, Hans Kohn, Otto Loewi, Joachim Maass, Thomas Mann, Walter Mehring, Karl O. Paetel, Jacob Picard, Kurt Pinthus, Heinz Politzer, Alexander Roda Roda, Max Roden, Albrecht Schaeffer, Anna Seghers, Friedrich Torberg, Fritz von Unruh, Ernst Waldinger, Alma Mahler-Werfel, Franz Werfel, Max Wertheimer, Kurt Wolff, Otto Zoff, Carl Zuckmayer, Friderike Zweig.

Congratulatory L. on receiving "Literaturpreis der Stadt Köln" and "Der große österreichische Preis für Literatur." 8 in.

"Kollegen, Künstler, Gelehrte. 1966." Birthday greetings.

"Freunde, Verwandte, Publikum. 1966." Birthday greetings.

"Offizielle. 1966." Birthday greetings.

"Zum 50. Geburtstag." Birthday greetings and newspaper cl.

"Zum 55. Geburtstag." Birthday greetings and cl.

"Zum 60. Geburtstag." Birthday greetings and cl.

B3   14 L., 1951-1971.

C1   Das Gold von Caramblu. Original and 2 c., ea. 80p.

C2   Untitled dramatic sketch, 1912/1913. 6p.

C3   Untitled poem, written as answer to L. from G. Schneider.

"Gegengedicht," for E. Waldinger. 1966. 2c.

"Zurückgestellt." Individual poems. Ca. 50p.

Poems, undated (mostly c.). Ca. 50p.

C4 "Bemerkungen," to missing text. 1967. 9p.
"Bist du es, Ronald?" Stories. 1967. Ca. 220p. (c.)
Outlines. 1967. Ca. 75p.
"Die Entführung und sieben andere Ereignisse." Undated.
225p. (c.)
"Die erbeuteten Frauen. Dramatische Geschichten. Ar-
chiv Leseexemplar." 1964-1965. 6 short Ms. 188p.
(c.)
"Grenzland. Eine Erzählung." 1954. 30p. (c.)
"Johannes Urzidil erzählt von der großen Finsternis zu
New York." 2c., ea. 22p.
"Stief und Halb. Eine Erzählung." 1955. 24p. (c.)

C7 28 Ms. (ca. 450p. plus cc.), on the following topics:
"Der Altar von Kefermarkt."
"Aus Italien."
"Autographen."
"Bildende Kunst."
"Brot und Wein."
"Defoe oder die Inselwelt der Träume."
"Der Dichter als Träger der Verantwortung."
"Einfall und Planung im literarischen Schaffen."
"Giottos Räume."
"Kritik der Kritik der Kritik."
"Literarische Reise durch Massachusetts."
"Michelangelos Fragmentarismus."
"Nicholas Vachel Lindsay, der Dichter aus Spring-
field, Illinois."
"Sisyphos war ein Junggeselle."
"Zentral Park."
"Leben mit Diplomaten", etc.
"Manuskripte politischer Artikel geschrieben in Amerika
ab März 1941." 1941-1945. Ca. 500p.
Essays on individuals (mostly authors):
Bryher McPherson. 19p.
Franz Kafka. 200p.
Heinz Risse. 21p.
Franz Werfel. 118p.
F. Thieberger. 46p.
Max Brod. 32p.
H. D. Thoreau. 62p.
Walt Whitman. 27p.
Vincent van Gogh. 21p.

Adalbert Stifter. 83p. plus notes.
Essays, book reviews, speeches. Ca. 350p. plus c.
"Akzeptionsrede anläßlich der Verleihung des großen
österreichischen Staatspreises für Literatur." 1964.
13p. (c.)
"Frühe Prosa." 7 short texts. Ca. 40p. (c.)
"Essays, Projekte." Undated. Ca. 30p. (c.), including:
"Die Sprache im Exil."
"Die Kunst des Übersetzens."

C8   Katalog der 1220 Werke des Wencelaus Hollar mit Addenda. Undated. Ca. 40p. (c.)

C9   Avon. Urzidil's tr. of the book by H. D., with the comment "geschrieben 1949-50." 116p. (c.)

C11   Da geht Kafka. "Archivexemplar." Ms. with additions for the DTV edition, 1961-1965. Ca. 100p.
Prag. Geist und Größe einer europäischen Hauptstadt. "Archivexemplar." 1965. 34p. (c.)

D7   "Hermann Broch." Probably a radio script. 1951. 2p.

G   Interview with Jean Starr Untermeyer, taken by Urzidil. 1957.

H5   Death notices. 8 in.

I   Invitations, newspaper reports, plans for European trips. 5 in.
List of materials that Urzidil donated to Leo Baeck Institute (Kafka letters, etc.).
Publishers' contracts, insurance papers, family and ancestral documents, tax records, receipts, honors, etc.

J   6 photo albums, plus 1 envelope of negatives.

K   Periodicals in Urzidil's library (most containing articles by Urzidil):
Czechoslovak London. 1940-1944.
The Central European Observer. 1940-1945.
OBZOR London. 1941-1944.

L   "Goethes Bibliothek." Card catalog assembled by Urzidil.
"Goethes Bibliographie." Card catalog assembled by Urzidil.
"Eigene Bemerkungen." Card catalog arranged by topics.

918

"Über Amerika." Card file.

"Zitate." Card file.

"Publikationsstatistiken." Card file.

"Eigene Werke." Card file.

"RARA-Bücher, Bilder Kunstobjekte." Card file.

"Geschenk-Exemplare." Card file.

"Dorothy Thompson." Newspaper cl., Christmas greetings.

"Petr Bezruc." Newspaper cl., stamps, 1 essay by Urzidil.

"Friedrich Thieberger." Newspaper cl., 20 L. of condolence.

"Henry David Thoreau." 30p.

"Die verlorene Geliebte." Cl. of interviews, reviews, some L. containing references. 1 B.

"Goethe Material. Studienmaterial zu Wilhelm Meisters Theatralische Sendung 1915/1916. Darin eigene Texte." 4 in.

"Kafka Material Sammlung." Cl., bibliographica, geographica, books and literature about Kafka, Kafka editions, Kafka/Felice, lectures on Kafka. 12 in.

"Italienische Kunst." Cl. 2 ft.

M   Graphics: drawings, lithographs, etc. 1 portfolio, probably received by Urzidil as a gift.

N   5 poems by Carl Zuckmayer. 1946.

1 poem by Rudolf Henz. Undated.

1 poem by Rudolf Kallir. 1957.

Kahler, Erich von. List of publications (German and English); 1 autobiographical comment (ca. 1968); "Besondere Freundschaften, Beziehungen."

2 poems by Ernst Waldinger.

1 essay by Franz Werfel: "Erinnerung an Karl Brand." 7p.

6 poems by Otto Pick.

1 essay by Jean Starr Untermeyer concerning her friendship with Hermann Broch. 1957. 9p.

Poems by Jean Starr Untermeyer. 9p.

10 poems by Hermann Kasack.

4 poems by Hermann Hesse.

Essay by Heinz Risse: "Ironischer Mythenbewahrer." 1951. 4p.

Essay by Hans Erich Nossack: "Der Tagesspiegel, Weihnachtsbeilage 1958." 2p.

JOHANNES URZIDIL

Essay by Bryher McPherson, a report about a Christmas
visit from Hermann Hesse, 1955.
33 poems by Christine Busta. 1960-1969.

Mrs. Elisabeth M. Stoerk and Mrs. Susanne B. Hoeller, 288
Ocean Drive West, Stamford, Connecticut 06902.

FRIDERIKE ZWEIG ARCHIVE

B1   76 L. 1944-1964, among them 75 to Friderike Zweig.

B3   7 L. 1966-1967, among them 2 L. from Gertrude Urzidil
      to Friderike Zweig.

C7   "An American Poetess and a Viennese Lady-writer remem-
      ber literary creators in the USA and in Europe. (The
      autobiographies of Jean Starr Untermeyer and Fri-
      derike Zweig)." 6p.
      "Goethe the Modern. 12 lectures by Johannes Urzidil."
      3p.
      "International Universities." 6p.

D7   Contributions in books and magazines. 13 items.

G   "A visit with Friderike Zweig. (A broadcast prepared
      on October 26, 1955, by the Austrian Service of the
      Voice of America)." 5p.

H5   1 F. in the files Lives and Outlines, assembled by
      Friderike Zweig.

Leo Baeck Institute, 129 East 73rd Street, New York, N.Y.
10021.

Most items catalogued under the call number AR 2319.

Die meisten Nummern finden sich unter der Signatur AR 2319.

A3   Curriculum vitae. 1p.

B1   L. to Manfred George. 1955.

B2   Ptc. from Franz Kafka. 1922.

C7   "Prag als geistiger Ausgangspunkt." 1965. 16p.

H3   3 newspaper cl. 1964, 1970, 1971.

H4   Entführung. 1 review.
      Bist du es, Ronald? 1 review.

I   Library of Congress catalog card (pc.).
      Death notice. 1970.
      Announcement, lecture and symposium, Texas Technical
         University, 1971.

J   2 photos of Urzidil. 1966 and undated.
      1 photo of Gertrude Urzidil.

Immigration History Research Center of the University of
Minnesota, 826 Berry Street, St. Paul, Minnesota 55101.

AMERICAN COUNCIL FOR EMIGRÉS IN THE PROFESSIONS ARCHIVES

A3   Questionnaire and short biography. 4p.

B1   Canby, Mrs. Henry. 4 L. 1944-1948.
      Wilkinson, Miss. 3 L. 1944.

B2   13 L. 1944-1949, among them 2 L. from Otto Zoff.

B3   22 L. 1944-1948, among them 3 L. from Otto Zoff.

C1   The Strangers. Outline. 2p. Synopsis. 2p. Also 2 short
         synopses (German and English tr.). 1p. ea.

C11   Der Trauermantel [Life of Adalbert Stifter]. Synopsis.
         1p.

H4   Nichtenhauser, D. Review of Urzidil's "Die Sprache im
         Exil." 1p.

Syracuse University, The George Arents Research Library,
Syracuse, New York 13210.

DOROTHY THOMPSON PAPERS

B1   37 L. to Dorothy Thompson. 1949-1960.

B2   2 L. from Dorothy Thompson. 1951, 1960.

B3   1 L. by Dorothy Thompson re: Johannes Urzidil. 1951.

C7   "Brot und Wein." T.cc.
      "Maxim Kopf's Prager Years." T.cc.
      "Polchau - Stenbock - Fermor." T.cc.

Mr. Hans Sahl, 800 West End Avenue, New York, N.Y. 10025.

B1   Many L. from Urzidil to Sahl. Unsorted and uncata-
         logued.

State University of New York at Albany, Department of Germanic Languages and Literatures, 1400 Washington Avenue,
Albany, New York 12222.

KARL O. PAETEL COLLECTION

B1   20 L. to Karl O. Paetel (xerox). 1946-1966.

University of Pennsylvania, The Charles Patterson Van Pelt
Library, Philadelphia, Pennsylvania 19104.

ALMA MAHLER-WERFEL COLLECTION

B1   4 L. to Alma Mahler-Werfel. 1941-1942.

New York Public Library, Manuscript Division, Fifth Avenue
and 42nd Street, New York, N.Y. 10018.

EMERGENCY COMMITTEE IN AID OF DISPLACED FOREIGN SCHOLARS,
1933-1945

*   File compiled, no assistance given. 1944.

Dr. Gustave O. Arlt, 13220-C Admiralty Way, Marina del Rey,
California 90291.

FRANZ WERFEL ARCHIVE

B1   2 L. to Franz Werfel. 1942, 1945.

922

Library of Congress, Manuscript Division, Independence Avenue and First Street S.E., Washington, D.C. 20540.

BENJAMIN W. HUEBSCH PAPERS

B2   1 L. from Benjamin W. Huebsch. c. 1960.

Mrs. Peter M. Lindt, 949 West End Avenue, New York, N.Y. 10025.

B1   Small amount of correspondence with Peter M. Lindt.

ALFRED VAGTS

Historian, 1892-

Prof. Alfred Vagts, Sherman, Connecticut 06784.

Private collection. / *Privatsammlung.*

A1   Diaries, 1934 to present. Microfilm c. at the Bundes-
      archiv in Koblenz.

A3   Memoirs (presently being compiled).

B1,2 Large amount of correspondence, including L. from:
      Karl Brandt, Fritz Epstein, Felix Gilbert, Hajo
      Holborn, Emil Lederer, Fritz Redlich, etc.

M   Memorabilia.

Leo Baeck Institute, 129 East 73rd Street, New York, N.Y.
10021.

Alfred Vagts materials are found in the following collec-
tions: EFRAIM FRISCH COLLECTION, THOMAS MANN COLLECTION,
AROLSEN MARC FAMILIE COLLECTION, ALBRECHT MENDELSSOHN-
BARTHOLDY COLLECTION, MARTIN SOMMERFELD COLLECTION, WARBURG
FAMILIE COLLECTION.

*Alfred Vagts Materialien finden sich in den folgenden Samm-
lungen: EFRAIM FRISCH COLLECTION, THOMAS MANN COLLECTION,
AROLSEN MARC FAMILIE COLLECTION, ALBRECHT MENDELSSOHN-
BARTHOLDY COLLECTION, MARTIN SOMMERFELD COLLECTION, WARBURG
FAMILIE COLLECTION.*

A1   Diary sketch. 3. Jan. 1934 - 6. Okt. 1934. 2p.

B1,2 Ca. 100 L., including correspondence with: Martin and
      Lela Sommerfeld, Albrecht Mendelssohn-Bartholdy,
      Felix Gilbert, Senator Georg Bortscheller, Leo Baeck
      Institute, etc.

C7   "Bericht über Martin Sommerfeld." 1966. T.cc. 4p.
      "Erinnerung an Albrecht Mendelssohn-Bartholdy." 1968.
        T. with h. corr. 43p. Also notes. Undated. 41p.
      "Die Familie Marc und der Durchbruch zur Malerei."
        T. 14p.
      "Über Th. Manns Artikel 'Zur jüdischen Frage'."

ALFRED VAGTS

Undated. T. 5p.
"Erinnerung an den Neuen Merkur." 2 versions. Undated
and 1967. T. 3p. ea.
"Zur Geschichte des Neuen Merkurs." 1967. T. 1p.

State University of New York at Albany, Department of Germanic Languages and Literatures, 1400 Washington Avenue,
Albany, New York 12222.

KARL O. PAETEL COLLECTION

B1   8 L. to Karl O. Paetel (xerox). 1947-1948.

Harvard University, Baker Library, Graduate School of Business, Soldiers Field, Boston, Massachusetts 02163.

FRITZ REDLICH COLLECTION

B2   2 L. from Fritz Redlich. 1969-1970.

Harvard University, Houghton Library, Cambridge, Massachusetts 02138.

OSWALD GARRISON VILLARD PAPERS

B2   2 L. from O. G. Villard. 1944.

New York Public Library, Manuscript Division, Fifth Avenue
and 42nd Street, New York, N.Y. 10018.

EMERGENCY COMMITTEE IN AID OF DISPLACED FOREIGN SCHOLARS,
1933-1945

*   File compiled, no assistance given. 1942.

VEIT VALENTIN

Historian, 1885-1947

Leo Baeck Institute, 129 East 73rd Street, New York, N.Y.
10021.

KURT KERSTEN COLLECTION, KURT GROSSMANN COLLECTION and general archive files.

KURT KERSTEN COLLECTION, KURT GROSSMANN COLLECTION und allgemeine Archivakten.

B1   1 L. to Kurt Kersten. 1946.

B1,2   Correspondence with Kurt Grossmann.

C11   Edward Lasker or The Tragedy of German Liberalism. T.
       568p. plus table of contents.

H3   1 cl.

Harvard University, Houghton Library, Cambridge, Massachusetts 02138.

OSWALD GARRISON VILLARD PAPERS

B1   9 L. to O. G. Villard. 1943.

B2   5 L. from O. G. Villard. 1943.

Immigration History Research Center of the University of Minnesota, 826 Berry Street, St. Paul, Minnesota 55101.

AMERICAN COUNCIL FOR EMIGRÉS IN THE PROFESSIONS ARCHIVES

A3   Curriculum vitae, biography. 12p.

B3   12 L. 1939-1940.

University of Texas, Humanities Research Center, Manuscripts Collection, Box 7219, Austin, Texas 78712.

B1   4 L.

B2   20 L.

<u>Columbia University</u>, Butler Library, New York, N.Y. 10027.

B1   2 L. to N. M. Butler. [1940-1941].

B2   2 L. from N. M. Butler. T.cc. 1939.

<u>Mrs. Elisabeth M. Stoerk and Mrs. Susanne B. Hoeller</u>, 288
Ocean Drive West, Stamford, Connecticut 06902.

FRIDERIKE ZWEIG ARCHIVE

B1   Several L. to Friderike Zweig, filed under Writers
      Service Center. 1943.

<u>New York Public Library</u>, Manuscript Division, Fifth Avenue
and 42nd Street, New York, N.Y. 10018.

EMERGENCY COMMITTEE IN AID OF DISPLACED FOREIGN SCHOLARS,
1933-1945

*   File compiled when assistance was granted. 1933-1944.

<u>University of Pennsylvania</u>, The Charles Patterson Van Pelt
Library, Philadelphia, Pennsylvania 19104.

ALMA MAHLER-WERFEL COLLECTION

B1   1 L. to Alma Mahler-Werfel. 1940.

<u>State University of New York at Albany</u>, Department of Ger-
manic Languages and Literatures, 1400 Washington Avenue,
Albany, New York 12222.

CARL MISCH PAPERS

H5   Misch, Carl. "Veit Valentin." Speech for memorial
      celebration in New York. Feb. 28, 1947. T. and cc.
      23p. ea.

<u>Mrs. Peter M. Lindt</u>, 949 West End Avenue, New York, N.Y. 10025.

Bl   Small amount of correspondence with Peter M. Lindt.

WALTHER VICTOR
Writer, 1895-

Mrs. Elisabeth M. Stoerk and Mrs. Susanne B. Hoeller, 288 Ocean Drive West, Stamford, Connecticut 06902.

FRIDERIKE ZWEIG ARCHIVE

B1   4 L. to Friderike Zweig. 1942, 1946-1947.

B3   3 L. from Maria Gleit Walther to Friderike Zweig. 1942, 1947-1948.

C7   Es ward Frühling 1848. Bilder aus einem großen Jahr. Chap. outline of essay volume. T. 2p.

H5   Materials in Friderike Zweig's Lives and Outlines files.

State University of New York at Albany, Department of Germanic Languages and Literatures, 1400 Washington Avenue, Albany, New York 12222.

CARL MISCH PAPERS, STORM PUBLISHERS ARCHIVE, KARL O. PAETEL COLLECTION

B1   7 L. to Karl O. Paetel. 1944-1945 and undated. Xerox.
      4 L. to Carl Misch. T. 1945-1948.
      2 L. and 1 Ptc. to Alexander Gode von Aesch. 1946.

B2   4 L. from Alexander Gode von Aesch. 1946.

Columbia University, Butler Library, New York, N.Y. 10027.

VARIAN FRY PAPERS

A3   "Notizen ueber die Bekanntschaft mit Herrn Berger." T. 8p.

I   2 documents mentioning Victor.

University of Southern California, Lion Feuchtwanger Memorial Library, 520 Paseo Miramar, Pacific Palisades, California 90272.

929

B1   1 L. to Lion Feuchtwanger. 1957.

B2   1 L. from Lion Feuchtwanger. 1957.

Harvard University, Houghton Library, Cambridge, Massachusetts 02138.

OSWALD GARRISON VILLARD PAPERS

B1   1 L. to Oswald Garrison Villard. 1944.

BERTHOLD VIERTEL

Writer, 1895-1953

University of Southern California, Lion Feuchtwanger Memorial
Library, 520 Paseo Miramar, Pacific Palisades, California
90272.

B1   7 L. to Lion Feuchtwanger. 1942-1953.

B2   9 L. from Lion Feuchtwanger. 1942-1953.

University of Texas, Humanities Research Center, Manuscripts
Collection, Box 7219, Austin, Texas 78712.

B1   8 L.

B2   4 L.

Yale University, Beinecke Rare Book and Manuscript Library,
New Haven, Connecticut 06520.

HERMANN BROCH ARCHIVE

B1   3 L. to Hermann Broch. 1943-1949.

B2   1 L. from Hermann Broch.

H5   Broch, Hermann. "Berthold Viertel: ein ethischer Dich-
       ter." 1942. T.cc. with some h. corr. 7p.

Immigration History Research Center of the University of
Minnesota, 826 Berry Street, St. Paul, Minnesota 55101.

AMERICAN COUNCIL FOR EMIGRÉS IN THE PROFESSIONS ARCHIVES

A3   Curriculum vitae. 3p.

B1   2 L. to Mrs. Henry Canby. 1945.
       1 L. to Else Staudinger. 1945.

B2   3 L. 1945.

B3   1 L. 1945.

H3   1 cl.

BERTHOLD VIERTEL

O   3 programs of 60th birthday celebration of Viertel, sponsored by the Austro-American Tribune.

University of New Hampshire, The Library, Department of Special Collections, Durham, New Hampshire 03824.

OSKAR MARIA GRAF COLLECTION

B1   3 L. to O. M. Graf. 1939.

Library of Congress, Manuscript Division, Independence Avenue and First Street S.E., Washington, D.C. 20540.

BENJAMIN W. HUEBSCH PAPERS

B1   1 L. to B. W. Huebsch. A. 1942.

B2   3 L. from B. W. Huebsch. T.cc. 1943-1944.
Transcripts of 2 L. from Stefan Zweig. 1941-1942.

Southern Illinois University, Morris Library, Department of Special Collections, Carbondale, Illinois 62901.

ERWIN PISCATOR PAPERS

B1   1 L. to Erwin Piscator. T. 1942.

C7   "Some Remarks and Suggestions Concerning the Re-Organization of the German Theater." Written together with Erwin Piscator. 1947-1948. T. with h. corr. by Piscator. Pc. 6p.

Academy of Motion Picture Arts and Sciences, Margaret Herrick Library, 9038 Melrose Avenue, Hollywood, California 90069.

J   1 photo of Berthold Viertel.

H3   1 obituary.

BERTHOLD VIERTEL

Indiana University, The University Libraries, The Lilly Library, Bloomington, Indiana 47401.

UPTON BEALL SINCLAIR MSS.

B1   1 L. to Upton Sinclair. 1930.

Mrs. Elisabeth M. Stoerk and Mrs. Susanne B. Hoeller, 288 Ocean Drive West, Stamford, Connecticut 06902.

FRIDERIKE ZWEIG ARCHIVE

D7   1 cl.

State University of New York at Binghamton, Center for Modern Theater Research, Binghamton, New York 13901.

MAX REINHARDT ARCHIVE

*   Uncatalogued materials concerning Viertel.

University of Pennsylvania, The Charles Patterson Van Pelt Library, Philadelphia, Pennsylvania 19104.

ALMA MAHLER-WERFEL COLLECTION

B1   1 L. to Alma Mahler-Werfel. A. 1940.

Mrs. Peter M. Lindt, 949 West End Avenue, New York, N.Y. 10025.

B1   Small amount of correspondence with Peter M. Lindt.

KARL VIËTOR

Writer, 1892-1951

Harvard University, University Archives, Widener Library, Cambridge, Massachusetts 02138.

Materials resulting from Viëtor's professorship at Harvard University.

Materialien aus Viëtors Zeit als Professor an der Harvard University.

B1,2   Correspondence concerning Viëtor's professorship at Harvard.

H3   Several obituaries and memorial addresses following Viëtor's death. 1951.

H5   List of doctoral dissertations written under Viëtor's direction.

Harvard University, Houghton Library, Cambridge, Massachusetts 02138.

GEORGE SARTON PAPERS, RICHARD BEER-HOFMANN COLLECTION

B1   3 L. to George Sarton. 1943-1948.
       Several L. to Richard Beer-Hofmann.

State University of New York at Albany, Department of Germanic Languages and Literatures, 1400 Washington Avenue, Albany, New York 12222.

KARL O. PAETEL COLLECTION

B1   2 L. to Karl O. Paetel (xerox). 1944, 1946.

Leo Baeck Institute, 129 East 73rd Street, New York, N.Y. 10021.

JACOB PICARD COLLECTION

KARL VIËTOR

B1,2   Correspondence between Karl Viëtor and Jacob Picard.

Immigration History Research Center of the University of Minnesota, 826 Berry Street, St. Paul, Minnesota 55101.

AMERICAN COUNCIL FOR EMIGRÉS IN THE PROFESSIONS ARCHIVES

B1   1 L. of recommendation for Jacob Picard. 1945.

American Philosophical Society, The Library, 105 South Fifth Street, Philadelphia, Pennsylvania 19106.

FRANZ BOAS PAPERS

B2   1 L. from Franz Boas. 1920.

KONRAD WACHSMANN

Architect, 1901-

Prof. Konrad Wachsmann, 805 South Genesee, Los Angeles, California 90036.

Private collection: inaccessible. / *Unzugängliche Privatsammlung.*

A3   Autobiographical Ms. (in progress 1976), written in the form of a history of architecture.

B1,2   Over 1,000 L., dating primarily from 1938- (except for 2 F. of pre-1938 correspondence). Includes correspondence with: Albert Einstein, Walter Gropius, Le Corbusier.

C7   Ms. of books, articles, lectures. Many pertaining to subject of industrialization in housing. 1920s-present. Ca. 500p.
Character analysis of Walter Gropius. 1975.

C7,   Tapes and texts of interviews made by Wachsmann of
F   acquaintances.

D7   Complete collection of offprints by Wachsmann (in several languages).

F   Films of Wachsmann's own work.

I   Documents, including passports, working papers, etc.

J   Over 2,000 photos.

K   Personal library. Ca. 2/3 still remains in this country.

M   Memorabilia such as awards and prizes.

N   Poem by Le Corbusier.

O   Ca. 50-60 posters, primarily concerning Wachsmann's work.

University of Illinois at Chicago Circle, The Library, Box 8198, Chicago, Illinois 60680.

INSTITUTE OF DESIGN RECORDS, 1927-1970

B1,2 Correspondence with Serge Chermayeff and Walter
      Paepcke. 1951-1954.

Library of Congress, Manuscript Division, Independence Avenue
and First Street S.E., Washington, D.C. 20540.

PAPERS OF LUDWIG MIES VAN DER ROHE

B1,2 Correspondence with Ludwig Mies van der Rohe. 1950-
      1965.

ERNST WALDINGER

Poet, Writer, 1896-1970

The literary estate, as well as various other materials in
the hands of relatives, friends and correspondents of Ernst
Waldinger, was transferred to Austria after his death (Dokumentationsstelle für Neuere österreichische Literatur, 1060
Wien, Gumpendorferstraße 15).

*Der literarische Nachlaß sowie andere Materialien aus dem
Besitz von Verwandten, Freunden und Briefwechselpartnern von
Ernst Waldinger wurden nach seinem Tode nach Österreich ge-
bracht (Dokumentationsstelle für Neuere Österreichische
Literatur, 1060 Wien, Gumpendorferstraße 15).*

Leo Baeck Institute, 129 East 73rd Street, New York, N.Y.
10021.

General archive files and JACOB PICARD COLLECTION.

*Materialien in allgemeinen Archivordnern und in der JACOB
PICARD COLLECTION.*

A3   Notes. A. 3p.

B1   2 L. 1967 and undated.

B1,2 Correspondence between Waldinger and Jacob Picard.

C3   Ich kann mit meinem Menschenbruder sprechen. Selected
        poems from the collection. T. 17p. with list.
      4 individual poems. T. 1946, 1949 and undated.

H3   1 obituary.

H5   Picard, Jacob. "Der Dichter Ernst Waldinger." 2p.

Immigration History Research Center of the University of
Minnesota, 826 Berry Street, St. Paul, Minnesota 55101.

AMERICAN COUNCIL FOR EMIGRÉS IN THE PROFESSIONS ARCHIVES

A3   Biographical sketches, applications, etc. 14p.

B1   15 L. to Mrs. Henry Canby. 1944-1948.
      2 L. to Else Staudinger. 1948.

B2   13 L. 1944-1948.

B3   19 L. 1944-1947.

C7   "Literature in Exile; an Opportunity and a Responsi-
      bility." 8p.

Mrs. Gertrude Urzidil, 83-39 116th Street, Richmond Hill,
New York 11418.

JOHANNES URZIDIL COLLECTION

B1   12 L. and 1 Ptc. to Johannes Urzidil. T. and A. 1947-
      1965.

C3   "Goethe und die Eisenzeit."
      "Schallplatte mit der Stimme Enrico Carusos."

Mrs. Elisabeth M. Stoerk and Mrs. Susanne B. Hoeller, 288
Ocean Drive West, Stamford, Connecticut 06902.

FRIDERIKE ZWEIG ARCHIVE

B1   3 L. and 3 Ptc. to Friderike Zweig. 1946-1947.

Library of Congress, Manuscript Division, Independence Avenue
and First Street S.E., Washington, D.C. 20540.

PAPERS OF SIEGFRIED BERNFELD

B1,2 Correspondence with Siegfried Bernfeld. 1943-1955.

C7   Research notes on the Freud family made by Waldinger
      and S. Bernfeld.

Yale University, Beinecke Rare Book and Manuscript Library,
New Haven, Connecticut 06520.

HERMANN BROCH ARCHIVE

B1   5 L. to Hermann Broch. 1945-1951.

1 L. to Erich von Kahler. 1951.

B2   1 L. from Hermann Broch. 1945.

University of New Hampshire, The Library, Department of Special Collections, Durham, New Hampshire 03824.

OSKAR MARIA GRAF COLLECTION, FRIEDRICH SALLY GROSSHUT COLLECTION

B1   3 L. to O. M. Graf. 1954-1967.
      1 L. to F. S. Grosshut. T. 1958.

State University of New York at Albany, Department of Germanic Languages and Literatures, 1400 Washington Avenue, Albany, New York 12222.

KARL O. PAETEL COLLECTION

B1   4 L. to Karl O. Paetel (xerox). 1944, 1945, 1952, 1953.

Harvard University, Houghton Library, Cambridge, Massachusetts 02138.

RICHARD BEER-HOFMANN COLLECTION and general archive files

B1   1 L. to Richard Beer-Hofmann. 1925.
C3   Poems. A. and T. 1919-1944. 107p.

New York Public Library, Manuscript Division, Fifth Avenue and 42nd Street, New York, N.Y. 10018.

THEO FELDMAN PAPERS

C3   "Dem Andenken Hermann Brochs." Undated. T.cc. Signed. 27 lines.

University of Kansas, Kenneth Spencer Research Library,

Department of Special Collections, Lawrence, Kansas 66045.

HENRY SAGAN COLLECTION

B1   1 L.

Princeton University, Firestone Library, Princeton, New Jersey 08540.

THE PAPERS OF ALBERT EINSTEIN (1879-1955). For details concerning the use of this collection, see description under Albert Einstein.

THE PAPERS OF ALBERT EINSTEIN (1879-1955). Nähere Angaben, den Zugang zu dieser Sammlung betreffend, finden sich unter: Albert Einstein.

B1,2 Unknown amount of correspondence between Einstein and Waldinger.

Mr. Francis Heilbut, 328 West 96th Street, New York, N.Y. 10025.

IVAN HEILBUT PAPERS

B2   Draft of a L. from Ivan Heilbut. A. 1942.

Mrs. Alice Loewy Kahler, 1 Evelyn Place, Princeton, New Jersey 08540.

ERICH VON KAHLER COLLECTION

B1   8 L. to Erich von Kahler. 1952-1965.

Mrs. Peter M. Lindt, 949 West End Avenue, New York, N.Y. 10025.

C   Ms. submitted to Lindt for use on his radio program.

BRUNO WALTER

Conductor, 1876-1962

<u>Bruno Walter Memorial Foundation</u>, c/o Miss Susie Danziger,
115 East 72nd Street, New York, N.Y. 10021.

The BRUNO WALTER COLLECTION was given to the Foundation
after the death of Walter's daughter, Lotte. Walter had no
other heirs. The collection will eventually be deposited in
the New York Public Library at Lincoln Center. The collection is closed at the present time; however, it will be made
accessible to researchers and scholars in the future with
the permission of the Foundation and Miss Susie Danziger.

*Die BRUNO WALTER COLLECTION wurde der Foundation nach dem
Tode von Lotte Walter, der Tochter des Dirigenten, überlassen. Bruno Walter hatte keine weiteren Erben. Die Sammlung
soll später einmal ihren endgültigen Platz in der New York
Public Library im Lincoln Center erhalten. Die Sammlung ist
zur Zeit geschlossen, sie wird aber später mit Erlaubnis der
Foundation bzw. Frau Susie Danzigers für Forschungszwecke
zugänglich gemacht werden.*

A3   Scrapbooks of trips, including cl. Dating from 1900.

B1,2 2 suitcases of correspondence. 1940s-1960s, including
      L. to and from: R. Coudenhove-Kalergi, Carl Ebert,
      Alfred Einstein, Karl Geiringer, Mascha Kaleko, Otto
      Klemperer, Ernst Křenek, Lotte Lehmann, Ernst Lothar,
      Alma Mahler-Werfel, Thomas Mann (pc.), Paul Nettl,
      Alfred Neumann, Alfred Polgar, Max Reinhardt, Rudolf
      Serkin, William Steinberg, Friedrich Torberg, Kurt
      Wolff, Friderike and Stefan Zweig.

F   Home movies.
      Records and tapes of discussions, interviews, perform-
      ances.

H1   Books about Walter.

I   Documents.

J   Family photos. Dating from 1900.

N   Musical Ms. of other composers, e.g., Gustav Mahler.

University of Pennsylvania, The Charles Patterson Van Pelt
Library, Philadelphia, Pennsylvania 19104.

ALMA MAHLER-WERFEL COLLECTION

B1   60 L., 6 Tel. and 1 Ptc. to Alma Mahler-Werfel. 1911-
         1960.

B2   Draft of a lengthy L. from Alma Mahler-Werfel.
         1 L. from Mary McLane.

H3   4 cl.

Leo Baeck Institute, 129 East 73rd Street, New York, N.Y.
10021.

SIEGFRIED ALTMANN COLLECTION, LUDWIG MISCH COLLECTION

B1   18 L. and 10 Ptc. to Siegfried Altmann. T. and A.
         1946-1961 and undated.
         2 L. to Ludwig Misch. 1948.

Detroit Public Library, 5201 Woodward Avenue, Detroit,
Michigan 48202.

OSSIP GABRILOWITSCH PAPERS

B1   20 L. to Ossip, Clara and Artur Gabrilowitsch. 1915-
         1939. Most pub.

University of California, Los Angeles, Music Library, 405
Hilgard Avenue, Los Angeles, California 90024.

ERNST TOCH ARCHIVE

B1   6 L. to Ernst Toch.

Syracuse University, The George Arents Research Library,
Syracuse, New York 13210.

FRANZ WAXMAN PAPERS

B1   Correspondence with Franz Waxman. 1943-1961.

University of Georgia, The University Libraries, Athens, Georgia 30601.

GUIDO ADLER PAPERS, OLIN DOWNES PAPERS

B1,2 Correspondence with Guido Adler. 9 L.
      Correspondence with Olin Downes. 14 L.

University of California, Santa Barbara, The Library, Santa Barbara, California 93105.

LOTTE LEHMANN COLLECTION

B1,2 Correspondence with Lotte Lehmann.

Dr. Harold von Hofe, Department of German, University of Southern California, Los Angeles, California 90007.

LUDWIG MARCUSE PAPERS

B1,2 Correspondence with Ludwig Marcuse.

Mrs. Vally Weigl, 50 West 95th Street, New York, N.Y. 10025.

B1,2 Correspondence with Karl Weigl.

Dr. Friedrich J. Hacker, The Hacker Clinic, 160 Lasky Drive, Beverly Hills, California 90212.

B1,2 Correspondence with Friedrich Hacker.

Princeton University, Firestone Library, Princeton, New Jersey 08540.

THOMAS MANN COLLECTION

B2   Correspondence with Thomas Mann.

<u>Mrs. Elisabeth M. Stoerk and Mrs. Susanne B. Hoeller</u>, 288
Ocean Drive West, Stamford, Connecticut 06902.

FRIDERIKE ZWEIG ARCHIVE

B1   3 L. to Friderike Zweig. 1957, 1961.

B3   2 Ptc. from Else Walter to Friderike Zweig. 1940-1941.

<u>University of Iowa</u>, The University Libraries, Special Collec-
tions, Iowa City, Iowa 52240.

B1   2 L. to Charles Eble. 1940.

<u>Metropolitan Opera Association, Inc.</u>, The Archives, Lincoln
Center Plaza, New York, N.Y. 10023.

H3   Newspaper and magazine cl., primarily from <u>Opera News</u>.
      1939-1958.

I   Contracts. 1941-1945.

<u>Museum of the City of New York</u>, Fifth Avenue at 103rd Street,
New York, N.Y. 10029.

H3   "Personality file" on Walter.

<u>Harvard University</u>, Houghton Library, Cambridge, Massachu-
setts 02138.

AUTOGRAPH FILE

B1   1 L. to Gisela Selden-Goth. A. 1938.

Mrs. Margrit Cartwright, Box 240, Mt. Hermon, Massachusetts 01354.

B1   1 L.

University of Texas, Humanities Research Center, Manuscripts Collection, Box 7219, Austin, Texas 78712.

B2   2 L.

Library of Congress, Manuscript Division, Independence Avenue and First Street S.E., Washington, D.C. 20540.

BENJAMIN W. HUEBSCH PAPERS

B2   1 L. from B. W. Huebsch. T.cc. 1940.

Mrs. Alice Loewy Kahler, 1 Evelyn Place, Princeton, New Jersey 08540.

ERICH VON KAHLER COLLECTION

B1   1 short note to Erich von Kahler. 1946.

FRANZ WAXMAN

Composer, 1906-1967

Syracuse University, The George Arents Research Library,
Syracuse, New York 13210.

The FRANZ WAXMAN PAPERS, 1922-1968, consist of 20 archive B.
and 31 packages of materials that were donated to the Library
in 1966 (described below), as well as additional materials
donated in 1976. Written permission to use the collection
must be obtained from Mr. John Waxman (8 Murvon Court, Westport, Connecticut 06880), son of Franz, who retains all
rights to the materials.

*Die FRANZ WAXMAN PAPERS, 1922-1968, umfassen 20 Archivkartons
und 31 Päckchen mit Materialien (Beschreibung s.u.), die der
Bibliothek im Jahre 1966 als Schenkung zukamen, sowie weitere Materialien, die der Bibliothek im Jahre 1976 geschenkt
wurden. Die Materialien können mit schriftlicher Genehmigung von dem Sohn Franz Waxmans, Herr John Waxman, 8 Murvon
Court, Westport, Connecticut 06880, eingesehen werden; die
literarischen Rechte ruhen ebenfalls bei Herrn John Waxman.*

A3   Biographical materials. 1956-1968.

B1   Numerous L., primarily cc. 1944-1966. 12 F.

B2   Correspondence. 1941-1967. 2+ B.   Including L. from:
     Ingrid Bergman, Leonard Bernstein, Rudolf Bing,
     Willy Brandt, Aaron Copland, Joan Crawford, Linda
     Darnell, Bette Davis, Dwight D. Eisenhower, Lion
     Feuchtwanger, Benny Goodman, Paul Henreid, Charlton
     Heston, Robert F. Kennedy, Erich Wolfgang Korngold,
     Lotte Lehmann, Erich Leinsdorf, Thomas Mann, Clif-
     ford Odets, Eugene Ormandy, Gregory Peck, Edward G.
     Robinson, Arnold Schoenberg, David O. Selznick,
     Rudolf Serkin, William Steinberg, Igor Stravinsky,
     Ernst Toch, Hal Wallis, Bruno Walter, Jack Warner,
     Orson Welles, Alma Mahler-Werfel, Darryl F. Zanuck.

C3   Lyric text to Richard Strauss' "Four Last Songs." Un-
     dated.

C5   Musical, based on Berkeley Square. Draft. 1961.

C7   Miscellaneous lecture texts. Ca. 1955-1961.
     Speeches:

"History of Motion Picture Music." Undated.
"On Jazz." Undated.
"On Music and the Composer's Inspiration." 1957.
"On Recent Experiences in Europe." Ca. 1955.
Miscellaneous essays, drafts, etc. Undated.
Narrations:
  Hamlet, Othello and Macbeth. Undated.
  King David. 1952.
  A Midsummer Night's Dream. Ca. 1964.
  Orpheus. Ca. 1964.
  The Prophet Isaiah. 1955.
Miscellaneous notes. Undated.

C9   Librettos for:
      Hugo von Hofmannsthal's Electra. Undated.
      Christoph Gluck's Orfeo ed Euridice. Undated.

C13a Bound scores for films:
      Air Force. 1943.
      Captains Courageous. 1937.
      A Christmas Carol. 1938.
      Dark Circle. Undated.
      The Edge of Darkness. 1943.
      The Emperor's Candlesticks. 1937.
      Florian. 1940.
      The Horn Blows at Midnight. 1945.
      In Our Time. 1944.
      Lady of the Tropics. Undated.
      Lure of the Wilderness. 1952.
      Objective Burma. 1945.
      Old Acquaintance. 1943.
      Pride of the Marines. 1945.
      Prince Valiant. 1954.
      Mr. Skeffington. 1944.
      To Have and to Have Not. 1943.
      Tortilla Flat. 1942.
      The Very Thought of You. 1944.
      Unbound scores, primarily intended as film scores:
      Absolute Quiet. 1936.
      "Ach, wie oft kommt die Liebe unverhofft!" 1932.
      All the Way. Undated.
      Beloved Infidel. Undated.
      Blue Veil. Undated.
      The Blue Danube. Undated.

948

The Bride of Frankenstein. Undated.
Count Your Blessings. 1959.
Crime in the Streets. Undated. 8 F.
Dark Passage. Undated.
Florian. Ballet-suite. 1939.
"Für'n Groschen Liebe" and "Ach, wie ist das Leben
    schön." 1932.
"Gruß und Kuß-Veronika." 1933.
He Ran All the Way. Undated. 3 F.
I, the Jury. Undated. 3 F.
The Indian Fighter. Undated.
Johnny Holiday. Undated. 21 F.
King David. Undated.
La belle Croisière. 1934.
La Crise est finie. 1934.
La Stella del Disidero. 1962.
Liliom. 1933.
Lion in the Streets. 1953.
Love in the Afternoon. Undated.
Love Music. 1947.
Men and Women. Undated.
Miracle in the Rain. Undated.
Mon Coeur Bat. 1932.
The Mysterious Deep. Undated.
On ne voit ça qu'à Paris. 1934.
Peyton Place. Undated.
Rebecca. Radio version. 1940. 9 F.
Sayonara. Undated.
Second Hungarian Rhapsody. Undated. 2 F.
The Song of Terezin. 1966.
"Theme, variations and Fugato." Music for jazz orches-
    tra. 1956.
This is My Love. Undated.
"Tchaikovsky Concerto." Op. 35. Undated.
Un peu d'amour. Undated.
The Virgin Queen. 1955.
Untitled unbound scores. Undated. 3 F.

C13b "Battle Hymn of the Republic." Undated.
      "Ein' feste Burg ist unser Gott." Undated.
      "Hartman Symphony." Undated.

H3   Newspaper cl. 1940-1961. 10 F.

I   Prizes, awards. 1938-1952 and undated.
Driver's licenses. 1950-1951.
Financial documents. 1962-1966.

J   Paintings.
Miscellaneous photos of actors, musicians, etc. Undated.
1 photo of Igor Stravinsky.
Individual photos of Waxman. Undated.
Group photos including Waxman. Undated.

L   Stage sketches:
    Gary Newton. "Carmen." 1958.
    Lisl Weil. "A Midsummer Night's Dream." Ca. 1964.
Printed materials on trips to Europe. 1951-1954. 2 F.
International Society for Contemporary Music materials. 1957.
Miscellaneous lists. Undated.
Materials concerning Waxman's concerts: cl., brochures, programs. 1943-1965.
"Joan of Arc at the Stake." Brochures, reviews, cl., etc.
Los Angeles Music Festival materials: cl., programs, pamphlets. 1949-1966. 10 F.
Paris concert materials: cl., programs, etc. 1949.
Requiem for John F. Kennedy. Nürnberg, Germany, 1964. Newspaper cl., etc.
Franklin D. Roosevelt Memorial. Hollywood Bowl, 1945. Programs, cl., etc.
Santa Catalina Festival of the Arts: pamphlets, programs, cl. 1961.
"The Song of Terezin." Cincinnati May Music Festival, 1965. Programs, cl., etc.
War Industry Concert, 1944. Programs, cl.

M   Scrapbooks. Undated.
Embroidery.
Funeral book. 1967.
Illustrations to: "Die schöne Melusine" and "Bremer Stadtmusikanten." 1967.
Autograph collection, including autographs of: Hector Berlioz, Charles Gounod, Jascha Heifetz, Engelbert Humperdinck, Arturo Toscanini, Dmitri Shostakovich.
"Memorial Concert to Franz Waxman." 1968. Memorabilia.

N   Ehlers, Alice. "Musical Days with Albert Schweitzer."
       Undated.
     Song texts to compositions by Waxman by: Clifford Gor-
       don, Man Kolpe and Fritz Rotter, Arthur Le Clerq,
       David Mack, Paul Novoix.
     Film scores:
       Jacques Brindejont Offenbach. Offenbach conduit le
        Bal.
       Paul Claudel and Arthur Honegger. Joan of Arc at the
        Stake.
       Wade Dent and Dino Yannopoulas. The Golden Curtain.
       James Forsythe. Christophe, Joshua, and Jocasta's
        Cry.
       Nelson Gidding. The Centurions.
       Kurt Kaiser. Jazz.
       Kathleen Millay. Persephone.
     Unidentified Ms. by others.
     2 poems.

O   Placards. 1960.

Library of Congress, Reference Department, Music Division,
Independence Avenue and First Street S.E., Washington, D.C.
20540.

C13a "Carmen Fantasie." Based on themes from the opera by
      Bizet. Violin and piano. A. 32p.
     "The Silver Chalice." Original sketches. [1955]. A.
      1 volume.
     "Taras Bulba." Condensed score. Reproduced in part
      from holograph. 1962.

Columbia University, Butler Library, New York, N.Y. 10027.

B1   31 L. to Daniel G. Mason. T. and A. 1931-1952.
     16 L. and Tel. to W. W. Norton. 1958-1961.
     3 L.

C7   Speech for Metropolitan Opera Guild. Undated. A. 2p.
     also T.

<u>University of Pennsylvania</u>, The Charles Patterson Van Pelt Library, Philadelphia, Pennsylvania 19104.

ALMA MAHLER-WERFEL COLLECTION

B1   1 L. and 1 Ptc. to Alma Mahler-Werfel. 1955 and un-dated.

C9   <u>Maximilian and Charlotte</u>. Adaptation of Werfel's drama. 35p.

<u>University of Georgia</u>, The University Libraries, Athens, Georgia 30601.

OLIN DOWNES PAPERS

B1,2   3 L.

JOSEPH WECHSBERG

Journalist, Writer, 1907-

<u>Columbia University</u>, Butler Library, New York, N.Y. 10027.

The PAUL R. REYNOLDS COLLECTION contains 9 archive boxes of materials of Joseph Wechsberg. Reynolds was Wechsberg's literary agent.

Die PAUL R. REYNOLDS COLLECTION enthält 9 Archivkartons Materialien von Joseph Wechsberg. Reynolds war Wechsbergs Agent.

B1,2 Correspondence between Joseph Wechsberg and Paul R. Reynolds. 1942-1968. Ca. 5,000 L.

B3   Over 750 L. concerning Wechsberg and his work. Primarily between publishers, editors and agent.

C7   Several Ms. of longer works. Ca. 100 Ms. of shorter prose works. Mostly from the 1940s.

D7   Some printed items among the correspondence.

I   Checks, receipts, accounts, other legal documents. 1942-1968. Ca. 1,000 items.

<u>Dr. Clementine Zernik</u>, 225-10 106th Avenue, Queens Village, New York 11429.

B1   Several L. to Arnold Höllriegel. 1938-1939.

EDITH WEIGERT

Psychoanalyst, 1894-

Dr. Edith Weigert, 12 Oxford Street, Chevy Chase, Maryland
20015.

Private papers: Ca. 10 in. / *Private Schriften: etwa 0,25 m.*

C7,8   Review of Anatomy of Human Destructiveness. 1973. 5p.
        "Goals in Psychotherapy." 1960.
        "Dissenting Psychotherapeutic Schools in the Early
          History of Psychoanalysis." Ca. 1940. 27p.
        "Psychoanalysis in a Psychiatric Hospital." 1941. 6p.
        "Discussion on Psychoanalysis." 1939. 13p.
        "Psychology of Women." 1973. 17p.
        "Reverence of Life." 1972. 13p.
        "Love and Respect." 1972. 16p.
        "Influence of Existentialism on Psychiatry." 1971. 31p.
        History of Psychoanalysis. Various Ms. versions. Ca.
          2 in.

Institute for Psychoanalysis, McLean Library, 180 N. Michigan Avenue, Chicago, Illinois 60601.

C7,8   5 articles by Weigert. Mimeo.:
        "The cult and mythology of the magna mater from the
          standpoint of psychoanalysis." 31p.
        "Emotional aspects of pregnancy." 30p.
        "Existentialism and its relations to psychotherapy."
          13p.
        "The psychoanalytic view of human personality." 3p.
        "The school and its students." 3p.

L   3 articles contained in collections of articles.
        Mimeo.:
        Cohen, Robert A. "Marital and parental patterns."
          11p.
        Coleman, Arthur D. "First-baby group: an investiga-
          tion into the psychology of pregnancy and mother-
          ing." 80p.
        Marcel, Gabriel. "Creative Voco ces Essence of
          Fatherhood in Homo Viator." 5p.

<u>Washington School of Psychiatry</u>, 1610 New Hampshire Avenue
N.W., Washington, D.C. 20009.

F   "Forty years of psychiatry." Series of taped lectures.
     (C. of tapes located also at: American Psychiatric
     Museum Association, 1700 18th Street N.W., Washing-
     ton, D.C. 20009.)

KARL WEIGL

Composer, 1881-1949

Mrs. Vally Weigl, 50 West 95th Street, New York, N.Y. 10025.

Mrs. Vally Weigl, the widow of Karl, has retained all materials, with the exception of the music manuscripts, from the papers of her late husband.

Frau Vally Weigl, die Witwe des Komponisten, befindet sich - mit Ausnahme der Notenmanuskripte - noch im Besitz aller Materialien aus der Sammlung ihres verstorbenen Mannes.

A2   Notebooks, mostly music.

B1,2 Correspondence, including L. to and from: Alfred Einstein, Gustav Mahler, Artur Schnabel, Bruno Walter, Zemlinsky.

C13a Musical sketches of several poems that Weigl had intended to set to music.

D7   Printed articles by Weigl.

F   Ca. 70 tapes and records of Weigl's performances.

H4   Reviews and cl. on Weigl's compositions, performances.

I   Miscellaneous documents.

J   Numerous photos.

K   Personal library.

M   Medals, prizes, etc.

New York Public Library at Lincoln Center, Library and Museum of the Performing Arts, 111 Amsterdam Avenue, New York, N.Y. 10023.

This collection of ca. 60 original manuscripts of Karl Weigl (1940-1949) was donated by Mrs. Vally Weigl in 1968. Copies of the materials are also located in the Edwin A. Fleischer Collection of Orchestral Music at the Free Library of Philadelphia, Logan Square, Philadelphia, Pennsylvania 19103.

Diese Sammlung von etwa 60 Originalmanuskripten von Karl Weigl (aus der Zeit von 1940 - 1949) ist eine Schenkung von

956

*Frau Vally Weigl aus dem Jahre 1968. Kopien der Materialien
befinden sich in der Edwin A. Fleischer Collection of Orchestral Music at the Free Library of Philadelphia, Logan Square,
Philadelphia, Pennsylvania 19103.*

C13a "Collection of chamber music." 4 pieces. [194-?]. A.
"Collection of choral music." 17 pieces. Undated. A.
"Collection of short orchestral works." 4 pieces.
[1922-1940]. A.
"Collection of organ music." 3 pieces. [1933-1939]. A.
"Aus Phantasus (Arno Holz) Gesänge für eine hohe
Frauenstimme." Feb. 1905. A. 13p.
"Konzert für Violine und Orchester." [1928]. A. 73p.,
21p., 61p.
"Konzert für Violoncello und mittleres Orchester."
[1939]. A. 34p., 11p., 37p.
"Festspielouvertüre für großes Orchester." Dated Feb.
1938. A. 58p. Earlier version. Dated Jan. 1938. A.
15p.
"4 Gedichte von Richard Dehmel, für eine tiefe Männerstimme." [1904?]. A.
["Gesänge, op. 1"]. "7 Gesänge für eine tiefe Männerstimme." [1903-1904]. A. 26p.
"5 Kinderlieder für eine Frauenstimme." [Ca. 1904-1906].
A.
["Lieder, op. 3"]. "5 Lieder für Tenor." [1903-1905].
A.
["Lieder, op. 23"]. "5 Lieder für eine hohe Männerstimme und Klavier." Ca. 1911. A.
"5 Lieder von Heinrich Heine." [1904]. A.
"10 Lieder von Heinrich Heine, für hohe Singstimme und
Klavier." [1906]. A.
"6 Lieder von O. J. Bierbaum, für eine hohe Singstimme."
Undated. A.
"3 Mädchenlieder für eine hohe Frauenstimme mit Kla-
vier." [Ca. 1900-1915]. A.
"Nachtphantasien für Klavier zu zwei Händen." [1911].
2 Exemplare. A.
["Old Vienna"]. "Tänze aus Wien/Dances from Vienna,
for big orchestra." [1939]. A. 64p. Another version.
A. 20p.
"Phantast. Zwischenspiel." [1921]. A. 91p.
["Quartet, strings, no. 2, E major"]. "Streichquartett

957

für 2 Violinen, Viola (auch Viola d'amour) und Violoncello." Undated. 28p.
["Quartet, strings, no. 3, A major"]. "Streichquartett für 2 Violinen, Viola, Violoncello." [1909]. A. 11p., 8p., 15p.
["Quartet, strings, no. 4, D minor"]. "Streichquartett d-moll, für zwei Violinen, Viola, Violoncello." [1924]. A. 8p., 7p., 11p.
["Quartet, strings, no. 6, C major"]. "6. Streichquartett, C dur, für 2 Violinen, Viola, Violoncello." [1939]. A. 51p.
["Quartet, strings, no. 7, F minor"]. "String quartet, f minor, for 2 violins, viola and violoncello." [1924]. A. 35p.
["Quartet, strings, no. 8, D major"]. "String quartet for 2 violins, viola and violoncello, D major." [1949]. A. 36p.
["Quartet, strings, no. 5, G major"]. "Streichquartett im leichten Stil für 2 Viol., Viola u. Violoncello." [1933]. A. 9p., 7p., 4p., 9p.
"Der Rattenfänger von Hameln." Opera. Undated. A.
"Rhapsody for piano and orchestra." 1940. A. 59p.
"Sextett für 2 Violinen, 2 Violen, 2 Violoncelli." [1906]. A. 48p., 1p.
"Sonata for violin and piano." [1940]. A. 19p.
"Sonate für Klavier u. Violine, C dur." [1923]. A. 18p. 11p., 21p.
"Sonate für Violine und Klavier, G dur." [1937]. A. 40p.
"Sonate für Violoncello und Klavier." [1923]. A. 20p., 18p.
"3 Gesänge für eine hohe Männerstimme u. Orchester." [1915]. A. Also English tr. by V. Weigl.
"3 Gesänge für eine Frauenstimme mit Orchester nach Gedichten von Ricarda Huch." [Ca. 1916]. A. 20p., 16p., 14p. Also English tr. by V. Weigl.
"3 Orchestergesänge für eine Männerstimme. Klavierauszug." [Ca. 1915]. A. 31p.
"3 Gesänge, für eine Frauenstimme mit Orchester. Klavierauszug [von Paul Frankl; Wörter von Ricarda Huch]." [Ca. 1916]. A. 16p., 6p. Also English tr. by V. Weigl.

"4 Lieder für eine tiefe Männerstimme." [1905-1907]. A.
"5 Lieder für eine tiefe Männerstimme." [1906-1907]. A.
"4 Lieder für eine hohe Singstimme und Klavier."
   [1908]. A.
"5 Lieder für eine hohe Singstimme und Klavier."
   [1908]. A.
"5 Lieder für eine hohe Männerstimme und Klavier."
   [1908?-1911]. A.
"7 Lieder für hohe Singstimme und Klavier." [1909]. A.
   18p.
Collection of songs. 27 pieces, primarily German.
   1912-1943. A.
"Sechs Gesänge für eine tiefe Frauenstimme und Klavier." [1925-1932]. A.
"5 Lieder für Sopranstimme mit Streichquartett."
   [1934]. A.
"3 Gesänge für Altstimme und Streichquartett." 1936. A.
   15p.
"3 Gesänge für Mezzosopran und Streichquartett."
   [1937]. A.
["Ein Stelldichein"]. "Gesang mit Streichsextett [sic].
   Streichsextett mit Gesang. Ein Stelldichein." [1904].
   A. 18p.
"Symphonische Phantasie für großes Orchester." [1905].
   A. 122p.
"Symphonische Phantasie für Orchester. Klavierauszug
   zu zwei Händen." Undated. A. 43p.
"Symphonisches Vorspiel zu einer Tragödie. Orchester
   Musik." [1933]. A. 63p. Also shortened version. A.
   23p.
"II. Symphonie." Score (4 movements). [1921-1922]. A.
"III. Symphonie B dur für großes Orchester." [1931]. A.
"IV. Symphonie für großes Orchester." [1936]. A. 72p.,
   48p., 26p.
"Trio für Violine, Violoncello und Klavier." 1939. A.
   23p., 11p., 17p.
"Weltfeier. Symphonische Kantate für Tenor und hohen
   Baß (Soli) gemischten Chor und Orchester. Text nach
   Gedichten von Heinrich Hart." Microfilm of Ms. in
   Toscanini Memorial Archives.
"Weltfeier. Symphonische Kantata für Chor, Soli, großes
   Orchester, nach Gedichten von Heinrich Hart." [Ca.
   1922]. A.

"Weltfeier II. Klavierauszug." [Ca. 1922]. Words from Heinrich Hart. A.

C13b Mendelssohn-Bartholdy, Felix. "Rondo capriccioso."
Adaptation. Ca. 1930s. 19p.
Schubert, Franz Peter. "Deux marches caractéristiques."
Adaptation. [1933]. A.
"Marche héroique." Adaptation. Undated. A. 12p.

American Composer's Alliance, 170 West 74th Street, New York, N.Y. 10023.

The American Composer's Alliance collects copyist manuscripts of compositions by its members, prepared either by the composer himself or by another. Weigl was a member of the American Composer's Alliance.

Die American Composer's Alliance sammelt Kopien von Originalmanuskripten von Kompositionen ihrer Mitglieder; diese Kopien werden entweder vom Komponisten selbst oder von einer anderen Person angefertigt. Weigl war Mitglied der American Composer's Alliance.

C13a "A Cradle Song" ("Schlummerlied"). 1946.
"And there you stood." 1945.
"4 Bagatelles." 1941; 1972.
"Bilder und Geschichten." Op. 2. 1909.
"Black Cat." 1946.
"Children's Songs" ("Kinderlieder"). 1916.
"6 Children's Songs on Poems by Vally Weigl." 1944.
"Comedy Overture." Op. 32. 1933.
"Concerto." Op. 21. 1931.
"Concerto for the Left Hand." 1924.
"Concerto in D major." 1928.
"Concerto (in G min.)." 1934.
"Dance of the Furies" ("Tanz der Erynnien"). 1938.
"Dances from Old Vienna." 1940.
"5 Duets." 1909.
"Ein Stelldichein"/"A Rendezvous." 1912.
"Ein Gleiches"/"Similitude." 1909.
"Fantastic Intermezzo." Op. 18. 1922.
"6 Fantasies." 1942.

"Festival Prelude." 1938.
"The Four Seasons." 1936.
"Frühlingsfeier."/"Spring Celebration." 1904.
"The Giant." 1927.
"The Glorious Hobo." 1939.
"Grey Years." 1942.
"In the MacDowell Woods." Op. 34. 1942.
"3 Intermezzi." 1944.
"The Invisible Light." 1942.
"Love Song"/"Liebeslied." 1938.
"6 Love Songs"/"Liebeslieder." Op. 22. 1946.
"Meditation."
"Men's Choruses." Op. 27-28. 1928.
"Nature." Op. 29. 1926.
"3 Night Phantasies." Op. 13. 1911.
"3 Odes on Poems by N. Lenau." Op. 6. 1909.
"Old Vienna." 1939.
"Passacaglia and Triple Fugue." 1934.
"Pictures and Tales." 1909-1922.
"Pictures from Childhood." 1943.
"2 Pieces." 1940.
"2 Pieces." 1942.
"The Pied Piper of Hamelin." 1936.
"Pied Piper Suite." 1936.
"4 Poems." 1909.
"Prelude and Fugue in the Old Style." 1933.
"Quartet No. 1 (C min.)." Op. 4. 1909.
"Quartet No. 2 (in E)." 1906.
"Quartet No. 3 (in A)." 1906.
"Quartet No. 4 (D min.)." 1924.
"String Quartet V in G Major." 1933.
"Quartet No. 6 (in C)." 1939.
"Quartet No. 7 (F min.)." 1939.
"Quartet No. 8 (in D)." 1949.
"The Refugee." 1939.
"2 Religious Songs." Op. 14. 1922.
"2 Religious Choruses." 1941-1942.
"Rhapsody." 1940.
"Rhapsody (in D min.)." Op. 30. 1940.
"Sextet (D min.)." 1906.
"4 short pieces." 1941.
"Shouting Sun (Early Easter Morning)." 1945.
"Sleeper's Wake." 1944.

"Sonata." 1940.
"Sonata (in G)." 1923.
"Sonata No. 1 (in C)." 1922.
"Sonata No. 2 (in G)." 1937.
"2 Songs of the Time." 1942.
"3 Songs." Op. 12. 1909.
"3 Songs." 1936.
"3 Songs." 1958.
"3 Songs from Op. 1." 1906.
"3 Songs for Baritone and Orchestra." 1916.
"3 Songs for High Woman's Voice and Orchestra." 1916.
"4 Songs." 1904-1908.
"4 Songs from 'Des Knaben Wunderhorn'." 1905.
"5 Songs." Op. 3.
"5 Songs." Op. 8. 1904.
"5 Songs." Op. 10. 1913.
"5 Songs"/"Fünf Lieder." Op. 23. 1955.
"5 Songs." 1934.
"5 Songs from 'Phantasus'." 1905.
"6 Songs." 1926.
"6 Songs on Poems of O. J. Bierbaum." 1905.
"7 Songs." Op. 1. 1908.
"10 Songs." 1906.
"Spring Overture (Music for the Young)." 1939.
"Summer Evening Music." 1940.
"Symphonic Fantasy (F min.)." 1905.
"Symphonic Prelude to a Tragedy." 1933.
"Symphony No. 1 (in E)." Op. 5. 1908.
"Symphony No. 2 in D minor." Op. 19. 1922.
"Symphony No. 3." 1931.
"Symphony No. 4 (F min.)." 1936.
"Symphony No. 5 (C min.), Apocalyptic." 1945.
"Symphony No. 6 (A min.)." 1947.
"To Baby Christine." 1941.
"Toteninsel"/"Island of the Dead." 1903.
"Trio." 1939.
"Variations on an Original Theme." Op. 15. 1910.
"The Watchman's Report." Op. 39. 1941.
"Wiegenlied"/"Lullaby for John." 1929.
"Women's Choruses." Op. 26. 1906-1927.
"World Festival"/"Weltfeier." Op. 17. 1924.

KARL WEIGL

<u>Immigration History Research Center of the University of Minnesota</u>, 826 Berry Street, St. Paul, Minnesota 55101.

AMERICAN COUNCIL FOR EMIGRÉS IN THE PROFESSIONS ARCHIVES

A3   Curriculum vitae, short biographies, questionnaires. 13p. Also 2 pamphlets. 8p. ea.

B1   2 L. to Else Staudinger. 1946-1947.

B2   5 L. 1945-1947.

B3   7 L., including 5 recommendations. 1945, 1971.

O   8 programs.

<u>University of Georgia</u>, The University Libraries, Athens, Georgia 30601.

GUIDO ADLER PAPERS

B1,2 Correspondence between Karl Weigl and Guido Adler. 14 L.

<u>New York Public Library</u>, Manuscript Division, Fifth Avenue and 42nd Street, New York, N.Y. 10018.

EMERGENCY COMMITTEE IN AID OF DISPLACED FOREIGN SCHOLARS, 1933-1945

*   File compiled when assistance was granted. 1938-1945.

Mrs. Lotte Lenya Weill-Detwiler, 404 East 55th Street, New
York, N.Y. 10022.

The materials in Mrs. Detwiler's possession are from the
estate of Kurt Weill. A catalog of the musical works and
manuscripts of Kurt Weill has been prepared by Mr. David
Drew: An Index and Catalog of Musical Works and Manuscripts
of Kurt Weill (Berlin: Akademie der Künste, expected publication date 1977/1978). The remaining materials from the
estate are being sorted, as of 1977, and are inaccessible
to researchers.

*Die Materialien im Besitz von Frau Detwiler stammen aus dem
Nachlaß von Kurt Weill. Herr David Drew hat ein Verzeichnis
der Werke und Manuskripte Kurt Weills erstellt: An Index and
Catalog of Musical Works and Manuscripts of Kurt Weill (Berlin: Akademie der Künste, die Veröffentlichung ist für 1977/
1978 geplant). Die übrigen Materialien aus dem Nachlaß werden geordnet und sind z.Zt. für Forschungszwecke nicht zugänglich.*

B1,2   Correspondence between Kurt Weill and Lotte Lenya.

B2   Correspondence, including L. from: Alfred Einstein,
       Bruno Frank, the Mann family.

C13   Orchestral scores to several Broadway shows, some with
       lyrics.

H3,4   Cl. about Weill and reviews of his work.
       Cl. about Lotte Lenya.

J   Production photos.
       Snapshots of Kurt Weill.
       Photos of Lotte Lenya.

O   Programs.

Library of Congress, Reference Department, Music Division,
Independence Avenue and First Street S.E., Washington, D.C.
20540.

B1,2   Extensive correspondence between Weill and Ira

Gershwin, including several p. of Gershwin's comments.

Cl3a   "Skizzen zur Musik für The Eternal Road." 1935. A.
"Highwind in Jamaica, no. 1." 1936. A.
"Der kleine Leutnant des lieben Gottes." [1959]. A. pc.

Cl3b   "Lady in the Dark." Arrangement by Weill. 1949. 80p.

Columbia University, Butler Library, New York, N.Y. 10027.

B1   18 L. to Leah Salisbury. T. and A. 1943-1950.
4 L. 1938-1939.

New York Public Library at Lincoln Center, Library and Museum of the Performing Arts, 111 Amsterdam Avenue, New York, N.Y. 10023.

Cl3   The Seven Deadly Sins. Original score. A.

State Historical Society of Wisconsin, 816 State Street, Madison, Wisconsin 53706.

PLAYWRIGHTS' COMPANY PAPERS

B   1 F. of correspondence by, about and to Kurt Weill.
1943-1950.

I   Weill's contract for Knickerbocker Holiday.

Southern Illinois University, Morris Library, Department of Special Collections, Carbondale, Illinois 62901.

ERWIN PISCATOR PAPERS

B1   1 L. to Erwin Piscator. A. 1939.

B2   1 L. from Erwin Piscator. cc. 1950.

D2   The Threepenny Opera. Written with Bertolt Brecht.
Script.

University of Texas, Humanities Research Center, Manuscripts
Collection, Box 7219, Austin, Texas 78712.

I   12 miscellaneous documents.

Harvard University, Houghton Library, Cambridge, Massachusetts 02138.

M   Pittkin, William. The Threepenny Opera. Drawing in ink
      and watercolor, signed. [New York], 1954. 1p.

University of California, Los Angeles, Music Library, 405
Hilgard Avenue, Los Angeles, California 90024.

ERNST TOCH ARCHIVE

B1   2 L. to Ernst Toch.

Boston University, Mugar Memorial Library, 771 Commonwealth
Avenue, Boston, Massachusetts 02215.

HELEN DEUTSCH PAPERS

B1   1 L. to Helen Deutsch. T. 1937.

B2   1 L. from Helen Deutsch. cc. 1947.

University of Pennsylvania, The Charles Patterson Van Pelt
Library, Philadelphia, Pennsylvania 19104.

ALMA MAHLER-WERFEL COLLECTION

B1   2 L. to Alma Mahler-Werfel. 1937, 1944.

Dr. Gustave O. Arlt, 13220-C Admiralty Way, Marina del Rey,
California 90291.

FRANZ WERFEL ARCHIVE

B2   1 L. from Louis B. Nizer. 1937.

Leo Baeck Institute, 129 East 73rd Street, New York, N.Y.
10021.

J   1 photo of Weill. Ca. 1929.

Metropolitan Opera Association, Inc., The Archives, Lincoln
Center Plaza, New York, N.Y. 10023.

H3   5 cl. from Opera News. 1950-1970.

Academy of Motion Picture Arts and Sciences, Margaret Herrick
Library, 9038 Melrose Avenue, Hollywood, California 90069.

H3   Newspaper cl. file.

Museum of the City of New York, Fifth Avenue at 103rd Street,
New York, N.Y. 10029.

H3   Newspaper cl. in the museum's "Personality File."

State University of New York at Binghamton, Center for Modern
Theater Research, Binghamton, New York 13901.

MAX REINHARDT ARCHIVE

*   Uncatalogued materials concerning Kurt Weill.

967

FRANZ CARL WEISKOPF

Writer, 1900-1955

The main collection of Weiskopf materials is located at the
Akademie der Künste, Ost-Berlin. There is no major collection of Weiskopf materials located in the U.S.

Die Hauptsammlung von Weiskopf-Materialien befindet sich in
der Akademie der Künste, Ost-Berlin. In den Vereinigten
Staaten gibt es keine bedeutende Weiskopf-Sammlung.

University of Southern California, Lion Feuchtwanger Memorial
Library, 520 Paseo Miramar, Pacific Palisades, California
90272.

B1   41 L. to Lion Feuchtwanger. 1937-1955.

B2   43 L. from Lion Feuchtwanger. 1937-1955.

New York Public Library, Manuscript Division, Fifth Avenue
and 42nd Street, New York, N.Y. 10018.

C1   The Firing Squad. T. with h. corr. 367p.

University of Texas, Humanities Research Center, Manuscripts
Collection, Box 7219, Austin, Texas 78712.

B1   6 L.

B2   9 L.

State University of New York at Albany, Department of Germanic Languages and Literatures, 1400 Washington Avenue,
Albany, New York 12222.

STORM PUBLISHERS ARCHIVE, CARL MISCH COLLECTION, KARL O.
PAETEL COLLECTION

B1   6 L. to Karl O. Paetel (xerox). 1944-1946.
      1 L. to Alexander Gode von Aesch. 1947.
      1 L. to Fritz von Unruh. 1947.

968

B2   1 L. from Alexander Gode von Aesch. 1947.
     1 L. from Carl Misch. T. 1946.

Library of Congress, Manuscript Division, Independence Avenue and First Street S.E., Washington, D.C. 20540.

BENJAMIN W. HUEBSCH PAPERS

B1   1 L. to B. W. Huebsch. T. 1945.
B2   2 L. from B. W. Huebsch. T.cc. 1945.
D7   Review of Stefan Zweig's The Royal Game. 1945.

Mr. Hans Sahl, 800 West End Avenue, New York, N.Y. 10025.

B1   Several L. to Hans Sahl.

University of Illinois at Urbana-Champaign, University Library, University Archives, Room 19, Urbana, Illinois 61801.

KERKER QUINN PAPERS

B1   Several L. to Kerker Quinn.

University of California, Los Angeles, Department of Special
Collections, 120 Lawrence Clark Powell Library, Los Angeles,
California 90024.

FRANZ WERFEL ARCHIVE

B1   1 L. to Franz Werfel. 1944.

Mrs. Peter M. Lindt, 949 West End Avenue, New York, N.Y.
10025.

C   Ms. submitted to Lindt for use on his radio program.

VICTOR F. WEISSKOPF

Physicist, 1908-

Prof. Victor F. Weisskopf, Center for Theoretical Physics, Massachusetts Institute of Technology, Cambridge, Massachusetts 02139.

Private collection: accessible with permission from Prof. Weisskopf.

Privatsammlung, die mit Erlaubnis von Prof. Weisskopf zugänglich ist.

A1   Notebooks of most important trips and events. Incomplete (war years missing, 1937-1950).

B1,2   Very large correspondence from the years at MIT, including c. of Weisskopf's own letters (only a small amount of scientific correspondence).

C7   Mss. of several talks.

C7,8   Several Mss. of articles. Also F. with working papers and notes to articles.
       Some course notes: quantum mechanics course, etc.

D7,8   Offprints of all of Weisskopf's writings.

E   Transcripts of interviews (including McCarthy investigating committee).

H3   Newspaper cl. concerning Weisskopf (1940-). Nearly complete collection.

I   Passport collection.

J   Large photo collection.

K   Large library of periodicals, such as: Physical Review, Nuclear Physics Review, etc. Complete from 1930- .

L   Materials used by Weisskopf to write articles.

M   Memorabilia, including awards and citations.

Library of Congress, Manuscript Division, Independence Avenue and First Street S.E., Washington, D.C. 20540.

J. ROBERT OPPENHEIMER PAPERS

B1   23 L. and 6 Tel. to J. Robert Oppenheimer. 1942-1965
      and undated.
      1 L. to Harlow Shapley. T.cc. 1949.

B2   7 L. and 4 Tel. from J. Robert Oppenheimer. 1942-1964.
      1 L. from Dr. Placzek. T.cc. 1949.
      1 L. from Eugene P. Wigner. T.cc. 1948.

C7   "Theoretical Physics at the Geneva Conference." [1955].
      T.cc. 6p.
      "Report on the Visa-Situation." 1952. 4p.

I   Recommendations for Weisskopf by J. Robert Oppenheimer.
      1956.

American Institute of Physics, Niels Bohr Library, 335 East
45th Street, New York, N.Y. 10017.

NIELS BOHR CORRESPONDENCE, ORAL HISTORY COLLECTION, PICTORIAL
FILE

B1   17 L. to Niels Bohr. 1931-1961. Microfilm.

B2   17 L. from Niels Bohr. 1931-1961. Microfilm.

F   Tapes of lectures:
      "Development of Recent Physics." 1967.
      "Fundamental Research - A Prerequisite." 1970.
      "The Los Alamos Years." 1967.
      "The Privilege of Being a Physicist." 1969.
      "Quantum Theory and Elementary Particles." 1965.
      "Role of Nuclear Structure Research in Modern Phys-
         ics." 1967.

G   Interview for Science and Technology Magazine: "Think-
         ing Ahead with..."
      6-hr. interview. Also transcript.

J   Uncatalogued photos. Portraits as well as group photos.

Archive for History of Quantum Physics (locations in U.S.:
Bancroft Library, University of California, Berkeley; Ameri-
can Philosophical Society, Philadelphia, Pennsylvania;
American Institute of Physics, New York, N.Y.).

B1   8 L. to Werner Heisenberg. [1934].
      1 L. ea. to H. A. Kramers, J. R. Oppenheimer, Arnold
      Sommerfeld.

B2   4 L. from: H. A. Kramers, Wolfgang Pauli. 1939, 1957.

C8   "Die Bose-Hyperquantelung der Schrö.-Gordongleichung."
      Undated. 7p.

G   Interview. 1963. 28p.

University of California, Los Alamos Scientific Laboratory,
P.O. Box 1663, Los Alamos, New Mexico 87544.

I   61 documents reporting work done at Los Alamos Scien-
      tific Laboratory.
      21 documents reporting work done at some location
      other than Los Alamos.

Duke University, William R. Perkins Library, Manuscript
Department, Durham, North Carolina 27706.

FRITZ WOLFGANG LONDON PAPERS

B1   6 L. to F. W. London. A. 1931-1938.
      2 L. from F. W. London. A. and cc. 1932.

University of Chicago, The Joseph Regenstein Library, 1100
East 57th Street, Chicago, Illinois 60637.

JAMES FRANCK PAPERS

B1,2 Correspondence between Weisskopf and James Franck.

B1,   L. of congratulations to Franck on his 70th birthday.
J   1952. Accompanied by photo of Weisskopf.

J   Group photo. Institute for Theoretical Physics. Copen-
      hagen, 1935.

University of California, San Diego, Mandeville Library,

VICTOR F. WEISSKOPF

Department of Special Collections, La Jolla, California
92037.

MARIA GOEPPERT MAYER COLLECTION

Bl   1 L. to Maria Mayer.

FRANZ WERFEL

Writer, 1890-1945

University of California, Los Angeles, Department of Special
Collections, 120 Lawrence Clark Powell Library, Los Angeles,
California 90024.

The FRANZ WERFEL ARCHIVE, which consists of 30 archive boxes
of materials (ca. 9 ft.), was donated to the library in 1948
by Alma Mahler-Werfel, widow of Franz.

*Das FRANZ WERFEL ARCHIVE, das etwa 30 Archivkartons Materia-
lien (ca. 2,70 m) umfaßt, ist eine Schenkung der Witwe Franz
Werfels, Alma Mahler-Werfel, an die Bibliothek.*

Al   Diary. 1919-1923. Contents: "Hofmeister Kaiser und die
      Hexe," Hoffmann stories (music), notes to readings,
      etc. 84p.
      "Tagebuch Franz Werfel 1925. Reise nach Ägypten und
      Palästina." A. 111p. Also dialog-fragment and notes
      to "Paulus unter den Juden." 5p.
      Diary. Begun Sept. 11, 1939. A. 3p.

A2   Large notebook. Hamburg, 1910. A. Poems. 40p. Der Be-
      such aus dem Elysium. Dialog. 6p. Prose fragment and
      notes. 3p.
      Pocket notebook. [1913]. A. Notes to Primadonna. 59p.
      List of works. 1p.
      Large notebook. [1914]. A. Draft of Einander. 39p.
      Poem titles. 1p.
      Large notebook. End of April 1915. A. "Traum von einer
      neuen Hölle" ("Gesang aus einer neuen Hölle"). 37p.
      Poems. 3p.
      Pocket notebook. 1916. A. 35p.
      Large notebook. Jan. and end of June 1917. A. Stock-
      leinen. Ein Schauspiel in 3 Aufzügen. 70p. Miscel-
      lany. 73p.
      Small notebook. 1917. A. Poems, political essay. 13p.
      Essay fragment. 5p. "Schlußwort von F.W.," Laurentin
      poems. 25p.
      Large notebook. A. Notes to Spiegelmensch, dialog,
      sketches. 14p. Prose and poetry drafts.
      Large notebook. A. "Klingsor. Eine Szene." 15p. "Der
      Spielhof. Ein Märchen." 32p. Miscellany. 4p.

974

Large notebook. 1918-1919. A. "Die Erschaffung des
Witzes." 20p. "Nachschrift zum Gerichtstag." 36p.
"Mittagsgöttin." 23p. Prose fragment, notes. 12p.
Large notebook. A. Dialog to Spiegelmensch, poetry and
prose fragments. 16p. "Der Dzhin. Ein Märchen." 29p.
Large notebook. 1919. A. "Die schwarze Messe." 126p.
"Spiegelmensch. Zaubermärchen. 1. Entwurf." 11p.
Large notebook. [Before May 1921]. A. Notes to "Fege-
feuer." 14p.
Large notebook. 1921. A. "19. Mai 1921. Franz Werfel.
Die Entdeckung der Seele. Fegefeuer. Eine mehr als
spiritistische Geschichte." 32p.
Large notebook. 1921. "Rest eines Traums." 1 leaf.
Large notebook. 1922. A. "Beschwörungen. Gedicht-
zyklus." 60p. "Die Hallen des Meeres." 4p. "Der
Massenmörder." 6p. Sketches. 1 leaf.
Pocket notebook. 1921-1922. A. Notes. 6p.
Large notebook. 1922-1923. A. Poems and sketches. 7p.
Drafts of "Schweiger." 7p. L. to Kurt Klaiber in
Alma's hand. 13p. Notes. 1p.
Large notebook. [Ca. 1923]. A. Aphorisms, poems. 2p.
Pocket notebook. 1923. A. Notes and sketches to "Verdi."
18p.
Large notebook. 1923. A. "Skizze. Totenaufruhr. Drama-
tische Ballade in neun Strophen." Dialog, notes. 37p.
"Erfolg." 8p.
Large notebook. 1923-1924. A. "Notizen zu einer 1923-24
historischen Tragödie." 50p. "Die Macht des Ge-
schicks." 12p.
Pocket notebook. [1925]. A. Miscellany. 15p.
Large notebook. 1925-1926. A. Essays. 28p.
Large notebook. July 1925 and April 1926. A. Notes and
drafts, primarily to "Paulus unter den Juden." 26p.
Pocket notebook. Ca. 1926. A. Notes. 7p.
Notebook. A. Poems. 1p.
Large notebook. July 1926. A. "Das Pogrom. Novelle."
63p.
Pocket notebook. Undated [1926-1929]. Miscellany. 24p.
Pocket notebook. Oct. 1927 - June 1928. A. Poetry and
notes. 17p.
Pocket notebook. 1928. A. Notes, poems, sketches. 15p.
Large notebook. Undated [fall 1929]. A. Notes to "Ge-
schwister von Neapel." 18p.

Pocket notebook. Ca. 1929. A. Religious-philosophic notes. 3p.

Large notebook. June 1930. A. Sketches and drawings to "Musa Dagh." 49p. plus 46 loose p.

Pocket notebook. 1931. A. Notes, poetry. 9p.

Pocket notebook. April/May 1932. A. Poetry, travel notes, dialog, etc. 26p.

Pocket notebook. Ca. 1935. A. Poetry, aphorism. 6p.

Large notebook. July 1935. A. "Die Fürbitterin der Tiere oder Die Erlösung der Tiere" and "Die Fürbitterin der Toten." 25p.

Pocket notebook. Aug. 3 [1935]. A. Notes and drawings. 12p.

Large notebook. 1936-1937. A. "Höret die Stimme." 82p.

Large notebook. 1937. A. "In einer Nacht. Schauspiel in 3 Akten. Skizzen." 24p. Miscellany. 6p.

Pocket notebook. Jan./Sept. 1938. A. Aphorisms, notes, dialog, poems, drawings. 148p.

Large notebook. 1938. A. "Krankheit, die zum Leben führt. Ich-Erzählung." 18p. "Nizza. Die Zukunft des Sozialismus. Ein Frage an die Weltgeschichte." 3p.

Small notebook. 1939, 1941. A. Sanary notes, poems, thoughts. 35p. "Bernadette." 13p. Personal notes. 2p.

Large notebook. A. "Grausamkeiten aus dem Exil." 10p. Notes. 2p.

Large notebook. July 1938 and Aug. 1942. A. "Beim Anblick eines Toten," "Porta Inferni," "Ist die Erde ein Strafort?" 15p. Notes, poem. 2p.

B1 Ca. 500 L., including L. to: Samuel Behrman, Gottfried Bermann-Fischer, Lazi Bus-Fekete, Lion Feuchtwanger, Herbert Fuchs-Robetin, Hamish Hamilton, Benjamin W. Huebsch, Heinrich Eduard Jacob, Lawrence Langner, Ludwig Lewisohn, Georg Marton, Heinrich Schnitzler, Edith Snow, Archbishop Francis Spellman, Friedrich Torberg.

264 L. and 36 Tel. to Alma Mahler-Werfel. A. 1918-1945.

B2 Ca. 300 L., including L. from: Hermann Bahr, Alban Berg, Gottfried Bermann-Fischer, Hermann Borchardt, Lazi Bus-Fekete, Alfred Döblin, Albert Einstein, Herbert Fuchs-Robetin, Willy Haas, Hugo von Hofmannsthal, Benjamin W. Huebsch, Heinrich Eduard Jacob, Alfred Kantorowicz, Annette Kolb, Lawrence Langner,

Else Lasker-Schüler, Peter M. Lindt, Jacques Maritain, Georg Marton, Erich Mühsam, Arthur Schnitzler, Friedrich Torberg, Ludwig Ullmann, Johannes Urzidil, F. C. Weiskopf, Anton Wildgans, Theodor Wolff, Arnold Zweig, Stefan Zweig.

C1   Das Lied von Bernadette. Roman. First volume. T.cc. with h. corr. 408p. Second volume. T.cc. with corr. 246p.

Reiseroman. In 3 parts. T. and cc. 802p.

"Die schwarze Messe. Romanfragment." 1919. T. 61p., 7p.

Stern der Ungeborenen. Working title: Reiseroman. In 3 parts. A. 142p., 183p., 163p.

C2   Jacobowsky und der Oberst. Komödie einer Tragödie in drei Akten. T. with h. corr. 158p. Dialog fragments and notes. 28p. Individual scenes in German. T. 272p. Individual scenes in English. T. 128p.

Paulus unter den Juden. Drawings, dialog fragments. A. 42p.

Schweiger. Drawings. A. 14p.

Der Weg der Verheißung. "Kleine Inszenierungs-Übersicht für das Bibelspiel Der Weg der Verheißung von Franz Werfel." [Ca. 1935]. Dialog fragment, description of plot. A. 58p.

C3   Botschaft vom irdischen Leben. Sammelmappe für ein künftiges Gedichtbuch. Erste Skizzen. A. with corr. 52p.

155 Ms. of poems. A. with corr. Also miscellaneous lists, etc. 10p.

"Der Tod Lenins. (Ballade oder kleines Epos). 1927. Erste Skizze (Sprachlich nur hingesetzt)." A. with corr. 16p. "Der Tod des Diktators." Aug. 1927. A. 3p.

C4   "Die andere Seite." 1916. T. 2p.

"Die arge Legende vom gerissenen Galgenstrick." Undated. [1938]. T. 24p.

"Der Arzt von Wien." Nov. 4, 1938. 3 versions. T. 7p., 8p., 5p.

"Bauernstuben. Erinnerung." Undated. T. 2p.

"Blasphemie eines Irren." Undated. T. 9p.

"Cabrinowitsch. Ein Tagebuch aus dem Jahre 1915. Erzählung." Undated. T. 7p.

"Der Dschin. Ein Märchen." Undated [1918]. A. 20p.

Another version. T. 14p.
"Die Ehe jenseits des Todes. Erzählung. 1. Skizze."
Undated [1925]. T. 17p.
"Ein wichtiges Erlebnis beim Hochschwebenden." Undated.
[194-?]. T. 8p.
"Erfolg." 1920/1921. T. 5p.
Fragments: "Theologie," "Skizze zu einem Gedicht,"
"Begegnung über einer Schlucht." Undated [191-?].
T. 3p., 1p., 2p.
"Die Geliebte." 1916. T. 6p.
"Geschichte von einem Hundefreund." 1916. T. 2 ver-
sions. 5p. ea.
"Géza de Varsany oder Wann wirst du endlich eine Seele
bekommen?" 1944. T. 3 versions. 27p., 24p., 25p.
"Die Katze (Erzählungen eines Kranken), meine dritte
Novelle." 1906. A. 9p.
"Par l'amour." Aug. 6-8, 1938. A. 2 versions. 7p. ea.
Another version. T. 9p.
"Pogrom." July 28, 1926. T. 38p.
"Revolution der Makulatur. Ein Märchen." 1917. T. 4p.
"Der Schauspieler." May 19, 1921. T. 17p.
"Die Schauspielerin." Undated. T. 1938. 2 versions.
4p., 6p.
"Die schlimme Legende vom gerissenen Galgenstrick."
Undated [1942]. A. 5p.
"Der Tode des Moses." Undated [191-?]. T. 5p.
"Traum von einem alten Mann." Undated. T. 7p.
"Das traurige Lokal." Nov. 1912. A. 7p.
"Die wahre Geschichte vom wiederhergestellten Kreuz."
Undated. A. 26p. Another version. Undated. T. 41p.
"Weissenstein der Weltverbesser." Undated [1939]. A.
8p. Another version. T. 8p.
"Zwei Legenden: Die Erschaffung der Musik. Die Erschaf-
fung des Witzes." 1913 and 1917. T. 2p., 5p.

C7 "Anläßlich eines Mauseblicks." Undated [1938]. T. 4p.
"Ansprache." Undated [1935]. A. 7p.
"Ansprache für den norwegischen Rundfunk." Undated
[1940]. A. 3p.
"Answers to Miss Dorothy Donnell, Department of Jus-
tice, Washington." Undated [1941]. A. 3p. Another
version. T. 4p.
"Aus der Dämmerung einer Welt." Undated. T. 16p.

"Beim Anblick eines Toten." 1938. T. 11p.

"Betrachtung über den Krieg von morgen (angestellt im Januar 1938)." T. 20p. Another version. A. 12p.

"Botschaft an das deutsche Volk." Undated [1945]. 3p.

"Das doppelte Deutschland." Undated. T. 7p.

"Ein Bildnis Giuseppe Verdis." Undated. T. 87p.

"Erguß und Beichte." Undated [after 1918]. A. 16p.

"Erinnerung an Brand." Undated [1920]. A. 6p.

"Festrede auf Schalom Asch." Undated [1920]. A. 9p.

"Fortsetzung der Bozener Tage (Seite 115-123)." Undated [1915]. T. 5p.

"Fragment gegen das männliche Geschlecht." Undated [1917]. T. 4p.

"Fragment zum Kapitel Theodizee (1914-1920)." A. 31p.

"Gustav Mahler (Zur Einführung in den Mahler-Zyklus der N.B.C.), 31. Dez. 1941." A. 2p. T. 2 versions. 4p., 3p.

"Heimkehr ins Reich." Undated [1938]. T. 6p.

Introduction to Hermann Borchardt's novel Die Verschwörung der Zimmerleute. Undated [194-?]. 3 versions. 7p., 4p., 9p.

Introduction to individual chap. of Twilight of the World. Undated. A. 16p.

"Jugend." Undated [early]. A. 1p.

"Kann die Menschheit ohne Religion leben?" March 3, 1932. A. 17p.

"Können wir ohne Gottesglauben leben? oder Die Wahrheit über die Krise unserer Zeit." Undated. T. 26p.

"Krisis der Ideale. Krieg, Revolution, Gesellschaft. Fragmente 1914-1917 [Der Snobismus als geistige Weltmacht]." A. 21p.

"Lebensdaten." Undated [before Fall 1921]. A. 5p.

"Max Reinhardt zum neunten September 1943." A. 3p. T. 3p.

"My Most Unforgettable Character." Undated. A. 8p. T. 9p. Another version with the title "Manon." T. 10p.

"Nur ein Weg zur deutschen Rettung." May 8, 1945. T. 2 versions. 3p., 2p.

"Ohne Divinität keine Humanität (Eine Ansprache gehalten in Paris am 14. I. 1939)." T. 2 versions. 9p., 10p.

"Pater Cyrill Fischer - ein Kaempfer in Wort und Tat." Sept. 21, 1944. T. 7p.

"Stefan Zweigs Tod." Undated [1942]. A. 6p. T. 8p.
"Die tanzenden Derwische." Undated [1925]. T. 11p.
Theologumena [1942-1944]. Preface. T. with numerous
    corr. and cc. 3c. 148p. ea.
    "Theologumena." Undated. A. 87p.
    "Theologumena. Skizzen und Vorarbeiten und Auszüge
      aus Notizbüchern 1937/38." A. 51p.
"Vorbericht." Introduction to "Verdi." Summer 1923.
    A. 3p. Another incomplete version. Undated [after
    1940]. A. 50p.
"Vortrag." Undated [after 1941]. A. 17p.
"Zemlinsky der Melodiker." Undated [1921]. A. 7p.
"Die Zukunft der Literatur." July 1937. A. 5p.
"Zum Judentum (1917)." A. 1p.
Untitled essays. 10 items. 27p.

D2   Der Weg der Verheißung. Ein Bibelspiel. Stage version.
        Mimeo. 105p.

D7   Ca. 50 newspaper and magazine cl. of articles by Wer-
        fel.

E   Embezzled Heaven. A Play in 4 Scenes by L. Bus-Fekete
        and Mary Helen Fay. From the Novel by Franz Werfel.
        T.cc. 90p.
        The Eternal Road by Franz Werfel. Revised Script,
        January 10, 1937. Alexander Leftwich, Jr. T.cc. 129p.
        The Forty Days of Musa Dagh. Franz Werfel. Dramatized
        by Iris English. T. 105p. + 6p.
        Franz Werfel's "The Song of Bernadette." Screen Play
        by George Seaton. 1st Draft Continuity. Jan. 20,
        1943. 232p. Final Script. February 19, 1943. 166p.
        Revised Final. March 8, 1943. Mimeo. 166p.
        The Song of Bernadette by Franz Werfel. Condensation
        by Charlotte Dieterle. T.cc. 69p.
        Jacobowsky and the Colonel. Comedy of a Tragedy in
        Three Acts. The Original Play by Franz Werfel. Trans-
        lated by Gustave O. Arlt. The Viking Press: New York
        1944. 144p. 6 additional English versions. 125p.,
        130p. (2c.), 137p. (3c.), 123p., 137p., 143p.
        Star of the Unborn. 3 parts. Tr. by Gustave O. Arlt.
        T. 767p.

H3   Ca. 60 articles about Werfel, partly interviews and
        partly reports on his activities.

H4   Jacobowsky und der Oberst. Ca. 100 cl.
Das Lied von Bernadette. Ca. 250 cl.
Der veruntreute Himmel. Ca. 70 cl.
Zwischen oben und unten. Ca. 80 cl.

I   Honorary doctorate. University of California, Los
Angeles, June 9, 1943.

K   Several books from Werfel's private library, including:
Verdi. With corr. by Werfel.
Der veruntreute Himmel. With corr. by Werfel.

L   Source materials to Stern der Ungeborenen.
Materials on the following subjects: anti-fascism,
pacifism, Judaism, Austria, Sudetendeutschtum.

M   Blue flask in the shape of the Lady of Lourdes.
Death mask, made by Werfel's stepdaughter, Anna Mahler.
Werfel's desk.
2 paintings of St. Bernadette.

O   Numerous programs and posters.

Dr. Gustave O. Arlt, 13220-C Admiralty Way, Marina del Rey,
California 90291.

The materials in Dr. Arlt's private collection will be deposited in the FRANZ WERFEL ARCHIVE at the University of
California, Los Angeles, sometime after 1979.

*Die Materialien in Dr. Arlts Privatsammlung werden nach 1979
dem FRANZ WERFEL ARCHIVE der University of California, Los
Angeles, eingegliedert werden.*

A2   Pocket notebook. A. Notes to "Paulus," "Zu Juarez."
15p.
Pocket notebook. A. Essay, poems, notes, drawings.
23p.
Pocket notebook. A. "Paulus unter den Juden/Notizen
zum Drama." 60p. + 1 loose p.
Large notebook. A. "2. Heft. Esther, Kaiserin von
Persien." 1914. 35p. "Nicht der Mörder, der Ermordete ist schuldig. Eine Novelle." 1919. 59p.

Large notebook. A. "Der Spielhof. 2tes Heft." p. 33-60. Notes. 1p.
Large notebook. A. 3p.
Large notebook. Nov. 1914. "1. Heft. Esther, Kaiserin von Persien. Dramatisches Gedicht von Franz Werfel." A. 80p.
Large notebook. A. "Paulus unter den Juden." Also notes. 44p. Poems, poem titles. 4p. "Argument." 3p. Notes. 3p.
Notebook. 1938-1941. A. "Die verlorene Mutter." 20p. Draft of "Jacobowsky." 16p.

B1   9 L. 1940-1943, including L. to: Bermann-Fischer Verlag, Benjamin W. Huebsch, Klaus Mann.

B2   Ca. 120 L., including L. from: Raoul Auernheimer, Albert Bassermann, Vicki Baum, Alban Berg, Hermann Borchardt, Max Brod, Jacques Chambrun, Herbert Fuchs-Robetin, Manfred George, Walter Gropius, Hans Habe, Hamish Hamilton, Wieland Herzfelde, Kurt Hiller, Benjamin W. Huebsch, Albrecht Joseph, Adolf Klarmann, Meyer Krakowski, Emil Ludwig, Klaus Mann, Georg Marton, Kurt Pinthus, Jacob Sonderling, Ludwig Ullmann, Fritz von Unruh, Johannes Urzidil, Guido Zernatto, Arnold Zweig.

B3   13 L., including L. to and from: Benjamin W. Huebsch, Louis Nizer, Edmond Pauker, Max Reinhardt, Edith A. Snow, Kurt Weill.

I   Werfel's family tree. "Zusammengestellt von Rabb. Dr. B. Wolf." 2p.
Contract between Werfel and Harold R. Peat, concerning lectures. Dated March 23, 1942. 2p.
Der Weg der Verheißung. Contract between Werfel and Viking Press. Feb. 14. 2p.
Certificate. Bundespolizeidirektion in Wien. Oct. 25, 1935. 1p.

University of Pennsylvania, The Charles Patterson Van Pelt Library, Philadelphia, Pennsylvania 19104.

The ALMA MAHLER-WERFEL ARCHIVE, consisting of 47 boxes of materials plus additional bound manuscripts, was received by the University of Pennsylvania in Feb. 1968. All publication rights to materials in the collection are held by Anna Mahler, daughter of Alma. Although the collection remains as yet uncatalogued, a catalog of the collection is presently being prepared for publication by Dr. Glyns Waldman of the University of Pennsylvania German Department. The following is a description of the Franz Werfel materials in the collection. For a description of the remainder of the materials, see Alma Mahler-Werfel.

Das ALMA MAHLER-WERFEL ARCHIVE, das 47 Kartons Materialien sowie zusätzliche gebundene Manuskripte umfaßt, wurde der University of Pennsylvania im Feb. 1968 übereignet. Alle Publikationsrechte ruhen bei Anna Mahler, der Tochter Alma Mahler-Werfels. Die Sammlung ist z.Zt. noch nicht völlig katalogisiert, es wird aber von Dr. Glyns Waldman vom German Department der University of Pennsylvania ein Katalog der Sammlung zur Veröffentlichung vorbereitet. Es folgt eine Beschreibung der Franz Werfel Materialien der Sammlung. Eine Beschreibung der übrigen Materialien findet sich unter "Alma Mahler-Werfel".

A1   "Zufalls Tagebuch." Beverly Hills, California, 1919-1920, 1922, 1923. T. with corr. 41p.

B1   Ca. 319 L., including L. to: Julius Bab, Samuel Behrman, Elisabeth Bergner, Hermann Borchardt, László Bus-Fekete, Albert Ehrenstein, Lion Feuchtwanger, Varian Fry, Manfred George, Theresa Helburn, Franz Horch, Benjamin W. Huebsch, Hans Janowitz, Albrecht Joseph, Alfred Kantorowicz, Oskar Karlweis, Frank Kingdon, Arnold Schoenberg, Gerhart Seger, Kurt Wolff, Heinrich Zimmer, Carl Zuckmayer.
    Xerox c. and cc. of L. to Alma Mahler-Werfel. 1920-1934, 1944-1945. Ca. 475p.
    1918-1945. T. with h. corr. 292p.
    1918. Cc. and xerox c. Ca. 100p.
    1919. Cc. and xerox c. Ca. 100p.
    4 L. A. Undated. 10p.
    12 L. Xerox c. and duplicates. 44p.

B2   Ca. 240 L., including L. from: Raoul Auernheimer, Julius Bab, Richard Beer-Hofmann, Elisabeth Bergner, Gottfried Bermann-Fischer, Hermann Borchardt, G. A.

Borgese, Hermann Broch, Richard Coudenhove-Kalergi,
Franz Csokor, Julius Deutsch, Marlene Dietrich,
Albert Ehrenstein, Fabricius, Lion Feuchtwanger,
Bruno Frank, Manfred George, Ivan Goll, Walter Gro-
pius, George Grosz, Hans Habe, Franz Horch, Benja-
min W. Huebsch, H. E. Jacob, Hans Janowitz, James
Joyce, Alfred Kantorowicz, Hermann Kesten, Otto von
Habsburg, Kurt Wolff, Friderike Zweig.

B3   Correspondences between Morton and Albine Werfel.
Wolff, Kurt. Miscellaneous L. concerning Werfel and
Werfel's publications.

C1   Barbara oder die Frömmigkeit. With the comment: "1ter
Entwurf." Dated June 22, 1929. Bound Ms. A. 651p.
"Die II. Niederschrift." Dated Sept. 25, 1929. In
notebook. A. 777p.
Bocksgesang. In fünf Akten. 1921. In large notebook.
A. 176p.
Cella oder die Überwinder. Versuch eines Romans. Dated
Sept. 1938, Jan. 31, 1939 and March 1, 1939. In 3
large notebooks. A. 281p. Another version. T. with
corr. 317p.
"Die Flucht aus dem Wintergarten." Synopsis of chap.
18-26 of Stern der Ungeborenen. T.
[Jeremias. Höret die Stimme]. Dated Nov. 12, 1936. In
small notebook. A. 723p.
Das Lied von Bernadette. Begun Jan. 14, 1941, ended
May 18, 1941. In 8 small notebooks. A. 530p.
"Bernadette Soubirous." Cc. with h. notes. 4p.
"Die Heiligsprechung." Early notes.
Love and Hatred of Zorah Pasha. Written with Friedrich
Torberg and Angela Stewart. Cc. 129p. Another version
written by Torberg and Werfel. 38p.
[Simone Bocanegra]. Untitled and undated. In notebook.
A. 244p.
Verdi. Roman. Dated Sept. 25, 1923. In large notebook.
A. 914p. Another untitled version, in small note-
book. A. 726p.
Die vierzig Tage des Musa Dagh. Roman. Dated Christmas
1933. 2 volumes. A. 888p.

C2   Bocksgesang. In fünf Akten. 1921. A. 176p.
Euripides: oder Über den Krieg. Unpub. A. pc. Ca. 40p.

Jacobowsky und der Oberst. Komödie einer Tragödie in
3 Akten. "3te Fassung." 1943. A. 172p. Third scene
only. T. 28p.

Juarez und Maximilian von Mexiko. Große Historie in
3 Phasen und dreizehn Bildern. Dated July 16, 1924.
In small notebook. A. 142p. Also in same notebook:
"Die Bestattung des Beins. Novelle." A. 5p.

Paulus unter den Juden. Dramatische Legende in sechs
Bildern. Undated [1926]. In notebook. A. 133p. Draft
of drama. 2p. Single scene. 4p. Stage directions,
notes, list of errors.

Das Reich Gottes in Böhmen. Tragödie eines Führers in
drei Teilen. 1ter Band. Undated [1930]. In 2 small
notebooks. A. 104p.

Schweiger. Ein Trauerspiel in 3 Akten. 1tes Heft.
Undated [1922]. In small notebook. A. 124p.

Spiegelmensch. Magische Trilogie. Fortsetzung des
zweiten Teils. Eins ums andre. Dated Feb. 11, 1920.
In small notebook. A. p. 146-292. "Nachtrag." 5p.
Another fragment. Cc. with h. corr. 88p. Bound c. of
book with notes and stage directions. 2p.

Der Weg der Verheißung. Ein Bibelspiel. Former title:
Das Volk. Dated Sept. 14, 1934. In 2 small notebooks.
A. 48p. and 28p.

C3   Der Erkennende. Composition by Alma Mahler-Werfel with
lyrics by Werfel. 49p.
Der Weltfreund. A. pc. 40p.
Miscellaneous poems. A. and T. Over 65p.
Poems by Werfel, copied in Alma's hand. A. Ca. 20p.

C4   "Aus der Dämmerung einer Welt. Versuch über das Kaiser-
tum Österreich." A. with corr. 35p.
"Die Entfremdung. Die Liebe der Schwester. Novelle von
Werfel No. 1." Undated. In notebook. A. 87p.
"Gabrinowitsch." Cc. with corr. 7p.
"Geheimnis eines Menschen. Novelle von Franz Werfel
No. 2." Undated. In notebook. A. 71p.
"Kleine Verhältnisse. Erzählung." 1930, with the com-
ment "Aus dem geplanten mehrbändigen Zyklus 'Die
Lebensalter'." A. 70p.
"Konto 2307." Story or individual chap. T. 6p.
"Nicht der Mörder, der Ermordete ist schuldig. Novelle.
Fortsetzung." Undated [1920]. In large notebook. A.

985

p. 59-230.

"Novellen 1927." Notebook containing:

"Die Hoteltreppe." A. 40p.

"Barbieri." A. 19p.

"Die Liebe der Schwester (oder vielleicht) Gabriele."
A. 79p.

"Das Trauerhaus." A. 63p.

"Der Spielhof." Draft. 2p.

"Der Tod des Kleinbürgers (1te Niederschrift). Skizze."
With the comment: "Angefangen 27. September, beendet
5. Oktober 1926." In small notebook. A. 76p.

"Wirrnisse eines Oktobertags. Erzählung." Dated April
24, 1940. In small notebook. A. 70p.

C5   Star of the Unborn. Film exposé of Stern der Ungeborenen. T.c. 26p.

C7   "Die Februarrevolte." 2 original German T. with comments. 25p., 19p. 2cc. 25p., 19p. English tr. by
Gustave O. Arlt.

"Gustav Mahler." Speech tr. by Gabriel Engel. T. with
h. corr. 3p. Also cc. 3p. 1 xerox of cl.

"Können wir ohne Gottesglauben leben?" Cc. 1p.

"Krisis des Ideals." Draft. 18p.

"Kunst und Gewissen." Draft. 10p.

"Metaphysik des Maximalismus." Draft. 7p.

"Ohne Divinität keine Humanität." Cc. 8p.

"Über den dichterischen Schaffensprozeß: aus einem Gespräch." Cc. with h. corr. 4p.

"Über den Rosenkranz." Cc. with h. notes. 11p.

"Verstreute Notizen." Lists, pieces of drafts, etc. Ca.
100p.

"Volk und Nation." Draft. 3p.

"Zusammenfassung der Gründe warum sich der Gottes-
glaube als notwendig und unüberwindlich erweist."
Draft. 1p.

"Zwischen zwei Kriegen." Original T. with corr. and 2
cc. 84p. ea.

Article on Ferdinand Rieser. Draft. 4p.

Essays on the refugee problem:

"The Jewish people..." T. 1p.

"Die Geschichte wiederholt sich..." T. with corr. 1p.

Preface to an article containing L. from Father Cyrill
Fischer to Werfel.

C14 Drawings in pencil. 4p.

D2 In einer Nacht. Pc. of printed 1937 edition. 110p.

D7 "Über die Sprache." Offprint. 5p.

E Abendgesang. Setting to music by Werner Wolf Glaser.
Forty Days of Musa Dagh. Dramatization by Iris English.
105p.
Maximilian and Charlotte. English version by Franz
Waxman. 35p.
Mirror Man. Magic Trilogy. English tr. and adaptation
by Gustave O. Arlt. 167p.
Der Tod des Kleinbürgers. Screen version by Conrad H.
Lester under the title "King of the Heart." 33p.

F Records by Werfel concerning Thomas Mann's relationship to Schoenberg.

H3 Klarmann, Adolf. "Franz Werfel und die Bühne." Undated.
7p. "Franz Werfel." Written for Collier's Encyclo-
pedia. 1947. 2p.
List of Werfel's pub. works.
"Gedenkblatt für Franz Werfel." Printed. 1960.
Ca. 15 cl. on Werfel.

H4 Abituriententag. 1 cl.
Barbara oder die Frömmigkeit. 1 cl.
Juarez und Maximilian. 1 cl., 1 playbill.
Das Lied von Bernadette. Misc. cl. and other materials.
Paulus unter den Juden. Cl. and page proofs.
Stern der Ungeborenen. 1 item.
Der veruntreute Himmel. Cl. and page proofs.
Die vierzig Tage des Musa Dagh. 1 cl.
Die wahre Geschichte vom wiederhergestellten Kreuz. 1
item.

H5 Horoscope of Franz Werfel, prepared by Carroll Righter.
1944.
Specht, Richard. "Franz Werfel. Versuch einer Zeitspiegelung." With a dedication by the author.
"Words and a Song." Re: Franz Werfel. Cc. 3p.

I Business documents between Werfel and the Bermann-
Fischer Verlag. 47p.
Business documents between Werfel and Boosey and
Hawkes.

Passports, birth certificates, safe conduct papers,
naturalization papers, other identification papers
for Franz and Alma.
Collection of documents of Werfel's family.
Contract between Werfel and the Kurt Wolff Verlag.
Various documents concerning the estate of Werfel. 8p.
Franz Werfel citations:
Patron of Record. Disabled American Veterans.
Fr. National Conference of Christians and Jews.
Recommendation for Grete Bach. Undated. 2p.

J   Snapshots of Alma and Franz Werfel.
        Snapshots and formal portraits of Werfel alone.
        Album photos and souvenir Ptc. from Palestine. Another
        album containing photos of scenes in and around Musa
        Dagh, compiled by A. A. Bedikian. Additional sundry
        photos not from the Middle East.

K   Approximately 1,200 of the original 5,000 books from
        the Werfel library were retained in the archive,
        including ca. 165 German editions and tr. of Wer-
        fel's works. In addition, many of the remaining
        books contain dedications by the authors.

M   Miscellaneous Werfel "cartes de visites."

N   Newlin, Dika. 2 songs in honor of Werfel. 10p.

O   3 programs.

Yale University, Beinecke Rare Book and Manuscript Library,
New Haven, Connecticut 06520.

KURT WOLFF ARCHIVE, HERMANN BROCH ARCHIVE, EDMOND PAUKER
COLLECTION

B1   103 L., 6 Ptc. and 184 Tel. to Kurt Wolff and the Kurt
        Wolff Verlag. 1912-1938.

B2   Ca. 150 Tel. and L. from: Martin Buber, Gustav Lan-
        dauer, Werfel's sister Albine, etc.

B2,3   Publisher's correspondence, including L. to and con-
        cerning Werfel from the Kurt Wolff Verlag.

B3   Correspondence between Rudolf Werfel (father of Franz) and Kurt Wolff, including 64 L. from and 46 L. to Rudolf Werfel.

C1   Die Troerinnen des Euripides. "Ausgewählte Szenen für die 'Weißen Blätter'." [1914]. A. 41p.

C3   Der Gerichtstag. 14 poems and 1 poem fragment. A. 15p.
Wir sind. Collection of poems. A. and T. 107p.
3 poems from the cycle "Beschwörungen." A. and T. 4p.

C7   "Der jüngste Tag. Neue Dichtungen." [1913]. A. 6p.
"Hasenclever," "Kurt Pinthus, der jüdische Bismarck," "Werfels verklärtes Selbstportrait." 3 sketches. 3p.

E   Broch, Hermann. Star of the Unborn. A film exposé of Franz Werfel's last novel. Draft of a film script. T. 27p.

H3   Several cl.

I   2 contracts between Werfel and the Kurt Wolff Verlag. c.
Embezzled Heaven. Contracts between Werfel and Edmond Pauker.

L   Miscellaneous publisher's materials and publicity on Werfel.

O   Lecture and theater programs.

Mrs. Adolf D. Klarmann, 1900 Rittenhouse Square, Apt. 6A, Philadelphia, Pennsylvania 19103.

The A. D. KLARMANN WERFELIANA collection will be deposited at the University of Pennsylvania Library sometime after 1978, according to the wishes of the late Dr. Adolf Klarmann. Until that time, the materials will remain at the apartment of Klarmann's widow, who plans to work with the materials after her retirement in 1978. The materials will be inaccessible until such time as they are transferred to the University of Pennsylvania.

Die A. D. KLARMANN WERFELIANA werden entsprechend dem Wunsch des verstorbenen Dr. Klarmann nach 1978 der University of Pennsylvania Library zukommen. Bis dahin bleiben die Materialien im Besitz der Witwe Dr. Klarmanns, die nach ihrer

Pensionierung mit den Materialien arbeiten wird. Bis zur Übergabe an die University of Pennsylvania bleiben die Materialien unzugänglich.

A3   Miscellaneous notes, thoughts.

B1   1 L. to Gottfried Bermann-Fischer. 1945.
       1 L., 1 Ptc. and 1 Tel. to A. D. Klarmann. 1935-1942.
       2 L. to Sigmund Freud. pc.

B1,2   Correspondence between Werfel and his sister, Mitzi
           Rieser. Pc.
       Correspondence between Werfel and Gertrud Spirk. pc.
       Miscellaneous Werfel correspondence. pc.

C3   Beschwörungen. A. Incomplete.
       Ms. of 35 poems, plus ca. 68 loose pages of poems
           (many untitled).
       Transcriptions of ca. 20 poems dedicated to Alma.

C5   Verdi. Film exposé of novel.

H3   Pc. of articles about Werfel.

I   Testament, Dated 28. IV. 1928.

Library of Congress, Manuscript Division, Independence Avenue
and First Street S.E., Washington, D.C. 20540.

BENJAMIN W. HUEBSCH PAPERS

B1   24 L., 1 fragment of a L., and 5 Tel. to B. W. Huebsch.
           T. and A. 1935-1945 and undated.

B2   14 L. and 4 Tel. from B. W. Huebsch. T.cc. 1936-1945.
       1 L. ea. from Jacques Chambrun and Victor Polzer.
           1944, 1940.

C1   Ein kleiner Roman. [1940]. T. with h. corr. 64p.
       Bernadette. French tr. by Alexander Clément. 1943.
           12p.
       Der veruntreute Himmel. 1939. T. with h. corr. 404p.

C4   "Die wahre Geschichte vom wiederhergestellten Kreuz."
           Undated. T. with h. corr. 41p.

C7   "United Jewish Appeal." 1945. 2p.

"Answers to the Book Cuties Questions April 1944." 2p.

H3   1 cl.

H4   1 cl.

<u>Leo Baeck Institute</u>, 129 East 73rd Street, New York, N.Y. 10021.

FRANZ WERFEL COLLECTION (20 items). Other materials located in the Institute's JULIUS BAB COLLECTION, ERICH KAHLER COLLECTION, and LEOPOLD SCHWARZSCHILD COLLECTION.

FRANZ WERFEL COLLECTION (20 Nummern). Andere Materialien befinden sich in den folgenden Sammlungen des Instituts: JULIUS BAB COLLECTION, ERICH KAHLER COLLECTION, LEOPOLD SCHWARZSCHILD COLLECTION.

A3   "Personalnachrichten für das Archiv der Akademie der Künste zu Berlin." pc. 4p.

B1   10 L., including L. to: Julius Bab, Ilse Blumenthal-Weiss, Erich Kahler, Eduard Korrodi, Max Reinhardt.

B1,2 Correspondence with Leopold Schwarzschild.

B3   C. of L. from Alma Mahler-Werfel to F. Zweig re: <u>Forty Days of Musa Dagh</u>.
      Correspondence with Werfel's family.

C3   1 poem.

C4   1 album page. A. 1922.

C7   "Alexander Moissi." A. 3p.

D7   Review of Schwarzschild's work.

H3   1 cl.

J   8 photos of Werfel. 1920-1959 and undated.
      Photo of Franz Werfel's mother.

O   2 programs.

<u>Mrs. Gertrude Urzidil</u>, 83-39 116th Street, Richmond Hill, New York 11418.

FRANZ WERFEL

JOHANNES URZIDIL COLLECTION

B1   4 L. to Johannes Urzidil. A. and pc. 1940-1942.
       Transcriptions of 2 L. to Gertrude Spitze. 1914, 1916.

B2   1 Ptc. from Karl Brand. A. 1916.

C4   "Weissenstein, der Weltverbesser." Undated. T. 8p.
       Also printed c.

C7   "Erinnerung an Karl Brand." Undated. A. 7p.

H3   1 cl. 1940.

New York Public Library at Lincoln Center, Library and
Museum of the Performing Arts, 111 Amsterdam Avenue, New
York, N.Y. 10023.

C2   English T. and scripts of:
       Schweiger. Adaptation by Jack Charash.
       Juarez and Maximilian.
       Paul among the Jews.
       God's Kingdom in Bohemia. Tr. by Ruth Langer.
       Jacobowsky and the Colonel. Adaptation by S. N.
          Behrman.
       Jacobowsky. Third version. T.

H3,4 Ca. 200 newspaper cl.

J   Numerous photos of performances of Werfel plays.

O   Several programs.

Indiana University, The University Libraries, The Lilly
Library, Bloomington, Indiana 47401.

LEWIS BROWNE MSS., UPTON BEALL SINCLAIR MSS.

B1   1 L. ea. to Lewis Browne and Upton Sinclair, signed
       also by: Lion Feuchtwanger, Bruno Frank, Max Hork-
       heimer, Erich Maria Remarque, Thomas Mann. 1942.

B3   1 L. from Thomas Mann to Lewis Browne re: Franz Wer-
       fel. 1942.

C2   Der Weg der Verheißung. Additions and corr. A. 13p.

Academy of Motion Picture Arts and Sciences, Margaret Herrick
Library, 9038 Melrose Avenue, Hollywood, California 90069.

H3   5 cl.

H4   Ca. 100 cl. concerning film versions of:
      Juarez.
      The Song of Bernadette.
      Me and the Colonel.
      Musa Dagh (never filmed).

Mr. Francis Heilbut, 328 West 96th Street, New York, N.Y.
10025.

IVAN HEILBUT PAPERS

B1,2 Correspondence with Ivan Heilbut.

H5   Heilbut, Ivan. Essay on Franz Werfel.

Mrs. Elisabeth M. Stoerk and Mrs. Susanne B. Hoeller, 288
Ocean Drive West, Stamford, Connecticut 06902.

FRIDERIKE ZWEIG ARCHIVE

B3   1 L. concerning Werfel.
     3 Tel. to Friderike Zweig concerning the death of
       Werfel.

C7   "Copie der von Werfel's mit eigener Hand geschriebenen
       Trauerrede für Stefan Zweig in Los Angeles." A. 6p.

University of Texas, Humanities Research Center, Manuscripts
Collection, Box 7219, Austin, Texas 78712.

B1   2 L.

C   3 bound Ms.

Harvard University, Houghton Library, Cambridge, Massachusetts 02138.

RICHARD BEER-HOFMANN COLLECTION, SCHWEIZER COLLECTION OF GERMAN AUTOGRAPHS

B1   3 L. to Richard Beer-Hofmann. 1940 and undated.

C3   "Ja, Du, Wir..." Poem from Beschwörungen. A. 1926.

Princeton University, Firestone Library, Princeton, New Jersey 08540.

THE PAPERS OF ALBERT EINSTEIN (1879-1955). For details concerning the use of this collection, see description under Albert Einstein. Further Werfel materials are located in the BARROWS MUSSY COLLECTION.

THE PAPERS OF ALBERT EINSTEIN (1879-1955). Angaben über den Zugang zu der Sammlung finden sich unter "Albert Einstein." Weitere Werfel Materialien befinden sich in der BARROWS MUSSY COLLECTION.

B1,2   Unknown amount of correspondence between Einstein and Werfel.

C2   Jacobowsky and the Colonel. German version with tr. by Barrows Mussy.

C   "A Portrait of Giuseppe Verdi." German version with tr. by Barrows Mussy.

Mrs. Alice Loewy Kahler, 1 Evelyn Place, Princeton, New Jersey 08540.

J   Photos of Franz and Alma Mahler-Werfel.

Southern Illinois University, Morris Library, Department of Special Collections, Carbondale, Illinois 62901.

ERWIN PISCATOR PAPERS

FRANZ WERFEL

B1   2 Tel. and 2 L. to Erwin Piscator. A. and T. 1940-1943.
B2   4 L. and several drafts of L. (3p.) from Erwin Pisca-
      tor. 1938-1944.

Yivo Institute, 1048 Fifth Avenue, New York, N.Y. 10028.

C4   "Begegnung über einer Schlucht." 3p.

Loyola University of Chicago, E. M. Cudahy Memorial Library,
6525 North Sheridan Road, Chicago, Illinois 60626.

B1   1 L. to Edgar R. Smothers. A. 1942.
H3   Article by Smothers about Werfel.

University of Southern California, Lion Feuchtwanger Memorial
Library, 520 Paseo Miramar, Pacific Palisades, California
90272.

B1   1 L. to Lion Feuchtwanger. Undated.

Columbia University, Butler Library, New York, N.Y. 10027.

ORAL HISTORY COLLECTION and general files

B1   1 L. to Bernardine Kielty Scherman. T. 1934.
H5   Recollections of Werfel by Benjamin W. Huebsch in an
      interview. 1955.

American Academy of Arts and Letters/National Institute of
Arts and Letters, 633 West 155th Street, New York, N.Y.
10032.

B1,2 Correspondence with the Academy and the National In-
      stitute of Arts and Letters. 1 F.

995

State University of New York at Binghamton, Center for Modern Theater Research, Binghamton, New York 13901.

MAX REINHARDT ARCHIVE

H4   Der Weg der Verheißung. Materials concerning the production.

New School for Social Research, Office of the Dean of the Graduate Faculty of Political and Social Science, 65 Fifth Avenue, New York, N.Y. 10003.

RECORDS OF THE UNIVERSITY IN EXILE

B3   3 L. about Werfel. 1940.

Mrs. Peter M. Lindt, 949 West End Avenue, New York, N.Y. 10025.

C   Ms. submitted to Lindt for use on his radio program.

ERIC WERNER

Musicologist, 1901-

Dr. Eric Werner, 900 West 190th Street, New York, N.Y. 10040.

Private collection. Dr. Werner intends to leave his materials to Hebrew Union College after his death.

Privatsammlung. Dr. Werner hat vor, seine Materialien nach seinem Tode dem Hebrew Union College zukommen zu lassen.

A1   Diary containing events of Dr. Werner's life (to be destroyed after his death).

A3   Family history, in preparation (1977). Ms.

B1,2 Thousands of L. including correspondences with: Curt Sachs, Alfred Einstein, Paul Pisk, A. Ringer, F. Shrenken, and others. 1925-. Also c. of Werner's own L. from 1950s on.

C7   Ms. to pub. writings.
     Ms. to unpub. writings, e.g., an interpretation of Plutarch's De Musica. Ca. 300p.
     Ms. to lectures.

H3   Cl. about Dr. Werner and his career (American years only).

H4   Numerous reviews.

I   Family documents.

J   Photos of Werner, from age 15 to present.

K   Large library: art, music, philosophy, literature.

L   Materials used in writing his 130 articles and 8 books.

Prof. Hans Tischler, 711 East First Street, Bloomington, Indiana 47401.

B1,2 Correspondence between Tischler and Eric Werner.

University of Georgia, The University Libraries, Athens, Georgia 30601.

OLIN DOWNES PAPERS

B1,2   11 L.

Harvard University, Houghton Library, Cambridge, Massachusetts 02138.

GEORGE SARTON PAPERS

B1   1 L. to George Sarton. 1946.

MAX WERTHEIMER

Psychologist, 1880-1943

New York Public Library, Manuscript Division, Fifth Avenue
and 42nd Street, New York, N.Y. 10018.

The MAX WERTHEIMER PAPERS, 9 archive boxes of materials,
were donated by Ann Hornbostel in 1960. All rights to the
materials are held by Mr. Valentin Wertheimer, son of Max.

*Die MAX WERTHEIMER PAPERS, 9 Archivkartons Materialien, sind
eine Schenkung von Ann Hornbostel aus dem Jahre 1960. Alle
Rechte ruhen bei dem Sohn, Herrn Valentin Wertheimer.*

A2   Notebooks in German:
          Unidentified. 1924 - Nov. 17, 1925.
          "Vorlesungen 1-5." Oct. 1 - Nov. 5, 1934.
          "Vorlesungen 6-9." Nov. 12 - Dec. 3, 1934.
          "Vorlesungen 10-12." Dec. 1 - Jan. 7, 1935.
       Unidentified. Nov. 6 - Dec. 10, 1934.
       Unidentified. Dec. 17, 1934 - Feb. 13, 1935.

B1   31 L. 1922-1943 and undated, including L. to: Albert
       Einstein, Wolfgang Köhler.

B2   Ca. 230 L. 1902-1943, including L. from: Rudolf Arn-
       heim, M. Born, Albert Einstein, C. G. Jung, Wolfgang
       Köhler, Kurt Lewin, K. Mannheim.

C7   "Liebe macht blind." Notes to a psychology course, in
          German. Ca. 1920s. 6 F.
       Notes, primarily in German, on psychology. Undated,
          unsorted. 75 F. (3 B.).
       Notes, primarily in German, on psychology, Gestalt
          theory. Ca. 1919, 1920s-1940s and undated. 25 F.
       Lectures and speeches, held in Europe and the U.S.
          1925-1942. Ca. 700p., including cc.

C7,8   Miscellaneous untitled and undated essays, in German
          and English. 22 F.
       Notes to the work by K. W. Spence on the learning
          ability of animals. Edited by Ilse Wertheimer, ca.
          1940-1943. 11 F.
       Productive Thinking. Original T. with corr. 280p. Mis-
          cellaneous chap., notes and corr. A. and cc. 5 F.
       Fragmentary dictation to the book. 1 F. Illustrations.

1 F. Proofs. 1 F.

C9   Unidentified essay on dictatorship, group theory, etc.
      Edited by Wertheimer. 170p.

I   Documents among the correspondence, including: finan-
      cial documents, bills and receipts, official docu-
      ments, cards, licenses, contracts, brochures, lists,
      travel documents, etc.
      Bills and receipts. 1926-1929. 1 F.
      Financial documents from Wertheimer and wife from
          Darmstädter National Bank. 1926-1929. 5 F.

K   Books, many with h. notations by Wertheimer, including
      books by: Annelies Argelander, Paul Frankel, Agos-
      tino Gemelli, Edmund Husserl, Alfred Rosenthal, Fr.
      von den Velden.

L   Miscellaneous cl., memorabilia, etc. Ca. 1925-1929. 1 F.
      New School for Social Research. Letter heads and enve-
          lopes. Ca. 1930s.
      Offprints, cl., etc. among the correspondence, col-
          lected by Wertheimer.
      E. M. von Hornbostel materials:
          Correspondence. 1907-1921, 1928-1931 and undated. 1 F.
          Cc. and proofs of 2 articles. 1929, 1931.
          "Über Geräuschhelligkeit." T., cc., proofs and pub.
              c. 2 F.
          Bibliographic notes. Ca. 1920s. 16 F.
          Miscellaneous. 1905-1906.
      Wilhelm Wertheimer materials. Ca. 1885-1900. Cl., some
          L.

N   Hauptmann, Gerhart. "Zum 70. Geburtstag von Baron
          Christian v. Ehrenfels am 20. VI. 1929." T.
      Essays on experimental and social psychology, includ-
          ing essays by: Theodor Adorno, Hans Friedlander,
          Jesse Orlansky, Hans Schneickert. 8 F.

EMERGENCY COMMITTEE IN AID OF DISPLACED FOREIGN SCHOLARS,
1933-1945

*   File compiled, no assistance given. 1933-1942.

MAX WERTHEIMER

Mr. Valentin Wertheimer, 383 Grand Street, Apt. M-1201, New York, N.Y. 10002.

Valentin Wertheimer is the son of Max Wertheimer.

Valentin Wertheimer ist der Sohn von Max Wertheimer.

B1,2   Correspondence of Max Wertheimer over the course of many years.

Archives of the History of American Psychology, University of Akron, Akron, Ohio 44325.

F   Tapes and transcriptions of interviews of Wertheimer's widow by Michael Wertheimer (son).

Princeton University, Firestone Library, Princeton, New Jersey 08540.

THE PAPERS OF ALBERT EINSTEIN (1879-1955). For details concerning the use of this collection, see description under Albert Einstein.

THE PAPERS OF ALBERT EINSTEIN (1879-1955). Angaben über den Zugang zu der Sammlung finden sich unter "Albert Einstein."

B1,2   Unknown amount of correspondence with Albert Einstein. 1920, 1937, 1943.
       Unknown amount of correspondence dealing with the League of Nations.

American Philosophical Society, The Library, 105 South Fifth Street, Philadelphia, Pennsylvania 19106.

WOLFGANG KÖHLER PAPERS

B1,2   Correspondence between Wolfgang Köhler and Max Wertheimer. 16 L. 1929-1932, 1956-1958 and undated.

1001

MAX WERTHEIMER

<u>Leo Baeck Institute</u>, 129 East 73rd Street, New York, N.Y. 10021.

B3   4 L., including 1 L. from Hans Staudinger.

H3   Article on Wertheimer for an encyclopedia. 1968.

H5   Ms. about Wertheimer by Mrs. Wertheimer. Undated. T. 4p.

<u>Yivo Institute</u>, 1048 Fifth Avenue, New York, N.Y. 10028.

HORACE M. KALLEN PAPERS

B1,2 Individual item(s) in folders: 64, 95, 348, 551, 553, 555, 877. 1934-1944.

<u>Mrs. Gertrude Urzidil</u>, 83-39 116th Street, Richmond Hill, New York 11418.

JOHANNES URZIDIL COLLECTION

B1   3 L. to Johannes Urzidil. T. and A. 1941.

HERMANN WEYL

Mathematician, 1885-1955

According to Prof. F. Joachim Weyl, son of Hermann, Weyl transferred all of his papers back to Zürich upon his retirement in 1950 from the Institute for Advanced Studies, Princeton. The papers are presently being kept at the Eidgenössische Technische Hochschule, where he taught from 1913 to 1930. The person most directly responsible for care of the papers is Prof. Benno Eckmann, Institut für Mathematik, Eidgenössische Technische Hochschule, Zürich, Switzerland.

Nach Auskunft von Prof. F. Joachim Weyl (der Sohn Hermann Weyls) hat sein Vater all seine Schriftstücke im Jahre 1950 mit zurück nach Zürich genommen, als er bei dem Institute for Advanced Studies, Princeton, in den Ruhestand trat. Die Schriften werden z.Zt. bei der Eidgenössische Technische Hochschule aufbewahrt, wo er von 1913 bis 1930 lehrte. Verantwortlich für diese Schriften ist Prof. Benno Eckmann, Institut für Mathematik, Eidgenössische Technische Hochschule, Zürich, Switzerland.

Library of Congress, Manuscript Division, Independence Avenue and First Street S.E., Washington, D.C. 20540.

SIMON FLEXNER PAPERS, OSWALD VEBLEN PAPERS

B1   37 L., 7 Tel. and 1 Ptc. to Oswald Veblen. 1928-1934.
       11 L. to Abraham Flexner. T. and A. 1932, 1942-1955.
       Ca. 500-600 L., signed by Weyl, during the time when
          he worked with Veblen for the Emergency Committee
          in Aid of Displaced German Scholars.
       Several L. filed under "Carl L. Siegel" in the Veblen
          correspondence.

B2   19 L. from Abrahem Flexner. T.cc. 1942-1955.
       11 L. from Oswald Veblen. 1928-1933.

B3   19 L. and 2 Tel. 1931-1933.

University of California, Berkeley, The Bancroft Library, Berkeley, California 94720.

E. O. LAWRENCE PAPERS

1003

B1   5 L. 1947-1948.

Archive for History of Quantum Physics (locations in the
U.S.: Bancroft Library, University of California, Berkeley;
American Philosophical Society, Philadelphia, Pennsylvania;
American Institute of Physics, New York, N.Y.).

B1   4 L. to Pascual Jordon. 1925.
       2 L. to A. Sommerfeld. 1911.

B2   1 L. from E. Schrödinger. 1943.

California Institute of Technology, Robert A. Millikan
Library, Pasadena, California 91109.

PAUL S. EPSTEIN PAPERS, THEODORE VON KARMAN CORRESPONDENCE

B1   3 L. to P. S. Epstein. 1924. Also additional items of
       correspondence. 1922-1924.

B1,2   Correspondence between Hermann, Hella and F. Joachim
       Weyl and Theodore von Karman. 1921-1952. 1 F.

Harvard University, Houghton Library, Cambridge, Massachusetts 02138.

GEORGE SARTON PAPERS

B1   3 L. to George Sarton. 1938-1940.

Harvard University, University Archives, Widener Library,
Cambridge, Massachusetts 02138.

RICHARD VON MISES COLLECTION

B1   2 L. to Richard von Mises. T. 1933, 1941.

B2   1 L. from Richard von Mises. T.cc. 1941.

Northwestern University, Mathematics Department, Evanston, Illinois 60201.

ERNST DAVID HELLINGER FILES

B1   1 L. to H. T. Davis. 1949.
       1 L. to Ernst David Hellinger. 1939.

New York Public Library, Manuscript Division, Fifth Avenue and 42nd Street, New York, N.Y. 10018.

EMERGENCY COMMITTEE IN AID OF DISPLACED FOREIGN SCHOLARS, 1933-1945

*   File compiled, no assistance given. 1933-1944.

Yale University, Beinecke Rare Book and Manuscript Library, New Haven, Connecticut 06520.

HERMANN BROCH ARCHIVE

B1   Several L. to Hermann Broch.

B2   2 L. from Hermann Broch. 1949-1950.

New York University, Courant Institute of Mathematical Sciences, Library, 251 Mercer Street, New York, N.Y. 10012.

B1,2 File "Hermann Weyl." 1947-1957.

University of Chicago, The Joseph Regenstein Library, 1100 East 57th Street, Chicago, Illinois 60637.

JAMES FRANCK PAPERS

B1,2 Correspondence with James Franck.

J   Group photo. Ninth Washington Conference on Theoretical Physics. Washington, D.C., Oct. 31 - Nov. 2, 1946.

1005

HERMANN WEYL

Princeton University, Firestone Library, Princeton, New Jersey 08540.

THE PAPERS OF ALBERT EINSTEIN (1879-1955). For details concerning the use of the collection, see description under Albert Einstein.

THE PAPERS OF ALBERT EINSTEIN (1879-1955). Angaben über den Zugang zu der Sammlung finden sich unter "Albert Einstein."

B1,2   Unknown amount of correspondence between Einstein and Weyl. 1916-1954.

EUGENE P. WIGNER

Physicist, 1902-

<u>Prof. Eugene P. Wigner</u>, 8 Ober Road, Princeton, New Jersey 08540.

Private collection: ca. 30 ft. Prof. Wigner is willing to respond to written questions concerning his materials.

Privatsammlung, etwa 9 m. Prof. Wigner hat sich bereiter-klärt, schriftliche Anfragen in Bezug auf seine Materialien zu beantworten.

B1,2 Correspondence, including L. to and from: Gregory Breit (1931-1971), Rudolf Ortvay, Karl Polanyi, Leo Szilard, Alvin Weinberg (1954-1973), and others.

C7   Notes to university lectures (Princeton). Some notes to speeches given.

D7,8 Complete collection of Wigner's publications.

H3   Newspaper and periodical cl. about Wigner, collected in albums.

I   Documents of various kinds.

J   Photos.

K   Private library, including some periodicals.

L   Over 100 F. containing materials on various topics, projects, etc. such as: "Manhattan Project," "Dirac Symposium," "Civil Defense," "AEC."

M   Honors received, medals, etc.

<u>American Institute of Physics</u>, Niels Bohr Library, 335 East 45th Street, New York, N.Y. 10017.

The EUGENE P. WIGNER CORRESPONDENCE was deposited by Eugene Wigner in 1966 and 1970. Some originals still remain in Prof. Wigner's possession.

Die EUGENE P. WIGNER CORRESPONDENCE wurde der Niels Bohr Library in den Jahren 1966 und 1970 von Prof. Wigner über-lassen. Einige Originale befinden sich noch in seinem Besitz.

B1,2   Correspondence. 1931-1942; 1958-1966. Ca. 800 L. (3 B.).
       Partially pc. of originals still in Wigner's posses-
       sion.

Library of Congress, Manuscript Division, Independence Avenue
and First Street S.E., Washington, D.C. 20540.

OSWALD VEBLEN PAPERS, J. ROBERT OPPENHEIMER PAPERS.

B1   7 L. and 1 Ptc. to J. R. Oppenheimer. T. and A. 1946-
       1963.
       14 L. to Oswald Veblen. T. and A. 1930-1946.
       6 L. 1936-1950, including 1 L. to Victor Weisskopf.

B2   3 L. from J. R. Oppenheimer. 1950-1952.
       8 L. from Oswald Veblen. T.cc. 1929-1946.

B3   2 L. 1933, 1938.

C8   "Atomic Energy." 1948. T.cc. 7p.

U.S. Atomic Energy Commission, Division of Classification,
Data Index System, Washington, D.C. 20545.

B1   2 memos by Wigner:
       Graphite Temperatures. University of Chicago, Metal-
          lurgical Labs, July 20, 1944.
       Nuclear Materials Production. E. I. DuPont de Nemours
          & Co., June 26, 1951.

C8   "LTR-Neutron Cross Sections." Princeton University,
       March 23, 1942.

I   2 patents:
       "Liquid Cooled 10,000 kw Neutronic Reaction Pin."
          Chicago Operations Office, Feb. 8, 1944.
       "Coffin for Vertical Type Pile." Chicago Operations
          Office, July 3, 1946.

Duke University, William R. Perkins Library, Manuscript Department, Durham, North Carolina 27706.

EUGENE P. WIGNER

FRITZ WOLFGANG LONDON PAPERS

B1   13 L. to F. W. London. A. 1928-1953.

B2   2 drafts of L. from F. W. London. 1935, 1938.

Archive for History of Quantum Physics (locations in U.S.:
Bancroft Library, University of California, Berkeley; Amer-
ican Philosophical Society, Philadelphia, Pennsylvania;
American Institute of Physics, New York, N.Y.).

B1   L. to Erwin Schrödinger. [1929-1930].

C7   Interview conducted by Wigner and T. S. Kuhn of P. A. M.
      Dirac. 1962.

C8   "Összetett Rendszerek Statisztikája As Új Quantum-
      mechanika Szerint." 1929. Proof sheets. 9p.

G   3 sessions of interview. Transcript. 1963. 65p.

Cornell University, John M. Olin Library, Department of Manuscripts and University Archives, Ithaca, New York 14850.

HANS BETHE PAPERS

B1,2 Correspondence between Eugene Wigner and Hans Bethe.

Smithsonian Institution, Dibner Library, Washington, D.C.
20560.

B1   4 L. 1971 and undated.

University of California San Diego, Mandeville Library,
Department of Special Collections, La Jolla, California 92037.

MARIA GOEPPERT MAYER COLLECTION

B1   5 L. to Maria Mayer.

California Institute of Technology, Robert A. Millikan Library, Pasadena, California 91109.

THEODORE VON KARMAN CORRESPONDENCE

B1,2   Correspondence between Wigner and Theodore von Karman.
       1950-1956. 1 F.

University of Chicago, The Joseph Regenstein Library, 1100 East 57th Street, Chicago, Illinois 60637.

JAMES FRANCK PAPERS

B1,2   Correspondence with James Franck.

B1,   L. of congratulations to Franck on his 70th birthday.
J   1952. Accompanied by photo of Wigner.

University of Illinois at Urbana-Champaign, University Library, University Archives, Room 19, Urbana, Illinois 61801.

FREDERICK SEITZ PAPERS

B1,2   Correspondence with Frederick Seitz. F. no. 24.

Lawrence Livermore Laboratory, P. O. Box 808, Livermore, California 94550.

B1,2   Correspondence between Eugene Wigner and Edward
       Teller.

American Philosophical Society, The Library, 105 South Fifth Street, Philadelphia, Pennsylvania 19106.

NIELS BOHR CORRESPONDENCE

B1   1 L. to Niels Bohr. 1946.

BILLY WILDER

Producer, Director, 1906-

Mr. Billy Wilder, Samuel Goldwyn Productions, 1041 North
Formosa Avenue, Hollywood, California 90046.

Billy Wilder has the bound Ms. of all of his film scripts in
his office at Samuel Goldwyn Productions.

*Billy Wilder bewahrt alle seine Filmscripts in seinem Büro
bei den Samuel Goldwyn Productions in gebundener Form auf.*

Academy of Motion Picture Arts and Sciences, Margaret Herrick
Library, 9038 Melrose Avenue, Hollywood, California 90069.

C5   Sunset Boulevard. 1950.
      Ace in the Hole. 1951.

H3,4 Newspaper and magazine cl. 3 F.

H5   Biographies of Wilder.

J   18 photos of Wilder.

Columbia University, Butler Library, New York, N.Y. 10027.

ORAL HISTORY COLLECTION and general files

B1   1 L. to Bennett Cerf. T. 1961.

H5   Recollections by Samson Raphaelson of Billy Wilder in
      an interview. 1959.

Boston University, Mugar Memorial Library, 771 Commonwealth
Avenue, Boston, Massachusetts 02215.

TOM WOOD PAPERS

H1   Wood, Tom. The Bright Side of Billy Wilder, Primarily.
      Setting c. 334p. Proofs.

EMANUEL WINTERNITZ

Musicologist, 1898-

<u>Dr. Emanuel Winternitz</u>, Metropolitan Museum of Art, Fifth
Avenue and 82nd Street, New York, N.Y. 10028.

Private collection: inaccessible. / *Unzugängliche Privatsammlung.*

B1,2   Correspondence over the course of many years.

C7   Several Ms. of books.
       Offprints of some of his articles.

F   Tapes of lectures and concerts.

H3,4   Cl. from European, Asian and American newspapers.
       Articles about Winternitz as well as reviews.

H4   Catalogs of exhibitions arranged by Winternitz.

J   Photos of exhibitions arranged by Winternitz.

K   Winternitz's personal library, including some rare
       items.

O   Programs of Winternitz exhibitions.

<u>Yivo Institute</u>, 1048 Fifth Avenue, New York, N.Y. 10028.

HORACE M. KALLEN PAPERS

B1,2   Individual item(s) in folders: 32, 104.

<u>University of Georgia</u>, The University Libraries, Athens,
Georgia 30601.

OLIN DOWNES PAPERS

B1,2   Correspondence with Olin Downes. 3 L.

<u>University of Pennsylvania</u>, The Charles Patterson Van Pelt
Library, Philadelphia, Pennsylvania 19104.

ALMA MAHLER-WERFEL COLLECTION

B1   2 L. to Alma Mahler-Werfel. 1947-1948.

New York Public Library, Manuscript Division, Fifth Avenue
and 42nd Street, New York, N.Y. 10018.

EMERGENCY COMMITTEE IN AID OF DISPLACED FOREIGN SCHOLARS,
1933-1945.

*   File compiled, no assistance given. 1933-1941.

Dr. Edward E. Lowinsky, Prof. Emeritus, Department of Music,
University of Chicago, Chicago, Illinois 60637.

B1   14 L. to Edward E. Lowinsky. 1954-1977.

B2   11 L. from Edward E. Lowinsky. 1954-1977.

KARL WITH

Art Historian, 1891-

Dr. Karl With, 3045 Kelton Avenue, Los Angeles, California
90034.

Private collection: inaccessible to researchers at present.
The entire collection (ca. 60 ft.) has been willed by With
to his son, Mr. Christopher With.

*Z. Zt. für Forschungszwecke unzugängliche Privatsammlung.
Die Sammlung (etwa 18 m) ist von Dr. Karl With vollständig
für seinen Sohn, Mr. Christopher With, testamentarisch bestimmt worden.*

B2   Large amount of correspondence, including numerous L.
     dating prior to World War I. Includes L. from: Bruno
     Adriani, Josef Albers, Alfred Neumeyer, Alfred Sal-
     mony.

C7   Ms. of pub. as well as unpub. writings. Ca. 3 ft.

C7, "Material on lectures." Notes and Ms. concerning con-
L   sultation work done by With (Rockefeller Foundation,
     etc.).

D7   Offprints of publications, incomplete for German per-
     iod.

I   Large number of documents concerning exhibitions done
     in the U.S., some on exhibitions in Germany.
     Honors received: Deutsches Verdienstkreuz, honorary
     doctorate (University of California, Los Angeles),
     etc.

J   Archive of photos and illustrations, including photos
     of exhibits, works of art, colleagues and friends.

K   Personal art library.

L   Files concerning exhibits and undertakings by With. Ca.
     3 ft.
     Large collection of cl. on all subjects.

M   Memorabilia.

N   Large collection of Ms. by others.

1014

KARL AUGUST WITTFOGEL

Social Scientist, Orientalist, 1896-

Prof. Karl A. Wittfogel, 420 Riverside Drive, New York, N.Y. 10025; and Dr. Gary L. Ulmen, 410 Riverside Drive, New York, N.Y. 10025.

The library and papers of Karl August Wittfogel are in the private holdings of Wittfogel and G. L. Ulmen. Of these materials, approximately 300 books, 30 notebooks and folders and some private correspondence date from the period prior to Wittfogel's first arrival in the U.S. in 1934. Copyrights to all published materials belong exclusively to Wittfogel; permission to use any of the unpublished materials for research must be obtained in the first instance from Wittfogel and in the second instance from Ulmen. A comprehensive bibliography of Wittfogel's published works and an analytical description of the unpublished manuscripts and some correspondence can be found in G. L. Ulmen, The Science of Society. Toward an Understanding of the Life and Work of Karl August Wittfogel (The Hague: Mouton, 1977).

Die Materialien und die Bibliothek Karl August Wittfogels befinden sich im Besitz Wittfogels und G. L. Ulmens. 300 Bücher, 30 Notizbücher und Mappen sowie eine Reihe von Briefe stammen aus der Zeit vor Wittfogels Ankunft in den U.S.A. im Jahre 1934. Das Copyright zu allen bereits veröffentlichten Arbeiten Wittfogels ruht bei dem Autor allein. Die Erlaubnis zur Benutzung des unveröffentlichten Materials muß von K. A. Wittfogel sowie von G. L. Ulmen eingeholt werden. Eine umfassende Bibliographie der Arbeiten von Wittfogel sowie eine Beschreibung der unveröffentlichten Arbeiten und anderer Materialien befindet sich in: G. L. Ulmen, The Science of Society. Toward an Understanding of the Life and Work of Karl August Wittfogel (The Hague: Mouton, 1977).

A3   Ms. about experiences in Nazi prisons and concentration camps during 1933, written in England in 1934. Ca. 300p.
      Autobiographical Ms., to be published as: "China und die osteurasische Kavalerie-Revolution. Sozialhistorische Einsichter gewonnen in Begegnungen mit Karl Heinrich Menges. Ein Beitrag zu Mengeses Biographie und eine Laudatio mit Fragmenten einer

Autobiographie des Laudators," <u>Ural-Altaische Jahr-bücher</u>, 49 (1977).

B1,2   4 filing cabinets of correspondence dating from the
1920s to the present. Aside from familial letters,
most of the correspondence before 1933 has been
either lost or destroyed.

B3   Correspondence between Ulmen and Georg Lukács, Ernst
Juenger, Upton Sinclair and others, relating to the
life and work of Wittfogel.

C2,7   Ca. 80 notebooks of unpub. papers, including:
Plays dating from the early 1920s.
<u>Wirtschaft und Gesellschaft Chinas</u>. Outlines and
   chap of a second volume. 1931.
Drafts of lectures and outlines of books planned
   but never completed.
"Russia and the Asiatic Restoration." Ms. 1947-1949.
   Ca. 1,000p.
400p. on Marx.
"China and Russia." Ca. 300p.
"Oriental Despotism and World History." Ca. 200p.
<u>Oriental Despotism</u>. Several drafts dating from 1940.
Memoranda on various scientific and political sub-
   jects dating from 1939 to the present.
Television lectures. University of Washington,
   Seattle.
Script: <u>From Marx to Mao. A Viewer's Guide. Tele-
courses</u>. University of Washington Press, Seattle,
   1960.

D,   The only complete set of Wittfogel's pub. writings
H   from 1917 to the present, and the fullest collection
of secondary literature concerned with Wittfogel's
life and work in Ulmen's library.

F   Ca. 50 hours of recorded tapes of university lectures.

G   50 notebooks of an oral history project.
10 hours of recorded interviews with Matthias Graefrat
for the Westdeutsche Rundfunk (1977).

H   Numerous books, articles and reviews.

J   1 volume of photos from the period prior to 1933.
15 volumes of photos 1935 to present.

K   Ca. 10,000 volumes.

L   Ca. 50 notebooks of original source materials.
Ca. 75 brief-folders of materials of the Chinese History Project.

O   Some theater programs of plays produced in the Weimar Republic.

Hoover Institution on War, Revolution and Peace, Stanford, California 94305.

F   100 hours of recorded tapes of the Memoirs of Karl August Wittfogel.

Indiana University, The University Libraries, The Lilly Library, Bloomington, Indiana 47401.

UPTON BEALL SINCLAIR MSS.

B1   2 L. to Upton Sinclair. 1925-1926.

State University of New York at Albany, Department of Germanic Languages and Literatures, 1400 Washington Avenue, Albany, New York 12222.

KARL O. PAETEL COLLECTION

B1   23 L. to Karl O. Paetel (xerox). 1942-1970.

B2   1 L. from Karl O. Paetel (xerox). 1961.

Harvard University, Houghton Library, Cambridge, Massachusetts 02138.

GEORGE SARTON PAPERS

B1   6 L. to George Sarton. 1947-1948.

B2   2 L. from George Sarton. 1947.

New York Public Library, Manuscript Division, Fifth Avenue and 42nd Street, New York, N.Y. 10018.

EMERGENCY COMMITTEE IN AID OF DISPLACED FOREIGN SCHOLARS, 1933-1945, ERICH FROMM PAPERS

B1,2   Correspondence with Erich Fromm.

*   File compiled by the Emergency Committee when assist-
       ance was granted. 1934-1944.

Yivo Institute, 1048 Fifth Avenue, New York, N.Y. 10028.

HORACE M. KALLEN PAPERS

*   Individual items in folders no.: 234, 886. Undated.

ARNOLD WOLFERS

Political Scientist, 1892-1968

The ARNOLD WOLFERS PAPERS were donated to the library by Mrs.
Arnold Wolfers in 1969 (6 B.).

*Die ARNOLD WOLFERS PAPERS sind eine Schenkung von Frau Wol-
fers aus dem Jahre 1969 (6 Kartons).*

A3   Bibliography of articles by Wolfers. 1916-1964.
      Curriculum vitae. Undated.
      Travel notes. 1924-1966.

B1   Denials of requests for articles, reviews, etc. 1960-
      1962.
      Denials of requests for speeches, conferences, etc.
      1962.

B1,2 Wolfers destroyed the major portion of his correspond-
      ence on three occasions: in 1949 when retiring as
      Master of Pierson College, in 1957 when leaving Yale
      University, and in 1966, the year after retiring as
      Director of the Johns Hopkins University Institute
      of Foreign Policy Research.
      Correspondence with Nicholas Kullmanns. 1921-1923.
      Correspondence with Julius Schmidhauser. 1923-1966.
      Correspondence with Paul Tillich. 1923-1963.
      Miscellaneous correspondence. 1933-1968. Ca. 1/2 B.

B2   L. to Wolfers, received after his death.

B3   Sympathy L. to Mrs. Wolfers. 1968.

C7   Ms. and T. of articles, speeches, etc. on international
      affairs. Germany, England, U.S.A. 1903-1967 and un-
      dated.
      Lectures on international economics. University of
      Berlin, 1931-1932. A.
      "Die Aufrichtung der Kapitalherrschaft in der abend-
      ländischen Geschichte." Ph.D. dissertation. Univer-
      sity of Giessen, 1924.
      Zoll und Preisniveau-Spanne. T. Berlin, 1926.
      "Power Politics and the Strategy of Peace." Draft of
      book. Undated.

D7   Newspaper and magazine cl., offprints, etc. of essays,
     articles. 1917-1965. Ca. 85 items.

H3   Newspaper cl. 1926-1965.
     Obituaries. Newspaper cl. 1968.
     Newspaper cl. concerning establishment of "Arnold O.
       Wolfers Professorship" at Yale University. 1968.
     Also several L.

I   Personal documents 1905-1966, including: birth certifi-
       cate, U.S. citizenship papers (1939), I.D. card
       (1934), passports and visas (1939-1966).
     Academic documents 1912-1925, including documents from
       the Universities at: Lausanne, Munich, Berlin, Zürich,
       Giessen.
     Military documents from the Swiss and American armies.
       1911-1945.
     Documents concerning Wolfers' career. 1919-1965.
     Academic degrees:
       Mount Holyoke College. Doctor of Letters diploma.
         1934.
       University of Rochester. Doctor of Laws diploma.
         1945.
     Military honors. 1942, 1962, 1964, 1965.
     Great Distinguished Service Cross of the Order of Dis-
       tinguished Service. West Germany, 1965.
     Professional honors. 1935, 1938 and undated.

J   Photos from childhood and boyhood years. 1903-1918.
     Photos of portraits.
     Photos of various academic activities. 1943-1965 and
       undated.

K   Books or sections of books, either authored or edited
       by Wolfers. 1930-1968.
     Books by other authors. 1938-1942.

L   Reports:
       "Report of the Civilian Advisory Group with Comments
         by the U.S. Army War College." 1962.
       "Report of the Yale Institute of International Stud-
         ies." 1948-1949.
       "The North Atlantic Area." Undated.
     Conferences:
       Conference on Theory of International Politics. 1954.

Franco-American Conference. Programs, lists, lec-
tures, correspondence. 1955-1958.
Third European-American Conference. 1966.
Conference of World Peace Foundation. 1956.
Deutsche Hochschule für Politik. Materials. 1930-1934.
Interim Council on Security and Defense Affairs. 1961.
International Red Cross. 1961-1967.
The U.S. Alliance System. Outline of lecture.
International Relations. Lectures. Undated.
World Peace Foundation. 1955-1956.
Yale Institute of International Studies. 1948-1951.
Bibliographies on international economics and affairs.
1931-1947.
Newspaper cl., offprints, etc. of articles by other
authors.

M   Memorial services and burial. Oct. 26 and 30, 1968.
Souvenirs of German inflation (bills). 1923.
Facsimile of a signature.

N   Schmidhauser, Julius. T. of books, essays, poems.
1927-1961.

State University of New York at Albany, Department of Germanic Languages and Literatures, 1400 Washington Avenue,
Albany, New York 12222.

KARL O. PAETEL COLLECTION

B1   7 L. to Karl O. Paetel (xerox). 1943-1946.

Leo Baeck Institute, 129 East 73rd Street, New York, N.Y.
10021.

JACOB PICARD COLLECTION

B1,2   Correspondence with Jacob Picard.

New York Public Library, Manuscript Division, Fifth Avenue
and 42nd Street, New York, N.Y. 10018.

ARNOLD WOLFERS

EMERGENCY COMMITTEE IN AID OF DISPLACED FOREIGN SCHOLARS, 1933-1945

*   File compiled, no assistance given. 1933-1944.

Harvard University, Houghton Library, Cambridge, Massachusetts 02138.

B1   1 L. to John Phillips Marquand. 1947.

Columbia University, Butler Library, New York, N.Y. 10027.

NICHOLAS MURRAY BUTLER PAPERS

B1   1 Tel. to N. M. Butler. 1931.

KURT WOLFF

Publisher, 1889-1963

Yale University, Beinecke Rare Book and Manuscript Library,
New Haven, Connecticut 06520.

The KURT WOLFF ARCHIVE, which consists of approximately
4,000 items, was purchased from Kurt Wolff in 1947. With
the exception of a small amount of materials, the collection
is open to the public. Permission to publish materials from
the collection must be obtained from Mrs. Helen Wolff, 230
East 48th Street, New York, N.Y. 10017.

*Das KURT WOLFF ARCHIVE, das aus etwa 4000 Nummern besteht,
wurde Kurt Wolff im Jahre 1947 abgekauft. Bis auf geringe
Ausnahmen sind die Materialien dieser Sammlung der Öffentlichkeit zugänglich. Erlaubnis zur Veröffentlichung von
Materialien aus dieser Sammlung muß von Frau Helen Wolff,
230 East 48th Street, New York, N.Y. 10017, eingeholt werden.*

B1,2 Correspondence with Walter Hasenclever. 510 L. 1911-
        1934. Also Wolff's correspondence with Marita (Hasen-
        clever) Kühn, sister of Walter. 53 L.
      Correspondence between Kurt Wolff (or the Kurt Wolff
        Verlag) and various individuals. 1910-1936. Ca.
        3,400 L., including L. to and from: Paul Amann,
        Johannes R. Becher, Gottfried Benn, Franz Blei, Ernst
        Bloch, Max Brod, Hans Carossa, Richard Coudenhove-
        Kalergi, Theodor Däubler, Richard Dehmel, Alfred
        Döblin, Kasimir Edschmid, Albert Ehrenstein, Herbert
        Eulenberg, Bruno Frank, Leonhard Frank, Salomo
        Friedländer (Mynona), Pola Gauguin, André Germain,
        Iwan Goll, Maxim Gorki, George Grosz, Ferdinand
        Hardekopf, Maximilian Harden, Gerhart Hauptmann,
        Wilhelm Herzog, Hermann Hesse, Kurt Hiller, Hugo von
        Hofmannsthal, Ricarda Huch, Richard Huelsenbeck,
        James Joyce, Franz Kafka, Georg Kaiser, Alfred Kerr,
        Paul Klee, Oskar Kokoschka, Annette Kolb, Käthe
        Kollwitz, Karl Kraus, Max Krell, Alfred Kubin, Gus-
        tav Landauer, Else Lasker-Schüler, Mechthilde Lich-
        nowsky, Sophie Liebknecht, Alma Mahler-Werfel, Hein-
        rich Mann, Thomas Mann, Frans Masereel, Walter Meh-
        ring, Erich Mühsam, Emil Nolde, Max Oppenheimer,
        Alfons Paquet, Alfred Polgar, Hans Reisinger, Rainer

Maria Rilke, Romain Rolland, René Schickele, Hans Siemsen, Georg Simmel, Carl Sternheim, Ernst Toller, Georg Trakl, Fritz von Unruh, Robert Walser, Jakob Wassermann, Frank Wedekind, Ernst Weiss, H. G. Wells, Franz Werfel, Alfred Wolfenstein, Karl Wolfskehl, Paul Zech, Carl Zuckmayer, Stefan Zweig.

B3   Ernst Rowohlt Verlag. Ca. 100 L. to and from Max Dauthendey and Georg Heym.
1 L. from Martin Buber to: Franz Werfel (1913), Erik-Ernst Schwabach (1914).

C7   Draft of a notice for Fritz von Unruh's book Ein Geschlecht. A.

I   Contracts, financial documents, etc., concerning the following individuals: Paul Amann, Max Brod, Alfred Brust (restricted), Herbert Eulenberg, Rudolf Fuchs, Pola Gauguin, Carl Ferdinand Hauptmann, Otto Janowitz, Ernst Ludwig Kirchner, Stefan J. Klein, Else Lasker-Schüler, Mechthilde Lichnowsky, Alma Mahler-Werfel, Gustav Meyrink, Erich Mühsam, René Schickele, Wilhelm August Schmidtbonn, Josef Anton Schneiderfranken, Richard Seewald, Carl Sternheim, Fritz von Unruh, H. G. Wells, Franz Werfel. Ca. 70 items.

L   Walter Hasenclever materials: several documents, a biography, programs, etc. 23 items.
Gustav Landauer. "Wie Hedwig Landauer starb." Pamphlet. 16p. Also newspaper cl. about Gustav and Hedwig Landauer.
Franz Werfel. Newspaper cl., advertising materials, lecture and theater programs, etc.

N   Borchardt, Rudolf. 6 items. A. and T. 72p.
Carossa, Hans. "Fahrt." Poem. A. 3p.
Dauthendey, Max. "Der Venusinenreim." A. 123p.
Eulenberg, Herbert. 8 dramas, several poems. 695p.
Fuchs, Rudolf. Poems and tr. of poems.
Gauguin, Paul. "Avant et après." 1903. Mimeo. 186p.
Grube, Max. 1 poem. T. 1p.
Hasenclever, Walter. 10 poems. 16p. Biography. 3p. Reviews. 6p.
Hauptmann, Carl Ferdinand Maximilian. "Zu Kriegsszenen" and "Zum Rübezahlbuch." T. 2p.

Kirchner, Ernst Ludwig. Wood carving.
Kölwel, Gottfried. 2 poems. A. 2p.
Meyrink, Gustav. Das grüne Gesicht. Novel fragment. A. 22p.
Scheerbart, Paul. Das Perpetuum Mobile. Novel. 101p. + 5p.
Schickele, René. Review, introduction, several advertisements.
Voigt, Hans Henning von. Die Schuldlosen. Novel fragment. A. 80p.
Walser, Robert. "Handharfe am Tag." Poem. A. 1p.
Werfel, Franz. 18 poems. 19p. 3 sketches. Outline of planned series. 6p. "Die 'Troerinnen des Euripides.' Ausgewählte Szenen für die 'Weißen Blätter'." 39p. Wir sind. 107p.
Zweig, Arnold. "Entwurf einer Ankündigung der Novellen um Claudia." 1p.

HERMANN BROCH ARCHIVE

B1   64 L. to Hermann Broch (some from Helen Wolff). 1943-1951.

B2   19 L. from Hermann Broch. 1943-1951.

Columbia University, Butler Library, New York, N.Y. 10027.

The Wolff materials are located primarily in the PANTHEON BOOKS COLLECTION, which was donated by Random House publishers in 1973.

Die Wolff-Materialien befinden sich hauptsächlich in der PANTHEON BOOKS COLLECTION, eine Schenkung des Random House-Verlagshauses aus dem Jahre 1973.

B1   Ca. 40 L. to Kurt Seligmann. T. and A. 1950-1958.
     75 L. to Richard and Mrs. Sterba. 1951-1965.
     1 L. ea. to Harry Scherman and Kurt Goldstein.
     Correspondence with Pantheon. 1952-1958. Also some contracts, lists, etc. enclosed.

B2   31 L. from Richard Sterba. T. and A. 1951-1958.
     22 L. from Kurt Seligmann. T. and A. 1951-1958.

1 L. from Kenneth Rexroth. 1954.

Mrs. Gertrude Urzidil, 83-39 116th Street, Richmond Hill,
New York 11418.

JOHANNES URZIDIL COLLECTION

B1   27 L. to Johannes Urzidil. T. and A. 1941-1955.

H5   5 cl.

I   Death notice.

University of Pennsylvania, The Charles Patterson Van Pelt
Library, Philadelphia, Pennsylvania 19104.

ALMA MAHLER-WERFEL COLLECTION

B1   8 L. and 6 Ptc. to Alma Mahler-Werfel. 1942-1961 and
         undated.
      3 L. to Franz Werfel.

B2   57 L. and 15 Ptc. from Franz Werfel. A.
      1 L. ea. from Alma Mahler-Werfel and Fritz von Unruh.
      Miscellaneous L., primarily concerning business affairs
         of Franz Werfel and Alma Mahler-Werfel.

I   Contract between Franz Werfel and the Kurt Wolff Ver-
         lag.

Mrs. Alice Loewy Kahler, 1 Evelyn Place, Princeton, New Jersey 08540.

ERICH VON KAHLER COLLECTION

B1   7 L., 3 Ptc. to Erich von Kahler. 1959-1963.
      1 L. ea. to: Wolfgang Pauli, Niels Bohr, Otto Loewi,
         Huberto A. Ph. Schoenfeldt, Erich Auerbach, P.
         Kirchgraber, Robert van Gelder, Arnando O. Reynal.

B2   1 L. ea. from: Arnando O. Reynal (1955), Robert van
         Gelder (1945).

KURT WOLFF

B3   4 L. from Helene Wolff to Erich von Kahler. 1959-1963.

Library of Congress, Manuscript Division, Independence Avenue
and First Street S.E., Washington, D.C. 20540.

BENJAMIN W. HUEBSCH PAPERS, HANNAH ARENDT PAPERS

B1   7 L. and 1 Ptc. to Benjamin W. Huebsch. T. and A.
      1941-1963.
B1,2 Correspondence with Hannah Arendt.
B2   1 L. from Benjamin W. Huebsch. T.cc. 1941.

Harvard University, Houghton Library, Cambridge, Massachusetts 02138.

GEORGE SARTON PAPERS, WITTER BYNNER PAPERS and general
archive files

B1   2 L. to George Sarton. 1944-1945.
      4 L. to E. E. Cummings. 1951-1958.
      1 L. to Howard Nelson. 1958.
B2   4 L. from Witter Bynner. 1958.
      1 L. from E. E. Cummings. 1951.

Mr. Hans Sahl, 800 West End Avenue, New York, N.Y. 10025.

B1   Numerous L. to Hans Sahl.

Bruno Walter Memorial Foundation, c/o Miss Susie Danziger,
115 East 72nd Street, New York, N.Y. 10021.

B1,2 Correspondence with Bruno Walter.

Harvard University, Harvard Divinity School, Andover-Harvard
Theological Library, 45 Francis Avenue, Cambridge, Massachusetts 02138.

PAUL TILLICH

Bl   2 L. to Paul Tillich. T. 1962.

B2   2 L. from Paul Tillich. T.cc. 1962-1963.

Leo Baeck Institute, 129 East 73rd Street, New York, N.Y.
10021.

ERICH KAHLER COLLECTION and general archive files

Bl   1 L. to Karl Wolfskehl.

B2   3 L. and 1 Ptc. from Franz Kafka. 1913-1920. pc.
        1 L. from Karl Wolfskehl.

H3   11 cl. 1958-1964.

Barthold Fles Literary Agency, 507 Fifth Avenue, New York,
N.Y. 10016.

Bl   1 L. to Barthold Fles. 1941.

Boston University, Mugar Memorial Library, 771 Commonwealth
Avenue, Boston, Massachusetts 02215.

JOSEPH SZIGETI PAPERS

Bl   1 L. to Joseph Szigeti. 1924.

Mr. Francis Heilbut, 328 West 96th Street, New York, N.Y.
10025.

IVAN HEILBUT PAPERS

B2   2 L. from Ivan Heilbut. 1942.

Yivo Institute, 1048 Fifth Avenue, New York, N.Y. 10028.

HORACE M. KALLEN PAPERS

B1,2   Individual item(s) in folders: 52, 349, 1034.

Mrs. Liselotte Stein, 115-25 Metropolitan Avenue, Kew Gardens, New York 11418.

FRED STEIN PAPERS

J   Photos of Kurt Wolff.

KURT H. WOLFF

Sociologist, 1912-

Prof. Kurt H. Wolff, 58 Lombard Street, Newton, Massachusetts 02158.

Private collection: inaccessible. / *Unzugängliche Privat-*
sammlung.

A1   Diaries. 1925-1935.

A2   Notebooks.

B1,2 Correspondence. 1920-1970, including L. from: Hermann
      Broch, John Dewey, Thomas Mann. Also c. of Wolff's L.

C1   Ms. of novels.

C2   Ms. of dramas.

C3   Ms. of poems.
      Opera text.

C7   Ms. of articles, radio lectures.

C9   Tr. of writings of others.

C14   Drawings and sketches.

D7   Numerous cl. of his own writings.

H4   Reviews of Wolff's books.

I   Personal documents.

J   Photos.

K   Substantial personal library. Ca. 5,000-6,000 volumes,
      including some rare editions.

N   1 Ms. by Elisabeth Langgässer.

Hoover Institution on War, Revolution and Peace, Stanford,
California 94305.

FRANZ SCHOENBERNER COLLECTION

B1   1 L. to Franz Schoenberner. 1941.

New York Public Library, Manuscript Division, Fifth Avenue

1030

and 42nd Street, New York, N.Y. 10018.

EMERGENCY COMMITTEE IN AID OF DISPLACED FOREIGN SCHOLARS,
1933-1945

*   File compiled, no assistance given. 1938-1939.

Mrs. Alice Loewy Kahler, 1 Evelyn Place, Princeton, New
Jersey 08540.

ERICH VON KAHLER COLLECTION

B1   18 L., 1 Ptc. to Erich von Kahler. 1950-1967.

B2   1 L. from Erich von Kahler. 1962.

D7   "Toward Communication between Sociology and Anthro-
      pology." Co-authored by John W. Bennett. Mimeo. p.
      329-351.
      3 offprints by Wolff.

Leo Baeck Institute, 129 East 73rd Street, New York, N.Y.
10021.

ERICH KAHLER COLLECTION

B1   1 L. to Erich Kahler. 1968.

GEORGE WUNDERLICH

Lawyer, 1883-1951

Library of Congress, Manuscript Division, Independence Avenue and First Street S.E., Washington, D.C. 20540.

The GEORGE WUNDERLICH PAPERS (Ac. 9649) were donated by Mrs. George Wunderlich in 1952. The materials, which consist of approximately 2,700 items or 4.5 shelf ft. of space, are arranged in folders, with a listing of the contents of the individual folders. Both the arrangement and the designation of contents of the individual folders have been kept basically as Wunderlich had arranged them.

Die GEORGE WUNDERLICH PAPERS (Ac. 9649) sind eine Schenkung von Frau Wunderlich aus dem Jahre 1952. Die Materialien, die annähernd 2700 Nummern (1,30 m) umfassen, sind in Ordnern zusammengefaßt, wobei der Inhalt eines jeden Ordners gesondert aufgeführt ist. Sowohl die Anordnung wie auch die Kennzeichnung der einzelnen Ordner sind im Prinzip so geblieben, wie Wunderlich selbst sie bestimmt hatte.

A1   Diary. July 9, 1900 - Oct. 6, 1901.

A2   Notebook concerning Wunderlich's career as junior barrister.

A3   Cash-book. Jan. 29 - July 1933.
      Concert and theater book. June 20, 1897 - Nov. 23, 1929.
      Personal cash-book.
      Biographical notes.
      "Reise Erinnerungen, 1898-99."
      London trip preparations. 1910.

B1,2 London trip correspondence. 1910.
      Colegio de Esribanas de la Provincia de Buenos Aires. Correspondence. Sept. 1922 - July 1924.
      American Society of International Law. Correspondence. 1928-1935.
      Correspondence with Malcolm MacDonald. 1933-1948.
      Correspondence with the Union of South Africa concerning Wunderlich's gift. 1933-1948.
      Correspondence concerning military activities and positions. 1938-1943.
      Correspondence. 1938-1944. Includes some reports, cl.

Correspondence concerning the article "Preparing an International Bill of Rights. The German Conception of Fundamental Rights." 1944.
Correspondence and applications for International Monetary Fund. Primarily 1947.
Correspondence between Wunderlich and Schätzel. 1946-1949.
Correspondence with the University of Pennsylvania Law Review concerning the article "Some Problems of Military Occupation."

B2   Miscellaneous correspondence, primarily recommendation L. 1935-1943. Also some cl.
L. from the American Association of Former European Jurists. 1941-1944.
Recommendation L. W. R. Bisschop, Dr. Hilmer Freiherr von dem Bussche-Haddenhausen, Dr. Max Gutzwiller, Manley O. Hudson, Dr. W. Kieszelback.

C7   First lecture.
"Some Problems of Military Occupation." Unpub. A. and T.
"Allegiance of a Resident Alien Enemy during Enemy Occupation." Unpub. T. and cc.
"Preparing an International Bill of Rights: the German Conception." T. and cc.

C8   Bound T. of technical work, written as junior barrister.

D7   Newspaper and magazine cl. of 15 articles plus numerous reviews.

I,   Documents from school years. Up to 1906.
L   Diploma from University of Leipzig, Dr. Utriusque juris. Also documents concerning dissertation, some L.
"Eigene Personalakten: Band I." Documents and notes, primarily 1904-1906.
"Eigene Personalakten: Band II." 1907 and 1909.
"Personalakten: Band III." Miscellaneous documents. 1912-1923.
"Eigene Personalakten, Band IV." Military and civil occupation of Belgium.
"Akten, betreffend: Meine Zulassung zur Rechtsanwalt-pflicht. Band I." 1910. 1 F.

"Generalakten, betreffend: Anwaltskammer. Band I."
1910-1922. 1 F.
"Generalakten, betreffend: Anwaltskammer, 1923-29." 1
F.
"Anwaltskammer, Band III, 1930-1933." 1 F.
"Anwaltskammer, Band IV, 1934-1935." 1 F.
"Generalakten, betreffend: Vorstand der Anwaltskammer,
Band I, 1933." 1 F.
"Vorstand der Anwaltskammer. Band II, 1933." 1 F.
"Reihe Zulassung zum Reichsgericht: Band I, 1928-33."
1 F.
"Reihe Zulassung zum Reichsgericht: Band II, 1933."
1 F.
"Generalakten, betreffend: Anträge auf Ernennung zum
Notar, Band I, Jan. 1919-1928." 1 F.
"Notar, Band II, 1928-1933." 1 F.
"Notar, Band IV, June 1933 - Nov. 1935." 1 F.
"Reichsnotarkammer, 30. Jan. 1935 - 2. Jan. 1936."
Nazification of Reichsnotarkammer.
"Militärpersonalakten, Band I." Up till Jan. 1, 1916.
"Eigene Militärpersonalakten, Band II." Bruxelles and
Jildirim, March 1916 - Jan. 1918.
"Eigene Militärpersonalakten, Band I." 1917-1918.
Career as civil law judge in Belgium. 1917-1919.
"Militärpersonalakten." Honorary mentions. Sept. 1916 -
Nov. 1918.
Documents re: Wunderlich's disbarment and loss of
notarial seal.
Naturalization of Wunderlich and his daughters.
Miscellaneous personal documents. 1 F.
Passports, police IDs.
"Britische Botschaft." 1923-1925.
"Stadtgemeinde Buenos Aires." 1926. 1 F.
"Deutsche Bank und Disconto-Gesellschaft, Band I,
1933."
"Deutsche Bank und Disconto-Gesellschaft, Band II,
1933-34." Soskin case.
"International Law Association, 1935." Termination of
memberships.
"International Law Association, 1935-1936."
"International Law Association, 1937-."
"International Law Association, 1938-1940."
"International Law Association, 1941-1944."

"International Law Association, American Branch, 1944-1948."
"International Law Association, American Branch." 1951.
FBI reports, committee reports. 1941-1944. Also several cl.
"American Association of European Lawyers, 1943-1945."
Department of State, Office of Foreign Liquidation Commissioner. Memos, some cl. 1945-1946.
U.S. Government official forms, memos, applications. 1943-1947.
"Second Potomac Investment Company."
Miscellaneous documents.

J   Photos.

H4   Reviews and notices of dissertation. Primarily 1906.

Columbia University, Butler Library, New York, N.Y. 10027.

NICHOLAS MURRAY BUTLER PAPERS

B1   2 L. to N. M. Butler. T. and A. 1941, 1945.

New York Public Library, Manuscript Division, Fifth Avenue and 42nd Street, New York, N.Y. 10018.

EMERGENCY COMMITTEE IN AID OF DISPLACED FOREIGN SCHOLARS, 1933-1945

*   File compiled, no assistance given. 1933-1941.

HANS ZEISEL

Social Scientist, 1905-

Prof. Hans Zeisel, 5825 South Dorchester, Chicago, Illinois
60637.

Private collection: inaccessible. / *Unzugängliche Privat-
                                     sammlung.*

B1,2 Correspondence over the past 20 years.

C7   Several Ms. of articles by Zeisel.
      Ms. of Zeisel's lectures.

D7   Complete collection of offprints of Zeisel's writings.

F   3 tapes of Zeisel lectures.

I   Documents.

J   Photos.

K   Personal library.

M   Memorabilia.

N   Ms. by other authors.

OTTO ZOFF

Writer, 1890-1963

Immigration History Research Center of the University of
Minnesota, 826 Berry Street, St. Paul, Minnesota 55101.

AMERICAN COUNCIL FOR EMIGRÉS IN THE PROFESSIONS ARCHIVES

A3   Curriculum vitae, biographical statements. 12p.

B1   42 L. 1944-1951, including L. to: Mrs. Henry S. Canby,
       Friedrich Sally Grosshut, Franz Schoenberner, Else
       Staudinger, Ludwig Ullmann, Johannes Urzidil, Ernst
       Waldinger.

B2   32 L. 1944-1951, including L. from: Ludwig Ullmann,
       Franz Schoenberner.

B3   8 L.

University of Minnesota, University Libraries, Social Welfare History Archives, Minneapolis, Minnesota 55455.

SURVEY ASSOCIATES PAPERS

B1,2   Correspondence with Survey Associates. 20 L. 1942-
       1945.

Mr. Hans Sahl, 800 West End Avenue, New York, N.Y. 10025.

B1   Several L. to Hans Sahl.

Yale University, Beinecke Rare Book and Manuscript Library,
New Haven, Connecticut 06520.

HERMANN BROCH ARCHIVE

B1   1 L. to Hermann Broch. 1948.

Mrs. Elisabeth M. Stoerk and Mrs. Susanne B. Hoeller, 288
Ocean Drive West, Stamford, Connecticut 06902.

FRIDERIKE ZWEIG ARCHIVE

B1   1 L. to Friderike Zweig. 1952.

Mrs. Gertrude Urzidil, 83-39 116th Street, Richmond Hill,
New York 11418.

JOHANNES URZIDIL COLLECTION

B1   1 L. to Johannes Urzidil. A. 1948.

Hoover Institution on War, Revolution and Peace, Stanford,
California 94305.

FRANZ SCHOENBERNER COLLECTION

B1   1 L. to Franz Schoenberner. 1952.

Harvard University, University Archives, Widener Library,
Cambridge, Massachusetts 02138.

RICHARD VON MISES COLLECTION

B1   1 L. to Richard von Mises. T. 1946.

State University of New York at Albany, Department of Germanic Languages and Literatures, 1400 Washington Avenue,
Albany, New York 12222.

KARL O. PAETEL COLLECTION

B1   1 L. to Karl O. Paetel (xerox). 1945.

Leo Baeck Institute, 129 East 73rd Street, New York, N.Y.
10021.

B1   1 L. to Dr. Lutz Weltmann. A. 1925.

OTTO ZOFF

University of Pennsylvania, The Charles Patterson Van Pelt Library, Philadelphia, Pennsylvania 19104.

ALMA MAHLER-WERFEL COLLECTION

B1   1 L. to Alma Mahler-Werfel.

New York Public Library, Manuscript Division, Fifth Avenue and 42nd Street, New York, N.Y. 10018.

EMERGENCY COMMITTEE IN AID OF DISPLACED FOREIGN SCHOLARS, 1933-1945

*   File compiled, no assistance given. 1942-1944.

University of Chicago, The Joseph Regenstein Library, 1100 East 57th Street, Chicago, Illinois 60637.

JAMES FRANCK PAPERS

B1,2 Correspondence with James Franck.

Mrs. Alice Loewy Kahler, 1 Evelyn Place, Princeton, New Jersey 08540.

ERICH VON KAHLER COLLECTION

B1   1 L. to Erich von Kahler. 1944.

CARL ZUCKMAYER

Dramatist, 1896-

Leo Baeck Institute, 129 East 73rd Street, New York, N.Y. 10021.

LEOPOLD SCHWARZSCHILD COLLECTION, KURT HIRSCHFELD COLLEC-
TION, JULIUS BAB COLLECTION

B1   Ca. 45 unpub. L. 1940s, including L. to: Julius Bab,
        Kurt Hirschfeld, Leopold Schwarzschild.

C   Ms.

Mrs. Gertrude Urzidil, 83-39 116th Street, Richmond Hill,
New York 11418.

JOHANNES URZIDIL COLLECTION

B1   11 L. and 13 Ptc. to Johannes Urzidil. T. and A. 1953-
        1968 and undated.

B2   2 L. from Johannes Urzidil. A.pc. 1956, 1957.

C3   5 poems, dedicated to Johannes Urzidil:
        "Aus dem Stegreif gesprochen." Sylvester 1932-1933.
        "Kleine Strophen von der Unsterblichkeit."
        "Mein Tod."
        "Römerode am Wallersee vorm Gewitter." 1937.
        "Trinkspruch für Gerhart Hauptmann." 1932.

Syracuse University, The George Arents Research Library,
Syracuse, New York 13210.

DOROTHY THOMPSON PAPERS

B1   25 L. to Dorothy Thompson. 1939-1955.

H5   Thompson, Dorothy. Ms. about Carl Zuckmayer. T.

University of Pennsylvania, The Charles Patterson Van Pelt
Library, Philadelphia, Pennsylvania 19104.

CARL ZUCKMAYER

ALMA MAHLER-WERFEL COLLECTION

B1   18 L., 6 Ptc., 3 short L. and 1 condolence L. to
      Alma Mahler-Werfel. 1944-1956.

B2   1 L. from Franz Werfel. cc.

C3   2 poems.

Southern Illinois University, Morris Library, Department of
Special Collections, Carbondale, Illinois 62901.

ERWIN PISCATOR PAPERS

B1   8 L. and 4 Tel. T. and A. 1939-1963.

B2   10 L. from Erwin Piscator. cc. 1939-1943.

C7   "Aufruf zum Leben." T. with corr. 4p.

Yale University, Beinecke Rare Book and Manuscript Library,
New Haven, Connecticut 06520.

KURT WOLFF ARCHIVE

B1   11 L. and 2 Tel. to the Kurt Wolff Verlag. 1920-1921.

B2   7 L. from Kurt Wolff. 1920-1921.

Library of Congress, Manuscript Division, Independence Avenue and First Street S.E., Washington, D.C. 20540.

BENJAMIN W. HUEBSCH PAPERS

B1   5 L. to B. W. Huebsch. T. 1932-1945.

B2   3 L. from B. W. Huebsch. T.cc. 1942-1945.

B3   1 L. from B. W. Huebsch to the U.S. Consul, Havana,
      Cuba. 1939.

Mrs. Elisabeth M. Stoerk and Mrs. Susanne B. Hoeller, 288

1041

CARL ZUCKMAYER

Ocean Drive West, Stamford, Connecticut 06902.

FRIDERIKE ZWEIG ARCHIVE

B1   7 L. to Friderike Zweig. 1942-1968.

State University of New York at Albany, Department of Germanic Languages and Literatures, 1400 Washington Avenue, Albany, New York 12222.

KARL O. PAETEL COLLECTION

B1   3 L. to Karl O. Paetel (xerox). 1945-1947.

Hoover Institution on War, Revolution and Peace, Stanford, California, 94305.

KARL BOROMAEUS FRANK COLLECTION

B1,2 Correspondence with Karl Frank.

Mr. Hans Sahl, 800 West End Avenue, New York, N.Y. 10025.

B1   Numerous L. to Hans Sahl.

Mrs. Gertrude Lederer, 372 Central Park West, Apt. 3B, New York, N.Y. 10024.

C7   Manuscript by Zuckmayer, sent to Lederer upon his 50th
      birthday.

Mrs. Liselotte Stein, 115-25 Metropolitan Avenue, Kew Gardens, New York 11418.

FRED STEIN PAPERS

J   Photos of Zuckmayer.

CARL ZUCKMAYER

State University of New York at Binghamton, Center for Modern Theater Research, Binghamton, New York 13901.

MAX REINHARDT ARCHIVE

J   Der Hauptmann von Koepenick. 2 production photos. Berlin, 1931.

Mrs. Alice Loewy Kahler, 1 Evelyn Place, Princeton, New Jersey 08540.

ERICH VON KAHLER COLLECTION

B1   1 L. to Erich von Kahler. 1957.

FRIDERIKE ZWEIG

Writer, 1882-1971

<u>Mrs. Elisabeth M. Stoerk and Mrs. Susanne B. Hoeller</u>, 288
Ocean Drive West, Stamford, Connecticut 06902.

The FRIDERIKE ZWEIG ARCHIVE, ca. 10.5 ft. of materials, is
located in the former residence of Friderike and is cared
for by her two daughters. Some of the materials, including
the correspondence between Friderike and Stefan Zweig, are
from the years before the war. Many papers from this period,
however, were either lost or destroyed by fire. The remaining materials were brought to the U.S. by Friderike and her
two daughters in 1940. The bulk of the materials in the
collection are from the U.S. years, 1940-1971. Permission
to use the collection may be obtained from either Mrs.
Stoerk or Mrs. Hoeller.

*Das FRIDERIKE ZWEIG ARCHIVE, etwa 3,15 m Materialien, befin-
det sich in der früheren Wohnung von Friderike Zweig und
wird von ihren beiden Töchtern betreut. Einige der Materialien, darunter auch der Briefwechsel zwischen Friderike und
Stefan Zweig, datieren aus der Zeit vor dem Krieg. Vieles
aus dieser Zeit ist jedoch entweder verlorengegangen oder
verbrannt. Alles noch existierende Material wurde von Friderike Zweig und ihren Töchtern im Jahre 1940 in die Vereinigten Staaten gebracht. Der größte Teil der Materialien in
diesem Archiv stammt aus der Zeit, die sie in den Vereinigten Staaten verbrachte, den Jahren 1940-1971. Erlaubnis,
Materialien der Sammlung zu benutzen, erteilt entweder Frau
Stoerk oder Frau Hoeller.*

A1   First diary, begun in Friderike's 10th year.
     Second diary, up to 1900.
     Diary. 1912-1914.

A3   Europe trip. 1958. Mimeo.
     Memoirs. Austria. A. and T.

B1   Ca. 30 L. 1935-1936, including L. to: Franz Csokor,
     Alfred Döblin, Alfred Einstein, René Fülöp-Miller,
     Emil Ludwig, Hertha Pauli, Joseph Roth, Josef Luit-
     pold Stern.
     353 L. to Stefan Zweig. 1912-1937.

B1,2 <u>Briefwechsel 1912-1942</u>. T.cc. of pub. correspondence

between Friderike and Stefan Zweig. German.
Altmann/Albermann correspondence. Re.: estate of Ste-
fan Zweig after his death in 1942.
Correspondence re: purchase of Friderike's autograph
collection.
Correspondence with the Connecticut Council to Abolish
Capital Punishment.
Correspondence re: Council for a Democratic Germany.
June-July 1944. Includes correspondence with Paul
Tillich.
Correspondence with Fredonia State University College,
New York, re: establishment of a Stefan Zweig Center.
1968.

B2   387 L. from Stefan and 5 L. from Lotte Zweig. 1915-
1942.
Congratulatory L., on Friderike's 70th, 80th and 85th
birthdays.
Condolence L. after the suicide death of Stefan Zweig.
1942.
Miscellaneous correspondence, including the awarding
of the Austrian "Verdienstkreuz" and honorary pro-
fessorship. Arranged chronologically or by individual
works.
Correspondence with publishers.
Writers Service Center correspondence, arranged in 4 B.:
I. 1942-1943.
II. 1944-1945.
IIa. 1946-1951.
III. Alfredo Cahn (Latin American editors of Fride-
rike's works). 1940-1954.
Includes L. from: Martin Beradt, Gottfried Bermann-
Fischer, Emil Bernhard (Cohn), Jacques Chambrun,
Albert Einstein, Barthold Fles, Paul Frank, René
Fülöp-Miller, Alexander Gode von Aesch, Claire
Goll, Felix Guggenheim, Gina Kaus, Hermann Kesten,
Heinrich Mann, Franz Molnar, Paul Nettl, Adrienne
Thomas, Veit Valentin, Fritz von Unruh.
Over 1,400 L. (some with Ms. and T. enclosed), includ-
ing L. from: Sir Norman Angell, Raoul Auernheimer,
Julius Bab, Hermann Broch, Max Brod, Martin Buber,
Pearl S. Buck, Henry and Marion Canby, Hans Carossa,
Franz Theodor Csokor, Alfred Döblin, Albert Ehren-

stein, Albert Einstein, Alfred Einstein, Clifton
Fadiman, Ernst Federn, Frederick J. Forell, Paul
Frank, Bella Fromm (Welles), René Fülöp-Miller,
Devora Ginzburg, Gerhart Hauptmann, Ivan Heilbut,
Hans Jaray, Heinrich Eduard Jacob, Hermann Kesten,
Erich Kästner, Annette Kolb, Alfred Kubin, Emil Lud-
wig, Joachim Maass, Alma Mahler-Werfel, Erika Mann,
Thomas Mann, Dmitri Mitropoulos, Soma Morgenstern,
Paul Nettl, John M. Oesterreicher, Hertha Pauli,
Gregor Piatigorsky, Erwin Piscator, Paul Pisk, Alfred
Polgar, Rainer Maria Rilke, Romain Rolland, Hans
Sahl, George Sarton, Arnold Schoenberg, Franz Schoen-
berner, George N. Shuster, Josef Luitpold Stern,
Richard Strauss, Siegfried Trebitsch, Ludwig Ullmann,
Johannes Urzidil, Walther Victor, Berthold Viertel,
Fritz von Unruh, Ernst Waldinger, Bruno Walter,
Franz Werfel, Thornton Wilder, Otto Zoff, Carl Zuck-
mayer.
17 L. from various individuals re: Joseph Roth Nachlaß
in Paris. 1945-1948, 1951-1952.

B3   Burger family correspondence.
     Refugee and Immigration Aid correspondence. 1941-1945.
     90 L. from Stefan Zweig to various individuals. 1913-
     1941.

C1   Riesen sind einsam. Rough versions. A. First and final
     versions. T. English synopsis and partial tr. by
     Richard Winston. T.
     Untitled, unfinished novel. 2c. 13p. ea.

C3   46 poems. A., T. and cc. 1913-1922, 1967-1969.

C4   Short stories and novellas. T. English and German. 4
     items.

C5   Geister um Verena: Exposé zu einem Tanzfilm. T.
     Herr Barton rettet sich selbst. Synopsis of story "Der
     Lebensretter" for film version. T. 3c. 12p.
     Rivalen. Draft of a film version of Stefan Zweig's
     "Schachnovelle." T. 2c. 24p. Incomplete version. cc.

C7   Introductions to works by others. T. 2 items.
     11 essays. T. and A.
     4 speech texts. T.

C9   Les Soleils Disparus. Tr. of work by Edmond Jaloux.
      Weiße Weihnacht. Tr. of work by Verhaeren.

C11   Erik Neergard und die Schwestern. T. German.
      Greatness Revisited. Rough drafts and final version. T.
      Pasteur. Rough drafts and materials. A. Incomplete
      English tr. by E. Camp-Huegli. T.
      Spiegelungen des Lebens. Rough drafts and T.
      Stefan Zweig: eine Bildbiographie. Rough drafts. A.
      German version. T.
      Stefan Zweig: wie ich ihn erlebte. Rough drafts and
      materials. A. German version. T. 2c. English version.
      T. English proofs. French tr. by Grossvogel. T. 2c.
      Wunder und Zeichen. Rough drafts and materials. A. Ger-
      man version. T. German proofs. Incomplete English
      version. T.

G   Several interviews.

H3   Recommendations, commemorative speeches, including:
      Liber Amicorum Friderike Zweig.

H4   Newspaper and magazine cl. of reviews.

I   Bank notes and other financial documents.
      3 F. 1892-1971, including: birth certificate, marriage
      certificate of first marriage with Fritz von Winter-
      nitz, divorce decree from Stefan (1937) and related
      documents from Paris, Montauban and Marseilles per-
      iods (1938-1940), lists of individuals, documents
      from the American years (1940-1971), documents per-
      taining to Europe trips (1958, 1963, 1969).

L   American/European Friendship Association materials.
      1950s-1960s.
      Summer vacation for writers. Cotuit, Massachusetts,
      July-Aug. 1943.
      Stefan Zweig Collection, including L., Ms. of essays,
      poems, novella, newspaper cl. by and about Zweig,
      interview, documents, programs, biographical mate-
      rials.
      Writers Service Center. Lives and Outlines files, in-
      cluding biographical materials on: Albert Ehrenstein,
      Paul Frank, Alexander Roda Roda, Ludwig Ullmann,
      Johannes Urzidil, Walther Victor.

N   Ms. of other authors filed under Writers Service Cen-
    ter. T. Ca. 5,200p. Includes Ms. by: Emil Bernhard
    (Cohn), Bella Fromm (Welles).

State University of New York at Albany, Department of Germanic Languages and Literatures, 1400 Washington Avenue,
Albany, New York 12222.

STORM PUBLISHERS ARCHIVE

B1   84 L. and 22 Ptc. and notes to Alexander Gode von
     Aesch. 1944-1958.
     1 L. ea. to Thomas Crowell and Patrick Mahoney.

B2   59 L. from Alexander Gode von Aesch. 1945-1948.

C7   "Veilchen." Notes to the work by Paul Nettl. 4p.

C11 Stefan Zweig. Biography. Notes. Ca. 10 items. Also
     miscellaneous chap. and tr. of chap. 33p.

J   6 photos of Friderike and Stefan Zweig. Pub. in the
     Stefan Zweig biography.

Leo Baeck Institute, 129 East 73rd Street, New York, N.Y.
10021.

The materials in the JOSEPH ROTH COLLECTION were originally
part of the Friderike Zweig Nachlaß. They were donated to
the Leo Baeck Institute by Friderike's heirs in 1972. Friderike Zweig materials are also located in the Institute's
PAUL AMANN COLLECTION.

Die Materialien in der JOSEPH ROTH COLLECTION waren ursprünglich ein Teil des Nachlasses von Friderike Zweig. Sie stellen
eine Schenkung an das Leo Baeck Institute durch Friderike
Zweigs Erben im Jahre 1972 dar. Weitere Friderike Zweig -
Materialien sind in der PAUL AMANN COLLECTION des Instituts
zu finden.

B1   1 L. and 1 Ptc. to Joseph Roth. A. 1935.
     6 L. 1944-1948.

FRIDERIKE ZWEIG

B1,2   Correspondence with Paul Amann. Uncatalogued.

B2   2 L. from Alma Mahler-Werfel. 1949 and undated.
       16 L. 1939-1957.

C7   Notes on Joseph Roth. Undated. A. 2p.

I   Visiting card, receipt.

N   Wittlin, Joseph. "Reminiscences of J. Roth." Undated.
       T.cc. 10p.

Mrs. Gertrude Urzidil, 83-39 116th Street, Richmond Hill,
New York 11418.

JOHANNES URZIDIL COLLECTION

B1   25 L. and 2 Ptc. to Johannes Urzidil. T. and A. 1946-
       1968 and undated.

B2   2 L. from Johannes Urzidil. 1954, 1959.

University of Pennsylvania, The Charles Patterson Van Pelt
Library, Philadelphia, Pennsylvania 19104.

ALMA MAHLER-WERFEL COLLECTION

B1   14 L. and 2 Ptc. to Alma Mahler-Werfel. 1941-1949.
       1 short L. to Franz Werfel.

B2   Draft of a L. from Alma Mahler-Werfel.

Library of Congress, Manuscript Division, Independence Avenue
and First Street S.E., Washington, D.C. 20540.

BENJAMIN W. HUEBSCH PAPERS

B1   8 L. and 4 Ptc. to B. W. Huebsch. 1928-1947 and undated.

B2   5 L. from B. W. Huebsch. T.cc. 1940-1945.

Harvard University, Houghton Library, Cambridge, Massachusetts 02138.

FRIDERIKE ZWEIG

RICHARD BEER-HOFMANN COLLECTION, GEORGE SARTON PAPERS

B1   1 L. to Paula Beer-Hofmann. Undated.
       3 L. to George Sarton. 1952-1953.

Immigration History Research Center of the University of Minnesota, 826 Berry Street, St. Paul, Minnesota 55101.

AMERICAN COUNCIL FOR EMIGRÉS IN THE PROFESSIONS ARCHIVES

B1   3 L. 1947, 1954 and undated.

B2   2 L. 1947.

Bruno Walter Memorial Foundation, c/o Miss Susie Danziger, 115 East 72nd Street, New York, N.Y. 10021.

B1,2 Correspondence with Bruno Walter.

Indiana University, The University Libraries, The Lilly Library, Bloomington, Indiana 47401.

MAX EASTMAN MSS.

B1   1 L. to Max Eastman. 1956.

B3   1 L. 1926.

University of California at Riverside, Riverside, California 92502.

RAOUL AUERNHEIMER ARCHIVE

B1   1 L. to Raoul Auernheimer. 1943.

University of Texas, Humanities Research Center, Manuscripts Collection, Box 7219, Austin, Texas 78712.

B2   1 L.

1050

Dr. Clementine Zernik, 225-10 106th Avenue, Queens Village, New York 11429.

B1   Several L. to Arnold Höllriegel. 1938-1939.

STEFAN ZWEIG

Writer, 1881-1942

Mrs. Elisabeth M. Stoerk and Mrs. Susanne B. Hoeller, 288
Ocean Drive West, Stamford, Connecticut 06902.

FRIDERIKE ZWEIG ARCHIVE, Appendix VII (Stefan Zweig Sammlung). For a more complete description of the entire collection, see Friderike Zweig.

*FRIDERIKE ZWEIG ARCHIVE, Appendix VII (Stefan Zweig Samm-
lung). Eine detailliertere Beschreibung der Sammlung findet sich unter "Friderike Zweig."*

A3   Die Welt von Gestern. 2 cl. of excerpts. German and
      English.

Bl   51 L. to Alfred Einstein. c. 1930-1941.
      44 L. to Joseph Roth. c. 1933-1938.
      387 L. to Friderike Zweig. 1913-1942.
      61 L. (all c.). 1917-1941, including L. to: Emil Lud-
      wig, Hans Sahl, Arturo Toscanini.

B2   353 L. from Friderike Zweig. 1912-1937.

C3   Poem Ms. A. and T.:
      "Winterabend im Zimmer."
      "Du."
      "Hand in Hand."
      "Dunkle Sehnsucht."
      "Weihnacht."
      "Spinoza."
      "Trugland."

C4   "Schachnovelle." With the notation "An L. B. Fischer,
      21. 2. 1942." T. 23p.
      "Legend of the Third Dove." Tr.
      "Escape in the Snow." Tr.
      "The Tower of Babel." Tr.

C7   4 essays. 1904-1929. T. and cc.
      "Thanks to Books." Tr.

D3   "Erfüllung." 1952.

D4   "Die spät bezahlte Schuld." Novella.

D7   11 articles on various topics. 1916-1951.

STEFAN ZWEIG

G   Interview, in French. 2c. 1941.

H3   93 cl. by various authors on Zweig, including: René
Fülöp-Miller, Oskar Maria Graf, Thomas Mann, Ludwig
Ullmann, Carl Zuckmayer, Friderike Zweig. 1942-1971
and undated.
Cl. re: "Gedenkfeier" and obituaries.

I   List of languages into which Zweig's works were tr.

L   Blätter der Stefan Zweig Gesellschaft.

O   Various programs.

Leo Baeck Institute, 129 East 73rd Street, New York, N.Y.
10021.

JULIUS BAB COLLECTION, GEORG HERMANN COLLECTION, HUGO WOLF
COLLECTION, JOHANNA MEYER COLLECTION, JACOB PICARD COLLEC-
TION and general archive files

B1   40 L. 1909-1941, including L. to: Julius Bab, Emil
Bernhard (Cohn), Georg Hermann, Jacob Picard.
4 cl. of pub. L.

B2   1 L. from Georg Altmann. T. 1961.

B3   1 L.

C7   "Dank an die Bücher." Undated. cc. 2p.
Draft of an address. 1937. A. pc. 1p.

D7   Newspaper cl. about Maximilian Harden. 1937.

H3   7 cl. 1931, 1942-1958.

H5   Meyer, Johanna. Lecture on Zweig. 1925. A. 9p.

H4   Book notice.

J   6 photos, including 4 of Stefan Zweig.
Photo of grave site, Rio de Janeiro. 1942.

L   Blätter der Stefan Zweig Gesellschaft. 1958. 8p.

O   Programs of "Berliner Festwochen" ("Jeremias"). 1962.

Harvard University, Houghton Library, Cambridge, Massachusetts 02138.

STEFAN ZWEIG

SCHWEIZER COLLECTION OF GERMAN AUTOGRAPHS, THEO FELDMAN
PAPERS, RICHARD BEER-HOFMANN COLLECTION, ZWEIG/SELDEN-GOTH
COLLECTION

B1   33 L. and 25 Ptc. to Julius Bab. A. and T. 1909-1934.
      7 L. to Richard Beer-Hofmann. 1931-1941 and undated.
      53 L. and 10 Ptc. to Mrs. Gisela Selden-Goth. 1935-
      1941.
      10 L. 1909-1942 and undated.

Indiana University, The University Libraries, The Lilly
Library, Bloomington, Indiana 47401.

MAX EASTMAN MSS., LUDWIG LEWISOHN MSS., MISCELLANEOUS MSS.

B1   1 L. to Max Eastman. 1932.
      1 Ptc. to Ludwig Lewisohn. 1925.

B3   1 L. from Friderike Zweig to Max Eastman. 1956.

C1   Die Welt von Gestern. German text. Undated.

C7   "Ein Blick auf Brasilien." German text. Undated.

Library of Congress, Manuscript Division, Independence Avenue and First Street S.E., Washington, D.C. 20540.

BENJAMIN W. HUEBSCH PAPERS

B1   93 L., 18 Ptc. and 9 Tel. to Benjamin W. Huebsch.
      T. and A. 1926-1934.
      299 L. to B. W. Huebsch. 1935-1942.
      Transcriptions of 2 L. to Berthold Viertel. 1941-1942.

B2   24 L. and 4 Tel. from Benjamin W. Huebsch. T.cc. 1931-
      1934.

C4   "Schachnovelle." cc. 62p.
      "Georg Friedrich Händels Auferstehung." T.cc. Undated.
      21p.

H3   The Royal Game. Review by F. C. Weiskopf. 1945.

I   1 document.

University of California at Riverside, Riverside, California
92502.

RAOUL AUERNHEIMER ARCHIVE

B1   77 L. and 1 Ptc. to Raoul Auernheimer. 1920-1941.
      Microfilm.

Yale University, Beinecke Rare Book and Manuscript Library,
New Haven, Connecticut 06520.

KURT WOLFF ARCHIVE

B1   10 L. and 2 Ptc. to the Kurt Wolff Verlag. 1921-1930.

B2   5 L. from the Kurt Wolff Verlag. 1921-1930.

University of Texas, Humanities Research Center, Manuscripts
Collection, Box 7219, Austin, Texas 78712.

B1   2 L. and 3 Ptc.

B2   28 L.

Columbia University, Butler Library, New York, N.Y. 10027.

B1   4 L. 1929-1939, including 1 L. to Benjamin W. Huebsch.

C7   Message at the opening of the Deutsches Haus. 1929. T.
      1p.

H5   Recollections of Stefan Zweig by Benjamin Huebsch in
      an interview. 1955.

Indiana University, University Libraries, Music Library,
Bloomington, Indiana 47401..

PAUL NETTL COLLECTION

H5   "Stefan Zweig und die Musik." T. German. 15p.

University of Pennsylvania, The Charles Patterson Van Pelt Library, Philadelphia, Pennsylvania 19104.

ALMA MAHLER-WERFEL COLLECTION

B1   7 L. and 3 Ptc. to Alma Mahler-Werfel. 1937-1941.

C7   "Zwischen zwei Kriegen." T. with corr. by Franz Werfel.

Dr. Marta Mierendorff, 8633 West Knoll Drive, Hollywood, California 90069.

SAMMLUNG WALTER WICCLAIR, WALTER WICCLAIR PRODUCTIONS: 4 F. of materials in total.

E   Jeremias. Partial English adaptation by Walter Wicclair.

H3,4 Cl. and other materials concerning Zweig, the Stefan Zweig "Festwoche" (20th anniversary of Zweig's death), productions of Jeremias.

J   Photo of Stefan Zweig's grave site. Jeremias. Several production photos.

Yale University Library, Manuscripts and Archives Research Room, 150 Sterling Memorial Library, New Haven, Connecticut 06520.

DECISION: A REVIEW OF FREE CULTURE. CORRESPONDENCE AND PAPERS OF KLAUS MANN

B1   4 L. to Klaus Mann. 1940-1942.

C7   Ms. written for publication in Decision magazine.

Mr. Hans Sahl, 800 West End Avenue, New York, N.Y. 10025.

B1   Numerous L. from Stefan Zweig to Hans Sahl.

Mrs. Erika Renon, 624 University Drive, Menlo Park, California 94025.

STEFAN ZWEIG

B1,2   Correspondence with René Fülöp-Miller.

Princeton University, Firestone Library, Princeton, New Jerset 08540.

THE PAPERS OF ALBERT EINSTEIN (1879-1955). For details concerning the use of the collection, see description under Albert Einstein.

THE PAPERS OF ALBERT EINSTEIN (1879-1955). Angaben über den Zugang zu der Sammlung finden sich unter "Albert Einstein."

B1,2   Unknown amount of correspondence between Einstein and Stefan Zweig.

Dr. Harold von Hofe, Department of German, University of Southern California, Los Angeles, California 90007.

LUDWIG MARCUSE PAPERS

B1,2   Correspondence with Ludwig Marcuse.

Bruno Walter Memorial Foundation, c/o Miss Susie Danziger, 115 East 72nd Street, New York, N.Y. 10021.

B1,2   Correspondence with Bruno Walter.

Mr. Francis Heilbut, 328 West 96th Street, New York, N.Y. 10025.

IVAN HEILBUT PAPERS

B1,2   Correspondence with Ivan Heilbut.

Barthold Fles Literary Agency, 507 Fifth Avenue, New York, N.Y. 10016.

B1   2 L. and 1 Ptc. to Barthold Fles. 1936-1941.

STEFAN ZWEIG

B2   1 L. from Barthold Fles. 1939.

Mr. Frederick Kohner, 12046 Coyne Street, Los Angeles, California 90049.

B1   1 L. and 1 Ptc. to Frederick Kohner.

Oberlin College Library, Oberlin, Ohio 44074.

B1   Pc. of Zweig's last L. to Friderike Zweig. Petropolis,
      Brazil, Feb. 18, 1942.
      1 L. to Mrs. Oscar Jaszi. Undated.

University of Southern California, Lion Feuchtwanger Memorial
Library, 520 Paseo Miramar, Pacific Palisades, California
90272.

B1   1 L. to Lion Feuchtwanger. Undated.

Hoover Institution on War, Revolution and Peace, Stanford,
California 94305.

FRANZ SCHOENBERNER COLLECTION

B1   1 L. to Franz Schoenberner. 1941.

University of California, Los Angeles, Department of Special
Collections, 120 Lawrence Clark Powell Library, Los Angeles,
California 90024.

FRANZ WERFEL ARCHIVE

B1   1 L. to Franz Werfel.

New York Public Library, Manuscript Division, Fifth Avenue
and 42nd Street, New York, N.Y. 10018.

STEFAN ZWEIG

THEO FELDMAN PAPERS

B1   1 L. to Theo Feldman. A. Undated.

Mrs. Peter M. Lindt, 949 West End Avenue, New York, N.Y.
10025.

C   Ms. submitted to Lindt for use on his radio program.

APPENDIXES

APPENDIX

List of individuals for whom (a) very small amounts of material could be found (under thirty units), or (b) whose collections could not be described early enough for inclusion in the Guide. The following names represent the remainder of the search list of ca. 700 names used as the basis of this survey.

Liste von Immigranten, von denen (a) nur sehr kleine Mengen an Material gefunden werden konnten (weniger als 30 Einheiten), oder (b) deren Sammlungen zu spät entdeckt wurden, um noch in dieses Handbuch aufgenommen werden zu können. Die folgenden Namen stammen aus der ursprünglichen Liste der Emigranten, nach deren Nachlässen gesucht wurde.

Adler, Kurt Herbert

Alexander, Franz

Alt, Franz

Apel, Willi

Ashton, E. B.

Auerbach, Erich

Baer, Reinhold

Baerensprung, Horst

Barnowsky, Victor

Barschak, Erna

Barth, Max

Bartsch, Hans

Bassermann, Albert

Bauchwitz, Kurt

Beck, Maximilian

Benesch, Otto

Beradt, Charlotte

Bergammer, Friedrich

Bergler, Edmund

Bergmann, Peter Gabriel

Bergner, Elisabeth

Bergsträsser, Arnold

Bernhard, Georg

Biel, Egon Vitalis

Bier, Justus

Block, Herbert

Blume, Bernhard

Bondy, Curt

Borgese, Giuseppe Antonio

Born, Max

Born, Wolfgang

Bothmer, Bernard von

Brauer, Max

Brauer, Richard

Braunstein, Josef

Breisach, Paul

Brentano, Felix

Brook, Warner F.

Brunswick, Egon

Brunswick, Else

Buch, Babette

Budzislawski, Hermann

Bühler, Charlotte

Bühler, Karl

Bunzel, Josef

Busch, Adolf

Canetti, Elias

Cohen, Frederic

Colm, Gerhard

Deri, Frances

Deutsch, Ernst

Deutsch, Julius

Deutsch, Karl

Dietrich, Marlene

Dolbin, B. F.

Eberhard, Wolfram

Ebert, Carl

Edelstein, Ludwig

Ehrenfest, Paul

Eisler, Gerhart

Eissler, Kurt

Eliasberg, George J.

Elow

Engel-Janosi, Friedrich

Epstein, Julius

Ernst, Max

Fabricius

Feigl, Herbert

Flechtheim, Ossip

Flesch, Rudolf

Forell, Frederick W.

Fraenkel-Conrat, Heinz

Frankl, Oskar Benjamin

Friedlander, Walter A.

Fröhlich, Paul

Fromm-Reichmann, Frieda

Gamow, George

Geiringer, Hilde

Gerhard, Dietrich

Gerth, Hans

Gilbert, Felix

Ginzburg, Toni

Gödel, Kurt

Goetz, Curt

Goldschmidt, Alfons

Golffing, Francis

Goll, Claire

Gong, Alfred

Grab, Hermann

Graf, Max

Guillemin, Bernard

Gumpert, Martin

Gurland, Arkadij

Haas, Willy

Haberler, Gottfried

Habsburg, Otto von

Halecki, Oscar

Hallgarten, Wolfgang

Hartmann, Heinz

Hauser, Heinrich

Heiden, Konrad

Hellmer, Kurt

Hempel, Carl Gustav

Henried, Paul von

Herma, John

Hermens, Ferdinand A.

Herz, John H.

Hesslein, Pablo

Heym, Stefan

Hiller, Kurt

Hippel, Arthur von

Hitschmann, Edward

Holborn, Louise

Höllering, Franz

Holde, Artur

Homolka, Oscar

Horch, Franz

Hoselitz, Bert F.

Huelsenbeck, Richard

Hula, Erich

Huth, Hans

Jackson, Felix

Jacobson, Edith

Jacoby, Kurt

Jahoda, Marie

Jalowetz, Hans

Janowitz, Hans

Jaray, Hans

Jekels, Ludwig

Jonas, Hans

Juchacz, Marie

Kafka, Hans

Kaleko, Mascha

Kalenter, Ossip

Kaskell, Joseph

Katz, Henry William

Katz, Rudolf

Katzenellenbogen, Adolf

Kaufmann, Edward

Kautsky, Karl

Kayser, Rudolf

Kelsen, Hans

Kieve, Rudolph

Kirchheimer, Otto

Kisch, Guido

Koestler, Arthur

Kohut, Heinz

Kortner, Fritz

Kotschnig, Walter Maria

Kracauer, Siegfried

Krautheimer, Richard

Kuh, Anton

Lampel, J. F. M.

Land, Gustav

Landsberger, Benno

Lang, Fritz

Lantz, Robert	Meyerhof, Otto
Lehmann, Fritz	Middeldorf, Ulrich
Lenya, Lotte	Moellenhoff, Fritz
Leonhard, Rudolf	Moldenhauer, Hans
Leschnitzer, Adolf	Morgenstern, Soma
Levy, Ernst	Morstein-Marx, Fritz
Liepe, Wolfgang	Nathan, Hans
Liepmann, Heinz	Nathan, Otto
Littauer, Rudolf	Natonek, Hans
Loewenstein, Karl	Neisser, Hans Philip
Loewi, Otto	Neumann, Franz
Lorre, Peter	Neumann, John von
Lothar, Ernst	Neumann, Robert
Löwith, Karl	Neumann, Sigmund
Maenchen-Helfen, Otto J.	Neumeyer, Alfred
Mahler, Fritz	Neurath, Hans
Mann, Elisabeth	Neurath, Otto
Mann, Fritz Karl	Neutra, Richard
Mann, Golo	Niebyl, Karl H.
Mann, Katia	Noether, Emmy
Marchwitza, Hans	Norden, Albert
Marck, Siegfried	Noth, Ernst Erich
Marcu, Valeriu	Nunberg, Herman
Marschak, Jacob	Nussbaum, Arthur
Massary, Fritzi	Oesterreicher, John M.
Massing, Paul	Oppler, Alfred
Masur, Gerhard	Osborn, Max
Meckauer, Walther	Paechter, Heinz
Meisel, Hans (James)	Pick, Robert
Meyer, Karl	Plant, Richard

Pol, Heinz

Politzer, Heinz

Porada, Edith

Prager, William

Preminger, Otto

Pringsheim, Peter

Proskauer, Eric S.

Rademacher, Hans

Rado, Sandor

Rauschning, Hermann

Redl, Fritz

Regler, Gustav

Reich, John

Rewald, John

Richter, Werner

Riess, Curt

Roda Roda, Alexander

Roden, Max

Rosenberg, Arthur

Rosenberg, Hans

Rosenfeld, Hans

Rosenfeld, Kurt

Rosenthal, Franz

Rothfels, Hans

Rudolf, Max

Sachs, Curt

Sachs, Hanns

Salmony, Alfred

Salomon, Albert

Saussure, Raymond de

Schaber, Will

Schaeffer, Albrecht

Schawinsky, Xanti

Schick, Rudolf

Schindler, Rudolf

Schirokauer, Arnold

Schlamm, Willi

Schlesinger, Rudolf

Schnabel, Artur

Schnitzler, Heinrich

Schocken, Theodore

Schoenberger, Guido

Schrade, Leo

Schück, Karl

Schütz, Alfred

Schwerin, Kurt

Seghers, Anna

Seidlin, Oskar

Serkin, Rudolf

Siemsen, Hans

Simson, Otto von

Singer, Kurt

Spiecker, Carl

Spitzer, Leo

Stampfer, Friedrich

Stechow, Wolfgang

Steinitz, Hans

Sterba, Richard

Stern, William

Sternberg, Fritz

Straus, Erwin Walter

Strauss, Leo

Stücklen, Hildegard

Sturmthal, Adolf

Swarzenski, Hanns

Tarski, Alfred

Tetens, Harens

Thalheimer, Siegfried

Thoeren, Robert

Thomas, Adrienne

Torberg, Friedrich

Trapp, Maria

Treviranus, Gottfried Reinhold

Urbanitzky, Grete von

Veidt, Conrad

Voegelin, Eric

Vordtriede, Werner

Wach, Joachim

Wachenheim, Hedwig

Weichmann, Herbert

Weigert, Hans W.

Weigel, Helene

Weigl, Vally

Weil, Bruno

Weinberger, Martin

Weiss, Maria

Weisskopf, Walter

Weitzmann, Kurt

Wildt, Rupert

Wilhelm, Hans

Wolff, Friedrich

Wolff, Victoria

Wolpe, Stefan

Wronkow, George

Wronkow, Ludwig

Württemburg, Odo von

Zech, Paul

Zeisl, Eric

Zernatto, Guido

Zimmer, Heinrich

APPENDIX

List of individuals for whom no materials were found in the United States.

Liste von Immigranten, von denen keine Materialien in den U.S.A. gefunden wurden.

Adler, Kurt

Auerbach, Frank

Baade, Walter

Baerwald, Friedrich

Becher, Ulrich

Berliner, Bernhard

Bernheimer, Richard

Buxbaum, Edith

Caspari, Fritz

Cori, Carl

Ebenstein, William

Elbau, Julius

Enoch, Kurt

Friedlaender, Walter

Glarner, Fritz

Goetze, Albrecht

Graetz, Paul

Grund, Peter

Haenel, Irene

Herzog, Wilhelm

Hirschman, Albert O.

Holländer, Friedrich

Ilberg, Werner

Infeld, Heinrich

Johnson, Walter

Jolles, Otto M.

Juhn, Erich

Koppell, H. G.

Kuczynski, Jürgen

Lehmann, Karl

Leser, Paul W.

Lisco, Hermann

Marton, George

Marx, Hilde

Michael, Franz

Moellenhoff, Anna

Ophüls, Max

Oppenheimer, Max

Papanek, Miriam Lewin

Plettl, Martin

Poebel, Arno

Polanyi, Karl

Praeger, Frederick Amos

Reich, Annie

Rinner, Erich

Rohrlich, George F.

Rommen, Heinrich

Rosenberg, Jakob

Scharl, Josef

Schoenheimer, Rudolf

Schreyer, Isaac

Schultz, H. Stefan

Schumacher, Joachim

Schulze, Suzanne

Siodmak, Robert

Sirk, Douglas

Stern, Max

Tintner, Gerhard

Ullstein, Hermann

Ungar, Frederick

Valtin, Jan

Waelder-Hall, Jenny

Wagner, Martin

Walcher, Jakob

Walther, Arnold

Walter, Hilde

Wangh, Martin

Wasow, Wolfgang

Wellek, René

Werner, Alfred

Wintner, Aurel

Wurmbrand, Michael

APPENDIX

Recent or Expected Changes in Locations
of Collections Listed in the Guide

Neue oder erwartete Standortänderungen von Sammlungen,
die in diesem Handbuch aufgeführt sind

The disposition of many private collections was uncertain at the time the reports were being prepared. In fact, as much as two years has elapsed between the completion of certain reports and the publication of the Guide. The following information is now available:

Die Weggabe vieler privater Sammlungen war zur Zeit der Zusammenstellung einzelner Berichte noch ungewiß. In manchen Fällen sind zwei Jahre seit der Fertigstellung des Berichts und der Veröffentlichung unseres Handbuches vergangen. Wir sind aber jetzt im Besitz folgender Informationen:

Martha Albrand	Remainder of private collection transferred to Boston University Library
Ludwig Bachofer	Acquired by the State University of New York at Albany library
Arnold Brecht	Originals to be deposited in the Bundesarchiv in Koblenz, copies in the library of the State University of New York at Albany
Moritz Goldstein	To be deposited in the Institut für Zeitungsforschung, Dortmund
Kurt R. Grossmann	53 additional boxes of materials deposited at the Hoover Institution on War, Revolution, and Peace, Stanford, California
Waldemar Gurian	To be deposited in the Library of Congress, Washington, D.C.

Julius Held	To be deposited in part at the Clark Institute, Williamstown, Massachusetts, and in part at the Leo Baeck Institute, New York
Arnold Höllriegel	Acquired by the Deutsche Bibliothek, Frankfurt am Main
Erich Kahler	Acquired by the State University of New York at Albany
Ludwig von Mises	Acquired by Grove City College, Grove City, Pennsylvania
Erwin and Dora Panofsky	Deposited in the Archives of American Art, Smithsonian Institution, Washington, D.C.
Yella Pessl-Sobotka	Acquired by the State University of New York at Albany
Hans Reichenbach	Acquired by the University of Pittsburgh
Hans Speier	To be deposited at the State University of New York at Albany
Johannes Urzidil	Transferred to the Leo Baeck Institute, New York, together with the materials of Gertrude Urzidil, his wife
Stefan Zweig	A collection of several thousand letters acquired by the Library of the State University College at Fredonia, New York

APPENDIX

Bibliography of Handbooks

Bibliographie der Handbücher

American Historical Association, Committee for the Study
of War Documents. Guides to German Records Microfilmed
at Alexandria, Va. Washington, D.C.: National Archives, National Archives and Records Service, General
Services Administration, 1958-1968. (Also known as
The Alexandria Guide to Captured German Documents.)

American Philosophical Society, Philadelphia. Guide to the
Archives and Manuscript Collections of the American
Philosophical Society. Compiled by Whitfield J. Bell,
Jr. and Murphy D. Smith. Philadelphia: American Philo-
sophical Society, 1966. vii, 182p. (Memoirs of the
American Philosophical Society, 66.)

Archiv der Sozialen Demokratie. Übersicht über die Archiv-
bestände. (Bearb. v. Jürgen Jensen u. Werner Krause.)
Bonn/Bad Godesberg: Forschungsinstitut der Friedrich-
Ebert-Stiftung, 1970. 34p.

Boeninger, Hildegard R. The Hoover Library Collection on
Germany. Stanford, Calif.: Stanford University Press,
1955. 56p.

Das Bundesarchiv und seine Bestände. Übersicht. bearb. von
Friedrich Facius, Hans Booms und Heinz Boberach.
[Boppard am Rhein: H. Boldt, 1961]. (Schriften des
Bundesarchivs, 10.).

_____. 3. Aufl. Boppard: Boldt, 1977. 940p.

Denecke, Ludwig. Die Nachlässe in den Bibliotheken der
Bundesrepublik Deutschland. Boppard: Boldt, 1969.
(Verzeichnis der Schriftlichen Nachlässe, 2: Biblio-
theken.) New edition in preparation.

Dictionary Catalog of the Manuscript Division. The Research
Libraries of the New York Public Library. 2 vols.
Robert W. Hill, Keeper of Manuscripts. Boston: G. K.
Hall & Co., 1967.

1073

Epstein, Fritz T. German Source Materials in American
Libraries. Milwaukee: Marquette University Press,
1958. 14p.

From Weimar to Hitler Germany, 1918-1933. London: Vallentine, Mitchell, 1964. 269p. (The Wiener Library,
Catalogue Series No. 2.)

German Jewry. Its History, Life and Culture. London:
Vallentine, Mitchell, 1958. 279p. (The Wiener Library,
Catalogue Series No. 3.)

Guide to the Swarthmore College Peace Collection. A Memorial to Jane Addams. Compiled by Ellen Starr Brinton
and Hiram Doty, with the assistance of Gladys Hill.
Swarthmore, Pennsylvania: Swarthmore College Press,
1947. 72p. (Swarthmore College Bulletin, Peace Collection Publication No. 1.)

Haase, Carl. The Records of German History in German and
Certain Other Record Offices with Short Notes on Libraries and Other Collections / Die Archivalien zur deutschen Geschichte in deutschen und einigen anderen
Archiven mit kurzen Bemerkungen über Bibliotheken und
andere Sammlungen. Boppard am Rhein: Boldt, 1975.
194p.

Heinz, Grete and Agnes F. Peterson. NSDAP Hauptarchiv.
Guide to the Hoover Institution Microfilm Collection.
Stanford, California: The Hoover Institution on War,
Revolution and Peace, Stanford University, 1974. 175p.
(Hoover Institution Bibliographical Series, XVII.)

Lenz, Wilhelm. Archivalische Quellen zur deutschen Ge-
schichte seit 1500 in Großbritanien / Manuscript
Sources for the History of Germany since 1500 in Great
Britain. Boppard am Rhein: Boldt, 1975. 372p.

Leo Baeck Institute of Jews from Germany. Katalog. Hrsg.
Max Kreutzberger unter Mitarb. v. Irmgard Foerg.
Tübingen: J. C. B. Mohr, 1970. xii, 623p. (Schriften-
reihe wissenschaftlicher Abhandlungen des Leo Baeck
Instituts, 22.)

APPENDIX

The Library Catalogs of The Hoover Institution on War, Revolution, and Peace. Boston: G. K. Hall. The subject
headings of greatest use to study of the German-speaking emigration include: Germans in Foreign Countries;
German Literature — Emigré Authors; Refugees, German;
Germany — Politics and Government, 1933-1945; Anti-Nazi
Movement — History.

Library of Congress. The National Union Catalogue of Manuscript Collections 1959-1961. Ann Arbor, Michigan:
J. W. Edwards, 1962. Updated by a yearly catalogue.

Meyer, Hans M. (Hrsg.). Dokumente deutscher Sozialisten.
Aus den Beständen der Handschriftenabteilung zusammengestellt und kommentiert von Hedwig Gunnemann. Dortmund: Stadt- und Landesbibliothek, 1974. 74p. (Mit-
teilungen und Folge, 9.)

Mommsen, Wolfgang J. Die schriftlichen Nachlässe in den
zentralen deutschen und preußischen Archiven. Koblenz:
Bundesarchiv, 1955. 139p. (Schriften des Bundesarchivs, 1.)

_____. Die Nachlässe in den deutschen Archiven (mit
Ergänzungen aud anderen Beständen). Boppard: Boldt,
1971. 582p. (Schriften des Bundesarchivs, 17.)

Die Nachlässe in den wissenschaftliche Allgemeinbibliothek.
Stand vom 1. 8. 1959. Im Auftrag d. Inst. f. Biblio-
thekswissenschaft u. wissenschaftlichen Information d.
Humboldt-Universität zu Berlin. Berlin: Dt. Staatsbibliothek, 1959. 103p.

Die Nachlässe in wissenschaftlichen Instituten und Museen
und in den allgemeinbildenden Bibliothek. Unter Mitw.
von Horst Wolf. Hrsg. von Hans Lülfing u. Ruth Unger.
Berlin: Dt. Staatsbibliothek, 1968. 102p.

_____. Nachträge, Ergänzungen, Register. Hrsg. von
Hans Lülfing u. Horst Wolf. Berlin: Dt. Staatsbibliothek, 1971. 248p.

Nachlässe und Sammlungen in der Handschriftenabteilung des
Schiller-Nationalmuseums und des Deutschen Literatur-

archivs. Ein Verzeichnis. Zusammengestellt von Mitar-
beitern der Handschriftenabteilung. Marbach am Neckar:
Dt. Literaturarchiv, 1972. 93p. (Deutsches Literaturarchiv: Verzeichnisse, Berichte, Informationen, 1.)

Persecution and Resistance under the Nazis. London: Vallentine, Mitchell, 1960. 208p. (The Wiener Library,
Catalogue Series, 1.)

Röder, Werner. "Quellen zur Geschichte der deutschsprachigen
Emigration 1933-1945 im Archiv des Instituts für Zeit-
geschichte," Jahrbuch für Internationale Germanistik,
VII, No. 2 (1975), 142-170.

Suchy, Viktor. "Die 'Dokumentationsstelle für neuere Österreichische Literatur' — ihr Entwicklungsgang und ihre
heutige Gestalt," in: Dichter zwischen den Zeiten.
Festschrift für Rudolf Henz zum 80. Geburtstag. Hrsg.
Viktor Suchy. Wien: Braumüller, 1977, 383-486.

Übersicht über die von der Deutschen Akademie der Künste
betreuten Schriftstellernachlässe. Abgeschlossen im
Februar 1962. Berlin: Deutsche Akademie der Künste
zu Berlin, 1962. 214p. (Schriftenreihe der Literatur-
Archive, 8.)

Weinberg, Gerhard L. Guide to Captured German Documents.
Prepared by Gerhard L. Weinberg and the WDP staff
under the direction of Fritz T. Epstein. New York:
The Bureau of Applied Social Research, Columbia Univer-
sity, December 1952. 90p. (Air University Resources
Research Institute, Maxwell Air Force Base, Alabama,
Research Memorandum, No. 2, Vol. 1.)

_____. Supplement to the Guide to Captured German Docu-
ments. Washington, D.C.: The National Archives and
Records Service, General Services Administration, 1959.
69p.

APPENDIX

Periodicals and Newsletters

Zeitschriften

Akademie der Künste. Mitteilungsblatt. 1000 Berlin 21,
    Hanseatenweg 10. So far published Nos. 1-10 (1972-
    1977). Contains information about the archives of
    the academy.

American Institute of Physics. Newsletter. Published by
    the American Institute of Physics, 335 East 45th Street,
    New York, N.Y. 10017. Contains information on collec-
    tions in the physical sciences acquired by the A.I.P.
    and other institutions.

Bulletin des Leo Baeck Instituts. Published by the Leo Baeck
    Institute, 129 East 73rd Street, New York, N.Y. 10021.
    Contains updated information on collections of the
    L.B.I. as well as about new acquisitions.

College and Research Libraries News. Published by the Asso-
    ciation of College and Research Libraries, 1201-05
    Bluff Street, Fulton, Missouri 65251. Gives informa-
    tion about acquisitions in all fields throughout the
    United States.

Internationale Wissenschaftliche Korrespondenz zur Geschichte
    der Arbeiterbewegung. Im Auftrage der Hist. Kommission
    zu Berlin beim Friedrich-Meinecke-Institut der Freien
    Universität Berlin, hrsg. von Henryk Skrzypczak. 1000
    Berlin 45, Tietzenweg 79.

Jahrbuch der Deutschen Schillergesellschaft. 7142 Marbach
    am Neckar, Postfach 57. Lists the annual acquisitions
    of the Deutsches Literaturarchiv in Marbach.

Library of Congress Information Bulletin. Published monthly.
    Gives information on acquisitions.

Survey of Sources Newsletter. Published by the American
    Philosophical Society, Library, 105 South Fifth Street,
    Philadelphia, Pennsylvania 91906. Contains information
    on new acquisitions in the fields of biochemistry and
    molecular biology at the A.P.S. as well as at other
    institutions.

INDEXES